MAJOR CRISES IN
AMERICAN HISTORY

UNDER THE GENERAL EDITORSHIP OF

Merrill D. Peterson &

University of Virginia

Leonard W. Levy

Brandeis University

T H E   E D I T O R S

JAMES MacGREGOR BURNS
JANET THOMPSON BURNS
Williams College

ALFRED D. CHANDLER, JR.
Massachusetts Institute of Technology

HOLMAN HAMILTON
University of Kentucky

SAMUEL P. HUNTINGTON
Columbia University

GORDON JENSEN
Massachusetts Institute of Technology

LEONARD W. LEVY
Brandeis University

DAVID S. LOVEJOY
University of Wisconsin

ERIC McKITRICK
Columbia University

ERNEST R. MAY
Harvard University

MERRILL D. PETERSON
University of Virginia

T. HARRY WILLIAMS
Louisiana State University

MAJOR CRISES
IN
AMERICAN
HISTORY

Documentary Problems

II

1865–1953

New York · San Francisco
Chicago · Atlanta

HARCOURT, BRACE & WORLD, INC.

© 1962 BY HARCOURT, BRACE & WORLD, INC.

Library of Congress Catalog Card Number: 62–15960

PRINTED IN THE UNITED STATES OF AMERICA

CONTENTS

Science, Religion, and Society: The Impact of Darwinism, 1859–1909

MERRILL D. PETERSON

Contents vii

Overseas Expansion: The Coming of War with Spain, 1895–1898

ERNEST R. MAY

Progressivism and the Trusts:
The Conflict of Freedom and Control, 1911–1914
GORDON JENSEN

World War I: Wilson and the Peace of Versailles, 1919

ERNEST R. MAY

The Depression Crisis and the
Emergence of the Welfare State, 1932–1935

ALFRED D. CHANDLER, JR.

World War II: Roosevelt and Intervention, 1940–1941

JAMES MacGREGOR BURNS
JANET THOMPSON BURNS

Democracy Fights a Limited War: Korea, 1950–1953

SAMUEL P. HUNTINGTON

PREFACE

M*ajor Crises in American History* offers a documentary approach in depth to the first college course in American history. It possesses a unifying theme in the general idea of historical crisis. Sixteen crucial events, episodes, or experiences in the history of the United States are treated intensively through primary sources, the raw data of historical knowledge. The eight topics grouped in Volume I range in time from the seventeenth century to the Civil War; the eight topics in Volume II begin with Reconstruction and end with the Korean War. While each topic has great intrinsic importance, it also offers a perspective on larger issues and developments. Utilizing different kinds of data, and calling for different kinds of analysis, each topic locates a problem, a problem that has a distinctly decisive aspect and that, from its focus in time, is subject to reasonably comprehensive, as well as intensive, coverage. Taken together, and within themselves, these chapters exhibit the standard fields of historical study—social, political, economic, diplomatic, constitutional, intellectual—and raise perennial questions of analysis and interpretation.

The structure of the present work has several distinguishing marks. *First*, it combines the interest in controversial problems and issues with the historian's fundamental responsibility to the record of events. Except as problems are delineated and explored in the thick, baffling context of specific situations and events, they cannot be grasped historically. As elementary as this truth is, the obligation to exchange the telescope, with its panoramic sweep, for the microscope, with its faithful attention to characteristic local contour and complexity, and so to examine the historical record in considerable depth and detail, needs to be brought home repeatedly. Narrative textbooks with centuries to account for are necessarily telescopic and if relied upon too heavily may convey the impression that history is a well-ordered march rather than a disheveled and spreading battle in which there are few certainties. The difficulty is but partially overcome by confronting students with issues and problems as sweeping in their scope as those disclosed in the chapters of the one- or even two-volume narrative text, since, in such a scheme, the contexts are vague and the quality of concreteness, so essential to historical understanding, is necessarily neglected. In the present volumes, the objectives of depth, fullness, and concreteness are sought through the study of a carefully selected series of critical cases as turning points in American history. No attempt is made to fill out an entire chronology; on the contrary, the deliberate intention is to place in focus a relatively few great moments in American history, each as dramatic as it is charged with significance.

Second, the method employed throughout the book makes a strong claim on the intelligence and initiative of the student in the reconstruction, analysis, and interpretation of the data. The aim is to provide the student not so much with a book of knowledge as with a tool of historical inquiry. Within reasonable limits, the goal is to make him the "doer" rather than the "taker." Only primary sources are used. The documents are accompanied by such editorial guidance and interpretation as may be necessary to assure coherence, but they are neither predigested nor prejudged for the student.

Confronted with primary sources—most of them entirely new to him—the student must work with their uncertainties and yield to their discipline, without the benefit or the hindrance of what historians have said at second hand about the events in question. He will learn from conflicting evidence, interest, and opinion that great historical events are susceptible to a number of interpretations, which are better or worse not according to their rightness or wrongness but according to their cogency in treating all the complexities of the problem at hand. It is no part of the editors' intention to create around the student what is as manifestly impossible as it is undesirable: a vacuum of accumulated historical knowledge. Classroom instruction and additional reading, either in standard texts or in specialized studies, may be relied upon to furnish this knowledge so far as it is wanted. But there is no substitute for the student making discoveries for himself; and in the instance of historical study this means there is no substitute for each student becoming, if only on a rudimentary level, his own historian.

Third, the work's focus on crises should convey to the student that American history is not lacking in turbulence and passion, that it has its share of dramatic conflict, great debate, and great decision, and that many contingencies attended the outcome. The editors believe that this emphasis is both pedagogically sound and a welcome antidote to the current tendency to view American history as one mellifluous and more or less predestined flow along an inevitable path of consensus. Without supposing that American history is adequately comprehended solely as a sequence of crises, they aim through these volumes to enrich the student's knowledge of the past, to give him a heightened awareness of the grave disturbances and dislocations that successive generations of Americans have experienced and of the responses they have made.

A number of considerations played a part in the actual choice of the topics included in each volume: the preferences of the general and contributing editors; the desire for freshness and variety and originality; the obvious needs of the course, both in terms of content and of coverage. Since it is assumed that the book will generally, if not exclusively, be used in conjunction with a standard text, efforts have been made to minimize repetition and to phase the topics chronologically so as to permit their assignment on a fairly regular basis—weekly in one semester courses, biweekly in two semester courses.

Each topic composes a chapter, and each chapter follows a uniform plan. The Chronology provides a useful guide to the progression of events in the particular crisis. The Introduction supplies, in narrative form, the immediate background and context of the crisis. The Documents, reproduced as they appear in the sources cited, are arranged in logical sequence, prefaced by Headnotes that explain the source or authorship and add other significant details. The Conclusion rounds out the documentary treatment in narrative fashion. The Study Questions, all of the essay type, are intended to contribute to the book's usefulness as a vehicle of undergraduate research. Each chapter is completed by a concise bibliography, Recommended Readings, which students may use most effectively in the writing of brief, critical essays or longer research papers. Maps, statistical tables, and similar aids are provided in so far as they seemed necessary. At the end of each volume there is a brief discussion—"Historical Aids"—of the chief standard bibliographical and historiographical works that facilitate the study of American history.

Within the limits of the format described, the historians responsible for the several chapters were free to make their own decisions. They wrote the original narratives, selected and edited the documents, and shaped each chapter. The general editors consider themselves fortunate to have obtained such excellent collaborators. They entered heartily into the spirit of the book, discharged their responsibilities cheerfully and skillfully, and responded to our gentle proddings and suggestions in a most gratifying fashion. The general editors shared equally in the responsibility of overseeing the entire work, from initial planning to final completion.

M.D.P.
L.W.L.

Brandeis University, March 1, 1962

The Decision to Reconstruct the South, 1865–1867:
A Question of Alternatives

ERIC McKITRICK

COLUMBIA UNIVERSITY

CONTENTS

CHRONOLOGY

1865

APRIL 15   Death of Lincoln; Andrew Johnson becomes seventeenth President of the United States.

MAY 29–JULY 13   Johnson issues reconstruction proclamations for seceded Southern states.

AUGUST 14   Mississippi holds convention as per proclamations; reorganization and elections there and in other states continue during remainder of summer and fall.

DECEMBER   "Black Codes" being described and discussed in Northern newspapers.

DECEMBER 4   Opening of Thirty-ninth Congress; exclusion of Southern members-elect; establishment of Joint Committee on Reconstruction.

1866

FEBRUARY 19   Veto of Freedmen's Bureau Bill.

FEBRUARY 22   Johnson's Washington's Birthday speech.

MARCH 27   Veto of Civil Rights Bill.

APRIL 6   Civil Rights veto overridden in Senate.

JUNE 13   Final passage of Fourteenth Amendment.

JUNE 21   Readmission of Tennessee.

AUGUST 14–16   National Union Convention at Philadelphia.

AUGUST 28–
SEPTEMBER 15   "Swing Around the Circle."

OCTOBER–
NOVEMBER   Heavy Republican victories in fall Congressional and state elections.

DECEMBER 3   Thirty-ninth Congress meets for second session.

1867

JANUARY   Breakdown of moderate position on Reconstruction. Southern states, exhorted by Northern Democrats and by President Johnson, refuse to act on Fourteenth Amendment. District commanders testify before Congressional committees on crime and lawlessness in the South.

FEBRUARY 20   Reconstruction bill reaches final form.

MARCH 2   Veto and repassage of First Reconstruction Bill.

INTRODUCTION

TODAY, almost any historical discussion of Reconstruction will hinge morally on the effort made by the North, during the two years following the Civil War and emancipation, to devise some satisfactory way of conferring citizenship upon the newly freed Negroes of the South. That the effort turned out badly is plain enough. But once past this, historical criticism proceeds with less and less assurance. The moral issues of Reconstruction are profoundly ambiguous; no amount of "plain talk" can do much to simplify them.

For instance, almost as soon as the Southern states were allowed any initiative to manage their own affairs, a number of them in 1865 produced codes of law that placed their Negroes in a status more closely resembling that of hired-out slaves than of freedmen, and the effect of these "Black Codes" on Northern public opinion was to inspire rage and distrust. And yet no one can be sure that such a step was in the nature of things foredoomed to occur; many of the South's own best men saw from the first what a foolish step it was. Subsequently, even with the codes set aside, by the winter of 1866–67 the state of law and order in the South, so far as it extended to Negroes and Unionists, was a matter of notoriety in even the most moderate of Northern newspapers. On the other hand, the best solution the North could find for this was the Military Reconstruction Acts of March, 1867, which introduced carpetbaggery. A strong note of vengeance ran through the business, and that too makes for a gloomy question: did circumstances absolutely require these measures? The North, as things turned out, could not exhibit its carpetbag governments as shining models of anything at all, and never seriously tried—meanwhile managing to corrupt all its best ideals while rubbing the Southerners' noses in their own worst prejudices. Whatever was "accomplished" here must be picked out of many impurities, whereas the aftermath of bitterness and frustration in Southern society is an enduring historical fact, even though our patience with it as a just historical grievance has about run out.

Retrospectively most historical events—particularly so extended an event as this one—look more and more "inevitable" as time goes on. Historians come across more and more reasons why things seemed bound to turn out exactly the way they did and, in the case of great miscarriages, more and more disreputable motives for the principals' failure to behave intelligently. This method can end by limiting the mind. The South's experience in the mid-twentieth century is a continuing reminder that this particular problem, Reconstruction, is one that might best remain open.

On the one hand, then, we are confronted with the excesses of carpetbaggery and, on the other, with the spirit of the Black Codes and a chronic legacy of barbarism and violence in Southern race relations. These are terrible extremes, and there is so wide a gulf between them that a prime question ought to be that of alternatives. A wide range of solutions should at some point have been possible in the interests of a principle that certainly came to be accepted in form if not in substance: the elimination of slavery and the absorption of black men into decent citizenship. The following problem has been organized on the assumption that the "inevitability" pattern of Reconstruction may for the moment be suspended, in order that the question of alternatives may again be opened up for discussion.

To make this a "legitimate" procedure, it will be necessary to limit the problem to some span of time during which conditions were in actual fact still fluid—a period when multiple choices were still thinkable and decisions were still being considered. There was such a period; it lasted nearly two years. From the end of the war in April, 1865, to the month of March, 1867, when the Reconstruction Acts were completed, it would not have been possible for anyone to predict just what "Reconstruction" would consist of, because the matter had not as yet been concluded. It was still in doubt, still being debated, right down to the end.

If men at the time could debate the choices they had before them, students of history ought to be able to do the same. The decision made was not the only possible one, though to recognize this does not mean that the range of choices was infinite. It may turn out to have been not so very wide after all, and we should at least be prepared for such a discovery in case we should make it. Our alternatives cannot be just any alternatives; they should be the same ones that were open to the men who considered them then, and it has to be borne in mind that the choices became progressively narrower as time went on.

What shape might the South's basic social prejudices have taken, given a Northern policy substantially different from that of carpetbag Reconstruction? That form of the question, with all its contingencies, may be somewhat beyond us; but it is not necessary to project a specific outcome in order to contemplate the possibility of one different from that which was actually arrived at. What was the best conceivable solution? There may not have been one. Still, it need not be supposed that the North was bound by circumstances to act vindictively no matter what, nor that the South was doomed by its own nature to respond to any sort of Northern policy with violence, terror, and persecution. It should be assumed, for the sake of the problem, that Southern compliance might have been undertaken in better faith had Northern policy been framed with greater intelligence. But greater or lesser "severity" might not in itself have made the difference. What most certainly would have mattered was a Reconstruction policy whose terms were clean and clear and laid down early.

The official and unofficial behavior of President Andrew Johnson appears to have had considerable effect on the shaping of Northern policy during this period, though the full nature and extent of this influence is a matter upon which historians still do not agree. Yet in any case the conflict, impasse, and eventual breakdown of communication between President and Congress over the issue of Reconstruction created untold obstacles to the making of any harmonious or reasonable decisions. From about February, 1866, on, Johnson openly insisted that reconstruction was at an end, that nothing further in that way was necessary and that, in effect, the only proper deciding authority on this entire question was himself. All but a handful of the Republican members of Congress, however, radicals and conservatives alike, were convinced that further federal supervision of the Southern states was required in some form, and they took for granted that it was as much the duty of Congress to make legislation on this subject as on any other. They spent months trying to decide what the nature of these laws should be. As these months passed, exactly which of two conditions had the greater influence on the Republican state of mind—the widening cross-purposes of legislative and executive or the increasing intransigence of the South—is hard to determine, because the one depended very much on the other.

Johnson never liked the idea of "reconstruction"; he always used the word restoration instead, though most people did not seem unduly troubled by the distinction. His first comprehensive step was the issuance of two proclamations on May 29, 1865. One, applying to individuals, dealt with amnesty and pardon; the other provided for the resumption of civil government in North Carolina. There was little public criticism of these measures. The pardoning plan seemed sensible and not excessively punitive; certain classes of rebels had to make special application for pardon, which conceivably meant that the President might keep certain ones waiting indefinitely if he so chose. The restoration plan likewise seemed, for the most part, a reasonable beginning. A provisional governor was appointed for the purpose of setting the state government in motion, and he was directed to call a convention which would amend the state constitution in accordance with the results of the war. It was understood that this should include the renouncing of secession, slavery, and the rebel debt. This done, the citizens might hold elections for a governor, legislature, and congressmen. Proclamations identical with that for North Carolina were shortly issued for the other states.

There were objections from some that the Johnson plan left the question of suffrage too fully up to the individual states, thereby leaving insufficient guarantee for a just settlement with regard to the Negroes. That such criticism did not immediately take serious form, however, was due to a general feeling that the solution of this as well as other questions was still very much open. The final settlement, which would presumably be made through the combined action of President and Congress later on, would depend both on what the states did of their own accord and on the spirit in which they did it: the President now was simply "testing" them. He regarded his plan—or so it was hoped—as an "experiment."

By the time Congress was ready to meet in December, 1865, events in the South had convinced a majority of the Northern public that the "experiment" was not working. Compliance with even the minimum conditions had been given with quibbling reservations and in some cases evaded entirely; the Black Codes, with severe discriminations on apprenticeship, vagrancy, land ownership, and other matters, had been enacted and published; and a considerable number of unpardoned Confederate leaders, military and civil, had been elected to public office. Yet all the Southern states assumed that they had, by then, qualified themselves for admission of their representatives to Congress. The editorial conviction of all Republican newspapers, however (every Northern state was governed by Republican majorities), was that they were not so qualified; and when the clerk of the House omitted from his roll call the names of the Southern members-elect, the step was greeted even in conservative circles with approval. Thaddeus Stevens, the extreme radical representative from Pennsylvania, moved the creation of a joint committee to study the question of a policy for the South, and nearly every Republican member voted for it. William Pitt Fessenden, a moderate senator from Maine, was appointed chairman.

It had meanwhile begun to dawn on Northern Republicans that Johnson himself had never regarded his policy as an experiment at all, though the Democrats had been joyfully saying this all along. The President had assumed, despite certain unfortunate slips in Southern behavior, that the policy was final and that when he relieved his provisional governors in December, 1865, reconstruction was at an end. Nor was he able to see, in telling the Southern leaders that their acts were "voluntary," what erratic and misleading instructions he was thus giving them. He was certainly not very emphatic—the tone of many of his dispatches was actually rather wheedling— nor did he represent to them with any accuracy the true state of Northern public opinion. The South Carolinians sent him full advance information about their Black Code, but so far as is known he made no move to warn them of how it might be received. Never in his communications with Southern leaders had he imputed any legitimacy to the idea that Congress would or should have something to say about reconstruction. Thus by the end of 1865 he had already got himself into a very bad box, having done things and made judgments which, unless modified, his party could not support.

Johnson's refusal to modify anything revealed itself during the early months of 1866 in a series of quarrels over the Freedmen's Bureau Bill, the Civil Rights Bill, and the Fourteenth Amendment, making the breach between himself and the Republican party formal and explicit. The two bills had been devised, under the sponsorship of Senator Lyman Trumbull of Illinois, for the purpose of extending certain forms of federal protection to the freedmen. Trumbull had assumed, from prior talks with the President, that he had the latter's support for these measures. He was much chagrined when Johnson vetoed them both. In his veto messages Johnson held that the bills were unconstitutional, but his chief objection proved in each case to be that no legislation should be made for the Southern states while they remained unrepresented in Congress. Greatly stung by hostile criticism of his Freedmen's Bureau veto, and especially by the abusive remarks of Thaddeus Stevens and Charles Sumner, Johnson made an extravagant public speech on the night of February 22 in which he attacked Stevens, Sumner, and certain others by name, accused Republican leaders of wrecking his policy, and hinted that there was a plot afoot to assassinate him. Moderate Republicans still hoping for harmony were very discouraged. The Freedmen's Bureau Bill failed of repassage in the Senate, but the Civil Rights veto was overridden in both houses.

The Joint Committee of Fifteen, under Fessenden's chairmanship, was meanwhile working on plans for a constitutional amendment that would represent the North's terms of reconstruction. There was a range of problems, such as representation, civil rights, citizenship, officeholding, and suffrage, that required some form of action. Remedies of every sort—including the sweeping formula of universal amnesty and universal suffrage—were considered and debated week after week in committee and in both houses of Congress. The President, however, would not lend his support to any of them. He said that under current circumstances he did not believe in adding further amendments to the Constitution. The amendment whose details were finally settled after five months of work—and which became the Fourteenth—conferred citizenship upon Negroes and forbade any state to make laws depriving citizens of life, liberty, and property, or equal protection of the laws; it specified penalties of reduced representation for former slave states that withheld the franchise from such citizens; it denied state and federal officeholding privileges to persons who had broken oaths of loyalty to the Constitution in order to support the rebellion; and it forbade any state to invalidate the federal debt or to validate the Confederate debt. Johnson, when he transmitted the amendment to the several states as required by law, sent Congress a message in which he gave all to understand that he did not approve of the document he was sending out and that he did not think the Southern states ought to ratify it.

The Fourteenth Amendment represented, in effect, the Republican party's campaign platform in the Congressional and state elections of 1866. It was understood by all except the extreme radicals that these were the North's terms: any Southern state ratifying them was virtually certain of readmission. It was also widely assumed that in case of a convincing Republican victory Johnson would see the light, hearken at last to the popular will, and proceed to work with, rather than against, the leaders of the party. The states, however, refused to ratify, and Johnson would not hearken to the popular will— even after his disastrous "Swing Around the Circle" of late summer when he campaigned against his own party, and even after the Republicans won crushing majorities in the fall. An abortive "National Union" movement had been organized earlier in the summer by a remnant of Johnson Republicans on the President's platform of immediate and unqualified readmission of the Southern states. A convention was held at Philadelphia in August, but the movement, whose main support came from the Democrats, was overwhelmingly repudiated in the elections. In his December message, despite all this, Johnson gave no concessions and announced that nothing whatever had happened to change his mind. The final critical period, then, was the one extending from the 1866 fall elections to the completion of the Reconstruction Acts in March, 1867.

When the Thirty-ninth Congress met for its second session in December, 1866, three Southern states had already rejected the amendment and prospects of acceptance by the others were not bright. Radical leaders like Stevens and Sumner had made it clear that they would press for measures that went beyond the amendment no matter what happened. Yet there were other Republicans—including radicals—who announced their willingness to stand by the amendment as a final settlement if the remaining states should see fit to accept it. Had those states actually done so, it is probable that this more moderate sector of party opinion would have commanded a majority.

Yet the Southern states were subjected during the crucial months of December and January to intense counterinfluences from the North, the effect of which was apparently to harden them in their resistance. One such influence was the leadership and press of the Northern Democratic party, whose interest was quite naturally to embarrass the Republicans in every way they could. The other was President Johnson. Democratic editorials, whose daily theme was "dead-lock," exhorted the South to stand fast and preserve its honor, insisting that if the amendment were not ratified the Republicans must either back down altogether or go to such extremes that their measures would be repudiated by public opinion or struck down by the Supreme Court. Southern editors found this reasoning immensely persuasive. Certain of the states, however, actually did consider ratifying. But Johnson himself, in at least two cases and possibly in others, intervened personally to discourage such movements, declaring that no possible good could come of them. Subsequently—except for Tennessee, which had ratified the amendment back in July—all the others rejected it, several without a dissenting vote. It was these developments, combined with reports from the South of increased lawlessness in the treatment of Negroes and Unionists, that cut much of the ground from moderate sentiment and opened the way for the Reconstruction Acts.

Even so, the issue was not decided until the last minute. Thaddeus Stevens, whose influence had been greatly increased by this course of events, favored a plan of straight military occupation. Discouraged in earlier efforts for a scheme of confiscation and disfranchisement, Stevens had come to think that if the South were once placed under military rule, the incoming Fortieth Congress (more radical than the Thirty-ninth) might be persuaded to enact more thorough measures. His logic was questionable, but a last-minute break prevented its being brought to a test.

One of the less-appreciated ironies of Reconstruction is that if Stevens had had his way, and Congress had passed a straight military bill, most of the distractions of the following decade would probably not have occurred. The military commanders were for the most part honest and just, and government under exclusive military control would probably have been relatively efficient. But straight military government for an indefinite period was regarded by moderate Republicans as too "radical": it should be so modified that the states might take the initiative to reconstruct themselves. Consequently, enough "moderate" influence was still at large to make the final product one of those grotesque "compromises" containing far more latent mischief than the thing it was designed to avoid. In the final version of the Reconstruction Act—together with the supplementary one passed later in the month—military rule would last only until the state government could be reorganized under civilian auspices and on the basis of universal manhood suffrage. The other side of the coin, however, was that most of the Southern men who had any sort of experience in public affairs would not be available for imparting legitimacy to the new regimes. They were not only disqualified from office but, for having taken part in the rebellion, were disfranchised as well. To an extent not fully appreciated at the outset, this would mean that new civil bureaucracies for those states, as well as political machinery, would have to be recruited from the outside.

Such then, in barest outline, are the principal facts. A problem peculiarly challenging to the analytical imagination emerges when it becomes apparent that at numerous points along this sequence there was a perfectly conceivable choice different from the one actually taken. Especially engaging is the question of what these "other" choices might have added up to.

Before turning to the documents, we should anticipate at least three general queries that are almost certain to come up in any consideration of this phase of Reconstruction. If we cannot know the answers, we can at least classify the questions.

The first of these is: *Was Reconstruction actually necessary in the first place?* What we say here depends very much on what we assume "Reconstruction" should mean. The word itself, with its implications of a "making over," may be misleading. On the one extreme, Thaddeus Stevens was convinced that the South's whole economic base would have to be revolutionized—that confiscation of property and its redistribution to the landless freedmen were needed to purge the Republic of all the poisons of slavery and to ensure its future stability and freedom. He may have been right. But since he had virtually no support for this, it becomes equivocal to speak of his plan as a true "alternative." The transformation of the South's political base, as done by the Reconstruction Acts, was "revolutionary" enough—indeed, too revolutionary—for most Southerners. And on the other extreme, the Johnson plan, which involved no more than the South's acquiescence to emancipation and to its own failure to achieve independence through war, was not enough for the North.

Yet the thing that was really at stake all along was a peace settlement; no matter what name were given it, this in the last analysis was the function which "Reconstruction" had to fulfill. Regardless of how much or how little it might consist of, there had to be something that was mutually recognized as a settlement before the war could be in every sense concluded and peace truly established. For it to have real meaning and legitimacy, the South could not be permanently alienated; but the other side of this was that the North, as victor, would have to be satisfied. The logic of emancipation as one of the war aims would probably have required Negro suffrage no matter how, in the end, it was achieved. Perhaps what the question really comes down to is whether a technique might have been found for making Negro suffrage stick better than, in actual fact, it did.

A second question is: *Who really precipitated the quarrel between Johnson and the Republican party?* Who created the provocations, the radical Republicans or Johnson himself? This point, highly debatable, is one which the student of these events must decide for himself. But the "alternatives" approach may help to transform the question into something more manageable: the result of the quarrel, rather than the "blame" for it, is perhaps what should matter. The President's stand, taken very early, meant that the influence of the executive branch was in effect removed from the making of legislative decisions. Had that influence been available, those decisions might have been wiser; they might, on the other hand, have been much more foolish. But they would almost certainly have been different.

A final question is: *Had Abraham Lincoln lived, what would he have done?* Were not Lincoln's and Johnson's plans the same, and might not Lincoln, as peacetime executive, have come to a fate similar to Johnson's? If there is any way out of this historical enigma, it should again be the concept of "alternatives" rather than "inevitability." Certain considerations may at least be borne in mind as we puzzle over it. For one thing, Lincoln's well-known "Ten Per Cent" plan was conceived as a war measure and formulated under wartime conditions. It would probably not have done for a peacetime policy, and how fully Lincoln himself appreciated this is a matter of doubt. But we do know that, unlike Johnson, he tended to think of this, and of whatever further measures he may have had in his mind at the time of his death, as "experimental." For another thing, we must picture a peacetime Lincoln who would be confronted, just as Johnson was, not with a single choice but with a series of choices. Yet we are not bound to picture him at each point taking the same ones Johnson took. And finally, Lincoln, unlike Johnson, never went it alone. He never worked without his party apparatus, and whatever he may have thought personally of his party leaders, he seems to have understood how little he could accomplish, for good or ill, without them. He took care that they should never be alienated quite to the point where he and they were not at least on terms of negotiation.

DOCUMENTS

1] President Lincoln States His Wartime Reconstruction Views

Whatever is to be said about Lincoln's plans for peacetime reconstruction, and how he might have responded to conditions developing after the close of hostilities, must of course rest on guesswork. His wartime plan, embodied in the "Ten Per Cent" proclamation of December 8, 1863, is one clue, though the governments organized under it (in Arkansas, Louisiana, and Tennessee) proved less effective than was originally hoped. (Special attention should be given to the proclamation's final paragraph.) Another clue is a letter which Lincoln wrote to General James Wadsworth, apparently early in 1864.*

A] THE "TEN PER CENT" PLAN

BY THE PRESIDENT OF THE UNITED STATES OF AMERICA.

A PROCLAMATION.

WHEREAS in and by the Constitution of the United States it is provided that the President "shall have power to grant reprieves and pardons for offenses against the United States, except in cases of impeachment;" and

Whereas a rebellion now exists whereby the loyal State governments of several States have for a long time been subverted, and many persons have committed and are now guilty of treason against the United States; and . . .

Whereas it is now desired by some persons heretofore engaged in said rebellion to resume their allegiance to the United States and to reinaugurate loyal State governments within and for their respective States:

Therefore, I, Abraham Lincoln, President of the United States, do proclaim, declare, and make known to all persons who have, directly or by implication, participated in the existing rebellion, except as hereinafter excepted, that a full pardon is hereby granted to them and each of them, with restoration of all rights of property, except as to slaves and in property cases where rights of third parties shall have intervened, and upon the condition that every such person shall take and subscribe an oath and thenceforward keep and maintain said oath inviolate, and which oath shall be registered for permanent preservation and shall be of the tenor and effect following, to wit:

* PRESIDENT LINCOLN STATES HIS WARTIME RECONSTRUCTION VIEWS: From James D. Richardson, ed., *A Compilation of the Messages and Papers of the Presidents, 1789–1897* (Washington, 1896–99), VI, 213–14; and Roy P. Basler, ed., *The Collected Works of Abraham Lincoln* (New Brunswick, N.J., 1953–55), VII, 101–02.

I, —— ——, do solemnly swear, in presence of Almighty God, that I will hence-forth faithfully support, protect, and defend the Constitution of the United States and the Union of the States thereunder; and that I will in like manner abide by and faithfully support all acts of Congress passed during the existing rebellion with reference to slaves, so long and so far as not repealed, modified, or held void by Congress or by decision of the Supreme Court; and that I will in like manner abide by and faithfully support all proclamations of the President made during the existing rebellion having reference to slaves, so long and so far as not modified or declared void by decision of the Supreme Court. So help me God.

The persons excepted from the benefits of the foregoing provisions are all who are or shall have been civil or diplomatic officers or agents of the so-called Confederate Government; all who have left judicial stations under the United States to aid the rebellion; all who are or shall have been military or naval officers of said so-called Confederate Government above the rank of colonel in the army or of lieutenant in the navy; all who left seats in the United States Congress to aid the rebellion; all who resigned commissions in the Army or Navy of the United States and afterwards aided the rebellion; and all who have engaged in any way in treating colored persons, or white persons in charge of such, otherwise than lawfully as prisoners of war, and which persons may have been found in the United States service as soldiers, seamen, or in any other capacity.

And I do further proclaim, declare, and make known that whenever, in any of the States of Arkansas, Texas, Louisiana, Mississippi, Tennessee, Alabama, Georgia, Florida, South Carolina, and North Carolina, a number of persons, not less than one-tenth in number of the votes cast in such State at the Presidential election of the year A. D. 1860, each having taken the oath aforesaid, and not having since violated it, and being a qualified voter by the election law of the State existing immediately before the so-called act of secession, and excluding all others, shall reestablish a State government which shall be republican and in nowise contravening said oath, such shall be recognized as the true government of the State, and the State shall receive thereunder the benefits of the constitutional provision which declares that "the United States shall guarantee to every State in this Union a republican form of government and shall protect each of them against invasion, and, on application of the legislature, or the executive (when the legislature can not be convened), against domestic violence."

And I do further proclaim, declare, and make known that any provision which may be adopted by such State government in relation to the freed people of such State which shall recognize and declare their permanent freedom, provide for their education, and which may yet be consistent as a temporary arrangement with their present condition as a laboring, landless, and homeless class, will not be objected to by the National Executive.

And it is suggested as not improper that in constructing a loyal State government in any State the name of the State, the boundary, the subdivisions, the constitution, and the general code of laws as before the rebellion be maintained, subject only to the modifications made necessary by the conditions hereinbefore stated, and such others, if any, not contravening said conditions and which may be deemed expedient by those framing the new State government.

To avoid misunderstanding, it may be proper to say that this proclamation, so far as it relates to State governments, has no reference to States wherein loyal State governments have all the while been maintained. And for the same reason it may be proper to further say that whether members sent to Congress from any State shall be admitted to seats constitutionally rests exclusively with the respective Houses, and not to any extent with the Executive. And, still further, that this proclamation is intended to present the people of the States wherein the national authority has been suspended and loyal State governments have been subverted a mode in and by which the national authority and loyal State governments may be reestablished within said States or in any of them; and while the mode presented is the best the Executive can suggest, with his present impressions, it must not be understood that no other possible mode would be acceptable.

ABRAHAM LINCOLN.

B] ABRAHAM LINCOLN TO JAMES S. WADSWORTH

[January, 1864?]

You desire to know, in the event of our complete success in the field, the same being followed by a loyal and cheerful submission on the part of the South, if universal amnesty should not be accompanied with universal suffrage.

Now, since you know my private inclinations as to what terms should be granted to the South in the contingency mentioned, I will here add, that if our success should thus be realized, followed by such desired results, I cannot see, if universal amnesty is granted, how, under the circumstances, I can avoid exacting in return universal suffrage, or, at least, suffrage on the basis of intelligence and military service.

How to better the condition of the colored race has long been a study which has attracted my serious and careful attention; hence I think I am clear and decided as to what course I shall pursue in the premises, regarding it a religious duty, as the nation's guardian of these people, who have so heroically vindicated their manhood on the battle-field, where, in assisting to save the life of the Republic, they have demonstrated in blood their right to the ballot, which is but the humane protection of the flag they have so fearlessly defended.

The restoration of the Rebel States to the Union must rest upon the principle of civil and political equality of both races; and it must be sealed by general amnesty.

2] President Johnson Pieces Out His Reconstruction Plan

President Johnson did not encompass the subjects of amnesty and recon-struction in a single proclamation, as Lincoln had done, but dealt with them in separate documents. His proclamation on amnesty and pardon, issued

May 29, 1865, was somewhat more detailed than Lincoln's had been. The other of that date provided for the reorganization of civil government in North Carolina, and in it the President appointed William W. Holden, a North Carolina Unionist, as provisional governor. Between June 13 and July 13 similar proclamations were issued for Mississippi, Georgia, Texas, Alabama, South Carolina, and Florida. The four other seceded states—Arkansas, Tennessee, Louisiana, and Virginia—were not brought under executive-appointed provisional governors. Of these, the first three had had "Ten Per Cent" governments. Virginia was a special case, a sort of loyalist government-in-exile for that state having maintained a precarious existence at Alexandria throughout most of the war. Johnson simply recognized these governments as already "restored," and allowed them to go on functioning.*

A] AMNESTY AND PARDON

BY THE PRESIDENT OF THE UNITED STATES OF AMERICA.

A PROCLAMATION.

. . . .

To THE end . . . that the authority of the Government of the United States may be restored and that peace, order, and freedom may be established, I, Andrew Johnson, President of the United States, do proclaim and declare that I hereby grant to all persons who have, directly or indirectly, participated in the existing rebellion, except as hereinafter excepted, amnesty and pardon, with restoration of all rights of property, except as to slaves and except in cases where legal proceedings under the laws of the United States providing for the confiscation of property of persons engaged in rebellion have been instituted; but upon the condition, nevertheless, that every such person shall take and subscribe the following oath (or affirmation) and thenceforward keep and maintain said oath inviolate, and which oath shall be registered for permanent preservation and shall be of the tenor and effect following, to wit:

I, ―― ――, do solemnly swear (or affirm), in presence of Almighty God, that I will henceforth faithfully support, protect, and defend the Constitution of the United States and the Union of the States thereunder, and that I will in like manner abide by and faithfully support all laws and proclamations which have been made during the existing rebellion with reference to the emancipation of slaves. So help me God.

The following classes of persons are excepted from the benefits of this proclamation:

First. All who are or shall have been pretended civil or diplomatic officers or otherwise domestic or foreign agents of the pretended Confederate government.

Second. All who left judicial stations under the United States to aid the rebellion.

Third. All who shall have been military or naval officers of said pretended

---

* PRESIDENT JOHNSON PIECES OUT HIS RECONSTRUCTION PLAN: From James D. Richardson, ed., *Messages and Papers of the Presidents* (Washington, 1896–99), VI, 310–12; 312–14.

Confederate government above the rank of colonel in the army or lieutenant in the navy.

Fourth. All who left seats in the Congress of the United States to aid the rebellion.

Fifth. All who resigned or tendered resignations of their commissions in the Army or Navy of the United States to evade duty in resisting the rebellion.

Sixth. All who have engaged in any way in treating otherwise than lawfully as prisoners of war persons found in the United States service as officers, soldiers, seamen, or in other capacities.

Seventh. All persons who have been or are absentees from the United States for the purpose of aiding the rebellion.

Eighth. All military and naval officers in the rebel service who were educated by the Government in the Military Academy at West Point or the United States Naval Academy.

Ninth. All persons who held the pretended offices of governors of States in insurrection against the United States.

Tenth. All persons who left their homes within the jurisdiction and protection of the United States and passed beyond the Federal military lines into the pretended Confederate States for the purpose of aiding the rebellion.

Eleventh. All persons who have been engaged in the destruction of the commerce of the United States upon the high seas and all persons who have made raids into the United States from Canada or been engaged in destroying the commerce of the United States upon the lakes and rivers that separate the British Provinces from the United States.

Twelfth. All persons who, at the time when they seek to obtain the benefits hereof by taking the oath herein prescribed, are in military, naval, or civil confinement or custody, or under bonds of the civil, military, or naval authorities or agents of the United States as prisoners of war, or persons detained for offenses of any kind, either before or after conviction.

Thirteenth. All persons who have voluntarily participated in said rebellion and the estimated value of whose taxable property is over $20,000.

Fourteenth. All persons who have taken the oath of amnesty as prescribed in the President's proclamation of December 8, A. D. 1863, or an oath of allegiance to the Government of the United States since the date of said proclamation and who have not thenceforward kept and maintained the same inviolate.

Provided, That special application may be made to the President for pardon by any person belonging to the excepted classes, and such clemency will be liberally extended as may be consistent with the facts of the case and the peace and dignity of the United States.

The Secretary of State will establish rules and regulations for administering and recording the said amnesty oath, so as to insure its benefit to the people and guard the Government against fraud.

ANDREW JOHNSON.

B] PROVISIONAL GOVERNMENT IN NORTH CAROLINA

BY THE PRESIDENT OF THE UNITED STATES OF AMERICA.

A PROCLAMATION.

WHEREAS the fourth section of the fourth article of the Constitution of the United States declares that the United States shall guarantee to every State in the Union a republican form of government and shall protect each of them against invasion and domestic violence; and

Whereas the President of the United States is by the Constitution made Commander in Chief of the Army and Navy, as well as chief civil executive officer of the United States, and is bound by solemn oath faithfully to execute the office of President of the United States and to take care that the laws be faithfully executed; and

Whereas the rebellion which has been waged by a portion of the people of the United States against the properly constituted authorities of the Government thereof in the most violent and revolting form, but whose organized and armed forces have now been almost entirely overcome, has in its revolutionary progress deprived the people of the State of North Carolina of all civil government; and

Whereas it becomes necessary and proper to carry out and enforce the obligations of the United States to the people of North Carolina in securing them in the enjoyment of a republican form of government:

Now, therefore, in obedience to the high and solemn duties imposed upon me by the Constitution of the United States and for the purpose of enabling the loyal people of said State to organize a State government whereby justice may be established, domestic tranquillity insured, and loyal citizens protected in all their rights of life, liberty, and property, I, Andrew Johnson, President of the United States and Commander in Chief of the Army and Navy of the United States, do hereby appoint William W. Holden provisional governor of the State of North Carolina, whose duty it shall be, at the earliest practicable period, to prescribe such rules and regulations as may be necessary and proper for convening a convention composed of delegates to be chosen by that portion of the people of said State who are loyal to the United States, and no others, for the purpose of altering or amending the constitution thereof, and with authority to exercise within the limits of said State all the powers necessary and proper to enable such loyal people of the State of North Carolina to restore said State to its constitutional relations to the Federal Government and to present such a republican form of State government as will entitle the State to the guaranty of the United States therefor and its people to protection by the United States against invasion, insurrection, and domestic violence: *Provided,* That in any election that may be hereafter held for choosing delegates to any State convention as aforesaid no person shall be qualified as an elector or shall be eligible as a member of such convention unless he shall have previously taken and subscribed the oath of amnesty as set forth in the President's proclamation of May 29, A. D. 1865, and is a voter qualified as prescribed by the constitution and laws of the State of North Carolina in force immediately before the 20th day of May, A. D. 1861, the date of the so-called ordinance of secession; and the said convention, when convened, or the legislature that may be thereafter assembled, will prescribe the qualification of electors and the eligibility of persons to hold office under the constitution and laws of the State —a power the people of the several States composing the Federal Union have rightfully exercised from the origin of the Government to the present time.

And I do hereby direct—

First. That the military commander of the department and all officers and persons in the military and naval service aid and assist the said provisional governor in carrying into effect this proclamation; and they are enjoined to abstain from in any way hindering, impeding, or discouraging the loyal people from the organization of a State government as herein authorized.

Second. That the Secretary of State proceed to put in force all laws of the United States the administration whereof belongs to the State Department applicable to the geographical limits aforesaid.

Third. That the Secretary of the Treasury proceed to nominate for appointment assessors of taxes and collectors of customs and internal revenue and such other officers of the Treasury Department as are authorized by law and put in execution the revenue laws of the United States within the geographical limits aforesaid. In making appointments the preference shall be given to qualified loyal persons residing within the districts where their respective duties are to be performed; but if suitable residents of the districts shall not be found, then persons residing in other States or districts shall be appointed.

Fourth. That the Postmaster-General proceed to establish post-offices and post routes and put into execution the postal laws of the United States within the said State, giving to loyal residents the preference of appointment; but if suitable residents are not found, then to appoint agents, etc., from other States.

Fifth. That the district judge for the judicial district in which North Carolina is included proceed to hold courts within said State in accordance with the provisions of the act of Congress. The Attorney-General will instruct the proper officers to libel and bring to judgment, confiscation, and sale property subject to confiscation and enforce the administration of justice within said State in all matters within the cognizance and jurisdiction of the Federal courts.

Sixth. That the Secretary of the Navy take possession of all public property belonging to the Navy Department within said geographical limits and put in operation all acts of Congress in relation to naval affairs having application to the said State.

Seventh. That the Secretary of the Interior put in force the laws relating to the Interior Department applicable to the geographical limits aforesaid.

ANDREW JOHNSON.

3] The Newspapers Respond to the President's Plan

During the summer and fall of 1865 it was assumed by most Republicans that President Johnson had intended his North Carolina proclamation of May 29 (and the subsequent ones for the other states) as simply an experimental beginning. They thought that the spirit in which the erstwhile Confederate states reorganized under this plan would serve as a test and indicator for Congress when it met that winter to devise a more detailed and comprehensive settlement. The Democratic party, on the other hand, took the position that the Johnson program was not experimental but final: once its terms were complied with, readmission would—or should—be automatic. Both parties thus supported the President during this period, each for the opposite reason. The following editorials, one Republican and the other Democratic, show how this was possible.*

A] "THE PRESIDENT'S EXPERIMENT"

WE ELSEWHERE call attention to a remarkable speech of General John A. Logan's in Jacksonville, Illinois. The General says that the policy of reconstruction adopted by the Administration is an experiment, and that it is the duty of all good citizens to stand heartily by the President until it is proved a failure.

That is precisely the ground which a true Conservatism now occupies. The Democratic Conventions, in breathless haste to eat their own words of the last few years, vociferate their adherence to the President's policy, and amiable poets of the morning press behold vast hosts of Jacobins marshaling under blood-red banners to oppose it. But as the President is merely trying an experiment, it is rather premature vehemently to support or rancorously to oppose his policy; nor is any country in a very "parlous state" when its Jacobins are the most intelligent, conservative, and substantial part of its population.

The President, acting from the necessity of the case and for the public safety, has set aside the civil officers elected in various States under their Constitutions, and has appointed provisional Governors of his own. He has further prohibited thirteen certain classes of voters under the Constitutions of those States from exercising the right of suffrage, and has authorized a certain number, who are also qualified by the State Constitutions, to vote for members of a Convention. This Convention is to remodel the existing State Constitutions, and to proceed, under them, to elect State officers and representatives in Congress. The Constitutions and, by consequence, the validity of the officers elected, are to be submitted to the Government for approval. In the President's words, the Convention is "to present such a republican form of State government as will entitle the State to the guaranty of the United States therefor, and the people to protection by the United States against invasion, insurrection, and domestic violence."

That is all that the President has done. This is his whole policy thus far. It is, as General Logan says, "an experiment." The President virtually says to certain persons in the States, "See what you can do. Suggest your plan." But he does not say that the plan shall be adopted. He does not promise that the Constitution shall be approved and the elections under it legitimated. The very object he has in view is to try the temper of the class of the population which he selects to prove whether the local political power of the State may be safely confided to them. Nor does he assume finally to decide so vital a question. He

---

* THE NEWPAPERS RESPOND TO THE PRESIDENT'S PLAN: From *Harper's Weekly* (R), IX (September 30, 1865), 610; and the Indianapolis *Sentinel* (D) (October 6, 1865).

leaves it, where it belongs, to the nation itself, to the representatives of the people.

The Democratic resolutions and the amiable chatter about opposition assume that it is not an experiment: that the President has declared the Constitution framed by the voters he has selected, and the elections held under it, to be the law without further process or approval. This is exactly what he has not done, and could have no pretense of authority for doing. If he had done it, if he had said that a certain class of persons in the States named by him should elect a convention, that that convention should frame a Constitution, that the elections should be held under the Constitution, and that thereupon the State should be recognized as having resumed all its relations in the Union, and its Representatives and Senators should be admitted to Congress as a matter of course, then, indeed, he would have laid down a policy, and the whole country would have crackled in opposition to it. . . .

B] "Not an Experiment"

THE ABOLITION press are consoling themselves and their leaders with the idea that the restoration policy of President Johnson is only an experiment. There is no foundation for such a representation of his views. Neither is it in character with his whole course in life. Firmness even to obstinacy has marked his career. And more than this, he has repeatedly stated that his plan of restoration was the policy of his administration, and upon it he would stand or fall. Certainly such expressions give no color to the contrary representations of the Abolition papers. Governor Morton endeavors to show, in his Richmond [Ind.] speech, that the policy of the late and the present Presidents are identical. This view only accumulates the evidence that the President's policy of restoration is fixed, not an experiment liable to change as the listless wind. There is no doubt that if Mr. Lincoln had lived, that his terms of amnesty to the Southern people would have been far more liberal than any his successor has yet proposed. Even Jeff. Davis and the leaders of the rebellion who are now incarcerated, would have been permitted to escape the country. "With malice toward none and charity for all," was the spirit which would have animated Mr. Lincoln in his treatment of the rebellion, after its military power had been crushed and the whole people subjugated. If, then, President Johnson intends to follow in the footsteps of his predecessor, as Governor Morton insists that he does, there is nothing whatever upon which to base the statement that his plan of restoration is only an experiment. Upon all questions of political economy President Johnson avows himself to be as thorough a Democrat now as he ever was. Slavery is no longer an issue, and Governor Morton declares that all fear of secession or resistance to the national authority is forever extinguished, hence there is no reason why the President should not guide the policy of his administration by the old Democratic landmarks. This he avows he intends to do; and the declaration is having a marked effect all over the country. Everywhere we find men who left the Democratic party on account of their opposition to African slavery, returning to the old banner; and conservative Republicans are rallying under the same standard. President Johnson looks to this class for his support and not to the men who, with honeyed words endorse his administration, but still adhere to the political organization which is guided by radical Abolitionists. In language unmistakable, the President declares that this is a white man's Government and such he intends it shall be, so far as his influence can maintain it. And this is the growing sentiment of the country. . . . Never was there a greater delusion than that President Johnson looks upon his restoration policy as an experiment.

4] South Carolina Passes a Black Code

It has been said in defense of the Southern states' Black Codes of 1865–66 that they were the logical response to certain inescapable social facts—that emancipation had created a problem of such massive dimensions as to require special (and thus by definition discriminatory) laws for dealing with it. Yet it might also be pointed out that a number of responsible Southerners foresaw immediately what effects the codes would have on Northern opinion and denounced them as the "sheerest folly."

A better defense of the states' behavior would be that no official or unofficial indication was ever conveyed to them, while the codes were being prepared, that such action might be displeasing to the administration. Indeed, it does not appear that the administration cared much one way or the other. For example, details of the South Carolina code—excerpts of which are given below—were known in some form for at least two months before its final enactment in December, 1865. The state convention, meeting in September, had ordered a committee to draw up the proposed laws, copies of which were duly submitted to President Johnson in October. So far as is known, they evoked no response from him.*

AN ACT PRELIMINARY TO THE LEGISLATION INDUCED BY THE
EMANCIPATION OF SLAVES

. . . .

III. All free negroes, mulattoes and mestizoes, all freedmen and freedwomen; and all descendants through either sex of any of these persons, shall be known as *persons of color,* except that every such descendant, who may have of Caucasian blood seven-eighths or more shall be deemed a white person.

IV. The Statutes and regulations concerning slaves are now inapplicable to persons of color; and although such persons are not entitled to social or political equality with white persons, they shall have the right to acquire, own and dispose of property; to make contracts; to enjoy the fruits of their labor; to sue and be sued; and to receive protection under the law in their persons and property.

V. All rights and remedies respecting persons or property, and all duties and liabilities under laws, civil and criminal, which apply to white persons, are

---

* SOUTH CAROLINA PASSES A BLACK CODE: From *Statutes at Large of South Carolina,* XIII (Columbia, S.C., 1875), 245–85, *passim.*

extended to persons of color, subject to the modifications made by this Act and the other Acts hereinbefore mentioned. . . .

An Act to Amend the Criminal Law

· · · · · · · · · · · · · · · · · · ·

I. Either of the crimes specified in this first Section shall be felony without benefit of clergy, to wit: For a person of color to commit any wilful homicide unless in self-defense; for a person of color to commit an assault upon a white woman with manifest intent to ravish her; for a person of color to have sexual intercourse with a white woman by personating her husband; for any person to raise an insurrection or rebellion in this State; for any person to furnish arms or ammunition to other persons who are in a state of actual insurrection or rebellion, or permit them to resort to his house for advancement of their evil purpose; for any person to administer, or cause to be taken by any other person, any poison, chloroform, soporific or other destructive thing, or to shoot at, stab, cut or wound any other person, or by any means whatsoever to cause bodily injury to any other person, whereby, in any of these cases, a bodily injury dangerous to the life of any other person is caused. . . .

· · · · · · · · · · · · · · · · · · ·

XIII. Persons of color constitute no part of the militia of the State, and no one of them shall, without permission in writing from the District Judge or Magistrate, be allowed to keep a fire arm, sword, or other military weapon; except that one of them, who is the owner of a farm, may keep a shot gun or rifle, such as is ordinarily used in hunting, but not a pistol, musket, or other fire arm or weapon appropriate for purposes of war. The District Judge or a Magistrate may give an order, under which any weapon unlawfully kept may be seized and sold, the proceeds of sale to go into the District Court fund. The possession of a weapon in violation of this Act shall be a misdemeanor, which shall be tried before a District Court or a Magistrate; and, in case of conviction, shall be punished by a fine equal to twice the value of the weapon so unlawfully kept; and if that be not immediately paid, by corporal punishment.

XIV. It shall not be lawful for a person of color to be the owner, in whole or in part, of any distillery where spirituous liquors of any kind are made, or of any establishment where spirituous liquors of any kind are sold by retail; nor for a person of color to be engaged in distilling any spirituous liquors, or in retailing the same in a shop or elsewhere. A person of color who shall do anything contrary to the prohibitions herein contained shall be guilty of a misdemeanor, and, upon conviction, may be punished by fine or corporal punishment and hard labor, as to the District Judge or Magistrate before whom he may be tried, shall seem meet. . . .

· · · · · · · · · · · · · · · · · · ·

XXII. No person of color shall migrate into and reside in this State, unless, within twenty days after his arrival within the same, he shall enter into a bond with two freeholders as sureties, to be approved by the Judge of the District Court or a Magistrate, in a penalty of one thousand dollars, conditioned for his good behavior, and for his support, if he should become unable to support himself. And in case any such person shall fail to execute the bond as aforesaid, the District Judge or any Magistrate is hereby authorized and required, upon complaint and due proof thereof, to issue his warrant commanding such person of color to leave the State within ten days thereafter. And if any such person, so ordered to leave the State, shall not leave the State within the time prescribed in such warrant, he shall, upon conviction thereof, be liable to such corporal punishment as the Court, in its discretion, shall think fit to order. And if any such person so convicted and punished shall still remain within the State more than fifteen days after the punishment shall have been inflicted, or having left the State, shall return to the same, he shall, upon conviction thereof, be transported beyond the limits of this State for life, or be kept to hard labor, with occasional solitary confinement, for a period not exceeding five years. And if any person of color who shall have been convicted of any infamous offense in any other state or country, shall come or be brought into this State, such person of color, on conviction thereof, shall be transported beyond the limits of this State for life, or be kept to hard labor, with occasional solitary confinement, for any period not exceeding fifteen years. . . .

.   .   .   .

XXVII. Whenever, under any law, sentence imposing a fine is passed, if the fine and costs be not immediately paid, there shall be detention of the convict, and substitution of other punishment. If the offense should not involve the *crimen falsi*,[1] and be infamous, the substitution shall be, in the case of a white person, imprisonment for a time proportioned to the fine, at the rate of one day for each dollar; and in the case of a person of color, enforced labor without unnecessary pain or restraint, for a time proportioned to the fine, at the rate of one day for each dollar. But if the offense should be infamous, there shall be substituted for a fine, for imprisonment, or for both, hard labor, corporal punishment, solitary confinement, and confinement in tread-mill or stocks, one or more, at the discretion of the Judge of the Superior Court, the District Judge, or the Magistrate who pronounces the sentence. In this Act, and in respect to all crimes and misdemeanors, the term servant shall be understood to embrace an apprentice as well as a servant under contract. . . .

.   .   .   .

XXIX. Upon view of a misdemeanor committed by a person of color, or by a white person toward a person of color, a Magistrate may arrest the offender, and, according to the nature of the case, punish the offender summarily, or bind him in recognizance, with sufficient sureties, to appear at the next monthly sitting of the District Court, or commit him for trial before the District Court.

XXX. Upon view of a misdemeanor committed by a person of color, any person present may arrest the offender and take him before a Magistrate, to be dealt with as the case may require. . . .

1 *crimen falsi*: the crime of falsifying.

An Act to Establish and Regulate the Domestic Relations
of Persons of Color, and to Amend the Law in Relation
to Paupers and Vagrancy.

. . . .

I. The relation of husband and wife amongst persons of color is established.

II. Those who now live as such are declared to be husband and wife.

III. In case of one man having two or more reputed wives, or one woman two or more reputed husbands, the man shall, by the first day of April next, select one of his reputed wives, or the woman one of her reputed husbands; and the ceremony of marriage between this man or woman, and the person so selected, shall be performed.

IV. Every colored child, heretofore born, is declared to be the legitimate child of his mother, and also of his colored father, if he is acknowledged by such a father.

V. Persons of color desirous hereafter to become husband and wife, should have the contract of marriage duly solemnized.

VI. A clergyman, the District Judge, a Magistrate, or any judicial officer, may solemnize marriages.

VII. Cohabitation, with reputation or recognition of the parties, shall be evidence of marriage in cases criminal and civil.

VIII. One who is a pauper or a charge to the public shall not be competent to contract marriage. Marriage between a white person and a person of color shall be illegal and void.

IX. The marriage of an apprentice shall not, without the consent of the master, be lawful.

X. A husband shall not, for any cause, abandon or turn away his wife, nor a wife her husband. Either of them that abandons or turns away the other may be prosecuted for a misdemeanor. . . .

. . . .

XV. A child, over the age of two years, born of a colored parent, may be bound by the father, if he be living in the District, or in case of his death or absence from the District, by the mother, as an apprentice to any respectable white or colored person who is competent to make a contract; a male until he shall attain the age of twenty-one years, and a female until she shall attain the age of eighteen years.

XVI. Illegitimate children, within the ages above specified, may be bound by the mother.

XVII. Colored children, between the ages mentioned, who have neither father nor mother living in the District in which they are found, or whose parents are paupers, or unable to afford to them maintenance, or whose parents are not teaching them habits of industry and honesty, or are persons of notoriously bad character, or are vagrants, or have been, either of them, convicted of an infamous offense, may be bound as apprentices by the District Judge, or one of the Magistrates, for the aforesaid term.

XVIII. Males of the age of twelve years, and females of the age of ten years, shall sign the indenture of apprenticeship, and be bound thereby.

XIX. When the apprentice is under these ages, and in all cases of compulsory apprenticeship, where the infant refuses assent, his signature shall not be necessary to the validity of the apprenticeship. The master's obligation of apprenticeship, in all cases of compulsory apprenticeship, and cases where the father or mother does not bind a child, shall be executed in the presence of the District Judge, or one of the Magistrates, certified by him, and filed in the office of the clerk of the District Court. . . .

.   .   .   .

XXII. The master or mistress shall teach the apprentice the business of husbandry, or some other useful trade or business, which shall be specified in the instrument of apprenticeship; shall furnish him wholesome food and suitable clothing; teach him habits of industry, honesty and morality; govern and treat him with humanity; and if there be a school within a convenient distance, in which colored children are taught, shall send him to school at least six weeks in every year of his apprenticeship, after he shall be of the age of ten years. *Provided,* That the teacher of such school shall have the license of the District Judge to establish the same.

XXIII. The master shall have authority to inflict moderate chastisement and impose reasonable restraint upon his apprentice, and to recapture him if he depart from his service. . . .

.   .   .   .

XXXV. All persons of color who make contracts for service or labor, shall be known as servants, and those with whom they contract, shall be known as masters.

XXXVI. Contracts between masters and servants, for one month or more, shall be in writing, be attested by one white witness, and be approved by the Judge of the District Court, or by a Magistrate.

XXXVII. The period of service shall be expressed in the contract; but if it be not expressed, it shall be until the twenty-fifth day of December next after the commencement of the service.

XXXVIII. If the rate of wages be not stipulated by the parties to the contract, it shall be fixed by the District Judge, or a Magistrate, on application by one of the parties, and notice to the other.

XXXIX. A person of color, who has no parent living in the District, and is ten years of age, and is not an apprentice, may make a valid contract for labor or service for one year of less.

XL. Contracts between masters and servants may be set aside for fraud or unfairness, notwithstanding they have been approved.

XLI. Written contracts between masters and servants shall be presented for approval within twenty days after their execution.

XLII. Contracts for one month or more shall not be binding on the servant, unless they are in writing, and have been presented for approval within the time aforesaid.

XLIII. For any neglect of the duty to make a contract as herein directed, or the evasion of that duty by the repeated employment of the same persons for periods less than one month, the party offending shall be guilty of a misdemeanor, and be liable, on conviction, to pay a sum not exceeding fifty dollars, and not less than five dollars, for each person so employed. No written contract shall be required when the servant voluntarily receives no remuneration except food and clothing. . . .

. . . .

LII. For any acts or things herein declared to be causes for the discharge of a servant, or for any breach of contract or duty by him, instead of discharging the servant, the master may complain to the District Judge or one of the Magistrates, who shall have power, on being satisfied of the misconduct complained of, to inflict, or cause to be inflicted, on the servant, suitable corporal punishment, or impose upon him such pecuniary fine as may be thought fit, and immediately remand him to his work; which fine shall be deducted from his wages, if not otherwise paid. . . .

. . . .

LXXII. No person of color shall pursue or practice the art, trade or business of an artisan, mechanic or shopkeeper, or any other trade, employment or business (besides that of husbandry, or that of a servant under a contract for service or labor,) on his own account and for his own benefit, or in partnership with a white person, or as agent or servant of any person, until he shall have obtained a license therefor from the Judge of the District Court; which license shall be good for one year only. This license the Judge may grant upon petition of the applicant, and upon being satisfied of his skill and fitness, and of his good moral character, and upon payment, by the applicant, to the Clerk of the District Court, of one hundred dollars, if a shopkeeper or pedlar, to be paid annually, and ten dollars, if a mechanic, artisan, or to engage in any other trade, also to be paid annually. *Provided, however,* That upon complaint being made and proved to the District Judge of an abuse of such license, he shall revoke the same: *And provided, also,* That no person of color shall practice any mechanical art or trade unless he shows that he has served an apprenticeship in such trade or art, or is now practicing such trade or art.

LXXIII. For violation of the prohibition contained in the Section next preceding, the offender, upon conviction thereof before the Judge of the District Court, shall pay, for each offense, a fine to double the amount of such license; one half whereof shall go to the informer, who shall be a competent witness. . . .

. . . .

XCVI. All persons who have not some fixed and known place of abode, and some lawful and reputable employment; those who have not some visible and known means of a fair, honest and reputable livelihood; all common prostitutes; those who are found wandering from place to place, vending, bartering or peddling any articles or commodities, without a license from the District Judge, or other proper authority; all common gamblers; persons who lead idle or disorderly lives, or keep or frequent disorderly or disreputable houses or places; those who, not having sufficient means of support, are able to work and do not work; those who (whether or not they own lands, or are lessees or mechanics,) do not provide a reasonable and proper maintenance for themselves and families; those who are engaged in representing, publicly or privately, for fee or reward, without license, any tragedy, interlude, comedy, farce, play or other similar entertainment, exhibition of the circus, sleight-of-hand, wax works, or the like; those who, for private gain, without license, give any concert or musical entertainment, of any description; fortune-tellers; sturdy beggars; common drunkards; those who hunt game of any description, or fish on the land of others, or frequent the premises, contrary to the will of the occupants, shall be deemed vagrants, and be liable to the punishments hereinafter prescribed. . . .

. . . .

XCVIII. The defendant, if sentenced to hard labor after conviction, may, by order of the District Judge or Magistrate, before whom he was convicted, be hired for such wages as can be obtained for his services, to any owner or lessee of a farm, for the term of hard labor to which he was sentenced, or be hired for the same labor on the streets, public roads or public buildings. The person receiving such vagrant shall have all the rights and remedies for enforcing good conduct and diligence at labor that are herein provided in the case of master and servant. . . .

5] Horace Greeley's Irritation Mounts

Throughout most of the summer of 1865 Horace Greeley, editor of the New York *Tribune*, had bubbled with optimism and general good will. He believed in moderate treatment for ex-rebels, strongly objecting to any punishment for Jefferson Davis; he was sure the President's "experiment" was wise and humane; and he hoped, amid the harmonious feeling which this should surely create everywhere, for the cheerful enactment of Negro suffrage. By mid-November, however, Greeley's increasing disappointment—not with Johnson, whom he warmly supported, but with the South—could no longer be concealed. Amid mounting irritation over unrepentant Southern behavior, Greeley and all other Republican editors had begun taking for granted that the Southern members-elect should not be entered on the clerk's roll call at the opening of Congress. Even Henry J. Raymond of the *Times*—who would continue supporting the President for nearly another year—said that the Southerners had better "keep the back seats in the lobby until they are sent for." *

We can best understand the success of the experiment of Reconstruction by looking at the results in many of the Southern States. It is six months since the President threw open the doors of the Union to the defeated Rebels, and invited all who were willing to become good citizens and obedient to the laws to enter and resume their seats at the old family board. History does not present an example of similar magnanimity. Men speak of the merciful revolution of

---

* **HORACE GREELEY'S IRRITATION MOUNTS**: Horace Greeley, "First Fruits of Reconstruction." From the New York *Tribune* (November 15, 1865).

William III, forgetting that William sent Fenwick to the scaffold, and bestowed the choicest estates of the Jacobites upon his supporters and favorites. We have punished no one for treason. Jefferson Davis was arrested for conspiring to commit murder, and, as that charge has never been abandoned, we presume it is as a "murderer" he is now at Fortress Monroe. Clement C. Clay was imprisoned on the same charge. The men executed were executed as murderers. Wirz died as one guilty of murder. All the confiscated lands have not quite been restored, but the pardon that embraces Tredgar Anderson will soon envelop in its consoling folds every remaining Rebel.

Those who have criticised that policy certainly admit that the President's motives were kind and charitable. Perhaps we can no better illustrate that kindness than by remembering that to gratify the South he was willing to postpone justice to the negro. Those who know how deeply and earnestly the honest Northern heart felt on this subject will appreciate the sacrifice that the President was willing to make to propitiate the South. If any statesman commanded their gratitude, their support, their undeviating kindness, it was the President. They made protestations. They were the President's most sincere friends. They would show him the true devotion of a Southern heart. He was their bulwark against Radicalism. He would stand between them and "Abolition ghouls." They, on their part, would be his most devoted supporters. They would take up arms for him as they took up arms against him, and under the fostering care of Andrew Johnson, poor white, but now President of all those States, they would assist in building up a Republic that would rival in imperial grandeur the proudest days of the Commonwealth of Rome.

Well, we have tried them, and what? Let us go down to Louisiana. Here is a State rich in resources—her great metropolis overflowing with the good things that commerce can bring. This peace gave its people, and how have they answered it. In the first place, we have a Governor like Wells, an accident of the war, who took advantage of the peace to hold his place by pandering to the worst Rebel feelings. We find the negro downtrodden. Men are imprisoned for speaking their opinions about Negro Suffrage. The worst features of the slave laws are revived, and a large party is, with difficulty, dissuaded—dissuaded, let us own it—by such men as Beauregard and Hays from going to Mexico and bringing the runaway Rebel Allen back as Governor. The good results of former administrations are wiped away in an instant, and the Rebels, headed by military popinjays like Fullerton, are rapidly rushing their State back to the terror and gloom of the ante-Rebellion period. If we go into Mississippi, we find not only a refusal to allow the negroes the rights of jurors, but even the rights of witnesses. In South Carolina, the Rebels almost force Wade Hampton in to the Gubernatorial chair, merely because such action would be a defiance to the President. As for the Rebel debt, she will pay her share, this rebellious Carolina, dollar for dollar. As for the Constitutional Amendment, it comes by compulsion. South Carolina will vote for it now, that she may kick open the doors of Congress and stand before the Speaker's chair with six electoral votes in her hand—six votes, to our shame be it spoken, that represent a power as great as Connecticut with eighty thousand white men less. Then we come to North Carolina, and find Jonathan Worth elected Governor because Holden was the choice of the President. Not one word about the Constitutional Amendment. As with these States it is everywhere throughout the South. What one State has come back frankly, and accepted all the issues of the war, even the issues of the President? For the temporary purpose of an argument, we will lay aside Manhood Suffrage. What Southern State has accepted all the Presidential propositions? Not one; and for this reason only that the Rebels will not concede one jot or tittle toward reconstructing a Union that does not eternalize Slavery and strengthen the power of the slaveholders. They know full well that if we leave the negro in their hands a freed man, and allow them to group around him laws as degrading as those of South Carolina, they will have little trouble in perpetuating a system more degrading than Slavery—in this, that it gives the master power over the negro, and at the same time releases him from any pecuniary or personal responsibility.

Let us emphasize these two points. The Rebels play for a winning game. "Let us," they say, "kick open the doors of Congress, and what then? We have our apportionment increased; for, the negro being free, he must be counted man for man. At home, we have negro labor at slave prices, and no responsibility. We may turn the negro out to the commons when he is seventy, just as we turn out horses. Our laws compel him to work for us—we may do as we please with him. The Government has released us from our obligation to the negro, and placed an obligation upon him. Altogether, we have made a jolly exchange and trumped the Yankees nicely in their own game." These gentlemen of the South mean to win. They meant it in 1861 when they opened fire on Sumter. They meant it in 1865 when they sent a bullet through the brain of Abraham Lincoln. They mean it now. The moment we remove the iron hand from the Rebels' throats they will rise and attempt the mastery. If South Carolina adopts the amendment, she does it under compulsion—the compulsion of a dispatch from Washington. South Carolina can well afford to adopt the amendment when she is permitted to reenact the slave-code. The power that compels this action on her part is the power that could have compelled her to grant Manhood Suffrage six months ago. The danger of our reconstruction is that we trifle with our own power—that, instead of waiting until the prodigal really comes home, we send the fatted calf to him. We do not give the true men of the South a chance. If with all our power we permit such men as Durant in Louisiana, Hamilton of Texas, and even the conservative Holden in North Carolina, to be overslaughed and beaten by returned Rebels, how can we expect Durants and Hamiltons and Holdens to rise up in the South? When Union men find they can only rise by eating Rebel dirt, we shall have a crop of Wells politicians over the South living on this unsavory diet. Therefore, we not only break faith with the negro, but with the true Union men— with those who went into the caves with Andrew Johnson, and with him suffered for their principles. The first fruits of reconstruction promise a most deplorable harvest, and the sooner we gather the tares, plow the ground again, and sow new seed, the better.

6] Governor Andrew Invokes "The Just Discretion of the Nation"

> John Andrew of Massachusetts had served his state with great distinction as war governor, and by the time he retired from office on January 5, 1866, after five successive terms, he had acquired considerable influence and respect not only in Massachusetts but throughout the country. His valedictory address, delivered on that occasion, was Andrew's version of what a wise and statesmanlike policy on reconstruction should consist of. In no state paper of the period is this subject considered with the subtlety and completeness that it is here. It should, of course, be remembered that these words were spoken while it was still possible to think of President Johnson's policy as an "experiment." *

THE STATES in rebellion tried, under the lead of their new Confederacy, to conquer the Union, but in the attempt they were themselves conquered.

They did not revert by their rebellion, nor by our conquest, into "Territories." They did not commit suicide. But they rebelled, they went to war; and they were *conquered*. . . .

The position of the rebel States is fixed by the Constitution, and by the laws, or rights, of war. If they had conquered the Union, they might have become independent, or whatever else it might have been stipulated they should become, by the terms of an ultimate treaty of peace. But being conquered, they failed in becoming independent, and they failed in accomplishing anything but their own conquest. They were still States,—though belligerents conquered. But they had lost their loyal organization as States, lost their present possession of their political and representative power in the Union. Under the Constitution they have no means nor power of their own to regain it. But the exigency is provided for by that clause in the Federal Constitution in which the Federal Government guarantees a republican form of government to every State. The regular and formal method would be, therefore, for the National Government to provide specifically for their re-organization.

The right and duty, however, of the General Government, under the circumstances of their present case, is not the single one of re-organizing these disorganized States. The war imposed rights and duties, peculiar to itself, and to the relations and the results of War. The first duty of the Nation is to regain its own *power*. It has already made a great advance in the direction of its power.

If ours were a despotic government, it might even now be thought that it had already accomplished the re-establishment of its power as a government. But, ours being a republican and a popular government, it cannot be affirmed, that the proper power of the government is restored, until a peaceful, loyal and

---

* GOVERNOR ANDREW INVOKES "THE JUST DISCRETION OF THE NATION": "Valedictory Address of His Excellency John A. Andrew." From Massachusetts *Governors' Speeches and Addresses, 1864–66* (Boston, 1866), II, 1–42, *passim*.

faithful state of mind gains a sufficient ascendancy in the rebel and belligerent States, to enable the Union and loyal citizens everywhere to repose alike on the purpose and the ability of their people, in point of numbers and capacity, to assert, maintain and conduct State Governments, republican in form, loyal in sentiment and character, with safety to themselves and to the national whole. If the people, or too large a portion of the people, of a given rebel State, are not willing and able to do this, then the state of war still exists, or at least, a condition consequent upon and incidental thereto exists, which only the exercise on our part of belligerent rights, or some of their incidents, can meet or can cure. The rights of war must continue until the objects of the war have been accomplished, and the nation recognizes the return of a state of peace. It is absolutely necessary then for the Union Government to prescribe some reasonable test of loyalty to the people of the States in rebellion. It is necessary to require of them conformity to those arrangements which the war has rendered, or proved to be, necessary to the public peace, and necessary as securities for the future. As the conquering party, the National Government has the right to govern these belligerent States meanwhile, at its own wise and conscientious discretion, subject: 1st. To the demands of natural justice, humanity and the usages of civilized nations. 2d. To its duty under the Constitution, to guarantee Republican governments to the States.

But there is no arbiter, save the people of the United States, between the Government of the Union and those States. Therefore the precise things to be done, the precise way to do them, the precise steps to be taken, their order, progress and direction, are all within the discretion of the National Government, in the exercise, both of its belligerent, and its more strictly constitutional, functions,—exercising them according to its own wise, prudent and just discretion. Its duty is not only to restore those States, but also to make sure of a lasting peace, of its own ultimate safety, and the permanent establishment of the rights of all its subjects. To this end, I venture the opinion that the Government of the United States ought to require the people of those States to reform their Constitutions,—

1. Guaranteeing to the people of color, now the wards of the Nation, their civil rights as men and women, on an equality with the white population, by amendments, irrepealable in terms.

2. Regulating the elective franchise according to certain laws of universal application, and not by rules merely arbitrary, capricious and personal.

3. Annulling the ordinances of Secession.

4. Disaffirming the Rebel Debt, and

5. To ratify the anti-slavery amendment of the United States Constitution by their legislatures.

And I would have all these questions, save the fifth—the disposition of which is regulated by the Federal Constitution—put to the vote of the *People* themselves. We should neither be satisfied with the action of the conventions which have been held, nor with what is termed the "loyal vote." We want the *popular* vote. And the rebel vote is better than the loyal vote, if on the right side. If it is not on the right side, then I fear those States are incapable at present of re-organization; the proper power of the Union Government is not restored; the people of those States are not yet prepared to assume their original functions with safety to the Union; and the state of war still exists; for they are contumacious and disobedient to the just demands of the Union, disowning the just conditions precedent to re-organization.

We are desirous of their re-organization, and to end the use of the war power. But I am confident we cannot re-organize political society with any proper security: 1. Unless we let in the *people* to a co-operation, and not merely an arbitrarily selected portion of them. 2. Unless we give those who are, by their intelligence and character, the natural leaders of the people, and who surely will lead them by-and-by, an opportunity to lead them now.

I am aware that it has been a favorite dogma in many quarters, *"No Rebel Voters."* But—it is impossible in certain States to have *any* voting by white men, if only "loyal men"—*i.e.,* those who continued so, during the rebellion, are permitted to vote. . . . Although there is some reason for assuming that the less conspicuous and less wealthy classes of men had less to do than their more towering neighbors in conducting the States into the Rebellion and through it—still I do not imagine that either wealth or conspicuous position, which are only the accidents of men, or at most, only external incidents, affect the substance of their characters. I think the poorer and less significant men who voted, or fought, for "Southern Independence" had quite as little love for "the Yankees," quite as much prejudice against "the Abolitionists," quite as much contempt for the colored man, and quite as much disloyalty at heart, as their more powerful neighbors.

The true question is, now, not of past disloyalty, but of present loyal purpose. We need not try to disguise the fact, that we have passed through a *great popular revolution*. Everybody in the Rebel States was disloyal, with exceptions too few and too far between to comprise a loyal force, sufficient to constitute the State, even now that the armies of the Rebellion are overthrown. Do not let us deceive ourselves. The truth is, the public opinion of the white race in the South was in favor of the rebellion. The colored people sympathized with the Union cause. To the extent of their intelligence, they understood that the success of the South meant their continued slavery; that an easy success of the North meant leaving slavery just where we found it; that the *War* meant, if it lasted long enough—their emancipation. The whites went to war and supported the war, because they hoped to succeed in it; since they wanted, or thought they wanted, separation from the Union, or "Southern Independence." There were, then, three great interests—there were the Southern whites, who as a body, wished for what they called "Southern Independence"; the Southern blacks, who desired emancipation; the people of the "loyal States" who desired to maintain the constitutional rights and the territorial integrity of the Nation. Some of us in the North had a strong hope, which by the favor of God has not been disappointed, out of our defence of the Union to accomplish the deliverance of our fellow-men in bondage. But the *"loyal" idea* included emancipation, not for its own sake, but for the sake of the Union—if the Union could be saved, or served, by it. There were many men in the South—besides those known as loyal—who did not like to incur the responsibility of war against the Union; or who did not think the opportune moment had arrived to fight "the North"; or in whose hearts there was "a divided allegiance." But, they were not the positive men. They were, with very few exceptions, not the leading minds, the courageous men, the impressive and powerful characters,—they were not the young and active men. And when the decisive hour came, they went to the wall. No matter what they thought, or how they felt, about it; they could not stand or they would not stand—certainly they did not stand, against the storm. The Revolution either converted them, or swept them off their feet. Their own sons volunteered. They became involved in all the work and in all the consequences of the war. The Southern people—as a people—fought, toiled, endured, and persevered, with a courage, a unanimity and a persistency, not outdone by any people in any Revolution. . . .

All honor to the loyal few! But I do not regard the distinction between loyal and disloyal persons of the white race, residing in the South, during the rebellion, as being, for present purposes, a practical distinction. It is even doubtful whether the comparatively loyal few (with certain prominent and honorable exceptions), can be well discriminated from the disloyal mass. . . .

When the day arrives, which must surely come, when an amnesty, substantially universal, shall be proclaimed, the leading minds of the South, who by temporary policy and artificial rules had been, for the while, disfranchised, will resume their influence and their sway. The capacity of leadership is a gift, not a device. They whose courage, talents, and will entitle them to lead, will lead. . . . If it is asked, in reply, "What can they do?" and "What can come of their discontent?" I answer, that while I do not know just what they can do, nor what may come of it, neither do I know what they may not attempt, nor what they may not accomplish. I only know that we ought to demand, and to secure, the co-operation of the strongest and ablest minds and the natural leaders of opinion in the South. If we cannot gain their support of the just measures needful for the work of safe re-organization, re-organization will be delusive and full of danger.

Why not try them? They are the most hopeful subjects to deal with, in the very nature of the case. They have the brain and the experience and the education to enable them to understand the exigencies of the present situation. They have the courage, as well as the skill, to lead the people in the direction their judgments point, in spite of their own and the popular prejudice. Weaker men, those of less experience, who have less hold on the public confidence, are comparatively powerless. Is it consistent with reason and our knowledge of human nature, to believe the masses of Southern men able to face about, to turn their backs on those they have trusted and followed, and to adopt the lead of those who have no magnetic hold on their hearts or minds? Re-organization in the South demands the aid of men of great moral courage, who can renounce their own past opinions, and do it boldly; who can comprehend what the work is, and what are the logical consequences of the new situation; men who have interests urging them to rise to the height of the occasion. They are not the strong men from whom weak, vacillating counsels come; nor are they the great men from whom come counsels born of prejudices and follies, having their root in an institution they know to be dead, and buried beyond the hope of resurrection.

Has it never occurred to us all, that we are now proposing the most wonderful and unprecedented of human transactions? The conquering government, at the close of a great war, is about restoring to the conquered rebels not only their local governments in the States, but their representative share in the general government of the country! They are, in their States, to govern themselves as they did before the rebellion. The conquered rebels are, in the Union, to help govern and control the conquering loyalists!! These being the privileges which they are to enjoy, when re-organization becomes complete, I declare that I know not any safeguard, precaution, or act of prudence, which wise statesmanship might not recognize to be reasonable and just. If we have no right to demand guarantees for the future; if we have no right to insist upon significant acts of loyal submission from the rebel leaders themselves; if we have no right to demand the positive, popular vote in favor of the guarantees we need; if we may not stipulate for the recognition of the just rights of the slaves, whom, in the act of suppressing the rebellion, we converted from slaves into freemen, then I declare that we had no right to emancipate the slaves, nor to suppress the rebellion.

It may be asked: Why not demand the suffrage for colored men, in season for their vote in the business of re-organization? My answer is—I assume that the colored men are in favor of those measures which the Union needs to have adopted. But it would be idle to re-organize those States by the colored vote. If the popular vote of the white race is not to be had in favor of the guarantees justly required, then I am in favor of holding on—just where we now are. I am not in favor of a surrender of the present rights of the Union to a struggle between a white minority aided by the freedmen on the one hand, against a majority of the white race on the other. I would not consent, having rescued those States by arms from secession and rebellion, to turn them over to anarchy and chaos. I have, however, no doubt—none whatever—of our *right* to stipulate for colored suffrage. The question is one of statesmanship, not a question of constitutional limitation.

If it is urged that the suffrage question is one peculiarly for the States, I reply: so also that of the abolition of slavery ordinarily would have been. But we are not now deciding what a loyal State, acting in its constitutional sphere, and in its normal relations to the Union, may do; but what a rebel, belligerent, conquered State must do, in order to be re-organized and to get back into those relations. And in deciding this, I must repeat that we are to be governed only by Justice, Humanity, the Public Safety, and our duty to re-organize those conquered, belligerent States, as we can and when we can, consistently therewith.

But, What of the policy of the President? I am not able to consider his future policy. It is undisclosed. He seems to me to have left to Congress alone the questions controlling the conditions on which the rebel States shall resume their representative power in the Federal Government. It was not incumbent on the President to do otherwise. He naturally leaves the duty of theoretical reasoning to those whose responsibility it is to reach the just practical conclusion. Thus far the President has simply used, according to his proper discretion, the power of commander-in-chief. . . . If he has assisted the people to re-organize their legislatures, and to re-establish the machinery of local State government; though his method may be less regular than if an act of Congress had prescribed it, still, it has permitted the people to feel their way back into the works and ways of loyalty, to exhibit their temper of mind, and to "show their hands." Was it not better for the cause of free government, of civil liberty, to incur the risk of error in that direction, than of error in the opposite one? It has proved that the national government is not drunk with power; that its four years' exercise of the dangerous rights of war has not affected its brain. . . .

The proceedings already had, are only certain acts in the great drama of Re-organization. They do not go for nothing; they were not unnecessary; nor do I approach them with criticism. But they are not the whole drama. Other acts are required for its completion. What they shall be, depends in part on the wisdom of Congress to determine.

The doctrine of the President that—in the steps preliminary to re-organizing a State which is not, and has not been theoretically cut off from the Union— he must recognize its own organic law, antecedent to the rebellion, need not be contested. I adhere, quite as strictly as he, to the logical consequences of that doctrine. . . .

But, yet, it may be, at the same time, needful and proper, in the sense of wise statesmanship, to require of them the amplification of certain privileges, the recognition of certain rights, the establishment of certain institutions, the re-distribution even of political power—to be by them accorded and executed through constitutional amendments, or otherwise—as elements of acceptable re-organization; and as necessary to the re-adjustment of political society in harmony with the new relations, and the new basis of universal freedom, re- sulting from the Rebellion itself. If these things are found to be required by wise statesmanship, then the right to exact them, as conditions of restoring those States to the enjoyment of their normal functions, is to be found, just where the Nation found the right to crush the Rebellion and the incidental right of emancipating Slaves. . . .

If the measures I have attempted to delineate are found to be impracticable, then Congress has still the right to refuse to the Rebel States re-admission to the enjoyment of their representative power, until amendments to the *Federal Constitution* shall have been obtained adequate to the exigency. Nor can the people of the rebel States object to the delay. They voluntarily withdrew from Congress; they themselves elected the attitude of disunion. They broke the agreements of the constitution: not we. They chose their own time, oppor- tunity and occasion to make war on the Nation, and to repudiate the Union. They certainly cannot now dictate to us the time nor the terms. Again, I re- peat, the just discretion of the nation—exercised in good faith towards all— must govern. . . .

7] Senator Fessenden Supports the Freedmen's Bureau Bill and Indirectly Addresses the President

These remarks, delivered in the Senate by William Pitt Fessenden of Maine on January 23, 1866, derive their interest from the role which Fessenden was playing at this period in trying to maintain harmony between President John- son and the Republican party in Congress. Fessenden was probably the most

influential member of the Senate, and he represented, along with Senators
Trumbull of Illinois and Sherman of Ohio, the forces of moderation in the
party. Those forces were thus given voice every time Fessenden spoke—and
the Senator chose his occasions carefully. Here, he is both explaining his
support of the pending Freedmen's Bureau Bill and denouncing the Democrats for presuming to use President Johnson for their own purposes. But
beneath this he is doing something else. Fessenden is letting the President
know, without addressing him directly, that if the latter's purposes are what
the party leaders hope and assume them to be, then he may have their support as long, and as fully, as he desires.*

. . . .

Now, sir, I will trust the Commissioner who stands at the head of this bureau
for his own calculations. I will trust him because I know his ability and I
know his integrity. He has examined this matter thoroughly and studied it well,
and knows what he wishes to accomplish, and unless I see something upon
the face of them that is in my judgment incorrect and wrong, I am willing
to take his calculations as a general rule.

. . . Senators will reflect that when we look upon measures we are very
apt to go back to previous days, when in a time of peace we guarded every
approach to an expenditure for which we could not find a specific warrant.

Sir, we have now been taught that the Government possesses much larger
and ampler powers than we had supposed. It was well at that day that such
was the prevailing notion. It is well and it will be well if we revert to it
as much as we possibly can; but if we attempt to hold that under an unexampled state of facts we cannot go beyond the rules that were laid down
for our action in time of profound peace in reference to appropriations from
the Treasury, we shall find ourselves utterly powerless to do what is absolutely
incumbent on us to do. So, then, the argument of money does not reach me,
nor does the argument drawn from the constitutionality of the act. . . .

With regard, therefore, to all these details of objection to the bill—and I
rose principally to say this—I see nothing which should trouble anybody
arising from the considerations which have been advanced to us with reference
to the constitutionality of the bill itself. We must meet it, and we must meet
it under some power. There is no positive prohibition. It is a thing to be done.
We have the power to appropriate money; and though we do not find a
specific power to appropriate money for this particular purpose, it is yet an
object of Government, a thing that the Government and country must provide
for, and there is no other way of doing it. . . .

Now, sir, having said this generally with regard to the bill—and although
in some of its details I might perhaps wish that we could get along without
doing what might seem to be offensive in some States, and what might be
used in an offensive sense against us, yet I am ready to vote for it, because
it is the result of the best thought that a very able committee has brought
to bear upon it, and it has been somewhat amended—I shall dismiss any
further remarks upon the bill itself, because really to speak of that was but one
of my objects in rising. . . .

* SENATOR FESSENDEN SUPPORTS THE FREEDMEN'S BUREAU BILL AND INDIRECTLY AD-
DRESSES THE PRESIDENT: From the *Congressional Globe*, 39 Cong., 1 Sess., pp. 366–67.

Senators, and able Senators, on both sides of the House have chosen, in the course of the debate, to talk a great deal about the policy of the President and the policy of Congress. I said a word or two before on that subject at the commencement of the session, when the matter was first broached here. I wish now to say a word or two more. I can understand why gentlemen on the other side of the House, and gentlemen of the same way of thinking out of this House, should be very anxious to get up the idea that there is a collision of opinion between the President and Congress. We have all sorts of rumors where "the wish is father to the thought." One day we hear that such a Cabinet minister is to be turned out or resign; another day we hear that something else is being done, that the President has said this, that the President means to ostracize people who do not support his policy, &c.—all idle, ridiculous rumors without the slightest foundation except the wish of those who invent them and give them currency. I understand the object. It will be a point for gentlemen on the other side of the Senate, and their friends outside, if they can make the people believe that there is or is likely to be some collision between the great party which elected the President and the President himself. I beg gentlemen not to flatter themselves with any such idea. I have not, as yet, seen the slightest indication of it, and I do not expect to see it. Why, sir, even suppose there is a difference of opinion, to a certain extent, as to the time and manner of accomplishing a great work, which we all desire to see accomplished at the earliest possible day, does it follow that . . . there is to be a collision? I know very well that gentlemen hang about the President and the White House, and very probably try to persuade him, and whispering in his ear, . . . insinuate that those who ought to be his best friends, and who are his friends and supporters, are not doing all they ought to do to sustain him. Do they in their secret souls pay the President the poor compliment to think that he does not see through all these suggestions of what they dare not openly speak? Do they think he is not a man of sense, that he is not a man of fixed opinions, that he does not know his friends? Let me say that, in my judgment, they mistake him. Sir, there is no collision. . . . Why? Because the President has done nothing that his friends complain of, and his friends in Congress have done nothing that he can complain of.

Sir, what was his authority? He was Commander-in-Chief of the Army, and as such, when the enemy ceased to exist, he had power necessarily to control the rebellious States which were thus reduced to subjection. It was his duty to control them, and to . . . keep order, to see that there was no anarchy; and if he chose to say to the confederate States, or to any portion of them, "I will appoint a provisional governor for you; if you choose to come together in a certain way and make a constitution of government for yourselves and take the power into your own hands of regulating your own domestic internal affairs, I will give you all the aid I can, and when you do it to my satisfaction and I think it is safe I will then withdraw the Army, or such portion of it as I see fit, and leave you to legislate for yourselves," he did what he had a perfect right to do and what nobody has a right to complain of. I might have done differently if I had been President, but I might probably not have done so wisely as he did. It is not for me to say that my opinion, had it differed from his, would have been wiser than his or better than his, but what I mean to say is that his policy went to the extent, and so far as he had the power to exercise it in a given way he exercised it rightfully, and we have no occasion to complain of it. He may think that these States are ready to come back altogether, and to send their Senators and Representatives to Congress. I do not know how that may be. I think they should come in at the earliest possible moment that they can come with safety. So he thinks. We may differ as to the time.

But mark me, sir, no man in this country, to my certain knowledge, has a greater respect for the Constitution or a more profound respect for the rights and privileges of the coordinate branches of this Government than the President of the United States. His life has illustrated it; and whatever gentlemen may think, he, in my judgment, would be the last man to complain of Congress for acting with reference to what is peculiarly incumbent upon them according to their own judgment and sense of propriety, so long as all the branches of the Government agree in this, that when it can be done safely, at the earliest possible moment, all the States should be restored to their position in the Union. So long as that is agreed upon, and we are all working together to that end, it is not to be expected that my friends here, there, or elsewhere, will quarrel with me for differing with him in opinion as to the time and as to the manner in doing it, and more especially shall I not think of quarreling with him when it belongs to him to decide, and not to me.

. . . Here are Congress, doing what? What they ought to do, what no man can dispute their perfect right to do, what no man can dispute their entire duty to do; and that is this: before taking a step which is perhaps to affect the welfare of this Government in all future time, and in acting upon a question that belongs peculiarly to them, the united wisdom of the nation as manifested through its agents in Congress, sees it a duty to deliberate quietly, calmly, and patiently upon what is best to do. Do you think anybody will quarrel with that? We do not mean to jump at conclusions; we mean to act as we can safely; but we do not mean to be hurried beyond what our judgment dictates as the necessary time for deliberation and for action. The nation will, however, understand, and does understand, that while Congress is doing this, it is anxious, as the people are anxious, that all these questions should be settled at the earliest possible day, that we may get rid of all this agitation, that we may be again a united people. . . .

But while I say this, I say that I trust our friends here will not allow themselves to be hurried or to be frightened by any talk about this policy or that policy, or this collision or that trouble anywhere. I do not fear it. I believe, and I know, that there is patriotism and magnanimity and love of country at both ends of the avenue. . . .

8] The Freedmen's Bureau Bill Is Vetoed

The Freedmen's Bureau was an agency established just before the war ended to deal with the many problems—relief, relocation, schools, asylums, employment, and so forth—created by the growing numbers of landless former slaves and dispossessed refugees. The Bureau operated under the War Department. After a few months of experience, the Bureau's commissioner, General O. O. Howard, came to feel that his agency required widened jurisdiction and extended powers. Senator Lyman Trumbull accordingly prepared a bill to meet these needs, and one of the new powers was that of convening special Bureau courts to hear certain kinds of cases involving racial discrimination. It passed the Senate on January 25 and the House on February 6, 1866.

President Johnson's veto, delivered on February 19, 1866, included a series of objections to the bill on its merits. He said it was unconstitutional because it contemplated the peacetime extension of military power and threatened the jurisdiction of the state civil courts and that it required great expenditures of money. His basic objections, however (set forth in the extract that follows), had only an indirect bearing on the bill's substance. Here, he announces for the first time his position on laws which Congress might pass in reference to the as yet unrepresented rebel states. It was this section of the message that attracted the most attention and evoked the sharpest criticism.*

. . . .

IN THIS connection the query presents itself whether the system proposed by the bill will not, when put into complete operation, practically transfer the entire care, support, and control of 4,000,000 emancipated slaves to agents, overseers, or taskmasters, who, appointed at Washington, are to be located in every county and parish throughout the United States containing freedmen and refugees. Such a system would inevitably tend to a concentration of power in the Executive which would enable him, if so disposed, to control the action of this numerous class and use them for the attainment of his own political ends.

I can not but add another very grave objection to this bill. The Constitution imperatively declares, in connection with taxation, that each State *shall* have at least one Representative, and fixes the rule for the number to which, in future times, each State shall be entitled. It also provides that the Senate of the United States *shall* be composed of two Senators from each State, and adds with peculiar force "that no State, without its consent, shall be deprived of its equal suffrage in the Senate." The original act was necessarily passed in the absence of the States chiefly to be affected, because their people were then contumaciously engaged in the rebellion. Now the case is changed, and some, at least, of those States are attending Congress by loyal representatives, soliciting the allowance of the constitutional right for representation. At the time, however, of the consideration and passing of this bill there was no Senator or Representative in Congress from the eleven States which are to be mainly affected by its provisions. The very fact that reports were and are made against the good disposition of the people of that portion of the country is an additional reason why they need and should have representatives of their own in Congress to explain their condition, reply to accusations, and assist by their local knowledge in the perfecting of measures immediately affecting themselves. While the liberty of deliberation would then be free and Congress would have full power to decide according to its judgment, there could be no objection urged that the States most interested had not been permitted to be heard. The principle is firmly fixed in the minds of the American people that there should be no

* THE FREEDMEN'S BUREAU BILL IS VETOED: From James D. Richardson, ed., *Messages and Papers of the Presidents* (Washington, 1896–99), VI, 398–405.

taxation without representation. Great burdens have now to be borne by all the country, and we may best demand that they shall be borne without murmur when they are voted by a majority of the representatives of all the people. I would not interfere with the unquestionable right of Congress to judge, each House for itself, "of the elections, returns, and qualifications of its own members;" but that authority can not be construed as including the right to shut out in time of peace any State from the representation to which it is entitled by the Constitution. . . .

The President of the United States stands toward the country in a somewhat different attitude from that of any member of Congress. Each member of Congress is chosen from a single district or State; the President is chosen by the people of all the States. As eleven States are not at this time represented in either branch of Congress, it would seem to be his duty on all proper occasions to present their just claims to Congress. There always will be differences of opinion in the community, and individuals may be guilty of transgressions of the law, but these do not constitute valid objections against the right of a State to representation. I would in no wise interfere with the discretion of Congress with regard to the qualifications of its members; but I hold it my duty to recommend to you, in the interests of peace and the interests of union, the admission of every State to its share in public legislation when, however insubordinate, insurgent, or rebellious its people may have been, it presents itself, not only in an attitude of loyalty and harmony, but in the persons of representatives whose loyalty cannot be questioned under any existing constitutional or legal test. It is plain that an indefinite or permanent exclusion of any part of the country from representation must be attended by a spirit of disquiet and complaint. It is unwise and dangerous to pursue a course of measures which will unite a very large section of the country against another section of the country, however much the latter may preponderate. The course of emigration, the development of industry and business, and natural causes will raise up at the South men as devoted to the Union as those of any other part of the land; but if they are all excluded from Congress, if in a permanent statute they are declared not to be in full constitutional relations to the country, they may think they have cause to become a unit in feeling and sentiment against the Government. Under the political education of the American people the idea is inherent and ineradicable that the consent of the majority of the whole people is necessary to secure a willing acquiescence in legislation.

The bill under consideration refers to certain of the States as though they had not "been fully restored in all their constitutional relations to the United States." If they have not, let us at once act together to secure that desirable end at the earliest possible moment. It is hardly necessary for me to inform Congress that in my own judgment most of those States, so far, at least, as depends upon their own action, have already been fully restored, and are to be deemed as entitled to enjoy their constitutional rights as members of the Union. Reasoning from the Constitution itself and from the actual situation of the country, I feel not only entitled but bound to assume that with the Federal courts restored and those of the several States in the full exercise of their functions the rights and interests of all classes of people will, with the aid of the military in cases of resistance to the laws, be essentially protected against unconstitutional infringement or violation. Should this expectation unhappily fail, which I do not anticipate, then the Executive is already fully armed with the powers conferred by the act of March, 1865, establishing the Freedmen's Bureau, and hereafter, as heretofore, he can employ the land and naval forces of the country to suppress insurrection or to overcome obstructions to the laws.

In accordance with the Constitution, I return the bill to the Senate, in the earnest hope that a measure involving questions and interests so important to the country will not become a law, unless upon deliberate consideration by the people it shall receive the sanction of an enlightened public judgment.

ANDREW JOHNSON.

9] The President Responds to the Serenaders

On the evening of February 22, 1866, a crowd of citizens gathered on the White House lawn to serenade the President in connection with the festivities of Washington's Birthday. Still burning over the criticism of his Freedmen's Bureau veto of three days before, and ignoring the warnings of his closest advisors, Johnson seized the occasion to make an impromptu speech which was fully reported in next day's newspapers. The speech is of particular interest since, despite the angry public reaction which greeted it, Johnson was to deliver virtually the same one at all of his appearances during the notorious "Swing Around the Circle" later that summer.*

．　．　．　．　．　．　．　．　．　．　．　．　．　．　．

WHO, I ASK, has suffered more for the Union than I have? I shall not now repeat the wrongs or suffering inflicted upon me; but it is not the way to deal with a whole people in the spirit of revenge. . . . There is no one who has labored harder than I have to have the principal conscious and intelligent traitors brought to justice; to have the law vindicated and the great fact vindicated that treason is a crime. Yet, while conscious, intelligent traitors are to be punished, should whole States, communities and people, be made to submit to and bear the penalty of death? I have, perhaps, as much hostility and as much resentment as a man ought to have; but we should conform our action and our conduct to the example of him who founded our holy religion, [not] that I would liken this to it or bring any comparison. . . .

But, gentlemen, I came into power under the constitution of the country and by the approbation of the people. And what did I find? I found eight millions of people who were in fact condemned under the law—and the penalty was death. Under the idea of revenge and resentment they were to be annihilated and destroyed. O, how different this from the example set by the holy founder of our religion. . . . What was His example? Instead of putting the world or a nation to death He went forth with grace and attested by His blood and His wounds that he would die and let the nation live.

* THE PRESIDENT RESPONDS TO THE SERENADERS: From the New York *Herald* (February 23, 1866).

[Applause.] Let them repent and let them acknowledge their allegiance. Let them become loyal and willing supporters and defenders of our glorious stripes and stars and the constitution of our country. *Let their leaders, the conscious, intelligent traitors suffer the penalty of the law,* but for the great mass who have been forced into this rebellion and misled by their leaders, I say *leniency, kindness, trust and confidence.* [Enthusiastic cheers.]

. . . The rebellion is put down by the strong arm of the government in the field, *but is it the only way in which we can have rebellion?* They struggled for the breaking up of the government, but before they are scarcely out of the battle field . . . we find ourselves almost *in the midst of another rebellion.* [Applause.] The war to suppress our rebellion was to prevent the separation of the States, and thereby change the character of the government and weakening its power. Now, what is this change? There is an attempt to concentrate the power of the government in the hands of a few, and *thereby bring about consolidation, which is equally dangerous and objectionable with separation.* [Enthusiastic applause.] We find that powers are assumed and attempted to be exercised of a most extraordinary character. . . .

We find that, in fact, by an irresponsible central directory, nearly all the powers of government are assumed without even consulting the Legislative or Executive departments of the government. Yes, and by resolution reported by a committee upon whom all the legislative power of the government has been conferred that [the] principle in the constitution which authorizes and empowers each branch of the legislative department to be judges of the election and qualifications of its own members has been virtually taken away from those departments and conferred upon a committee, who must report before they can act under the constitution and allow members duly elected to take their seats. By this rule they assume that there must be laws passed; that there must be recognition in respect to a State in the Union, with all its practical relations restored before the respective houses of Congress, under the constitution, shall judge of the election and qualifications of its own members. What position is that? You have been struggling for four years to put down the rebellion. You denied in the beginning of the struggle that any State had the right to go out. You said that they had neither the right nor the power. The issue has been made, and it has been settled that a State has neither the right nor the power to go out of the Union. And when you have settled that by the executive and military power of the government, and by the public judgment, you *turn around and assume that they are out and shall not come in.* [Laughter and cheers.]

I am free to say to you, as your Executive, that *I am not prepared to take any such position.* . . . I say that when these States comply with the constitution, when they have given sufficient evidence of their loyalty, and that they can be trusted, when they yield obedience to the law, I say, *extend to them the right hand of fellowship,* and let peace and union be restored. [Loud cheers.] I have fought traitors and treason in the South; I opposed the Davises and Toombses, the Slidells, and a long list of others whose names I need not repeat; and now, when I turn around at the other end of the line, I find men—I care not by what name you call them—[a Voice, "Call them traitors"] who still stand opposed to the restoration of the Union of these States, and I am free to say to you that I am still for the preservation of this compact; I am still for the restoration of this Union; I am still in favor of this great government of ours going on and following out its destiny. [A Voice—"Give us the names."]

A gentleman calls for their names. Well, suppose I should give them. [A Voice—"We know them."] I look upon them—I repeat it, as President or citizen—as being as much opposed to the fundamental principles of the government, and believe they are as much laboring to prevent or destroy them as were the men who fought against us. [A Voice—"What are the names?"] *I say Thaddeus Stevens, of Pennsylvania*—[tremendous applause]—*I say Charles Sumner*—[great applause] *I say Wendell Phillips and others of the same stripe are among them.* [A Voice—"Give it to Forney."] Some gentleman in the crowd says, "Give it to Forney." I have only just to say that *I do not waste my ammunition upon dead ducks.* [Laughter and applause.]

I stand for my country, I stand for the constitution, where I placed my feet from my entrance into public life. They may traduce me, they may slander me, they may vituperate; but let me say to you that it has no effect upon me. . . . I know, my countrymen, that it has been insinuated . . . that if such a usurpation of power had been exercised two hundred years ago in a particular reign it would have cost a certain individual his head. What usurpation has Andrew Johnson been guilty of? ["None, none."] The usurpation I have been guilty of has always been standing between the people and the encroachments of power. And because I dared to say in a conversation with a fellow citizen, and a Senator too, that I thought amendments to the constitution ought not to be so frequent . . . —it was a usurpation of power that would have cost a king his head at a certain time. . . . What positions have I held under this government? Beginning with an alderman and running through all branches of the Legislature. [A Voice—"From a tailor up."] Some gentleman says I have been a tailor. [Tremendous applause.] Now, that did not discomfit me in the least; for when I used to be a tailor I had the reputation of being a good one, and making close fits—[great laughter]—always punctual with my customers and always did good work. . . . I was saying that I had held nearly all positions, from alderman, through both branches of Congress, to that which I now occupy, and who is there that will say Andrew Johnson ever made a pledge that he did not redeem, or made a promise he did not fulfill? Who will say that he has ever acted otherwise than in fidelity to the great mass of the people? They may talk about beheading and usurpation; but when I am beheaded I want the American people to witness. I do not want by innuendoes, by indirect remarks in high places, to see the man who has assassination brooding in his bosom, exclaim, "This presidential obstacle must be gotten out of the way." I make use of a very strong expression when I say that I have no doubt the *intention was to incite assassination* and so get out of the way the obstacle from place and power. Whether by assassination or not, there are individuals in this government, I doubt not, who want to destroy our institutions and change the character of the government. Are they not satisfied with the blood which has been shed? Does not the murder of

Lincoln appease the vengeance and wrath of the opponents of the government? Are they still unslaked? Do they still want more blood? Have they not got honor and courage enough to attain their objects otherwise than by the hands of the assassin? . . . If my blood is to be shed because I vindicate the Union and the preservation of this government in its original purity and character, let it be shed; let an altar to the Union be erected, and then, if it is necessary, take me and lay me upon it, and the blood that now warms and animates my existence shall be poured out as a fit libation to the Union of these States. [Great applause.] But let the opponents of this government remember that when it is poured out "the blood of the martyrs will be the seed of the Church." [Cheers.] . . .

10] Senator Fessenden Defends the Joint Committee and Responds to the President

> After Johnson's Freedmen's Bureau veto, and particularly after his Washington's Birthday speech, Fessenden's mood was no longer what it had been back in January. These remarks were made in the Senate on February 23, the day following the speech, after a clerk had read extracts from reports of what the President had said. Fessenden here deals with the charges Johnson had made against the Joint Committee on Reconstruction, of which he was chairman, and with the crucial closing section of the President's veto message.*

.   .   .   .

BUT THE President undertakes to say that legislative power has been granted to this committee. . . .

Sir, is this committee of fifteen anything more than a servant of Congress? Is any committee, either joint or special, which is appointed, anything more than the mere servant of Congress? Can any member of it, or the whole of it, set up its will for a single day or a single hour or a single moment against the will of the body which constituted it? We were appointed for a special purpose, to make inquiries, and report to Congress the result of our inquiries; and for what reason? . . . Simply that neither branch, acting without sufficient information, might take a course from which the other branch would differ, and thus bring about a collision between the two bodies which constitute the Congress. Under those circumstances, is it quite fair to designate the committee of fifteen as a central directory, as a power assuming to judge and to decide questions which belong to the bodies which the committee represents? Is it quite fair to designate it as a central power sitting here with a view to get up the government of a few against government of the many? I can understand the allusion in no other way; and if any gentleman can place a different construction upon it, I should like to have him do so. I am unwilling myself, individually, to rest under such an imputation. I have the honor to be one of that

* SENATOR FESSENDEN DEFENDS THE JOINT COMMITTEE AND RESPONDS TO THE PRESIDENT: From the *Congressional Globe*, 39 Cong., 1 Sess., pp. 985–87.

committee. I never understood myself as anything but the servant of Congress, or of the body which sent me there, to endeavor to obtain information and to come to a conclusion upon which the body might act understandingly; and that we have not come to a conclusion yet, is only a proof that the question is a much larger one than gentlemen might have supposed, and involves more consideration and more examination than might possibly have been apparent to those who looked only upon the surface and judged only from what they could gather from common report.

If the Executive—and I mean to speak of the President with respect, because I entertain for him respect—has an idea that the several points which he has suggested are preliminaries to the admission of Senators and Representatives from these States, the question arises, who is to exercise that power of judgment? Does it belong to us, if a Senator presents himself here, to ascertain in the first place if those conditions have been complied with on the part of these States, or does it belong to him? . . .

. . . If the President had confined himself in the objections which he stated to a criticism of the bill itself, it is very possible that I might have been quite willing to waive my own feelings and opinions in regard to the bill as it passed, and to sustain his veto. But on looking at the veto message, and the reasons given in it, it struck me, that after passing from the consideration of the provisions of the bill which was sent to him, he gave other reasons which rendered it impossible, in my judgment, for any member of this Senate with a due respect to himself and to the rights of the Senate and of Congress, to vote otherwise than to sustain the bill they had sent to him; because a vote in the negative on the question of its passage seems to indorse all his opinions whatever they may be, as expressed in the veto message. I considered it so. At any rate, I did not mean to put myself in the position of indorsing, or being supposed for a single instant to give my assent to the closing parts of the veto message. What do I understand by the closing parts of that message? Simply, that, in the judgment of the President, Congress, as at present organized, has no right to pass any bill affecting the interests of the late confederate States while they are not represented in Congress. . . .

. . . If I have mistaken the view of the President, I shall be very glad to be corrected by him or by anybody that is authorized to speak for him; and one would think there are plenty of those gentlemen about; but what he says is, substantially, in my judgment, this: "I have come to the conclusion that these States are in the Union to be represented in the councils of the nation. . . . I admit that certain things must be done; they must show their loyalty, but I am the person to decide upon whether those things have been done . . . and when I have decided that question with reference to these States, Congress may take up the questions of elections, qualifications, and returns of the members who present themselves to them, inquire into that, and have nothing to do but to settle the question whether they come within the description of the Constitution or not." . . .

Looking, therefore, upon these two arguments in this part of the veto message as I did, one distinctly indicating that no legislation affecting the States which have recently been in rebellion would meet with the approval of the

President while those States were not represented here, the other that all the consideration that we as members of the Senate had a right to give to this subject was to look at the papers presented and say whether men coming here had the proper credentials from somebody, leaving the question to be settled at the other end of the avenue whether or not the States themselves had a right to be represented on this floor—while I considered those two things as not only shadowed forth, but distinctly stated in the veto message, I could not hesitate for a single instant to say that where such reasons were given for the veto of a bill, I could not, without sacrificing all my self-respect, and what is of more consequence as far as I am concerned, sacrificing all the rights and honors of the body of which I am a member, vote to sustain that message, whatever good reasons might be given in other parts of it. . . .

11] The President Vetoes the Civil Rights Bill

The Civil Rights Bill was Senator Trumbull's other measure for the benefit of the Negroes, and it was introduced together with the Freedmen's Bureau Bill on January 5, 1866. It passed the Senate and House on February 2 and March 13, respectively. It specifically conferred citizenship on the freedmen and provided protection for their civil rights in the federal district courts. The occasion for its passage was legislation of a discriminatory nature then being enacted in the Southern states; in the opinion of the Republican majority in Congress the situation required special federal action.

President Johnson's veto of this bill rested on essentially the same grounds as his Freedmen's Bureau veto, unconstitutional extension of federal power and nonrepresentation of the states principally concerned. With this message, sent in on March 27, 1866, working relations between President and Congress were brought to a virtual standstill.*

· · · · · · · · · · · · · · · · · · · ·

THE RIGHT of Federal citizenship thus to be conferred on the several excepted races before mentioned is now for the first time proposed to be given by law. If, as is claimed by many, all persons who are native born already are, by virtue of the Constitution, citizens of the United States, the passage of the pending bill can not be necessary to make them such. If, on the other hand, such persons are not citizens, as may be assumed from the proposed legislation to make them such, the grave question presents itself whether, when eleven of the thirty-six States are unrepresented in Congress at the present time, it is sound policy to make our entire colored population and all other excepted classes citizens of the United States. Four millions of them have just emerged from slavery into freedom. Can it be reasonably supposed that they possess the requisite qualifications to entitle them to all the privileges and immunities of citizens of the United States? Have the people of the several States expressed such a conviction? It may also be asked whether it is necessary that they should

* THE PRESIDENT VETOES THE CIVIL RIGHTS BILL: From James D. Richardson, ed., *Messages and Papers of the Presidents* (Washington, 1896–99), VI, 405–13.

be declared citizens in order that they may be secured in the enjoyment of the civil rights proposed to be conferred by the bill. . . .

I do not propose to consider the policy of this bill. To me the details of the bill seem fraught with evil. The white race and the black race of the South have hitherto lived together under the relation of master and slave—capital owning labor. Now, suddenly, that relation is changed, and as to ownership capital and labor are divorced. They stand now each master of itself. In this new relation, one being necessary to the other, there will be a new adjustment, which both are deeply interested in making harmonious. Each has equal power in settling the terms, and if left to the laws that regulate capital and labor it is confidently believed that they will satisfactorily work out the problem. Capital, it is true, has more intelligence, but labor is never so ignorant as not to understand its own interests, not to know its own value, and not to see that capital must pay that value.

This bill frustrates this adjustment. It intervenes between capital and laboi and attempts to settle questions of political economy through the agency of numerous officials whose interest it will be to foment discord between the two races, for as the breach widens their employment will continue, and when it is closed their occupation will terminate.

In all our history, in all our experience as a people living under Federal and State law, no such system as that contemplated by the details of this bill has ever before been proposed or adopted. They establish for the security of the colored race safeguards which go infinitely beyond any that the General Government has ever provided for the white race. In fact, the distinction of race and color is by the bill made to operate in favor of the colored and against the white race. They interfere with the municipal legislation of the States, with the relations existing exclusively between a State and its citizens, or between inhabitants of the same State—an absorption and assumption of power by the General Government which, if acquiesced in, must sap and destory our federative system of limited powers and break down the barriers which preserve the rights of the States. It is another step, or rather stride, toward centralization and the concentration of all legislative powers in the National Government. The tendency of the bill must be to resuscitate the spirit of rebellion and to arrest the progress of those influences which are more closely drawing around the States the bonds of union and peace. . . .

ANDREW JOHNSON.

12] Senator Trumbull Responds

Noting that "a standing objection in all the veto messages of the President" was that "no bill is to be passed because certain States are unrepresented, [even though] their being unrepresented is their own fault," Lyman Trumbull on April 4, 1866, made a minute analysis of the Civil Rights veto. Trumbull's long experience with the law, both as lawyer and as judge, gave his words much authority and effectiveness. He made something of a sensation at one point when he quoted—revealing the source after a challenge from the floor

—from an angry speech that Johnson himself had made as a senator six years before, upon President Buchanan's veto of his own homestead bill. What follows is the closing portion of Trumbull's speech. The veto was overriden two days later.*

.   .   .   .

MR. PRESIDENT, I have . . . gone through this veto message, replying with what patience I could command to its various objections to the bill. Would that I could stop here, . . . but justice to myself, justice to the State whose representative I am, justice to the people of the whole country, in legislation for whose behalf I am called to participate, justice to the Constitution I am sworn to support, justice to the rights of American citizenship it secures, and to human liberty, now imperiled, requires me to go further. Gladly would I refrain from speaking of the spirit of this message, of the dangerous doctrines it promulgates, of the inconsistencies and contradictions of its author, of his encroachments upon the constitutional rights of Congress, of his assumption of unwarranted powers, which, if persevered in and not checked by the people, must eventually lead to a subversion of the Government and the destruction of liberty.

Congress, in the passage of the bill under consideration, sought no controversy with the President. So far from it, the bill was proposed with a view to carry out what were supposed to be the views of the President, and was submitted to him before its introduction into the Senate. I am not about to relate private declarations of the President, but it is right that the American people should know that the controversy which exists between him and Congress in reference to this measure is of his own seeking. Soon after Congress met it became apparent that there was a difference of opinion between the President and some members of Congress in regard to the condition of the rebellious States, and the rights to be secured to freedmen.

The President in his annual message had denied the constitutional power of the General Government to extend the elective franchise to negroes, but he was equally decided in the assertion of the right of every man to life, liberty, and the pursuit of happiness. This was his language:

"But while I have no doubt that now, after the close of the war, it is not competent for the General Government to extend the elective franchise in the several States, it is equally clear that good faith requires the security of the freedmen in their liberty and their property."

There were some members of Congress who expressed the opinion that in the reorganization of the rebellious States the right of suffrage should be extended to the colored man, though this was not the prevailing sentiment of Congress. All were anxious for a reorganization of the rebellious States and their admission to full participation in the Federal Government as soon as these relations could be restored with safety to all concerned. Feeling the importance

* SENATOR TRUMBULL RESPONDS: From the *Congressional Globe*, 39 Cong., 1 Sess., p. 1760.

of harmonious action between the different departments of the Government, and an anxious desire to sustain the President, for whom I had always entertained the highest respect, I had frequent interviews with him during the early part of the session. Without mentioning anything said by him, I may with propriety state that, acting from the considerations I have stated, and believing that the passage of a law by Congress, securing equality in civil rights when denied by State authorities to freedmen and all other inhabitants of the United States, would do much to relieve anxiety in the North, to induce the southern States to secure these rights by their own action, and thereby remove many of the obstacles to an early reconstruction, I prepared the bill substantially as it is now returned with the President's objections. After the bill was introduced and printed a copy was furnished him, and at a subsequent period, when it was reported that he was hesitating about signing the Freedmen's Bureau bill, he was informed of the condition of the civil rights bill then pending in the House, and a hope expressed that if he had objections to any of its provisions he would make them known to its friends, that they might be remedied, if not destructive of the measure; that there was believed to be no disposition on the part of Congress, and certainly none on my part, to have bills presented to him which he could not approve. He never indicated to me, nor, so far as I know, to any of its friends, the least objection to any of the provisions of the bill till after its passage. And how could he, consistently with himself? The bill was framed, as was supposed, in entire harmony with his views, and certainly in harmony with what he was then and has since been doing in protecting freedmen in their civil rights all through the rebellious States. It was strictly limited to the protection of the civil rights belonging to every freedman, the birthright of every American citizen, and carefully avoided conferring or interfering with political rights or privileges of any kind.

The bill neither confers nor abridges the rights of any one, but simply declares that in civil rights there shall be an equality among all classes of citizens, and that all alike shall be subject to the same punishment. Each State, so that it does not abridge the great fundamental rights belonging, under the Constitution, to all citizens, may grant or withhold such civil rights as it pleases; all that is required is that, in this respect, its laws shall be impartial.

And yet this is the bill now returned with the President's objections, and such objections! What are they? That—

"In all our history, in all our experience as a people, living under Federal and State laws, no such system as that contemplated by the details of this bill has ever before been proposed or adopted." . . .

[3] Framing the Fourteenth Amendment

Framing the Fourteenth Amendment was a long-drawn-out process, characterized by pulling and hauling and endless debate. The final product evolved out of several previous versions, two of which are reproduced here.

On March 16, 1866, Senator William M. Stewart of Nevada offered his "universal amnesty and universal suffrage" plan, which was at first received with much enthusiasm. It was offered not as a constitutional amendment but as an immediate settlement which the South might accept or reject as it chose, though the form was later changed to that of an amendment. The enthusiasm for Stewart's plan, however, lasted only a few days; it was killed by Johnson's Civil Rights veto. The Robert Dale Owen plan, presented to the Joint Committee on Reconstruction April 21, 1866, differed in certain important respects from the final version. Consisting of an amendment plus an enabling act, the plan made direct, rather than indirect, provision for Negro suffrage after a ten-year period if such suffrage had not been enacted voluntarily in the meantime. This was what made the Owen plan vulnerable: not enough men were yet ready to insist on a direct and universal prescription of Negro suffrage. This ambivalence may be seen in section 2 of the completed Fourteenth Amendment, which reached final form on June 13, 1866.*

A] The Stewart Plan

Be it resolved by the Senate and House of Representatives of the United States in Congress assembled, 1. That each of said States, whose people were lately in insurrection, as aforesaid, shall be recognized as having fully and validly resumed its former relations with this Government, and its chosen representatives shall be admitted into the two Houses of the national Legislature whenever said State shall have so amended its constitution as, first, to do away all existing distinctions as to civil rights and disabilities among the various classes of its population by reason either of race or color, or previous condition of servitude; second, to repudiate all pecuniary indebtedness which said State may have heretofore contracted, incurred, or assumed in connection with the late unnatural and treasonable war; third, to yield all claim to compensation on account of the liberation of its slaves; and fourth, to provide for the extension of the elective franchise to all persons upon the same terms and conditions, making no discrimination on account of race, color, or previous condition of servitude: *Provided,* That those who were qualified to vote in the year 1860 by the laws of their respective States shall not be disfranchised by reason of any new tests or conditions which have been or may be prescribed since that year.

2. *Resolved,* That after the aforesaid conditions shall have been complied with and the same shall have been ratified by a majority of the present voting population of the State, including all those qualified to vote under the laws thereof as they existed in 1860, a general amnesty shall be proclaimed in regard to all persons in such State who were in any way connected with armed opposition to the Government of the United States, wholly exonerating them from all pains, penalties, or disabilities to which they may have become liable by reason of their connection with the rebellion.

3. *Resolved,* That in view of the importance of the thorough assimilation of the basis of suffrage in the various States of the Union, all other States not above specified be respectfully requested to incorporate an amendment in their

* FRAMING THE FOURTEENTH AMENDMENT: From the *Congressional Globe,* 39 Cong., 1 Sess., p. 1437; Benjamin B. Kendrick, *The Journal of the Joint Committee of Fifteen on Reconstruction* (New York, 1914), pp. 83–84; U.S. Constitution, Article XIV.

State constitutions respectively, corresponding with the one above described.

4. *Resolved,* That in the adoption of the aforesaid resolutions it is not intended to assert a coercive power on the part of Congress in regard to the regulation of the right of suffrage in the different States of the Union, but only to make a respectful and earnest appeal to their own good sense and love of country, with a view to the prevention of serious evils now threatened, and to the peaceful perpetuation of the repose, the happiness, and true glory of the whole American people.

b] The Owen Plan

ARTICLE —

SECTION 1. No discrimination shall be made by any state, nor by the United States, as to the civil rights of persons because of race, color, or previous condition of servitude.

SEC. 2. From and after the fourth day of July, in the year one thousand eight hundred and seventy-six, no discrimination shall be made by any state, nor by the United States, as to the enjoyment by classes of persons of the right of suffrage, because of race, color, or previous condition of servitude.

SEC. 3. Until the fourth day of July, one thousand eight hundred and seventy-six, no class of persons, as to the right of any of whom to suffrage discrimination shall be made by any state, because of race, color, or previous condition of servitude, shall be included in the basis of representation.

SEC. 4. Debts incurred in aid of insurrection or of war against the Union, and claims of compensation for loss of involuntary service or labor, shall not be paid by any state nor by the United States.

SEC. 5. Congress shall have power to enforce by appropriate legislation, the provisions of this article.

And be it further resolved, That whenever the above recited amendment shall have become part of the Constitution, and any state lately in insurrection shall have ratified the same, and shall have modified its constitution and laws in conformity with the first section thereof, the Senators and Representatives from such State, if found duly elected and qualified, shall, after having taken the usual oath of office, be admitted as such:

Provided, That no person who, having been an officer in the army or navy of the United States, or having been a member of the Thirty-sixth Congress, or of the Cabinet in the year one thousand eight hundred and sixty, took part in the late insurrection, shall be eligible to either branch of the national legislature until after the fourth day of July, one thousand eight hundred and seventy-six.

c] The Fourteenth Amendment

SECTION 1. All persons born or naturalized in the United States, and subject to the jurisdiction thereof, are citizens of the United States and of the

State wherein they reside. No State shall make or enforce any law which shall abridge the privileges or immunities of citizens of the United States; nor shall any State deprive any person of life, liberty, or property, without due process of law; nor deny to any person within its jurisdiction the equal protection of the laws.

Section 2. Representatives shall be apportioned among the several States according to their respective numbers, counting the whole number of persons in each State, excluding Indians not taxed. But when the right to vote at any election for the choice of electors for President and Vice-President of the United States, Representatives in Congress, the Executive and Judicial officers of a State, or the members of the Legislature thereof, is denied to any of the male inhabitants of such State, being twenty-one years of age, and citizens of the United States, or in any way abridged, except for participation in rebellion, or other crime, the basis of representation therein shall be reduced in the proportion which the number of such male citizens shall bear to the whole number of male citizens twenty-one years of age in such State.

Section 3. No person shall be a Senator or Representative in Congress, or elector of President and Vice-President, or hold any office, civil or military, under the United States, or under any State, who, having previously taken an oath, as a member of Congress, or as an officer of the United States, or as a member of any State legislature, or as an executive or judicial officer of any State, to support the Constitution of the United States, shall have engaged in insurrection or rebellion against the same, or given aid or comfort to the enemies thereof. But Congress may by a vote of two-thirds of each House, remove such disability.

Section 4. The validity of the public debt of the United States, authorized by law, including debts incurred for payment of pensions and bounties for services in suppressing insurrection or rebellion, shall not be questioned. But neither the United States nor any State shall assume or pay any debt or obligation incurred in aid of insurrection or rebellion against the United States, or any claim for the loss or emancipation of any slave; but all such debts, obligations, and claims shall be held illegal and void.

Section 5. The Congress shall have the power to enforce, by appropriate legislation, the provisions of this article.

14] The President Comments on the "National Union" Platform

In the spring and summer of 1866 a group of Johnson supporters in Washington, with Johnson's active assistance, organized a movement to campaign for the Presidential position in the fall elections. The "National Union" movement, a quasi-third-party affair which would soon be absorbed by the Democrats, held a three-day convention at Philadelphia opening on August 14. Its principal object was the immediate readmission of the Southern states without conditions or qualifications. Here is part of what the President said

to a delegation that came to present a copy of the platform to him. In referring to this platform, the President is in effect commenting on his own
work.*

• • • • • • • • • • • • • • • • •

MR. CHAIRMAN, I consider the proceedings of this Convention equal to, if
not more important than, those of any convention that ever assembled in the
United States. [Great applause.] When I look upon that collection of citizens
coming together voluntarily, and sitting in council, with ideas, with principles
and views commensurate with all the States, and co-extensive with the whole
people, and contrast it with a Congress whose policy, if persisted in, will destroy the country, I regard it as more important than any convention that has
sat—at least since 1787. [Renewed applause.] I think I may also say that the
declarations that were there made are equal to those contained in the Declaration of Independence itself, and I here to-day pronounce them a second Declaration of Independence. [Cries of "Glorious!" and most enthusiastic and prolonged applause.]

Yes, I will go further, and say that the declarations you have made, that the
principles you have enunciated in your address, are a second proclamation of
emancipation to the people of the United States. [Renewed applause.] For in
proclaiming and reproclaiming these great truths you have laid down a constitutional platform on which all, without reference to party, can make common
cause, engage in a common effort to break the tyranny which the dominant
party in Congress has so unrelentingly exercised, and stand united together
for the restoration of the States and the preservation of the Government. The
question only is the salvation of the country; for our country rises above all
party considerations or influences. [Cries of "Good!" and applause.] How
many are there in the United States that now require to be free? They have
the shackles upon their limbs and are bound as rigidly by the behests of party
leaders in the National Congress as though they were in fact in slavery. I repeat, then, that your declaration is the second proclamation of emancipation to
the people of the United States, and offers a common ground upon which all
patriots can stand. [Applause.]

In this connection, Mr. Chairman and gentlemen, let me ask what have I
to gain more than the advancement of the public welfare? . . . I have been
placed in the high office which I occupy by the Constitution of the country,
and I may say that I have held, from lowest to highest, almost every station
to which a man may attain in our Government. I have passed through every
position, from alderman of a village to the Presidency of the United States. . . .

* THE PRESIDENT COMMENTS ON THE "NATIONAL UNION" PLATFORM: From Edward Mc-
Pherson, *The Political History of the United States of America During the Period of
Reconstruction* (Washington, 1871), pp. 126–29.

15] The President Transmits the Fourteenth Amendment to the States and Advises the Former Governor of Alabama

> Johnson expressed himself at several critical points on the question of whether the Southern states should ratify the amendment, and it seems clear that the President's views made considerable difference in those states. The following documents include the message Johnson sent to Congress on June 22, 1866, when he transmitted the amendment for ratification, and his advice to ex-Governor Parsons of Alabama on January 17, 1867, regarding what action that state ought to take.*

A] MESSAGE OF TRANSMITTAL

WASHINGTON, D.C., *June 22, 1866.*

To the Senate and House of Representatives:

I submit to Congress a report of the Secretary of State, to whom was referred the concurrent resolution of the 18th instant, respecting a submission to the legislatures of the States of an additional article to the Constitution of the United States. It will be seen from this report that the Secretary of State had, on the 16th instant, transmitted to the governors of the several States certified copies of the joint resolution passed on the 13th instant, proposing an amendment to the Constitution.

Even in ordinary times any question of amending the Constitution must be justly regarded as of paramount importance. This importance is at the present time enhanced by the fact that the joint resolution was not submitted by the two Houses for the approval of the President and that of the thirty-six States which constitute the Union eleven are excluded from representation in either House of Congress, although, with the single exception of Texas, they have been entirely restored to all their functions as States in conformity with the organic law of the land, and have appeared at the national capital by Senators and Representatives, who have applied for and have been refused admission to the vacant seats. Nor have the sovereign people of the nation been afforded an opportunity of expressing their views upon the important questions which the amendment involves. Grave doubts, therefore, may naturally and justly arise as to whether the action of Congress is in harmony with the sentiments of the people, and whether State legislatures, elected without reference to such an issue, should be called upon by Congress to decide respecting the ratification of the proposed amendment.

---

* THE PRESIDENT TRANSMITS THE FOURTEENTH AMENDMENT TO THE STATES AND ADVISES THE FORMER GOVERNOR OF ALABAMA: From James D. Richardson, ed., *Messages and Papers of the Presidents* (Washington, 1896–99), VI, 391–92; and Edward McPherson, *The Political History of the United States of America During the Period of Reconstruction* (Washington, 1871), pp. 352–53.

Waiving the question as to the constitutional validity of the proceedings of Congress upon the joint resolution proposing the amendment or as to the merits of the article which it submits through the executive department to the legislatures of the States, I deem it proper to observe that the steps taken by the Secretary of State, as detailed in the accompanying report, are to be considered as purely ministerial, and in no sense whatever committing the Executive to an approval or a recommendation of the amendment to the State legislatures or to the people. On the contrary, a proper appreciation of the letter and spirit of the Constitution, as well as of the interests of national order, harmony, and union, and a due deference for an enlightened public judgment may at this time well suggest a doubt whether any amendment to the Constitution ought to be proposed by Congress and pressed upon the legislatures of the several States for final decision until after the admission of such loyal Senators and Representatives of the now unrepresented States as have been or as may hereafter be chosen in conformity with the Constitution and laws of the United States.

ANDREW JOHNSON.

B] THE PARSONS-JOHNSON TELEGRAMS

Montgomery, Alabama, January 17, 1867

LEGISLATURE in session. Efforts making to reconsider vote on constitutional amendment. Report from Washington says it is probable an enabling act will pass. We do not know what to believe. I find nothing here.

LEWIS E. PARSONS

Washington, D.C., January 17, 1867

WHAT possible good can be obtained by reconsidering the constitutional amendment? I know of none in the present posture of affairs; and I do not believe the people of the whole country will sustain any set of individuals in attempts to change the whole character of our government by enabling acts or otherwise. I believe, on the contrary, that they will eventually uphold all who have patriotism and courage to stand by the Constitution, and who place their confidence in the people. There should be no faltering on the part of those who are honest in their determination to sustain the several coordinate departments of the government in accordance with its original design.

ANDREW JOHNSON

16] General Wood Testifies on Enforcing the Law in Mississippi

Acting upon reports from the various military departments concerning the frequency of crimes against Union men and Negroes in the South, a House committee in January, 1867, asked Generals Sickles, Baird, Wood, Schofield, and Thomas to appear and give testimony. All testified in substantially similar vein on the difficulty of having this class of cases prosecuted in the civil courts. The testimony of General Thomas J. Wood is typical.*

WASHINGTON, *January* 28, 1867.

Testimony of Brevet Major General THOMAS J. WOOD.

.　.　.　.　.　.　.　.　.　.　.　.　.　.　.

Q. During your residence in the State I wish to inquire as to the frequency of criminal offences against Union men, United States soldiers and freedmen?

A. During the time I was in command in Mississippi the commission of such crimes as are described in the question have been frequent. It might be well to add that the commission of crime generally has been frequent, but more particularly against persons of Union proclivities, and of northern men who have emigrated to Mississippi since the termination of the troubles, and against freed people. Murder was quite a frequent affair against freedmen everywhere in that community, and the commission of crimes of a lesser grade was still more frequent than the commission of murder, such as beating and assaults.

.　.　.　.　.　.　.　.　.　.　.　.　.　.

Q. So far as you can judge, was the number of offences of this description on the increase or decrease?

A. I could not say. There was a great deal of variation; some months more cases were reported and others less. My impression is that the number of cases of killing was on the increase; although without a reference to my reports I could not state that fact with certainty. . . . I recollect that about September or October the number of cases so reported to me of offences committed was greater than it had been any months previous. But that may have been merely one of those fluctuating periods when bad men gratified their revenge, and did not indicate any regular increase of crime.

Q. You say the measures heretofore taken for the suppression of crime do not seem to have effected sensibly the diminution of crime?

A. No, sir; it seemed to me that the condition of things remained about the same.

.　.　.　.　.　.　.　.　.　.　.　.　.　.

Q. Do you know of any cases where citizens of Mississippi had been punished for high offences against freedmen?

A. I have never heard of but one. That was, I think, in Madison county, where a white man was tried for killing a freedman and convicted of manslaughter, and was sentenced to the penitentiary for one year.

.　.　.　.　.　.　.　.　.　.　.　.　.　.

* GENERAL WOOD TESTIFIES ON ENFORCING THE LAW IN MISSISSIPPI: "Murder of Union Soldiers." From *House Reports,* No. 23, 39 Cong., 2 Sess. (1866–67), pp. 29–31.

Q. Would you say that, with the present condition of things, there is encouragement to believe they will be improved in the future?

A. In the present unsettled condition of a great portion of the southern
country—and I speak now particularly in reference to Mississippi—the want
of a due administration of justice by civil authorities, taken as a whole, in
cases in which Union men or freedmen are concerned, taken in connection
with the failure of the crops and the destitution that prevails, I do not think
matters are likely to grow better; my observation in life having been that
whenever crime goes unpunished, it becomes more instead of less frequent.

.   .   .   .

Q. In the present condition of popular feeling in Mississippi, can any adequate redress be obtained for crimes against freedmen, Union men, and United
States soldiers, through the civil courts?

A. In the present state of public feeling in Mississippi, taking the bulk of
the people, I do not think there is a certain reliance that crime would be punished, when committed against United States soldiers, Union men, or freedmen, or at least that a full measure of justice would be dealt out. I have known
cases in which I think justice had been fairly administered, in civil cases,
where a freedman or Union man was one of the litigants. But there is a want
of assurance that justice will be fairly meted out, whether in civil or criminal
cases, and that of itself tends to create a restless feeling on the part of emi-
grants there. It keeps away capital, and prevents further immigration, of course.
There are there, as everywhere, people who were willing to go there, for the
sake of money, and take the risk. I may repeat, that it is not the better class of
people who commit these crimes; they are committed by the rabble, or by the
lower order. The poorer classes, who still retain the malignant prejudices generated before and during the war, against northern men and freedmen, they
commit these crimes. But the complaint is made against the better classes of
people that they are not diligent in bringing these men to justice; they are
apathetic in their feelings, and do not give the information which would
enable the authorities to bring offenders to justice.

17] Congress at Loggerheads on a Reconstruction Bill

This speech by Thaddeus Stevens, made on February 13, 1866, gives some
idea of how hopelessly far from agreement Republican congressmen still were
on a policy for the South. Stevens had by this time come to support a straight
military-government bill which would simply suspend Southern political life
until further notice, and he was fighting to keep the bill from being weighted
down by amendments. An amendment proposed by James G. Blaine had
changed the character of the bill by offering readmission to the states after
they had, on their own initiative, ratified the Fourteenth Amendment and
guaranteed a general Negro suffrage. It contained no provision for disfranchisement; indeed, according to Stevens, it was a "step toward universal
amnesty and universal Andy-Johnsonism." Stevens here is arguing against a
motion that would refer Blaine's bill to the Judiciary Committee with instruc-

tions to report it out immediately; should the motion be defeated, Stevens could then bring his own unamended bill to a vote.*

. . . .

I F, S I R, I might presume upon my age, without claiming any of the wisdom of Nestor, I would suggest to the young gentlemen around me, that the deeds of this burning crisis, of this solemn day, of this thrilling moment, will cast their shadows far into the future and will make their impress upon the annals of our history, and that we shall appear upon the bright pages of that history, just in so far as we cordially, without guile, without bickering, without small criticisms, lend our aid to promote the great cause of humanity and universal liberty.

I know that the gentlemen upon the other side of the House believe that this is a harsh measure; and so does the gentleman from Ohio on this side, who to-day, and the other day, made beautiful appeals to our sense of humanity, and depicted the glory of a great nation forgiving great criminals for unrepented crimes. . . .

Mr. Speaker, I desire to say what perhaps had better not be said, that gentlemen who are thus, either by direction or indirection, defending the cause or palliating the conduct of these rebel traitors are making for themselves no good record with posterity. They, sir, who while preaching this doctrine are hugging and caressing those whose hands are red and whose garments are dripping with the blood of our and their murdered kindred, are covering themselves with indelible stains, which all the waters of the Nile cannot wash out.

Mr. Speaker, a single word as to the number of amendments. There are seven of them; and I am satisfied that any one of them, if ingrafted upon this bill will be sure to kill it. This bill proposes to do certain things. If there is anything further desired, let it be accomplished in some other way. . . .

The amendment of the gentleman from Maine [Mr. BLAINE,] as I said before, lets in a vast number of rebels, and shuts out nobody. All I ask is that when the House comes to vote upon that amendment it shall understand that the adoption of it would be an entire surrender of those States into the hands of the rebels. . . .

18] The First Reconstruction Act Becomes Law

Stevens did persuade the House to pass his military bill, but the Senate refused to take it without reinserting the Blaine amendment, somewhat modified by Senator Sherman. The House, however, would not concur in the Senate's version until two more amendments, proposed by Representatives Wilson of Iowa and Shellabarger of Ohio, were added to the Sherman substitute. Those last-minute amendments, which imposed wide-scale disfranchisement and defined the existing civil governments as not only subject

* CONGRESS AT LOGGERHEADS ON A RECONSTRUCTION BILL: From the *Congressional Globe*, 39 Cong., 2 Sess., pp. 1213–14.

to military control but entirely provisional and temporary in character, brought the bill to its final form. This was on February 20, 1866. On March 2 the bill became law, having been vetoed by President Johnson and repassed the same day.*

WHEREAS no legal State governments or adequate protection for life or property now exists in the rebel States of Virginia, North Carolina, South Carolina, Georgia, Mississippi, Alabama, Louisiana, Florida, Texas, and Arkansas; and whereas it is necessary that peace and good order should be enforced in said States until loyal and republican State governments can be legally established: Therefore,

Be it enacted . . . That said rebel States shall be divided into military districts and made subject to the military authority of the United States as hereinafter prescribed, and for that purpose Virginia shall constitute the first district; North Carolina and South Carolina the second district; Georgia, Alabama, and Florida the third district; Mississippi and Arkansas the fourth district; and Louisiana and Texas the fifth district.

SEC. 2. *And be it further enacted,* That it shall be the duty of the President to assign to the command of each of said districts an officer of the army, not below the rank of brigadier-general, and to detail a sufficient military force to enable such officer to perform his duties and enforce his authority within the district to which he is assigned.

SEC. 3. *And be it further enacted,* That it shall be the duty of each officer assigned as aforesaid, to protect all persons in their rights of person and property, to suppress insurrection, disorder, and violence, and to punish, or cause to be punished, all disturbers of the public peace and criminals; and to this end he may allow local civil tribunals to take jurisdiction of and to try offenders, or, when in his judgment it may be necessary for the trial of offenders, he shall have power to organize military commissions or tribunals for that purpose, and all interference under color of State authority with the exercise of military authority under this act, shall be null and void.

SEC. 4. *And be it further enacted,* That all persons put under military arrest by virtue of this act shall be tried without unnecessary delay, and no cruel or unusual punishment shall be inflicted, and no sentence of any military commission or tribunal hereby authorized, affecting the life or liberty of any person, shall be executed until it is approved by the officer in command of the district, and the laws and regulations for the government of the army shall not be affected by this act, except in so far as they conflict with its provisions: *Provided,* That no sentence of death under the provisions of this act shall be carried into effect without the approval of the President.

SEC. 5. *And be it further enacted,* That when the people of any one of said rebel States shall have formed a constitution of government in conformity with the Constitution of the United States in all respects, framed by a convention of delegates elected by the male citizens of said State, twenty-one years old and upward, of whatever race, color, or previous condition, who have been

---

* THE FIRST RECONSTRUCTION ACT BECOMES LAW: "An act to provide for the more efficient Government of the Rebel States." From *U.S. Statutes at Large,* XIV, 428–29.

resident in said State for one year previous to the day of such election, except such as may be disfranchised for participation in the rebellion or for felony at common law, and when such constitution shall provide that the elective franchise shall be enjoyed by all such persons as have the qualifications herein stated for electors of delegates, and when such constitution shall be ratified by a majority of the persons voting on the question of ratification who are qualified as electors for delegates, and when such constitution shall have been submitted to Congress for examination and approval, and Congress shall have approved the same, and when said State, by a vote of its legislature elected under said constitution, shall have adopted the amendment to the Constitution of the United States, proposed by the Thirty-ninth Congress, and known as article fourteen, and when said article shall have become a part of the Constitution of the United States, said State shall be declared entitled to representation in Congress, and senators and representatives shall be admitted therefrom on their taking the oath prescribed by law, and then and thereafter the preceding sections of this act shall be inoperative in said State: *Provided,* That no person excluded from the privilege of holding office by said proposed amendment to the Constitution of the United States, shall be eligible to election as a member of the convention to frame a constitution for any of said rebel States, nor shall any such person vote for members of such convention.

Sec. 6. *And be it further enacted,* That, until the people of said rebel States shall be by law admitted to representation in the Congress of the United States, any civil governments which may exist therein shall be deemed provisional only, and in all respects subject to the paramount authority of the United States at any time to abolish, modify, control, or supersede the same; and in all elections to any office under such provisional governments all persons shall be entitled to vote, and none others, who are entitled to vote, under the provisions of the fifth section of this act; and no person shall be eligible to any office under any such provisional governments who would be disqualified from holding office under the provisions of the third article of said constitutional amendment.

CONCLUSION

Thus, by a process far more haphazard than is realized today, was patched together the notorious Reconstruction Act. The three supplementary acts which later had to be passed (March 23, 1867, July 19, 1867, and March 11, 1868) reflect the jerry-built quality of the original.

The resulting Southern governments are themselves best described as "patched together." Quite aside from the question of how heavy a proportion of Negroes participated in them, or how callous the carpetbaggers were, or what a disreputable lot the Southern scalawags turned out to be, the primary fact was that the officialdom in every jurisdiction of government was essentially new and unfamiliar to the people. This in itself required a whole new network of arrangements and produced much disruption. In the course of it, moreover, the sanctions of "legitimacy"—invisible and dimly appreciated when working normally—which any government needs simply to lumber through its daily routine, slipped almost completely away. It was in this setting of tainted legitimacy that the first strokes for racial justice had to be taken, and this may have had a great deal to do with their lack of permanency.

During the Grant administration, the extent to which the North was willing to support the carpetbag regimes gradually ebbed, which meant that the native citizenry of the several states could take greater and greater initiative in pushing them out of office. The last of these regimes departed in 1877. With the Jim Crow movement of the nineties, nearly all the civil and political rights gained by the Negro during Reconstruction were obliterated.

STUDY QUESTIONS

The basic study problem—implicit in the arrangement of the documents and explicit in the introductory essay—is to formulate "a question of alternatives" to Reconstruction as it was actually carried out by Congress. More specific questions along these lines might include the following:

1] What was the "moderate" Republican position as implied in the speeches of Fessenden and Trumbull?
2] Consider the plan of Governor Andrew and prepare a critique of it.
3] Was it possible for President Johnson to have retained his influence without abandoning his principles during the critical spring of 1866? If so, how?
4] In an effort to shed light on Johnson's uncompromising position, various historians have formulated "psychologi-

cal" explanations of his behavior, based on such matters as his background, the influence of this or that adviser, etc. Using the documents here provided (especially numbers 9 and 14), attempt a theory of your own.

5] Profiting from the lessons of 1865–67, draw up the most sensible plan of Reconstruction you yourself can think of, and say when you think it would have had to be put into effect in order to achieve maximum results. Anticipate whatever criticisms your plan might receive from Andrew Johnson and Thaddeus Stevens, and defend it accordingly.

RECOMMENDED READINGS

PRIMARY SOURCES

KENDRICK, BENJAMIN B. *The Journal of the Joint Committee of Fifteen on Reconstruction* (New York, 1914).

McPHERSON, EDWARD. *The Political History of the United States of America During the Period of Reconstruction* (Washington, 1871).

RICHARDSON, JAMES D., ed. *A Compilation of the Messages and Papers of the Presidents, 1789–1897* (Washington, 1896–99), Vol. VI.

SHERMAN, JOHN, AND WILLIAM T. SHERMAN. *The Sherman Letters: Correspondence Between General and Senator Sherman from 1837 to 1891*, Rachel Sherman Thorndike, ed. (New York, 1894).

STRONG, GEORGE TEMPLETON. *The Diary of George Templeton Strong*, Allan Nevins and Milton H. Thomas, eds., 4 vols. (New York, 1952), Vol. IV.

U.S. CONGRESS. *Congressional Globe*, 39 Cong.

U.S. CONGRESS. *Report of the Joint Committee on Reconstruction*, 39 Cong. 1 Sess. (1866).

WELLES, GIDEON. *Diary of Gideon Welles, Secretary of the Navy Under Lincoln and Johnson*, Howard K. Beale, ed., 3 vols. (New York, 1960), Vols. II–III.

SECONDARY SOURCES

BEALE, HOWARD K. *The Critical Year: A Study of Andrew Johnson and Reconstruction* (New York, 1930).

BLAINE, JAMES G. *Twenty Years of Congress: From Lincoln to Garfield*, 2 vols. (Norwich, Conn., 1884).

BRODIE, FAWN M. *Thaddeus Stevens: Scourge of the South* (New York, 1959).

DORRIS, JONATHAN T. *Pardon and Amnesty under Lincoln and Johnson: The Restoration of the Confederates to Their Rights and Privileges* (Chapel Hill, N.C., 1953).

DUNNING, WILLIAM A. *Reconstruction, Political and Economic* (New York, 1907).

HESSELTINE, WILLIAM. *Lincoln's Plan of Reconstruction* (Tuscaloosa, Ala., 1960).

LOMASK, MILTON. *Andrew Johnson: President on Trial* (New York, 1960).

McKITRICK, ERIC L. *Andrew Johnson and Reconstruction* (Chicago, 1960).

MILTON, GEORGE F. *The Age of Hate: Andrew Johnson and the Radicals* (New York, 1930).

RANDALL, JAMES G., AND DAVID DONALD. *The Civil War and Reconstruction*, rev. ed. (Boston, 1961).

RHODES, JAMES F. *History of the United States from the Compromise of 1850*, 7 vols. (New York, 1893–1906), Vols. V–VI.

WINSTON, ROBERT W. *Andrew Johnson, Plebeian and Patriot* (New York, 1928).

WOODWARD, C. VANN. *The Strange Career of Jim Crow*, rev. ed. (New York, 1958).

Science, Religion, and Society: The Impact of Darwinism, 1859–1909

MERRILL D. PETERSON

UNIVERSITY OF VIRGINIA

CONTENTS

CHRONOLOGY

1859

Publication in England of Charles Darwin's *Origin of Species*.

1860

First American edition of *Origin of Species*; Asa Gray's review in the *American Journal of Science*; and Agassiz's criticism.

1864

Herbert Spencer's *First Principles* lays the basis of the "synthetic philosophy" to be developed in subsequent volumes.

1869

Charles W. Eliot, a chemist, inaugurated president of Harvard; John Fiske invited to lecture on evolution at Harvard.

1871

Publication of Darwin's *The Descent of Man*.

1872

Edward L. Youmans establishes the *Popular Science Monthly*, which popularizes evolutionary science.
William Graham Sumner appointed professor of political and social science at Yale.

1873

Death of Louis Agassiz.

1874

Yale paleontologist O. C. Marsh publishes scientific paper on the evolution of the horse, acclaimed by Darwin the best proof yet advanced of natural selection.
Spencer's *The Study of Sociology*, introduced by Sumner at Yale, lays foundations of the academic discipline in the United States.
James Dwight Dana endorses natural selection in the final edition of his *Manual of Geology*.
John Fiske publishes *Outlines of Cosmic Philosophy*.
John W. Draper, American historian and scientist, publishes *The Conflict Between Religion and Science*, a historical study.
Charles Hodge publishes *What Is Darwinism?*

1876

Thomas H. Huxley makes American lecture tour; speaks at the inauguration of The Johns Hopkins University.

1879

Henry George's *Progress and Poverty* bases reform proposals on an evolutionary view of economic society.

1882

Spencer makes American tour, concluded by banquet in his honor in New York City.

1883

Lester F. Ward publishes *Dynamic Sociology*.

1885

Henry Ward Beecher's *Evolution and Religion* published.

1888

Princeton President James McCosh endorses Darwinism in *The Religious Aspects of Evolution*.

1890

William James's *Principles of Psychology* gives a new, non-Spencerian turn to the study of psychology.

1893

Huxley delivers famous lecture, "Evolution and Ethics."

1900

The rediscovery of Gregor Mendel's work on inheritance in plants lays the basis of the modern science of genetics and proves valuable adjunct to natural selection theory.

1902

Peter Kropotkin's *Mutual Aid* supplies fruitful new emphasis on the role of cooperation in natural evolution.

1909

Celebration of the fiftieth anniversary of *Origin of Species*.

INTRODUCTION

A CRISIS in the history of thought is less readily apprehended than a crisis of state. It originates in a startling new theory or idea that shatters the image men have of their world and forces them to revise all their conceptions. Because it challenges customary canons of thought and belief, the innovative theory makes its way slowly into the way men think. Once accepted, however, there are no limits to its influence. It escapes from its original confines within a specific field of knowledge and pervades the entire intellectual atmosphere. The law of gravitation, as set forth by Isaac Newton in 1685, was a turning point in the history of civilization, transforming not only physics but also politics, theology, and art, ultimately giving rise to the comprehensive world view known as Newtonianism. Yet, Newton's great theory was but grudgingly accepted at first and only finally triumphant after three-quarters of a century. It is not surprising, therefore, that the Darwinian theory of natural selection, which symbolizes the crucial shift of thought in the nineteenth century, was elaborately denounced and debated before it was so thoroughly assimilated in the minds of thinking men as to be, in the words of an eminent champion, "part and parcel of their daily thoughts and an element in every investigation."

Charles Darwin's *Origin of Species* appeared in 1859. The result of thirty years' unremitting investigation by the English naturalist, the book attempted to demonstrate the genetic relationships of life forms—their transmutation and the development of progressively higher forms over vast time—and the fundamental cause of this evolutionary process in nature. The idea of organic evolution had appealed for some decades to the imagination of poets, naturalists, and philosophers. Perceiving the delicate shadings among the classes and orders of plants and animals, they had speculated on the possibility of genetic relationship mounting from the lowest to the highest forms in the grand "chain of being." But, as such men approached the threshold of the theory of evolution, they were checked by religious piety and the limits of scientific knowledge. Within the system devised by the eighteenth-century Swedish naturalist Linnæus, scientists made great progress in ordering and classifying plants and animals. The Linnæan system was harmonious with the Newtonian world view: it kept the phenomena of life as neatly and surely in place as the Newtonian scheme fixed the planets in their motions. In addition, it conformed to Christian belief. "We reckon," said Linnæus, "as many species as issued in pairs from the hands of the Creator." Science and theology tended to agree that the God who created the world in six days, probably about four thousand years before Christ, created the species as well; that being an omnipotent and omniscient God, none of the work of His mind and hand could be obliterated; that the species known to science were, therefore, permanently fixed from the moment of creation, the only change being in their dispersion over the world.

But nineteenth-century discoveries slowly undermined this conception. Paleontologists turned up more and more fossil specimens that could not be fitted into the Linnæan scheme or reconciled with the Bible. The French zoologist Lamarck, convinced there were no absolute separations between species, advanced a theory of evolution that explained the process in terms of the adjustment of plants and animals to changed environments which caused the development of useful variations and the hereditary transmission of these "acquired characteristics" to offspring. Lamarck's theory was suggestive but far from convincing. More influential was the masterly work of Charles Lyell in geology. Lyell, an Englishman and elder friend of Darwin's, set forth in his *Principles of Geology* (1830) the theory that the earth as presently known is the result of the operation of uniform natural causes over vast stretches of time. The "uniformitarianism" of Lyell not only explained the past by forces operative in the present, thus shaking the notion of a universe sprung complete from the mind of the Creator, but it also made available to scientific inquiry the factor of the immensity of time, the *sine qua non* of a theory of organic evolution. Lyell was the principal agent in smoothing the road for Darwin. The shock of Darwin's theory was at least partially absorbed, in America as in Europe, by the quarter-century controversy between Genesis and Geology. During the same period, moreover, the hold of Scriptural authority on the mind of Christendom was further relaxed by the comparative study of religions and the so-called "higher criticism" of the Bible. The former eroded historic conceptions of the uniqueness of Christianity, while the latter threw grave doubts on acceptance of the Bible as the literal word of God. Nevertheless, despite scientific and theological inroads, despite the unmistakable drift toward naturalistic and evolutionary viewpoints in all fields of knowledge, the prevailing opinion among scientists and laymen alike, right down to 1859, was that the species are fixed and immutable.

By the massive array of evidence in his *Origin of Species*, Darwin first provided mankind with impressive scientific grounds for believing in evolution. Equally important in winning that belief was Darwin's explanation of *how* evolution occurred: natural selection. The key insight came to Darwin in 1838 when he was casually reading Thomas Malthus' forty-year-old *Essay on Population*. He was struck by Malthus' formulation of the "law of population": that in human groups population increases at a much more rapid rate than the means of subsistence, thus causing a relentless "struggle for existence." Darwin discovered in this idea, which Malthus, a political economist, had directed against eighteenth-century visionaries of the progress and perfectibility of mankind, the very mechanism of progress in the kingdoms of plants and animals. Those organisms that best adapt to their environment —the fittest—survive and flourish, while the unfit are eliminated. Since slight variations occur almost at random in nature, those variations that prove most useful in the "struggle for existence" tend to be perpetuated through hereditary transmission. Accumulated and perfected through countless generations, the favorable variations eventuate in new species. This selection process was, Darwin thought, nature's equivalent of the plant or animal breeder's artificial selection. Natural selection was the fundamental force in the origin and evolution of all the multitudinous forms of life. Darwin did not shrink from embracing *homo sapiens* in his scheme, though he deferred the subject to a later volume, *The Descent of Man*, published in 1871.

Like other great seminal works in the history of ideas, Darwin's work was subject to different interpretations only the fullness of time would disclose. But, on the face of it, the Darwinian theory ran headlong against well-fortified convictions about man and his place in nature. Man was no longer "the final cause of the universe, the Heaven-descended heir of all the ages." So far from being but a little lower than the angels, man was, on Darwin's reckoning, but a little higher than the apes. Nothing in the evolutionary process decreed the creation of man, nor was there any assurance that it would end in man. Evolution was aimless in its movements and fortuitous in its results. Nature, in which even the gravest skeptics had seen the workings of a divine mind, was an endless scene of famine, rape, and slaughter—inevitable accompaniments of the mighty thrust of evolution. Of course, Darwin reduced the whole process to a law of nature, natural selection, and thus suggested to many an ordered and directed course in evolution akin to the precision of Newtonian law. Actually, the Darwinian law could only explain the transformation of species in terms of a congeries of accidents. Given a favorable variation, its selection for survival could be explained; but how was the variation generated? About this first and invisible phase of the evolutionary process, Darwin confessed ignorance. Variations were indeterminate, spontaneous, accidental, which is to say lawless. In the final accounting, the existence of man himself was an accident.

The public reception of Darwinism has been described in three stages: first, "It is absurd"; second, "It's contrary to the Bible"; and third, "We always knew it was so." The final stage was reached in England within a decade of the publication of *Origin of Species*. In America the controversy was only approaching its climax in 1870, and another decade was needed to secure the triumph. On this side of the Atlantic, particularly, the triumph was, as Darwin had predicted, the work of the younger generation of scientists and intellectuals: men who came to maturity around 1860, whose minds were ripe for receiving the new vision of the universe, whose sense of discontinuity with the past of their elders was accentuated by the Civil War and the well-nigh incredible social change that followed. Many such men could say, with Henry Adams, that they began as confident children of Darwin, that they were Darwinists before the letter and providential followers of the tide that swept up their generation.

In the initial discussion evoked by Darwin's book in the United States, the outstanding contribution came from the foremost American botanist, professor of natural history at Harvard University, Asa Gray. Pioneering the cause of evolution in this country, Gray at once, and repeatedly, addressed himself to the clamorous objections that came from both scientific and religious quarters. Many scientists on first encounter with Darwin found his theory, if not "absurd," at least implausible. There were enormous gaps—"missing links"—in the line of descent sketched by Darwin, who reasoned that the gaps, if filled up, would show the continuous progression of species. But others thought this curious logic for a scientist, and reasoned that the gaps defeated the theory. It was better, then, to await a more coherent account of evolution, meanwhile adhering to the old theory of the immutability of species, whose great champion was Louis Agassiz, Gray's colleague at Harvard and the most celebrated American scientist of the generation. Gray knew that Agassiz would throw his enormous prestige into the battle against Darwin. He therefore did not hesistate, in his initial American review of *Origin of Species*, to draw the issue keenly between Darwin and Agassiz. Agassiz accepted the challenge. Three months later he denounced the Darwinian theory as "a scientific mistake, untrue in its facts, unscientific in its method, and mischievous in its tendency." Death alone silenced Agassiz's opposition. When it came, in 1873, there were no disciples to champion his cause.

Gray realized, however, that Darwinism would never command a sympathetic hearing, even among scientists, unless it could be shown—and this was more important than scientific soundness—to be perfectly compatible with the enlarged purposes of a Christian universe. Darwin, an easygoing agnostic, had not anticipated the great outcry that religious men raised against his work. Among the orthodox of all sects, it was treated with downright contempt. One writer even called the book a hoax, perpetrated to make money, and he imagined Darwin laughing up his sleeve "at the stupidity of the numbers he has gulled into believing it as true." A bit more respectful, but equally censorious, was the learned Princeton divine Charles Hodge. Posing the question "What is Darwinism?" in a little book of that title, Hodge answered flatly, "It is Atheism." Of course, Darwinism could not possibly be squared with Scripture, but the same was true of many scientific theories. What really stabbed the sensibilities of religious men was the denial of *design* in nature. In the accommodation that had been worked out between religion and science over the previous century, God continued to be viewed as the Creator of the universe, which in His wisdom and beneficence He superintended through the agency of natural laws as revealed by science. Science had made notable progress within this system of "natural religion" and, excepting the hard core of orthodoxy, religion was satisfied, since every advance of science added to the power and the glory of the Deity.

Then along came Darwin with his picture of a universe distressingly without design or purpose. On Darwin's accounting, even such a wonderfully complex organ as the eye, seemingly irrefutable proof of design in nature, had neither been created in its perfect state nor been purposely evolved toward the useful end of sight. "There seems to be no more design in the variability of organic beings, and in the action of natural selection," Darwin observed, "than in the course which the wind blows." If Darwin was willing to settle for this, Gray, with nine-tenths of mankind, was not. Darwinism would be infinitely more palatable if it were sweetened with the old certainties of religious faith. Pressing his views on Darwin himself, Gray outlined a grand strategy for the reconciliation of Darwinism with "theistic" Christianity. "The important thing to do," he wrote,

is to develop aright evolutionary teleology, and to present the argument for design from the exquisite adaptations in such a way as to make it tell on both sides; with Christian men, that they may be satisfied with, and perchance may learn to admire, Divine works effected step by step, if need be, in a system of nature; and the antitheistic people, to show that without the implication of a superintending wisdom nothing is made out, and nothing credible.

Nothing in Darwinism called for the abandonment of design. On the contrary, Gray argued, once the fundamental idea of design was separated from outmoded notions of special creation and immutability, God could be seen at work in the evolutionary process itself. It was no longer necessary to imagine that man was suddenly flung into the universe by some inscrutable power or that creation was inalterably fixed from the beginning of time. Was the magnificence of the Divine Creator dimmed by the knowledge that He operated piecemeal? Gray thought not. His conciliatory proposition would never satisfy either the Christians whose faith was grounded in Biblical revelation or the Darwinian "irreconcilers" on the opposite side who refused to traffic in religious sentiment; but for the mass of liberal-minded men, not indifferent to religion, it provided a convenient bridge for the passage into Darwinism.

Rehabilitation of the old idea of design made possible the development of an evolutionary cosmology—an all-encompassing view of the universe as a grand and harmonious system, alien neither to the religious nor to the moral feelings of mankind. The key—almost the philosophers' stone—was furnished by Darwin's English contemporary, Herbert Spencer. The evolutionary theory in biology did not arise in a vacuum. Evolutionary ideas were germinating in many fields of knowledge in the middle of the nineteenth century. For example, Auguste Comte (1798–1857), the founder of sociology, offered a theory of the evolution of society through historical stages culminating in the Positivist stage of the future, when society would be organized, not theologically or metaphysically as before, but scientifically. Spencer felt Comte's influence along with others, and he had actually already commenced his gigantic project to unite all natural and human phenomena under one fundamental law of evolution when Darwin's work appeared. Recasting the Darwinian theory for his system, which he called the "synthetic philosophy," Spencer provided it with the appealing gloss of science. Superficially, at least, the progression in nature as observed by Darwin corresponded to Spencer's cosmic law, Persistence of Force: everything develops from a state of "incoherent homogeneity" toward a state of "coherent heterogeneity"—the protozoic mass to civilized man.

Spencer won an immense vogue in the United States. If John Locke was "America's philosopher" in the Revolutionary era, Spencer was his successor in the late nineteenth century. In part, his popularity stemmed from his political and economic ideas, which buttressed the regime of *laissez-faire* capitalism. More generally, however, Americans subscribed to the Spencerian philosophy because it drew the sting of chance, disorder, and uncertainty from evolutionary science, and because it reaffirmed in the language of science the traditional ideals of progress and perfectibility in creation. As John Dewey wrote of Spencer's philosophy:

Nature never parts with its eighteenth century function of effecting approximation to the goal of ultimate perfection and happiness, but nature no longer proffers itself as a pious reminiscence of the golden age of Rousseau, or a prophetic inspiration of the millenium of Condorcet, but as that most substantial, most real of all forces guaranteed and revealed to us at every turn by the advance of scientific inquiry.

Spencer's leading disciple and interpreter in America was John Fiske. Discovering Spencer while still an undergraduate at Harvard, Fiske soon came to believe that the "synthetic philosophy" was the greatest intellectual achievement of all history. But whereas the master was an agnostic, insensible to theological questions, the disciple felt the gnawing religious concern of his New England forebears. He set out, therefore, to enthrone God in Spencer's secular system. Spencer acknowledged that even he could not explain the power that originated and sustained the great law of evolution through all the workings of nature. He gave it the name of the "Unknowable." Fiske saw in this "infinite and eternal Energy from which all things proceed" the attributes of divinity. It was not the anthropomorphic God of the Christian epic, described by a later philosopher as "a great celestial King, wise and good, surrounded by a court of winged musicians and messengers"; it was not the God who set the stars in the heavens or placed Adam in the orchard or gave His son to mankind; but it was, in Fiske's view, a God the more credible for being glorified by science. The true Darwinian, Fiske wrote, "sees that in the deadly struggle for existence, which has raged through eons of time, the whole creation has been groaning and travailing together in order to bring forth the last consummate specimen of God's handiwork, the Human Soul."

Such doctrine carried Darwinism into the bosom of the church itself. In 1882, at the celebrity-studded banquet held in New York in honor of Herbert Spencer, Henry Ward Beecher, the most powerful Protestant minister of the time, announced his conversion to the new gospel. Thereafter, he preached evolution from his influential pulpit in Brooklyn's Plymouth Church. Of course, Beecher's formula for reconciling Christianity with Darwinism, differing from Fiske's, kept a place for Biblical revelation. But men like Beecher, seeing the inroads of science upon the traditional province of religion, opened up the wide and edifying avenues which modern, or liberal, Protestantism has traveled. Only the shriveling remnant of the old orthodoxy, the so-called fundamentalists, kept to the back roads.

Inseparable from the problem of religion in the Darwinian universe was the problem of morality. The provision of a moral code had always been one of the functions of religion. Operating through the church, religion had given the sanctions of morality; and in the case of Christianity, the virtues of peace, love, and mercy had stood foremost. But if men were now to take their cue from nature, what was to become of these virtues? What was to check the strong from oppressing the weak, the rich from robbing the poor, the poor from plundering the rich? If all life is a brute "struggle for existence," if "survival of the fittest" is the law of progress, did not the "fittest" have a right, even a duty, to eliminate the "unfit" by whatever force and cunning were at their disposal? The Darwinian theory neither asked these questions nor answered them. But men who were caught in its charmed circle sought a unifying vision of life and conduct on its terms, which, in their ethical import, appeared to negate the humane other-regarding virtues of Christianity.

The moral gulf thus opened up, though it scarcely daunted the hardiest Spencerians, created a nagging dilemma from which escape was found along three main routes. One claimed to be a scientific correction, or clarification, of the Darwinian emphasis on competition and strife among animals of the same species almost to the exclusion of the factors of cooperation and affection in evolution. The Russian naturalist Peter Kropotkin published the principal work, *Mutual Aid, a Factor in Evolution,* in 1902; but the notion that altruism figured prominently in evolution had been tossed about for some time. Darwin's great advocate, Thomas Huxley, projected a widely traveled route in a dramatic address, "Evolution and Ethics," in 1893. Huxley drew an absolute dualism between the "cosmic process" in nature and the "ethical process" in society. "Let us understand once and for all that the ethical progress of society depends, not in imitating the cosmic process, still less in running away from it, but in combatting it." Thus the standard for man was just the opposite of the jungle standard, and the farther man traveled away from the "struggle for existence" the more moral he became. Many American thinkers, however, were uncomfortable with Huxley's dualism, since it forced a return to the split universe and the split mind it had been the great achievement of the Spencerian philosophy to overcome. John Fiske, for example, took direct issue with Huxley. His retreat from Darwinism, Fiske said, gave joy to the enemies of science. Reflecting on the fact that one of the principal distinctions between man and the lower animals is the long duration of human infancy, Fiske had been led to work out its implications for evolution in *The Meaning of Infancy* (1883). When man came into nature, he found it necessary to develop institutions and to cultivate attitudes that would serve the survival of his helpless offspring; thus there arose, out of evolution itself, the family and the clan, socialized habits of behavior, and ultimately, Fiske thought, religion. Evolution did not negate the ethics of Christianity but actually placed them on the footing of scientific truth!

In its application to society, Darwinism had a "double potential." On the one hand, the law of natural selection could be taken as the model for the law of society, the forces of social progress could be deduced from the "cosmic process," and men could be abjured from interference. The true science of society would thus be laid in obedience to nature's law. On the other hand, conclusions of another order could be drawn from the elements of chance, freedom, and spontaneity in Darwinian evolution, as well as from the Darwinian method, which called for meticulous investigation of the processes of adaptation and change in the organism-environment relationship. On this reckoning, human freedom and intelligence to shape the environment toward specifically human goals would become the first principle of social science. The American philosopher and psychologist William James, in his essay "Great Men and Their Environment" (1880), clearly discerned the contradictory readings of Darwinism that were implicit in the two different cycles of operation in nature.

The first potential of "Social Darwinism" was practically realized in the last quarter of the nineteenth century. Largely contained in the social philosophy of Herbert Spencer, it provided the moral and intellectual underpinning of competitive business enterprise in the heroic age of American capitalism. The Yale professor William Graham Sumner was the leading advocate of this philosophy in the United States. The ideas of economic individualism, free competition, protection of property, and *laissez faire*, originally got from Adam Smith and the classical political economists, were triumphant in evolutionary science. "Rugged individualism" became the guarantor of "survival of the fittest" in modern industrial society. Many of the so-called robber barons justified their work by appeal to the law of evolution. "The growth of large business is merely a survival of the fittest . . . ," John D. Rockefeller declared, "it is merely the working out of a law of nature and a law of God." Spencerian doctrine penetrated the Supreme Court, where it acted as a hidden premise in the justices' attack on legislation intended to correct the evils of an unruly industrial order. In 1905 Mr. Justice Holmes, himself a Darwinist, filed a famous dissent against the court's practice, declaring that "the fourteenth amendment does not enact Mr. Herbert Spencer's *Social Statics.*"

The Spencerian philosophy was increasingly challenged after 1890 as the second potential of Darwinism for society disclosed itself in the minds of a new generation. Sometimes called Reform Darwinism, it set out to free men from the prison of social determinism by applying scientific intelligence to the solution of problems that arose in the course of evolution. While Sumner denounced "the absurd effort to make the world over," reformers like Henry George, who could see nothing in Sumner's philosophy but "a sort of hopeful fatalism," held that men might consciously direct their steps to the promised land. George, with his apocalyptic vision, still had one foot in the eighteenth century. The later Reform Darwinists, associated with the Progressive movement at the turn of the century, studied the problems of society as problems of adaptation of man to his environment, as specific obstacles to life goals which intelligence might overcome, not wholesale and once for all, but piecemeal and gradually in the way of evolution.

The finished philosophy of Reform Darwinism was put together in the twentieth century by the American pragmatist John Dewey. The logic of evolution, Dewey argued, dismissed the ancient and fruitless search for the end and being of the universe at large, and directed intelligence to the more useful investigation of the multitude of concrete problems that intelligence might solve. The real issue raised by Darwin's work, Dewey said on its fiftieth anniversary, was not the issue between religion and science, or any other question of belief; it was the issue between pseudo-Darwinists and true Darwinists, between men who, fearing to face nature directly, sought in Darwinism "the claim to formulate *a priori* the legislative constitution of the universe," and men who adopted the scientific mode of thinking in place of the old speculative mania of philosophy, converting philosophy, at least potentially, into "a method of moral and political diagnosis and prognosis."

DOCUMENTS

1] Professor Gray Lays the Groundwork

The *Origin of Species* was avidly discussed in literary and scientific circles when the first American edition appeared in 1860. The first and historically most significant review came from Asa Gray. Darwin esteemed Gray as a botanist, knew him personally, and made him privy to the *Origin* prior to publication. While never a thoroughgoing Darwinist, Gray classed himself among the converts when he wrote his review in America's leading scientific journal; but he purposely curbed his enthusiasm, thinking, as he said to Darwin, "I do your theory more good here, by bespeaking for it a fair and favorable consideration." Only two sections of the review appear below.*

. . . .

WHO, UPON a single perusal, shall pass judgment upon a work like this, to which twenty of the best years of the life of a most able naturalist have been devoted? And who among those naturalists who hold a position that entitles them to pronounce summarily upon the subject, can be expected to divest himself for the nonce of the influence of received and favorite systems? In fact, the controversy now opened is not likely to be settled in an off-hand way, nor is it desirable that it should be. A spirited conflict among opinions of every grade must ensue, which—to borrow an illustration from the doctrine of the book before us—may be likened to the conflict in Nature among races in the struggle for life, which Mr. Darwin describes; through which the views most favored by facts will be developed and tested by "Natural Selection," the weaker ones be destroyed in the process, and the strongest in the long-run alone survive. . . .

Between the doctrines of this volume and those of the other great naturalist whose name adorns the title-page of this journal [Mr. Agassiz], the widest divergence appears. It is interesting to contrast the two, and, indeed, is necessary to our purpose; for this contrast brings out most prominently, and sets in strongest light and shade, the main features of the theory of the origination of species by means of Natural Selection.

The ordinary and generally-received view assumes the independent, specific creation of each kind of plant and animal in a primitive stock, which reproduces its like from generation to generation, and so continues the species. Taking the idea of species from this perennial succession of essentially similar individuals, the chain is logically traceable back to a local origin in a single stock, a single pair, or a single individual, from which all the individuals composing the species have proceeded by natural generation. Although the similar-

---

* PROFESSOR GRAY LAYS THE GROUNDWORK: Asa Gray, "The Origin of Species by Means of Natural Selection." From the *American Journal of Science*, XXIX (March, 1860), in Asa Gray, *Darwiniana* (New York, 1876), pp. 10–15, 20–21, 53–58.

ity of progeny to parent is fundamental in the conception of species, yet the likeness is by no means absolute; all species vary more or less, and some vary remarkably—partly from the influence of altered circumstances, and partly (and more really) from unknown constitutional causes which altered conditions favor rather than originate. But these variations are supposed to be mere oscillations from a normal state, and in Nature to be limited if not transitory; so that the primordial differences between species and species at their beginning have not been effaced, nor largely obscured, by blending through variation. Consequently, whenever two reputed species are found to blend in Nature through a series of intermediate forms, community of origin is inferred, and all the forms, however diverse, are held to belong to one species. Moreover, since bisexuality is the rule in Nature (which is practically carried out, in the long-run, far more generally than has been suspected), and the heritable qualities of two distinct individuals are mingled in the offspring, it is supposed that the general sterility of hybrid progeny interposes an effectual barrier against the blending of the original species by crossing. . . .

That of Agassiz differs fundamentally from the ordinary view only in this, that it discards the idea of a common descent as the real bond of union among the individuals of a species, and also the idea of a local origin—supposing, instead, that each species originated simultaneously, generally speaking, over the whole geographical area it now occupies or has occupied, and in perhaps as many individuals as it numbered at any subsequent period.

Mr. Darwin, on the other hand, holds the orthodox view of the descent of all the individuals of a species not only from a local birthplace, but from a single ancestor or pair; and that each species has extended and established itself, through natural agencies, wherever it could; so that the actual geographical distribution of any species is by no means a primordial arrangement, but a natural result. He goes farther, and this volume is a protracted argument intended to prove that the species we recognize have not been independently created, as such, but have descended, like varieties, from other species. Varieties, on this view, are incipient or possible species: species are varieties of a larger growth and a wider and earlier divergence from the parent stock; the difference is one of degree, not of kind.

The ordinary view—rendering unto Cæsar the things that are Cæsar's—looks to natural agencies for the actual distribution and perpetuation of species, to a supernatural for their origin.

The theory of Agassiz regards the origin of species and their present general distribution over the world as equally primordial, equally supernatural; that of Darwin, as equally derivative, equally natural.

The theory of Agassiz, referring as it does the phenomena both of origin and distribution directly to the Divine will—thus removing the latter with the former out of the domain of inductive science (in which efficient cause is not the first, but the last word)—may be said to be theistic to excess. The contrasted theory is not open to this objection. Studying the facts and phenomena in reference to proximate causes, and endeavoring to trace back the series of cause and effect as far as possible, Darwin's aim and processes are strictly scientific, and his endeavor, whether successful or futile, must be regarded as a legitimate attempt to extend the domain of natural or physical science. For, though it well may be that "organic forms have no physical or secondary cause," yet this can be proved only indirectly, by the failure of every attempt to refer the phenomena in question to causal laws. But, however originated, and whatever be thought of Mr. Darwin's arduous undertaking in this respect, it is certain that plants and animals are subject from their birth to physical influences, to which they have to accommodate themselves as they can. How literally they are "born to trouble," and how incessant and severe the struggle for life generally is, the present volume graphically describes. Few will deny that such influences must have gravely affected the range and the association of individuals and species on the earth's surface. Mr. Darwin thinks that, acting upon an inherent predisposition to vary, they have sufficed even to modify the species themselves and produce the present diversity. Mr. Agassiz believes that they have not even affected the geographical range and the actual association of species, still less their forms; but that every adaptation of species to climate, and of species to species, is as aboriginal, and therefore as inexplicable, as are the organic forms themselves. . . .

In a word, the whole relations of animals, etc., to surrounding Nature and to each other, are regarded under the one view as ultimate facts, or in their ultimate aspect, and interpreted theologically; under the other as complex facts, to be analyzed and interpreted scientifically. The one naturalist, perhaps too largely assuming the scientifically unexplained to be inexplicable, views the phenomena only in their supposed relation to the Divine mind. The other, naturally expecting many of these phenomena to be resolvable under investigation, views them in their relations to one another, and endeavors to explain them as far as he can (and perhaps farther) through natural causes.

. . . We are thus, at last, brought to the question, What would happen if the derivation of species were to be substantiated, either as a true physical theory, or as a sufficient hypothesis? What would come of it? The inquiry is a pertinent one, just now. For, of those who agree with us in thinking that Darwin has not established his theory of derivation many will admit with us that he has rendered a theory of derivation much less improbable than before; that such a theory chimes in with the established doctrines of physical science, and is not unlikely to be largely accepted long before it can be proved. Moreover, the various notions that prevail—equally among the most and the least religious—as to the relations between natural agencies or phenomena and efficient cause, are seemingly more crude, obscure, and discordant, than they need be.

It is not surprising that the doctrine of the book should be denounced as atheistical. What does surprise and concern us is, that it should be so denounced by a scientific man, on the broad assumption that a material connection between the members of a series of organized beings is inconsistent with the idea of their being intellectually connected with one another through the Deity, i. e., as products of one mind, as indicating and realizing a preconceived plan. An assumption the rebound of which is somewhat fearful to contemplate, but fortunately one which every natural birth protests against.

It would be more correct to say that the theory in itself is perfectly compatible with an atheistic view of the universe. That is true; but it is equally true of physical theories generally. Indeed, it is more true of the theory of gravitation, and of the nebular hypothesis, than of the hypothesis in question. The latter merely takes up *a particular, proximate cause,* or set of such causes, from which, it is argued, the present diversity of species has or may have *contingently* resulted. The author does not say *necessarily* resulted; that the actual results in mode and measure, and none other, must have taken place. On the other hand, the theory of gravitation and its extension in the nebular hypothesis assume a *universal and ultimate* physical cause, from which the effects in Nature must *necessarily* have resulted. Now, it is not thought, at least at the present day, that the establishment of the Newtonian theory was a step toward atheism or pantheism. Yet the great achievement of Newton consisted in proving that certain forces (blind forces, so far as the theory is concerned), acting upon matter in certain directions, must *necessarily* produce planetary orbits of the exact measure and form in which observation shows them to exist—a view which is just as consistent with eternal necessity, either in the atheistic or the pantheistic form, as it is with theism.

Nor is the theory of derivation particularly exposed to the charge of the atheism of fortuity; since it undertakes to assign real causes for harmonious and systematic results. . . .

How the author of this book harmonizes his scientific theory with his philosophy and theology, he has not informed us. Paley in his celebrated analogy with the watch, insists that if the timepiece were so constructed as to produce other similar watches, after a manner of generation in animals, the argument from design would be all the stronger. What is to hinder Mr. Darwin from giving Paley's argument a further *a-fortiori* extension to the supposed case of a watch which sometimes produces better watches, and contrivances adapted to successive conditions, and so at length turns out a chronometer, a town clock, or a series of organisms of the same type? From certain incidental expressions at the close of the volume . . . we judge it probable that our author regards the whole system of Nature as one which had received at its first formation the impress of the will of its Author, foreseeing the varied yet necessary laws of its action throughout the whole of its existence, ordaining when and how each particular of the stupendous plan should be realized in effect, and—with Him to whom to will is to do—in ordaining doing it. Whether profoundly philosophical or not, a view maintained by eminent philosophical physicists and theologians . . . will hardly be denounced as atheism. Perhaps Mr. Darwin would prefer to express his idea in a more general way, by adopting the thoughtful words of one of the most eminent naturalists [Agassiz] of this or any age, substituting the word *action* for "thought," since it is the former (from which alone the latter can be inferred) that he has been considering. "Taking Nature as exhibiting thought for my guide, it appears to me that while human thought is consecutive, Divine thought is simultaneous, embracing at the same time and forever, in the past, the present and the future, the most diversified relations among hundreds of thousands of organized beings, each of which may present complications again, which to study and understand even imperfectly—as for instance man himself—mankind has already spent thousands of years." In thus conceiving of the Divine Power in act as coetaneous with Divine Thought, and of both as far as may be apart from the human element of time, our author may regard the intervention of the

Creator either as, humanly speaking, *done from all time,* or else as *doing through all time.* In the ultimate analysis we suppose that every philosophical theist must adopt one or the other conception.

A perversion of the first view leads toward atheism, the notion of an eternal sequence of cause and effect, for which there is no first cause—a view which few sane persons can long rest in. The danger which may threaten the second view is pantheism. We feel safe from either error, in our profound conviction that there is order in the universe; that order presupposes mind; design, will; and mind or will, personality. Thus guarded, we much prefer the second of the two conceptions of causation, as the more philosophical as well as Christian view—a view which leaves us with the same difficulties and the same mysteries in Nature as in Providence, and no other. Natural law, upon this view, is the human conception of continued and orderly Divine action.

2] Professor Agassiz Files a Dissent

Louis Agassiz, Gray's colleague at Harvard, was the titan of American science in 1860. Vain and egocentric, powerful, charming, casting an almost hypnotic spell over his students, he was, in the words of one of them, "one of those folio copies of nature" who looked upon the vastness of living things "as if he were there to take possession of them all." Born in Switzerland, he had studied with the French zoologist Cuvier, the great antagonist of Lamarck. and his *Essay on Classification* (1857) carried forward Cuvier's work. Agassiz's reputation as a scientist was bound up with the doctrine of immutability; thus he could not help but see in Darwin a threat to himself. His religious feelings were also involved. In June, 1860, the *American Journal of Science* published Agassiz's answer to Darwin (and Gray) from the advance sheets of the third volume of his *Contributions to the Natural History of the United States.**

.   .   .   .

IT SEEMS to me that there is much confusion of ideas in the general statement of the variability of species so often repeated lately. If species do not exist at all, as the supporters of the transmutation theory maintain, how can they vary? and if individuals alone exist, how can the differences which may be observed among them prove the variability of species? The fact seems to me to be that while species are based upon definite relations among individuals which differ in various ways among themselves, each individual, as a distinct being, has a definite course to run from the time of its first formation to the end of its existence, during which it never loses its identity nor changes its individuality, nor its relations to other individuals belonging to the same species, but preserves all the categories of relationship which constitute specific or generic or family affinity, or any other kind or degree of affinity. *To prove that species vary it should be proved that individuals born from common ancestors change the different categories of relationship which they bore primitively to*

* PROFESSOR AGASSIZ FILES A DISSENT: "Prof. Agassiz on the Origin of Species." From the *American Journal of Science,* XXX (June, 1860), 143–47, 149–50.

one another. While all that has thus far been shown is, that there exists a considerable difference among individuals of one and the same species. This may be new to those who have looked upon every individual picked up at random, as affording the means of describing satisfactorily any species; but no naturalist who has studied carefully any of the species now best known, can have failed to perceive that it requires extensive series of specimens accurately to describe a species, and that the more complete such series are, the more precise appear the limits which separate species. Surely the aim of science cannot be to furnish amateur zoölogists or collectors, a *recipe* for a ready identification of any chance specimen that may fall into their hands. And the difficulties with which we may meet in attempting to characterize species do not afford the first indication that species do not exist at all, as long as most of them can be distinguished, as such, almost at first sight. I foresee that some convert to the transmutation creed will at once object that the facility with which species may be distinguished is no evidence that they were not derived from other species. It may be so. But as long as no fact is adduced to show that any one well known species among the many thousands that are buried in the whole series of fossiliferous rocks, is actually the parent of any one of the species now living, such arguments can have no weight; and thus far the supporters of the transmutation theory have failed to produce any such facts. Instead of facts we are treated with marvelous bear, cuckoo, and other stories. Credat Judaeus Apella! [1]

Had Mr. Darwin or his followers furnished a single fact to show that individuals change, in the course of time, in such a manner as to produce at last species different from those known before, the state of the case might be different. But it stands recorded now as before, that the animals known to the ancients are still in existence, exhibiting to this day the characters they exhibited of old. The geological record, even with all its imperfections, exaggerated to distortion, tells now, what it has told from the beginning, that the supposed intermediate forms between the species of different geological periods are imaginary beings, called up merely in support of a fanciful theory. The origin of all the diversity among living beings remains a mystery as totally unexplained as if the book of Mr. Darwin had never been written, for no theory unsupported by fact, however plausible it may appear, can be admitted in science.

It seems generally admitted that the work of Darwin is particularly remarkable for the fairness with which he presents the facts adverse to his views. It may be so; but I confess that it has made a very different impression upon me. I have been more forcibly struck by his inability to perceive when the facts are fatal to his argument, than by anything else in the whole work. His chapter on the Geological Record, in particular, appears to me, from beginning to end, as a series of illogical deductions and misrepresentations of the modern results of Geology and Palæontology. I do not intend to argue here, one by one, the questions he has discussed. Such arguments end too often in special pleading, and any one familiar with the subject may readily perceive where the truth lies by confronting his assertions with the geological record itself. But since the question at issue is chiefly to be settled by palæontological evi-

1 Credat Judaeus Apella!: Let the Jew, Apella, believe! (From the Roman poet Juvenal.)

dence, and I have devoted the greater part of my life to the special study of the fossils, I wish to record my protest against his mode of treating this part of the subject. Not only does Darwin never perceive when the facts are fatal to his views, but when he has succeeded by an ingenious circumlocution in overleaping the facts, he would have us believe that he has lessened their importance or changed their meaning. He would thus have us believe that there have been periods during which all that had taken place during other periods was destroyed, and this solely to explain the absence of intermediate forms between the fossils found in successive deposits, for the origin of which he looks to those missing links; whilst every recent progress in Geology shows more and more fully how gradual and successive all the deposits have been which form the crust of our earth. . . . He would have us believe that the oldest organisms that existed were simple cells, or something like the lowest living beings now in existence; when such highly organized animals as Trilobites and Orthoceratites are among the oldest known.—He would have us believe that these lowest first-born became extinct in consequence of the gradual advantage some of their more favored descendants gained over the majority of their predecessors; when there exist now, and have existed at all periods in past history, as large a proportion of more simply organized beings, as of more favored types, and when such types as Lingula were among the lowest Silurian fossils, and are alive at the present day.—He would have us believe that each new species originated in consequence of some slight change in those that preceded; when every geological formation teems with types that did not exist before.—He would have us believe that animals and plants became gradually more and more numerous; when most species appear in myriads of individuals, in the first bed in which they are found. He would have us believe that animals disappear gradually; when they are as common in the uppermost bed in which they occur as in the lowest, or any intermediate bed. Species appear suddenly and disappear suddenly in successive strata. That is the fact proclaimed by Palæontology; they neither increase successively in number, nor do they gradually dwindle down; none of the fossil remains thus far observed show signs of a gradual improvement or of a slow decay. . . . He would also have us believe that the most perfect organs of the body of animals are the product of gradual improvement, when eyes as perfect as those of the Trilobites are preserved with the remains of these oldest animals. He would have us believe that it required millions of years to effect any one of these changes; when far more extraordinary transformations are daily going on, under our eyes, in the shortest periods of time, during the growth of animals.—He would have us believe that animals acquire their instincts gradually; when even those that never see their parents, perform at birth the same acts, in the same way, as their progenitors. . . . And all these, and many other calls upon our credulity, are coolly made in the face of an amount of precise information, readily accessible, which would overwhelm any one who does not place his opinions above the records of an age eminently characterized for its industry, and during which, that information was laboriously accumulated by crowds of faithful laborers.

It would be superfluous to discuss in detail the arguments by which Mr. Darwin attempts to explain the diversity among animals. Suffice it to say, that he has lost sight of the most striking of the features, and the one which pervades the whole, namely, that there runs throughout Nature unmistakable evidence of thought, corresponding to the mental operations of our own mind, and therefore intelligible to us as thinking beings, and unaccountable on any other basis than that they owe their existence to the working of intelligence; and no theory that overlooks this element can be true to nature.

There are naturalists who seem to look upon the idea of creation, that is, a manifestation of an intellectual power by material means, as a kind of bigotry; forgetting, no doubt, that whenever they carry out a thought of their own, they do something akin to creating, unless they look upon their own elucubrations as something in which their individuality is not concerned, but arising without an intervention of their mind, in consequence of the working of some "bundles of forces," about which they know nothing themselves. And yet such men are ready to admit that matter is omnipotent, and consider a disbelief in the omnipotence of matter as tantamout to imbecility; for, what is the assumed power of matter to produce all finite beings, but omnipotence? And what is the outcry raised against those who cannot admit it, but an insinuation that they are *non-compos?* The book of Mr. Darwin is free of all such uncharitable sentiments towards his fellow-laborers in the field of science; nevertheless his mistake lies in a similar assumption that the most complicated system of combined thoughts can be the result of accidental causes; for he ought to know, as every physicist will concede, that all the influences to which he would ascribe the origin of species are accidental in their very nature, and he must know, as every naturalist familiar with the modern progress of science does know, that the organized beings which live now, and have lived in former geological periods, constitute an organic whole, intelligibly and methodically combined in all its parts. As a zoölogist he must know in particular, that the animal kingdom is built upon four different plans of structure, and that the reproduction and growth of animals takes place according to four different modes of development, and that unless it is shown that these four plans of structure, and these four modes of development, are transmutable one into the other, no transmutation theory can account for the origin of species. The fallacy of Mr. Darwin's theory of the origin of species by means of natural selection, may be traced in the first few pages of his book, where he overlooks the difference between the voluntary and deliberate acts of selection applied methodically by man to the breeding of domesticated animals and the growing of cultivated plants, and the chance influences which may effect animals and plants in the state of nature. To call these influences "natural selection," is a misnomer which will not alter the conditions under which they may produce the desired results. Selection implies design; the powers to which Darwin refers the order of species, can design nothing. Selection is no doubt the essential principle on which the raising of breeds is founded, and the subject of breeds is presented in its true light by Mr. Darwin; but this process of raising breeds by the selection of favorable subjects, is in no way similar to that which regulates specific differences. Nothing is more remote from the truth than the attempted parallelism between the breeds of domesticated animals and the species of wild ones. . . .

All attempts to explain the origin of species may be brought under two cat-

egories: viz. 1st, some naturalists admitting that all organized beings are created, that is to say, endowed from the beginning of their existence with all
their characteristics, while 2d, others assume that they arise spontaneously. This
classification of the different theories of the origin of species, may appear objectionable to the supporters of the transmutation theory; but I can perceive
no essential difference between their views and the old idea that animals may
have arisen spontaneously. They differ only in the modes by which the spontaneous appearance is assumed to be effected; some believe that physical agents
may so influence organized beings as to modify them—this is the view of De-
Maillet and the Vestiges of Creation; others believe that the organized beings
themselves change in consequence of their own acts, by changing their mode
of life, etc., this is the view of Lamarck; others still assume that animals and
plants tend necessarily to improve, in consequence of the struggle for life, in
which the favored races are supposed to survive; this is the view lately propounded by Darwin. I believe these theories will, in the end, all share the fate
of the theory of spontaneous generations so called, as the facts of nature shall
be confronted more closely with the theoretical assumptions. The theories of
DeMaillet, Oken, and Lamarck are already abandoned by those who have
adopted the transmutation theory of Darwin; and unless Darwin and his followers succeed in showing that the struggle for life tends to something beyond
favoring the existence of certain individuals over that of other individuals, they
will soon find that they are following a shadow. . . .

Until the facts of Nature are shown to have been mistaken by those who
have collected them, and that they have a different meaning from that now
generally assigned to them, I shall therefore consider the transmutation theory
as a scientific mistake, untrue in its facts, unscientific in its method, and mischievous in its tendency.

3] Professor Hodge Declares "Darwinism Is Atheism"

The college at Princeton, New Jersey, a Presbyterian institution, was the
citadel of traditional theology and philosophy in America. Princeton divines
were always on guard against new forms of "infidelity," which they exposed
in the *Biblical Repository and Princeton Review*. Editor of the *Review* was
Charles Hodge, professor of systematic theology at Princeton. His little volume *What Is Darwinism?*, intended for popular consumption, stated the
case of the more orthodox Protestants for whom the God of Scripture and
the miraculous story of Christianity were the crucial elements of Christian
belief. At the very time Hodge wrote, however, Princeton's President James
McCosh was following the path of reconciliation.*

THE SCRIPTURAL SOLUTION OF THE PROBLEM OF THE UNIVERSE.

THAT solution is stated in words equally simple and sublime: "In the beginning God created the heavens and the earth." We have here, first, the idea

* PROFESSOR HODGE DECLARES "DARWINISM IS ATHEISM": From Charles Hodge, *What
Is Darwinism?* (New York, 1874), pp. 3–7, 40–48, 52–53, 57–62.

of God. The word God has in the Bible a definite meaning. It does not stand for an abstraction, for mere force, for law or ordered sequence. God is a spirit, and as we are spirits, we know from consciousness that God is, (1.) A Substance; (2.) That He is a person; and, therefore, a self-conscious, intelligent, voluntary agent. He can say I; we can address Him as Thou; we can speak of Him as He or Him. This idea of God pervades the Scriptures. It lies at the foundation of natural religion. It is involved in our religious consciousness. It enters essentially into our sense of moral obligation. It is inscribed ineffaceably, in letters more or less legible, on the heart of every human being. The man who is trying to be an atheist is trying to free himself from the laws of his being. He might as well try to free himself from liability to hunger or thirst.

The God of the Bible, then, is a Spirit, infinite, eternal, and unchangeable in his being, wisdom, power, holiness, goodness, and truth. As every theory must begin with some postulate, this is the grand postulate with which the Bible begins. This is the first point.

The second point concerns the origin of the universe. It is not eternal either as to matter or form. It is not independent of God. It is not an evolution of his being, or his existence form. He is extramundane as well as antemundane. The universe owes its existence to his will.

Thirdly, as to the nature of the universe; it is not a mere phenomenon. It is an entity, having real objective existence, or actuality. This implies that matter is a substance endowed with certain properties, in virtue of which it is capable of acting and of being acted upon. These properties being uniform and constant, are physical laws to which, as their proximate causes, all the phenomena of nature are to be referred.

Fourthly, although God is extramundane, He is nevertheless everywhere present. That presence is not only a presence of essence, but also of knowledge and power. He upholds all things. He controls all physical causes, working through them, with them, and without them, as He sees fit. As we, in our limited spheres, can use physical causes to accomplish our purposes, so God everywhere and always coöperates with them to accomplish his infinitely wise and merciful designs.

Fifthly, man a part of the universe, is, according to the Scriptures, as concerns his body, of the earth. So far, he belongs to the animal kingdom. As to his soul, he is a child of God, who is declared to be the Father of the spirits of all men. God is a spirit, and we are spirits. We are, therefore, of the same nature with God. We are God-like; so that in knowing ourselves we know God. No man conscious of his manhood can be ignorant of his relationship to God as his Father.

The truth of this theory of the universe rests, in the first place, so far as it has been correctly stated, on the infallible authority of the Word of God. In the second place, it is a satisfactory solution of the problem to be solved,— (1.) It accounts for the origin of the universe. (2.) It accounts for all the universe contains, and gives a satisfactory explanation of the marvellous contrivances which abound in living organisms, of the adaptations of these organisms to conditions external to themselves, and for those provisions for the future, which on any other assumption are utterly inexplicable. (3.) It is in conflict with no truth of reason and with no fact of experience. (4.) The Scriptural doctrine accounts for the spiritual nature of man, and meets all his spiritual necessities. It gives him an object of adoration, love, and confidence. It reveals the Being on whom his indestructible sense of responsibility terminates. The truth of this doctrine, therefore, rests not only on the authority of the Scriptures, but on the very constitution of our nature. The Bible has little charity for those who reject it. It pronounces them to be either derationalized or demoralized, or both.

The Sense in which Mr. Darwin uses the Word "Natural."

WE HAVE not yet reached the heart of Mr. Darwin's theory. The main idea of his system lies in the word "natural." He uses that word in two senses: first, as antithetical to the word artificial. Men can produce very marked varieties as to structure and habits of animals. This is exemplified in the production of the different breeds of horses, cattle, sheep, and dogs; and specially, as Mr. Darwin seems to think, in the case of pigeons. Of these, he says, "The diversity of breeds is something astonishing." Some have long, and some very short bills; some have large feet, some small; some long necks, others long wings and tails, while others have singularly short tails; some have thirty, and even forty, tail-feathers, instead of the normal number of twelve or fourteen. They differ as much in instinct as they do in form. Some are carriers, some pouters, some tumblers, some trumpeters; and yet all are descendants of the Rock Pigeon which is still extant. If, then, he argues, man, in a comparatively short time, has by artificial selection produced all these varieties, what might be accomplished on the boundless scale of nature, during the measureless ages of the geologic periods.

Secondly, he uses the word natural as antithetical to supernatural. Natural selection is a selection made by natural laws, working without intention and design. It is, therefore, opposed not only to artificial selection, which is made by the wisdom and skill of man to accomplish a given purpose, but also to supernatural selection, which means either a selection originally intended by a power higher than nature; or which is carried out by such power. In using the expression Natural Selection, Mr. Darwin intends to exclude design, or final causes. All the changes in structure, instinct, or intelligence, in the plants or animals, including man, descended from the primordial germ, or animalcule, have been brought about by unintelligent physical causes. On this point he leaves us in no doubt. He defines nature to be "the aggregate action and product of natural laws; and laws are the sequence of events as ascertained by us." . . . It is denied that it is a process originally designed, or guided by intelligence, such as the activity which foresees an end and consciously selects and controls the means of its accomplishment. Artificial selection, then, is an intelligent process; natural selection is not.

There are in the animal and vegetable worlds innumerable instances of at least apparent contrivance, which have excited the admiration of men in all ages. There are three ways of accounting for them. The first is the Scriptural doctrine, namely, that God is a Spirit, a personal, self-conscious, intelligent agent; that He is infinite, eternal, and unchangeable in his being and per-

fections; that He is ever present; that this presence is a presence of knowledge and power. . . . This universal and constant control of God is not only
one of the most patent and pervading doctrines of the Bible, but it is one of
the fundamental principles of even natural religion.

The second method of accounting for contrivances in nature admits that
they were foreseen and purposed by God, and that He endowed matter with
forces which He foresaw and intended should produce such results. But here
his agency stops. He never interferes to guide the operation of physical causes.
He does nothing to control the course of nature, or the events of history. On
this theory it may be said, (1.) That it is utterly inconsistent with the Scriptures. (2.) It does not meet the religious and moral necessities of our nature.
It renders prayer irrational and inoperative. It makes it vain for a man in any
emergency to look to God for help. (3.) It is inconsistent with obvious facts. . . .

This banishing God from the world is simply intolerable, and, blessed be
his name, impossible. An absent God who does nothing is, to us, no God.
Christ brings God constantly near to us. He said to his disciples, "Consider the
ravens, for they neither sow nor reap; which have neither store-house nor
barn; and God feedeth them; how much better are ye than the fowls. And
which of you by taking thought can add to his stature one cubit? Consider
the lilies how they grow; they toil not, neither do they spin; and yet I say
unto you that Solomon in all his glory was not arrayed like one of these. If
then God so clothe the grass, which is to-day in the field, and to-morrow is
cast into the oven; how much more will He clothe you, O ye of little faith."
"And seek ye not what ye shall eat, or what ye shall drink, neither be ye of
doubtful mind. For all these things do the nations of the world seek after;
and your Father knoweth that ye have need of these things." It may be said
that Christ did not teach science. True, but He taught truth; and science, so
called, when it comes in conflict with truth, is what man is when he comes
in conflict with God. . . .

The third method of accounting for the contrivances manifested in the
organs of plants and animals, is that which refers them to the blind operation
of natural causes. They are not due to the continued coöperation and control of
the divine mind, nor to the original purpose of God in the constitution of
the universe. This is the doctrine of the Materialists, and to this doctrine, we
are sorry to say, Mr. Darwin, although himself a theist, has given in his ad-
hesion. It is on this account the Materialists almost deify him. . . .

DARWINISM EXCLUDES TELEOLOGY.

IT IS however neither evolution nor natural selection, which give Darwinism
its peculiar character and importance. It is that Darwin rejects all teleology,
or the doctrine of final causes. He denies design in any of the organisms in the
vegetable or animal world. He teaches that the eye was formed without any
purpose of producing an organ of vision. . . .

The point to be proved is that it is the distinctive doctrine of Mr. Darwin,
that species owe their origin, not to the original intention of the divine mind;
not to special acts of creation calling new forms into existence at certain epochs;
not to the constant and everywhere operative efficiency of God, guiding phys-

ical causes in the production of intended effects; but to the gradual accumulation of unintended variations of structure and instinct, securing some advantage to their subjects.

That such is Mr. Darwin's doctrine we prove from his own writings. And the first proof from that source is found in express declarations. When an idea pervades a book and constitutes its character, detached passages constitute a very small part of the evidence of its being inculcated. In the present case, however, such passages are sufficient to satisfy even those who have not had occasion to read Mr. Darwin's books. In referring to the similarity of structure in animals of the same class, he says, "Nothing can be more hopeless than to attempt to explain this similarity of pattern in members of the same class, by utility or the doctrine of final causes." . . .

What, however, perhaps more than anything, makes clear his rejection of design is the manner in which he deals with the complicated organs of plants and animals. Why don't [*sic*] he say, they are the product of the divine intelligence? If God made them, it makes no difference, so far as the question of design is concerned, how He made them: whether at once or by a process of evolution. But instead of referring them to the purpose of God, he laboriously endeavors to prove that they may be accounted for without any design or purpose whatever.

"To suppose," he says, "that the eye with all its inimitable contrivances for adjusting the focus to different distances, for admitting different degrees of light, and for the correction of spherical and chromatic aberration, could have been formed by natural selection, seems, I freely confess, absurd in the highest degree." Nevertheless he attempts to explain the process. "It is scarcely possible," he says, "to avoid comparing the eye with the telescope. We know that this instrument has been perfected by the long continued efforts of the highest of human intellects; and we naturally infer that the eye has been formed by a somewhat analogous process. But may not this inference be presumptuous? Have we any right to assume that the Creator works by intellectual powers like those of man? If we must compare the eye to an optical instrument, we ought in imagination to take a thick layer of transparent tissue, with spaces filled with fluid, and with a nerve sensitive to light beneath, and then suppose every part of this layer to be continually changing slowly in density, so as to separate into layers of different densities and thicknesses, placed at different distances from each other, and with the surfaces of each layer slowly changing in form. Further, we must suppose that there is a power represented by natural selection, or the survival of the fittest, always intently watching each slight alteration in the transparent layers, and carefully preserving each, which, under varied circumstances, tends to produce a distinct image. We must suppose each new state of the instrument to be multiplied by the million; each to be preserved until a better is produced, and the old ones to be all destroyed. In living bodies, variations will cause the slight alterations, generations will multiply them almost infinitely, and natural selection will pick out with unerring skill each improvement." "Let this process," he says, "go on for millions of years," and we shall at last have a perfect eye.

It would be absurd to say anything disrepectful of such a man as Mr. Darwin, and scarcely less absurd to indulge in any mere extravagance of language;

yet we are expressing our own experience, when we say that we regard Mr. Darwin's books the best refutation of Mr. Darwin's theory. He constantly shuts us up to the alternative of believing that the eye is a work of design or the product of the unintended action of blind physical causes. To any ordinarily constituted mind, it is absolutely impossible to believe that it is not a work of design. Darwin himself, it is evident, dear as his theory is, can hardly believe it. "It is indispensable," he says, "to arrive at a just conclusion as to the formation of the eye, that the reason should conquer the imagination; but I have felt the difficulty far too keenly to be surprised at any degree of hesitation in extending the principle of natural selection to so startling an extent."

It will be observed that every step in his account of the formation of the eye is an arbitrary assumption. . . . In like manner we may suppose a man to sit down to account for the origin and contents of the Bible, assuming as his "working hypothesis," that it is not the product of mind either human or divine, but that it was made by a typesetting machine worked by steam, and picking out type hap-hazard. In this way in a thousand years one sentence might be produced, in another thousand a second, and in ten thousand more, the two might get together in the right position. Thus in the course of "millions of years" the Bible might have been produced, with all its historical details, all its elevated truths, all its devout and sublime poetry, and above all with the delineation of the character of Christ, the ἰδέα τῶν ἰδεῶν, the ideal of majesty and loveliness, before which the whole world, believing and unbelieving, perforce bows down in reverence. And when reason has sufficiently subdued the imagination to admit all this, then by the same theory we may account for all the books in all languages in all the libraries in the world. Thus we should have Darwinism applied in the sphere of literature. This is the theory which we are told is to sweep away Christianity and the Church!

4] John Fiske Embraces Evolution and Religion

Already an intellectual prodigy, well versed in evolutionary philosophy when the *Origin of Species* appeared in his twentieth year, John Fiske blazed the trail of Darwinism for the younger generation. His mind, like that of his master Herbert Spencer, ranged nimbly if somewhat superficially through all realms of knowledge. The most definitive statement of his theistic evolution will be found in *Outlines of Cosmic Philosophy* (1874), but more popular were the little volumes and addresses written, all in Fiske's mellifluous manner, over many years. The address which follows was delivered at the farewell dinner given to Spencer in New York City, November 9, 1882. It exhibits the American adulation of Spencer as well as Fiske's remarkably successful translation of Darwinism into religion.*

. . . WE HAVE met here this evening to do homage to a dear and noble teacher and friend, and it is well that we should choose this time to recall the various aspects of the immortal work by which he has earned the gratitude of a world.

* JOHN FISKE EMBRACES EVOLUTION AND RELIGION: John Fiske, "Evolution and Religion." From John Fiske, *Excursions of an Evolutionist* (Boston, 1884), pp. 295–305.

The work which Herbert Spencer has done in organizing the different departments of human knowledge, so as to present the widest generalizations of all the sciences in a new and wonderful light, as flowing out of still deeper and wider truths concerning the universe as a whole; the great number of profound generalizations which he has established incidentally to the pursuit of this main object; the endlessly rich and suggestive thoughts which he has thrown out in such profusion by the wayside all along the course of this great philosophical enterprise,—all this work is so manifest that none can fail to recognize it. It is work of the calibre of that which Aristotle and Newton did. Though coming in this latter age, it as far surpasses their work in its vastness of performance as the railway surpasses the sedan-chair, or as the telegraph surpasses the carrier-pigeon.

But it is not of this side of our teacher's work that I wish to speak, but of a side of it that has hitherto met with less general recognition. There are some people who seem to think that it is not enough that Mr. Spencer should have made all these priceless contributions to human knowledge, but actually complain of him for not giving us a complete and exhaustive system of theology into the bargain. What I wish, therefore, to point out is that Mr. Spencer's work on the side of religion will be seen to be no less important than his work on the side of science, when once its religious implications shall have been fully and consistently unfolded.

If we look at all the systems or forms of religion of which we have any knowledge, we shall find that they differ in many superficial features. They differ in many of the transcendental doctrines which they respectively preach, and in many of the rules of conduct which they respectively lay down for men's guidance. They assert different things about the universe, and they enjoin or prohibit different kinds of behaviour on the part of their followers. The doctrine of the Trinity, which to many Christians is the most sacred of mysteries, is to all Mohammedans the foulest of blasphemies. The Brahman's conscience would be more troubled if he were to kill a cow by accident than if he were to swear to a lie or steal a purse. The Turk, who sees no wrong in bigamy, would shrink from the sin of eating pork. But, amid all such surface differences we find throughout all known religions two points of substantial agreement. And these two points of agreement will be admitted by modern civilized men to be of far greater importance than the innumerable differences of detail. All religions agree in the two following assertions, one of which is of speculative and one of which is of ethical import. One of them serves to sustain and harmonize our thoughts about the world we live in and our place in that world; the other serves to uphold us in our efforts to do each what we can to make human life more sweet, more full of goodness and beauty, than we find it. The first of these assertions is the proposition that the things and events of the world do not exist or occur blindly or irrelevantly, but that all, from the beginning to the end of time, and throughout the farthest sweep of illimitable space, are connected together as the orderly manifestations of a divine Power, and that this divine Power is something outside of ourselves, and upon it our own existence from moment to moment depends. The second of these assertions is the proposition that men ought to do certain things, and ought to refrain from doing certain other things; and that the reason why some things are wrong to do and other things are right to do is in some mysterious but very real way connected with the existence and nature of this divine Power, which reveals itself in every great and every tiny thing, without which not a star courses in its mighty orbit, and not a sparrow falls to the ground. Matthew Arnold once summed up these two propositions very well, when he defined God as "an eternal Power, not ourselves, that makes for righteousness." This twofold assertion, that there is an eternal Power that is not ourselves, and that this Power makes for righteousness, is to be found, either in a rudimentary or in a highly developed state, in all known religions. In such religions as those of the Eskimos . . . this assertion is found in a rudimentary shape on each of its two sides,—the speculative side and the ethical side; in such religions as Buddhism or Judaism, it is found in a highly developed shape on both its sides. But the main point is that in all religions you find it in some shape or other.

I said, a moment ago, that modern civilized men will all acknowledge that this two-sided assertion in which all religions agree is of far greater importance than any of the superficial points in which religions differ. It is really of much more concern to us that there is an eternal Power, not ourselves, that makes for righteousness, than that such a Power is onefold or threefold in its metaphysical nature, or that we ought not to play cards on Sunday or to eat meat on Friday. No one, I believe, will deny so simple and clear a statement as this. . . . In spite of all this, however, it is true that in the mind of the uncivilized man the great central truths of religion are so densely overlaid with hundreds of trivial notions respecting dogma and ritual that his perception of the great central truths is obscure. These great central truths, indeed, need to be clothed in a dress of little rites and superstitions, in order to take hold of his dull and untrained intelligence. But, in proportion as men become more civilized, and learn to think more accurately, and to take wider views of life, just so do they come to value the essential truths of religion more highly, while they attach less and less importance to superficial details.

Having thus seen what is meant by the essential truths of religion, it is very easy to see what the attitude of the doctrine of evolution is toward these essential truths. It asserts and reiterates them both; and it asserts them not as dogmas handed down to us by priestly tradition, not as mysterious intuitive convictions of which we can render no intelligible account to ourselves, but as scientific truths concerning the innermost constitution of the universe, truths that have been disclosed by observation and reflection, like other scientific truths, and that accordingly harmonize naturally and easily with the whole body of our knowledge. The doctrine of evolution asserts, as the widest and deepest truth which the study of nature can disclose to us, that there exists a Power to which no limit in time or space is conceivable, and that all the phenomena of the universe, whether they be what we call material or what we call spiritual phenomena, are manifestations of this infinite and eternal Power. Now, this assertion, which Mr. Spencer has so elaborately set forth as a scientific truth,— nay, as the ultimate truth of science, as the truth upon which the whole structure of human knowledge philosophically rests,—this assertion is identical with the assertion of an eternal Power, not ourselves, that forms the speculative basis of all religions. When Carlyle speaks of the universe as in very truth the star-domed city of God, and reminds us that through every crystal and through every grass-blade, but most through every living soul, the glory of a present God still beams, he means pretty much the same thing that Mr. Spencer means, save that he speaks with the language of poetry, with language coloured by emotion, and not with the precise, formal, and colourless language of science. By many critics who forget that names are but the counters rather than the hard money of thought, objections have been raised to the use of such a phrase as the Unknowable whereby to describe the power that is manifested in every event of the universe. Yet, when the Hebrew prophet declared that "by Him were laid the foundations of the deep," but reminded us, "Who by searching can find Him out?" he meant pretty much what Mr. Spencer means when he speaks of a Power that is inscrutable in itself, yet is revealed from moment to moment in every throb of the mighty rhythmic life of the universe.

And this brings me to the last and most important point of all. What says the doctrine of evolution with regard to the ethical side of this twofold assertion that lies at the bottom of all religion? Though we cannot fathom the nature of the inscrutable Power that animates the world, we know, nevertheless, a great many things that it does. Does this eternal Power, then, work for righteousness? Is there a divine sanction for holiness and a divine condemnation for sin? Are the principles of right living really connected with the intimate constitution of the universe? If the answer of science to these questions be affirmative, then the agreement with religion is complete, both on the speculative and on the practical sides; and that phantom which has been the abiding terror of timid and superficial minds—that phantom of the hostility between religion and science—is exorcised now and for ever.

Now science began to return a decisively affirmative answer to such questions as these, when it began, with Mr. Spencer, to explain moral beliefs and moral sentiments as products of evolution. For clearly, when you say of a moral belief or a moral sentiment that it is a product of evolution, you imply that it is something which the universe through untold ages has been labouring to bring forth, and you ascribe to it a value proportionate to the enormous effort that it has cost to produce it. Still more, when with Mr. Spencer we study the principles of right living as part and parcel of the whole doctrine of the development of life upon the earth; when we see that, in an ultimate analysis, that is right which tends to enhance fulness of life, and that is wrong which tends to detract from fulness of life,—we then see that the distinction between right and wrong is rooted in the deepest foundations of the universe; we see that the very same forces, subtle and exquisite and profound, which brought upon the scene the primal germs of life and caused them to unfold, which through countless ages of struggle and death have cherished the life that could live more perfectly and destroyed the life that could only live less perfectly, until Humanity, with all its hopes and fears and aspirations, has come into being as the crown of all this stupendous work,—we see that these very same subtle and exquisite forces have wrought into the very fibres of the universe those principles of right living which it is man's highest function to put into practice. The theoretical sanction thus given to right living is incomparably the most powerful that has ever been assigned in any philosophy of ethics. Human responsibility is made more strict and solemn than ever, when the eternal Power that lives in every event of the universe is thus seen to be in the deepest possible sense the author of the moral law that should guide our lives, and in obedience to which lies our only guarantee of the happiness which is incorruptible,—which neither inevitable misfortune nor unmerited obloquy can ever take away.

I have here but barely touched upon a rich and suggestive topic. When this subject shall once have been expounded and illustrated with due thoroughness,—as I earnestly hope it will be within the next few years,—then I am sure it will be generally acknowledged that our great teacher's services to religion have been no less signal than his services to science, unparalleled as these have been in all the history of the world.

5] Reverend Beecher Preaches "The Two Revelations"

Henry Ward Beecher became a national figure during the antislavery agitation—it was his sister who wrote *Uncle Tom's Cabin* (1852). He was one of the galaxy of notables to pay tribute to Spencer at the conclusion of his American tour. In his closing remarks at the banquet, Beecher promised to meet Spencer beyond the grave. An ebullient personality and a great rhetorician, Beecher commanded a national audience through the *Christian Union*, a magazine edited from his Brooklyn church, and through books and lectures. Several of his modernist sermons were collected in *Evolution and Religion*. The most significant of these is printed below.*

"All things were made by Him, and without Him was not anything made that was made."—JOHN i:3.

THAT the whole world and the universe were the creation of God is the testimony of the whole Bible, both Jewish and Christian; but how he made them—whether by the direct force of a creative will or indirectly through a long series of gradual changes—the Scriptures do not declare. The grand truth is that this world was not a chance, a creative fermentation, a self-development, but that it was the product of an Intelligent Being, that the divine will in the continuance of this world manifests itself under the form of what are called natural laws, and that the operations of normal and legitimate laws are the results of divine will.

There are two records of God's creative energy. One is the record of the unfolding of *man* and of the race under the inspiration of God's nature: this is a mere sketch; of the ancient periods of man there is almost nothing known. The other of these records or revelations—if you choose to call them so—pertains to the physical globe, and reveals the divine thought through the unfolding history of *matter;* and this is the older. So we have two revelations: God's thought in the evolution of matter, and God's thought in the evolution of

* REVEREND BEECHER PREACHES "THE TWO REVELATIONS": Henry Ward Beecher, "The Two Revelations." From Henry Ward Beecher, *Evolution and Religion* (New York, 1885), pp. 44–55.

mind; and these are the Old Testament and the New—not in the usual sense of those terms, but in an appropriate scientific use of them.

In that great book of the Old there is a record of the progress, order, and result of God's thought in regard to the globe as a habitation for man. Though not every stage, yet the chief stages of preparation of this dwelling for man have been discovered and are now being deciphered and read. The crude, primitive material of the world of matter, the igneous condition, the aqueous stages, the dynamic and chemical periods, the gradual formation of the soil, the mountain-building, the dawn of life, vegetable and animal, the stages of their progress—are not all these things written in the scientific revelation of God's history of creation? When I reflect upon the range of the invisible and the silent God, with the vast and well-nigh incomprehensible stretch of time, and of his compassionate waiting and working through illimitable ages and periods, compared with which a million years as marked by the clock are but seconds; when I reflect that the silent stones and the buried strata contain the record of God's working, and that the globe itself is a sublime history of God as an engineer and architect and as a master-builder, I cannot but marvel at the indifference with which good men have regarded this stupendous revelation of the ages past, and especially at the assaults made by Christian men upon scientific men who are bringing to light the long-hidden record of God's revelation in the material world.

. . . Science is but the deciphering of God's thought as revealed in the structure of this world; it is a mere translation of God's primitive revelation. If to reject God's revelation of the Book is infidelity, what is it to reject God's revelation of himself in the structure of the whole globe? There is as much infidelity in regard to the great history that science unfolds today, as there is in regard to the record of the Book—and more! The primitive prefatory revelation of the structural thought of God in preparing a dwelling for the human race—is that nothing? Man had a cradle represented to antiquity as the poetical Eden; but the globe itself had a different Eden, one of fire, convulsions, clouds and storms, of grinding ice and biting chemistry preparing the soil.

To be sure, the history of man in the Bible is more important than the history of the globe. The globe was created for man as a house is created to serve the family. But both are God's revelations; both are to be received with intelligent reverence; both are to be united and harmonized; both are to be employed in throwing light, the one upon the other. That noble body of investigators who are deciphering the hieroglyphics of God inscribed upon this temple of the earth are to be honored and encouraged. As it is now, vaguely bigoted theologians, ignorant pietists, jealous churchmen, unintelligent men, whose very existence seems like a sarcasm upon creative wisdom, with leaden wit and stinging irony swarm about the adventurous surveyors who are searching God's handiwork and who have added to the realm of the knowledge of God the grandest treasures. Men pretending to be ministers of God, with all manner of grimace and shallow ridicule and witless criticism and unproductive wisdom, enact the very feats of the monkey in the attempt to prove that the monkey was not their ancestor.

It is objected to all assertions of the validity of God's great record in matter, that science is uncertain and unripe; that men are continually changing the lines of science, that it will not do to rest upon the results of scientific investigation. It will be time to consider science when it has ripened into a certainty, say men, but not now. Well, as the case stands, how is the record of the book any more stable and intelligible than the record of the rock? The whole Christian world for two thousand years, since the completion of the canons, has been divided up like the end of a broom into infinite splinters, quarreling with each other as to what the book did say, and what it did mean. Why then should men turn and say that scientific men are unsettled in their notions? . . .

It is said, or thought, that a layman should not meddle with that which can be judged by only scientific experts: that science demands a special training before one can discern correctly its facts, or judge wisely of the force of its conclusions. This is true; it is true both of those who accept and those who deny its results. But, when time and investigation have brought the scientific world to an agreement, and its discoveries pass into the hands of all men, there comes an important duty, which moral teachers, parents, and especially clergymen, are perhaps as well or better fitted to fulfill than mere scientists, viz., to determine what effect the discoveries of science will have upon questions of morality and religion. It is to this aspect that the best minds of the Christian ministry are now addressing themselves.

It may be well before going further to expose some popular errors regarding the Evolutionary philosophy—now so widely accepted by the scientific world—and to point out some of the changes which it will work out in the schools of theology, as a new interpreter of God's two revelations.

A vague notion exists with multitudes that science is infidel, and that Evolution in particular is revolutionary—that is, revolutionary of the doctrines of the Church. Men of such views often say, "I know that religion is true. I do not wish to hear anything that threatens to unsettle my faith." But faith that can be unsettled by the access of light and knowledge had better be unsettled. The intensity of such men's faith in their own thoughts is deemed to be safer than a larger view of God's thoughts. Others speak of Evolution as a pseudo-science teaching that man descended from monkeys, or ascended as the case may be. They have no conception of it as the history of the divine process in the building of this world. They dismiss it with jests, mostly ancient jests; or, having a smattering of fragmentary knowledge, they address victorious ridicule to audiences as ignorant as they are themselves.

Now the ascent of man from the anthropoid apes is a mere hypothesis. It has not been proved; and in the broader sense of the word "proved," I see certainly no present means of proving it. It stands in the region of hypothesis, pressed forward by a multitude of probabilities. The probabilities are so many, and the light which this hypothesis throws upon human history and human life and phenomena is such that I quite incline to the supposition that it is, in the order of nature, in analogy with all the rest of God's work, and that in the ascending scale there was a time unknown, and methods not yet discovered, in which man left behind his prior relatives, and came upon the spiritual ground which now distinguishes him from the whole brute creation. Of one thing I am certain, that whatever may have been the origin, it does not change either the destiny or the moral grandeur of man as he stands in the full light of civilization today. The theory of the evolution of the human race from an inferior race, not proved and yet probable, throws light upon many obscure points of doctrine and of theology that have most sadly needed light and solution.

First, then, what is Evolution, and what does it reveal? The theory of Evolution teaches that the creation of this earth was not accomplished in six days of twenty-four hours; that the divine method occupied ages and ages of immense duration; that nothing, of all the treasures of the globe as they now stand, was created at first in its present perfectness; that everything has grown through the lapse of ages into its present condition; that the whole earth, with their development in it, was, as it were, an egg, a germ, a seed; that the forests, the fields, the shrubs, the vineyards, all grasses and flowers, all insects, fishes, and birds, all mammals of every gradation, have had a long history, and that they have come to the position in which they now stand through ages and ages of gradual change and unfolding. Also that the earth itself went through a period of long preparation, passing from ether by condensation to a visible cloud form with increasing solidity, to such a condition as now prevails in the sun; that it condensed and became solid; that cold congealed its vapor; that by chemical action and by mechanical grinding of its surface by ice a soil was prepared fit for vegetation, long before it was fit for animal life; that plants simple and coarse came first and developed through all stages of complexity to the present conditions of the vegetable kingdom; that aquatic, invertebrate animals were the earliest of animals, according to the testimony of fossils in the earth. Fishes came next in order, then amphibians, then reptiles. "All these tribes were represented by species before the earliest of the mammals appeared. The existence of birds before the earliest mammal is not proved, though believed by some paleontologists upon probable evidence. The early mammals were marsupial, like the opossum and the kangaroo, and lived in the same era called by Agassiz the reptilian period. True mammals came into geologic history in the tertiary era. Very long after the appearance of the first bird came man, the last and grandest of the series, it is doubtful whether in the tertiary period or immediately sequent. It is not established whether his bones or relics occur as far back as the tertiary era." . . .[1]

Second. As thus set forth, it may be said that Evolution is accepted as *the method* of creation by the whole scientific world, and that the period of controversy is passed and closed. A few venerable men yet live, with many doubts; but it may be said that ninety-nine per cent—as has been declared by an eminent physicist—ninety-nine per cent of scientific men and working scientists of the world are using this theory without any doubt of its validity. While the scientific world is at agreement upon this *order* of occurrence, it has been much divided as to the *causes* which have operated to bring about these results. There is a diversity of opinion still, but with every decade scientific men are drawing together to a common ground of belief.

Third. The theory of Evolution is the *working* theory of every department of physical science all over the world. Withdraw this theory, and every depart-

1 Quoted from James Dwight Dana.

ment of physical research would fall back into heaps of hopelessly dislocated facts, with no more order or reason or philosophical coherence than exists in a basket of marbles, or in the juxtaposition of the multitudinous sands of the seashore. We should go back into chaos if we took out of the laboratories, out of the dissecting-rooms, out of the fields of investigation, this great doctrine of Evolution.

Fourth. This science of Evolution is taught in all advanced academies, in all colleges and universities, in all medical and surgical schools, and our children are receiving it as they are the elements of astronomy or botany or chemistry. That in another generation Evolution will be regarded as uncontradictable as the Copernican system of astronomy, or the Newtonian doctrine of gravitation, can scarcely be doubted. Each of these passed through the same contradiction by theologians. They were charged by the Church, as is Evolution now, with fostering materialism, infidelity, and atheism. We know what befell Galileo for telling the truth of God's primitive revelation. We know, or do not know, at least, how Newton stood charged with infidelity and with atheism when he announced the doctrine of gravitation. Who doubts the heliocentric theory today? Who doubts whether it is the sun which is moving round the earth or the earth round the sun? Who doubts that the law of attraction, as developed by Newton, is God's material law universally? The time is coming when the doctrine of Evolution, or the method of God in the creation of the world, will be just as universally accepted as either of these great physical doctrines. The whole Church fought them; yet they stand, conquerors.

Fifth. Evolution is substantially held by men of profound Christian faith. . . .

Sixth. To the fearful and the timid let me say, that while Evolution is certain to oblige theology to reconstruct its system, it will take nothing away from the grounds of true religion. It will strip off Saul's unmanageable armor from David, to give him greater power over the giant. Simple religion is the unfolding of the best nature of man toward God, and man has been hindered and embittered by the outrageous complexity of unbearable systems of theology that have existed. If you can change theology, you will emancipate religion; yet men are continually confounding the two terms, religion and theology. They are not alike. Religion is the condition of a man's nature as toward God and toward his fellow-men. That is religion—love that breeds truth, love that breeds justice, love that breeds harmonies of intimacy and intercommunication, love that breeds duty, love that breeds conscience, love that carries in its hand the scepter of pain, not to destroy and to torment, but to teach and to save. Religion is that state of mind in which a man is related by his emotions, and through his emotions by his will and conduct, to God and to the proper performance of duty in this world. Theology is the philosophy of God, of divine government, and of human nature. The philosophy of these may be one thing; the reality of them may be another and totally different one. Though intimately connected, they are not all the same. Theology is a science; religion, an art.

Evolution will multiply the motives and facilities of righteousness, which was and is the design of the whole Bible. It will not dull the executive doctrines of religion, that is, the forms of them by which an active and reviving ministry arouses men's consciences, by which they inspire faith, repentance, reformation, spiritual communion with God. Not only will those great truths be unharmed, by which men work zealously for the reformation of their fellow-men, but they will be developed to a breadth and certainty not possible in their present philosophical condition. At present the sword of the spirit is in the sheath of a false theology. Evolution, applied to religion, will influence it only as the hidden temples are restored, by removing the sands which have drifted in from the arid deserts of scholastic and medieval theologies. It will change theology, but only to bring out the simple temple of God in clearer and more beautiful lines and proportions.

Seventh. In every view of it, I think we are to expect great practical fruit from the application of the truths that flow now from the interpretation of Evolution. It will obliterate the distinction between natural and revealed religion, both of which are the testimony of God; one, God's testimony as to what is best for man in his social and physical relations, and the other, what is best for man in his higher spiritual nature. What is called morality will be no longer dissevered from religon. Morals bear to spirituality the same relation which the root bears to the blossom and the fruit. Hitherto a false and imperfect theology has set them in two different provinces. We have been taught that morality will not avail us, and that spirituality is the only saving element: whereas, there is no spirituality itself without morality; all true spirituality is an outgrowth, it is the blossom and fruit on the stem of morality. It is time that these distinctions were obliterated, as they will be, by the progress and application of the doctrine of Evolution.

In every view, then, it is the duty of the friends of simple and unadulterated Christianity to hail the rising light and to uncover every element of religious teaching to its wholesome beams. Old men may be charitably permitted to die in peace, but young men and men in their prime are by God's providence laid under the most solemn obligations to thus discern the signs of the times, and to make themselves acquainted with the knowledge which science is laying before them. And above all, those zealots of the pulpit—who make faces at a science which they do not understand, and who reason from prejudice to ignorance, who not only will not lead their people, but hold up to scorn those who strive to take off the burden of ignorance from their shoulders—these men are bound to open their eyes and see God's sun shining in the heavens.

That Evolution applied will greatly change the reading and the construction of the earlier periods of the Scripture history cannot be doubted. The Bible itself is one of the most remarkable monuments of the truth of the Evolutionary process. There has been an immense amount of modern ignorance imported into the Bible. Again the Lord is turning out the money-changers, and those who sell oxen and doves, from the temple. But that operation of old left the temple cleansed and pure for religious uses. With many thoughtful Christian men, large tracts of the Bible lie uncultivated and unused. They do not use the whole; yet if any should take out a single text there would be screams of fear. There is not one Christian man in a hundred, nor in a thousand, that thinks that the whole Bible is necessary to his spiritual development and growth. Men pick and choose, and, in a sort of unconscious way, reject portions constantly. We must save them from throwing it all over. For the growth of knowledge, and of intelligence, will not permit men any longer to hold it as a talisman, an idol; and unless guided by a wiser teaching they will reject the Sacred Scriptures not only as false in science, but as a guide to conduct and to character!

We of this age have come to the mountain-top; yet we can only see the promised land of the future. Our children shall go over to the land flowing with milk and honey. Great has been the past; the future shall be yet greater. Instead of doubts and dread of ill-omened prophecies, and railings and murmurings, the Church should write upon her banner in this day of the orient, "Rise, shine; Thy light has come. The glory of the Lord is risen upon thee."

The last years of my life I dedicate to this work of religion, to this purpose of God, to this development, on a grander scale, of my Lord and Master Jesus Christ. I believe in God. I believe in immortality. I believe in Jesus Christ as the incarnated representative of the spirit of God. I believe in all the essential truths that go to make up morality and spiritual religion. I am neither an infidel, nor an agnostic, nor an atheist; but if I am anything, by the grace of God I am a lover of Jesus Christ, as the manifestation of God under the limitations of space and matter; and in no part of my life has my ministry seemed to me so solemn, so earnest, so fruitful, as this last decade will seem if I shall succeed in uncovering to the faith of this people the great truths of the two revelations—God's building revelation of the material globe, and God's building revelation in the unfolding of the human mind. May God direct me in your instruction!

6] Goldwin Smith Foresees a "Moral Interregnum"

> The implications of Darwinism for the accepted standards of morality were discussed by the English-born author, editor, and historian, Goldwin Smith. Professor of history at Cornell University for a number of years, later a resident of Canada, Smith wrote and lectured widely on American and British affairs. In the following essay, Smith expresses the apprehension many felt about Darwinism, touches on most of the moral issues it raised, and foresees an interregnum such as followed on the Roman collapse and the beginning of the Reformation.*

IN A PAPER on the results of universal suffrage which appeared a short time ago in the *Atlantic Monthly,* among the adverse influences for which allowance ought to be made was mentioned the disturbance of morality, political and general, at the present juncture by the breaking of religious belief. The writer has since been struck, on more than one occasion, by the unsuspecting complacency with which thinkers of the materialist or the Agnostic school seem to regard the immediate future; as though religion had been merely an obstruction in the way of science, and its removal were sure to be followed by a happy acceleration of scientific progress without danger to morality, or to

---

* GOLDWIN SMITH FORESEES A "MORAL INTERREGNUM": Goldwin Smith, "The Prospect of a Moral Interregnum." From the *Atlantic Monthly,* XXXIV (November, 1879), 629–30, 635–37, 640–42.

anything else in human life. Some of them speak as if the peculiar moral code of Christianity would remain unaffected, or would even practically gain influence, by the total destruction of the Christian faith. They seem almost to think that under the reign of evolution, natural selection, and the struggle for existence the Sermon on the Mount will still be accepted as perfectly true; that the Christian beatitudes will retain their place; and that meekness, humility, poverty of spirit, forgiveness, unworldliness, will continue to be regarded as virtues. Much less do they suspect that the brotherhood of man may fall when its present foundation fails, or that the weak things of this world may miss the protection which the life and death of Christ and the consecration of his character have hitherto afforded them against the strong. The truth is that many who have renounced Christianity have not yet ceased to be Christians, or begun to regard human nature and society from any but an essentially Christian point of view. In the next generation Evolutionists and the belief in the struggle for existence will be clear of the penumbra of gospel morality, and the world will then have their Sermon on the Mount.

It is commonly assumed by positivists (if that is the appropriate name for the anti-theological school) that the religions of the world have been merely so many primitive and unscientific attempts to explain the origin of things and the phenomena of nature by reference to the arbitrary action of a divinity or a group of divinities. Were it so, we might see the last of them go to its grave without misgiving, or rather with a jubilant sense of final emancipation. But the fact surely is quite otherwise. The religions have been much more than infantine cosmogonies or explanations of physical phenomena: each of them in its turn has been the basis of moral life, and especially of the moral life of the community; each of them after its fashion has been the support of righteousness and the terror of unrighteousness. Overlaid and disguised by fable, ceremony, and priestcraft the moral element has been, but it has always been present in everything that could be called a religious system. Particularly is this true of the great religions and above all of Christianity, which is clearly an effort to improve morality and to give it a consecrated type and a divine foundation, not to explain phenomena of any kind. Apart, indeed, from miracles, which belong to a totally different category, the gospel says very little about the physical world; it rebukes an excessive belief in special interpositions of Providence by the apologue of the Tower of Siloam, and in the single petition "Give us this day our daily bread" it hardly implies anything more than sustaining care.

So with the doctrine of the immortality of the soul. This may have been always mixed up more or less with animistic fancy, but animistic fancy is not the essence of it; the essence of it is, to righteousness assured reward, to unrighteousness inevitable retribution.

It may be that morality is now about to disengage itself finally from religion, and to find a new basis in science; but in the past it has rested on religious belief, and the collapse of religious belief has accordingly been always followed by a sort of moral interregnum. . . .

What then, we ask, is likely to be the effect of this revolution on morality? Some effect it can hardly fail to have. Evolution is force, the struggle for existence is force, natural selection is force. It is not possible, at all events, that their enthronement in place of the Christian theory should leave untouched a type of character which is a renunciation of force,—which is weakness, humility, poverty of spirit, self-abnegation. But what will become of the brotherhood of men and of the very idea of humanity? Historically these beliefs are evidently Christian. Will they survive the doctrines with which in the Christian creed they are inseparably connected of the universal Fatherhood of God and of the fraternal relation of all men to Christ? On what other basis do they rest? God, says the New Testament, "hath made of one blood all nations of men, for to dwell on all the face of the earth." Blot out the name of the Creator, and on what does this assertion of the unity and virtual equality of mankind rest? What principle forbids the stronger races and those that have superior fire-arms to prey upon the weaker? What guards the sanctity of human life, if there is nothing more divine in man than in any other animal? Mr. Roebuck says, "The first business of a colonist is to clear the country of wild beasts, and the most noxious of all the wild beasts is the wild man." What is to be said in answer to this, and why is it not to be extended in principle to all the human lives which may stand in the way of the elect of nature, the strong and cunning masters of their kind? Nothing, we must recollect, can in any but a figurative sense be henceforth *sacred;* everything must present its natural title to existence, which, according to the theory of evolution, must apparently be some sort of force. It may be the collective force of a community, not that of an individual; but if the individual gets the better of the community, as a successful tyrant does, it would seem that there is no more to be said. Science is not neglectful of the need. She is presenting us with elaborate delineations of the origin, growth, and dissolution of human communities, from the point of view and in the terms of evolution, that is, of force. But these delineations, supposing them to square with the facts of history,—which we venture to think some of the most elaborate of them are far from doing,—scarcely touch our moral being; much less do they furnish a new motive power, either impelling or restraining, for the actions of the individual man. Being theories of which the principle is force, they in fact exclude morality in the common acceptation and practical sense of the term. Being necessarian, they, according to the existing perceptions of the human mind, exclude responsibility and effort, that is, the elements of moral life. Hereafter the difficulty of reconciling necessarianism with responsibility and effort may be overcome; it has not been overcome yet. . . .

The world is in no danger of another Peloponnesian war, or of a repetition of the convulsions of the fifteenth and sixteenth centuries; but it is in considerable danger of a desperate conflict between different classes of society for the good things of that which people are coming to believe is the only world. Is it likely that the passions of such a conflict will be controlled by any motive derived from scientific definitions of evolution; by any consideration connected with the rhythm of motion, the instability of the homogeneous, or the multiplication of effects? Force is force, and its own warrant: so the strong will say, and upon this principle they will act in the struggle for existence and for the enjoyments of existence; they will be restrained only by something to which force must bow, and which no alembic, apparently, can extract from force itself. . . .

That the history of religion has closed, and that no more efforts will ever be made by the human mind to penetrate beyond the veil of sense and approach the Spirit of the Universe, is an opinion which rests mainly on the belief that religions are mere crude interpretations of natural phenomena; and that this is not their essence we have already ventured to submit. Suppose supernaturalism to be discarded; this does not put out of the question natural manifestations of Deity in the spiritual conceptions, efforts, and experiences of men. Christianity itself, though it may cease to be accepted as a miraculous revelation, remains the central fact of history; and as such it, in connection with other religions, seems to call for an examination which it has not yet received. It is true that religious thought is employed on objects not like those of science, perceived by the bodily sense. But let evolution itself, which presents all things as in course of development, say whether exhaustive apprehension and final authority can be claimed for the nerves of sight, touch, hearing, taste, and smell. Let evolution itself say, too, whether it is certain that organized matter is the ultimate goal of progress, and that nothing answering to the name of spirit can have been evolved. To the Eozoon the limits of the knowable were narrow. We are pleading merely for circumspection, and for a careful examination of the phenomena of religious history, which are phenomena like the rest. Religious sentiment is still strong in the minds of many scientific men, who find nothing in the pure monotheistic hypothesis that contradicts the results of science. At any rate, it is vain to bid men exclude these subjects from their minds, and think only of making the best of this world. The question in what hands we are—in those of goodness, of something other than goodness, or of blind force—is not one concerning the nature of things, of which we might be content to remain in ignorance; it is one concerning the estate of man, and it swallows up all others in its practical importance; the truth about it, if known, would affect all our conceptions, all our estimates of the value of objects, every action of our lives. It cannot be in its own nature insoluble; and on the hypothesis that we are in the hands of goodness there seems to be reason to hope for a solution, and to believe that the delay and the necessity of effort are part of a moral plan. Mankind are not bees; they have learned to look before and after, and will never be cured of the habit. The present will not satisfy or engross them. Let the place of their brief sojourn be made as commodious as possible by science, and, what is more, enriched as much as possible by affection. "Aye, sir," said Johnson, after being shown over a luxurious mansion, "these are the things that make death bitter." Upon the materialist hypothesis of life, the pessimist has the best of the argument; and the effect of his unsparing scrutiny will soon appear. . . .

Again, the question which is perhaps at the bottom of all, tainted as it has been by logomachy, the question of human free agency, seems to claim the benefit of the same consideration. It may be very difficult to reconcile our sense of free agency and of the responsibility attaching to it with the apparent arguments in favor of necessarianism, automatism, or whatever the opposite theory is to be called. But the difficulty is equally great of conceiving moral responsibility not to exist, or to exist without free agency. To ignore one element of our perplexity is merely to cut the logical knot with a sword. Have we an exhaustive knowledge of the possibilities of being, and can we say that free agency is excluded? If not, and if it must be allowed to be possible that in the ascending scale of being human free agency might at last emerge, we have to consider how its appearance could be manifested in any other way than those in which it is apparently manifested now,—our sense of a qualified freedom of choice before action, our consciousness of responsibility founded on the same belief after action, and our uniform treatment of our fellows as free and responsible agents. . . .

But these questions are beyond our present scope. The object of this short paper is only to call attention to the fact that, if we may judge by the experience of history, a crisis in the moral sphere, which will probably bring with it a political and social crisis, appears to have arrived.

7] Professor Sumner Faces the Facts

William Graham Sumner was the paramount American philosopher of "Social Darwinism." Born in Paterson, New Jersey, the son of a working-class English immigrant, he entered Yale College in 1859 and, after an interlude in the Episcopal ministry, returned to Yale to become professor of political and social science in 1872. He quarreled bitterly with Yale's clergyman president Noah Porter over the use of Spencer's *The Study of Sociology* in his classes. Spencer's theory, the doctrines of Malthus and the classical political economists, the Protestant ethic of individualism and industry—these blended in Sumner's mind to create an outlook on society that was hard, bleak, and impervious to the reforming passions of mankind. A tremendously influential teacher at Yale, Sumner reached a larger audience through his many pungent essays, one of which is abridged below.*

SOCIALISM is no new thing. In one form or another it is to be found throughout all history. It arises from an observation of certain harsh facts in the lot of man on earth, the concrete expression of which is poverty and misery. These facts challenge us. It is folly to try to shut our eyes to them. We have first to notice what they are, and then to face them squarely.

Man is born under the necessity of sustaining the existence he has received by an onerous struggle against nature, both to win what is essential to his life and to ward off what is prejudicial to it. He is born under a burden and a necessity. Nature holds what is essential to him, but she offers nothing gratuitously. He may win for his use what she holds, if he can. Only the most meager and inadequate supply for human needs can be obtained directly from nature. There are trees which may be used for fuel and for dwellings, but labor is required to fit them for this use. There are ores in the ground, but labor is necessary to get out the metals and make tools or weapons. For any real satisfaction, labor is necessary to fit the products of nature for human use. In this struggle every individual is under the pressure of the necessities for food, clothing, shelter, fuel, and every individual brings with him more or less

---

* PROFESSOR SUMNER FACES THE FACTS: William Graham Sumner, "The Challenge of Facts." From *Essays of William Graham Sumner*, Albert G. Keller and Maurice R. Davie, eds. (New Haven, 1934), II, 87–122, *passim*. Reprinted by permission of the Yale University Press.

energy for the conflict necessary to supply his needs. The relation, therefore, between each man's needs and each man's energy, or "individualism," is the first fact of human life. . . .

The next great fact we have to notice in regard to the struggle of human life is that labor which is spent in a direct struggle with nature is severe in the extreme and is but slightly productive. To subjugate nature, man needs weapons and tools. These, however, cannot be won unless the food and clothing and other prime and direct necessities are supplied in such amount that they can be consumed while tools and weapons are being made, for the tools and weapons themselves satisfy no needs directly. A man who tills the ground with his fingers or with a pointed stick picked up without labor will get a small crop. To fashion even the rudest spade or hoe will cost time, during which the laborer must still eat and drink and wear, but the tool, when obtained, will multiply immensely the power to produce. Such products of labor, used to assist production, have a function so peculiar in the nature of things that we need to distinguish them. We call them capital. A lever is capital, and the advantage of lifting a weight with a lever over lifting it by direct exertion is only a feeble illustration of the power of capital in production. The origin of capital lies in the darkness before history, and it is probably impossible for us to imagine the slow and painful steps by which the race began the formation of it. Since then it has gone on rising to higher and higher powers by a ceaseless involution, if I may use a mathematical expression. Capital is labor raised to a higher power by being constantly multiplied into itself. Nature has been more and more subjugated by the human race through the power of capital, and every human being now living shares the improved status of the race to a degree which neither he nor any one else can measure, and for which he pays nothing. . . .

So far as I have yet spoken, we have before us the struggle of man with nature, but the social problems, strictly speaking, arise at the next step. Each man carries on the struggle to win his support for himself, but there are others by his side engaged in the same struggle. If the stores of nature were unlimited, or if the last unit of the supply she offers could be won as easily as the first, there would be no social problem. If a square mile of land could support an indefinite number of human beings, or if it cost only twice as much labor to get forty bushels of wheat from an acre as to get twenty, we should have no social problem. If a square mile of land could support millions, no one would ever emigrate and there would be no trade or commerce. If it cost only twice as much labor to get forty bushels as twenty, there would be no advance in the arts. The fact is far otherwise. So long as the population is low in proportion to the amount of land, on a given stage of the arts, life is easy and the competition of man with man is weak. When more persons are trying to live on a square mile than it can support, on the existing stage of the arts, life is hard and the competition of man with man is intense. In the former case, industry and prudence may be on a low grade; the penalties are not severe, or certain, or speedy. In the latter case, each individual needs to exert on his own behalf every force, original or acquired, which he can command. In the former case, the average condition will be one of comfort and the population will be all nearly on the average. In the latter case, the average condition will not be one of comfort, but the population will cover wide extremes of comfort and misery. Each will find his place according to his ability and his effort. The former society will be democratic; the latter will be aristocratic.

The constant tendency of population to outstrip the means of subsistence is the force which has distributed population over the world, and produced all advance in civilization. To this day the two means of escape for an overpopulated country are emigration and an advance in the arts. The former wins more land for the same people; the latter makes the same land support more persons. If, however, either of these means opens a chance for an increase of population, it is evident that the advantage so won may be speedily exhausted if the increase takes place. The social difficulty has only undergone a temporary amelioration, and when the conditions of pressure and competition are renewed, misery and poverty reappear. The victims of them are those who have inherited disease and depraved appetites, or have been brought up in vice and ignorance, or have themselves yielded to vice, extravagance, idleness, and imprudence. In the last analysis, therefore, we come back to vice, in its original and hereditary forms, as the correlative of misery and poverty.

The condition for the complete and regular action of the force of competition is liberty. Liberty means the security given to each man that, if he employs his energies to sustain the struggle on behalf of himself and those he cares for, he shall dispose of the product exclusively as he chooses. It is impossible to know whence any definition or criterion of justice can be derived, if it is not deduced from this view of things; or if it is not the definition of justice that each shall enjoy the fruit of his own labor and self-denial, and of injustice that the idle and the industrious, the self-indulgent and the self-denying, shall share equally in the product. Aside from the *a priori* speculations of philosophers who have tried to make equality an essential element in justice, the human race has recognized, from the earliest times, the above conception of justice as the true one, and has founded upon it the right of property. The right of property, with marriage and the family, gives the right of bequest. . . .

Private property, also, which we have seen to be a feature of society organized in accordance with the natural conditions of the struggle for existence produces inequalities between men. The struggle for existence is aimed against nature. It is from her niggardly hand that we have to wrest the satisfactions for our needs, but our fellow-men are our competitors for the meager supply. Competition, therefore, is a law of nature. Nature is entirely neutral; she submits to him who most energetically and resolutely assails her. She grants her rewards to the fittest, therefore, without regard to other considerations of any kind. If, then, there be liberty, men get from her just in proportion to their works, and their having and enjoying are just in proportion to their being and their doing. Such is the system of nature. If we do not like it, and if we try to amend it, there is only one way in which we can do it. We can take from the better and give to the worse. We can deflect the penalties of those who have done ill and throw them on those who have done better. We can take the rewards from those who have done better and give them to those who have done worse. We shall thus lessen the inequalities. We shall favor the survival of the unfittest, and we shall accomplish this by destroying liberty. Let it be understood that we cannot go outside of this alternative: liberty, inequality, survival of the fittest; not-liberty, equality, survival of the unfittest. The former carries society forward and favors all its best members; the latter carries society downwards and favors all its worst members.

For three hundred years now men have been trying to understand and realize liberty. Liberty is not the right or chance to do what we choose; there is no such liberty as that on earth. No man can do as he chooses: the autocrat of Russia or the King of Dahomey has limits to his arbitrary will; the savage in the wilderness, whom some people think free, is the slave of routine, tradition, and superstitious fears; the civilized man must earn his living, or take care of his property, or concede his own will to the rights and claims of his parents, his wife, his children, and all the persons with whom he is connected by the ties and contracts of civilized life.

What we mean by liberty is civil liberty, or liberty under law; and this means the guarantees of law that a man shall not be interfered with while using his own powers for his own welfare. It is, therefore, a civil and political status; and that nation has the freest institutions in which the guarantees of peace for the laborer and security for the capitalist are the highest. Liberty, therefore, does not by any means do away with the struggle for existence. We might as well try to do away with the need of eating, for that would, in effect, be the same thing. What civil liberty does is to turn the competition of man with man from violence and brute force into an industrial competition under which men vie with one another for the acquisition of material goods by industry, energy, skill, frugality, prudence, temperance, and other industrial virtues. Under this changed order of things the inequalities are not done away with. Nature still grants her rewards of having and enjoying, according to our being and doing, but it is now the man of the highest training and not the man of the heaviest fist who gains the highest reward. It is impossible that the man with capital and the man without capital should be equal. To affirm that they are equal would be to say that a man who has no tool can get as much food out of the ground as the man who has a spade or a plough; or that the man who has no weapon can defend himself as well against hostile beasts or hostile men as the man who has a weapon. If that were so, none of us would work any more. We work and deny ourselves to get capital just because, other things being equal, the man who has it is superior, for attaining all the ends of life, to the man who has it not. Considering the eagerness with which we all seek capital and the estimate we put upon it, either in cherishing it if we have it, or envying others who have it while we have it not, it is very strange what platitudes pass current about it in our society so soon as we begin to generalize about it. If our young people really believed some of the teachings they hear, it would not be amiss to preach them a sermon once in a while to reassure them, setting forth that it is not wicked to be rich, nay even, that it is not wicked to be richer than your neighbor.

It follows from what we have observed that it is the utmost folly to denounce capital. To do so is to undermine civilization, for capital is the first requisite of every social gain, educational, ecclesiastical, political, æsthetic, or other.

It must also be noticed that the popular antithesis between persons and capital is very fallacious. Every law or institution which protects persons at the expense of capital makes it easier for persons to live and to increase the number of consumers of capital while lowering all the motives to prudence and frugality by which capital is created. Hence every such law or institution tends to produce a large population, sunk in misery. All poor laws and all eleemosynary institutions and expenditures have this tendency. On the contrary, all laws and institutions which give security to capital against the interests of other persons than its owners, restrict numbers while preserving the means of subsistence. Hence every such law or institution tends to produce a small society on a high stage of comfort and well-being. It follows that the antithesis commonly thought to exist between the protection of persons and the protection of property is in reality only an antithesis between numbers and quality. . . .

We have now before us the facts of human life out of which the social problem springs. These facts are in many respects hard and stern. It is by strenuous exertion only that each one of us can sustain himself against the destructive forces and the ever recurring needs of life; and the higher the degree to which we seek to carry our development the greater is the proportionate cost of every step. For help in the struggle we can only look back to those in the previous generation who are responsible for our existence. In the competition of life the son of wise and prudent ancestors has immense advantages over the son of vicious and imprudent ones. The man who has capital possesses immeasurable advantages for the struggle of life over him who has none. The more we break down privileges of class, or industry, and establish liberty, the greater will be the inequalities and the more exclusively will the vicious bear the penalties. Poverty and misery will exist in society just so long as vice exists in human nature.

I now go on to notice some modes of trying to deal with this problem. There is a modern philosophy which has never been taught systematically, but which has won the faith of vast masses of people in the modern civilized world. For want of a better name it may be called the sentimental philosophy. It has colored all modern ideas and institutions in politics, religion, education, charity, and industry, and is widely taught in popular literature, novels, and poetry, and in the pulpit. The first proposition of this sentimental philosophy is that nothing is true which is disagreeable. If, therefore, any facts of observation show that life is grim or hard, the sentimental philosophy steps over such facts with a genial platitude, a consoling commonplace, or a gratifying dogma. The effect is to spread an easy optimism, under the influence of which people spare themselves labor and trouble, reflection and forethought, pains and caution—all of which are hard things, and to admit the necessity for which would be to admit that the world is not all made smooth and easy, for us to pass through it surrounded by love, music, and flowers.

Under this philosophy, "progress" has been represented as a steadily increasing and unmixed good; as if the good steadily encroached on the evil without involving any new and other forms of evil; and as if we could plan great steps in progress in our academies and lyceums, and then realize them by resolution. To minds trained to this way of looking at things, any evil which exists is a reproach. We have only to consider it, hold some discussions about it, pass resolutions, and have done with it. Every moment of delay is, therefore, a social crime. It is monstrous to say that misery and poverty are as constant as vice and evil passions of men! People suffer so under misery and poverty! Assuming, therefore, that we can solve all these problems and eradicate all these evils by expending our ingenuity upon them, of course we cannot hasten too soon to do it.

A social philosophy, consonant with this, has also been taught for a century. It could not fail to be popular, for it teaches that ignorance is as good as knowledge, vulgarity as good as refinement, shiftlessness as good as painstaking, shirking as good as faithful striving, poverty as good as wealth, filth as good as cleanliness—in short, that quality goes for nothing in the measurement of men, but only numbers. Culture, knowledge, refinement, skill, and taste cost labor, but we have been taught that they have only individual, not social value, and that socially they are rather drawbacks than otherwise. In public life we are taught to admire roughness, illiteracy, and rowdyism. The ignorant, idle, and shiftless have been taught that they are "the people," that the generalities inculcated at the same time about the dignity, wisdom, and virtue of "the people" are true of them, that they have nothing to learn to be wise, but that, as they stand, they possess a kind of infallibility, and that to their "opinion" the wise must bow. It is not cause for wonder if whole sections of these classes have begun to use the powers and wisdom attributed to them for their interests, as they construe them, and to trample on all the excellence which marks civilization as on obsolete superstition.

Another development of the same philosophy is the doctrine that men come into the world endowed with "natural rights," or as joint inheritors of the "rights of man," which have been "declared" times without number during the last century. The divine rights of man have succeeded to the obsolete divine right of kings. If it is true, then, that a man is born with rights, he comes into the world with claims on somebody besides his parents. Against whom does he hold such rights? There can be no rights against nature or against God. A man may curse his fate because he is born of an inferior race, or with an hereditary disease, or blind, or, as some members of the race seem to do, because they are born females; but they get no answer to their imprecations. But, now, if men have rights by birth, these rights must hold against their fellow-men and must mean that somebody else is to spend his energy to sustain the existence of the persons so born. What then becomes of the natural rights of the one whose energies are to be diverted from his own interests? If it be said that we should all help each other, that means simply that the race as a whole should advance and expand as much and as fast as it can in its career on earth; and the experience on which we are now acting has shown that we shall do this best under liberty and under the organization which we are now developing, by leaving each to exert his energies for his own success. The notion of natural rights is destitute of sense, but it is captivating, and it is the more available on account of its vagueness. It lends itself to the most vicious kind of social dogmatism, for if a man has natural rights, then the reasoning is clear up to the finished socialistic doctrine that a man has a natural right to whatever he needs, and that the measure of his claims is the

wishes which he wants fulfilled. If, then, he has a need, who is bound to satisfy it for him? Who holds the obligation corresponding to his right? It must
be the one who possesses what will satisfy that need, or else the state which
can take the possession from those who have earned and saved it, and give it
to him who needs it and who, by the hypothesis, has not earned and saved
it. . . .

The origin of socialism, which is the extreme development of the sentimental philosophy, lies in the undisputed facts which I described at the outset. The socialist regards this misery as the fault of society. He thinks that
we can organize society as we like and that an organization can be devised
in which poverty and misery shall disappear. He goes further even than this.
He assumes that men have artificially organized society as it now exists. Hence
if anything is disagreeable or hard in the present state of society it follows,
on that view, that the task of organizing society has been imperfectly and
badly performed, and that it needs to be done over again. These are the assumptions with which the socialist starts, and many socialists seem also to believe that if they can destroy belief in an Almighty God who is supposed to
have made the world such as it is, they will then have overthrown the belief
that there is a fixed order in human nature and human life which man can
scarcely alter at all, and, if at all, only infinitesimally.

The truth is that the social order is fixed by laws of nature precisely analogous to those of the physical order. The most that man can do is by ignorance and self-conceit to mar the operation of social laws. The evils of society
are to a great extent the result of the dogmatism and self-interest of statesmen, philosophers, and ecclesiastics who in past time have done just what the
socialists now want to do. Instead of studying the natural laws of the social
order, they assumed that they could organize society as they chose, they made
up their minds what kind of a society they wanted to make, and they planned
their little measures for the ends they had resolved upon. It will take centuries of scientific study of the facts of nature to eliminate from human society
the mischievous institutions and traditions which the said statesmen, philosophers, and ecclesiastics have introduced into it. Let us not, however, even then
delude ourselves with any impossible hopes. The hardships of life would not
be eliminated if the laws of nature acted directly and without interference.
The task of right living forever changes its form, but let us not imagine that
that task will ever reach a final solution or that any race of men on this earth
can ever be emancipated from the necessity of industry, prudence, continence,
and temperance if they are to pass their lives prosperously. If you believe the
contrary you must suppose that some men can come to exist who shall know
nothing of old age, disease, and death. . . .

The newest socialism is, in its method, political. The essential feature of its
latest phases is the attempt to use the power of the state to realize its plans and
to secure its objects. These objects are to do away with poverty and misery,
and there are no socialistic schemes yet proposed, of any sort, which do not,
upon analysis, turn out to be projects for curing poverty and misery by making those who have share with those who have not. Whether they are paper-
money schemes, tariff schemes, subsidy schemes, internal improvement schemes,
or usury laws, they all have this in common with the most vulgar of the com-

munistic projects, and the errors of this sort in the past which have been committed in the interest of the capitalist class now furnish precedents, illustration, and encouragement for the new category of demands. The latest socialism divides into two phases: one which aims at centralization and despotism —believing that political form more available for its purposes; the other, the anarchical, which prefers to split up the state into townships, or "communes," to the same end. The latter furnishes the true etymology and meaning of "communism" in its present use, but all socialism, in its second stage, merges into a division of property according to the old sense of communism. . . .

The sound student of sociology can hold out to mankind, as individuals or as a race, only one hope of better and happier living. That hope lies in an enhancement of the industrial virtues and of the moral forces which thence arise. Industry, self-denial, and temperance are the laws of prosperity for men and states; without them advance in the arts and in wealth means only corruption and decay through luxury and vice. With them progress in the arts and increasing wealth are the prime conditions of an advancing civilization which is sound enough to endure. The power of the human race to-day over the conditions of prosperous and happy living are sufficient to banish poverty and misery if it were not for folly and vice. The earth does not begin to be populated up to its power to support population on the present stage of the arts; if the United States were as densely populated as the British Islands, we should have 1,000,000,000 people here. If, therefore, men were willing to set to work with energy and courage to subdue the outlying parts of the earth, all might live in plenty and prosperity. But if they insist on remaining in the slums of great cities or on the borders of an old society, and on a comparatively exhausted soil, there is no device of economist or statesman which can prevent them from falling victims to poverty and misery or from succumbing in the competition of life to those who have greater command of capital. The socialist or philanthropist who nourishes them in their situation and saves them from the distress of it is only cultivating the distress which he pretends to cure.

8] Professor James Cracks the Spencerian "Block Universe"

William James was educated at Harvard and in Germany for a scientific career. Among his teachers was Louis Agassiz. Appointed to the Harvard faculty in 1872, James moved from physiology to psychology and then from psychology to philosophy. Until his own great work on psychology appeared in 1890, James used Spencer's *Principles of Psychology* in his course at Harvard. It served for him, as he confessed, all the purposes of "an intellectual punching bag." Whereas Spencer conceived of mind as mechanically adapting to environment, James held that intelligence was molded in constant interaction with the environment. Against all deterministic "block universes," James envisioned a universe consonant with man's desire for freedom, spontaneity, and change. The final result of this line of thinking was the philosophy of pragmatism, but James developed the pivotal conception as early as 1880 in an essay which dealt with the general problem of the great man in history. It was first presented as a lecture before the Harvard Natural History Society and then published in the *Atlantic Monthly* for October, 1880.*

A REMARKABLE parallel, which I think has never been noticed, obtains between the facts of social evolution on the one hand, and of zoological evolution as expounded by Mr. Darwin on the other.

It will be best to prepare the ground for my thesis by a few very general remarks on the method of getting at scientific truth. It is a common platitude that a complete acquaintance with any one thing, however small, would require a knowledge of the entire universe. Not a sparrow falls to the ground but some of the remote conditions of his fall are to be found in the milky way, in our federal constitution, or in the early history of Europe. That is to say, alter the milky way, alter the federal constitution, alter the facts of our barbarian ancestry, and the universe would so far be a different universe from what it now is. One fact involved in the difference might be that the particular little street-boy who threw the stone which brought down the sparrow might not find himself opposite the sparrow at that particular moment; or, finding himself there, he might not be in that particular serene and disengaged mood of mind which expressed itself in throwing the stone. But, true as all this is, it would be very foolish for any one who was inquiring the cause of the sparrow's fall to overlook the boy as too personal, proximate, and, so to speak, anthropomorphic an agent, and to say that the true cause is the federal constitution, the westward migration of the Celtic race, or the structure of the milky way. If we proceeded on that method, we might say with perfect legitimacy that a friend of ours, who had slipped on the ice upon his doorstep and cracked his skull, some months after dining with thirteen at the table, died because of that ominous feast. I know, in fact, one such instance; and I might, if I chose, contend with perfect logical propriety that the slip on the ice was no real accident. "There are no accidents," I might say, "for science. The whole history of the world converged to produce that slip. If anything had been left out, the slip would not have occurred just there and then. To say it would is to deny the relations of cause and effect throughout the universe. The real cause of the death was not the slip, *but the conditions which engendered the slip*—and among them his having sat at a table, six months previous, one among thirteen. *That* is truly the reason why he died within the year."

It will soon be seen whose arguments I am, in form, reproducing here. I would fain lay down the truth without polemics or recrimination. But unfortunately we never fully grasp the import of any true statement until we have a clear notion of what the opposite untrue statement would be. The error is needed to set off the truth, much as a dark background is required for exhibiting the brightness of a picture. And the error which I am going to use as a foil to set off what seems to me the truth of my own statements is contained in the philosophy of Mr. Herbert Spencer and his disciples. Our prob-

---

* PROFESSOR JAMES CRACKS THE SPENCERIAN "BLOCK UNIVERSE": William James, "Great Men and Their Environment." From William James, *The Will to Believe, and Other Essays in Popular Philosophy* (New York, 1908), pp. 216–54.

lem is, What are the causes that make communities change from generation to generation—that make the England of Queen Anne so different from the England of Elizabeth, the Harvard College of to-day so different from that of thirty years ago?

I shall reply to this problem, The difference is due to the accumulated influences of individuals, of their examples, their initiatives, and their decisions. The Spencerian school replies, The changes are irrespective of persons, and independent of individual control. They are due to the environment, to the circumstances, the physical geography, the ancestral conditions, the increasing experience of outer relations; to everything, in fact, except the Grants and the Bismarcks, the Joneses, and the Smiths.

Now, I say that these theorizers are guilty of precisely the same fallacy as he who should ascribe the death of his friend to the dinner with thirteen, or the fall of the sparrow to the milky way. Like the dog in the fable, who drops his real bone to snatch at its image, they drop the real causes to snatch at others, which from no possible human point of view are available or attainable. Their fallacy is a practical one. Let us see where it lies. Although I believe in free-will myself, I will waive that belief in this discussion, and assume with the Spencerians the predestination of all human actions. On that assumption I gladly allow that were the intelligence investigating the man's or the sparrow's death omniscient and omnipresent, able to take in the whole of time and space at a single glance, there would not be the slightest objection to the milky way or the fatal feast being invoked among the sought-for causes. Such a divine intelligence would see instantaneously all the infinite lines of convergence towards a given result, and it would, moreover, see impartially: it would see the fatal feast to be as much a condition of the sparrow's death as of the man's; it would see the boy with the stone to be as much a condition of the man's fall as of the sparrow's.

The human mind, however, is constituted on an entirely different plan. It has no such power of universal intuition. Its finiteness obliges it to see but two or three things at a time. If it wishes to take wider sweeps it has to use "general ideas," as they are called, and in so doing to drop all concrete truths. Thus, in the present case, if we as men wish to feel the connection between the milky way and the boy and the dinner and the sparrow and the man's death, we can do so only by falling back on the enormous emptiness of what is called an abstract proposition. We must say, All things in the world are fatally predetermined, and hang together in the adamantine fixity of a system of natural law. But in the vagueness of this vast proposition we have lost all the concrete facts and links; and in all practical matters the concrete links are the only things of importance. The human mind is essentially partial. It can be efficient at all only by *picking out* what to attend to and ignoring everything else—by narrowing its point of view. Otherwise, what little strength it has is dispersed, and it loses its way altogether. Man always wants his curiosity gratified for a particular purpose. If, in the case of the sparrow, the purpose is punishment, it would be idiotic to wander off from the cats, boys, and other possible agencies close by in the street, to survey the early Celts and the milky way: the boy would meanwhile escape. And if, in the case of the unfortunate man, we

lose ourselves in contemplation of the thirteen-at-table mystery, and fail to notice the ice on the step and cover it with ashes, some other poor fellow, who
never dined out in his life, may slip on it in coming to the door, and fall and
break his head too. . . .

There are, in short, *different cycles of operation* in nature; different departments, so to speak, relatively independent of one another, so that what goes
on at any moment in one may be compatible with almost any condition of
things at the same time in the next. The mould on the biscuit in the store-
room of a man-of-war vegetates in absolute indifference to the nationality of
the flag, the direction of the voyage, the weather, and the human dramas that
may go on on board; and a mycologist may study it in complete abstraction
from all these larger details. Only by so studying it, in fact, is there any chance
of the mental concentration by which alone he may hope to learn something
of its nature. On the other hand, the captain who in manœuvring the vessel
through a naval fight should think it necessary to bring the mouldy biscuit
into his calculations would very likely lose the battle by reason of the excessive "thoroughness" of his mind.

The causes which operate in these incommensurable cycles are connected with
one another only *if we take the whole universe into account*. For all lesser
points of view it is lawful—nay, more, it is for human wisdom necessary—
to regard them as disconnected and irrelevant to one another.

And this brings us nearer to our special topic. If we look at an animal or
a human being, distinguished from the rest of his kind by the possession of
some extraordinary peculiarity, good or bad, we shall be able to discriminate
between the causes which originally *produced* the peculiarity in him and the
causes that *maintain* it after it is produced; and we shall see, if the peculiarity
be one that he was born with, that these two sets of causes belong to two such
irrelevant cycles. It was the triumphant originality of Darwin to see this, and
to act accordingly. Separating the causes of production under the title of "tendencies to spontaneous variation," and relegating them to a physiological cycle
which he forthwith agreed to ignore altogether, he confined his attention to the
causes of preservation, and under the names of natural selection and sexual
selection studied them exclusively as functions of the cycle of the environment.

Pre-Darwinian philosophers had also tried to establish the doctrine of descent
with modification; but they all committed the blunder of clumping the two
cycles of causation into one. What preserves an animal with his peculiarity,
if it be a useful one, they saw to be the nature of the environment to which the
peculiarity was adjusted. The giraffe with his peculiar neck is preserved by the
fact that there are in his environment tall trees whose leaves he can digest. But
these philosophers went further, and said that the presence of the trees not only
maintained an animal with a long neck to browse upon their branches, but also
produced him. They *made* his neck long by the constant striving they aroused
in him to reach up to them. The environment, in short, was supposed by these
writers to mould the animal by a kind of direct pressure, very much as a seal
presses the wax into harmony with itself. Numerous instances were given of the
way in which this goes on under our eyes. The exercise of the forge makes
the right arm strong, the palm grows callous to the oar, the mountain air

distends the chest, the chased fox grows cunning and the chased bird shy, the arctic cold stimulates the animal combustion, and so forth. Now these changes, of which many more examples might be adduced, are at present distinguished by the special name of *adaptive* changes. Their peculiarity is that that very feature in the environment to which the animal's nature grows adjusted, itself produces the adjustment. The "inner relation," to use Mr. Spencer's phrase, "corresponds" with its own efficient cause.

Darwin's first achievement was to show the utter insignificance in amount of these changes produced by direct adaptation, the immensely greater mass of changes being produced by internal molecular accidents, of which we know nothing. His next achievement was to define the true problem with which we have to deal when we study the effects of the visible environment on the animal. That problem is simply this: Is the environment more likely to *preserve or to destroy him,* on account of this or that peculiarity with which he may be born? In giving the name "of accidental variations" to those peculiarities with which an animal is born, Darwin does not for a moment mean to suggest that they are not the fixed outcome of natural law. If the total system of the universe be taken into account, the causes of these variations and the visible environment which preserves or destroys them, undoubtedly do, in some remote and roundabout way, hang together. What Darwin means is, that, since that environment is a perfectly known thing, and its relations to the organism in the way of destruction or preservation are tangible and distinct, it would utterly confuse our finite understandings and frustrate our hopes of science to mix in with it facts from such a disparate and incommensurable cycle as that in which the variations are produced. This last cycle is that of occurrences before the animal is born. It is the cycle of influences upon ova and embryos, in which lie the causes that tip them and tilt them towards masculinity or femininity, towards strength or weakness, towards health or disease, and towards divergence from the parent type. What are the causes there?

In the first place, they are molecular and invisible—inaccessible, therefore, to direct observation of any kind. Secondly, their operations are compatible with any social, political, and physical conditions of environment. The same parents, living in the same environing conditions, may at one birth produce a genius, at the next an idiot or a monster. The visible external conditions are therefore not direct determinants of this cycle; and the more we consider the matter, the more we are forced to believe that two children of the same parents are made to differ from each other by causes as disproportionate to their ultimate effects as is the famous pebble on the Rocky Mountain crest, which separates two rain-drops, to the Gulf of St. Lawrence and the Pacific Ocean toward which it makes them severally flow.

The great mechanical distinction between transitive forces and discharging forces is nowhere illustrated on such a scale as in physiology. Almost all causes there are forces of *detent,* which operate by simply unlocking energy already stored up. They are upsetters of unstable equilibria, and the resultant effect depends infinitely more on the nature of the materials upset than on that of the particular stimulus which joggles them down. Galvanic work, equal to unity, done on a frog's nerve will discharge from the muscle to which the nerve belongs mechanical work equal to seventy thousand; and exactly the same muscular effect will emerge if other irritants than galvanism are employed. The irritant has merely started or provoked something which then went on of itself,—as a match may start a fire which consumes a whole town. And qualitatively as well as quantitatively the effect may be absolutely incommensurable with the cause. We find this condition of things in all organic matter. Chemists are distracted by the difficulties which the instability of albuminoid compounds opposes to their study. Two specimens, treated in what outwardly seem scrupulously identical conditions, behave in quite different ways. You know about the invisible factors of fermentation, and how the fate of a jar of milk—whether it turn into a sour clot or a mass of koumiss—depends on whether the lactic acid ferment or the alcoholic is introduced first, and gets ahead of the other in starting the process. Now, when the result is the tendency of an ovum, itself invisible to the naked eye, to tip towards this direction or that in its further evolution,—to bring forth a genius or a dunce, even as the rain-drop passes east or west of the pebble—is it not obvious that the deflecting cause must lie in a region so recondite and minute, must be such a ferment of a ferment, an infinitesimal of so high an order, that surmise itself may never succeed even in attempting to frame an image of it?

Such being the case, was not Darwin right to turn his back upon that region altogether, and to keep his own problem carefully free from all entanglement with matters such as these? The success of his work is a sufficiently affirmative reply.

And this brings us at last to the heart of our subject. The causes of production of great men lie in a sphere wholly inaccessible to the social philosopher. He must simply accept geniuses as data, just as Darwin accepts his spontaneous variations. For him, as for Darwin, the only problem is, these data being given, How does the environment affect them, and how do they affect the environment? Now, I affirm that the relation of the visible environment to the great man is in the main exactly what it is to the "variation" in the Darwinian philosophy. It chiefly adopts or rejects, preserves or destroys, in short *selects* him. And whenever it adopts and preserves the great man, it becomes modified by his influence in an entirely original and peculiar way. He acts as a ferment, and changes its constitution, just as the advent of a new zoological species changes the faunal and floral equilibrium of the region in which it appears. We all recollect Mr. Darwin's famous statement of the influence of cats on the growth of clover in their neighbourhood. We all have read of the effects of the European rabbit in New Zealand, and we have many of us taken part in the controversy about the English sparrow here—whether he kills most canker-worms or drives away most native birds. Just so the great man, whether he be an importation from without like Clive in India or Agassiz here, or whether he spring from the soil like Mahomet or Franklin, brings about a rearrangement, on a large or a small scale, of the pre-existing social relations.

The mutations of societies, then, from generation to generation, are in the main due directly or indirectly to the acts or the example of individuals whose genius was so adapted to the receptivities of the moment, or whose accidental position of authority was so critical that they became ferments, initiators of movement, setters of precedent or fashion, centres of corruption, or destroyers of other persons, whose gifts, had they had free play, would have led society in another direction. . . .

But the indeterminism is not absolute. Not every "man" fits every "hour." Some incompatibilities there are. A given genius may come either too early or too late. Peter the Hermit would now be sent to a lunatic asylum. John Mill in the tenth century would have lived and died unknown. Cromwell and Napoleon need their revolutions, Grant his civil war. An Ajax gets no fame in the day of telescopic-sighted rifles; and, to express differently an instance which Spencer uses, what could a Watt have effected in a tribe which no precursive genius had taught to smelt iron or to turn a lathe? . . .

Thus social evolution is a resultant of the interaction of two wholly distinct factors—the individual, deriving his peculiar gifts from the play of physiological and infra-social forces, but bearing all the power of initiative and origination in his hands; and, second, the social environment, with its power of adopting or rejecting both him and his gifts. Both factors are essential to change. The community stagnates without the impulse of the individual. The impulse dies away without the sympathy of the community. . . .

To conclude: The evolutionary view of history, when it denies the vital importance of individual initiative, is, then, an utterly vague and unscientific conception, a lapse from modern scientific determinism into the most ancient oriental fatalism. The lesson of the analysis that we have made (even on the completely deterministic hypothesis with which we started) forms an appeal of the most stimulating sort to the energy of the individual. Even the dogged resistance of the reactionary conservative to changes which he cannot hope entirely to defeat is justified and shown to be effective. He retards the movement; deflects it a little by the concessions he extracts; gives it a resultant momentum, compounded of his inertia and his adversaries' speed; and keeps up, in short, a constant lateral pressure, which, to be sure, never heads it round about, but brings it up at last at a goal far to the right or left of that to which it would have drifted had he allowed it to drift alone. . . .

The plain truth is that the "philosophy" of evolution (as distinguished from our special information about particular cases of change) is a metaphysical creed, and nothing else. It is a mood of contemplation, an emotional attitude, rather than a system of thought—a mood which is old as the world, and which no refutation of any one incarnation of it (such as the spencerian philosophy) will dispel; the mood of fatalistic pantheism, with its intuition of the One and All, which was, and is, and ever shall be, and from whose womb each single thing proceeds. Far be it from us to speak slightingly here of so hoary and mighty a style of looking on the world as this. What we at present call scientific discoveries had nothing to do with bringing it to birth, nor can one easily conceive that they should ever give it its *quietus,* no matter how logically incompatible with its spirit the ultimate phenomenal distinctions which science accumulates should turn out to be. It can laugh at the phenomenal distinctions on which science is based, for it draws its vital breath from a region which—whether above or below—is at least altogether different from that in which science dwells. A critic, however, who cannot disprove the truth of the metaphysic creed, can at least raise his voice in protest against its disguising itself in "scientific" plumes. I think that all who have had the patience to follow me thus far will agree that the spencerian "philosophy" of social and intellectual progress is an obsolete anachronism, reverting to a pre-darwinian type of thought, just as the spencerian philosophy of "Force," effacing all the previous distinctions between actual and potential energy, momentum, work, force, mass, etc., which physicists have with so much agony achieved, carries us back to a pre-galilean age.

9] Lester F. Ward Announces a "Philosophy of Action"

> Lester Frank Ward, Sumner's contemporary, was the first serious American thinker to revolt against "Social Darwinism" and, on Darwinian assumptions, to project a social philosophy serviceable to reform. Largely self-educated, publishing his first book, *Dynamic Sociology*, in 1883, Ward spent most of his life in government service, principally with the United States Geological Survey. Only in 1906, when he was appointed professor of sociology at Brown University, did he receive the academic recognition he had for so long deserved. Ward founded his sociology on the distinction between *genetic*, or physical, phenomena, which are the result of natural forces, and *telic*, or psychic, phenomena, which are the result of human intelligence and purpose. The latter arose in the course of evolution and made it possible for man to shape nature to his purposes. It followed from this that deductions of *laissez faire* from Darwinian science were wholly fallacious. The selection below is from a paper that Ward read before the American Anthropological Society in 1884 and subsequently published in the journal *Mind*.*

AFTER many centuries of exclusive study of the soul, the thinkers of the world turned their attention for some centuries more to the study of the intellect. During all this time, the true influence of mind as a social factor was left quite out of view. At last there rose up the scientific philosophy which essayed to explain the nature of mind. Its dependence upon organisation in general and upon brain in particular was proved by scientific experimentation, and the domain of metaphysics became that of psychology. Mind was shown to be a function of body and psychology became a department of biology. Man has now taken his true position in the animal world as a product of development. Brain, which alone raises him above other animals, has been developed in the same manner as the other anatomical characters. The brain is the organ of the mind, its physical seat and cause. Mind is therefore a natural product of evolution, and its achievements are to be classed and studied along with all other natural phenomena. Such is the scientific conception of mind.

The modern scientist places all objects in the midst of an infinite series of antecedents and consequents. Organic forms as well as inorganic must take

---

* LESTER F. WARD ANNOUNCES A "PHILOSOPHY OF ACTION": Lester F. Ward, "Mind as a Social Factor." From Lester F. Ward, *Glimpses of the Cosmos* (New York, 1915), III, 361–77.

their places in this series—the animal no less than the plant, the man no less than the beast. Mind itself is a link of this endless chain. Its activities consist in the transmission of the properties of its antecedents to its consequents. The quantity of force in the universe is constant. No power can increase or diminish it. All attempts on the part of the creatures of this constant and unchangeable force to modify its normal effects are not less vain because such creatures happen to have acquired the faculty of observing the changes going on in nature.

The protracted study of nature's processes leads to admiration of them, and the belief has become prevalent that they are not only unalterable but also in some way necessarily beneficent. Nature has made great progress in developing organised beings and is assumed to be still working in this direction. The natural method is always the true method, and to find it out is the aim of all scientific investigation. Out of this earnest and laudable strife to discover the true method of nature has grown, logically enough, the assumption that when found it must be something of great worth. It is commonly supposed that the highest wisdom of man is to learn and then to follow the ways of nature. Those dissatisfied people who would improve upon the natural course of events are rebuked as meddlers with the unalterable. Their systems are declared utopian, their laws *bruta fulmina*.[1] All efforts in this direction are held to be trifling and are stigmatised as so many ignorant attempts to nullify the immutable laws of nature.

This general mode of reasoning is carried into all departments of human life.

In government every attempt to improve the condition of the state is condemned and denounced. Curiously enough, here the claim is illogically made that such measures are harmful. In fact, unfortunately for the whole theory, they have often been proved to be so. But this, of course, proves their efficacy. This glaring inconsistency is, however, overlooked, and government is implored, not to adopt wise and successful measures, but to refrain from adopting any, to let society alone, and thus allow the laws of nature to work out their beneficent results.

In commerce and trade absolute freedom is insisted upon. Free trade is the watchword of this entire school. The laws of trade, they maintain, are natural laws. As such they must be better than any human rules. And here again we find them insisting that regulation is injurious to trade, although it is at the same time declared to be nugatory.

In social affairs these doctrines are carried to their extreme logical outcome. The laws of nature as they manifest themselves in society must be left wholly untouched. The passions of men will neutralise and regulate themselves. Competition can be depended upon to correct abuses. The seller must be allowed to exaggerate and misstate the nature of his wares. This has the effect to sharpen the wits of the buyer, and this develops the brain. To dilute, adulterate, or even poison food and medicine for personal gain is not objectionable, since the destruction thereby of a few unwary consumers only proves their unfitness to survive in society. As in general commerce, so in private business,

---

1 *bruta fulmina*: stupid fulminations.

competition must be free. If a dealer, by selling at a loss, can hold out until all his competitors have been driven from the field, in order then to recover more than his losses by the monopoly he will enjoy, his right to do this must not be questioned. It is under such conditions and by the aid of such discipline that man and society have developed.

Education must be that of experience. Knowledge must be gained by efforts to avoid the consequences of ignorance already felt. The intellectual development of the child must be an epitome of that of the race. It is thus only that nature operates, and surely nature is greater and wiser than man.

All schemes of social reform are unscientific. Public charities tend to bolster up unworthy elements in society that nature has declared unfit to survive. Temperance reforms tend only to abridge individual liberty—for even the liberty to destroy one's self should be respected. Philanthropy is zeal without knowledge, while humanitarianism is fanaticism.

This general class of views antedated by many years the publication by Spencer and Darwin of their formulated doctrines of the "survival of the fittest" and "natural selection." But it cannot be denied that these doctrines, supported as they were by facts fresh from nature, have greatly strengthened this habit of thought. Nature's method is now much better known than formerly, and it is now well understood that an utterly soulless competition constitutes its fundamental characteristic. Surely man cannot go astray in following in the footsteps of nature. Let him learn from the animal world. He has descended from some of the humble stocks which he is now studying. Nature's plan has raised him from the condition of a beast to that of a rational being. It has created and developed society and civilisation. Unless tampered with by "reformers" all the operations of society would be competitive. Competition is the law of nature out of which progress results. Sociology, as its founder insisted, must be based on biology, and the true sociologist must understand this biologic law. Those who propose to apply methods to society which are opposed to the methods of nature are supposed to be ignorant of these fundamental truths and are called empiricists, "meddlers," and "tinkers."

Such, I say, is the tenor and tendency of modern scientific thought. I do not say that all scientific men hold these views. I merely maintain that leading ones have formulated and inculcated them as natural deductions from the established facts of science, and that the public mind is rapidly assimilating them, while scarcely any attempts are being made to check their advance.

Is there any way of answering these arguments? Can the *laissez faire* doctrine be successfully met? That all attempts to do this have been timidly made cannot be denied. That these have been few and feeble is equally certain. While there has existed in the minds of many rational persons a vague sense of some hidden fallacy in all this reasoning, none have felt competent to formulate their objections with sufficient clearness and force to warrant pitting them against the resistless stream of concurrent science and philosophy of the nineteenth century. There has, however, been developing of late a more or less marked apprehension with regard to the possible consequences of this mode of thought. The feeling is distinct in the best minds, and to a large extent in the public mind, that the tendency of modern ideas is nihilistic. It is clear that if they become universally accepted they must work stagnation in society. The *laissez faire* doctrine is a gospel of inaction, the scientific creed is struck with sterility, the policy of resigning all into the hands of Nature is a surrender. . . .

The *laissez faire* doctrine fails to recognise that, in the development of mind, a virtually *new power* was introduced into the world. To say that this has been done is no startling announcement. It is no more than has taken place many times in the course of the evolution of living and feeling beings out of the tenuous nebulæ of space. For, while it is true that nature makes no leaps, while, so long as we consider their beginning, all the great steps in evolution are due to minute increments repeated through vast periods, still, when we survey the whole field, as we must do to comprehend the scheme, and contrast the extremes, we find that nature has been making a series of enormous strides, and reaching from one plane of development to another. It is these independent achievements of evolution that the true philosopher must study.

Not to mention the great steps in the cosmical history of the solar system and of the earth, we must regard the evolution of protoplasm, the "physical basis of life," as one of those gigantic strides which thenceforth completely revolutionised the surface of our planet. The development of the cell as the unit of organisation was another such stride. The origin of vertebrate life introduced a new element, and the birth of man wrought still another transformation. These are only a few of nature's revolutions. Many more will suggest themselves. And although, in no single one of these cases can it be said at what exact point the new essence commenced to exist, although the development of all these several expressions of Nature's method of concentrating her hitherto diffused forces was accomplished through an unbroken series of minute transitional increments continued through eons of time, still, it is not a whit less true that each of these grand products of evolution, when at length fully formed, constituted a new cosmic energy, and proceeded to stamp all future products and processes with a character hitherto wholly unknown upon the globe.

It is in this sense, and in this only, that I claim the development of mind —of the thinking, reasoning, inventing faculty of the human brain—as another, and one of the best marked, of the great cosmic strides that have characterised the course of evolution and belong to the legitimate methods of nature.

It is, for example, only to a limited extent and in the most general way that we can apply the same canons to the organic as to the inorganic world. It is usually, but falsely, supposed that the student of biology need know nothing of physics, the assumption being that they have nothing in common. While this error is fatal to all fundamental acquaintance with the laws of life, it well illustrates the immensity of the advance from one realm to the other. The same could be said, in varying degrees of obviousness, of every one of the ascending steps to which reference has been made. I freely admit that the theologians and metaphysicians commit the most fatal error in treating the soul, or mind, as independent of the body, but this enormous fallacy is scarcely greater than that of the modern evolutionist, who, finding out their dependence, ignores the *magnitude* of the step by which mind was made a property of body, and proceeds as though no new factor had entered into the world. . . .

If we analyse mind into its two departments, sense and intellect, we shall see that it is through this latter faculty that these results are accomplished. If we inquire more closely into the mode by which intellect operates, we shall find that it serves as a guiding power to those natural forces with which it is acquainted (and no others), directing them into channels of human advantage. If we seek for a single term by which to characterise with precision the nature of this process, we find this in *Invention*. The essential characteristic of all intellectual action is invention.

Glancing now at the *ensemble* of human achievement, which may be collectively called civilisation, we readily see that it is all the result of this inventive process. All practical art is merely the product of successful invention, and it requires no undue expansion of the term, nor extraordinary power of generalisation, to see in all human institutions only modified forms of arts, and true products of the intellectual, or inventive, faculty.

But what is the general result of all this? An entirely new dispensation has been given to the world. All the materials and forces of nature have been thus placed completely under the control of one of the otherwise least powerful of the creatures inhabiting the earth. He has only to know them in order to become their master. Nature has thus been made the servant of man. Thus only has man succeeded in peopling the entire globe while all other animals are restricted to narrow faunal areas. He has also peopled certain portions far more densely than any other species could have done, and he seems destined to continue multiplying his numbers for a long time yet in the future. But this quantitative proof is even less telling than the qualitative. When we confine our attention to the *élite* of mankind we do not need to have the ways specified in detail by which the powers of mind have exalted the intellectual being above all other products of creation. At the present moment the most dense and the most enlightened populations of the globe occupy what are termed temperate latitudes, which means latitudes in which for from three to five months each year vegetation ceases entirely, the waters are locked in ice, and the temperature frequently sinks far below the zero of the Fahrenheit thermometer. Imagine the thin-skinned, furless animal man subsisting in such a climate. Extinguish his fires, banish his clothing, blot out the habitations that deck the civilised landscape. How long would the puny race survive? But these are not products of nature, they are products of *art*, the wages of thought —fruits of the intellect.

When a well-clothed philosopher on a bitter winter's night sits in a warm room well lighted for his purpose and writes on paper with pen and ink in the arbitrary characters of a highly developed language the statement that civilisation is the result of natural laws, and that man's duty is to let nature alone so that untrammeled it may work out a higher civilisation, he simply ignores every circumstance of his existence and deliberately closes his eyes to every fact within the range of his faculties. If man had acted upon his theory there would have been no civilisation, and our philosopher would have remained a troglodyte.

But how shall we distinguish this human, or anthropic, method from the method of nature? Simply by reversing all the definitions. Art is the antithesis of nature. If we call one the natural method we must call the other the artificial method. If nature's process is rightly named natural selection, man's process is artificial selection. The survival of the fittest is simply the survival of the strong, which implies, and might as well be called, the destruction of the weak. And if nature progresses through the destruction of the weak, man progresses through the *protection* of the weak. This is the essential distinction.

In human society the psychic power has operated to secure the protection of the weak in two distinct ways: first, by increasing the supply of the necessities of life, and, secondly by preventing the destruction of life through the enemies of man. The immediate instrumentality through which the first of these processes is carried on is art, the product of invention. The second process takes place through the establishment of positive institutions. . . .

The truth thus comes forth from a rational study of nature and human society that social progress has been due only in very slight degree to natural evolution as accomplished through the survival of the fittest, and its chief success has resulted from the reduction of competition in the struggle for existence and the protection of the weaker members. Such competition, in so far as it has been permitted to operate, has tended to lower the standard of the fittest and to check advancement. It is not, of course, claimed that the natural method has ever been fully overcome. It has always operated, and still operates, powerfully in many ways. It has been chiefly in the simpler departments of physical and mechanical phenomena that the psychic, or anthropic, method has superseded it. The inventive arts have been the result. Vital forces have yielded to some extent to the influence of mind in bringing about improved stocks of animals and vegetables, and even certain social laws have come under rational control through the establishment of institutions. Still, every step in this progress has been contested. It was not enough that the intellect was feeble and ill-fitted to grapple with such problems. It was not enough that ignorance of nature's laws should cause unnumbered failures. A still stronger barrier was presented by the intellect itself in the form of positive error embodied in philosophy. As already remarked, philosophy has always been negative and nihilistic, and has steadily antagonised the common sense of mankind. It is only quite recently that there has come into existence anything like a truly *positive* philosophy, *i.e.,* a philosophy of *action.* The intellectual power of enlightened man has at length become sufficient to grasp the problems of social life. A large body of truth has been accumulated by which to be guided in their solution. Positive error in the drawing of false conclusions from established facts is now the chief obstacle. Rational interpretation has come to prevail in all the lower departments of phenomena. It is chiefly in the complex departments of psychic and social action that error still holds sway. Nothing remains to be done but to apply the established canons of science to these higher fields of activity. Here there is still competition. Here the weaker still go to the wall. Here the strong are still the fittest to survive. Here Nature still practises here costly selection which always involves the destruction of the defenceless. The demand is for still further reduction of competition, still greater interference with the operations of natural forces, still more complete control of the laws of nature, and still more absolute supremacy of the psychic over the natural method of evolution.

These ends will be secured in proportion as the true nature of mind is understood. When nature comes to be regarded as passive and man as active, instead of the reverse as now, when human action is recognised as the most important of all forms of action, and when the power of the human intellect over vital, psychic and social phenomena is practically conceded, then, and then only, can man justly claim to have risen out of the animal and fully to have entered the human stage of development.

10] Professor Dewey Assesses Darwin's Influence

> John Dewey, born in Burlington, Vermont, in the year of *Origin of Species*, devoted most of his long and productive life to working out the implications of post-Darwinian science for mind and society. Darwin and the course of modern science opened Dewey's eyes to the sterility of the philosophical tradition and turned them not only toward a philosophy of action but toward a life of action in the world of real problems. The Darwinian revolution overthrew "the sacred ark of absolute permanency" and impressed upon man the conviction that mind is "an organ of service for the control of environment in relation to ends of the life process." Dewey, a professor at Columbia University, stated this view in a lecture delivered there in commemoration of the fiftieth anniversary of *Origin of Species*. As reproduced below, the introductory passage is omitted, and Dewey is describing the pre-Darwinian attitude toward permanence and change.*

II

. . . .

THE CONCEPTION of εἶδος, species, a fixed form and final cause, was the central principle of knowledge as well as of nature. Upon it rested the logic of science. Change as change is mere flux and lapse; it insults intelligence. Genuinely to know is to grasp a permanent end that realizes itself through changes, holding them thereby within the metes and bounds of fixed truth. Completely to know is to relate all special forms to their one single end and good: pure contemplative intelligence. Since, however, the scene of nature which directly confronts us is in change, nature as directly and practically experienced does not satisfy the conditions of knowledge. Human experience is in flux, and hence the instrumentalities of sense-perception and of inference based upon observation are condemned in advance. Science is compelled to aim at realities lying behind and beyond the processes of nature, and to carry on its search for these realities by means of rational forms transcending ordinary modes of perception and inference.

There are, indeed, but two alternative courses. We must either find the appropriate objects and organs of knowledge in the mutual interactions of changing things; or else, to escape the infection of change, we *must* seek them in some transcendent and supernal region. The human mind, deliberately as it

---

* PROFESSOR DEWEY ASSESSES DARWIN'S INFLUENCE: John Dewey, "The Influence of Darwin on Philosophy." From John Dewey, *The Influence of Darwin on Philosophy and Other Essays* (New York, 1910), pp. 4–19. Copyright © 1910, 1937, Holt, Rinehart and Winston, Inc. Reprinted by permission.

were, exhausted the logic of the changeless, the final, and the transcendent, before it essayed adventure on the pathless wastes of generation and transformation. We dispose all too easily of the efforts of the schoolmen to interpret nature and mind in terms of real essences, hidden forms, and occult faculties, forgetful of the seriousness and dignity of ideas that lay behind. We dispose of them by laughing at the famous gentleman who accounted for the fact that opium put people to sleep on the ground it had a dormitive faculty. But the doctrine, held in our day, that knowledge of the plant that yields the poppy consists in referring the peculiarities of an individual to a type, to a universal form, a doctrine so firmly established that any other method of knowing was conceived to be unphilosophical and unscientific, is a survival of precisely the same logic. This identity of conception in the scholastic and anti-Darwinian theory may well suggest greater sympathy for what has become unfamiliar as well as greater humility regarding the further unfamiliarities that history has in store.

Darwin was not, of course, the first to question the classic philosophy of nature and of knowledge. The beginnings of the revolution are in the physical science of the sixteenth and seventeenth centuries. When Galileo said: "It is my opinion that the earth is very noble and admirable by reason of so many and so different alterations and generations which are incessantly made therein," he expressed the changed temper that was coming over the world; the transfer of interest from the permanent to the changing. When Descartes said: "The nature of physical things is much more easily conceived when they are beheld coming gradually into existence, than when they are only considered as produced at once in a finished and perfect state," the modern world became self-conscious of the logic that was henceforth to control it, the logic of which Darwin's *Origin of Species* is the latest scientific achievement. Without the methods of Copernicus, Kepler, Galileo, and their successors in astronomy, physics, and chemistry, Darwin would have been helpless in the organic sciences. But prior to Darwin the impact of the new scientific method upon life, mind, and politics, had been arrested, because between these ideal or moral interests and the inorganic world intervened the kingdom of plants and animals. The gates of the garden of life were barred to the new ideas; and only through this garden was there access to mind and politics. The influence of Darwin upon philosophy resides in his having conquered the phenomena of life for the principle of transition, and thereby freed the new logic for application to mind and morals and life. When he said of species what Galileo had said of the earth, *e pur se muove*,[1] he emancipated, once for all, genetic and experimental ideas as an organon of asking questions and looking for explanations.

III

THE EXACT bearings upon philosophy of the new logical outlook are, of course, as yet, uncertain and inchoate. We live in the twilight of intellectual transition. One must add the rashness of the prophet to the stubbornness of the partizan to venture a systematic exposition of the influence upon philosophy

1 *e pur se muove:* and yet it moves.

of the Darwinian method. At best, we can but inquire as to its general bearing—the effect upon mental temper and complexion, upon that body of half-conscious, half-instinctive intellectual aversions and preferences which determine, after all, our more deliberate intellectual enterprises. In this vague inquiry there happens to exist as a kind of touchstone a problem of long historic currency that has also been much discussed in Darwinian literature. I refer to the old problem of design *versus* chance, mind *versus* matter, as the causal explanation, first or final, of things.

As we have already seen, the classic notion of species carried with it the idea of purpose. In all living forms, a specific type is present directing the earlier stages of growth to the realization of its own perfection. Since this purposive regulative principle is not visible to the senses, it follows that it must be an ideal or rational force. Since, however, the perfect form is gradually approximated through the sensible changes, it also follows that in and through a sensible realm a rational ideal force is working out its own ultimate manifestation. These inferences were extended to nature: (*a*) She does nothing in vain; but all for an ulterior purpose. (*b*) Within natural sensible events there is therefore contained a spiritual causal force, which as spiritual escapes perception, but is apprehended by an enlightened reason. (*c*) The manifestation of this principle brings about a subordination of matter and sense to its own realization, and this ultimate fulfillment is the goal of nature and of man. The design argument thus operated in two directions. Purposefulness accounted for the intelligibility of nature and the possibility of science, while the absolute or cosmic character of this purposefulness gave sanction and worth to the moral and religious endeavors of man. Science was underpinned and morals authorized by one and the same principle, and their mutual agreement was eternally guaranteed.

This philosophy remained, in spite of sceptical and polemic outbursts, the official and regnant philosophy of Europe for over two thousand years. The expulsion of fixed first and final causes from astronomy, physics, and chemistry had indeed given the doctrine something of a shock. But, on the other hand, increased acquaintance with the details of plant and animal life operated as a counterbalance and perhaps even strengthened the argument from design. The marvelous adaptations of organisms to their environment, of organs to the organism, of unlike parts of a complex organ—like the eye—to the organ itself; the foreshadowing by lower forms of the higher; the preparation in earlier stages of growth for organs that only later had their functioning—these things were increasingly recognized with the progress of botany, zoology, paleontology, and embryology. Together, they added such prestige to the design argument that by the late eighteenth century it was, as approved by the sciences of organic life, the central point of theistic and idealistic philosophy.

The Darwinian principle of natural selection cut straight under this philosophy. If all organic adaptations are due simply to constant variation and the elimination of those variations which are harmful in the struggle for existence that is brought about by excessive reproduction, there is no call for a prior intelligent causal force to plan and preordain them. Hostile critics charged Darwin with materialism and with making chance the cause of the universe. Some naturalists, like Asa Gray, favored the Darwinian principle and attempted to reconcile it with design. Gray held to what may be called design on the installment plan. If we conceive the "stream of variations" to be itself intended, we may suppose that each successive variation was designed from the first to be selected. In that case, variation, struggle, and selection simply define the mechanism of "secondary causes" through which the "first cause" acts; and the doctrine of design is none the worse off because we know more of its *modus operandi*.

Darwin could not accept this mediating proposal. He admits or rather he asserts that it is "impossible to conceive this immense and wonderful universe including man with his capacity of looking far backwards and far into futurity as the result of blind chance or necessity." But nevertheless he holds that since variations are in useless as well as useful directions, and since the latter are sifted out simply by the stress of the conditions of struggle for existence, the design argument as applied to living beings is unjustifiable; and its lack of support there deprives it of scientific value as applied to nature in general. If the variations of the pigeon, which under artificial selection give the pouter pigeon, are not preordained for the sake of the breeder, by what logic do we argue that variations resulting in natural species are pre-designed?

IV

So MUCH for some of the more obvious facts of the discussion of design *versus* chance, as causal principles of nature and of life as a whole. We brought up this discussion, you recall, as a crucial instance. What does our touchstone indicate as to the bearing of Darwinian ideas upon philosophy? In the first place, the new logic outlaws, flanks, dismisses—what you will—one type of problems and substitutes for it another type. Philosophy forswears inquiry after absolute origins and absolute finalities in order to explore specific values and the specific conditions that generate them.

Darwin concluded that the impossibility of assigning the world to chance as a whole and to design in its parts indicated the insolubility of the question. Two radically different reasons, however, may be given as to why a problem is insoluble. One reason is that the problem is too high for intelligence; the other is that the question in its very asking makes assumptions that render the question meaningless. The latter alternative is unerringly pointed to in the celebrated case of design *versus* chance. Once admit that the sole verifiable or fruitful object of knowledge is the particular set of changes that generate the object of study together with the consequences that then flow from it, and no intelligible question can be asked about what, by assumption, lies outside. To assert—as is often asserted—that specific values of particular truths, social bonds and forms of beauty, if they can be shown to be generated by concretely knowable conditions, are meaningless and in vain; to assert that they are justified only when they and their particular causes and effects have all at once been gathered up into some inclusive first cause and some exhaustive final goal, is intellectual atavism. Such argumentation is reversion to the logic that explained the extinction of fire by water through the formal essence of aqueousness and the quenching of thirst by water through the final cause of aqueousness. Whether used in the case of the special event or that of life as a whole, such logic only abstracts some aspect of the existing course of events in order to reduplicate it as a petrified eternal principle by which to explain the very changes of which it is the formalization.

When Henry Sidgwick casually remarked in a letter that as he grew older his interest in what or who made the world was altered into interest in what kind of a world it is anyway, his voicing of a common experience of our own day illustrates also the nature of that intellectual transformation effected by the Darwinian logic. Interest shifts from the wholesale essence back of special changes to the question of how special changes serve and defeat concrete purposes; shifts from an intelligence that shaped things once for all to the particular intelligences which things are even now shaping; shifts from an ultimate goal of good to the direct increments of justice and happiness that intelligent administration of existent conditions may beget and that present carelessness or stupidity will destroy or forego.

In the second place, the classic type of logic inevitably set philosophy upon proving that life *must* have certain qualities and values—no matter how experience presents the matter—because of some remote cause and eventual goal. The duty of wholesale justification inevitably accompanies all thinking that makes the meaning of special occurrences depend upon something that once and for all lies behind them. The habit of derogating from present meanings and uses prevents our looking the facts of experience in the face; it prevents serious acknowledgment of the evils they present and serious concern with the goods they promise but do not as yet fulfill. It turns thought to the business of finding a wholesale transcendent remedy for the one and guarantee for the other. One is reminded of the way many moralists and theologians greeted Herbert Spencer's recognition of an unknowable energy from which welled up the phenomenal physical processes without and the conscious operations within. Merely because Spencer labeled his unknowable energy "God," this faded piece of metaphysical goods was greeted as an important and grateful concession to the reality of the spiritual realm. Were it not for the deep hold of the habit of seeking justification for ideal values in the remote and transcendent, surely this reference of them to an unknowable absolute would be despised in comparison with the demonstrations of experience that knowable energies are daily generating about us precious values.

The displacing of this wholesale type of philosophy will doubtless not arrive by sheer logical disproof, but rather by growing recognition of its futility. Were it a thousand times true that opium produces sleep because of its dormitive energy, yet the inducing of sleep in the tired, and the recovery to waking life of the poisoned, would not be thereby one least step forwarded. And were it a thousand times dialectically demonstrated that life as a whole is regulated by a transcendent principle to a final inclusive goal, none the less truth and error, health and disease, good and evil, hope and fear in the concrete, would remain just what and where they now are. To improve our education, to ameliorate our manners, to advance our politics, we must have recourse to specific conditions of generation.

Finally, the new logic introduces responsibility into the intellectual life. To idealize and rationalize the universe at large is after all a confession of inability to master the courses of things that specifically concern us. As long as mankind suffered from this impotency, it naturally shifted a burden of responsibility that it could not carry over to the more competent shoulders of the transcendent cause. But if insight into specific conditions of value and into specific consequences of ideas is possible, philosophy must in time become a method of locating and interpreting the more serious of the conflicts that occur in life, and a method of projecting ways for dealing with them: a method of moral and political diagnosis and prognosis.

The claim to formulate *a priori* the legislative constitution of the universe is by its nature a claim that may lead to elaborate dialectic developments. But it is also one that removes these very conclusions from subjection to experimental test, for, by definition, these results make no differences in the detailed course of events. But a philosophy that humbles its pretensions to the work of projecting hypotheses for the education and conduct of mind, individual and social, is thereby subjected to test by the way in which the ideas it propounds work out in practice. In having modesty forced upon it, philosophy also acquires responsibility.

Doubtless I seem to have violated the implied promise of my earlier remarks and to have turned both prophet and partisan. But in anticipating the direction of the transformations in philosophy to be wrought by the Darwinian genetic and experimental logic, I do not profess to speak for any save those who yield themselves consciously or unconsciously to this logic. No one can fairly deny that at present there are two effects of the Darwinian mode of thinking. On the one hand, there are making many sincere and vital efforts to revise our traditional philosophic conceptions in accordance with its demands. On the other hand, there is as definitely a recrudescence of absolutistic philosophies; an assertion of a type of philosophic knowing distinct from that of the sciences, one which opens to us another kind of reality from that to which the sciences give access; an appeal through experience to something that essentially goes beyond experience. This reaction affects popular creeds and religious movements as well as technical philosophies. The very conquest of the biological sciences by the new ideas has led many to proclaim an explicit and rigid separation of philosophy from science.

Old ideas give way slowly; for they are more than abstract logical forms and categories. They are habits, predispositions, deeply engrained attitudes of aversion and preference. Moreover, the conviction persists—though history shows it to be a hallucination—that all the questions that the human mind has asked are questions that can be answered in terms of the alternatives that the questions themselves present. But in fact intellectual progress usually occurs through sheer abandonment of questions together with both of the alternatives they assume—an abandonment that results from their decreasing vitality and a change of urgent interest. We do not solve them: we get over them. Old questions are solved by disappearing, evaporating, while new questions corresponding to the changed attitude of endeavor and preference take their place. Doubtless the greatest dissolvent in contemporary thought of old questions, the greatest precipitant of new methods, new intentions, new problems, is the one effected by the scientific revolution that found its climax in the *Origin of Species*.

CONCLUSION

By 1909, when Dewey spoke, Darwin's theory of natural selection had returned to the possession of biological scientists. For fifty years they had worked patiently with the theory, adding to it and subtracting from it, never able to *prove* its truth, yet less and less able to carry on without it. As August Weismann, one of Darwin's successors, remarked, "We must *assume* natural selection to be the principle of the explanation of the metamorphoses, because all other apparent principles of explanation fail us." During the same period Darwinism had cast its shadow over the entire intellectual landscape; but the point was reached at which the theory of evolution ceased to offer a fruitful source of generalization about man and society. Not only had society changed and men been captivated by new ideas, but the truth had finally been driven home that Darwinism had no *cosmic* significance. At that point, scientists were left at peace to refine the theory in the technical aspects that were of little interest to laymen and, accordingly, of little consequence in the broad stream of intellectual history.

The enormous fecundity, variability, and adaptability of Darwin's theory in the history of thought were reminiscent of his account of the species in the history of nature. Having fathered the theory, Darwin had no control over its diffusion and development, and he lived long enough (until 1882) to feel bewildered and dismayed by some of his amazing progeny. The theory was one thing, the uses men made of it—Darwin*ism*—quite another. Nothing in the theory itself called for its extension to fields of knowledge remote from biology, its transformation into a new secular religion, its reduction to a social ideology that claimed scientific sanction for everything from compulsory sterilization of the unfit to imperial domination of "backward races." What, then, explains the phenomenon? The answer must be sought in the mind and the society of the generation that discovered in the generous outlines of Darwinian evolution a philosophy responsive to its experience, its questions, and its needs. Men who knew change as an almost daily fact of life were excited by the vision of a universe not only constantly changing but becoming better with each creative innovation. Men who felt the steady erosion of an old supernatural faith also felt the need for a substitute, answerable to the modern mind, yet neither alienating man from the cosmos nor undermining the moral foundations of the community. And men who struggled for survival in the fiercely competitive jungle of industrial capitalism found in Darwinism the supreme vindication of what they were doing.

But, as the record shows, every attempt to turn the Darwinian theory into a rule for man and society encountered opposition from competing versions of Darwinism. In the final reckoning, the very proliferation of Darwinism, its malleability to almost any creed, supplied the proof of its absurdity; and, thus, out of the long struggle of opinion which, as Gray had anticipated, offered an analogue to the process of natural selection, what was selected to survive was the naked scientific proposition itself. It alone had the integrity to endure.

STUDY QUESTIONS

1] With respect to Darwinism in America, is there validity in the concept of "intellectual crisis"? If Darwinism produced a crisis, how did it differ from other crises Americans had faced, and what made it one?

2] It has been said that ideas have a radiation and development of their own in which their originators play the part of unwitting godfathers rather than of legitimate parents. Was this true of Darwin's theory? Discuss.

3] Discuss the different uses and applications American thinkers made of Darwinian evolution in the areas of (1) religion and (2) society.

4] It is generally assumed that changes in thought are associated with changes in society and its institutions. In the case of Darwinism, what contemporaneous developments in American society encouraged acceptance of the new ideas? Did the ideas, in turn, shape social and institutional growth? Discuss.

RECOMMENDED READINGS

PRIMARY SOURCES

DEWEY, JOHN. *Characters and Events*, 2 vols. (New York, 1929).

DRUMMOND, HENRY. *The Ascent of Man* (New York, 1894).

FISKE, JOHN. *The Destiny of Man* (Boston, 1884).

————. *Outlines of Cosmic Philosophy*, 2 vols. (Boston, 1874).

GEORGE, HENRY. *Progress and Poverty* (New York, 1879).

————. *Social Problems* (New York, 1883).

GRAY, ASA. *Darwiniana: Essays and Reviews Pertaining to Darwinism* (New York, 1876).

HUXLEY, THOMAS H. *Evolution and Ethics and Other Essays* (New York, 1894).

KROPOTKIN, PETER. *Mutual Aid, A Factor in Evolution* (London, 1902, 1915).

McCOSH, JAMES. *The Religious Aspects of Evolution* (New York, 1888).

SPENCER, HERBERT. *The Man Versus the State*, Truxton Beale, ed. (New York, 1916).

————. *The Study of Sociology* (New York, 1874).

SUMNER, WILLIAM GRAHAM. *What Social Classes Owe to Each Other* (New York, 1883).

VEBLEN, THORSTEIN. "Why Is Economics Not an Evolutionary Science?" in Max Lerner, ed., *The Portable Veblen* (New York, 1948).

WARD, LESTER F. *The Psychic Factors of Civilization* (Boston, 1893).

SECONDARY SOURCES

CLARK, JOHN SPENCER. *The Life and Letters of John Fiske*, 2 vols. (Boston, 1917).

DUPREE, A. HUNTER. *Asa Gray* (Cambridge, Mass., 1959).

EISLEY, LOREN. *Darwin's Century* (New York, 1957).

GABRIEL, RALPH H. *The Course of American Democratic Thought* (New York, 1940).

HIMMELFARB, GERTRUDE. *Darwin and the Darwinian Revolution* (London, 1959).

HOFSTADTER, RICHARD. *Social Darwinism in American Thought, 1860–1915* (Philadelphia, 1945).

JORDY, WILLIAM H. *Henry Adams: Scientific Historian* (New Haven, 1952).

LOEWENBERG, BERT JAMES. "The Controversy over Evolution in New England, 1859–1873," *New England Quarterly*, VIII (1935), 232–57.

————. "Darwinism Comes to America," *Mississippi Valley Historical Review*, XXVIII (1941), 339–69.

————. "The Reaction of American Scientists to Darwinism," *American Historical Review*, XXXVIII (1933), 687–701.

LURIE, EDWARD. *Louis Agassiz: A Life in Science* (Chicago, 1960).

MAY, HENRY F. *The Protestant Churches and Industrial America* (New York, 1949).

PERSONS, STOW, ed. *Evolutionary Thought in America* (New Haven, 1950).

PRATT, JULIUS W. *The Expansionists of 1898* (Baltimore, 1936).

WHITE, MORTON. *Social Thought in America: The Revolt Against Formalism* (Boston, 1957).

Overseas Expansion: The Coming of War with Spain, 1895–1898

ERNEST R. MAY

HARVARD UNIVERSITY

CONTENTS

CHRONOLOGY

1895

FEBRUARY 28   Rebels in Cuba proclaim war for independence from Spain.

SEPTEMBER–
OCTOBER   Rallies in various U.S. cities ask action by the government in behalf of the rebels.

DECEMBER 17   Cleveland's message to Congress on the Venezuelan boundary issue precipitates a crisis with Britain.

1896

JANUARY–
FEBRUARY   Negotiations end Anglo-American crisis.

FEBRUARY 10   Weyler becomes commander of Spanish forces in Cuba.

FEBRUARY 28   Senate votes a concurrent resolution for recognition of Cuban belligerency.

APRIL 4   Cleveland offers to mediate between Spain and the rebels.

APRIL 6   House approves the concurrent resolution.

JUNE 4   Spain refuses Cleveland's good offices.

NOVEMBER 3   McKinley elected President.

DECEMBER 7   Cleveland's annual message warns that the United States cannot refrain indefinitely from acting on the Cuban problem.

DECEMBER   Widespread and massive demonstration throughout the United States in favor of assistance to the rebels.

1897

MARCH 4   McKinley inaugurated.

MAY 20   Senate votes a joint resolution for recognition of Cuban belligerency.

JULY 16   McKinley dispatches General Woodford as minister to Spain.

AUGUST 8   Spanish Premier Cánovas assassinated.

OCTOBER 4   Sagasta, leader of the Liberal party, becomes Premier of Spain.

NOVEMBER 25   Spain decrees autonomy for Cuba.

DECEMBER 6   McKinley's annual message warns Spain that the Cuban war must end in the "near future."

1898

JANUARY 12   Riots in Havana.

JANUARY 24   *Maine* dispatched to Havana.

FEBRUARY 8   Papers publish indiscreet letter by Spanish Minister de Lôme.

FEBRUARY 15	*Maine* blows up in Havana harbor.
FEBRUARY–MARCH	Mounting public agitation for intervention in Cuba.
MARCH 11	Spanish queen regent appeals to European powers for support.
MARCH 26–28	McKinley makes demands on Spain.
APRIL 6	European powers urge preservation of peace.
APRIL 10	Spain announces an armistice in Cuba.
APRIL 11	McKinley asks Congress for power to intervene in Cuba.
APRIL 19	Congress votes power asked and recognizes independence of Cuba.
APRIL 20	Spain severs diplomatic relations.
APRIL 25	United States formally declares war.

INTRODUCTION

WHEN THE Spanish-American War was almost over, John Hay wrote Theodore Roosevelt that it had been a "splendid little war." Hay's letter came to light in 1920, when Joseph Bucklin Bishop published an authorized biography of Roosevelt. With the First World War just ended, the word war brought to mind pictures of the shell-pocked hills around Verdun, the corpse-littered fields in Flanders, the sound of shrapnel on a concrete bunker, and the smell of mustard gas and decaying flesh. Hay's adjectives seemed shockingly wrong. So they continued to seem later when the word conjured up images of Monte Cassino, Guadalcanal, Hiroshima, the retreat from the Yalu, or the smoky track of a missile in flight.

Americans of the earlier day had, it is true, lived through the bloody war for union. But by the 1890's that was three decades in the past; recollections had softened, turned romantic; memoirs reached the best-seller rank by telling of dashing exploits, gallantry, and romance, not of boredom, suffering, and death. Military and naval experts wrote of new tactics and weapons, such as the needle gun and the all-steel warship, calculated to make future wars short, sharp, and decisive. In the 1890's it was easier than it was ever to be again for men to contemplate war as a possible solution for moral or political problems. That is the first fact that must be borne in mind about the period.

The second is that, on the whole, the nineties were neither naughty nor gay. The depression of 1893 was one of the most severe in the nation's history. Over fifteen thousand business failures occurred during its first twelve months. Farmers, who had been witnessing declining prices ever since the seventies, saw the market for their products shrink just as banks began to call in loans and otherwise tighten credit. Protesting their plight and the increasing political, economic, and social dominance of industrialists and financiers, some had joined the Populist movement even before the panic. Afterward, millions turned to the nostrum of free coinage of silver; William Jennings Bryan, a thirty-six-year-old silverite, captured the Democratic nomination for the Presidency. Meanwhile, labor violence broke out in many urban or semi-urban areas of the country, culminating in 1894 in the bloody Pullman strike that temporarily paralyzed half the nation's railroads.

The panic, coupled with these uprisings among farmers and workingmen, rattled the businessmen, lawyers, clergymen, teachers, and journalists who were molders and leaders of public opinion. Speeches, news stories, magazine articles, and sermons dwelt on dangers. Some predicted a new sectional conflict, this time between the industrial East and the agricultural West; others warned of impending class conflict; still others put forward the pessimistic view that the economy had grown too fast, that it produced too much, and that new markets would have to be found if industry were to continue its progress, capital to grow, and jobs to be provided for the nation's expanding population. A number of native Americans blamed the country's ills on an influx of immigrants from southern and eastern Europe who, they said, not only crowded the labor market but also introduced inferior and unassimilable strains into the "American race." Hostility toward aliens merged with fear of radicalism; strikes and other signs of disquiet were attributed to foreign agitators and anarchists. Some Protestant clergymen seized upon these trends of thought to intensify their campaign against Catholicism, the religion of many immigrants. They did so with special fervor because the Catholic population grew while church attendance by Protestants declined. Clergymen, teachers, journalists, and other intellectuals were also occupied in trying to reconcile with old beliefs the newer scientific and social dogmas derived from Darwinian biology. For nearly all Americans, the nineties were agitated, unquiet, fearful years.

Paradoxically, however, they were also years when Americans began to realize how far their country actually had progressed. Always boastful, they had long described their nation grandiloquently. But in the 1880's and 1890's they saw that vanity had solid foundations. The growth in population, while cause for some concern, was also cause for pride, because Americans now outnumbered the people of all other industrial states except Russia. Their nation's agricultural output exceeded that of all other countries, as did its railroad mileage and the total number of its schools, newspapers, churches, and banks. In output of coal, iron, and steel, it bade fair soon to surpass England, the industrial leader of the world. An American of the 1890's had only to flip through an almanac to see that his country had indeed become one of the greatest on earth.

Realization of this fact merged with the general disquiet to produce attentive audiences for speakers and writers prophesying America's future. Traveling about the country in the mid-1880's, John Fiske, a popularizer of history and Darwinian biology, drew large crowds with a lecture entitled "Manifest Destiny," a phrase first applied to the American experience by John L. O'Sullivan in 1845. Fiske proclaimed that America would expand "until every land on the earth's surface that is not already the seat of an old civilization shall become English in its language, in its political habits and traditions, and to a predominant extent in the blood of its people." Another popular lecturer, the Reverend Josiah Strong of the American Home Missionary Society and the Evangelical Alliance, declared:

. . . this race of unequaled energy, with all the majesty of numbers and the might of wealth behind it—the representative, let us hope, of the largest liberty, the purest Christianity, the highest civilization—having developed peculiarly aggressive traits calculated to impress its institutions upon mankind, will spread itself over the earth. If I read not amiss, this powerful race will move down upon Mexico, down upon Central and South America, out upon the islands of the sea, over upon Africa and beyond. . . .

Is there room for reasonable doubt that this race, unless devitalized by alcohol and tobacco, is destined to dispossess many weaker races, assimilate others, and mold the remainder, until, in a very true and important sense, it has Anglo-Saxonized mankind?

Captain Alfred Thayer Mahan, U.S.N., became a national figure almost overnight when in 1890 he published a book, *The Influence of Sea Power upon*

History, 1660–1783, and an article in the *Atlantic Monthly* entitled "The United States Looking Outward." In the latter he wrote:

Whether they will or no, Americans must now begin to look outward. The growing population of the country demands it. An increasing volume of public sentiment demands it. The position of the United States, between the two Old Worlds and the two greatest oceans, makes the same claim.

In order to fulfill its destiny, however, the nation would have to copy England, he argued: build up its navy and merchant marine, establish naval bases in distant seas, and acquire colonies.

That voices such as Fiske's, Strong's, and Mahan's moved at least a segment of public opinion was evidenced in the late eighties and early nineties. Significant support developed for a large, modern navy, and Congress appropriated enough money so that by the mid-1890's the United States fleet ranked above those of several European powers. In addition, controversies with other nations became increasingly important issues in American politics. Trouble with Canada over the Newfoundland fisheries led in 1888 to a near crisis, with numerous members of Congress talking of teaching the Canadians and English a lesson. Though most observers dismissed these words as meant for Irish voters, the same construction was not so easily put on outbursts in 1889–90, for their target was not England but Germany. Rumor that the Germans meant to take over Samoa, where the United States had an ill-defined zone of influence, brought dozens of congressmen to their feet shouting for militant defense of the nation's rights. In the following winter, President Benjamin Harrison almost precipitated war with Chile over that government's failure to apologize for the death of some American seamen in a riot in Santiago.

In 1893 a powerful movement arose for the annexation of Hawaii. In Honolulu American settlers overthrew the native queen, set up a provisional government, and appealed for annexation by the United States. Two decades earlier, when President Ulysses Grant proposed acquiring nearby Santo Domingo, Congress and public opinion killed the project. Now, however, when Mahan's notions of strategic necessity fused with ideas for beneficent American expansionism, public opinion seemed to favor taking these more distant lands. President Harrison submitted an annexation treaty to the Senate, and Washington correspondents predicted ratification by well over the requisite two-thirds. But the Harrison administration was leaving office; the incoming Democratic President, Grover Cleveland, asked time to study the proposition and withdrew the treaty. When Cleveland decided later in 1893 to abandon it, he met a torrent of criticism, some of it from members of his own party.

Public enthusiasm for a "vigorous foreign policy" found much expression during Cleveland's remaining years in office. In 1895, in the aftermath of a war between China and Japan, local uprisings in China menaced American mission property. Before the Chinese government punished the rioters, some demand appeared in the American press and the pulpit for armed intervention. Even louder cries rose during the same year when Turks massacred Christians in Armenia and aroused fear for American missionaries in the Ottoman Empire. Churches and church-sponsored rallies urged stern measures, including the use of the navy in the Mediterranean.

At the same time, many congressmen and newspaper editors called on the executive branch to assert America's supremacy in the Western Hemisphere. The Republic of Venezuela had long disputed with Britain about its boundary with British Guiana. Owing to gold strikes, English settlers and officials were moving in force into the controverted zone. Orators, pamphleteers, and editorial writers spoke of British aggression against Venezuela and demanded that the President invoke that portion of the Monroe Doctrine which forbade European states to acquire new territory in the Americas.

Fat, lethargic, and unimaginative, Cleveland had grown increasingly conservative since his first term in office (1885–89). Nevertheless, he possessed a stern Presbyterian conscience and believed strongly that the United States should follow and uphold a strict moral code. (He turned against Hawaiian annexation because he became convinced that Harrison's minister in Honolulu had helped the revolutionaries, not because he opposed imperialism in principle.) Reading over the documents on the Venezuelan boundary dispute, he became convinced that Britain was morally wrong. When the British ignored his suggestion that the dispute be submitted to arbitration, he had his Secretary of State send to London a note virtually making it a demand. The British still refused, and he went before Congress to declare that the United States would draw a boundary line and then compel Britain to respect it.

This message produced a real crisis. Both Washington and London heard talk of possible war. But though the public seemed at first to support the President enthusiastically, this backing soon melted away. Prominent businessmen, clergymen, and educators attacked his course, declaring that conflict with Britain would wreck the American economy and that war between Anglo-Saxons would be catastrophic for civilization. Lord Salisbury's government, shocked into realization that intransigence might actually bring war, meanwhile opened negotiations, and presently agreement was reached in submitting the boundary dispute to arbitration. The crisis had been weathered, but it had shown not only that large numbers of Americans were vaguely though excitedly in favor of the nation's somehow manifesting its new power, but also that chauvinism, when carried to excess, could excite a conservative reaction.

Such forms the background of the Cuban controversy of 1895–98. And when in 1895 bands of Cubans proclaimed a war for independence from Spain, a rebel junta, or committee, in New York then sent agents all over the United States to seek money and agitate for recognition of Cuban belligerency or, better still, of independence. Owing partly to the natural American sympathy for such a cause and partly to the fact that wire services were still in their infancy and newspapers were hungry for copy to fill space between advertisements, rebel propaganda releases became staples even in the most conservative dailies. Sensational papers, like William Randolph Hearst's New York *Journal* and Joseph Pulitzer's New York *World*, exploited the evident public interest and printed increasingly lurid tales about Spanish atrocities. By the winter of 1895–96, many individuals were enthusiastic partisans of the rebels. Huge rallies were held in various cities to raise funds and urge action by the American government.

President Cleveland was unresponsive. Though his informants reported the war in Cuba to be on a much larger scale than in the previous insurrection of Yara of 1868–78, they also indicated that the rebels had no central government and no well-defined area of control. It was not clear how many of the island's 800,000 whites and mestizos and 600,000 Negroes were participating in the revolt or were loyal to Spain. Moreover, the Spaniards were taking resolute measures. They sent over nearly 100,000 troops during 1895 and at the end of the year dispatched their toughest general, Valeriano Weyler, to command them. Weyler, known in Spain as "Butcher," announced that he would reconcentrate the rural population in fortified towns. The rebels would thus be left to roam the land when no crops grew, and, Weyler declared, they would be starved into surrender. Though newspaper editorials in America almost unanimously condemned such inhumane tactics, and Cleveland privately expressed his horror, the treatment of Cuba was still clearly Spain's affair. The President saw no compelling reason for recognition. He endeavored to enforce American laws and prevent the rebels from outfitting expeditions to the United States. Otherwise, he took no action for or against the Cubans; he merely bided his time.

Both Cleveland and his successor, William McKinley, saw the Cuban problem, however, as one that could not indefinitely be left alone. Later, when the word war came to have new connotations, many Americans could not comprehend why this had been so—why any President should have felt compelled to meddle in the affair at the risk of precipitating an international conflict.

Some early writers protested that the United States had had no right in international law to intervene in a dispute between a European state and its colony. Others were to analyze the exaggerations and sensationalism in Hearst's and Pulitzer's accounts of Spanish atrocities, blaming the war that came in 1898 on the aroused state of public opinion and laying that in turn to unscrupulous "yellow journalism."

Some writers in the 1920's and 1930's expressed doubt that the explanation was so simple. Looking back with the cool Marxist-inspired skepticism that was common among intellectuals of those decades, they asked who had made money out of the war. Many people had, they found: sugar refiners became able not only to buy Cuban sugar more cheaply but also to acquire possession of the island's canefields; tobacco interests similarly profited; so did arms manufacturers and others who supplied goods for war. In addition, agitation over Cuba distracted public attention from farmer and labor grievances.

These largely economic-determinist and quasi-Marxist historians pointed out that bankers and big businessmen surrounded both Cleveland and McKinley. The former had been a partner in a Wall Street law firm in the interval between his two presidencies, and in office he had distinguished himself by calling out federal troops to break a strike against the Pullman Company and by standing fast for the gold standard. McKinley was elevated to the White House by certain industrialists, notably Mark Hanna of Cleveland, who plotted and financed his nomination and campaign. These were the very men who benefited from the war, and historians like Charles A. Beard inferred that they must therefore have planned it and brought it about. Yellow journalism in the view of Beard and his followers was but an instrument in a capitalist conspiracy.

This reasoning remained neat and satisfying until other scholars poked at its underpinning. Concluding a three-volume history of the Monroe Doctrine with a study of the years 1867–1905, Dexter Perkins of the University of Rochester pointed out that bankers and businessmen had reacted against Cleveland's jingoism in the Venezuelan boundary affair and, for the most part, had opposed all controversy with other nations, partly on the ground that international complications might unsettle the securities market. In *Expansionists of 1898* (1936), Julius W. Pratt of the University of Buffalo explored the files of business periodicals, including not only the *Wall Street Journal* but also esoteric monthlies and weeklies like the *American Grocer* and the *Dry Goods Economist*. He found that spokesmen for the business community had been almost unanimously averse to expansionism and chauvinism and had opposed war with Spain until the last moment.

Richard Hofstadter of Columbia University later pointed out in a thoughtful contribution to Daniel Aaron's *America in Crisis* (1952) that enthusiasm for expansion and war had been most marked among spokesmen for Southern and Western agrarians—the people most hostile to big business and most critical of Cleveland and McKinley. He was the first to suggest that Americans in the nineties were going through a psychological crisis of which both yellow journalism and the war with Spain were symptoms. In *Imperial Democracy* (1961) the present author examined this psychological crisis, singling out evidence of the near hysteria that arose not so much in rural areas as in cities and towns. Big businessmen were not only not swept up in it, as Pratt indicated, but were actually frightened, seeing in the agitation for war a revolt against their own leadership of public opinion. The problem that faced Cleveland and McKinley was not, as Beard argued, to carry out the wishes of businessmen and put something over on the people. On the contrary, their dilemma was to find some means of satisfying the public without alienating the bankers and industrialists who were their supporters and without widening the social and class conflict that seemed imminent.

To appreciate the agony of spirit which both Presidents suffered, it is necessary to understand the mounting pressure on them. Some of the documents that follow illustrate the moods of the people, but no selections can quite convey the atmosphere. Day in and day out, over a period of three years, not just the yellow journals but even the most conservative newspapers recited for their readers the horrors that were occurring in Cuba. Tens of thousands were dying there, mostly of disease and starvation. The hearts of Americans were wrenched time and again. Already in explosive temper because of unsettled economic and social conditions, people felt that their government should do something to stop these horrors. As time passed, they became impatient, then angry. All over the land there were speeches, sermons, meetings, and rallies demanding action. The clamor would fade, then rise again, louder and more insistent than before. Politicians in Washington could not ignore it.

Nor were domestic considerations the only ones that pressed on Cleveland and McKinley. In the late 1890's European powers were thrusting outward, engrossing the remainder of Africa, erecting naval and trading outposts in the Pacific, and threatening to partition China. Cleveland and McKinley believed that the United States had important interests in these distant parts of the world, especially the Far East. But the United States could do little to protect these faraway interests if it appeared unwilling to act for those nearer at hand, specifically in Cuba. Indeed, despite Cleveland's utterances about the Venezuelan boundary, continued inaction seemed likely to encourage European adventures in the Western Hemisphere itself. Each week's dispatches from abroad, like each week's reports of agitation at home, made it more difficult for the American government to withhold intervention in the Cuban imbroglio.

Spain could have freed Cleveland and McKinley from their predicament by coming to terms with the Cuban rebels or making the island independent. After the first year of fighting, it became increasingly clear that she could not subdue the insurrection. But important groups in Spain would not acknowledge this fact. The army would not own up to its inability to cope with Cuban guerrillas, and many Spaniards could not bring themselves to believe that Spain, once the mistress of all Latin America, no longer possessed the power to hold one island there. The Spanish constitutional monarchy had existed for barely two decades. Republicans on one side and adherents of the exiled Carlist dynasty on the other threatened at any moment to launch a revolution. Successive Spanish cabinets simply could not afford to offend the pride of the army and the nation. Many ministers in Madrid agreed, indeed, with one of the Spanish commanders in Cuba who said that a war with the United States might be welcome: "We would have real battles instead of ambushes . . .; and . . . if luck were to go against us, if we were to be defeated, if we were to lose the island of Cuba, we would have lost it with honor."

In *History and Human Relations* (1951), Sir Herbert Butterfield writes that behind most international conflicts "is a terrible human predicament which lies at the heart of the story . . . a terrible knot almost beyond the ingenuity of man to untie." The conflict between the United States and Spain was to be short and, as wars go, relatively bloodless. Nevertheless, behind it did lie one of these terrible human predicaments. The documents that follow are intended to give some sense of this predicament and also to illustrate the complexities that may inhere in any critical international issue.

~~~~~~

DOCUMENTS

1] Impatience in Congress: Henry Cabot Lodge Espouses Intervention

When Congress convened in December, 1895, several resolutions for recognition of Cuban belligerency or Cuban independence were introduced. Cleveland delivered his message on the Venezuelan boundary issue on December 17, and more than a month passed before the crisis was clearly at an end. Almost as soon as it was over, however, the Senate Foreign Relations Committee reported out a concurrent resolution counseling the President to recognize Cuban belligerency. Many speeches were made, among them one on February 20, 1896, by young Henry Cabot Lodge, a shrill-voiced, somewhat supercilious New England aristocrat, who was already a power in the Republican party.*

MR. LODGE. . . . Mr. President, I united with the rest of the Committee on Foreign Relations, with a single exception, in reporting the concurrent resolution which is now before the Senate. I will say, however, with perfect frankness, that I for one should be very glad if the Senate should see fit to go further in this direction, for I believe that the time has come when the United States should use their good offices to bring to an end the deplorable condition of affairs which now exists in the Island of Cuba. In my opinion the course which would meet with universal approbation of our own people and command the respect of the world would be to offer our good offices to mediate between Spain and the Cubans in order to restore peace and give independence to the island which Spain can no longer hold.

I think there are very few matters which are of more immediate importance to the people of the United States than this, not merely because their sympathies are engaged, but also because in the condition of that island and in its future are involved large and most serious interests of the United States. . . .

Now, Mr. President, the question arises, and I think the time has come and more than come to decide it. What are the duties of the United States in the presence of this war? What action should we take in regard to a condition of affairs which lies right at our threshold[?] We have heard a good deal in some of the recent debates [on the Venezuelan issue] of the ties of kindred, of our gratitude to other nations with whom we happen to be in controversy, and of how much consideration we should show for the nations of Europe in regard to matters where the interests of the United States are involved. Whatever may be said as to our relations to some other countries, I think the relations of this country to Spain offer no ties of gratitude or of blood. If that for

* HENRY CABOT LODGE ESPOUSES INTERVENTION: From the *Congressional Record*, 54 Cong., 1 Sess., pp. 1971-72.

which the Spanish Empire has stood since the days of Charles V is right, then everything for which the United States stands and has always stood is wrong. If the principles that we stand for are right, then the principles of which Spain has been the great exponent in history are utterly wrong.

Among the people who first settled in the United States, whose blood flows in American veins to-day, were to be found Hollanders, who, weak in numbers, but strong of heart, there among their dikes on the borders of the North Sea, first made head against the oppression of the Spanish Empire. Mr. President, in . . . Delaware the first settlers were the men who had followed the "Lion of the North," the Protestant champion, when he stayed the oncoming of Spain and Austria on the plains of Germany. The great English-speaking people who settled here and who largely outnumber all others are the descendants of the men who stood with Drake and with Hawkins, of that small band of English Protestant seamen who curbed the power of Spain in the days of her greatest authority. . . .

Such are the men, such are the races which have done most to settle and build up the United States. It is from those people that we derive all that we hold dear and all in which we most believe, and they fought their way to liberty against the power and bigotry of Spain, which was then the great force of the European world. . . .

No, Mr. President, we owe Spain nothing. We have the right to look at this thing purely from the point of view of the interests of humanity and the interests of the United States. . . .

Now turn to the other party in this conflict. Turn to the Cubans battling for their liberties. I think, Mr. President, that even the most bitter opponent of the Spanish-Americans would admit that free Cuba, under the constitution which now exists, would be an immense advance in civilization, in all that makes for the progress of humanity, over the government which Spain has given to that island.

The Cubans offer a free press and free speech. Both are suppressed there by Spain. Spain closed a Protestant chapel in the city of Matanzas. The Cubans by their constitution guarantee a free church in a free state. They guarantee liberty of conscience. Those are things in which Americans believe, and the Cubans, whatever their faults or deficiencies may be, stand also for those principles.

Our immediate pecuniary interests in the island are very great. They are being destroyed. Free Cuba would mean a great market to the United States; it would mean an opportunity for American capital, invited there by signal exemptions; it would mean an opportunity for the development of that splendid island.

Cuba is but a quarter smaller than the island of Java, and the island of Java sustains 23,000,000 people. Cuba has a population of a million and a half, and she is one of the richest spots on the face of the earth. She has not grown or prospered, because the heavy hand of Spain has been upon her.

Those, Mr. President, are some of the more material interests involved in this question, but we have also a broader political interest in the fate of Cuba. The great island lies there across the Gulf of Mexico. She commands the Gulf, she commands the channel through which all our coastwise traffic between the

Gulf and our Northern and Eastern States passes. She lies right athwart the line which leads to the Nicaragua Canal. Cuba in our hands or in friendly hands, in the hands of its own people, attached to us by ties of interest and gratitude, is a bulwark to the commerce, to the safety, and to the peace of the United States.

We should never suffer Cuba to pass from the hands of Spain to any other European power. We may dismiss that aspect of the subject. The question is whether we shall permit the present condition of affairs to continue. The island to-day is lost to Spain. They may maintain a guerilla warfare for years. They may wipe out every plantation and deluge the island in blood. . . .

Spain may ruin the island. She can never hold it or govern it again. Cuba now is not fighting merely for independence. Those men are fighting, every one of them, with a price on their heads and a rope around their necks. They have shown that they could fight well. They are now fighting the battle of despair. That is the condition to-day in that island. And here we stand motionless, a great and powerful country not six hours away from these scenes of useless bloodshed and destruction.

I have spoken of our material interests. I have referred to our political interests in the future of Cuba. But, Mr. President, I am prepared to put our duty on a higher ground than either of those, and that is the broad ground of a common humanity. No useful end is being served by the bloody struggle that is now in progress in Cuba, and in the name of humanity it should be stopped.

We have had a good deal to say in this Chamber and elsewhere about Armenia. We know very well that Armenia is far beyond our sphere of influence or of action. . . . The words we utter on Armenia are mere words, the words of sympathy, and that is all. . . . To-day those massacres go on in Armenia, and the civilization of western Europe has stood by paralyzed and helpless. . . . England, to whom Turkey owes her very existence as a nation among nations, has not stirred. The recent utterances of Lord Salisbury in regard to Armenia can only be described as pitiful. . . .

But, Mr. President, Lord Salisbury obeys a stronger force, a mightier will, than his own. In the last resort, the power which controls in Europe and in England is the great power of money and of the money lender. The money lenders do not care how many Armenians are butchered; . . . but they care very much . . . that nothing shall be done to disturb values. . . .

Now, Mr. President, we have right here an Armenia at our own doors. In Cuba there is useless bloodshed, brutality, cruelty, and destruction of life and property—all the horrors that can accompany a savage war which is not submitted to the rules of civilized warfare. Is our civilization in the United States to break down as the civilization of western Europe has broken down before Armenia? I do not believe it to be possible. Of the sympathies of the American people, generous, liberty loving, I have no question. They are with the Cubans in their struggle for freedom. I believe our people would welcome any action on the part of the United States to put an end to the terrible state of things existing there. . . .

Recognition of belligerency as an expression of sympathy is all very well. I think it is fully justified by the facts in Cuba, but I should like to see some

more positive action taken than that. I think we can not escape the responsibility which is so near to us. We can not shrug our shoulders and pass by
on the other side. If that war goes on in Cuba, with the added horrors which
this new general brings with him, the responsibility is on us; we can not escape it. We should exert every influence of the United States. Standing, as I
believe the United States stands, for humanity and civilization, we should exercise every influence of our great country to put a stop to that war which is
now raging in Cuba and give to that island once more peace, liberty, and independence.

2] Cleveland Tries to Mediate

> The Senate passed the concurrent resolution 64–6; the House passed it
> 247–27. Not being a joint resolution, it had no legal force; it merely repre-
> sented the sentiment of Congress. Nevertheless, the speeches that had been
> made, coupled with newspaper editorials and other indices of public opinion,
> made it clear that this sentiment might soon become so strong that the
> executive branch would have difficulty resisting it. Consequently, Cleveland
> and his Secretary of State, Richard Olney, on April 4, 1896, presented the
> following note to the Spanish minister in Washington.*

IT MIGHT well be deemed a dereliction of duty to the Government of the
United States, as well as a censurable want of candor to that of Spain, if I
were longer to defer official expression as well of the anxiety with which the
President regards the existing situation in Cuba as of his earnest desire for the
prompt and permanent pacification of that island. Any plan giving reasonable
assurance of that result and not inconsistent with the just rights and reasonable demands of all concerned would be earnestly promoted by him by all
means which the Constitution and laws of this country place at his disposal.

It is now some nine or ten months since the nature and prospects of the
insurrection were first discussed between us. In explanation of its rapid and,
up to that time, quite unopposed growth and progress, you called attention to
the rainy season which from May or June until November renders regular
military operations impracticable. Spain was pouring such numbers of troops
into Cuba that your theory and opinion that, when they could be used in an
active campaign, the insurrection would be almost instantly suppressed, seemed
reasonable and probable. In this particular you believed, and sincerely believed,
that the present insurrection would offer a most marked contrast to that which
began in 1868, and which, being feebly encountered with comparatively small
forces, prolonged its life for upward of ten years.

It is impossible to deny that the expectations thus entertained by you in the
summer and fall of 1895, and shared not merely by all Spaniards but by most
disinterested observers as well, have been completely disappointed. The insurgents seem to-day to command a larger part of the island than ever before.

---

* CLEVELAND TRIES TO MEDIATE: From U.S. Department of State, *Papers Relating
to the Foreign Relations of the United States,* 1897 (Washington, 1898), pp. 540–44.

Their men under arms, estimated a year ago at from ten to twenty thousand, are now conceded to be at least two or three times as many. Meanwhile, their discipline has been improved and their supply of modern weapons and equipment has been greatly enlarged, while the mere fact that they have held out to this time has given them confidence in their own eyes and prestige with the world at large. In short, it can hardly be questioned that the insurrection, instead of being quelled, is to-day more formidable than ever, and enters upon the second year of its existence with decidedly improved prospects of successful results.

Whether a condition of things entitling the insurgents to recognition as belligerents has yet been brought about may, for the purposes of the present communication, be regarded as immaterial. . . .

Even if it be granted that a condition of insurgency prevails and nothing more, it is on so large a scale and diffused over so extensive a region, and is so favored by the physical features and the climate of the country, that the authority of Spain is subverted and the functions of its Government are in abeyance or practically suspended throughout a great part of the island. Spain still holds the seaports and most, if not all, of the large towns in the interior. Nevertheless, a vast area of the territory of the island is in effect under the control of roving bands of insurgents, which, if driven from one place to-day by an exhibition of superior force, abandon it only to return to-morrow when that force has moved on for their dislodgment in other quarters.

The consequences of this state of things can not be disguised. Outside of the towns still under Spanish rule, anarchy, lawlessness, and terrorism are rampant. The insurgents realize that the wholesale destruction of crops, factories, and machinery advances their cause in two ways. It cripples the resources of Spain on the one hand. On the other, it drives into their ranks the laborers who are thus thrown out of employment. The result is a systematic war upon the industries of the island and upon all the means by which they are carried on, and whereas the normal annual product of the island is valued at something like eighty or a hundred millions, its value for the present year is estimated by competent authority as not exceeding twenty millions.

Bad as is this showing for the present year, it must be even worse for the next year and for every succeeding year during which the rebellion continues to live. . . . Not only is it certain that no fresh money is being invested on the island, but it is no secret that capital is fast withdrawing from it, frightened away by the utter hopelessness of the outlook. Why should it not be? What can a prudent man foresee as the outcome of existing conditions except the complete devastation of the island, the entire annihilation of its industries, and the absolute impoverishment of such of its inhabitants as are unwise or unfortunate enough not to seasonably escape from it?

The last preceeding insurrection lasted for ten years and then was not subdued, but only succumbed to the influence of certain promised reforms. . . . It may well be feared, therefore, that if the present is to be of shorter duration than the last insurrection, it will be because the end is to come sooner or later through the inability of Spain to prolong the conflict, and through her abandonment of the island to the heterogeneous combination of elements and of races now in arms against her.

Such a conclusion of the struggle can not be viewed even by the most devoted friend of Cuba and the most enthusiastic advocate of popular government except with the gravest apprehension. There are only too strong reasons to fear that, once Spain were withdrawn from the island, the sole bond of union between the different factions of the insurgents would disappear; that a war of races would be precipitated, all the more sanguinary for the discipline and experience acquired during the insurrection, and that, even if there were to be temporary peace, it could only be through the establishment of a white and a black republic, which, even if agreeing at the outset upon a division of the island between them, would be enemies from the start, and would never rest until the one had been completely vanquished and subdued by the other.

The situation thus described is of great interest to the people of the United States. They are interested in any struggle anywhere for freer political institutions, but necessarily and in special measure in a struggle that is raging almost in sight of our shores. They are interested, as a civilized and Christian nation, in the speedy termination of a civil strife characterized by exceptional bitterness and exceptional excesses on the part of both combatants. They are interested in the noninterruption of extensive trade relations which have been and should continue to be of great advantage to both countries. They are interested in the prevention of that wholesale destruction of property on the island which, making no discrimination between enemies and neutrals, is utterly destroying American investments that should be of immense value, and is utterly impoverishing great numbers of American citizens.

On all these grounds and in all these ways the interest of the United States in the existing situation in Cuba yields in extent only to that of Spain herself, and has led many good and honest persons to insist that intervention to terminate the conflict is the immediate and imperative duty of the United States. It is not proposed now to consider whether existing conditions would justify such intervention at the present time, or how much longer those conditions should be endured before such intervention would be justified. That the United States can not contemplate with complacency another ten years of Cuban insurrection, with all its injurious and distressing incidents, may certainly be taken for granted.

The object of the present communication, however, is not to discuss intervention, nor to propose intervention, nor to pave the way for intervention. The purpose is exactly the reverse—to suggest whether a solution of present troubles can not be found which will prevent all thought of intervention by rendering it unnecessary. What the United States desires to do, if the way can be pointed out, is to cooperate with Spain in the immediate pacification of the island on such a plan as, leaving Spain her rights of sovereignty, shall yet secure to the people of the island all such rights and powers of local self-government as they can reasonably ask. To that end the United States offers and will use her good offices at such time and in such manner as may be deemed most advisable. Its mediation, it is believed, should not be rejected in any quarter, since none could misconceive or mistrust its purpose.

Spain could not, because our respect for her sovereignty and our determination to do nothing to impair it have been maintained for many years at great cost and in spite of many temptations. The insurgents could not, because anything assented to by this Government which did not satisfy the reasonable demands and aspirations of Cuba would arouse the indignation of our whole people. It only remains to suggest that, if anything can be done in the direction indicated, it should be done at once and on the initiative of Spain. . . .

Thus far Spain has faced the insurrection sword in hand, and has made no sign to show that surrender and submission would be followed by anything but a return to the old order of things. Would it not be wise to modify that policy and to accompany the application of military force with an authentic declaration of the organic changes that are meditated in the administration of the island with a view to remove all just grounds of complaint?

It is for Spain to consider and determine what those changes would be. But should they be such that the United States could urge their adoption, as substantially removing well-founded grievances, its influence would be exerted for their acceptance, and it can hardly be doubted, would be most potential for the termination of hostilities and the restoration of peace and order to the island. One result of the course of proceeding outlined, if no other, would be sure to follow, namely, that the rebellion would lose largely, if not altogether, the moral countenance and support it now enjoys from the people of the United States.

In closing this communication it is hardly necessary to repeat that it is prompted by the friendliest feelings toward Spain and the Spanish people. To attribute to the United States any hostile or hidden purposes would be a grave and most lamentable error. The United States has no designs upon Cuba and no designs against the sovereignty of Spain. Neither is it actuated by any spirit of meddlesomeness nor by any desire to force its will upon another nation. Its geographical proximity and all the considerations above detailed compel it to be interested in the solution of the Cuban problem whether it will or no. Its only anxiety is that that solution should be speedy, and, by being founded on truth and justice, should also be permanent.

To aid in that solution it offers the suggestions herein contained. They will be totally misapprehended unless the United States be credited with entertaining no other purpose toward Spain than that of lending its assistance to such termination of a fratricidal contest as will leave her honor and dignity unimpaired at the same time that it promotes and conserves the true interests of all parties concerned.

3] Spain Refuses: A Note from Premier Cánovas

To the Spaniards there was nothing new about the idea of trying to end the insurrection by offering reforms to Cuba. But the Premier, Conservative party leader Antonio Cánovas del Castillo, did not believe that the rebels would accept anything short of independence. He also assumed, cynically though realistically, that those Cubans who would accept a compromise would be disappointed by the reforms that were within the power of the

Spanish government to effect. He was loath to say more than that Cuba could someday expect reforms. On June 4, 1896, two months after receiving the American note, he responded through the Spanish minister in Washington.*

THE GOVERNMENT of His Majesty appreciates to its full value the noble frankness with which that of the United States has informed it of the very definite opinion it has formed in regard to the legal impossibility of granting the recognition of belligerency to the Cuban insurgents. . . .

His Majesty's Government has read with no less gratification the explicit and spontaneous declarations to the effect that the Government of the United States seeks no advantage in connection with the Cuban question, its only wish being that the ineluctable and lawful sovereignty of Spain be maintained and even strengthened, through the submission of the rebels, which, as your excellency states in your note, is of paramount necessity to the Spanish Government for the maintenance of its authority and its honor. . . .

It is unnecessary, as your excellency remarks, and in view of so correct and so friendly an attitude, to discuss the hypothesis of intervention, as it would be utterly inconsistent with the above views. . . .

The Island of Cuba has been exclusively Spanish since its discovery; the great normal development of its resources, whatever it is, whatever its value, and whatever it represents in the community of mankind, it owes in its entirety to the mother country; and even at this day, among the various groups of people that inhabit it, whatever be the standpoint from which the question be examined, the natives of the peninsula are there absolutely necessary for the peace and advancement of the island.

All these reasons fully and clearly demonstrate that it is not possible to think that the island of Cuba can be benefited except through the agency of Spain, acting under her own impulse, and actuated, as she has long been, by the principles of liberty and justice.

The Spanish Government is aware of the fact that far from having justice done it on all sides on these points, there are many persons, obviously deceived by incessant slanders, who honestly believe that a ferocious despotism prevails in our Antilles, instead of one of the most liberal political systems in the world, being enjoyed there now as well as before the outbreak of the insurrection. . . .

The Government of His Majesty and the people of Spain wish and even long for the speedy pacification of Cuba. In order to secure it, they are ready to exert their best efforts and at the same time to adopt such reforms as may be useful or necessary and compatible, of course, with their inalienable sovereignty, as soon as the submission of the insurgents be an accomplished fact. . . .

The insurgents, elated by the strength which they have acquired through the aid of a certain number of citizens of the United States, have contemptuously repelled, by the medium of the Cubans residing in this Republic, any idea that the Government of Washington can intervene in the contest, either

---

* SPAIN REFUSES: A NOTE FROM PREMIER CÁNOVAS: From *Foreign Relations, 1897* (Washington, 1898). pp. 544–48.

with its advice or in any other manner, on the supposition that the declarations of disinterestedness on the part of the Government of the United States are false and that it wishes to get possession of the island one of these days. Hence it is evident that no success would attend such possible mediation, which they repel, even admitting that the mother country would condescend to treat with its rebellious subject as one power with another, thus surely jeopardizing its future authority, detracting from its national dignity, and impairing its independence for which it has at all times shown such great earnestness, as history teaches. In brief, there is no effectual way to pacify Cuba unless it begins with the actual submission of the armed rebels to the mother country. . . .

When the Government of the United States shall once be convinced of our being in the right, and when that honest conviction shall in some manner be made public, but little more will be required in order that all those in Cuba who are not merely striving to accomplish the total ruin of the beautiful country in which they were born, being then hopeless of outside help and powerless by themselves, will lay down their arms.

Until that happy state of things has been attained Spain will, in the just defense not only of her rights but also of her duty and honor, continue the efforts for an early victory which she is now exerting regardless of the greatest sacrifices.

4] Cleveland Voices a Warning

The Presidential contest in 1896, turning mainly that November on the issue of free coinage of silver, took the Cuban problem temporarily out of the headlines in the United States. When it was over, however, with William McKinley the victor over Bryan, agitation for some governmental action revived. As Congress prepared to open its winter session, rumors were rife that various representatives and senators intended to introduce resolutions for the recognition of Cuban independence or for intervention to end the island's civil war, and the talk this time was not of concurrent resolutions but of joint resolutions that would have the force of law. Cleveland greeted the convening Congress with his last annual message, which dwelt on the Cuban question.*

. . . .

THE INSURRECTION in Cuba still continues with all its perplexities. It is difficult to perceive that any progress has thus far been made towards the pacification of the island or that the situation of affairs . . . has in the least improved. If Spain still holds Havana and the seaports and all the considerable towns, the insurgents still roam at will over at least two-thirds of the inland country. If the determination of Spain to put down the insurrection seems but to strengthen with the lapse of time, and is evinced by her unhesitating devotion of largely increased military and naval forces to the task, there is much reason to believe that the insurgents have gained in point of numbers, and

* CLEVELAND VOICES A WARNING: From *Foreign Relations*, 1896 (Washington, 1897), pp. xxix–xxxvi.

character, and resources, and are none the less inflexible in their resolve not to succumb, without practically securing the great objects for which they took up arms. If Spain has not yet reestablished her authority, neither have the insurgents yet made good their title to be regarded as an independent state. Indeed, as the contest has gone on, the pretense that civil government exists on the island, except so far as Spain is able to maintain it, has been practically abandoned. Spain does keep on foot such a government, more or less imperfectly, in the large towns and their immediate suburbs. But, that exception being made, the entire country is either given over to anarchy or is subject to the military occupation of one or the other party. . . .

Were the Spanish armies able to meet their antagonists in the open, or in pitched battle, prompt and decisive results might be looked for, and the immense superiority of the Spanish forces in numbers, discipline, and equipment, could hardly fail to tell greatly to their advantage. But they are called upon to face a foe that shuns general engagements, that can choose and does choose its own ground, that from the nature of the country is visible or invisible at pleasure, and that fights only from ambuscade and when all the advantages of position and numbers are on its side. In a country where all that is indispensable to life in the way of food, clothing, and shelter is so easily obtainable, especially by those born and bred on the soil, it is obvious that there is hardly a limit to the time during which hostilities of this sort may be prolonged. Meanwhile, as in all cases of protracted civil strife, the passions of the combatants grow more and more inflamed and excesses on both sides become more frequent and more deplorable. They are also participated in by bands of marauders, who, now in the name of one party and now in the name of the other, as may best suit the occasion, harry the country at will and plunder its wretched inhabitants for their own advantage. Such a condition of things would inevitably entail immense destruction of property even if it were the policy of both parties to prevent it as far as practicable. But while such seemed to be the original policy of the Spanish Government, it has now apparently abandoned it and is acting upon the same theory as the insurgents, namely, that the exigencies of the contest require the wholesale annihilation of property, that it may not prove of use and advantage to the enemy.

It is to the same end that in pursuance of general orders, Spanish garrisons are now being withdrawn from plantations and the rural population required to concentrate itself in the towns. The sure result would seem to be that the industrial value of the island is fast diminishing, and that unless there is a speedy and radical change in existing conditions, it will soon disappear altogether. That value consists very largely, of course, in its capacity to produce sugar—a capacity already much reduced by the interruptions to tillage, which have taken place during the last two years. It is reliably asserted that should these interruptions continue during the current year and practically extend, as is now threatened, to the entire sugar-producing territory of the island, so much time and so much money will be required to restore the land to its normal productiveness that it is extremely doubtful if capital can be induced to even make the attempt.

The spectacle of the utter ruin of an adjoining country, by nature one of the most fertile and charming on the globe, would engage the serious attention of the Government and people of the United States in any circumstances. In point of fact, they have a concern with it which is by no means of a wholly sentimental or philanthropic character. It lies so near to us as to be hardly separated from our territory. Our actual pecuniary interest in it is second only to that of the people and Government of Spain. It is reasonably estimated that at least from $30,000,000 to $50,000,000 of American capital are invested in plantations and in railroad, mining, and other business enterprises on the island. The volume of trade between the United States and Cuba, which in 1889 amounted to about $64,000,000, rose in 1893 to about $103,000,000, and in 1894, the year before the present insurrection broke out, amounted to nearly $96,000,000. Besides this large pecuniary stake in the fortunes of Cuba, the United States finds itself inextricably involved in the present contest in other ways both vexatious and costly.

Many Cubans reside in this country and indirectly promote the insurrection through the press, by public meetings, by the purchase and shipment of arms, by the raising of funds, and by other means, which the spirit of our institutions and the tenor of our laws do not permit to be made the subject of criminal prosecutions. Some of them, though Cubans at heart and in all their feelings and interests, have taken out papers as naturalized citizens of the United States, a proceeding resorted to with a view to possible protection by this Government, and not unnaturally regarded with much indignation by the country of their origin. The insurgents are undoubtedly encouraged and supported by the widespread sympathy the people of this country always and instinctively feel for every struggle for better and freer government, and which, in the case of the more adventurous and restless elements of our population, leads in only too many instances to active and personal participation in the contest. The result is that this Government is constantly called upon to protect American citizens, to claim damages for injuries to persons and property, now estimated at many millions of dollars, and to ask explanations and apologies for the acts of Spanish officials, whose zeal for the repression of rebellion sometimes blinds them to the immunities belonging to the unoffending citizens of a friendly power. It follows from the same causes that the United States is compelled to actively police a long line of seacoast against unlawful expeditions, the escape of which the utmost vigilance will not always suffice to prevent.

These inevitable entanglements of the United States with the rebellion in Cuba, the large American property interests affected, and considerations of philanthropy and humanity in general, have led to a vehement demand in various quarters, for some sort of positive intervention on the part of the United States. It was at first proposed that belligerent rights should be accorded to the insurgents. . . . It has since been and is now sometimes contended that the independence of the insurgents should be recognized. But imperfect and restricted as the Spanish government of the island may be, no other exists there—unless the will of the military officer in temporary command of a particular district, can be dignified as a species of government. It is now also suggested that the United States should buy the island—a suggestion possibly worthy of consideration if there were any evidence of a desire or willingness on the part of Spain to entertain such a proposal. It is urged, finally, that, all other methods failing, the existing internecine strife in Cuba should be terminated by our intervention, even at the cost of a war between the United States and Spain—a war which its advocates confidently prophesy could be neither large in its proportions nor doubtful in its issue.

The correctness of this forecast need be neither affirmed nor denied. The United States has nevertheless a character to maintain as a nation, which plainly dictates that right and not might should be the rule of its conduct. Further, though the United States is not a nation to which peace is a necessity, it is in truth the most pacific of powers, and desires nothing so much as to live in amity with all the world. Its own ample and diversified domains satisfy all possible longings for territory, preclude all dreams of conquest, and prevent any casting of covetous eyes upon neighboring regions, however attractive. . . . No other great power, it may safely be said, under circumstances of similar perplexity, would have manifested the same restraint and the same patient endurance. It may also be said that this persistent attitude of the United States towards Spain in connection with Cuba, unquestionably evinces no slight respect and regard for Spain on the part of the American people. They in truth do not forget her connection with the discovery of the Western Hemisphere, nor do they underestimate the great qualities of the Spanish people, nor fail to fully recognize their splendid patriotism and their chivalrous devotion to the national honor. . . .

It would seem that if Spain should offer to Cuba genuine autonomy—a measure of home rule which, while preserving the sovereignty of Spain, would satisfy all rational requirements of her Spanish subjects—there should be no just reason why the pacification of the island might not be effected on that basis. Such a result would appear to be in the true interest of all concerned. It would at once stop the conflict which is now consuming the resources of the island and making it worthless for whichever party may ultimately prevail. It would keep intact the possessions of Spain without touching her honor, which will be consulted rather than impugned by the adequate redress of admitted grievances. It would put the prosperity of the island and the fortunes of its inhabitants within their own control, without severing the natural and ancient ties which bind them to the mother country, and would yet enable them to test their capacity for self-government under the most favorable conditions. . . . The friendly offices of the United States will always be at the disposal of either party.

Whatever circumstances may arise, our policy and our interests would constrain us to object to the acquisition of the island or an interference with its control by any other power.

It should be added that it can not be reasonably assumed that the hitherto expectant attitude of the United States will be indefinitely maintained. While we are anxious to accord all due respect to the sovereignty of Spain, we can not view the pending conflict in all its features, and properly apprehend our inevitably close relations to it, and its possible results, without considering that by the course of events we may be drawn into such an unusual and unprecedented condition, as will fix a limit to our patient waiting for Spain to end the contest, either alone and in her own way, or with our friendly cooperation.

When the inability of Spain to deal successfully with the insurrection has become manifest, and it is demonstrated that her sovereignty is extinct in Cuba for all purposes of its rightful existence, and when a hopeless struggle for its reestablishment has degenerated into a strife which means nothing more than the useless sacrifice of human life and the utter destruction of the very subject-matter of the conflict, a situation will be presented in which our obligations to the sovereignty of Spain will be superseded by higher obligations, which we can hardly hesitate to recognize and discharge. . . .

A contemplation of emergencies that may arise should plainly lead us to avoid their creation, either through a careless disregard of present duty or even an undue stimulation and ill-timed expression of feeling. But I have deemed it not amiss to remind the Congress that a time may arrive when a correct policy and care for our interests, as well as a regard for the interests of other nations and their citizens, joined by considerations of humanity and a desire to see a rich and fertile country, intimately related to us, saved from complete devastation, will constrain our Government to such action as will subserve the interests thus involved and at the same time promise to Cuba and its inhabitants an opportunity to enjoy the blessings of peace.

5] Moderates and Jingoes Clash

Cleveland's words did not satisfy those who wanted immediate action by the government. Senator J. Donald Cameron, Republican of Pennsylvania, soon introduced a joint resolution calling upon the President to recognize Cuban independence. At about the same time, the reported ambushing and slaying in Cuba of rebel general Antonio Maceo produced waves of sympathetic demonstrations all over the country. But the President still refused to stir. Recognition, he declared, was an executive act and could not be forced by Congress, even through a joint resolution.

McKinley now had to give guidance to the Republicans. Erect, handsome, and poised, he looked like a leader, but was not. Spending most of his public life in the House, he had developed skill as a manipulator and compromiser. He had hoped at first that Congress would pass the resolution so that the issue would be resolved before he took office. But he saw that if Cleveland would not act, passage of it would embarrass him. He therefore changed front and asked the senators of his party to wait and allow him time to study the problem. Agitation among Republicans noticeably subsided. Democrats came to the fore, offering resolutions of their own, and debate continued intermittently in the upper chamber until well into the spring of 1897. Moderates who had previously been quiet found the courage to state their views, as Republicans Justin S. Morrill of Maine and George L. Wellington of Maryland did on May 11 and May 17. But they were answered not only by Democrats but also by members of their own party, as Wellington was on May 18 and May 19 by William E. Mason of Illinois and Frank G. Cannon of Utah.*

MR. MORRILL. . . . On the other side of the Atlantic our Republic is regarded, by the so-called right-divine rulers of European nations, as an arrogant

* MODERATES AND JINGOES CLASH: From the *Congressional Record*, 55 Cong., 1 Sess., pp. 994–95, 1089–91, 1130–35, 1150–51.

American experiment, the success of which contributes nothing to their glory or happiness. Whether they have ever graciously accepted of the original "Monroe doctrine" or not, certainly they are unlikely to accept of a new and botched version of that doctrine with all the apocryphal additions presented by our most intrepid jingoists.

Already our action . . . has excited the deep-toned sympathy of all the neighbors-in-law of Spain, who might, after all, in case of a war on account of a premature recognition by the United States of the independence of Cuba, prefer a war as allies of overmatched Spain to a war which has long been supposed to be brewing among themselves. . . . We are in danger of being led . . . to . . . a grave departure from the great doctrine of Washington's Farewell Address, which taught that the United States should "beware of entangling alliances with foreign nations." This doctrine, with a luster and veracity unimpeachable, has bestowed upon our country long years of peace with honor, secured the comforts of happy homes with many remunerative industries, and the exemption of our American people from the extreme taxation required to support a force of not inferior magnitude to any of the great armed hosts of European nations.

This peace policy of Washington would seem to be often threatened by the Senate with abandonment or to be superseded by something supposed to be more heroic; that is to say, by a flatulent exaggeration of the Monroe doctrine. . . .

Cuba is now, as it was in 1823, an existing dependency of Spain, such as President Monroe then pledged the United States not to interfere with. Is this half of the Monroe doctrine to be repudiated by us? How can we ever expect to enforce that doctrine when we are the first to treat as obsolete and as having no binding force the pledge made in behalf of the United States?

The inhabitants of Cuba up to this time have not established and of course have not maintained their independence, and there has been no provocation to us . . . which would justify warlike interference on our part or that can entangle our peace and happiness. . . .

As warmly as we may sympathize with any heroic efforts upon the part of any of the inhabitants of Cuba for independence and self-government, we can not afford their union or annexation as a State to the United States, nor can we afford in any form to become responsible for its debts or its statesmanship as an independent government. . . .

In the climate of Cuba only the full-blooded negro appears to be equal to much outdoor labor with impunity. As insurgents, they have won the chief honors. . . . The heterogeneous character of the great mass of the inhabitants, their total inexperience in any autonomous government where the rights of man have been recognized, and the differences of race, language, and religion offer no encouragement for any political union. . . .

Now some of our teachers of jingo statesmanship do not conceal the fact that some of their prominent acquisitive Cuban propositions . . . may portend war, which they seem to covet as a panacea for all of our political, financial, and industrial woes, claiming that it would promote the general prosperity by making cheap money in the United States plentiful, . . . and by giving employment and a uniform to all the idle.

I confess I do not look in this direction for the return of prosperity which can only come from the years of peace now promised, and years of industry now most desired, that will give to labor the American standard of remuneration, to capital some exemption from a sudden collapse, and to our whole country an era of good common sense and conservatism like that of Washington and Monroe.

. . . .

Mr. WELLINGTON. . . . Our first duty is to the American people, not to Cuba, not as against Spain, not with respect to Turkey or England or any foreign nation. It is to the American people that the Senate of the United States owes present, aye, immediate, attention. We should faithfully perform that duty, and with due celerity find a remedy for the sad plight and unhappy environments which have retarded advancement and progress for four years, and from which the American people desire succor and relief, and if it be not afforded them, they will hold the Administration responsible for the failure of its mission, and hurl the Republican party from the throne of power. . . .

We must demonstrate to the people of the world that the American Republic is a conservative government. We must not go out as a Bombastes Furioso among the nations of the earth, nor yet as Don Quixote, seeking to attack windmills that are beyond our boundary. . . .

Why was it that the great depression of four years ago came? It was because European nations were losing confidence in this Republic, and deemed that the people of American were about to break their promises as to obligations incurred. What we must do in the Senate, what we must do in the House of Representatives, what we must do in this Administration, is to appeal to the nations of the earth in a manner which will inspire in them an abiding faith not only in our willingness to keep every promise, but also in our caution and desire for peaceful growth. This will assure them that in this great Republic there is as much conservatism as in the monarchies of Europe. . . .

What information has the Senate in regard to affairs in Cuba? We have newspaper reports. What are newspaper reports? Are they always true? Is that the kind of information upon which the Senate of the United States should act? I think not. . . .

Where is the civil government upon the Island of Cuba? Where is the capital of the government? Where is the congress that is there assembled? Where are the legislatures? Where is the president of the republic? Where is its judiciary? Where the many things that would denominate and demonstrate the fact that there is in Cuba to-day a civil government? Nowhere. They exist only in the imagination of those who are carried away by sentiment and sympathy. . . .

Make haste slowly. . . . You may say Spain is a weak power; that Spain can be demolished and annihilated by our forces in thirty minutes, as has been suggested in the newspapers. I doubt it. . . . Is the American Republic ready for war? I do not believe it is. If one of the great nations of Europe were to come here to-day, they could demolish every port you have on the Atlantic coast from the rock-bound isle of Maine to the headlands of Florida before you could gather strength to prevent or resist an invasion. . . . I think no action should be taken.

.   .   .   .

Mr. MASON. . . . Day after day the papers have been full of the announcement that this country was at last to speak, and that the barbarities inflicted by the Spaniard on the Cuban were to have some rebuke at least in the Senate of the United States. . . . I am here to say as a Republican . . . that there is no question before the American people so much demanded by the hearts of the intelligent Christian people of this country as the demand made upon us here and now that we shall lift our voices and our hands in defense of liberty in the Island of Cuba. . . . Those people suffer exactly as our fathers suffered in 1770 and on until we relieved ourselves of the yoke of England. . . .

My friend says that the four years of depression came from a lack of confidence in Europe. It is true to a certain extent. . . . but it was not produced by anything we had done by way of demanding our rights among the nations of the world. Fear of Europe! Afraid of war! He suggested how gunboats would clean our frontier.

Mr. President, if we did not have a ship in the world, if every gun was melted into a plowshare, if every bayonet was buried, if every ship we ever had was sunk in the middle of the sea, there is no nation in the world, much less Spain, that would ever dare strike our colors or invade American soil. . . .

Mr. President, no one expects war, but if to keep our promises with Cuba and protect her means war, let it come. If to protest against the butchery of women and children means war, let it come. If to defend the honest daughters of brave patriots means an insult to Spain and war, in the name of God, let it come, and come quickly. Whether you sleep bound hand and foot by the rules of order, or whether you speak like American brave men, the march of the Nazarene is upon us; liberty shall prevail, and the Island of Cuba, under the providence of God, shall be free.

.   .   .   .

Mr. CANNON. . . . Mr. President, jingoism in this country is a fluctuating characteristic. When I had the honor to be admitted to a seat in this Chamber there were, I believe, but three defenders of the then existing Administration; and therefore there were but three anti-jingoes in the Senate. So long as a Democratic President sat in the White House, it was the general impression in this body that no Republican could be quite loyal to his party and the people and the traditions of America unless he outjingoed jingoism. . . . But no sooner does the triumphant party come into its own than it begins to pursue in this body the tactics which it reprehended when another Administration was in power.

Parties may come and parties may go in their control in the United States Senate and in the affairs of Government in this country, but jingoism among the people of the United States will go on forever. If it be jingoism, Mr. President, to desire that the United States shall stretch out the arm of its power and seize that mad dog, Weyler, . . . the ravisher of women, the assassin of men, the crucifier of children—if it be jingoism to hope that no longer will we write words of cowardice in chapters of American history, then 71,000,000 Americans are jingoes. The remaining 263,000 of our population are, some of them, engaged in trade, in counting houses; a few of them, a very few, thank Heaven, in newspaper offices; and a few, still fewer in number, but, alas, greater in power, are in the Senate of the United States. . . .

We can not stand alone, we are told, Mr. President. . . . We can not stand alone! when we are the most prosperous, the most intelligent, the most industrious nation under the sun. The only thing needed to enable us to stand alone, patriotically, politically, commercially, financially, is a little more of the jingoism which has fallen into disrepute in this body. . . .

Mr. President, Cuba is lost to Spain. . . . She will be banished from the island, and with her will go the last tyranny that infests the Western Hemisphere. If we shall do our duty, we shall aid Cuba in throwing off the yoke. . . . If the Senate of the United States will rise to the wonderful opportunity now afforded for an assertion of the dignity of Americanism, and if . . . there shall be such aggressive action on the part of the people of the United States as shall serve notice on tyranny that faith is absolved, . . . Cuban independence will be resurrected to be mighty and powerful, as a further example to the liberty loving of all lands of what the Western Hemisphere can do under the providence of God.

6] McKinley Prompts the Spaniards: A Directive from the State Department

> The new President soon decided that he should continue the line of policy that Cleveland had initiated in his appeal to Spain in April, 1896. After some delay, McKinley selected Stewart Lyndon Woodford, a former Union general and well-known New York lawyer, to be his minister in Madrid. He asked Woodford to stop en route to his post for conversations with the American ambassadors to Britain, France, and Germany. On July 16, 1897, just before the general departed, the Secretary of State gave him the following formal directive.*

BEFORE you go to your post it is proper to state to you the President's views on the relation of your Government to the contest which is now being waged in Cuba. The same occasion requires that you should be made acquainted with the course which has been deemed best for the United States to follow under existing conditions. . . .

For more than two years a wholly unexampled struggle has raged in Cuba between the discontented native population and the mother power. Not only has its attendant ruin spread over a larger area than in any previous contest,

* MCKINLEY PROMPTS THE SPANIARDS: A DIRECTIVE FROM THE STATE DEPARTMENT: From *Foreign Relations*, 1898 (Washington, 1899), pp. 558–61.

but its effects have been more widely felt and the cost of life and treasure to Spain has been far greater. The strife continues on a footing of mutual destruction and devastation. Day by day the conviction gathers strength that it is visionary for Spain to hope that Cuba, even if eventually subjugated by sheer exhaustion, can ever bear to her anything like the relation of dependence and profit she once bore. The policy which obviously attempts to make Cuba worthless to the Cubans, should they prevail, must inevitably make the island equally worthless to Spain in the event of reconquest, whether it be regained as a subject possession or endowed with a reasonable measure of self-administration.

The recuperative processes, always painfully slow in an exhausted community, would necessarily be doubly remote in either of the latter contingencies, for in the light of events of the past twenty-nine years capital and industry would shrink from again engaging in costly enterprises in a field where neither proximate return nor permanent security is to be expected. To fix the truth of this assertion one need only regard the fate of the extraordinary efforts to rehabilitate the fortunes of Cuba that followed the truce of 1878. The capital and intelligence contributed by citizens of the United States and other countries, which at that time poured into Cuba seeking to endow the island with the marvelous resources of modern invention and advanced industrial processes, have now become submerged in the common ruin. The commerce of Cuba has dwindled to such unprofitable proportions that its ability for self-support is questionable even if peace was restored to-day. Its capacity to yield anything like adequate return toward the support of the mother country, even granting the disposition to do so, is a matter of the gravest doubt.

Weighing all these facts carefully and without prejudice, in the judgment of the President the time has come for this Government to soberly consider and clearly decide the nature and methods of its duty both to its neighbors and itself.

This Government has labored and is still laboring under signal difficulties in its administration of its neutrality laws. It is ceaselessly confronted with questions affecting the inherent and treaty rights of its citizens in Cuba. It beholds the island suffering an almost complete paralysis of many of its most necessary commercial functions by reason of the impediments imposed and the ruinous injuries wrought by this internecine warfare at its very doors; and above all, it is naturally and rightfully apprehensive lest some untoward incident may abruptly supervene to inflame mutual passions beyond control and thus raise issues which, however deplorable, can not be avoided.

In short, it may not be reasonably asked or expected that a policy of mere inaction can be safely prolonged. There is no longer question that the sentiment of the American people strongly demands that if the attitude of neutrality is to be maintained toward these combatants it must be a genuine neutrality as between combatants, fully recognized as such in fact as well as in name. The problem of recognition of belligerency has been often presented, but never perhaps more explicitly than now. Both Houses of Congress, nearly a year ago, adopted by an almost unanimous vote a concurrent resolution recognizing belligerency in Cuba, and latterly the Senate, by a large majority, has voted a joint resolution of like purport, which is now pending in the House of Representatives.

At this juncture our Government must seriously inquire whether the time has not arrived when Spain, of her own volition, moved by her own interests and by every paramount sentiment of humanity, will put a stop to this destructive war and make proposals of settlement honorable to herself and just to her Cuban colony and to mankind. The United States stands ready to assist her and tender good offices to that end.

It should by no means be forgotten that besides and beyond the question of recognition of belligerency, with its usual proclamation of neutrality and its concession of equal rights and impartial imposition of identical disabilities in respect to the contending parties within our municipal jurisdiction, there lies the larger ulterior problem of intervention, which the President does not now discuss. It is with no unfriendly intent that this subject has been mentioned, but simply to show that this Government does not and can not ignore the possibilities of duty hidden in the future, nor be unprepared to face an emergency which may at any time be born of the unhappy contest in Cuba. The extraordinary, because direct and not merely theoretical or sentimental, interest of the United States in the Cuban situation can not be ignored, and if forced the issue must be met honestly and fearlessly, in conformity with our national life and character. Not only are our citizens largely concerned in the ownership of property and in the industrial and commercial ventures which have been set on foot in Cuba through our enterprising initiative and sustained by their capital, but the chronic condition of trouble and violent derangement in that island constantly causes disturbance in the social and political condition of our own people. It keeps up a continuous irritation within our own borders, injuriously affects the normal functions of business, and tends to delay the condition of prosperity to which this country is entitled.

No exception can be taken to the general proposition that a neighboring nation, however deeply disturbed and injured by the existence of a devastating internal conflict at its doors, may be constrained, on grounds of international comity, to disregard its endangered interests and remain a passive spectator of the contest for a reasonable time while the titular authority is repressing the disorder. The essence of this moral obligation lies in the reasonableness of the delay invited by circumstances and by the effort of the territorial authority to assert its claimed rights. The onlooking nation need only wait "a reasonable time" before alleging and acting upon the rights which it, too, possesses. This proposition is not a legal subtlety, but a broad principle of international comity and law.

The question arises, then, whether Spain has not already had a reasonable time to restore peace and been unable to do so, even by a concentration of her resources and measures of unparalleled severity which have received very general condemnation. The methods which Spain has adopted to wage the fight give no prospect of immediate peace or of a stable return to the conditions of prosperity which are essential to Cuba in its intercourse with its neighbors. Spain's inability entails upon the United States a degree of injury and suffering which can not longer be ignored. Assuredly Spain can not expect this Government to sit idle, letting vast interests suffer, our political elements disturbed, and the country perpetually embroiled, while no progress is being made in the settlement of the Cuban problem. Such a policy of inaction would in reality prove of no benefit to Spain, while certain to do the United States incalculable harm. This Government, strong in its sense of right and duty, yet keenly sympathetic with the aspirations of any neighboring community in close touch with our own civilization, is naturally desirous to avoid, in all rational ways, the precipitation of a result which would be painfully abhorrent to the American people.

For all of the reasons before stated the President feels it his duty to make the strongest possible effort to help bring about a result which shall be in conformity alike with the feelings of our people, the inherent rights of civilized man, and be of advantage both to Cuba and to Spain. Difficult as the task may seem now, it is believed that frankness, earnestness, perseverance, and a fair regard for the rights of others will eventually solve the problem.

It should be borne in mind from the start that it is far removed from the feelings of the American people and the mind of the President to propose any solution to which the slightest idea of humiliation to Spain could in any way be attached. But no possible intention or occasion to wound the just susceptibilities of the Castilian nation can be discerned in the altogether friendly suggestion that the good offices of the United States may now be lent to the advantage of Spain.

You are hereby instructed to bring these considerations as promptly as possible, but with due allowance for favorable conditions, to the attention of the Government of Her Majesty the Queen Regent, with all the impressiveness which their importance demands, and with all the earnestness which the constantly imperiled national interests of the United States justifies. You will emphasize the self-restraint which this Government has hitherto observed until endurance has ceased to be tolerable or even possible for any longer indefinite term. You will lay especial stress on the unselfish friendliness of our desires, and upon the high purpose and sincere wish of the United States to give its aid only in order that a peaceful and enduring result may be reached, just and honorable alike to Spain and to the Cuban people, and only so far as such aid may accomplish the wished-for ends. In so doing, you will not disguise the gravity of the situation, nor conceal the President's conviction that, should his present effort be fruitless, his duty to his countrymen will necessitate an early decision as to the course of action which the time and the transcendent emergency may demand.

As to the manner in which the assistance of the United States can be effectively rendered in the Cuban situation, the President has no desire to embarrass the Government of Spain by formulating precise proposals. All that is asked or expected is that some safe way may be provided for action which the United States may undertake with justice and self-respect, and that the settlement shall be a lasting one, honorable and advantageous to Spain and to Cuba and equitable to the United States.

7] The View from Havana: A Spanish Liberal Assesses the Situation

Before Woodford arrived in Madrid, Cánovas was assassinated by a young anarchist. The minister presented the substance of his instruction to a care-taker Conservative government, but within a few days the Conservatives were out of office; the queen regent, Doña María Cristina de Habsburgo-Lorena, installed in its place a Liberal cabinet headed by Práxedes Mateo Sagasta. Since Liberal leaders had already spoken out for extensive reforms for Cuba, it was not long before Sagasta proclaimed that an autonomous regime would be set up there. He also brought about Weyler's recall, replacing him with General Ramón Blanco. But the reports that came to him from Blanco and from the traveling Liberal journalist José Canalejas were not encouraging. The following extract is from a biography of Sagasta by a fellow Liberal statesman.*

Sagasta's body was beginning to become round, the decline in his physique was visible, when, for the sixth time in his life, he received, without being able to refuse, the confidence of the ruler. And in what conditions! Not a ray of hope illuminated the horizon.

Sagasta didn't like to keep papers . . . , but he saved a few, chosen with special care, in a folder on which is written in his own hand: "The situation at our entry into power." In it there is a letter from Blanco, the Captain General in Cuba, of three pages, and two from Canalejas, very long, dated from Washington and from Havana. . . .

They are so long that, in spite of their great interest, it is not possible to produce them in their entirety in these pages. If Sagasta at that time had been able to make them public, what weapons he would have had with which to defend himself against the charges that were flung at him.

We see how Blanco describes the situation which he found on the island: "The administration has reached the last stage of disarray and disorder; the army, exhausted and bloodless, filling the hospitals, without the power to fight or hardly even to lift their arms; more than three hundred thousand concen-trados suffering or starving, dying of hunger and misery all around the towns; the people frightened, in the grip of real terror, obliged to abandon their homes and properties in order to suffer under even more terrible tyranny, with no opportunity to escape this fearful situation except by going to join the ranks of the rebels." In other paragraphs he makes a strong attack on the con-stitutional party for resisting the establishment of autonomy, and, undoubtedly in order to end his report on a note which will give some comfort to Sagasta, but with a tremendous equivocation, he affirms: "Almost all the country is on the side of the government; the insurrection, which was strong and dominated

* THE VIEW FROM HAVANA: A SPANISH LIBERAL ASSESSES THE SITUATION: From Conde de Romanones, *Sagasta o El Político* (Madrid, 1930), pp. 191–94. Translation by Ernest R. May. Reprinted by permission of Sr. D. Agustín de Figueroa, Marqués de Santo Floro.

all the country at the advent of the present government, *hardly exists today."* This is what Blanco affirmed in February of '98, that is to say, four months before the total defeat of Spain.

If the information given by Blanco was true in its first part, his blindness in believing in good faith that the rebellion was overcome is something dismaying. Such were the official informants of the President of the Council.

Contrast with the optimistic statements of Blanco the judgments contained in the two letters from Canalejas. . . .

We read, even though anguish grips his soul: "Priests and soldiers, radicals and conservatives, all agree that the war and the reconcentration have caused the death of at least a third of the rural population, that is to say, more than four hundred thousand human beings; add to this figure the increasing number of reconcentrados who are going to die each day in terrifying proportions. Taking into account the civil population and armed rebels and soldiers, the war, even if it ends soon, will represent a loss of more than six hundred thousand lives! What a horror!. . . . And think that this most beautiful of islands, without the war and with good government, would be a treasure house!"

In discounting the dangers of a war with the United States, Spain revealed almost total ignorance of America's military and naval power. Canalejas, six months before the landing at Santiago, draws aside the veil and presents to Sagasta the naked truth. . . . "The Yankee generals do not have to have a war to win laurels; but they are certain, absolutely certain, of winning. . . . The United States has a real navy, with four first-class battleships very superior to ours, and in number and quality the other ironclads they possess are also very superior." "To oppose them," he adds, "we have our army, which is very large but disorganized and debilitated by sickness and suffering, and a squadron. . . . [sic]"

Canalejas showed his pessimism about the establishment of autonomy and observed that, for lack of preparation, it was going to end in disaster; however, there was now no course open except to concede it; thus the first act of the government was to proclaim it in the *Gazeta*. It arrived late; . . . political therapy rests on the same fundamentals as medical: it is not enough that the remedy be appropriate; it is also necessary to administer it in time. The Cuban people, certain of obtaining independence by their own power and counting on the help of the United States, rejected the concessions that Spain offered them.

8] The Scene in Madrid: A French Journalist Describes His Observations

But Sagasta could not base his policy solely on the facts reported from Havana. Like his predecessor, he had to recognize that Republicans, Carlists, and others might seize upon any intense public disappointment to foment a revolution. The attitudes of the Spanish people were described at the end

of 1897 by an astute and experienced French journalist who reported on
Spain for the Paris *Revue de deux mondes.**

CONSERVATIVES, Liberals, republicans, or Carlists, parties, ministries, dynasties,
and even the forms of government, these pass; but it is necessary that Spain
live on. And Cuba is the flesh of the flesh of Spain; it is part of the history,
the glory, and the grandeur of Spain; it is the last evidence of Spain in that
New World which has been torn from her by the strangers from the sea.
So, in that language rich above all others, made, as the Emperor said, for conversation with God, in which so many appeals have been addressed to Him
against institutions and men, now only three words are heard: *"Viva Cuba
española!"* Little rancors, little hatreds, little ambitions, little passions, at least
during these grave times, become silent. If you pick up a newspaper at random:
La Época, the *Imparcial,* the *Liberal,* the *Heraldo*—perhaps it is *La Época*
—Cuban affairs occupy the first, the second, the third page. Articles, fillers,
dispatches, news stories, rumors from political circles and the stock market:
everywhere . . . Cuba. Two full columns at the top of the *Imparcial* list
each day names and figures: contributions for the wounded and ill in Cuba;
farther on, other names, other figures: contributions to the 400 million peseta
loan for the expenses of the war in Cuba; all the headlines call attention
to . . . Cuba. On Sunday mornings, special illustrated supplements are attached to the *Liberal,* devoted one week to the army, another week to the
navy, another to some other patriotic or military topic, but always on the
single subject, Cuba. Prose, poetry, pictures describe, sing of, portray Cuba.
These service records fully recited, these portraits, are the service records and
portraits of generals who command in Cuba. At the bottom of the Calle
Mayor, in front of the door of a cafe, and it need not be the most popular, stands
someone selling songs; go up to his stand and read: "The War in Cuba,"
—"Dialogue between Spain and Cuba."

Some soldiers pass by, dressed in blue and white striped duck trousers, in
streets swept in November by the wind of the Guadarrama; people look at
them and say, "soldiers for Cuba." Twenty thousand have just gone, and if
necessary they will not be the last who go. That company that goes on maneuvers, this battery of artillery that returns to its barracks, they have only
three very young lieutenants and three very old captains—lieutenants of
eighteen, captains of fifty. Where are the others? In Cuba. Thus, what is seen
in Madrid and what is not seen, presences, absences, departures, at every minute and on every side call to mind Cuba. . . .

"Understand this well," said to me one of the best known orators in the
two chambers, "We *cannot* give up Cuba; we absolutely cannot. . . . You
Frenchmen, if one of your colonies is lost, can console yourselves with the
thought that you have new ones, and Africa will more than fill the void left
by any loss in Asia or America. But we have no new colonies, and, among the

---

* THE SCENE IN MADRID: A FRENCH JOURNALIST DESCRIBES HIS OBSERVATIONS: From
Charles Benoist, *L'Espagne, Cuba et les États-Unis* (Paris, 1898), pp. 3–5, 10–12. Translation by Ernest R. May.

old ones, what do we still have in comparison with what we used to have? Furthermore, colonies are more useful to us than to you because of our geographic position at the end of Europe and between two seas. You stand on the continent; you are tied to it by a long land frontier connecting with four or five countries and, across it, with all the others. We are a peninsula, locked in on the land side by high mountains. We do not have an opening except toward the ocean and the Mediterranean, one western sea and one eastern sea. . . . As a peninsular state, we have to have a navy; since we have a navy, we must have ports for them to the east and to the west; that is why Cuba and the Philippines have ties to us which we *cannot* permit to be broken. Life depends on it, honor depends on it, and, why hide the fact, money depends on it too. However poor, however weak or backward, however little developed she may be from the economic point of view, Spain has at least three provinces that are rich and industrious. She has the iron of Biscay, the textiles of Catalonia, and the grain of Andalusia; even though all the domestic market is protected, it is not enough. In sum, Cuba and the Philippines are for us at one and the same time historically sacred, politically necessary, and economically desirable." Thus spoke . . . a man who is justly reputed to speak the truth and speak it well.

9] McKinley Asserts That Time Is Running Out

> Even though American officials were as pessimistic as Spaniards about the prospect that the autonomy decree would end the Cuban war, the fact that the decree had been issued tended to quiet public agitation in the United States. The winter session of Congress in December, 1897, was preceded by few demonstrations and editorial demands on behalf of the Cuban rebels. Nevertheless, McKinley greeted the session with stern words on the Cuban problem.*

. . . .

THE MOST important problem with which this Government is now called upon to deal pertaining to its foreign relations concerns its duty toward Spain and the Cuban insurrection. . . .

The instructions given to our new Minister to Spain before his departure for his post directed him to impress upon that Government the sincere wish of the United States to lend its aid toward the ending of the war in Cuba by reaching a peaceful and lasting result, just and honorable alike to Spain and to the Cuban people. . . .

The reply to our note was received on the 23rd day of October. It is in the direction of a better understanding. It appreciates the friendly purposes of this Government. It admits that our country is deeply affected by the war in Cuba and that its desires for peace are just. It declares that the present Spanish Government is bound by every consideration to a change of policy that should satisfy the United States and pacify Cuba within a reasonable time. To this

---

* MCKINLEY ASSERTS THAT TIME IS RUNNING OUT: From *Foreign Relations, 1897* (Washington, 1898), pp. xi–xxi.

end Spain has decided to put into effect the political reforms heretofore advocated by the present Premier without halting for any consideration in the path
which in its judgment leads to peace. The military operations, it is said,
will continue but will be humane and conducted with all regard for private
rights, being accompanied by political action leading to the autonomy of Cuba
while guarding Spanish sovereignty. This, it is claimed, will result in investing
Cuba with a distinct personality; the Island to be governed by an Executive
and by a Local Council or Chamber, reserving to Spain the control of the
foreign relations, the army and navy and the judicial administration. To
accomplish this the present Government proposes to modify existing legislation by decree, leaving the Spanish Cortes, with the aid of Cuban Senators
and Deputies, to solve the economic problem and properly distribute the
existing debt. . . .

The immediate amelioration of existing conditions under the new administration of Cuban affairs is predicted, and therewithal the disturbance and all
occasion for any change of attitude on the part of the United States. . . .

Throughout all these horrors and dangers to our own peace this Government has never in any way abrogated its sovereign prerogative of reserving
to itself the determination of its policy and course according to its own high
sense of right and in consonance with the dearest interests and convictions
of our own people should the prolongation of the strife so demand.

Of the untried measures there remain only: Recognition of the insurgents
as belligerents; recognition of the independence of Cuba; neutral intervention
to end the war by imposing a rational compromise between the contestants,
and intervention in favor of one or the other party. I speak not of forcible
annexation, for that can not be thought of. That by our code of morality
would be criminal aggression.

Recognition of the belligerency of the Cuban insurgents has often been
canvassed as a possible if not inevitable step both in regard to the previous
ten years' struggle and during the present war. I am not unmindful that the
two Houses of Congress in the spring of 1896 expressed the opinion by concurrent resolution that a condition of public war existed requiring or justifying
the recognition of a state of belligerency in Cuba, and during the extra session
the Senate voted a joint resolution of like import, which however was not
brought to a vote in the House of Representatives. In the presence of these
significant expressions of the sentiment of the Legislative branch it behooves
the Executive to soberly consider the conditions under which so important
a measure must needs rest for justification. It is to be seriously considered
whether the Cuban insurrection possesses beyond dispute the attributes of
Statehood which alone can demand the recognition of belligerency in its
favor. Possession, in short, of the essential qualifications of sovereignty by the
insurgents and the conduct of the war by them according to the received code
of war are no less important factors toward the determination of the problem
of belligerency than are the influences and consequences of the struggle upon
the internal polity of the recognizing State. . . .

Turning to the practical aspects of a recognition of belligerency and review-
ing its inconveniences and positive dangers, still further pertinent considerations appear. In the code of nations there is no such thing as a naked rec-

ognition of belligerency unaccompanied by the assumption of international neutrality. Such recognition without more will not confer upon either party to a domestic conflict a status not theretofore actually possessed or affect the relation of either party to other States. The act of recognition usually takes the form of a solemn proclamation of neutrality which recites the de facto condition of belligerency as its motive. It announces a domestic law of neutrality in the declaring State. It assumes the international obligations of a neutral in the presence of a public state of war. It warns all citizens and others within the jurisdiction of the proclaimant that they violate those rigorous obligations at their own peril and can not expect to be shielded from the consequences. The right of visit and search on the seas and seizure of vessels and cargoes and contraband of war and good prize under admiralty law must under international law be admitted as a legitimate consequence of a proclamation of belligerency. While according the equal belligerent rights defined by public law to each party in our ports disfavors would be imposed on both, which while nominally equal would weigh heavily in behalf of Spain herself. Possessing a navy and controlling the ports of Cuba her maritime rights could be asserted not only for the military investment of the Island but up to the margin of our own territorial waters, and a condition of things would exist for which the Cubans within their own domain could not hope to create a parallel; while its creation through aid or sympathy from within our domain would be even more impossible than now, with the additional obligations of international neutrality we would perforce assume.

The enforcement of this enlarged and onerous code of neutrality would only be influential within our own jurisdiction by land and sea and applicable by our own instrumentalities. It could impart to the United States no jurisdiction between Spain and the insurgents. It would give the United States no right of intervention to enforce the conduct of the strife within the paramount authority of Spain according to the international code of war.

For these reasons I regard the recognition of the belligerency of the Cuban insurgents as now unwise and therefore inadmissible. Should that step hereafter be deemed wise as a measure of right and duty the Executive will take it.

Intervention upon humanitarian grounds has been frequently suggested and has not failed to receive my most anxious and earnest consideration. But should such a step be now taken when it is apparent that a hopeful change has supervened in the policy of Spain toward Cuba? A new government has taken office in the mother country. It is pledged in advance to the declaration that all the effort in the world can not suffice to maintain peace in Cuba by the bayonet; that vague promises of reform after subjugation afford no solution of the insular problem; that with a substitution of commanders must come a change of the past system of warfare for one in harmony with a new policy which shall no longer aim to drive the Cubans to the "horrible alternative of taking to the thicket or succumbing in misery;" that reforms must be instituted in accordance with the needs and circumstances of the time, and that these reforms, while designed to give full autonomy to the colony and to create a virtual entity and self-controlled administration, shall yet conserve and affirm the sovereignty of Spain by a just distribution of powers and burdens upon a basis of mutual interest untainted by methods of selfish expediency.

The first acts of the new government lie in these honorable paths. The policy of cruel rapine and extermination that so long shocked the universal sentiment of humanity has been reversed. Under the new military commander a broad clemency is proffered. Measures have already been set on foot to relieve the horrors of starvation. The power of the Spanish armies it is asserted is to be used not to spread ruin and desolation but to protect the resumption of peaceful agricultural pursuits and productive industries. That past methods are futile to force a peace by subjugation is freely admitted, and that ruin without conciliation must inevitably fail to win for Spain the fidelity of a contented dependency.

That the Government of Sagasta has entered upon a course from which recession with honor is impossible can hardly be questioned; that in the few weeks it has existed it has made earnest of the sincerity of its professions is undeniable. I shall not impugn its sincerity, nor should impatience be suffered to embarrass it in the task it has undertaken. It is honestly due to Spain and to our friendly relations with Spain that she should be given a reasonable chance to realize her expectations and to prove the asserted efficacy of the new order of things to which she stands irrevocably committed. . . .

The near future will demonstrate whether the indispensable condition of a righteous peace, just alike to the Cubans and to Spain as well as equitable to all our interests so intimately involved in the welfare of Cuba, is likely to be attained. If not, the exigency of further and other action by the United States will remain to be taken. When that time comes that action will be determined in the line of indisputable right and duty. It will be faced, without misgiving or hesitancy in the light of the obligation this Government owes to itself, to the people who have confided to it the protection of their interests and honor, and to humanity.

Sure of the right, keeping free from all offense ourselves, actuated only by upright and patriotic considerations, moved neither by passion nor selfishness, the Government will continue its watchful care over the rights and property of American citizens and will abate none of its efforts to bring about by peaceful agencies a peace which shall be honorable and enduring. If it shall hereafter appear to be a duty imposed by our obligations to ourselves, to civilization and humanity to intervene with force, it shall be without fault on our part and only because the necessity for such action will be so clear as to command the support and approval of the civilized world.

10] The Spanish Minister Calls McKinley "Weak": The De Lôme Letter

Congress seemed content with these statements, as it had not a year earlier with those of Cleveland. Riots in Havana in January, 1898, aroused some fear that the United States might have to act to protect American citizens, but it was announced that the battleship *Maine* would be posted to the port in case Americans had to be evacuated, and public concern appeared to subside. Then in the second week of February, newspapers suddenly blazoned on their front pages the text of a private letter from the Spanish minister in Washington, Enrique Dupuy de Lôme, to Canalejas. It had been intercepted at the Havana post office; its authenticity was conceded by the minister, who was promptly recalled by the Spanish government. The following is the somewhat awkward translation of his letter released by the Department of State.*

THE SITUATION here remains the same. Everything depends on the political and military outcome in Cuba. The prologue of all this, in this second stage . . . of the war, will end the day when the colonial cabinet shall be appointed and we shall be relieved in the eyes of this country of a part of the responsibility for what is happening in Cuba, while the Cubans, whom these people think so immaculate, will have to assume it.

Until then, nothing can be clearly seen, and I regard it as a waste of time and progress, by a wrong road, to be sending emissaries to the rebel camp, or to negotiate with the autonomists who have as yet no legal standing, or to try to ascertain the intentions and plans of this Government. The [Cuban] refugees will keep on returning one by one, and as they do so will make their way into the sheepfold, while the leaders in the field will gradually come back. Neither the one nor the other class had the courage to leave in a body and they will not be brave enough to return in a body.

The message has been a disillusionment to the insurgents, who expected something different; but I regard it as bad . . .

Besides the ingrained and inevitable bluntness (*groseria*) with which is repeated all that the press and public opinion in Spain have said about Weyler, it once more shows what McKinley is, weak and a bidder for the admiration of the crowd, besides being a would-be politician (*politicastro*) who tries to leave a door open behind himself while keeping on good terms with the jingoes of his party.

Nevertheless, whether the practical results of it [the message] are to be injurious and adverse depends only upon ourselves.

I am entirely of your opinions; without a military end of the matter nothing will be accomplished in Cuba, and without a military and political settlement there will always be the danger of encouragement being given to the insurgents by a part of the public opinion if not by the Government. . . .

11] The *Maine* Blows Up

On February 15, a few days after the publication of the De Lôme letter, the nation was electrified with the news that the U.S.S. *Maine* had suddenly blown up in the harbor at Havana, with 260 of her crew killed or mortally wounded. Jingo newspapers declared Spain responsible and urged war. But administration leaders asked time for a naval board of inquiry to investigate the disaster, and a surprisingly large number of editors, politicians, and other public figures called for patience and calm. After an interval of about four

* THE SPANISH MINISTER CALLS MC KINLEY "WEAK": THE DE LÔME LETTER: From *Foreign Relations*, 1898 (Washington, 1899), pp. 1007–08.

weeks, Albert Shaw, the perceptive, if erratic, editor of a monthly digest magazine, summed up the situation as follows.*

... THE AMERICAN people saw the fairness and the necessity of suspending judgment until proof had been substituted for mere probability. And there was in no part of the country any disposition to take a snap judgment or to act precipitately. No other such spectacle of national forbearance has been witnessed in our times. Unquestionably the whole community has been intensely eager for news; and it is perhaps true that certain newspapers which have devoted themselves for a month or more to criticizing the sensational press, might as well have been occupied in a more energetic effort to supply their readers with information. The fact is that the so-called "war extras" which for many days were issued from certain newspaper offices at the rate of a dozen or more a day have not seemed to communicate their hysteria to any considerable number of the American people, East or West, North or South, so far as our observation goes.

The situation has simply been one of a very absorbing and profound interest, while the suspense has been very trying to the nerves. The possibility that our country might soon be engaged in war with a foreign power has been a preoccupying thought not to be dismissed for a single hour. . . . The papers which have printed the largest number of extras and sold the most copies per day have simply been doing what they could to supply the almost insatiate demand of the public for news about the war preparations. To say that these newspapers have been creating a war feeling is altogether to put the cart before the horse. Some of them are accused of grave misconduct. Our contention simply is that their behavior has not seemed to bias the judgment of the American people, which has been sensible and shrewd enough to discount all the exaggeration and froth of the bold head-line writers. . . .

Probably the report of the commission on the *Maine* will have become public news before this issue of the REVIEW is distributed. . . . That being the case, any attempt at forecast would be hazardous. Nevertheless, certain factors in the situation are not likely to be affected to any extent by the nature of the commission's report. In any case, the American people will have now to decide, through their responsible representatives at Washington, whether or not they will interfere in Cuba. . . . Even if . . . the *Maine* should be reported . . . to have been blown up by a Spanish mine, the really essential question would seem to us not to be altered. Our Government would merely be able to say that the destruction of the *Maine* was a very aggravating proof of Spain's inability to maintain order, and therefore a clinching reason why this country ought to intervene and ought to consider that no further probation should be granted. Interference in the affairs of another country is not a holiday undertaking. It is neither safe nor pleasant. It is for the conscience and the firm will of the American people to say whether or not they will interfere in Cuba. . . .

Quite regardless of the responsibilities for the *Maine* incident, it is apparently

* THE MAINE BLOWS UP: Albert Shaw, "The Progress of the World." From the *American Monthly Review of Reviews*, XVII (April, 1898), 389–06.

true that the great majority of the American people are hoping that President McKinley will promptly utilize the occasion to secure the complete pacification and independence of Cuba.

12] A Moderate Explains the Reasons for War

> The cool-headedness of the public, on which Shaw commented, gradually began to disappear. The early weeks of March saw mounting frenzy for war. Newspapers whose editorials were pacific admitted regretfully that the public mood was otherwise, and this was as true of dailies on the Eastern seaboard as of those in the South and Middle and Far West. Then on March 17, Redfield Proctor of Vermont, an erstwhile moderate, rose in the Senate and reported on a trip which he had recently made to the island of Cuba.*

THERE ARE six provinces in Cuba, each, with the exception of Matanzas, extending the whole width of the island, and having about an equal sea front on the north and south borders. Matanzas touches the Caribbean Sea only at its southwest corner, being separated from it elsewhere by a narrow peninsula of Santa Clara Province. The provinces are named, beginning at the west, Pinar del Rio, Habana, Matanzas, Santa Clara, Puerto Principe, and Santiago de Cuba. My observations were confined to the four western provinces, which constitute about one-half of the island. The two eastern ones are practically in the hands of the insurgents, except the few fortified towns. These two large provinces are spoken of to-day as "Cuba Libre."

Habana, the great city and capital of the island, is, in the eyes of the Spaniards and many Cubans, all Cuba, as much as Paris is France. . . . Everything seems to go on much as usual in Habana. Quiet prevails, and except for the frequent squads of soldiers marching to guard and police duty and their abounding presence in all public places, one sees few signs of war.

Outside Habana all is changed. It is not peace nor is it war. It is desolation and distress, misery and starvation. Every town and village is surrounded by a "trocha" (trench), a sort of rifle pit. . . .

The purpose of these trochas is to keep the reconcentrados in as well as to keep the insurgents out. From all the surrounding country the people have been driven in to these fortified towns and held there to subsist as they can. They are virtually prison yards, and not unlike one in general appearance, except that the walls are not so high and strong; but they suffice, where every point is in range of a soldier's rifle, to keep in the poor reconcentrado women and children.

Every railroad station is within one of those trochas and has an armed guard. Every train has an armored freight car, loopholed for musketry and filled with soldiers. . . . There are frequent blockhouses inclosed by a trocha and with a guard along the railroad track. With this exception there is no human life or habitation between these fortified towns and villages, and throughout

* A MODERATE EXPLAINS THE REASONS FOR WAR: From the *Congressional Record*, 55 Cong., 2 Sess., pp. 2916–19.

the whole of the four western provinces, except to a very limited extent among the hills where the Spaniards have not been able to go and drive the people to the towns and burn their dwellings. I saw no house or hut in the 400 miles of railroad rides from Pinar del Rio Province in the west across the full width of Habana and Matanzas provinces . . . except within the Spanish trochas.

There are no domestic animals or crops on the rich fields and pastures except such as are under guard in the immediate vicinity of the towns. In other words, the Spaniards hold in these four western provinces just what their army sits on. Every man, woman, and child, and every domestic animal, wherever their columns have reached, is under guard and within their so-called fortifications. To describe one place is to describe all. To repeat, it is neither peace nor war. It is concentration and desolation. This is the "pacified" condition of the four western provinces. . . .

All the country people in the four western provinces, about 400,000 in number, remaining outside the fortified towns when Weyler's order was made were driven into these towns, and these are the reconcentrados. . . .

Their huts are about 10 by 15 feet in size, and for want of space are usually crowded together very closely. They have no floor but the ground, no furniture, and, after a year's wear, but little clothing except such stray substitutes as they can extemporize; and with large families, or more than one, in this little space, the commonest sanitary provisions are impossible. Conditions are unmentionable in this respect. Torn from their homes, with foul earth, foul air, foul water, and foul food or none, what wonder that one-half have died and that one-quarter of the living are so diseased that they can not be saved? A form of dropsy is a common disorder resulting from these conditions. Little children are still walking about with arms and chest terribly emaciated, eyes swollen, and abdomen bloated to three times the natural size. The physicians say these cases are hopeless.

Deaths in the streets have not been uncommon. I was told by one of our consuls that they have been found dead about the markets in the morning, where they had crawled, hoping to get some stray bits of food from the early hucksters, and that there had been cases where they had dropped dead inside the market surrounded by food. . . . I went to Cuba with a strong conviction that the picture had been overdrawn; that a few cases of starvation and suffering had inspired and stimulated the press correspondents, and that they had given free play to a strong, natural, and highly cultivated imagination. . . . I could not believe that out of a population of 1,600,000, two hundred thousand had died within these Spanish forts, practically prison walls, within a few months past from actual starvation and diseases caused by insufficient and improper food. My inquiries were entirely outside of sensational sources. They were made of our medical officers, of our consuls, of city alcaldes (mayors), of relief committees, of leading merchants and bankers, physicians, and lawyers. Several of my informants were Spanish born, but every time the answer was that the case had not been overstated. What I saw I can not tell so that others can see it. It must be seen with one's own eyes to be realized. . . .

General Blanco's order of November 13 last somewhat modifies the Weyler order, but is of little or no practical benefit. Its application is limited to farms "properly defended," and the owners are obliged to build "centers of defense."

Its execution is completely in the discretion of the local military authorities, and they know the terrible military efficiency of Weyler's order in stripping the country of all possible shelter, food, or source of information for an insurgent, and will be slow to surrender this advantage. In fact, though the order was issued four months ago, I saw no beneficent results from it worth mentioning.

I do not impugn General Blanco's motives, and believe him to be an amiable gentleman, and that he would be glad to relieve the condition of the reconcentrados if he could do so without loss of any military advantage; but he knows that all Cubans are insurgents at heart, and none now under military control will be allowed to go out from under it. . . .

The dividing lines between parties are the straightest and clearest cut that have ever come to my knowledge. The division in our war was by no means so clearly defined. It is Cuban against Spaniard. It is practically the entire Cuban population on one side and the Spanish army and Spanish citizens on the other.

I do not count the autonomists in this division, as they are so far too inconsiderable in numbers to be worth counting. General Blanco filled the civil offices with men who had been autonomists and who were still classed as such. But the march of events had satisfied most of them that the chance for autonomy came too late. . . .

Most of my informants were business men, who had taken no sides and rarely expressed themselves. I had no means of guessing in advance what their answers would be, and was in most cases greatly surprised by their frankness.

I inquired in regard to autonomy of men of wealth and men as prominent in business as any in the cities of Habana, Matanzas, and Sagua, bankers, merchants, lawyers, and autonomist officials, some of them . . . still believers in autonomy if practicable, but without exception they replied that it was "too late" for that.

Some favored a United States protectorate, some annexation, some free Cuba; not one has been counted favoring the insurrection at first. They were business men and wanted peace, but said it was too late for peace under Spanish sovereignty. . . .

I have endeavored to state in not intemperate mood what I saw and heard, and to make no argument thereon, but leave everyone to draw his own conclusions. To me the strongest appeal is not the barbarity practiced by Weyler nor the loss of the *Maine,* if our worst fears should prove true, terrible as are both of these incidents, but the spectacle of a million and a half of people, the entire native population of Cuba, struggling for freedom and deliverance from the worst misgovernment of which I ever had knowledge. . . .

I am not in favor of annexation: not because I would apprehend any particular trouble from it, but because it is not wise policy to take in any people of foreign tongue and training, and without any strong guiding American element. . . .

But it is not my purpose at this time, nor do I consider it my province, to suggest any plan. I merely speak of the symptoms as I saw them, but do not undertake to prescribe. Such remedial steps as may be required may safely be left to an American President and the American people.

13] The Immoderates Increase Their Pressure

> After Proctor's speech, newspapers all over the country reported conservative
> men changing front and declaring that they would back the President if he
> decided upon intervention. In the Senate, jingoes abandoned their temporary
> silence and began to exhort McKinley to act. Two who did so were members
> of his own party, Jacob H. Gallinger of New Hampshire and John M.
> Thurston of Nebraska. The former spoke on March 23, the latter on March
> 24.*

MR. GALLINGER. . . . . I will be called a jingo, whatever that may mean, but
. . . I would infinitely rather be a jingo than a Tory; I would infinitely rather
stand here as the defender of human rights than as the apologist of cruelty and
oppression. A vigorous foreign policy is necessary to the strength and dignity
of any nation, and it is the best possible assurance of peace that can be
given. . . .

During the four hundred years of Spain's rise and fall her invariable record
has been one of cruelty, of persecution, of bigotry, of hostility to every sentiment of human freedom, common justice, and enlightenment. The slavery to
which she doomed her subjects in the Western Hemisphere was not more cruel
than her oppression of Holland or her tyranny over her own people at home.
The bigotry, the fanaticism, the intolerance, and the gloomy superstition of
her tone of mind are unrelieved by one single gleam of recognition of human
rights. . . .

Mr. President, it is not accident or chance which has brought about the
present situation. It is inexorable destiny, which decrees that the last of
Spain's ill-gotten possessions in this hemisphere will be lifted to freedom by
the one Republic which represents everything that Spain has antagonized during her whole history.

Fortunately the people of this great Republic are thoroughly aroused to the
situation, and the great heart of the American populace is in full sympathy
with Cuba.

Religion and humanity alike demand that this unholy war shall cease, and
cease it should, even though the glitter and glamour of military rule shall end
and a decaying and dissolute throne shall pass away never to return. . . .

The Senator from Vermont closed his speech by a declaration that he does
not favor annexation; but for myself, looking to the demands of advancing
civilization and the future peace and prosperity of the island, I am of opinion
that sooner or later this great Government will of necessity absorb Cuba. And
if it is to come, why not now?

It is argued that we do not want territory peopled by a race different in
nationality and habits of life from our own. Is it forgotten that when we absorbed California, Florida, and Texas that the same problem confronted our
Government? The problem was soon solved. . . .

* THE IMMODERATES INCREASE THEIR PRESSURE: From the *Congressional Record*, 55
Cong., 2 Sess., pp. 3131-32, 3164-65.

But, Mr. President, if annexation can not be accomplished, let Cuban independence speedily come. American interests in Cuba have already suffered enough. We have patrolled our coast in the interest of Spain as long as we should, and we have spent quite too much money in protecting our people from epidemic diseases coming to our shores because of the unsanitary condition of the harbor and city of Havana. Spain has failed to meet the requirements of an age of advanced civilization. Let the United States or Cuba take up the problem and solve it. . . .

Mr. President, for Cuba the present is dark and foreboding, but we must not forget that God reigns, and that the mighty sweep of human progress will not rest until oppression and cruelty are overcome, and the aspirations and hopes of all people struggling for better conditions and a higher life are realized. Poor Cuba! Crushed and bleeding, I commend her to the great heart of the American people. [Applause in the galleries.]

.   .   .   .

Mr. Thurston. . . . The time for action has . . . come. No greater reason for it can exist to-morrow than exists to-day. Every hour's delay only adds another chapter to the awful story of misery and death. Only one power can intervene—the United States of America. Ours is the one great nation of the New World, the mother of American republics. She holds a position of trust and responsibility toward the peoples and the affairs of the whole Western Hemisphere.

It was her glorious example which inspired the patriots of Cuba to raise the flag of liberty in her eternal hills. We can not refuse to accept the responsibility which the God of the universe has placed upon us as the one great power in the New World. We must act! What shall our action be . . . ?

Mr. President, there is only one action possible, if any is taken; that is, intervention for the independence of the island; intervention that means the landing of an American army on Cuban soil, the deploying of an American fleet off Habana; intervention which says to Spain, Leave the island, withdraw your soldiers, leave the Cubans, these brothers of ours in the New World, to form and carry on government for themselves. Such intervention on our part would not of itself be war. It would undoubtedly lead to war. But if war came it would come by act of Spain in resistance of the liberty and the independence of the Cuban people. . . .

Mr. President, there was a time when "jingoism" was abroad in the land; when sensationalism prevailed, and when there was a distinct effort to inflame the passions and prejudices of the American people and precipitate a war with Spain. That time has passed away. "Jingoism" is long since dead. The American people have waited and waited in patience; yea, in patience and confidence—confidence in the belief that decisive action would be taken in due season and in a proper way. To-day all over this land the appeal comes up to us; it reaches us from every section and from every class. That appeal is now for action. . . .

Mr. President, against the intervention of the United States in this holy cause there is but one voice of dissent; that voice is the voice of the money changers. They fear war! Not because of any Christian or ennobling sentiment against war and in favor of peace, but because they fear that a declaration of war, or the intervention which might result in war, would have a depressing effect upon the stock market. . . . They do not represent American sentiment; they do not represent American patriotism. Let them take their chances as they can. Their weal or woe is of but little importance to the liberty-loving people of the United States. They will not do the fighting; their blood will not flow; they will keep on dealing in options on human life. Let the men whose loyalty is to the dollar stand aside while the men whose loyalty is to the flag come to the front.

14] McKinley and the Moderates Agree on Terms for an Ultimatum

The President and his advisers had become convinced that the Cuban war could not be allowed to continue. Though the report on the *Maine*, submitted to Congress on March 28, was inconclusive, its publication set off new rounds of public agitation for war. Increasingly, too, reports told of criticism of the President: his picture was hissed in theaters; he was even on occasion burned in effigy. But before McKinley sent any kind of ultimatum to Madrid, he needed to be sure of the approval of the conservative clique that really dominated the Senate, the Congress, and to some extent the whole Republican party. Late in March his close collaborator, Assistant Secretary of State William R. Day, appears to have met with the principal members of this clique. The following document is a penciled memorandum dated April 11 in the handwriting of Senator William E. Chandler of New Hampshire, the chairman of the Naval Affairs Committee and a leader among the jingoes. The persons referred to are Senators Orville H. Platt of Connecticut, Charles W. Fairbanks of Indiana, John C. Spooner of Wisconsin, Marcus A. Hanna of Ohio, William B. Allison of Iowa, Eugene Hale of Maine, and Nelson W. Aldrich of Rhode Island.*

SENATOR Platt of Conn says that at Senator Fairbank's house, shortly before the verdict of the Maine Court of Inquiry, there was a meeting of the friends of peace. There were present Senators Spooner, Hanna, Allison, Hale, Aldrich, Platt (Ct) and Secretary Day, with Senator Fairbanks.

The understanding was that an armistice would be agreed to and negotiations opened with Spain for an autonomous government to the insurgents in Cuba, Spain not to relinquish her sovereignty. The final arbitration was to be left to the President of the United States if Spain and the Cubans couldn't agree.

At that meeting Secretary Day chilled those present in their hopes of success by informing them that the report of the Court of Inquiry, then unknown to the public, would show the explosion on the MAINE to have been caused from the outside, but that the Court would not fix the responsibility on Spain or Spanish agents. The meeting adjourned much discouraged but in the understanding that the armistice and negotiations plan was to be sought for.

* MC KINLEY AND THE MODERATES AGREE ON TERMS FOR AN ULTIMATUM: From the Private Papers of William E. Chandler, Manuscripts Division, Library of Congress. Reprinted by permission of the Library of Congress.

15] The American Ultimatum Is Delivered

After this conference, Assistant Secretary Day dispatched the following cable-grams to Minister Woodford in Madrid.*

[March 26, 1898]

THE PRESIDENT's desire is for peace. He can not look upon the suffering and starvation in Cuba save with horror. The concentration of men, women, and children in the fortified towns and permitting them to starve is unbearable to a Christian nation geographically so close as ours to Cuba. All this has shocked and inflamed the American mind, as it has the civilized world, where its extent and character are known. It was represented to him in November that the Blanco government would at once release the suffering and so modify the Weyler order as to permit those who were able to return to their homes and till the fields from which they had been driven. There has been no relief to the starving except such as the American people have supplied. The reconcentration order has not been practically superseded. There is no hope of peace through Spanish arms. The Spanish Government seems unable to conquer the insurgents. More than half of the island is under control of the insurgents; for more than three years our people have been patient and forbearing; we have patrolled our coast with zeal and at great expense, and have successfully prevented the landing of any armed force on the island. The war has disturbed the peace and tranquility of our people. We do not want the island. The President has evidenced in every way his desire to preserve and continue friendly relations with Spain. He has kept every international obligation with fidelity. He wants an honorable peace. He has repeatedly urged the Government of Spain to secure such a peace. She still has the opportunity to do it, and the President appeals to her from every consideration of justice and humanity to do it. Will she? Peace is the desired end.

For your own guidance, the President suggests that if Spain will revoke the reconcentration order and maintain the people until they can support themselves and offer to the Cubans full self-government, with reasonable indemnity, the President will gladly assist in its consummation. If Spain should invite the United States to mediate for peace and the insurgents would make like request, the President might undertake such office of friendship.

[March 27, 1898]

BELIEVED the MAINE report will be held in Congress for a short time without action. A feeling of deliberation prevails in both houses of Congress. See if the following can be done:

FIRST. Armistice until October 1. Negotiations meantime looking for peace between Spain and insurgents through friendly offices of President United States.

* THE AMERICAN ULTIMATUM IS DELIVERED: From *Foreign Relations*, 1898 (Washington, 1899), pp. 711–13.

SECOND. Immediate revocation of reconcentrado order so as to permit people to return to their farms, and the needy to be relieved with provisions and supplies from United States cooperating with authorities so as to afford full relief.

Add, if possible:

THIRD. If terms of peace not satisfactorily settled by October 1, President of the United States to be final arbiter between Spain and insurgents.

If Spain agrees, President will use friendly offices to get insurgents to accept plan. Prompt action desirable.

[March 28, 1898]

FULL self-government with indemnity would mean Cuban independence. As to other matters see Sunday's [yesterday's] telegram. Very important to have definite agreement for determining peace after armistice, if negotiations pending same fail to reach satisfactory conclusions.

16] The Spanish Queen Appeals to Europe

> Well before McKinley decided to dispatch the ultimatum to Madrid, Spanish statesmen foresaw that a crisis was probably inevitable. From the beginning of the insurrection, they had hoped that, if such a crisis came, they would have at least moral support from the European powers and that evidence of this backing would deter the Americans from intervention. They had hinted in first one capital and then another at a possible collective note by the powers. Each government had indicated, however, that while it sympathized with Spain, it was unable to act on its own. María Cristina, increasingly concerned about her ability to preserve the monarchy for her twelve-year-old son, Alfonso XIII, finally called in the Austro-Hungarian ambassador, Count Viktor Dubsky, and through him appealed to her kinsman, Emperor Franz Josef.*

SECRET:

Queen Regent advises me that Ambassador León y Castillo has brought assurances from Paris that, even though France cannot seize the initiative for representations in Washington, on account of the Russian-American intimacy, she will be happy to take part if the lead comes from Austria-Hungary.

With tears in her eyes, the Queen Regent described her situation and continued as follows:

"I have thus far carefully avoided causing His Majesty the Emperor the least concern for my affairs. At this moment, however, the agony which presses on the heart of this mother is so great as to overcome any fear of seeming importunate.

"Moreover, all that is needed is merely a first step, for I already have the firmest promises from Berlin as well as Paris that it will immediately be joined in by them.

* THE SPANISH QUEEN APPEALS TO EUROPE: Count Viktor Dubsky to Count Agenor Goluchowski, March 11, 1898. From Liasse No. 20 (Spanien), LXVIII, Archives of the Austro-Hungarian Foreign Ministry, Haus- Hof- und Staatsarchiv, Vienna. Translation by Ernest R. May.

"Thus I ask you to report this to Vienna and to add my earnest hope that in my need I will not be forgotten.

"General Blanco definitely believes that within at least three months he will be master of the situation unless the insurgents continue to receive fresh encouragement from the Americans. Indeed, as things are now, in spite of the fact that this support is being manifested increasingly shamelessly, it appears that the insurrection may be overcome anyway.

"For that very reason, however, a calamitous conflict becomes inevitable and therefore I implore mediation and assistance.

"It is not at all improbable that McKinley, who, I would like to believe, maintains a properly pacific attitude, would also welcome the opportunity to be able to point out to certain groups that my fate was not a matter of indifference to the rest of the world. In any event, I leave it up to the Emperor and his heart."

17] The Powers Counsel Peace

> After long and complex negotiations, the powers agreed to make collective representations in Washington. On April 6 their ambassadors in Washington called on the President and read a joint note; he in turn read a formal response to it.*

THE UNDERSIGNED representatives of Germany, Austria-Hungary, France, Great Britain, Italy, and Russia, duly authorized in that behalf, address, in the name of their respective Governments, a pressing appeal to the feelings of humanity and moderation of the President and of the American people in their existing differences with Spain. They earnestly hope that further negotiations will lead to an agreement which, while securing the maintenance of peace, will afford all necessary guaranties for the reestablishment of order in Cuba.

The Powers do not doubt that the humanitarian and purely disinterested character of this representation will be fully recognized and appreciated by the American nation.

> JULIAN PAUNCEFOTE,
>   For Great Britain.
> HOLLEBEN,
>   For Germany.
> JULES CAMBON,
>   For France.
> VON HENGELMÜLLER,
>   For Austria-Hungary.
> DE WOLLANT,
>   For Russia.
> G. C. VINCI,
>   For Italy.

* THE POWERS COUNSEL PEACE: *Foreign Relations*, 1898 (Washington, 1899), pp. 740–41.

[The President's reply.]

THE GOVERNMENT of the United States recognizes the good will which has prompted the friendly communication of the representatives of Germany, Austria-Hungary, France, Great Britain, Italy, and Russia, as set forth in the address of your excellencies, and shares the hope therein expressed that the outcome of the situation in Cuba may be the maintenance of peace between the United States and Spain by affording the necessary guaranties for the re-establishment of order in the island, so terminating the chronic condition of disturbance there, which so deeply injures the interests and menaces the tranquillity of the American nation by the character and consequences of the struggle thus kept up at our doors, besides shocking its sentiment of humanity.

The Government of the United States appreciates the humanitarian and disinterested character of the communication now made on behalf of the powers named, and for its part is confident that equal appreciation will be shown for its own earnest and unselfish endeavors to fulfill a duty to humanity by ending a situation the indefinite prolongation of which has become insufferable.

18] The Dilemma in Madrid: Spanish Liberals Invoke the National Honor

> After taking this step in Washington, the European powers turned to Madrid. Their ambassadors urged the Spanish government to proclaim an armistice in Cuba. Their advice was seconded by the Pope. At first, the Spaniards took the stand that they would concede an armistice only if it were requested by the rebels. Then they suggested doing so if the Americans would in turn promise to withdraw all naval forces from the Caribbean. The ambassadors and the Pope advised, however, that Spain should not set conditions and warned that failure to grant an armistice would make it impossible for the powers to lend further support. The queen pressed the cabinet. But the ministers were keeping a fearful eye on public opinion. They were reading newspaper editorials like the following from the moderate, independent Madrid *Imparcial* of March 28, 1898.*

. . . WHEN PERILS are inevitable, fear of them constitutes the greatest danger.

This is what the government must not forget. If it does not identify itself with the national spirit, it is lost and it may lose many things.

No one is so foolish as to demand victory. Even with a little disequilibrium of force, triumph is always problematical. But there is no good son of Spain who does not demand of the government the maintenance of the nation's dignity, cost what it may.

This is not only a question of honor, it is most of all a matter of internal order. To end the Cuban war humiliatingly would be equivalent to touching off a civil war in the peninsula.

* THE DILEMMA IN MADRID: SPANISH LIBERALS INVOKE THE NATIONAL HONOR: From the Madrid *Imparcial* (March 28, 1898). Translation by Ernest R. May.

The army, which would have to return from the Great Antilles in consequence of a shameful peace, would not consider itself defeated, but betrayed. Can it not be foreseen what this army, upon setting foot on peninsular territory, would do with a government that had forced upon it such a lamentable retreat? What feelings would there be among their brothers in arms who have remained with us?

In addition, it would provide the Carlists with the opportunity of which they have dreamed so long. . . . The partisans of Don Carlos would take the field under the banner of national honor. Is not all that more dangerous than a war with the United States? The only way of avoiding war is to withdraw our troops; the lesser evil is to fight the United States. This emerges with perfect clarity as the course of honor, duty, and convenience.

19] Spain Grants an Armistice

> Nevertheless, the powers, the Pope, and the queen were insistent. Fearfully, the cabinet agreed to proclaim an armistice and end reconcentration. On April 10, Polo de Bernabé, De Lôme's successor, formally notified the Department of State.*

THE MINISTER plenipotentiary of Spain has the honor to state to the honorable Secretary of State of the United States of America that Her Majesty the Queen Regent, acceding to the reiterated desires of His Holiness, and inspired by the sentiments of concord and peace which animate her, has given appropriate instructions to the general in chief of the army of Cuba, to the end that he shall concede an immediate suspension of hostilities for such time as he shall deem prudential, in order to prepare and facilitate peace in that island. . . .

The Government of Her Majesty, by this most important step, has set the crown to her extraordinary efforts to obtain the pacification of Cuba through the instrumentalities of reason and of right.

The autonomic constitution, which gives to the inhabitants of the island of Cuba a political system at least as liberal as that which exists in the Dominion of Canada, will within a short time enter upon the stage of complete development, when, after the elections have been held, the insular parliament will meet at Habana on the 4th of May next; and the franchise and liberties granted to the Cubans are such that no motive or pretext is left for claiming any fuller measure thereof. . . .

No one knowing the liberal spirit of the majority in the recently elected Spanish Cortes and the patriotic attitude of the principal parties in opposition can doubt that the Cubans will obtain whatever changes they may justly desire, within the bounds of reason and of the national sovereignty. . . .

The abrogation of the decree of reconcentration and the assistance of every kind which the Government of Her Majesty has granted and permitted to be extended to the reconcentrados have at last terminated a lamentable condition

* SPAIN GRANTS AN ARMISTICE: From *Foreign Relations, 1898* (Washington, 1899), pp. 747–48.

of things, which was the unavoidable consequence of the sanguinary strife provoked by a small minority of the sons of Cuba, and who have been mainly led and sustained by foreign influences.

No impartial mind, having full knowledge of the facts, which have never on any occasion been perverted, as those relating to the Cuban question have been and are now perverted, can justly impute to Spain remissness in endeavoring to reach the means of pacification of the island nor illiberality in granting privileges, liberties, and franchises for the welfare and happiness of its inhabitants. The Government of Her Majesty doubts not that this will be recognized by the United States Government. . . .

20] McKinley Turns to Congress

Jingoes in Congress had meanwhile given warning to the President that, if he did not act soon, they would take the initiative and perhaps vote a declaration of war. To appease them, he drew up a special message, allowed some of them to read it, then locked it in his safe on the pretext that the consul general in Havana needed a few days in which to arrange for the evacuation of Americans. He was able to postpone its delivery, however, only until April 11, the day after he received notice of the armistice. He discussed with his Cabinet the question of whether or not he should revise the message but finally decided merely to add a postscript. At the appointed time, therefore, the words he had written a week earlier were read before a joint session of the two houses.*

Obedient to that precept of the Constitution which commands the President to give from time to time to the Congress information of the state of the Union and to recommend to their consideration such measures as he shall judge necessary and expedient, it becomes my duty now to address your body with regard to the grave crisis that has arisen in the relations of the United States to Spain by reason of the warfare that for more than three years has raged in the neighboring island of Cuba.

I do so because of the intimate connection of the Cuban question with the state of our own Union and the grave relation the course which it is now incumbent upon the nation to adopt must needs bear to the traditional policy of our Government if it is to accord with the precepts laid down by the founders of the Republic and religiously observed by succeeding Administrations to the present day.

The present revolution is but the successor of other similar insurrections which have occurred in Cuba against the dominion of Spain, extending over a period of nearly half a century, each of which, during its progress, has subjected the United States to great effort and expense in enforcing its neutrality laws, caused enormous losses to American trade and commerce, caused irritation, annoyance, and disturbance among our citizens, and, by the exercise of

* MCKINLEY TURNS TO CONGRESS: From *Foreign Relations, 1898* (Washington, 1899), pp. 750–60.

cruel, barbarous, and uncivilized practices of warfare, shocked the sensibilities and offended the humane sympathies of our people.

Since the present revolution began, in February, 1895, this country has seen the fertile domain at our threshold ravaged by fire and sword in the course of a struggle unequaled in the history of the island and rarely paralleled as to the numbers of the combatants and the bitterness of the contest by any revolution of modern times where a dependent people striving to be free have been opposed by the power of the sovereign state.

Our people have beheld a once prosperous community reduced to comparative want, its lucrative commerce virtually paralyzed, its exceptional productiveness diminished, its fields laid waste, its mills in ruins, and its people perishing by tens of thousands from hunger and destitution. We have found ourselves constrained, in the observance of that strict neutrality which our laws enjoin, and which the law of nations commands, to police our own waters and watch our own seaports in prevention of any unlawful act in aid of the Cubans.

Our trade has suffered; the capital invested by our citizens in Cuba has been largely lost, and the temper and forbearance of our people have been so sorely tried as to beget a perilous unrest among our own citizens which has inevitably found its expression from time to time in the National Legislature, so that issues wholly external to our own body politic engross attention and stand in the way of that close devotion to domestic advancement that becomes a self-contained commonwealth whose primal maxim has been the avoidance of all foreign entanglements. All this must needs awaken, and has, indeed, aroused the utmost concern on the part of this Government, as well during my predecessor's term as in my own.

The war in Cuba is of such a nature that short of subjugation or extermination a final military victory for either side seems impracticable. The alternative lies in the physical exhaustion of the one or the other party, or perhaps of both. . . . The prospect of such a protraction and conclusion of the present strife is a contingency hardly to be contemplated with equanimity by the civilized world, and least of all by the United States, affected and injured as we are, deeply and intimately, by its very existence.

Realizing this, it appeared to be my duty, in a spirit of true friendliness, no less to Spain than to the Cubans who have so much to lose by the prolongation of the struggle, to seek to bring about an immediate termination of the war. To this end I submitted, on the 27th ultimo, as a result of much representation and correspondence, through the United States minister at Madrid, propositions to the Spanish Government looking to an armistice until October 1 for the negotiation of peace with the good offices of the President.

In addition, I asked the immediate revocation of the order of reconcentration, so as to permit the people to return to their farms and the needy to be relieved with provisions and supplies from the United States, cooperating with the Spanish authorities, so as to afford full relief.

The reply of the Spanish cabinet was received on the night of the 31st ultimo. It offered, as the means to bring about peace in Cuba, to confide the preparation thereof to the insular parliament, inasmuch as the concurrence of that body would be necessary to reach a final result, it being, however, understood that the powers reserved by the constitution to the central Government are not lessened or diminished. As the Cuban parliament does not meet until the 4th of May next, the Spanish Government would not object, for its part, to accept at once a suspension of hostilities if asked for by the insurgents from the general in chief, to whom it would pertain, in such case, to determine the duration and conditions of the armistice.

The propositions submitted by General Woodford and the reply of the Spanish Government were both in the form of brief memoranda, the texts of which are before me, and are substantially in the language above given. The function of the Cuban parliament in the matter of "preparing" peace and the manner of its doing so are not expressed in the Spanish memorandum; but from General Woodford's explanatory reports of preliminary discussions preceding the final conference it is understood that the Spanish Government stands ready to give the insular congress full powers to settle the terms of peace with the insurgents—whether by direct negotiation or indirectly by means of legislation does not appear.

With this last overture in the direction of immediate peace, and its disappointing reception by Spain, the Executive is brought to the end of his effort.

In my annual message of December last I said:

Of the untried measures there remained only: Recognition of the insurgents as belligerents; recognition of the independence of Cuba; neutral intervention to end the war by imposing a rational compromise between the contestants, and intervention in favor of one or the other party. I speak not of forcible annexation, for that can not be thought of. That, by our code of morality, would be criminal aggression.

Thereupon I reviewed these alternatives. . . . I commented especially upon . . . the inconveniences and positive dangers of a recognition of belligerence which, while adding to the already onerous burdens of neutrality within our own jurisdiction, could not in any way extend our influence or effective offices in the territory of hostilities.

Nothing has since occurred to change my view in this regard, and I recognize as fully now as then that the issuance of a proclamation of neutrality, by which process the so-called recognition of belligerents is published, could, of itself and unattended by other action, accomplish nothing toward the one end for which we labor—the instant pacification of Cuba and the cessation of the misery that afflicts the island.

Turning to the question of recognizing at this time the independence of the present insurgent government in Cuba, we find safe precedents in our history from an early day. . . .

I said in my message of December last, "It is to be seriously considered whether the Cuban insurrection possesses beyond dispute the attributes of statehood which alone can demand the recognition of belligerency in its favor." The same requirement must certainly be no less seriously considered when the graver issue of recognizing independence is in question, for no less positive test can be applied to the greater act than to the lesser; while, on the other hand, the influences and consequences of the struggle upon the internal policy of the recognizing State, which form important factors when the recognition of belligerency is concerned, are secondary, if not rightly eliminable, factors when the real question is whether the community claiming recognition is or is not independent beyond peradventure.

Nor from the standpoint of expediency do I think it would be wise or prudent for this Government to recognize at the present time the independence of the so-called Cuban Republic. Such recognition is not necessary in order to enable the United States to intervene and pacify the island. To commit this country now to the recognition of any particular government in Cuba might subject us to embarrassing conditions of international obligation toward the organization so recognized. In case of intervention our conduct would be subject to the approval or disapproval of such government. We would be required to submit to its direction and to assume to it the mere relation of a friendly ally.

When it shall appear hereafter that there is within the island a government capable of performing the duties and discharging the functions of a separate nation, and having, as a matter of fact, the proper forms and attributes of nationality, such government can be promptly and readily recognized and the relations and interests of the United States with such nation adjusted.

There remain the alternative forms of intervention to end the war, either as an impartial neutral by imposing a rational compromise between the contestants, or as the active ally of the one party or the other.

As to the first it is not to be forgotten that during the last few months the relation of the United States has virtually been one of friendly intervention in many ways, each not of itself conclusive, but all tending to the exertion of a potential influence toward an ultimate pacific result, just and honorable to all interests concerned. The spirit of all our acts hitherto has been an earnest, unselfish desire for peace and prosperity in Cuba, untarnished by differences between us and Spain, and unstained by the blood of American citizens.

The forcible intervention of the United States as a neutral to stop the war, according to the large dictates of humanity and following many historical precedents where neighboring States have interfered to check the hopeless sacrifices of life by internecine conflicts beyond their borders, is justifiable on rational grounds. It involves, however, hostile constraint upon both the parties to the contest as well to enforce a truce as to guide the eventual settlement.

The grounds for such intervention may be briefly summarized as follows:

FIRST. In the cause of humanity and to put an end to the barbarities, bloodshed, starvation, and horrible miseries now existing there, and which the parties to the conflict are either unable or unwilling to stop or mitigate. It is no answer to say this is all in another country, belonging to another nation, and is therefore none of our business. It is specially our duty, for it is right at our door.

SECOND. We owe it to our citizens in Cuba to afford them that protection and indemnity for life and property which no government there can or will afford, and to that end to terminate the conditions that deprive them of legal protection.

THIRD. The right to intervene may be justified by the very serious injury to the commerce, trade, and business of our people, and by the wanton destruction of property and devastation of the island.

FOURTH, and which is of the utmost importance. The present condition of affairs in Cuba is a constant menace to our peace, and entails upon this Government an enormous expense. With such a conflict waged for years in an island so near us and with which our people have such trade and business relations; when the lives and liberty of our citizens are in constant danger and their property destroyed and themselves ruined; where our trading vessels are liable to seizure and are seized at our very door by war ships of a foreign nation, the expeditions of filibustering that we are powerless to prevent altogether, and the irritating questions and entanglements thus arising—all these and others that I need not mention, with the resulting strained relations, are a constant menace to our peace, and compel us to keep on a semiwar footing with a nation with which we are at peace.

These elements of danger and disorder already pointed out have been strikingly illustrated by a tragic event which has deeply and justly moved the American people. I have already transmitted to Congress the report of the naval court of inquiry on the destruction of the battle ship MAINE in the harbor of Havana during the night of the 15th of February. The destruction of that noble vessel has filled the national heart with inexpressible horror. Two hundred and fifty-eight brave sailors and marines and two officers of our Navy, reposing in the fancied security of a friendly harbor, have been hurled to death, grief and want brought to their homes, and sorrow to the nation.

The naval court of inquiry, which, it is needless to say, commands the unqualified confidence of the Government, was unanimous in its conclusion that the destruction of the MAINE was caused by an exterior explosion, that of a submarine mine. It did not assume to place the responsibility. That remains to be fixed.

In any event the destruction of the MAINE, by whatever exterior cause, is a patent and impressive proof of a state of things in Cuba that is intolerable. That condition is thus shown to be such that the Spanish Government can not assure safety and security to a vessel of the American Navy in the harbor of Havana on a mission of peace, and rightfully there. . . .

The long trial has proved that the object for which Spain has waged the war can not be attained. The fire of insurrection may flame or may smolder with varying seasons, but it has not been and it is plain that it can not be extinguished by present methods. The only hope of relief and repose from a condition which can no longer be endured is the enforced pacification of Cuba. In the name of humanity, in the name of civilization, in behalf of endangered American interests which give us the right and the duty to speak and to act, the war in Cuba must stop.

In view of these facts and of these considerations, I ask the Congress to authorize and empower the President to take measures to secure a full and final termination of hostilities between the Government of Spain and the people of Cuba, and to secure in the island the establishment of a stable government, capable of maintaining order and observing its international obligations, insuring peace and tranquillity and the security of its citizens as well as our own, and to use the military and naval forces of the United States as may be necessary for these purposes. . . .

The issue is now with the Congress. It is a solemn responsibility. I have exhausted every effort to relieve the intolerable condition of affairs which is at our doors. Prepared to execute every obligation imposed upon me by the Constitution and the law, I await your action.

Yesterday, and since the preparation of the foregoing message, official information was received by me that the latest decree of the Queen Regent of Spain directs General Blanco, in order to prepare and facilitate peace, to proclaim a suspension of hostilities, the duration and details of which have not yet been communicated to me.

This fact with every other pertinent consideration will, I am sure, have your just and careful attention in the solemn deliberations upon which you are about to enter. If this measure attains a successful result, then our aspirations as a Christian, peace-loving people will be realized. If it fails, it will be only another justification for our contemplated action.

21] Europe Refuses to Aid Spain

The President's failure even to mention Spain's representations in favor of peace angered European diplomats. The ambassadors in Washington met and decided to recommend that their foreign ministries send identical notes to the American government condemning the proposed intervention and saying that it would not have the approval of the civilized world. Though several of the powers were willing to take this action, the British cabinet expressed doubt about its wisdom, and the German government refused. The project, which might conceivably have produced grave complications, collapsed. The following communication from the German foreign minister, Count Bernhard von Bülow, to Kaiser Wilhelm II indicates some of the attitudes of the German and Russian courts. The italicized words in brackets are comments written on the margin of the letter by the German Kaiser.*

YOUR IMPERIAL and Royal Majesty's Ambassador in St. Petersburg has just telegraphed the following concerning a conversation which he has had with Count Muraviev about the opportuneness of new representations by the powers to the American government: "Count Muraviev will ask the decision of the Tsar tomorrow on the question of whether or not it appears indicated that Russia should join in an identical or collective note. His purely personal view (he remarked especially that he does not speak as Minister for Foreign Affairs and that if necessary he will deny having said this) [*He does this now as always*] would be that both steps are pointless, for they would surely not be accepted by America and would only injure the credit of the powers in America, [*Absolutely right! just what I have thought*] since to him war seems inevitable. These notes would be useless and would irritate America. Count Muraviev fears in addition that the whole proceeding, which is sponsored by England, has as its aim to divide the monarchical powers from America. [*?*]

---

* EUROPE REFUSES TO AID SPAIN: From Johannes Lepsius, Albrecht Mendelssohn Bartholdy, and Friedrich Thimme, eds., *Die Grosse Politik der Europäischen Kabinette, 1871–1914* (Berlin, 1922–26), XV, No. 4141, 25–26. Translation by Ernest R. May.

If ill-feeling once develops, it would be very difficult for us to become close to America again—something that under certain circumstances could become necessary. For purely parliamentary states a rapprochement would not be so difficult as for the monarchies, Russia and Germany. . . . That the first note from the ambassadors found no mention in the President's words proves that America does not want the concurrence of the powers. Count Muraviev would regard it as dangerous to force upon America the interference of the powers, for it could cause her to think in future of mixing in *European* affairs [*not improbably*], something which could not be permitted.

"As concerns Spain, commented Count Muraviev, she must be dealt with primarily in the interest of the dynasty; this can, in his view, only be preserved if the Queen herself becomes head of the movement and, cost what it may, leads the war, even if there is no chance of a happy outcome. [*yes*] Only thus can the dynasty maintain itself and be protected; in the contrary case the Queen would unquestionably be overthrown by revolution. Count Muraviev used the words: 'If the Queen is wise, moderate, and truly patriotic, she will fall and be exiled [*not very likely*]; if, on the other hand, she puts herself at the head of the movement and is neither wise nor patriotic, she can save her crown; this is cynical, but it is true.' [*then, however, they may not wait a minute longer*]

"Count Muraviev summarized his view by saying that he, from his personal standpoint, expected no success from either an identical or a collective note [*good*]; non-interference appeared to him therefore as the best policy [*yes*]" . . .

22] War!

> McKinley had thrown to Congress the question of whether or not the United States should recognize the Cuban rebels, and debate on this issue caused some delay in the framing of a joint resolution. It was not until April 19 that the two houses concurred on a text. The final sentence of it had been proposed in the Senate by Henry M. Teller, an Independent Silver Republican from Colorado.*

WHEREAS the abhorrent conditions which have existed for more than three years in the island of Cuba, so near our own borders, have shocked the moral sense of the people of the United States, have been a disgrace to civilization, culminating as they have in the destruction of a United States battle ship, . . . and can not longer be endured . . . Therefore,

Resolved by the Senate and House of Representatives of the United States of America in Congress assembled, FIRST. That the people of the island of Cuba are, and of right ought to be, free and independent.

SECOND. That it is the duty of the United States to demand, and the Government of the United States does hereby demand, that the Government of Spain

---

* WAR!: From *Foreign Relations*, 1898 (Washington, 1899), p. 763.

at once relinquish its authority and government in the island of Cuba, and withdraw its land and naval forces from Cuba and Cuban waters.

THIRD. That the President of the United States be, and he hereby is, directed and empowered to use the entire land and naval forces of the United States, and to call into the actual service of the United States the militia of the several States, to such extent as may be necessary to carry these resolutions into effect.

FOURTH. That the United States hereby disclaims any disposition or intention to exercise sovereignty, jurisdiction, or control over said island, except for the pacification thereof, and asserts its determination, when that is accomplished, to leave the government and control of the island to its people.

CONCLUSION

UP TO THE last moment the Spaniards hoped that Congress would merely authorize intervention and that McKinley would say, in view of the armistice, that he did not need to use this power. But the recognition of Cuban independence and the demand for Spanish withdrawal was more than Spain could bear. Sagasta's cabinet directed Minister Polo to ask for his passports as soon as McKinley signed the resolution. Spain thus severed diplomatic relations, refusing to receive the demands that Congress had made. Spanish officials were informed that hostilities had begun, and on April 25 Congress voted a formal declaration of war.

The conflict that ensued justified one of Hay's adjectives: it was little. The United States lost fewer men in battle than it had lost through the explosion of the *Maine*. The Spanish fleet was utterly destroyed in engagements at Manila and Santiago. American ground forces invaded and occupied a small bit of the southeastern coast of Cuba. The Spanish garrison at Santiago surrendered, and on August 12 Spain and the United States agreed to an armistice. Spain was to abandon Cuba, surrender Puerto Rico and Guam, and leave the ultimate disposition of the Philippines to be decided at an eventual peace conference. In the final treaty, signed at Paris on December 8, 1898, and ratified by the Senate on February 6, 1899, these islands, too, came to the victorious power. Since in the course of the war Congress had by joint resolution annexed Hawaii, the United States stood as unquestioned master of the Caribbean and possessor of a vast Pacific empire. From the standpoint of those who had wanted the nation to prove its new might, the results of the war seemed "splendid."

But upon the war itself Americans soon began to look back with a certain uneasiness. The *Nation* had contended at the time that it had been unnecessary: Spain had conceded all that McKinley asked for or could have wanted. As time passed, more and more people reached the same conclusion. Within a few decades it was almost universally believed that the United States had behaved shamefully and that the war had been needless.

The preceding documents should make it clear that any such judgment is at least subject to many qualifications. The question of whether any event was necessary or inevitable is, of course, one involving some subjective judgment. The reader of these selections may come away convinced that the *Nation* was right, or he may equally well conclude that the principal actors on both sides faced a dilemma from which they could not escape. There is no question that, however "little" the war may have been, the events that brought it on had elements of high tragedy. But whether the tragedy resulted from mistakes or was classical, in the sense of having been wrought by ineluctable fate, must be left for the reader to decide.

STUDY QUESTIONS

1] What was the predicament of the Spanish government? Why was it incapable either of suppressing the rebellion in Cuba or of making peace with the rebels?

2] Describe the Cuban policies of Cleveland and McKinley. Were there significant differences? Were the Presidents firmly in control of American policy toward Cuba, or were they moved by forces outside their control?

3] What were the arguments both for and against intervention and the assumptions that underlay them?

4] Why did President McKinley finally ask for power to intervene in Cuba, and why did Congress finally declare war on Spain?

RECOMMENDED READINGS

PRIMARY SOURCES

Spanish Diplomatic Correspondence and Documents, 1896–1900, Presented to the Cortes by the Minister of State (Washington, 1905).

U.S. CONGRESS. *Congressional Record*, 54–55 Congs.

U.S. DEPARTMENT OF STATE. *Papers Relating to the Foreign Relations of the United States, 1895–1898* (Washington, 1896–99).

SECONDARY SOURCES

CHADWICK, FRENCH ENSOR. *The Relations of the United States and Spain: Diplomacy* (New York, 1909).

DULLES, FOSTER RHEA. *The Imperial Years* (New York, 1956).

FERNÁNDEZ ALMAGRO, MELCHOR. *Historia Política de la España Contemporanea,* Vol. II (Madrid, 1960).

FERRARA, ORESTES. *The Last Spanish War* (New York, 1937).

HOFSTADTER, RICHARD. "Manifest Destiny and the Philippines," in Daniel Aaron, ed., *America in Crisis* (New York, 1952), pp. 173–202.

LEECH, MARGARET. *In the Days of McKinley* (Boston, 1959).

MAY, ERNEST R. *Imperial Democracy: The Emergence of America as a Great Power* (New York, 1961).

MILLIS, WALTER. *The Martial Spirit: A Study of Our War with Spain* (Boston, 1931).

OLCOTT, CHARLES S. *William McKinley*, 2 vols. (Boston, 1916).

PRATT, JULIUS W. *Expansionists of 1898* (Baltimore, 1936).

WEINBERG, ALBERT K. *Manifest Destiny* (Baltimore, 1935).

WILKERSON, MARCUS M. *Public Opinion and the Spanish-American War* (Baton Rouge, La., 1932).

WISAN, J. E. *The Cuban Crisis as Reflected in the New York Press (1895–1898)* (New York, 1934).

Progressivism and the Trusts: The Conflict of Freedom and Control,

1911–1914

GORDON JENSEN

MASSACHUSETTS INSTITUTE OF TECHNOLOGY

CONTENTS

4] Congress Legislates
(The Federal Trade Commission Act and the Clayton Antitrust
Act, *Statutes at Large*)

CHRONOLOGY

1911

JANUARY 21   National Progressive Republican League formed.

MAY 15   Supreme Court orders Standard Oil Company dissolved and enunciates rule of reason.

MAY 27   Stanley Committee of the House begins investigation of United States Steel (completed April 13, 1912).

MAY 29   Supreme Court orders American Tobacco Company dissolved and reaffirms rule of reason.

OCTOBER 26   Government brings suit against United States Steel.

NOVEMBER 16   Senate Interstate Commerce Committee begins hearings on control of interstate corporations (completed March 27, 1912).

NOVEMBER 18   Roosevelt's editorial in *Outlook*.

DECEMBER 5   Taft, in message to Congress, contends that Sherman Antitrust Law, as modified by rule of reason, provides final solution to trust problem and only supplementary legislation is needed.

1912

FEBRUARY 21   Roosevelt announces that his hat is in the ring.

MAY 16   House Pujo Committee begins investigation of "money trust" (completed February 26, 1913).

JUNE 14   Subcommittee of Senate Committee on Privileges and Elections begins investigation of campaign contributions and corporate influence in elections of 1904, 1908, and 1912 (completed February 25, 1913).

JUNE 22   Republicans nominate Taft.

JULY 2   Democrats nominate Wilson.

AUGUST 5-7   Formation of Progressive party and nomination of Roosevelt as its candidate.

NOVEMBER 5   Wilson elected President.

1913

APRIL 8   Wilson asks Congress for reform of tariff.

JUNE 23   Wilson explains his program for banking reform to Congress.

OCTOBER 2   Congress passes Underwood Tariff.

DECEMBER 9   House Judiciary Committee begins hearings on trust legislation (completed April 6, 1914).

DECEMBER 23   Congress passes Federal Reserve Act.

1914

JANUARY 20 Wilson explains his program for trust control to Congress.

SEPTEMBER 26 Congress passes Federal Trade Commission Act.

OCTOBER 15 Congress passes Clayton Antitrust Act.

NOVEMBER 17 Wilson declares New Freedom complete.

INTRODUCTION

I N MAY, 1911, the Supreme Court decided the Standard Oil and American
Tobacco Company antitrust cases. In September and October, 1914, Congress passed the Federal Trade Commission Act and the Clayton Antitrust
Act. During the intervening years, the long-standing issue of the regulation of
trusts culminated in a great national debate that dominated the politics and
discussion of the time. Long subject to controversy, but as yet unsettled, the
issue of trust control now moved to the forefront of the public consciousness. A decisive confrontation of opinion occurred; and legislative action was
taken which resolved the issue in the minds of most Americans. Progressive
reform reached its crest as a national movement focused, in large part, about
the question of the place of the large corporation, or "trust," in American
life.

How had the emergence of the large corporation affected the "promise of
American life"? Did the large corporation represent a natural or an unnatural
economic growth? What attitude, or stance, ought the nation to adopt toward
it? These were the questions that seemed important to the American people
as, "stirred by a solemn passion, stirred by the knowledge of wrong, of ideals
lost," they sought, in the language of Wilson's first inaugural address, "to
cleanse . . . to restore . . . to purify and humanize . . . to square every
process of our national life again with the standards we so proudly set up at
the beginning and have always carried at our hearts."

Behind the ferment of 1911–14 lay nearly a generation of antecedent development, embracing, on the one hand, the gradual emergence of the reform
spirit and of public concern about the growth of big business; and, on the other
hand, the transformation of American life by the coming of industrial maturity
during the last decade of the nineteenth century and the early years of the
twentieth century—that larger tendency in American affairs which gave rise
both to the issue of the trusts and to the progressive movement.

The decade of the nineties witnessed a decisive transition in the sequence
of American industrialization. Many of the tendencies set in motion by the
onset of industrialization during the decade preceding the Civil War now
reached a maximum of scale and intensity of action. The consequence was
to bring to completion, with comparative suddenness, a variety of long-foreshadowed changes in industry and in the relation of industry to the economy as a whole and to society. By 1900, or shortly thereafter, many of the
conditions that we have come to think of as characteristic of an advanced,
or "mature," level of industrial development had appeared in more or less
complete form.

The American industrial system had come to maturity in the sense that, by
1900, its basic plant and resources had been built and its basic institutional
structure and organizational forms established. During the course of the nine-

ties, the United States took over world leadership in the production of the fundamental commodities of industrialism—iron, steel, and coal. By 1900, the American railroad network had been brought substantially to completion. During the latter part of the nineties, the scarcity of capital typical of the early stages of industrialization began to ease, and capital imports declined markedly while American bankers undertook their first significant ventures in foreign investment. The coming of big business during the 1890's and early 1900's brought into existence the essential institutional unit and the characteristic competitive pattern of modern industry.

Considered from a broader perspective, the American industrial system had come to maturity in the sense that, to one degree or another, the conditions of industrialism had come to embrace the whole, or very nearly the whole, of American economic and social life. Industry, by 1900, had become far and away the most important sector of the total economy, although agricultural products still accounted for a large share of American exports. As a result of the completion of the nation's railroad network, the many limited, and largely independent, local markets typical of an earlier day had knit together to form a unified national market; by 1900, most of the major lines of industry were dominated by firms transacting a nationwide business, and few localities in the country were completely independent of the influence of the national market. The lengthy process of urbanization, which had begun early in the nineteenth century and quickened noticeably after 1880, now was approaching the time at which its accumulated action finally would tip the balance between rural and urban elements in American life. In 1900 the proportion of Americans living in cities and towns had reached the 40-per-cent mark; by 1910 the figure would rise to 45.8 per cent, and by 1920 to 51.4 per cent. Lastly, the formal closing-off of the frontier during the nineties foretold the imminent disappearance of the once-great reservoir of unoccupied land, or its contraction to insignificant proportions. As a consequence, a classic conditioning factor of American history—and the major force sustaining agrarianism and localism against the advance of industrialism, urbanism, and interdependence—was decisively weakened in effect.

In all countries, the transition from an agricultural and commercial to an industrial economy has induced profound changes in society. It has unsettled the relations among classes, heightened extremes of wealth and poverty, transformed the pattern and texture of the individual's existence, brought about the breakdown of political and administrative processes under the impact of headlong economic change, and created the unprecedented social and governmental problems of the modern city. With the coming of industrial maturity, these changes became so widespread, so sharpened, and so palpable in the United States as to affect the lives and interests and penetrate the consciousness of a majority of Americans. The ensuing national reaction called into being, during the years between 1901 and 1916, that vast and diffuse collective effort to subordinate the hitherto-unregulated course of industrialization to social ends which we know as the progressive movement.

Various movements looking toward the control or reform of industrialism, or protesting its consequences, had appeared before 1900. Obvious examples are the utopian literature of the late nineteenth century, or the endemic labor conflicts and the recurrent waves of agrarian dissent that stretched over the entire post-Civil War nineteenth century. Moreover, proposals first advanced by nineteenth-century reformers, such as the device of the regulatory commission, the broad precedent of government intervention in economic and social matters, and the whole scheme of direct democracy, were later taken over by the progressive reformers.

But the reform movements of the nineteenth century, deriving from an earlier and less complete stage of industrialization, by and large had appealed only to isolated groups or scattered individuals in American society; moreover they had usually divided national opinion, as in the campaign of 1896, and, generally speaking, had failed. The progressive movement, by contrast, though in no sense a unitary affair, drew support from a more or less general public concern with reform; issued in a rough national consensus, at least of mood and aspiration; and left a permanent impress upon the policies, politics, thought, and legislation of the country.

In addition to revolutionizing the circumstances of their material existence, the coming of industrial maturity profoundly challenged the ideas, values, and attitudes of the American people. The American ideology had evolved, in large part, during an agrarian and commercial age and had taken much of its concrete meaning and characteristic tone from the conditions typical of such an age. As a consequence, the new environment of industrialism inevitably came into conflict with values and attitudes—such as equality of opportunity, economic individualism, popular democracy, antipathy to caste, or fear of unchecked power—to which the American people were deeply committed. The terms of progressive reform were set not only by the material imperatives of industrial maturity, but also by the intellectual and emotional pull of pre-industrial beliefs, attitudes, and values.

Out of the interplay between an industrial environment and a pre-industrial ideology arose the distinctive mood of the period—its sense of conscience and duty, its feeling of something gone wrong, its conviction that the reality of American life no longer corresponded to the ideal. Here lay an important source of the impulse to reform. Out of this interplay arose, also, the era's characteristic approach to reform. In defining the problems of reform, Americans at the time tended strongly to interpret the new conditions of industrialism in terms of pre-industrial conceptions and to judge them by pre-industrial values. Thus, they often attributed conditions they disapproved of to the evil-doings of individuals, rather than to impersonal social or economic process. In formulating proposals for reform, they often drew upon ideas and precedents of the past. To many, for example, the proper solution to the trust problem lay in restoring the unimpeded competition of nineteenth-century economic theory. In proposing innovations in policy, Americans of the progressive era often were thinking of the achievement of old ends. The initiative, referendum, and recall introduced new forms into the American political system, but their purpose was to strengthen the old ideal of democracy.

Of the many revolutionary changes brought about by the coming of industrial maturity, none attracted so much public attention or aroused so much public concern as the emergence of the trusts. No other change was so striking and so obvious. No other change was so widely felt by all classes of society and in all sections of the nation. No other change brought to a focus so many lines of tension between the new economy and the old values.

Originally, the term trust referred to a specific legal form of corporate combination common during the 1880's. But, by the time of the progressive era, Americans had come to use the term in a wide variety of senses, to refer to a number of different facts of the contemporary economic scene. Depending upon the circumstances, they might be speaking about large-scale business enterprise per se; about corporate combination and consolidation; about agreements among competing companies to restrict competition; about the general decline of price competition evident in American business; or about the high degree of control that they believed the large banking houses exercised over American business. Each of these meanings, and the conditions to which they referred, derived from a single underlying phenomenon: the emergence of the modern corporation as the essential new administrative unit in American industry.

The new—or "modern"—corporations which had come to dominate most of the important areas of American industry by the first decade of the twentieth century exhibited three distinguishing characteristics. First, and most obviously, they were large in size. They possessed huge assets, were heavily capitalized, conducted operations on a nationwide scale, and, usually, transacted a large share of the business in their respective fields. Secondly, most of them had come into being as combinations of smaller, formerly independent companies, and sometimes as combinations of combinations. Thirdly, and most significantly, they exhibited a distinctive pattern of administrative organization. The main features of this pattern, developing usually in close association with one another, were centralization, functional departmentalization, and vertical integration. Centralization consisted in the establishment of a unified administrative system encompassing the entire firm and converging on a single central office, which formulated and supervised the execution of over-all policy. Functional departmentalization consisted in the more or less elaborate articulation of the company's administrative apparatus into distinct, centrally controlled departments, each of which was responsible for handling some one of the company's major operating functions, such as manufacturing, sales, purchasing, finance, or statistics. Vertical integration consisted in the concentration within one concern of all or most of the major operations involved in the fabrication and distribution of a product, beginning with the purchasing or production of raw materials and ending with the selling of the finished goods.

The coming of the large, centralized, departmentalized, and integrated corporation radically altered the nature of business activity in those areas of industry that it affected. Within the context of the individual firm, the emergence of the modern corporation brought into being a new environment of bureaucracy, characterized by sophisticated techniques of management, hierarchical lines of authority, and specialization of duties and career. Externally, the modern corporation established in American industry the structural pattern later to be known as oligopoly, and the forms of "imperfect" competition peculiar to it. The typical pattern in many areas of industry became one in which a few very large concerns transacted the bulk of the business in their particular line and, by virtue of this fact, exercised a large measure of control over the course of prices. In some cases, prices might be administered in common by the dominant firms; in other cases, one particular firm might be large enough and strong enough to become a "price leader" and, by the prices it set, determine prices for the industry as a whole. As price competition declined, competition came to center about such things as advertising, differentiation of product, diversification of output, and cost-cutting.

In the widest sense, the modern corporation developed in response to long-term requirements of largeness of scale and complexity of operation imposed by the emergence of the national market and the advance of urbanization. That is to say, the modern corporation came into being in American industry because only great size and elaborate organization could solve the administrative problems of doing business on a nationwide scale and supplying the diverse needs of the large, new urban centers. The relation was direct and clearly visible in industries manufacturing newer types of consumers' goods, or, in other words, in those industries that came into existence sufficiently late to be subject to the influence of the national and urban market from the beginning of their development. Here, the modern large corporation emerged from a process of internal growth within a single company, centering usually about the building of a nationwide marketing and distributing organization. In such cases combination played only a minor role or occurred comparatively late.

In a narrower sense, the modern corporation developed in response to short-term problems of excess capacity and intensified competition, which sprang up among established industries as the market widened. Thus it was that the large corporation most often originated as a combination intended to control prices and production. But in a majority of cases, it was the suitability of the large corporation to the new national and urban market that created conditions favorable to combination and made the combinations viable once they had come into existence. Combination usually was soon followed by centralization, departmentalization, and integration. By 1909, of the fifty industrial companies possessing the largest assets, only two or three remained purely combinations.

Industrial combination appeared in two main waves, one running from the late 1880's to the end of 1893, the other, from 1898 to the end of 1903. The first and smaller of these waves affected primarily the consumers' goods industries, which felt the effects of the national and urban market sooner than the producers' goods industries. In all, some sixty-nine combinations were organized during the years 1887–93 in the clothing, food-processing, kerosene, and fertilizer industries. Most of them took the form of combination by merger or purchase of property. The most important combinations, however, and the ones that most attracted the attention of the general public were the "trusts" proper—the Standard Oil trust, organized in 1879 and reorganized in 1882; the American Cotton Oil trust, organized in 1884; the National Linseed Oil trust, organized in 1885; and the Whiskey trust, the Sugar trust, the National Lead Trust, and the Cordage trust, all organized in 1887.

The later wave of combination, that of 1898–1903, was a far more spectacular affair than the earlier wave and differed from it in a number of other important respects as well. First, it involved an important new legal form of combination, the holding company, the use of which was made possible by New Jersey's revisions of its incorporation law in 1889 and 1893. Secondly, the combination movement of 1898–1903 centered upon the producers' goods industries, such as mining, metals, and machinery, which had become ripe for combination by the late 1890's. Thirdly, it was strongly stimulated by an influence from outside industry, that of investment banking. Where the combinations of 1887–93 had been accomplished, for the most part, by the industries concerned, the combinations of 1898–1903 often were engineered and financed by the large banking houses of Wall Street.

The convergence of pressures generated by conditions within the producers' goods industries, on the one hand, and by bankers in search of new investment opportunities, on the other, produced a combination movement of huge proportions. Between the beginning of 1898 and the end of 1903, some 280 new industrial combinations were organized. So great a momentum did the movement develop that combination came to be sought as an end in itself and carried over into areas of business other than industry, particularly railroads and utilities. By 1904, according to the classic study of the veteran Wall Street analyst John Moody, "about 445 active trusts" had been formed, with a total capitalization of $20,379,162,551.

Nor was this all. An even higher level of combination resulted from banker participation, or so it appeared to the American people. In the course of promoting combinations, the bankers often placed their own personnel on the boards of the newly formed companies and, by this means, established centers of influence over large areas of American business. Thus, the Pujo Committee, in 1913, calculated that the members of J. P. Morgan and Company held seventy-two directorships in forty-seven of the greater corporations. To the American people, facts such as these seemed to point to the existence of a trust of all trusts, or, as it came to be known, the "money trust."

Comparatively few Americans, during the late nineteenth and early twentieth centuries, had a clear conception of the complexities involved in the evolution of the modern corporation. For the most part, they were aware only of the surface contours of that evolution. Above all, they were aware of the eye-catching sequence of combination.

In attempting to understand the modern corporation as an economic phenomenon, most Americans instinctively took as their norm the business world of the earlier nineteenth century, in which small, individually owned firms competed in local markets. This norm, derived from experience, was buttressed intellectually by the individualistic social ethic of nineteenth-century America and by the principles of nineteenth-century economic thought, with their emphasis upon a natural economic order, competition, and the unfettered play of the market. The effect of these beliefs was to create in the minds of

Americans a deep suspicion of anything resembling combined economic action. Such action smacked of "restraint of trade," as the long-established phrase of the common law had it, of conspiracy, monopoly, and subversion of the market place.

The rise of the modern corporation challenged the nineteenth-century norm at almost every point—by replacing price competition with the administered prices of oligopoly, by subordinating the local market to the national market, and by substituting for the activity of individual entrepreneurs the activity of impersonal organizations. But the fact that the modern corporation so often originated in combination, thus invoking the taboo of restraint of trade, gave a peculiar intensity to the challenge and predetermined the public's perception of it. When they looked at the modern corporation, what most Americans saw was not a distinctive new administrative form made essential by a changing economic order, or even necessarily a large-scale business concern; what they saw was, first and foremost, a combination of formerly competing firms, which, simply because it was a combination, probably had been contrived in order to promote monopoly and destroy the small entrepreneur in his legitimate local market.

Political belief reinforced the effect of economic belief. Industrial combination represented precisely that kind of amassment of power in society which their entire political tradition had taught Americans to fear. In addition, the values of the American political tradition had become closely connected, in the minds of most Americans, with the existence of an individualistic, competitive economic order; for such an order seemed to them to provide the economic opportunity for the individual on which liberty, equality, and democracy depended. In threatening the free economy, it followed, industrial combination also threatened free government.

Thus it was that the emergence of the modern corporation struck a peculiarly sensitive nerve in the thought and feeling of the American people. The formation of the original trusts during the late 1880's touched off an immediate public outcry. Many of the states instituted legal proceedings against the new concerns as soon as they appeared; many others enacted laws prohibiting trusts and combinations. The most important result of this agitation was the passage, in 1890, of the Sherman Antitrust Law, a rather carelessly drawn statute, hastily put together by Congress to quiet the public clamor. In its major provisions, the law declared illegal all contracts or combinations in restraint of trade and declared guilty of misdemeanor all persons attempting to monopolize trade. Though lively, this early controversy over the modern corporation was short-lived. Public interest in the trust problem fell off sharply after 1890, as the first wave of industrial combination subsided, and remained at a low level throughout most of the nineties. Little effort was made to enforce the Sherman Antitrust Law.

The spectacular combination movement of 1898–1903, however, by its suddenness and enormous scale, had an impact that penetrated deeply into the consciousness of the American people. Where during the late 1880's they had been disturbed by a comparative handful of combinations, they now were overwhelmed by a flood of literally hundreds of new combinations, which seemed likely to change the entire fabric of American life overnight. Their concern was correspondingly acute.

Important groups in American society feared that their positions would be undermined in an America dominated by large corporations. The commercial travelers, who lost their selling "territories" in large numbers as the trusts established their own centralized marketing organizations, believed themselves and other middle-class Americans to be slipping into a "galling . . . serfdom to the monopolistic class." The Western wheat farmer saw himself as more than ever the "helpless victim of the numerous combines through which his products pass . . . from the farm to the consumer." Labor leaders drew from capital's drive "to monopolize" the conclusion that it had become "absolutely compulsory" for the worker to "form a combination with his fellow worker."

Fundamental questions were raised in the minds of Americans as to where the nation was going and where it should be going. Could the freedom from caste that had distinguished American society survive in the face of what amounted to a "commercial feudalism"? Could impartial government be preserved in the face of economic organizations so large that they dwarfed many state governments? It was in this period of shock, as it were, that the problem of the trusts took root as a major issue before the American people. The combination movement, more than any other event, awakened the American people to an awareness of their new industrial environment.

Intellectually, the reaction to the combination movement was confused. The changes that it brought with it were too great to be absorbed or assessed in a short time. The public discussion threw up a bewildering variety of ill-assorted diagnoses and remedies, including, among other things, tariff reform, the adoption of the single tax, the repeal of all laws permitting incorporation, the abolition of "special privilege," the outlawing of specific unfair practices, the enforcement of full public disclosure of the component parts of organization (both financial and administrative), the substitution of federal for state incorporation, and the establishment of a federal regulatory commission. However great their concern, the initial reaction of the American people to the triumph of the modern corporation resulted in a scattering of opinion so great as to preclude agreement on a national policy, or even meaningful debate on possible lines of policy. Not until after the long improvisation and experimentation in policy conducted by the administrations of Theodore Roosevelt and William Howard Taft did the thinking of the American people become sufficiently focused to permit them to come to grips with the problem of framing a national policy toward the trusts.

But the lines along which their opinion was to converge were already apparent in 1900. Generally speaking, Americans tended to adopt one or the other of two rough approaches in discussing the combination movement. Either they thought in terms of somehow breaking up the large corporation, or they thought in terms of somehow controlling it. At bottom, this distinction reflected emotional attitudes of either rejection or acceptance of the large corporation as a feature of American life. The subsequent history of the trust issue turns about the gradual sharpening of these contrasting approaches and the elaboration of policies intended to implement them.

Much of this process took place during the Presidency of Theodore Roosevelt, who, here as elsewhere, dramatized the issues and shaped the opinion of the early progressive era. Each approach was reflected in the policy that Roosevelt improvised in order to calm the fears aroused by the combination movement. On the one hand, his vitalization and enforcement of the Sherman Antitrust Law, beginning with the Northern Securities suit in 1902, served, over the years, to educate the American people in the techniques and possibilities of doing away with the trusts by dissolving them into their constituent parts. On the other hand, Roosevelt's use of the Bureau of Corporations—established in 1903 on his recommendation—to investigate the activities of big business and, even more, Roosevelt's words pointed in an opposite direction. From the beginning, Roosevelt had had little real faith in a policy of dissolution. By the time of his final message to Congress, delivered in December, 1908, he was advocating that the effort to prohibit all combinations be given up and a policy of continuous federal regulation put in its place.

From the beginning, the control of the trusts stood out as the major national issue of reform; no other, except that of railroad regulation, so clearly depended upon the action of the federal government for solution. But, as the reform movement spread outward from its first seizures of power in the cities and states and gained ascendancy in the federal government, the issue of trust control took on an additional dimension. Always considered important in itself, it now came to be seen as the central problem underlying the whole reform effort, as the grand reform on which all others depended. Urban reformers had encountered the large corporation in their struggles over utilities franchises. Social workers and those interested in humanitarian legislation had found themselves dealing with conditions that they could trace back to the actions of large corporations. And political reformers on all levels had come to see behind the corruption that they fought in their particular spheres a "system" of corporate power and influence by which, in the words of Lincoln Steffens, "our government, city, state, and federal, is made to represent not the common, but the special interests." In the end, the trust, the large corporation, became for Americans the symbol of those massive industrial changes which, they sensed, lay behind the conditions they sought to reform.

The events of Taft's administration brought about the simultaneous maturing of the national reform movement and the issue of the trusts. On the one hand, the controversies that disturbed Taft's administration, the increasing amount of reform legislation passed by Congress under Taft, the progressive rebellion within the Republican party, and the Democratic victories in the Congressional elections of 1910, brought the reform impulse throughout the nation to such a pitch of strength that it became plain that the election of 1912 would bring to power an administration openly committed to reform. On the other hand, Taft's trust policies led to a decisive sharpening of public thinking about the trust problem.

Where Roosevelt, by word or by deed, had incorporated both the policy of dissolution and the policy of regulation into his handling of the trust problem, Taft moved determinedly toward the alternative of dissolution. In particular, Taft greatly stepped up the pace of antitrust prosecutions, undertaking more than twice as many proceedings in his four years as had Roosevelt in his seven. By its vigor and its pace, Taft's trust program attracted a degree of controversy that Roosevelt's more moderate and ambiguous program had not. The consequence was to put the as yet unresolved question of the nation's trust policy before the people as a matter of public policy on which decision could not much longer be deferred. By its espousal of one of the policy alternatives that had emerged during Roosevelt's administration, Taft's program brought about a direct confrontation of these policies and of the differing attitudes toward the large corporation that lay behind them. The consequence was to put the question of the nation's trust policy before the people in the form of a choice, thus making possible a genuine national debate.

The debate was precipitated by the Supreme Court's enunciation of the so-called rule of reason in deciding the Standard Oil and American Tobacco cases in May, 1911. By distinguishing between combinations that were an "undue restraint" of trade and those that were not, the Court changed, in effect, the meaning of the Sherman Antitrust Law and aroused fears in many that the law had been fatally weakened and the nation left without any protection against the trusts.

The ensuing national debate occupied the attention of the American people for the next three years. The debate was given impetus and direction by a number of important and widely followed Congressional investigations and hearings, including hearings on the revision of the Sherman Law, an investigation of the United States Steel Corporation, an investigation of the connection between campaign contributions and corporate influence, and an investigation of the "money trust." During the course of this wide-ranging examination of the trust considered as the central problem of American life, the American people made their nearest approach to coming to grips with the implications and meaning of industrial maturity. The debate reached its climax in the campaign of 1912, in which the three main candidates, two of them (Wilson and Roosevelt) avowed progressives and the third (Taft) running on what amounted to a progressive platform, discussed the issue of trust control as the one on which, above all, the election turned. The debate came to an end with the passage, in 1914, of the Federal Trade Commission Act and the Clayton Antitrust Act, which stand as the progressive era's final answer to the question that had so long concerned it.

~~~~~~

DOCUMENTS

1] The Supreme Court Considers

A] THE GOVERNMENT PRESENTS ITS CASE

> On March 14, 1910, the Supreme Court began to hear arguments on an
> appeal by the Standard Oil Company for the reversal of a decree entered
> against it in 1909 by the circuit court of the eastern division of the eastern
> judicial district of Missouri. The decree, which issued from an antitrust suit
> brought against Standard Oil in November, 1906, by the administration of
> Theodore Roosevelt, had found Standard Oil to be in violation of the Sher-
> man Antitrust Law and had ordered that it be dissolved. More than any
> other company, Standard Oil exemplified for Americans the evils they asso-
> ciated with the term trust (by 1907, the Standard had nearly a thousand
> legal indictments standing against it throughout the country). The Govern-
> ment, in the brief that it presented to the Supreme Court urging denial of
> Standard Oil's appeal, undertook, by reviewing the company's history, to
> demonstrate what some of these evils were.*

SUMMARY OF THE FACTS

FROM the bill, the answers, and the testimony the following facts appear:
About 1870 John D. Rockefeller, William Rockefeller, and Henry M. Flagler
conceived the purpose of controlling the petroleum trade, both domestic and
export, and obtaining a monopoly thereof. We believe the evidence fully justifies the statement that these men entered into a conspiracy which from time to
time took the form of various combinations; that shortly thereafter they were
joined in the conspiracy by Henry H. Rogers, John D. Archbold, Oliver H.
Payne, Charles M. Pratt, and various other persons. For the purposes of this
case, the history of this conspiracy is naturally divided into three periods.

In the first period, from 1870 to 1882, it took the form of combination between a large number of manufacturers, who acted in harmony and whose
stock interests were pooled in the hands of three trustees in 1879.

In the second period, from 1882 to 1899, it took the form of a trust under
the Trust Agreement of 1882, whereby the stocks of a large number of corporations and limited partnerships were placed in the hands of nine trustees,
of which these individual defendants were the majority, who controlled the
various separate corporations and limited partnerships.

In the third period, from 1899 to the present time, the conspiracy has taken
the form of a holding corporation, the Standard Oil Company of New Jersey,

---

* THE GOVERNMENT PRESENTS ITS CASE: From *In the Supreme Court of the United
States. October Term, 1909. Standard Oil Company of New Jersey et al., Appellants,* v.
United States of America, Appellee: Brief for the United States, I, 6–7, 33–34, 43–47,
94–97, 134–35, 164–65, 169, 187–92.

which has controlled the principal corporations, limited partnerships, and co-partnerships engaged in the business, by stock ownership, agreements in restraint of trade, and otherwise.

It appears from the allegations of the petition, the admissions in the answers, and the testimony taken in this case that interstate trade and commerce has thus been controlled and monopolized. The business involves the production and purchase of crude petroleum at the wells in the various States where oil has been discovered; its transportation from said States by rail, and in modern times principally by pipe lines controlled by the combination, to the various refining points throughout the United States, where the same is refined and manufactured into various products; the transportation of these products into the various States by rail and by water, and the marketing thereof. . . .

THE STANDARD OIL COMPANY IS THE RESULT OF ABSORPTION OF
PREVIOUSLY COMPETING CONCERNS

CONCERNS ABSORBED BY STOCK INTERESTS

IT APPEARS to be the contention of counsel for the defense in this case that the properties of the Standard combination as it now exists have for the most part either been built and established by the Standard interests or bought outright by Standard interests many years ago. The facts do not justify this position. We now propose to show just how the present companies comprising the Standard combination have come to possess the properties which they own and operate, and to what a great extent those properties are the properties of previously competing concerns in which the Standard Oil Company or the Standard interests bought stock or united stock interests instead of buying properties outright. To be sure, in a large number of cases where such stock interests were acquired the companies were subsequently liquidated (usually many years later) and their physical properties turned over to other Standard concerns, but this does not alter the fact that these concerns were brought together by a combination and held together through stock ownership for a long period of time. Moreover, as we shall show, a large number of the present existing companies in the combination were originally independent concerns. . . .

. . . the Standard Oil Company at present controls through direct stock ownership 37 companies (including the Standard of New Jersey itself) engaged in refining, manufacturing, marketing, and pipe-line transportation in the United States. *Of these 37 companies, 28 were in existence prior to 1892, and their stock was held by the Standard Oil trustees at that time.* . . .

Again, of the 37 companies, 11 were not in the first instance organized by Standard interests, but were competitors of the Standard prior to the original acquisition of their stocks by the trustees or other Standard concerns, while 6 were organized by Standard interests but took over at the time of their acquisition concerns which prior thereto had been competitors of the Standard.

These 37 companies, however, have succeeded to the property of 61 other concerns now out of existence, . . . making 98 in all. We find these 98 are classified as follows: (1) 47 concerns which were not organized by the Standard interests, but which prior to the acquisition of stock interests therein were competitors of the Standard interests; (2) 22 concerns which, although organized by Standard interests, were organized to take over concerns which were competitors of the Standard immediately prior to such organization; (3) 29 concerns which were organized by Standard interests, but many of which have, however, from time to time, taken over the property of some of the other concerns in the first two classes.

In the case of the refining and marketing concerns, the proportion which were not organized by the Standard, or which, if so organized, were organized for the purpose of taking over competing concerns, is much greater than for the companies as a whole; while, conversely, the proportion of the pipe-line concerns which have been organized by the Standard interests is quite large. This latter fact is the natural result of the practical monopoly which the Standard Oil Company has had of the pipe-line business since about 1877. . . .

It is perfectly clear from these figures that these defendants have undertaken during the long history of their combination to bring together, under the cloak of stock ownership, an exceedingly large number of previously competing concerns. There can be no explanation of this large number of acquisitions of stock interests except the purpose of monopoly. . . .

SECRECY OF COMBINATION DURING FIRST PERIOD

No ONE can read the testimony of Mr. Rockefeller and Mr. Archbold and the other witnesses (particularly Messrs. Emery, Irwin, Lee, and Lombard) and not come to a conclusion that this combination during all the years up to 1882 was secret and designed to hold together various competing concerns without actually acquiring their properties, and for the very purpose of securing a monopoly. We now desire to briefly refer to some of this testimony.

In the first place, as already stated, the original owners of the concerns which joined the combination in most cases remained in charge of the business, which tended to conceal the fact that the control had changed hands. In the second place, the parties to the combination denied its existence, or at least concealed its form.

During all of the examinations of these defendants before various committees of Congress, the legislature of New York, masters in chancery in cases pending in Pennsylvania and Ohio, not only did the defendants evade in every possible way showing how these companies were combined prior to 1882, but in many instances swore directly that they were in no way owned, or controlled by, or affiliated with the Standard Oil Company of Ohio, and that they were separate, competing concerns. In all these disclosures this Trust Agreement of 1879 was never made public, and it was not made public until brought into court in this case. . . .

It further appears, by the testimony of Mr. Emery, Mr. Lee, and the other gentlemen, that while the people in the oil regions generally knew there was some sort of a combination, because they felt the effect of it, they did not know exactly the form it took. It is a fact that notwithstanding all of these investigations in the New York legislature, in the courts, and before the committees of Congress, the exact condition of this early combination was never disclosed until the present time, and that the parties undertook to hold out that these concerns were separate, competing concerns prior to 1882. This very secrecy is evidence that it was a conspiracy to restrain trade, and not an open purchase of property or stocks, as these defendants are now trying to claim. . . .

ACQUISITION AND CONSOLIDATION OF PIPE LINES BY STANDARD INTERESTS DURING THE FIRST PERIOD, 1873–1882

IT APPEARS in the testimony in this case that the Standard Oil Company did not originate the idea of pipe-line transportation or construct the original lines in existence during the years from 1873 to about 1877. These lines were constructed by various individuals and corporations and partnerships. The Standard, however, early realized the importance of getting control of these lines, and as early as 1874 obtained an interest in the most important ones, namely, the United Pipe Lines and the American Transfer Company. It appears also that these associated other pipe lines with them in the pool agreement of 1874 [and] . . . by 1877 the Standard interests had obtained control through stock ownership of substantially all of the pipe lines in the oil regions. . . .

This acquisition of pipe lines was an enormous aid to the Standard Oil Company in securing and maintaining its monopoly of the refining business of the country. . . . The Standard at that time and ever since has used every means possible to get control of or prevent the construction and operation of independent pipe lines.

It appears also that the Standard Oil Company, having secured a system of pipe lines practically throughout the oil region, uniformly opposed the passage of legislation which would facilitate the construction of competing pipe lines, namely, the so-called free pipe-line bill, which would confer the power of eminent domain upon the pipe-line companies throughout the State of Pennsylvania. Bills of this character were introduced in the Pennsylvania legislature year after year from 1870 on, but were not finally passed until 1883. Mr. Lee and Mr. Emery, who were members of the legislature during this period, testified that the Standard as well as the railroads opposed the passage of this legislation, and Mr. Lee states that his reelection was opposed by the Standard Oil interests because of his attitude on this matter. . . .

CONTROL OF THE PRICES OF CRUDE OIL AND ITS PRODUCTS IN THE UNITED STATES

SO FAR as the crude oil is concerned, it appears that in the Pennsylvania, Lima-Indiana, and Mid-Continent fields, which are the principal fields producing oil suitable for refining, the Standard Oil Company absolutely fixes the price, publishes it daily, and its price is the public market price of crude oil. The producer has nothing whatever to say about it. It appears by the testimony that the Standard Oil Company produces only about 25 per cent of the crude oil which it manufactures. The rest, of course, it buys from a large number of independent producers. The significance, therefore, of fixing the price is apparent. It shows the strength of this monopoly. P. S. Trainor, the purchasing agent of the Standard for crude oil, admitted that, in consultation with Mr. Archbold, he fixed the price of crude oil, which was published from day to day. . . .

Mr. Archbold undertook to explain the Standard's manner of fixing the price. He said they took into consideration the availability of the oil, the yield of the various products, the different kinds of crude, the volume of production, and the world's supply, but he admitted on cross-examination that he and his associates were the only ones who took it into consideration. No one else had anything to do about it. . . .

Prior to 1895 there were oil exchanges at Pittsburg, Oil City, and New York, where oil was bought and sold the same as other products of the country. These exchanges have been discontinued for the reason that the Standard announced about 1895 that it would no longer purchase oil on the basis of the prices quoted thereon, and from that date to the present time the Standard has named the price. . . .

MARKETING BUSINESS

THE MARKETING business is a very important branch of the Standard Oil business. It will be hereafter treated when we come to show its effect upon the monopoly, but we will now give a general description, principally with reference to the marketing of refined oil and naphtha, which two products are handled in the same way and are the most important.

The marketing business is kept entirely distinct from the other branches of the business. The companies marketing buy the oil at the several refineries, whence it is transported to main and substations of the marketing companies scattered throughout the United States. It is unloaded into tanks at these stations, and from these stations is distributed, principally by tank wagons, to the retail dealers; in some places and in some instances the marketing companies deliver direct to the consumer either by tank wagons or in tin cans. The Standard also sells a large amount of bulk oil to peddlers, who peddle it out by tank wagons. It also sells considerable quantities in barrels and in cases. Of all the Standard's sales of refined oil and naphtha in the United States, about two-thirds are made in the tank wagons of the Standard itself.

The Standard organization has divided the United States into marketing districts, and there is an understanding, which is effectively carried out, that no other Standard company shall market in the territory thus awarded to a particular company. . . .

VARIOUS MEANS USED BY THE STANDARD OIL COMPANY TO MONOPOLIZE COMMERCE

UNQUESTIONABLY the principal means used by the defendants to monopolize and restrain trade and commerce in petroleum has been the combination of previously independent concerns in the manner fully set forth hitherto in this brief. The opinion of the court below rests practically upon the fact of combination. Nevertheless, the defendants have strengthened the monopolistic power of their combination by various other means which we desire very briefly to call to the attention of the court, both because we conceive that these means are themselves violations of section 2 of the Sherman Antitrust Act and because they throw light upon the intent of the combination to secure and maintain a monopoly.

These means, other than the combination itself, may be classified as follows: Control of pipe lines and abuse thereof; railroad discrimination; unfair competition; contracts in restraint of trade with concerns outside the combination proper. . . .

UNFAIR COMPETITION

THE TESTIMONY in this case shows that the various defendants have pursued a system of unfair competition against their competitors, whereby the independent companies selling and marketing petroleum have either been driven out of business or their business so restricted that the Standard Oil Company has practically controlled the prices and monopolized the commerce in the products of petroleum in the United States. This system has taken the form of price cutting in particular localities while keeping up high prices, or raising them still higher, in other localities where no competition exists; of paying rebates to customers as a part of said system of price cutting; of obtaining secret information as to competitive business largely through bribing railway employees, and using said secret information to procure the countermanding of orders of independents, and to facilitate the price-cutting policy; of the use of so-called bogus independent companies—that is, companies held out by the Standard Oil Company as independent which are engaged in price cutting, while the Standard Oil Company maintains the prices through its well-known companies—and other abusive competitive methods against the independents. . . .

The Standard Oil Company is particularly able to carry on this predatory competition for the reason that it does not sell its product at central markets or through ordinary channels like most other large manufacturers. It markets its product to the retailer in every village and community in the United States and often directly to consumers. It does from 85 to 90 per cent of the business in the United States, leaving about 10 or 15 per cent to all its competitors. It is perfectly obvious, therefore, that if all the balance of the trade in the United States were in one concern it could not afford to have marketing stations and facilities in every part of the United States. In order to market in effective competition with the Standard Oil Company the independents must of course ship by tank cars, which is much cheaper than shipping by barrel, especially in less than carload lots, and they must also have stations for unloading where tanks are available, and tank wagons to meet the trade in competition with the Standard. It would be obviously impossible for such a concern to afford to spread its product over the whole United States. Even if all the balance of trade were in the hands of one concern it would have to confine itself to particular districts where it could have adequate facilities equal to the Standard's, and therefore since the 10 or 15 per cent is in the hands of a large number of independents these independents must all the more confine themselves to small districts. This gives the Standard an opportunity to attack the particular district, as it does, and either to keep the independent concern down to a minimum of business or to destroy it entirely. It has undoubtedly been the policy of the Standard Oil Company to permit the independents to do a small percentage of the business, and this percentage has run from 10 to 15 per cent for many years. By thus keeping the independents within reasonable bounds it may control the prices, permit them to make a moderate profit and not allow their competition to get beyond control, and in most parts of the country make enormous profits itself. There is no question that if this court holds the Standard combination to be a legal organization and not guilty of monopoly —in other words, gives it carte blanche to pursue its own methods—it can eliminate every competitor within two years.

We desire here to describe briefly the various devices to which the Standard has resorted in the pursuit of its methods of unfair competition. The Standard Oil Company keeps a secret department in New York, known as the statistical department. Through this department it has a complete system of espionage upon its competitors all over the United States. It was with great difficulty that the Government succeeded in finally uncovering this system. Many of the leading men connected with the Standard Oil Company were placed on the stand and denied knowing anything about the department until they were confronted with certain reports and statements which had come into the Government's hands. It appears by this testimony that the Standard Oil Company has a system of reports whereby every salesman and local agent procures information as to shipments of oil by independents into his district. . . . These reports are sent in immediately to the head office of the Standard's marketing division. From such reports the local salesmen and agents throughout the country are informed of the shipments made into their territory. This information is also reported to the head sales agents of the several Standard marketing companies at their New York headquarters and is preserved in the statistical department at 26 Broadway, to which we have referred. The greatest secrecy is maintained in regard to this entire system. . . .

On the basis of this information regarding competitive shipments the Standard Oil Company at this central statistical department keeps complete records showing the percentage of the business done by independent concerns in each of its large territories and in each of its smaller subdivisions and in individual cities. . . . This information is obviously of the greatest advantage to the Standard in determining where and how far it will cut prices in order to destroy competition. Moreover, it appears that the information of competitive shipments is often used in advance of the arrival of the shipments to secure the countermanding of orders and to facilitate other methods of unfair competition.

This same statistical department at New York keeps records showing the prices at which the Standard sells oil at each town throughout the United States, together with the margin of profit of the marketing company on such oil. Summaries of these records were introduced by the Government. They show in a most startling manner the practice of local price cutting and price discrimination, the widest possible differences appearing in the prices and profits per gallon at different towns even in the same general vicinity, to say nothing of still greater differences between different parts of the country. These statistics corroborate the testimony of numerous witnesses for the Government regarding local price cutting.

The statistics show that in many places where there is a large percentage of independent business and sharp competition, the Standard Oil companies sell oil at a loss, and in most places where there is any considerable competition at low prices with a small margin of profit, whereas throughout the larger

percentage of the territory where competition is substantially or entirely eliminated the Standard companies sell at very high prices with a large margin of
profit. . . .

B] STANDARD OIL REPLIES

> Standard Oil's appeal was argued by the opposing lawyers March 14–16,
> 1910, and reargued January 12–17, 1911. The lawyers for Standard Oil, in
> the brief that they presented to the Court, also reviewed the history of Stand-
> ard Oil, but they reached quite different conclusions.*

Origin, development and ownership of the Standard Oil business and
properties down to 1882.

FIRST: EARLY CONDITIONS IN THE OIL INDUSTRY.

I. *The uncertainty as to the supply of crude oil and the conditions under
which the oil business was carried on necessarily rendered the business for
many years highly speculative.*

1. In the early days of the oil industry, the supply of crude oil was obtained
entirely from the oil region of New York and Pennsylvania. Production in
the various local fields within the oil region was invariably characterized by
a great output at the start followed by a rapid decline, until in many instances
the production became insignificant. . . . While the total production of the
New York and Pennsylvania Oil Region increased rapidly and, on the whole,
steadily until the year 1882, yet the wide variations in the output of the local
fields and the resulting fluctuations in the prices of crude oil made the business
both of producers and of refiners most uncertain and speculative.

2. Throughout the early period of the business, and down even to the early
eighties, there was general apprehension that the total available supply of
crude oil would be soon exhausted, and that the value of all investments dependent upon such supply would be destroyed. . . .
Unwillingness further to encounter the hazards which would ensue from
failure of the oil fields, on which the value of their investments was dependent,
led many to retire from the oil business.

3. In the earlier days of the oil industry, the prices of crude oil were subject
to tremendous fluctuations. The prices of oil in the field prior to 1865 went
down as low as ten cents a barrel, and oil from the same well was sold at
$16.00 a barrel. Between 1865 and 1870 oil sold as high as $7.25 per barrel and
as low as $1.90 per barrel; the price of the barrels themselves being upwards of
$2.50 each. The first oil exchanges were established in 1870–71. A large amount
of speculation in oil took place on these exchanges, where daily prices fluctuated
widely. For instance, on February 7, 1874, the price ranged from $1.60 to $2.10
a barrel; in October of the same year, oil sold as low as $.70 a barrel. Many wild-

---

* STANDARD OIL REPLIES: From *Supreme Court of the United States. October Term,
1909. Standard Oil Company of New Jersey et al., Appellants, Against United States of
America, Appellee: Brief for Appellants*, II, 13–19, 26, 73–74, 88–97.

cat companies were established, ostensibly to engage in the production of oil, and the stocks of these companies were disposed of to the public, with the result of utterly demoralizing the business of production. . . .

II. *Over-production of refineries, inferior business methods of refiners, and the results.*

1. Prior to 1870, numerous small refineries had been established at many different places. A great part of these refineries, at least in the oil regions, were very primitive concerns, "often with single little goose-neck stills, hastily constructed and ineligibly located as a rule, put up just in the hurry of the mining excitement of the early days without much knowledge of what the business could or would develop into—mere make-shifts of concerns." *The total capacity of the refineries was from 2 to 5 times the amount of the crude oil to be refined.* Many of those who went into the refining business were without general business experience or special knowledge of the oil business. *By 1870 or 1871 the profits of refining had become so reduced that it was necessary for any refining concern to increase its volume of business in order to live.*

2. The business methods of the earlier refiners were as primitive as their equipment. The by-products of petroleum were not utilized. In 1870 benzine derived from the crude petroleum was burned under the stills. The tars produced by the refining processes were run into the river. The refined oil was disposed of by advertising and often by sending samples to remote points with a view to inducing customers. The product of the refineries was of very uncertain quality as to color, test and burning qualities, and its introduction for domestic use made slow progress. The refiners as a rule had no warehouses or shipping facilities at sea-board points, so that oil destined for export had to bear warehousing and lighterage charges there.

3. Before 1870, when the Standard Oil Company of Ohio was organized, many of the weaker refineries had gone out of business. . . . Consolidation of the business was hastened by the improvidence of the early refiners in putting too much of their capital into refining plants and by the attitude of capitalists, among whom had grown up a great distrust of the oil business and who were unwilling to risk their money in it because of the wildcat oil schemes which had been so largely exploited. *All these changes had taken place without the agency of the Standard Oil Company or of its projectors* and they show persuasively how necessary to the continued existence of any concern at that time in the oil business was the policy of strengthening itself and increasing its volume of business which the Standard Oil Company pursued through its earlier years.

SECOND: THE RISE OF THE STANDARD OIL COMPANY AND THE DEVELOPMENT OF ITS BUSINESS DOWN TO THE TRUST AGREEMENT OF 1882.

I. *The Standard Oil business from its inception showed the qualities of permanence and stability and had the elements for successful development.*

. . . The members of the firm were constantly adopting new ideas and putting them into practice. Prior to 1867, they had purchased their barrels, which were often of inferior quality, causing loss by leakage, and the supply of which was insufficient. The cost was as high as $2.50 per barrel. In 1867, the firm established its own plant to make barrels by machinery, with the result that they secured an adequate and regular supply of barrels of good quality, so that the loss by leakage was saved and the cost per barrel was reduced to less than one-half of the former cost. Other innovations in the business of the firm were the establishment of its own warehouses in New York and the purchase there of its own lighters for transporting its own oil from the cars to the warehouses. In short, the method pursued by the firm from the beginning was to provide its own facilities rather than to hire the facilities of others, and this was done as fast as capital could be obtained. . . .

Perhaps the most important element in the success of the business in its early days and subsequently was the ability of its owners to obtain the necessary capital. From the beginning, they enjoyed high credit and were large borrowers, and the establishment of their branch house in New York enabled them to obtain larger sums of money at lower rates than was possible in the West. This borrowed capital enabled them to avoid tying up all their available resources in the construction of refineries.

In 1870, the Standard Oil Co. of Ohio was organized with a capital of $1,000,000., and took over the business and properties of the firm of Rockefeller, Andrews & Flagler. Various large capitalists, who had watched the progress of the firm and had confidence in its members, subscribed largely to the stock of the new company, and their connection with the concern greatly increased its ability to borrow the capital necessary for the further expansion and development of the business. The refineries of the new company were already not only much the largest in Cleveland but the largest in the entire country. Their business was probably fully 10 per cent of the entire petroleum business of the country. By reason of the various innovations they had introduced, the new company was able to save a large part of the expenses which their competitors had to bear. They had ample capital outside of that invested in their refineries. The ability of the new company to conduct the business economically and its strong financial position gave it the best chance to survive in the impending struggle for existence due to the over-construction of refining plants, with the necessary resulting decline in profits. . . .

IV. *Extension of the Standard's domestic marketing business necessarily attended its increase of refining capacity.*

From the beginning the Standard Oil interests had not been idle in seeking to extend their domestic markets. . . .

Concerning the local marketing concerns, Mr. Archbold testified:

"Prior to that time (1890) the business had been done largely in barrels, which was an expensive and wasteful method. The inauguration of bulk stations, the transportation in bulk cars, and the distribution that came about in bulk wagons, tank wagons, of course worked a radical change in all respects in the doing of the business, and it tended irresistibly toward the elimination of the jobber or small dealer in oil in the various sections of the country. They realized that the change was occurring and that their facilities were rapidly becoming valueless because of the introduction of these better methods, and for that reason they, in numberless cases, desired to treat for such properties as they had, whether teams, platform, wagons, or whatever, and through that period that was the reason of the many trades that were made with different small dealers throughout the country. It was largely—

I should say in the great majority of instances—their own wish that they be dealt with in that way; for the march of progress in the business showed perfectly clearly that their facilities were becoming old fashioned and obsolete." . . .

Reasons for the remarkable success of the Standard Oil business.

The success of the Standard Oil business, broadly considered, is due to extraordinary foresight, energy and boldness and to a policy of investment on an immense scale, displayed and carried out in every branch of the petroleum industry. This industry may be analyzed under four great heads: (1) ensuring a constant and adequate supply of crude oil; (2) getting the crude oil to the refineries; (3) maintaining extensive, up-to-date, well situated refineries and employing the latest and most economical refining methods; and (4) developing and extending markets domestic and foreign by improved marketing methods.

FIRST: MEANS FOR ENSURING A CONSTANT AND ADEQUATE SUPPLY OF CRUDE OIL.
  I. From the beginning, the Standard interests have been liberal buyers, offering high prices for practically unlimited quantities of crude and paying cash unless the seller preferred otherwise. . . .
  II. The amount of the Standard's purchases has not been limited by its immediate needs, but only by the utmost capacity of its pipe lines and storage facilities.
  1. *Over-production of crude.* In the early days of every oil field, there has been great over-production due to the peculiar conditions of oil mining. . . .
  3. *Storage of crude surplus.* Overproduction followed by exhaustion could only result in enormous waste at one period, and in extreme shortage in another. To save the oil for producers and at the same time to secure a uniform supply for their own refineries, the Standard interests early began to store crude oil during the fat years, to an extent measured only by the utmost limit of their available capital. These stores were heavily drawn on during the lean years. . . .
  How necessary this policy of storage has been is shown by the fact that the total present annual production in the States of New York and Pennsylvania, about 11,000,000 barrels, even if all available, would be inadequate for one year's consumption of the Bayonne refinery alone. In fact, independent refineries take a large part of this greatly reduced production from a waning field. . . .
  III. The Standard has been at great pains and expense from time to time to develop processes for successfully refining refractory crude oils, which by reason of their chemical composition could not be refined by ordinary methods. . . .
  IV. *Extension of pipe lines to new fields.*
  The Standard Oil Co. alone early adopted and has always pursued the policy of extending its pipe lines without delay and regardless of cost to new oil fields upon their discovery. . . .

This story of the development and use of pipe lines emphasizes the position taken by numerous witnesses of the defendant, that pipe lines are adjuncts to refineries, having been built, substantially without exception, to carry crude oil to the refineries belonging to the real owners of the pipe lines. On this point Mr. Archbold says:

"The pipe lines are an absolutely necessary adjunct, a necessary part of the business as a whole. The volume of the business as a whole has entirely outgrown the possibilities of railroad transportation, and the transportation by pipe is a more convenient method in every way; and in the construction of the large refineries necessary for the doing of the business, pipe lines of a necessity had to be created in order to insure them a regular supply, a sure supply, of crude oil. They have become a part of the great scheme of the business with reference to reaching the markets and they are essential in their use."

. . . .

THIRD: THE MAINTENANCE OF EXTENSIVE, UP-TO-DATE AND WELL SITUATED REFINERIES EMPLOYING THE LATEST AND MOST ECONOMICAL REFINING METHODS.

I. The policy of the Standard from the beginning in refinery building has been to construct large central refineries and, further, to enlarge these as the growth of the business required. . . . The collective capacity of all the Standard's refineries has increased from 16,592,593 barrels in 1882 to over 70,000,000 in 1908. The investment in refineries has grown from $17,000,000 in 1882 to over $57,000,000 in 1906. Nor do the various refinery properties purchased from others form any substantial part of this great investment. Some of the greatest refineries were built entirely with Standard Oil capital,—as at Whiting and Sugar Creek. . . . And even where the nucleus of a refinery consists or ever consisted of a plant purchased from some other concern, that nucleus has been so added to as to form but an insignificant part of the existing plants. . . .

II. Nor has money been spared in making every refinery the very best of its class, the equipment frequently being renewed as improved methods and machinery have succeeded each other.

III. While it is not claimed that the Standard Oil Co. in all or most cases was the first to locate refineries at advantageous points, yet it has always been the Company's policy to concentrate its manufacturing at the best selected points. . . .

FOURTH: DEVELOPMENT AND EXTENSION OF MARKETS, DOMESTIC AND FOREIGN.

I. The introduction of the system of marketing stations, to which oil is transported in bulk from the refineries by means of tank cars and from which the oil is distributed to the retail trade by tank wagons, has revolutionized the methods of marketing illuminating oil. In 1882, there were but 130 marketing stations operated by Standard Oil interests, which were located in the larger cities and towns. The trade was supplied largely through jobbers at the more important points and through general merchants at the smaller points. In 1888, the number of stations had increased to 313, and, in 1906, to 3,573, distributed throughout the United States according to the density of population. Almost without exception, these stations are the creation of the Sandard Oil interests.

Of these stations, 2,552 were established subsequent to July, 1890, of which only 16 were acquired from outside interests—all the rest being the creation of one or the other of the Standard Oil companies. From every one of these stations, one or more tank wagons make frequent visits to the retail dealers in the town in which the station is situated and in the smaller towns and villages in its vicinity and fill their oil tanks, without charge for cartage or service, and without leakage or other loss through the use of barrels. There has thus resulted great saving in cost and trouble to the smaller dealers, a great increase in the consumption of oil and a great extension of the Standard's own business. . . .

c] THE COURT DECIDES

On May 15, 1911, the Court rejected Standard Oil's appeal and upheld the decree of the lower court without dissent. More important, at the insistence of Chief Justice White, who wrote the decision, the Court also discussed at length the meaning of the Sherman Antitrust Law. The Court's interpretation, commonly capsuled as the "rule of reason," held that the Sherman Act was intended to outlaw only "undue" or "unreasonable" restraints of trade and, in effect, left it to the Court to determine in each particular case whether such a restraint had occurred. To this portion of the decision, Justice Harlan entered a vigorous dissent, arguing that the Court had indulged in judicial legislation. The ruling represented a great personal triumph for White, who had contended for such an interpretation as long ago as 1897, in the dissenting opinion that he wrote as associate justice in the Trans-Missouri Freight Association case. It also changed the long-range impact of the nation's antitrust laws: during the next several decades, the rule of reason supplied the ground on which the Court repeatedly found large corporate combinations, such as the United Shoe Machinery Company, United States Steel, and International Harvester, innocent of violation of the Sherman Antitrust Law. Two weeks after the Standard Oil decision, on May 29, the Court reaffirmed the rule in rejecting an appeal by the American Tobacco Company from a lower-court antitrust decree.*

. . . .

LET US consider the language of the first and second sections, guided by the principle that where words are employed in a statute which had at the time a well-known meaning at common law or in the law of this country they are presumed to have been used in that sense unless the context compels to the contrary.

As to the first section, the words to be interpreted are: "Every contract, combination in the form of trust or otherwise, or conspiracy in restraint of trade or commerce . . . is hereby declared to be illegal." As there is no room for dispute that the statute was intended to formulate a rule for the regulation of interstate and foreign commerce, the question is what was the rule which it adopted?

In view of the common law and the law in this country as to restraint of

---

* THE COURT DECIDES: From *The Standard Oil Company of New Jersey et al.* v. *The United States*, 221 U.S., 59–62.

trade, which we have reviewed, and the illuminating effect which that history must have under the rule to which we have referred, we think it results: . . .

b. That in view of the many new forms of contracts and combinations which were being evolved from existing economic conditions, it was deemed essential by an all-embracing enumeration to make sure that no form of contract or combination by which an undue restraint of interstate or foreign commerce was brought about could save such restraint from condemnation. The statute under this view evidenced the intent not to restrain the right to make and enforce contracts, whether resulting from combination or otherwise, which did not unduly restrain interstate or foreign commerce, but to protect that commerce from being restrained by methods, whether old or new, which would constitute an interference that is an undue restraint.

c. And as the contracts or acts embraced in the provision were not expressly defined, since the enumeration addressed itself simply to classes of acts, those classes being broad enough to embrace every conceivable contract or combination which could be made concerning trade or commerce or the subjects of such commerce, and thus caused any act done by any of the enumerated methods anywhere in the whole field of human activity to be illegal if in restraint of trade, it inevitably follows that the provision necessarily called for the exercise of judgment which required that some standard should be resorted to for the purpose of determining whether the prohibitions contained in the statute had or had not in any given case been violated. Thus not specifying but indubitably contemplating and requiring a standard, it follows that it was intended that the standard of reason which had been applied at the common law and in this country in dealing with subjects of the character embraced by the statute, was intended to be the measure used for the purpose of determining whether in a given case a particular act had or had not brought about the wrong against which the statute provided.

And a consideration of the text of the second section serves to establish that it was intended to supplement the first and to make sure that by no possible guise could the public policy embodied in the first section be frustrated or evaded. The prohibitions of the second embrace "Every person who shall monopolize, or attempt to monopolize, or combine or conspire with any other person or persons, to monopolize any part of the trade or commerce among the several states, or with foreign nations, . . ." By reference to the terms of § 8 it is certain that the word person clearly implies a corporation as well as an individual.

. . . when the second section is thus harmonized with and made as it was intended to be the complement of the first, it becomes obvious that the criteria to be resorted to in any given case for the purpose of ascertaining whether violations of the section have been committed, is the rule of reason guided by the established law and by the plain duty to enforce the prohibitions of the act and thus the public policy which its restrictions were obviously enacted to subserve. And it is worthy of observation, as we have previously remarked concerning the common law, that although the statute by the comprehensiveness of the enumerations embodied in both the first and second sections makes it certain that its purpose was to prevent undue restraints of every kind or nature, nevertheless by the omission of any direct prohibition against monopoly in the concrete it indicates a consciousness that the freedom of the individual right to contract when not unduly or improperly exercised was the most efficient means for the prevention of monopoly, since the operation of the centrifugal and centripetal forces resulting from the right to freely contract was the means by which monopoly would be inevitably prevented if no extraneous or sovereign power imposed it and no right to make unlawful contracts having a monopolistic tendency were permitted. In other words that freedom to contract was the essence of freedom from undue restraint on the right to contract.

2] Congress Investigates

A] A Self-Styled "Student" of the Trust Problem States the Alternatives

By revising the meaning of the Sherman Antitrust Law—weakening the law in the opinion of some, making it vague and uncertain of application in the opinion of others—the Court's enunciation of the rule of reason gave the issue of trust control a new urgency in the minds of Americans. A typical reaction was that of the Senate, which on July 26, 1911, adopted a resolution authorizing its Committee on Interstate Commerce to inquire into what changes were "necessary or desirable" in the nation's laws concerning "corporations, persons, and firms engaged in interstate commerce." The committee began its hearings on November 16, 1911, and, during the next three months, took testimony from a total of 103 witnesses of all descriptions. One of the early witnesses was Eugene G. Hay of New York City, a member of the Board of United States General Appraisers, who attempted to take a large view of the trust problem.*

MR. HAY. I do not know that any explanation or excuse of any kind is necessary for one's being here. I have no doubt every gentleman who accepts your chairman's invitation to come before you hopes to add something to the sum of wisdom on the subject. It happened that I was United States district attorney at the time of the passage of the so-called Sherman law, the antitrust law. It fell to my lot, as a part of my official duties, to prepare and try one of the earlier indictments under that law, and I have watched with a great deal of interest all the litigation since. That earlier study of the law prompted and stimulated me to a study of the questions that are embraced within your inquiry, stimulated me in a general way as a lawyer and as a student. . . .

I have been impressed by all that has been written and said in the newspapers, magazine articles, and public speeches that there was too generally a disposition to confine the inquiry as to the effect of both present laws and proposed legisla-

---

* A SELF-STYLED STUDENT OF THE TRUST PROBLEM STATES THE ALTERNATIVES: Testimony of Eugene G. Hay. From "Control of Corporations, Persons, and Firms Engaged in Interstate Commerce: Report of the Committee on Interstate Commerce, U.S. Senate," *Senate Reports*, No. 1326, 62 Cong., 3 Sess. (Washington, 1913), I, 424–26, 428–32.

tion, to what is or would be their effect upon business. . . . It seems to me that there are considerations of importance before that. Regarding any legislation and the effect of any law, the first thing to be considered by anyone proposing the law, a Congressman or a citizen, is what will be its effect upon our institutions, upon the fundamental principles that underlie our form of government. And, next, its effect upon the interests of the people en masse and individually; and the effect upon business stability and prosperity, although of very great importance should come afterwards. Any legislation that is destructive of, or affects in any way detrimentally, the institutions of our country, or affects for ill the people of the country, is unwise legislation, even if it will stimulate and improve business.

The fact that you gentlemen are making this inquiry, perhaps establishes the general fact that there is something wrong with commercial conditions. The very fact of your inquiring about it indicates that.

I believe that most of the political troubles that we have had in the last 40 years have grown out of the same source—the Granger movement, the Greenback and the free silver agitation, the Populist Party, the war against the boss in politics, the election reforms, the recall and the referendum, were and are, all of them, attempts on the part of those who advocate them, who believe in them, to alleviate the conditions of the great mass of the people. All of these political movements have, it seems to me, as I have watched them through the years that they have flourished, simply scratched the surface of things and have not gone deep enough to find the source.

It was apparent that the great mass of people did not have their share in the country's wealth, nor even in the wealth that their industry and their energy produced. Hence it has at various times been proposed to print more greenbacks, coin more silver, organize the masses against the classes, drive the boss out of politics, bring the Government nearer to the people—all for the purpose of relieving an evil condition that was perfectly apparent but without, as I believe, fully understanding or at least appreciating the cause.

Sometimes I think, too, we have lost sight of ideals. The great ideal that underlies our form of government is the equality of opportunity. For the first hundred years of our country's life political economists believe that we were realizing that great ideal, but a study of public events for the last 25 years will, I believe, disclose that that ideal has been day by day and year by year slipping away from us. The consensus of opinion is now centering upon the belief that the institution that we call the trust has worked the disintegration of that ideal. . . .

The antitrust law was passed during the administration of President Harrison, and the Department of Justice immediately sought to put the law in force. I speak advisedly, because I was connected with the department at that time. But for the two succeeding administrations, the administrations between those of Harrison and Roosevelt, the law was permitted to fall into desuetude. . . .

In the first place, public sentiment had not crystallized in favor of that legislation. It is true, I think, that the law was passed responsive to a general public sentiment, responsive to a public sentiment that found voice in the Republican platform of 1888, but that public sentiment had not definitely settled upon the trusts as the one great danger that the country was threatened with, and that public sentiment favored a vigorous enforcement of that law, can not be said.

Another thing, there was no machinery at hand to enforce it; there was no Department of Commerce and Labor; there was no Bureau of Corporations; there was [*sic*] no inspectors available for the Department of Justice to investigate with reference to trusts. . . .

But, by the failure to enforce the law, the Government, as such, without criticizing any department of it, is in some measure responsible for the great growth of the trusts, and that fact should, I think, be taken into consideration in connection with any remedy that might be suggested.

Now, the three courses which seem to me logically possible for our Government to follow relative to the trusts are: First, let them alone to work out their own destiny. Second, foster and control them. Third, prohibit and destroy them. One or the other of these courses is a necessity, and whatever may be the legislation upon the subject, the logic of the situation will eventually drift the Nation into one or the other of these policies.

In my judgment the first policy is economically unsound. Society, drawn together in that concrete form we call government, should, in a certain sense, have a monopoly of organization. Those things which the Government does not undertake to do should be performed as largely as possible by the individual. Commerce is one of those. Not but what men may properly group themselves together either in copartnerships or in corporations for the conduct of business, but it is economically unsound to permit any association of men to exist that have in the form of their association the possibilities of becoming more powerful than the government which society has ordained.

The second policy, to foster and control the trusts, would, in my judgment, lead, when carried to its logical conclusion, to the disintegration of representative democracy. President Taft was absolutely right in one of his western speeches when he said that the abandonment of competition leads unerringly to socialism. I heard Senator Cummins say substantially the same thing in a most eloquent speech before the Republican Club in the city of New York last winter. The most minute study of the history of the commerce of the world, from the Phœnecian traders upon the Mediterranean down to the present hour, reveals but two forces that can control that greed and ambition which are the great moving power in commerce. The one is law and the other is competition. . . .

To foster and control the trusts, therefore, if the control is to be effective, means to go deep into all interstate business, to regulate the capital stock, the wages of employees, and the profits. This would be effectually distributing the proceeds of labor, and logically lead us into socialism and change our form of government in fact, if not in name. Representative democracy, which is the form of government we have established, is based upon individualism, and experience teaches that this can only exist where there is free and open competition.

All that brings me to what has seemed to me the wisest course and what I believe is the best remedy; and it is because I have believed that that I am here in answer to the invitation of the chairman to present such views as I have.

The antitrust law I never have looked upon as constructive legislation, or as intended to be so. It is a remedial statute and a penal statute, and as such it impresses me as being about as near perfect as human wits can devise. I might say, I hope without being charged with using too strong language, that I would just as leave, if I was charged with the responsibility, undertake to amend the decalogue, or the commerce clause of the Constitution, which I have always considered the most all-embracing and comprehensive provision in human law as to amend the antitrust law. But this law does not pretend to create anything. It simply prescribes a punishment, a penalty, for certain things. It is remedial purely.

. . . My suggestion is the enactment of a law that would define the charter powers of such corporations as may engage in interstate commerce and prohibit the engaging in interstate commerce of all other corporations.

In going into detail with reference to any such law, I appreciate the danger and particularly if one is not charged with the responsibility, as you gentlemen are and as I am not, of framing a law. But if you will permit me I shall make a few suggestions as to what I think such a law should contain, not with any thought that the suggestions I make are perfect or that I would act upon them without giving much more deliberation to them than I have if I were going to prepare a law.

My suggestion is a law requiring every corporation organized after the passage of the law to file with the Secretary of Commerce and Labor its charter or articles of incorporation, and to secure from that official a certificate which would entitle them to engage in interstate commerce; that this certificate should be issued by the Secretary when, and only when, the charter or articles of incorporation of the company shall fully describe the business which it is chartered to engage in, and expressly confine its operations to the business so stated, . . .

The law should prohibit all corporations not complying with its provisions from engaging in interstate commerce, and affix a severe penalty to be enforced against the corporations and also against the officers and directors for violating this prohibition. It should provide further that the certificate, issued by the Secretary of Commerce and labor to any corporation which shall thereafter do any act or engage in any business that is in violation of or in excess of its charter, shall be, ipso facto, annulled, and said corporation forever thereafter prohibited from engaging in interstate commerce, and declare invalid and nonenforceable all contracts made in interstate commerce by such corporations.

In a word, my thought is that the commerce of this country ought to be brought back to a competitive system; that such a law would make this the declared policy of the Government, but that existing business should be given ample time to adjust itself thereto. I would leave the antitrust law unamended, to deal with corporations which may violate its provisions.

B] THE AMERICAN ANTITRUST LEAGUE ACCUSES

One of the most vehement witnesses called by the committee was Henry B. Martin of New York City, national secretary of the American Antitrust

League. Since its founding in 1899, the League had lobbied persistently in Washington for punitive legislation and vigorous action against the trusts.*

Mr. Martin. Mr. Chairman, personally I am in the mining business. I appear before the committee, however, as a representative of my organization.

. . . while our organization is favorably disposed toward any new steps that Congress may see fit to take wisely for the regulation of the great corporations engaged in interstate commerce—the great aggregations of capital—we believe that the matter is of such large importance that in any steps that Congress takes, the greatest deliberation should be observed and nothing done hastily. In starting on a voyage or a process of manufacture of any legislation governing this great subject, we believe there are certain great rules—landmarks of our Government and of our principle of government—that should be observed in this legislation. We are adherents of the idea laid down in the Constitution of the United States that the purpose of this Government and of its founders was the establishment of freedom and equality, and we believe that all legislation now to be enacted affecting these matters should have that purpose mainly in mind, and be directed principally to that end.

The objection that we have or that the Antitrust League has and the great mass of the people of the United States have to the operations of the so-called trusts and great corporations and aggregations of capital in interstate commerce, is that they destroy the principle of freedom and equality in commerce and industry and labor. For that reason the antitrust act of 1890, which our members were very actively in favor of, was passed and is on the statute books. . . .

. . . We believe, and we desire to urge upon this committee, the necessity of giving a very thorough trial to the antitrust law with all its provisions before it is further amended. We believe that one of the most dangerous things that Congress could do to-day would be to amend the antitrust law. There is a statute which was drawn by some of the greatest legal minds in the history of this Republic—men of both parties who worked harmoniously and earnestly in the preparation of that statute; some of the greatest men in the history of the country of both parties united in the preparation of that statute, and it was reported, I believe, from the Judiciary Committee unanimously. Those men were bright men, and I believe that statute is a very excellent instrument for the protection of the people's right against trusts if it is enforced, for no matter how good a statute is, if it is not enforced the people get no relief. That is the only trouble with this situation to-day, we believe. For instance, President Taft said in his speech in Chicago, and we agreed with him heartily, that the business men complained that they were unable to understand when they were violating and when they were not violating the antitrust act. We believe that the business men who made that protest are either extremely innocent or intentionally deceptive—one of the two—because, as the President said, he doubted the soundness of their contention, and that any jury could tell in two minutes whether a man was intending to establish a monopoly or a corporation, or

* THE AMERICAN ANTITRUST LEAGUE ACCUSES: Testimony of Henry B. Martin. From *Ibid.*, I, 102–03, 106–07, 122–24.

whether they were not, and our only suggestion to the President now, and to the members of this committee, is that it would be a good thing to give them a chance before the juries. There are very few of them who have ever been brought before any jury to try whether they are guilty or innocent, and when there was a late attempt to bring them before a jury they were so sure of their innocence that they resorted to the extraordinary proceeding, habeas corpus, to avoid getting before the jury. I suppose that was an evidence in their minds of their innocence, that they had not violated the law. We believe the criminal clauses of the law certainly ought to be given much more full and thorough trial than they have been given so far, before anyone passed his judgment as to whether the law ought to be amended in that respect.

As to the civil provisions of the law, in the latest case, the Tobacco Trust case, the Attorney General expressed his hesitancy about invoking the drastic remedies of the civil clauses of the antitrust act, and as a matter of fact those drastic remedies, I believe, with one lone exception in 21 years, have never been invoked.

Now, if we have a law, that even in its civil provisions, without going to the criminal provisions, provides such drastic remedies that the Attorney General was afraid to invoke them, I think it well for this committee to have the Attorney General to come here and explain why he is afraid to invoke them. I think the people of the United States are interested to know if we have a law that in its civil provisions and so effective upon the violators [*sic*], that the great Attorney General of the United States is afraid to invoke it against them, that by the instrumentality of the law of 1890 against trusts, a provision is inserted in the civil clause of the act—not one but several provisions—that the giant, seasoned, rhinocerous [*sic*] hided corporation, like the Tobacco Trust and Standard Oil, become tender about it, and the Attorney General is afraid to invoke it, it seems to me we ought to know why. They have not been tender in other respects. They have not been tender of the consumers. They have taken the last drop of blood and the last pound of flesh wherever they could get it, but it seems to me the law should take its course with these men, and the failure or neglect of our Attorneys General for 21 years to make use of this law, I think and it is the belief of our organization that it is ample reason why something should be done now on the part of Congress in the exercise of its supervisory power to see that more active steps are taken by the executive departments in that direction.

Now, when we come to the matter of new legislation, our organization, the Antitrust League, is strenuously opposed to amending the antitrust law at this time. . . . it has never been given a full and fair trial, either as to its civil or criminal provisions. . . .

Senator CUMMINS. Well, there has been a great deal of activity in recent years in the enforcement of the law, has there not?

Mr. MARTIN. We are pleased to note that there has been.

Senator CUMMINS. You understand that the chief purpose, if not the only purpose, of the antitrust laws is to preserve competition in business, do you not?

Mr. MARTIN. I think that would be a correct statement . . .

Senator CUMMINS. . . . During the 21 years that the antitrust law has been an enactment of the United States more has been accomplished in the way of destroying competition over the entire country than before that time, has there not?

Mr. MARTIN. And much more would have been done had the antitrust law not been in existence.

Senator CUMMINS. I am simply asking you if it is not openly known by everybody that there has been more done in the way of destroying competition in the last 21 years than ever before in the history of the United States?

Mr. MARTIN. In the aggregate, and roughly, that is true. . . .

Senator CUMMINS. I did not mean to suggest that all competition in the United States has been destroyed, because I am sure that it has not been in many of the fields of industry and business. But it is still true that notwithstanding the existence of the antitrust law, competition has been throttled and strangled during the last 21 years so that now there is less of it than there was then.

Mr. MARTIN. In the aggregate, I should say yes.

Senator CUMMINS. Now you attribute that fact, or you explain that fact, by the suggestion that the law has not been enforced as it should have been enforced.

Mr. MARTIN. Exactly.

Senator CUMMINS. Do you think that if the law had been enforced vigorously and properly that we would have been able to preserve competition in our business?

Mr. MARTIN. I do.

Senator CUMMINS. Do you rely on the criminal or the civil remedies of the statute chiefly in reaching that conclusion?

Mr. MARTIN. Both are substantially equal in effect if thoroughly enforced.

Senator CUMMINS. The criminal remedies have not hitherto been very deterrent, have they?

Mr. MARTIN. They have been but partially invoked.

Senator CUMMINS. That is, you say the judges have been rather slow to impose penalties other than fines for the violation of the law.

Mr. MARTIN. They have not been as slow as the Department of Justice has been in asking for the imposition of those penalties. . . .

Senator CUMMINS. That brings us to the point that I had in mind. When you find a consistent course of that sort pursued by a great many people, officials in high stations and in low stations, over a long period of time, there are but two conclusions that can be reached, as it seems to me. One is that there is something essentially weak in the law that needs strengthening, the other is that the officers of the United States over a period of 20 years have been a band of rascals.

Mr. MARTIN. Not a band; there are isolated cases, but there has been a remarkable coincidence in their inactivity in this matter.

Senator CUMMINS. It is hardly believable that all our judges, and all our district attorneys, and all our Attorneys General, and all our Presidents have been in conspiracy to defeat the operation of this law during the 21 years that it has been in existence. It is hardly a fair conclusion, is it?

Mr. Martin. Senator, that is a very serious question and a very grave one, and I want to ask your permission to answer it as deliberately and as fairly as I can.

Senator Cummins. The time is yours, and the opportunity, Mr. Martin.

Mr. Martin. I do not charge, nor does the organization which I represent, that all these executive officers and courts, charged with the enforcement of the antitrust law during the last 20 years, have been in a conspiracy together. What we do charge and what we stand ready to prove to this committee, or to any other committee of Congress, is that the enormous wealth and power over the commerce and industries and politics of the United States by the conspiracies of great wealth who control these trusts has been so great, so insidious, and so far-reaching that no man to-day can tell how far it has gone in bending executive or judicial officers, by direct or indirect influences, in the direction they desire them to be bent. It is easier always, Senator, if you will pardon me, to prevent something from being done than it is to get it done. It is easier to defeat the passage of a bill than it is to pass one. It is a good deal easier to prevent the enforcement of a law than to get it enforced, and when you consider the enormous discipline and powers of these great trust conspiracies that have been erected in every great industry in the United States and which dominate the railroads and the banks and the coal mines as well as the manufacturing and merchandising industries—when you consider their enormous extent and the cunning and the power with which they have been directed, it is no wonder at times that they have been able to resist, by one means or another, the enforcement of the law. That is what we charge, and what we ask of Congress is that it now rise and exercise its great supervisory power over the executive and judicial branches of the Government and see to it that when these officials do not enforce the law that their conduct is inquired into and adequate steps taken to deal with the situation. . . .

c] A Member of the New York Board of Trade Calls for a New Policy

At the opposite pole from the position of Martin and the Antitrust League was that taken by C. U. Carpenter, chairman of the Sherman Antitrust Committee of the New York Board of Trade, and vice president and general manager of the American Stamp and Ticket Vending Machine Company. The position was one which was particularly common among big business men. Its most active public advocates were the chairman of the board of United States Steel, E. H. Gary, and the former Morgan partner and later financial backer of Theodore Roosevelt and the Progressive party, George W. Perkins.*

That the business of this country is in a greatly disturbed condition can not be denied. This applies not only to the great corporations known as the monopolies, but also to the smaller businesses operated by the average Ameri-

---

* A member of the new york board of trade calls for a new policy: Testimony of C. U. Carpenter. From *Ibid.*, I, 1027–31.

can business man. Anyone who has traveled throughout the country and observed conditions carefully can not but note that this general business distress
is becoming alarming. . . .

Business men generally place the largest share of blame for this condition
upon the feeling of uncertainty over the Sherman antitrust law, its interpretation, and method of enforcement of the Sherman Act.

In my conversation with business men throughout the country I find that
they have now come to believe that there is a stern necessity for a regulating
act which will control the greed of these monopolies. There is no question
about it, but in my opinion much of the business distress occurs through the
lawsuits which have been instituted by the Government against corporations,
or threatened lawsuits against corporations, which appear to be willing to
adjust their businesses to whatever Congress shall decide. . . .

Now, gentlemen, of course it is not my province to criticize Congress or any
of the messages, but it must be admitted that there still exists the greatest
uncertainty as to where legality ends and illegality begins in our industrial
corporations of to-day. Now, that is the feeling of business men generally.
Whether it is warranted or not is another question, but they certainly feel it.
Mere bigness of plant, no matter what the size, may not be illegal, but when
this "bigness" incidentally results in elimination of competition the result,
apparently, would be an illegal corporation, no matter what the intent. . . .

Now, we refer to the old era of competition sometimes as very desirable.
I do not agree with that. Any set of business men who have been through that
era of competition know just what it means. The old era of competition was
fraught with unfair practices, with attempts and intent to suppress competitors
by any methods, no matter how unfair. In fact, in our "good old era of competition" the big fellows were suppressing and swallowing up the little fellows
by using all the means at their command. As a matter of fact, many of these
large combinations of to-day were welcomed by the little fellow, for thus he
was absorbed at a profit instead of being swallowed at a loss.

There is no business corporation to-day which is in the nature of monopoly
now that was formed not because of the greed of the men to make large profits,
but because of the desire of the men to escape being ruined from the effects of
competition.

I consider, therefore, that the business men of the country are dissatisfied,
and have a right to be dissatisfied with the Sherman law as it stands and as it
is being enforced. They feel that general prosecutions of corporations should
be withheld until some amendment is offered that will make it possible for
them to reorganize their industries without any further disturbance.

There is a point that I wish to emphasize, that it is not a question of the
changing of the Sherman Act; it is not a question of the Sherman Act being
unjust. We need the Sherman Act, or need something like the Sherman Act.
In my opinion, though, I think it bears the aspect of unfairness to prosecute
these large corporations which were formed under the Sherman Act, which
corporations are perfectly willing to disintegrate and reorganize according to
any legal method that might be defined, and there, in my opinion, is the great
reason for the disturbance to-day, the fact that the business men do not know
what to do.

Many feel that inasmuch as the Government has never really interpreted this law for over 20 years, that the Government should give due consideration to the fact that they have allowed these corporate practices to exist and these corporations to grow up without protest. Therefore, that in these widespread prosecutions there is a certain element of unfairness. Hence these suggestions that Congress enact a statute which will give the fair business men of this country a chance to comply with the law, and at the same time protect their business interests.

If one believes in the rigorous enforcement of the present law, and the suing under it, then naturally one must believe that unrestricted competition is a good thing for the country at large. Fairminded business men do not approve of unrestricted competition as an economically correct condition. We can not convince ourselves that the bitter costly fights, the cutting of prices too close to cost, business worries and failures, and the low wages resulting from such conditions represent conditions which are good for the country at large.

The average business man of this country is as much opposed to unrestricted competition as he is to unrestricted monopoly.

We can not but recognize the enormous advantages and economies to be gained through combinations. The possibility of savings in both the selling and manufacturing ends of the business are too great to be neglected. This question has been so elucidated by men of great prominence, such as Mr. Gary and others, that this point needs no further elaboration.

The question of the enormous savings to be gained through combinations is undisputed.

It is my belief that one of the greatest mistakes has been made by our large corporate interests in failing to give to the public the benefit of at least a portion of the savings resulting from these large combinations. The public hears much about the economies and savings that can be and have been made, but they see little or no evidence of it in the prices which they have to pay for the articles themselves, and naturally they are dissatisfied. They resent bitterly the fact that most large corporations have not given them at least some slight share in these savings and economies. In my opinion this condition explains much of the bitter attitude of the public against these large corporations.

It seems to me that the managers of the large corporations to-day have expended their energies largely in "capitalizing their possibilities," and have failed to recognize the rights as well as the demands of the public.

Managers of corporations of all sizes recognize now that the insistent demand of the public for a proper and thorough degree of control over their corporations is a fair demand, a just demand, and one that must be complied with.

We have had the suggested remedy, first, of Federal incorporation for all corporations doing an interstate business. In case it is desired to avoid conflict with the States, these corporations might be formed under State laws, with the provision for a Federal license, a Government fee, and Government supervision. The regular State taxes should be paid to the State.

Second. In my opinion a commission similar to the Interstate Commerce Commission should be appointed. This commission should have control over the question of the issuance of the stocks and bonds of such corporations, basing

their calculations upon actual net assets, plus an allowance of, say, 20 per cent
for good will. Their work should include not only the control of the primary
issues of all stocks, bonds, etc., but also of any such issues that might be proposed after the company was incorporated. . . .

Personally I think it would be wise to take these steps first and then stop
all further legislation until the Government officials could note the effect of
these steps.

Now, when such eminent men as Mr. Wickersham and Mr. Gary speak of
Government control of prices, no American can fail to recognize that we are
moving very rapidly and going very far. It seems to me that this is a most
serious plunge. But Government control of prices means that we would take
some steps that we could never retrace, and it is a plunge, in my belief, that
would prove most serious.

In my opinion, the question of the Government setting prices, notwithstanding the fact that the theory has been advanced by very eminent men, would
be impracticable. It might do in some of the necessities of life, but you will
have to go beyond that if you pass a law that will be general in its application—
you get into fields where you are wandering in a jungle. . . .

d] A New Organization Calls Attention to the Plight of Small Business

> One month before the committee began its hearings, 233 representatives from
> fifteen different lines of retail trade met in Chicago and, discovering that they
> were "thinking along the same lines . . . facing the same conditions and . . .
> attempting to solve similar problems," founded the National Federation of
> Retail Merchants. The national secretary of the new organization, J. R.
> Moorehead, of Lexington, Missouri, came before the committee to explain
> small business' interest in the trust problem.*

. . . I have come here to submit for your consideration some observations
relative to some of the conditions that confront the small business men of the
country, and it is for these 212,000 officially, and for five times that many more,
I shall speak. . . .

You will all agree that there are grave problems confronting big business
of this country, and there are grave problems confronting Congress and the
people of the country in dealing with big business. I want to say that although
it may not have been intentional on the part of those who are responsible for
the present situation—and I have no reason to believe that it is—there are also
grave problems confronting the small business men of the country. I want to
say in the beginning that many of the stones that are being cast at the big
fellows are missing the mark and crossing the street and breaking the windows
of the little fellows. In other words, the efforts that are being made to curb
the powerful, the rich, and the grasping are recoiling upon that class of men
in this country for whom we believe it was not intended, those who are the

* A NEW ORGANIZATION CALLS ATTENTION TO THE PLIGHT OF SMALL BUSINESS: Testimony
of J. R. Moorehead. From *Ibid.*, I, 913–19.

least able and the least organized to secure their rights and combat the opposition. In other words, we know that the antitrust law of the Nation and the States as well is being perverted and is being used for ends that were never intended, and should present conditions continue would bring about a situation that can not be later on remedied. There are no longer any uncertain theories confronting the little man in business. We have a condition, and had we come here oftener and made our wants known and our influence in politics felt, long since, perhaps, the status of these I have the honor to represent could be better determined.

First. There is a great outcry in this country just now for the elimination of the "middle man," better known as the retail merchant, although the wholesaler and jobber may be classed as such. Our answer to this demand is that we do not propose to be eliminated if concerted action on our part should be able to show the Congress and the legislatures of the several States that we have a place in the economy of the country and that our preservation is for the best interest of the greatest number; best for their economical, political, and social welfare. This outcry emanates from four principal sources: First. The great aggregations of capital known as mail-order houses; second, almost all of what are known as farm journals; third, a great part of the metropolitan press; fourth, many politicians seeking to curry favor with the farming and laboring classes. These elements in our national make-up, along with others of lesser influence, have brought about a condition in the minds of the public adverse to the retail merchants, especially among the farmers and laboring men, that is no less than criminal. To my mind, this is the most serious side of the whole question. Just to think that it has been possible in this country of ours to so organize and conduct a campaign of advertising to so poison the minds of hundreds of thousands of people scattered all over the country against their neighbors, the home merchant, that they will not even give us a chance to meet outside competition. Under these false representations, carried on for so long, the public seems not able to distinguish between our efforts to obtain a fair living and the practice of extortion. They set us down as extortionists, without argument or chance to be heard. . . .

. . . I have mentioned four of the principal elements that are just now, intentionally or not, working to the undoing of the little man in business. Gentlemen, the attempt at combination or concentration of business into the hands of a few is no more manifest or real than is now being brought about in the distribution of merchandise of every kind, known as the retail business. This country has been wonderfully prosperous in the last 10 years. I venture to assert that there never was a time in the history of this country, taking into account the last five years or more, when there were so many people in every walk of life who were doing so well, making such a good living, getting such prices for farm products and live stock, making better wages, better housed, better fed, better clothed, and, taking all things into consideration, no greater general prosperity ever existed in the country. We can and do rejoice in this fact. Not one of us would reduce the price of a single item raised upon our farms or produced by our labor; but I am confident that I am within the truth when I say that the million or more retail merchants of this country have received less of the benefits growing out of this great era of prosperity than any one other class of our people. I feel safe in saying that the little merchants of the country have not reaped their share of the reward. Their business nor their profits have grown in proportion to the general prosperity that surrounds us. Certainly there has been a greater consumption of merchandise in the shape of clothing, food, and every other class of goods used by humanity; but the increase has not fallen into the lap of the small retailer.

When you have the opportunity to go amongst your constituents, who are the retailers of merchandise, you will surely find that the great majority of them have done little more than hold their own. Many of them do not do that well. Farm lands have increased beyond all expectations, and I am not saying they are too high. Wages have increased, but I do not say that labor is too well paid. No one knows better than those for whom I speak that upon these two elements rest our security and prosperity, and they have no better friends or defenders in the country than their home merchants, but we do assert, with emphasis, that the business, the storehouses, the homes, the stocks of goods, and the profits of the retailers have not grown in proportion to that obtained by either of the above-mentioned class or any others. Where has it gone? Who has gathered the harvest? I have said that "mail-order houses" are one of the factors that has brought about this condition of affairs. What are some of the facts? It has gone the rounds of the press, and is no doubt a fact, that one of these houses alone sold more than $63,000,000 of merchandise by mail last year. The business of one increased, it is said, 1,000 per cent in three years—so much business that they were scarcely able to take care of it. And while the "control of trusts" and the influence of Wall Street are pertinent questions for debate at this time, I venture to remind you that it is not disputed that the chairman of the board of directors of the largest mail-order house in this country is the president of one of the largest banks in New York. It might not be out of place to suggest that this would be a fruitful field for investigation. If the business of this class is to go on increasing, how long will it be before there will be dictation to the jobber, wholesaler, and manufacturer as to whom they shall sell, and we can imagine what would happen to the little fellows in business.

I have referred to the feeling of public sentiment which has obtained in the public mind against the retail merchant. Ever since this method of merchandising by mail began to take root in this country a great part of their advertising has not been in praise of their wares, but has been a tirade of insinuation, misrepresentation, and abuse for the home merchants, as being nothing more than robbers and thieves, and when we attempt to get together to protect our business, our homes, and our families we find out how they are able to invoke in their own behalf the antitrust laws of the country. Almost without exception the greater part of the advertising revenue of the farm journals comes from the mail-order house, just as the daily press is largely supported by revenues from the large department stores. I think you can readily see why there is rarely ever a good word spoken for the little man in business from these sources. . . .

. . . We believe we have a just complaint, when we find ourselves involved in this already unequal struggle and the Government steps in and says, "Stop;

you are restraining the trade of the mail-order house, the manufacturers and the big fellows. You are operating a new kind of trust, a trust of power." What greater trust of power could there be than that of a great aggregation of capital to spread it broadcast through the daily and farm press and catalogues that they can sell their wares at half the price charged by the home merchants?

To be more specific, a United States grand jury in Chicago recently indicted 14 secretaries of as many retail lumber associations, and I am informed upon good authority, by the parties themselves, that the retail implement dealers' association and the retail coal dealers' association are undergoing the same kind of an investigation. . . . what is the charge? In short, it is that these retail merchants have been guilty of "restraining the trade of certain companies and corporations by furnishing information to its membership." . . . If it is unlawful to furnish information of this character to each other as to the action or practices of a manufacturer, wholesaler, or mail-order house, why is it not also unlawful for Dun's or Bradstreet's to furnish the manufacturers or wholesalers with the information that will enable them to avoid great loss in the sale of merchandise to the retailer. What is the difference? . . . this situation resolves itself into the only solution possible, that this is a fight for the retail business of the country between the little fellows and the mail-order house and, unfortunately for the little fellows, the Government is furnishing the stronger with the ammunition and the attorneys to fight their battles. . . . The retail merchants, for whom I speak, do not ask you to pass any law or make any amendments to the present law that will in any way curtail the rights of those who are surely working to the reduction of the little merchants to nothing more than makeshifts; to serve as an accommodation when the people have no money to send away from home for what they want, when crops fail and when the strike is on. All that we ask is a chance for a fair fight and no favors, but we do insist that this law shall in some way be made so plain along these lines that the threat of being sent to jail will not be hanging over us when we join hands to fight for our business existence, upon which so much depends, our happiness and the welfare of our families and everyone in the communities in which we are perchance doing business. It is out of all reason to think that the business man has to submit, or work under a law the uncertainties of which are such that he has no idea or conception of his standing before such a law until he has been brought into court and tried. Therefore, it would seem that it should be the aim of Congress to make it so plain in so far as it affects voluntary associations of business men not formed for making prices or profits that "he who runs may read." Does this seem to be an unreasonable demand, although the exact terms in which it is to be expressed may not at this time be clear? We are restless under suspicion and surveillance, when Government and State officials are upon our heels and delving into our business.

. . . The retail merchant is not going to be put out of business, but he will be reduced to a mere means of accommodation to those who have not the cash to send away from home to supply their wants. We believe we have a right to more than this. We believe that we are of as much a necessity to the community as the farmer, laborer, the doctor, lawyer, or postmaster. We believe that a good live town, with live merchants making something more than a living, are as much of a necessity in our economy as is the farmer. For you can not deny that every acre of land is increased in value in proportion to its proximity to a good town or city, and depreciates in value just in proportion to its distance from a good town or city. A good town or city is as much of a necessity to the farmer as the farmer to a good town. It appears to us that such a condition would be ideal in this country and should not be in anywise disturbed or discounted, even though it might be admitted that the farmer or any other citizen might save in a small way upon his purchases when sent to a city. In this connection I want to say, although it might not be germane to the question to be decided by you, that the new shibboleth is the demand for a parcels post, a new link to be forged into the chain. I might not be competent to give advice, but, gentlemen, look well and you will find that the demand for this law emanates from the sources about which I have been speaking, and is desired for the purpose of further crippling the small communities of this country to the advantage of the mail-order house and the city department store. Have we not already enough problems growing out of the drift of the population to the great centers? Do we want to increase our social, economical, and political problems along this line? . . .

E] A Farm Leader Asks Consideration for the Farmer

> To speak for the farmers and, in particular, for the new cooperative organizations that they were developing during the early twentieth century, a farmer from Atwood, Tennessee, T. J. Brooks, took the stand.*

Mr. Chairman and gentlemen of the committee, the particular phase of this question which it is our purpose to discuss relates to that portion of the antitrust law which might be construed to apply to organizations of farmers.

I represent the Farmers' Educational Cooperative Union, the largest organization of farmers in the world. It extends from Virginia to California and from the State of Washington to Florida, including about 30 States.

The efforts upon the part of the farmer to adjust his business to the commercial demands of the age necessarily compel him to organize. When he is organized, for commercial purposes, the object of his organization should be proclaimed without reserve, and understood thoroughly by the public.

The advantages of combination are the advantages of better organization and more effective operation, cheaper production and distribution. The disadvantages of combination have arisen chiefly from the misuse of the power of combination which develops into monopoly.

There is a great deal of difference between a monopoly whose purpose is to coerce and oppress, and cooperative organization whose purpose is to eliminate useless expense without in any degree practicing extortion by withholding from

---

* A FARM LEADER ASKS CONSIDERATION FOR THE FARMER: Testimony of T. J. Brooks. From *Ibid.*, II, 2336–38, 2353.

the consumer, regardless of the law of supply and demand, in order to create fictitious values.

A great deal has been said about an elastic system of currency that would meet those periodic demands for enormous amounts of capital to move the great staple crops of the country from the producer to the consumer. In other words, when wheat is thrown on the market at harvest time, a great deal of money is required to purchase this wheat from the farmer, hold it till it is needed by the mills, and finally sold to the consumer—and the same way with cotton. In the fall of the year something over $800,000,000 are required to purchase from the farmer his cotton crop. He usually markets it so fast that this volume of money is taken from other channels of trade to the inconvenience of our financial institutions in order to hold this cotton until the mills can use it. Now, an organization of farmers who grow wheat or who grow cotton, which has for its purpose the establishing of a system whereby the farmers can assume the carrying function, and gradually market his wheat and his cotton throught the year, should be exempt from any law that would hinder its operation. The purpose of the organization which I represent is to facilitate marketing according to the normal operation of the law of supply and demand, and is in no sense of the word an attempt to corner the market and create artificial prices. It takes a great deal less money to finance the holding of a crop than it does to purchase it outright; and by gradual marketing the periodic disturbance in our commercial world would be lessened, and the evils of the exchanges mitigated.

None of the evils of overcapitalization, oppression of employees, or extortion of the public are inherent in the class of organizations to which we refer. A law whose purpose is to prevent injustice to the public should be so worded as to exempt all legitimate enterprises where there is no attempt to misuse the public confidence or destroy or pervert the natural operation of the law of supply and demand in the markets of the world. We believe that all corporations doing interstate business should be required to come to the strictest standard of account as to their tangible assets and methods of operation. We wish it to be clearly provided for in any antitrust law that no penalty shall attach to those promoting any organization or combination upon the part of producers having as its purpose the gradual marketing of farm products. We think it would be performing a great public service to so arrange the delivery of our staple crops each year as consumption called for them, instead of dumping them on the market regardless of the demands of trade. This is the basis of our contention, and upon this contention we rest our plea for exemption from antitrust legislation.

I do not claim that the present law makes the farmers' organizations now in existence subject to its penal provisions. I do not say that any amendments proposed would interfere with any business organization of the farmer. But what I do suggest is, that if such provisions could by technical construction be construed to interfere, that they should be eliminated, and when amendments are passed, that they should be so worded as to exempt the organizations to which I refer from any liabilities to its prohibitory features. I suppose there never would have been an antitrust law passed had it not been that there were combinations being formed which were calculated to do an injustice to the public. If any such organization has ever been formed by the agricultural classes I have not seen any notice of it; I have not heard of any organization of farmers being accused of plotting for such a purpose. The condition of the farmer financially, as compared with that of other vocations, would indicate that he has not heretofore made use of any unfair means by which he could extort from his patrons. He is in a sense a manufacturer. He manufactures the soil, the sunshine, and the showers into the raw materials that feed and clothe the people of the world. He has never arrogated to himself the prerogatives that his power might indicate that he could if he so chose. Beginning with 90 per cent of the wealth, when this Government was first launched among the sovereignties of the world, he has now only about one-fifth of the aggregate wealth of the Nation; and only a part of the farmers own this percentage. A great per cent of them are propertyless. In fact, one-half of the plowmen of this Nation have no home. We have, approximately, 93,000,000 people who are supported by about twelve and one-half million actual field hands, who produce the food and raiment that feeds and clothes the 93,000,000 people at home and millions beyond the seas. Is it not an alarming state of affairs that one-half of these producers have no place on this planet that they can call their own? So a combination of the farmers when organized for mutual benefit should not run against some national statute intended for public protection. According to the census of 1910 the manufacturers of the United States are worth approximately twenty billions of dollars, and their yearly output is valued at the same figures, employing 6,500,000 hands and paying them $3,427,000,000. How is it that the farmer, who has something like twenty-eight billions invested, twice as many hands, and the annual value of his crop, at farm prices, is only $9,000,000,000? We may see here some indication of the cause of the exits from the country to the towns and cities. The cry of "back to the farm," of which we have seen so much in the press of late, is invariably a command to "go" and not an entreaty to "come." In other words, the farmer is not begging the people to come from the city to help him farm, but the city man is urging people to go back to the country, but seldom does he take his own advice. I mention these things merely to show that the farmer is not holding his own in the race of life. We have about one million corporations in the United States, which control 82 per cent of the wealth of the nation. . . .

The CHAIRMAN.[1] I understand, in concrete form, that your plan would be to enable the holding of an annual product so that it might be distributed over the year, leaving the price to be governed by the demand as it met that distribution?

Mr. BROOKS. You have got it exactly. . . .

Senator WATSON. You are not much of an individualist, I believe, from your statement?

Mr. BROOKS. It is owing to how you define it. We have people who have various constructions of what constitutes an individualist. I believe that individualism, so far as it stimulates individual efforts, ought to be encouraged.

1 Moses E. Clapp, of Minnesota.

f] The President of the AFL Demands Freedom of Action for Labor

In addition to his professional role as a trade-union leader, Samuel Gompers played another and larger role during the early decades of the twentieth century—that of labor's advocate before the American people. In this role, he devoted himself unflaggingly to explaining the interests of the working class and to defending its place in American society. Both roles are apparent in this attack on the use of the Sherman Antitrust Law to restrict the activities of labor unions, the most notable instances of which had occurred in the Danbury Hatters and the Bucks Stove and Range cases.*

Mr. Chairman and gentlemen, of course you understand that, as a representative of an organization of working people, and assuming to speak in the interests of all the working people, we have, in the Sherman antitrust law the additional interest as it has been made to apply to the working people as such and though we may have some views upon the trust law in its general aspect, we have particular views as that law has been made to affect the working people, and made to affect the working people by reason of the interpretation placed upon that law by the courts of the United States and finally adjudged by the Supreme Court of the United States.

I think it were best if such of my colleagues who may have the opportunity of appearing before you, and myself, would apply ourselves to the effect the antitrust law has upon the working people rather than dealing with the subject as it applies to others. I might say that we do not feel averse to expressing our opinion upon even its general aspect, too, but I think that we would then express our personal views rather than any views as officially expressed in any concrete form by the men of labor. . . .

We are interested in securing relief from the interpretation placed upon the Sherman antitrust law by the Supreme Court of the United States, and the restoration of the working people, either as individuals or in association, to their status before the enactment of the law as interpreted by the court. In so far as the Sherman antitrust law is concerned, as now held as the law of the land, voluntary associations of the working people are regarded as combinations coming under the provisions of the antitrust law and amenable to its civil and penal provisions. . . .

The Sherman antitrust law, as it has been interpreted, brings the men and women of labor under its civil and penal sections. As a consequence, any person or persons who may be injured in their business by reason of the normal and rightful action of working people, the person or persons so injured may bring suit and recover threefold damages. . . .

The men of labor want to know their status in society in the United States. They hold that their organizations are essential to their safety and well-being. It is not a matter of mere desire; nor are these organizations the growth of a desire on the part of those who are designated "labor leaders." Under modern

* THE PRESIDENT OF THE AFL DEMANDS FREEDOM OF ACTION FOR LABOR: Testimony of Samuel Gompers. From *Ibid.*, II, 1728-29, 1757-59, 1776-77.

industry there is no factor in all our governmental or civic life that undertakes to protect the working people against the power which wealth possesses in the hands of employers, corporations, combinations, and trusts of employers.

With the power of wealth and concentration of industry, the tremendous development in machinery, and power to drive machinery; with the improvement of the tools of labor, so that they are wonderfully tremendous machines, and with these all on the one hand; with labor, the workers, performing a given part of the whole product, probably an infinitesimal part, doing the thing a thousand or thousands of times over and over again in a day—labor divided and subdivided and specialized, so that a working man is but a mere cog in the great industrial modern plant; his individuality lost, alienated from the tools of labor; with concentration of wealth, concentration of industry, I wonder whether any of us can imagine what would be the actual condition of the working people of our country to-day without their organizations to protect them.

What would be the condition of the working men in our country in our day by acting as individuals with as great a concentrated wealth and industry on every hand? It is horrifying even to permit the imagination full swing to think what would be possible. Slavery! Slavery! Demoralized, degraded slavery. Nothing better.

To say that the men and women of labor may not do jointly what they may do in the exercise of their individual lawful right is an anomaly. . . .

Gentlemen, the individual workingmen accept conditions as they are, until driven to desperation. Then they throw down their tools and strike, without experience, without the knowledge of how best to conduct themselves, and to secure the relief which they need and demand. But the workingmen know where to go. It may be true that there are some workers who are opposed to organizations of labor, but they are very, very few. Those that do not come to us are either too helpless or too ignorant. But let no man fool himself. When in sheer desperation, driven to the last, where they can no longer submit to the lording of the master, they strike, they quit, and all the pent up anger gives vent in fury—they then come to us and ask us for our advice and our assistance, and we give it to them, whether they were indifferent to us or whether they were antagonistic to us. They are never questioned. We come to their assistance as best we can.

I do not pretend to say that with organizations of labor that strikes are entirely eliminated. I do not fool myself with any such beliefs, and I would not insult the intelligence of any other man by pretending to believe, much less to make, such a statement. But this one fact is sure: That in all the world there is now an unrest among the people, and primarily among the working people, with the present position they occupy in society—their unrequited toil; the attitude of irresponsibility of the employer toward the workers; the bitter antagonism to any effective attempt on the part of workers to protect themselves against aggression and greed, and the failure of employers to realize their responsibilities.

The demand of the workers is to be larger sharers in the product of their labor. In different countries they have unrest and this dissatisfaction takes on different forms. In our own country it takes on the form of the trade-union movement, as exemplified by the American Federation of Labor—a movement and a federation founded as a replica of the American governments, both the Federal Government and the State and city governments. It is formed to conform as nearly as it is possible to the American idea, and to have the crystallized unrest and discontent manifested under the Anglo-Saxon or American fashion; to press it home to the employers; to press it home to the lawmakers; to press it home to the law administrators, and possibly to impregnate and influence the minds of judges who may accord to us the rights which are essential to our well being rather than guaranteeing to us the academic rights which are fruitless and which we do not want. . . .

Senator TOWNSEND. Do you believe in the Sherman antitrust law, so far as it prohibits contracts and conspiracies in restraint of trade and prohibits attempts to monopolize and monopolizations?

Mr. GOMPERS. I am expressing my own opinion. I quoted a statement of one of our statesmen made a decade ago who said that it was perhaps the crudest piece of legislation ever enacted by the Congress of the United States. It not only prohibits combinations but it is a curb upon individual initiative. If you will read carefully section 2, I think it will disclose what I have in mind.

Senator TOWNSEND. That is in reference of monopolies.

Mr. GOMPERS. "Every person who shall monopolize, or attempt to monopolize," and so forth. It does not require a combination to be illegal under this law—"any person who shall monopolize or attempt to monopolize." In other words, anyone—any person—who shall attempt to extend his business, his enterprise, to the fullest, is doing an unlawful act.

Senator TOWNSEND. Well, that construction has never been put upon it. Let us take the one that has been followed. Do you believe it is right for a number of concerns, corporations, to combine to monopolize?

Mr. GOMPERS. May I answer in this way, Senator, that it matters little what I think upon that subject, and I imagine that it matters very little what others may think, combinations of capital will go on, and there can be very little successful attempt to disrupt or even to curb it.

Senator TOWNSEND. Do you believe there ought to be any attempts to do so?

Mr. GOMPERS. I believe that industry is going to grow, and combinations will grow.

Senator TOWNSEND. Well, is it correct to state, then, frankly, that you think we ought not to deal with that proposition?

Mr. GOMPERS. I prefer not to express that opinion, but I am free to express this opinion, that if you do you will fail.

Senator TOWNSEND. Well, in view of your position on that, it is not necessary for me to ask some other questions that I wanted to ask with reference to it. I know you said at the beginning that you did not care to express yourself on that subject as to whether it ought to be dealt with or not, but I was in hopes that you would feel like giving us your views, because while you say it matters little what your opinion may be on this subject, you are here for the purpose of creating some impression on this committee.

Mr. GOMPERS. I do not want to underestimate, I am not vain, nor am I overmodest, and I do not think that I would care to have it appear that I have no opinion as to that, or that I underestimate my own opinion. What I intended to say was that any opinion I had on the subject would have no avail in so far as the effect of the development and growth of the combinations of capital was concerned. That is what I had in mind.

Senator TOWNSEND. I think I am not doing any violence to your statement when I put the question in this way: Why would not your logical position be to repeal the Sherman antitrust law?

Mr. GOMPERS. If I had a vote—either as a Member of Congress or the referendum obtained—I should vote for it.

Senator TOWNSEND. Vote to repeal it?

Mr. GOMPERS. I would. I would go to the fullest length of my rights as a citizen to have the lawful and inherent rights of man restored to the working people of our country. . . .

3] The Candidates Debate

A] ROOSEVELT STATES THE CASE FOR REGULATION

Two days after the Senate Interstate Commerce Committee began its hearings, the following editorial by Theodore Roosevelt appeared in the *Outlook* magazine and attracted widespread attention. In it, Roosevelt pulled together ideas that had been taking shape in his mind since at least 1900 and gave what is probably his most concise and coherent discussion of the trust problem. The editorial appeared at a time when Roosevelt was just beginning to incline toward running again for the Presidency. It sets forth clearly the position on which he later campaigned as the candidate of the Progressive party.*

THE SUIT against the Steel Trust by the Government has brought vividly before our people the need of reducing to order our chaotic Government policy as regards business. As President, in Messages to Congress I repeatedly called the attention of that body and of the public to the inadequacy of the Anti-Trust Law by itself to meet business conditions and secure justice to the people, and to the further fact that it might, if left unsupplemented by additional legislation, work mischief, with no compensating advantage; and I urged as strongly as I knew how that the policy followed with relation to railways in connection with the Inter-State Commerce Law should be followed by the National Government as regards all great business concerns; and therefore that, as a first step, the powers of the Bureau of Corporations should be greatly enlarged, or else that there should be created a Governmental board or commission, with powers somewhat similar to those of the Inter-State Commerce Commission, but covering the whole field of inter-State business, exclusive of transportation (which should, by law, be kept wholly separate from ordinary industrial business, all common ownership of the industry and the railway being

---

* ROOSEVELT STATES THE CASE FOR REGULATION: "The Trusts, the People, and the Square Deal: Editorial by Theodore Roosevelt." From the *Outlook* (November 18, 1911); 649, 651–56.

forbidden). In the end I have always believed that it would also be necessary to give the National Government complete power over the organization and capitalization of all business concerns engaged in inter-State commerce. . . .

. . . When my Administration took office, I found, not only that there had been little real enforcement of the Anti-Trust Law and but little more effective enforcement of the Inter-State Commerce Law, but also that the decisions were so chaotic and the laws themselves so vaguely drawn, or at least interpreted in such widely varying fashions, that the biggest business men tended to treat both laws as dead letters. The series of actions by which we succeeded in making the Inter-State Commerce Law an efficient and most useful instrument in regulating the transportation of the country and exacting justice from the big railways without doing them injustice—while, indeed, on the contrary, securing them against injustice—need not here be related. The Anti-Trust Law it was also necessary to enforce as it had never hitherto been enforced; both because it was on the statute-books and because it was imperative to teach the masters of the biggest corporations in the land that they were not, and would not be permitted to regard themselves as, above the law. Moreover, where the combination has really been guilty of misconduct the law serves a useful purpose, and in such cases as those of the Standard Oil and Tobacco Trusts, if effectively enforced, the law confers a real and great good.

Suits were brought against the most powerful corporations in the land, which we were convinced had clearly and beyond question violated the Anti-Trust Law. These suits were brought with great care, and only where we felt so sure of our facts that we could be fairly certain that there was a likelihood of success. As a matter of fact, in most of the important suits we were successful. It was imperative that these suits should be brought, and very real good was achieved by bringing them, for it was only these suits that made the great masters of corporate capital in America fully realize that they were the servants and not the masters of the people, that they were subject to the law, and that they would not be permitted to be a law unto themselves; and the corporations against which we proceeded had sinned, not merely by being big (which we did not regard as in itself a sin), but by being guilty of unfair practices towards their competitors, and by procuring unfair advantages from the railways. But the resulting situation has made it evident that the Anti-Trust Law is not adequate to meet the situation that has grown up because of modern business conditions and the accompanying tremendous increase in the business use of vast quantities of corporate wealth. As I have said, this was already evident to my mind when I was President, and in communications to Congress I repeatedly stated the facts. But when I made these communications there were still plenty of people who did not believe that we would succeed in the suits that had been instituted against the Standard Oil, the Tobacco, and other corporations, and it was impossible to get the public as a whole to realize what the situation was. Sincere zealots who believed that all combinations could be destroyed and the old-time conditions of unregulated competition restored, insincere politicians who knew better but made believe that they thought whatever their constituents wished them to think, crafty reactionaries who wished to see on the statute-books laws which they believed unenforceable, and the almost solid "Wall Street crowd" or representatives of "big business" who at that time opposed with equal violence both wise and necessary and unwise and improper regulation of business—all fought against the adoption of a sane, effective, and far-reaching policy.

It is a vitally necessary thing to have the persons in control of big trusts of the character of the Standard Oil Trust and Tobacco Trust taught that they are under the law, just as it was a necessary thing to have the Sugar Trust taught the same lesson in drastic fashion by Mr. Henry L. Stimson when he was United States District Attorney in the city of New York. But to attempt to meet the whole problem not by administrative governmental action but by a succession of lawsuits is hopeless from the standpoint of working out a permanently satisfactory solution. Moreover, the results sought to be achieved are achieved only in extremely insufficient and fragmentary measure by breaking up all big corporations, whether they have behaved well or ill, into a number of little corporations which it is perfectly certain will be largely, and perhaps altogether, under the same control. Such action is harsh and mischievous if the corporation is guilty of nothing except its size; and where, as in the case of the Standard Oil, and especially the Tobacco, trusts, the corporation has been guilty of immoral and anti-social practices, there is need for far more drastic and thoroughgoing action than any that has been taken, under the recent decree of the Supreme Court. In the case of the Tobacco Trust, for instance, the settlement in the Circuit Court, in which the representatives of the Government seem inclined to concur, practically leaves all of the companies still substantially under the control of the twenty-nine original defendants. Such a result is lamentable from the standpoint of justice. The decision of the Circuit Court, if allowed to stand, means that the Tobacco Trust has merely been obliged to change its clothes, that none of the real offenders have received any real punishment, while, as the New York "Times," a pro-trust paper, says, the tobacco concerns, in their new clothes, are in positions of "ease and luxury," and "immune from prosecution under the law."

Surely, miscarriage of justice is not too strong a term to apply to such a result when considered in connection with what the Supreme Court said of this Trust. That great Court in its decision used language which, in spite of its habitual and severe self-restraint in stigmatizing wrong-doing, yet unhesitatingly condemns the Tobacco Trust for moral turpitude, saying that the case shows an "ever-present manifestation . . . of conscious wrong-doing" by the Trust, whose history is "replete with the doing of acts which it was the obvious purpose of the statute to forbid, . . . demonstrative of the existence from the beginning of a purpose to acquire dominion and control of the tobacco trade, not by the mere exertion of the ordinary right to contract and to trade, but by methods devised in order to monopolize the trade by driving competitors out of business, which were ruthlessly carried out upon the assumption that to work upon the fears or play upon the cupidity of competitors would make success possible." The letters from and to various officials of the Trust, which were put in evidence, show a literally astounding and horrifying indulgence by the Trust in wicked and depraved business methods—such as the "endeavor to cause a strike in their [a rival business firm's] factory," or the "shutting off the market" of an independent tobacco firm by "taking the necessary steps to give them a warm reception," or forcing importers into a price agreement by causing and continuing "a demoralization of the business for such length of time as may be deemed desirable" (I quote from the letters). A Trust guilty of such conduct should be absolutely disbanded, and the only way to prevent the repetition of such conduct is by strict Government supervision, and not merely by lawsuits.

The Anti-Trust Law cannot meet the whole situation, nor can any modification of the principle of the Anti-Trust Law avail to meet the whole situation. The fact is that many of the men who have called themselves Progressives, and who certainly believe that they are Progressives, represent in reality in this matter not progress at all but a kind of sincere rural toryism. These men believe that it is possible by strengthening the Anti-Trust Law to restore business to the competitive conditions of the middle of the last century. Any such effort is foredoomed to end in failure, and, if successful, would be mischievous to the last degree. Business cannot be successfully conducted in accordance with the practices and theories of sixty years ago unless we abolish steam, electricity, big cities, and, in short, not only all modern business and modern industrial conditions, but all the modern conditions of our civilization. The effort to restore competition as it was sixty years ago, and to trust for justice solely to this proposed restoration of competition, is just as foolish as if we should go back to the flintlocks of Washington's Continentals as a substitute for modern weapons of precision. The effort to prohibit all combinations, good or bad, is bound to fail, and ought to fail; when made, it merely means that some of the worst combinations are not checked and that honest business is checked. Our purpose should be, not to strangle business as an incident of strangling combinations, but to regulate big corporations in thoroughgoing and effective fashion, so as to help legitimate business as an incident to thoroughly and completely safeguarding the interests of the people as a whole. Against all such increase of Government regulation the argument is raised that it would amount to a form of Socialism. This argument is familiar; it is precisely the same as that which was raised against the creation of the Inter-State Commerce Commission, and of all the different utilities commissions in the different States, as I myself saw, thirty years ago, when I was a legislator at Albany, and these questions came up in connection with our State Government. Nor can action be effectively taken by any one State. Congress alone has power under the Constitution effectively and thoroughly and at all points to deal with inter-State commerce, and where Congress, as it should do, provides laws that will give the Nation full jurisdiction over the whole field, then that jurisdiction becomes, of necessity, exclusive—although until Congress does act affirmatively and thoroughly it is idle to expect that the States will or ought to rest content with non-action on the part of both Federal and State authorities. This statement, by the way, applies also to the question of "usurpation" by any one branch of our Government of the rights of another branch. It is contended that in these recent decisions the Supreme Court legislated; so it did; and it had to; because Congress had signally failed to do *its* duty by legislating. For the Supreme Court to nullify an act of the Legislature as unconstitutional except on the clearest grounds is usurpation; to interpret such an act in an obviously wrong sense is usurpation; but where the legislative body persistently leaves open a field which it is absolutely imperative, from the public standpoint, to fill, then no possible blame attaches to the official or officials who step in because they have to, and who then do the needed work in the interest of the people. The blame in such cases lies with the body which has been derelict, and not with the body which reluctantly makes good the dereliction. . . .

Few will dispute the fact that the present situation is not satisfactory and cannot be put on a permanently satisfactory basis unless we put an end to the period of groping and declare for a fixed policy, a policy which shall clearly define and punish wrong-doing, which shall put a stop to the iniquities done in the name of business, but which shall do strict equity to business. We demand that big business give the people a square deal; in return we must insist that when any one engaged in big business honestly endeavors to do right he shall himself be given a square deal; and the first, and most elementary, kind of square deal is to give him in advance full information as to just what he can, and what he cannot, legally and properly do. It is absurd, and much worse than absurd, to treat the deliberate lawbreaker as on an exact par with the man eager to obey the law, whose only desire is to find out from some competent Governmental authority what the law is, and then to live up to it. Moreover, it is absurd to treat the size of a corporation as in itself a crime. As Judge Hook says in his opinion in the Standard Oil Case: "Magnitude of business does not alone constitute a monopoly . . . the genius and industry of man when kept to ethical standards still have full play, and what he achieves is his . . . success and magnitude of business, the rewards of fair and honorable endeavor [are not forbidden] . . . [the public welfare is threatened only when success is attained] by wrongful or unlawful methods." Size may, and in my opinion does, make a corporation fraught with potential menace to the community; and may, and in my opinion should, therefore make it incumbent upon the community to exercise through its administrative (not merely through its judicial) officers a strict supervision over that corporation in order to see that it does not go wrong; but the size in itself does not signify wrong-doing, and should not be held to signify wrong-doing.

Not only should any huge corporation which has gained its position by unfair methods, and by interference with the rights of others, by demoralizing and corrupt practices, in short, by sheer baseness and wrong-doing, be broken up, but it should be made the business of some administrative governmental body, by constant supervision, to see that it does not come together again, save under such strict control as shall insure the community against all repetition of the bad conduct—and it should never be permitted thus to assemble its parts as long as these parts are under the control of the original offenders, for actual experience has shown that these men are, from the standpoint of the people at large, unfit to be trusted with the power implied in the management of a large corporation. But nothing of importance is gained by breaking up a huge inter-State and international industrial organization *which has not offended otherwise than by its size,* into a number of small concerns without any attempt to regulate the way in which those concerns as a whole shall do business. Nothing is gained by depriving the American Nation of good weapons wherewith to fight in the great field of international industrial competition. Those who would seek to restore the days of unlimited and uncontrolled competition, and who believe that a panacea for our industrial and economic ills is to be found in the mere breaking up of all big corporations, simply because they are big, are attempting not only the impossible, but what, if possible, would be undesirable. They are acting as we should act if we tried to dam the Mississippi, to stop its flow outright. The effort would be certain to result in failure and disaster; we would have attempted the impossible, and so would have achieved nothing, or worse than nothing. But by building levees along the Mississippi, not seeking to dam the stream, but to control it, we are able to achieve our object and to confer inestimable good in the course of so doing.

This Nation should definitely adopt the policy of attacking, not the mere fact of combination, but the evils and wrong-doing which so frequently accompany combination. The fact that a combination is very big is ample reason for exercising a close and jealous supervision over it, because its size renders it potent for mischief; but it should not be punished unless it actually does the mischief; it should merely be so supervised and controlled as to guarantee us, the people, against its doing mischief. We should not strive for a policy of unregulated competition and of the destruction of all big corporations, that is, of all the most efficient business industries in the land. Nor should we persevere in the hopeless experiment of trying to regulate these industries by means only of lawsuits, each lasting several years, and of uncertain result. We should enter upon a course of supervision, control, and regulation of these great corporations—a regulation which we should not fear, if necessary, to bring to the point of control of monopoly prices, just as in exceptional cases railway rates are now regulated. Either the Bureau of Corporations should be authorized, or some other governmental body similar to the Inter-State Commerce Commission should be created, to exercise this supervision, this authoritative control. When once immoral business practices have been eliminated by such control, competition will thereby be again revived as a healthy factor, although not as formerly an all-sufficient factor, in keeping the general business situation sound. Wherever immoral business practices still obtain—as they obtained in the cases of the Standard Oil Trust and Tobacco Trust—the Anti-Trust Law can be invoked; and wherever such a prosecution is successful, and the courts declare a corporation to possess a monopolistic character, then that corporation should be completely dissolved, and the parts ought never to be again assembled save on whatever terms and under whatever conditions may be imposed by the governmental body in which is vested the regulatory power. Methods can readily be devised by which corporations sincerely desiring to act fairly and honestly can on their own initiative come under this thoroughgoing administrative control by the Government and thereby be free from the working of the Anti-Trust Law. But the law will remain to be invoked against wrong-doers; and under such conditions it could be invoked far more vigorously and successfully than at present.

. . . But punishment should not be the only, or indeed the main, end in view. Our aim should be a policy of construction and not one of destruction. Our aim should not be to punish the men who have made a big corporation successful merely because they have made it big and successful, but to exercise such thoroughgoing supervision and control over them as to insure their business skill being exercised in the interest of the public and not against the public interest. Ultimately, I believe that this control should undoubtedly indirectly or directly extend to dealing with all questions connected with their treatment of their employees, including the wages, the hours of labor, and the like. Not only is the proper treatment of a corporation, from the standpoint of the managers, shareholders, and employees, compatible with securing from that corporation the best standard of public service, but when the effort is wisely made it results in benefit both to the corporation and to the public. . . .

. . . The National Government exercises control over inter-State commerce railways, and it can in similar fashion, through an appropriate governmental body, exercise control over all industrial organizations engaged in inter-State commerce. . . .

B] WILSON CALLS FOR REGULATED COMPETITION

> Unlike Roosevelt, who had been dealing with the trust problem for a decade, Wilson, at the time of his nomination, had no clearly thought-out or well-fixed views on the trusts. Not until after he met with and was instructed by the progressive lawyer Louis D. Brandeis, in August and September of 1912, did he develop a coherent position. Once he had found a program, however, Wilson made the trusts the main issue of his campaign.*

SPEECH AT SIOUX FALLS, SOUTH DAKOTA, SEPTEMBER 17, 1912

• • • • • • • • • • • • • • • •

THERE was a time when we could indulge in all sorts of pleasantries at each other's expense in politics. But every time I find myself tempted to pleasantry there comes over me a feeling of the critical seriousness of the choice to be made in the year 1912, not the critical seriousness, ladies and gentlemen, of choosing between one man and another man, for there is no indispensable man, but the criticalness of choosing between one policy and another. We are at the parting of the ways. As we determine the direction which we take in 1912 we shall determine the future political development and the future economic development of the United States of America. It looks like a very small difference sometimes when you state it, but you know that where roads come together the separation is small but where they end the separation is not small. Although it may seem that they are choosing just to deviate a little in this direction or a little in that, remember where they are going to lead. Remember where the finger of that road points and make up your mind what the goal is at the other end.

There is one proposition upon which this campaign turns. I have repeated it very often already in other speeches and I am going to repeat it until I am sure everybody's heard it. That proposition is this: that monopoly is inevitable. That is what some of the people who want us to adopt a certain purpose maintain, and that is what I deny. If monopoly is inevitable, then the thing to

* WILSON CALLS FOR REGULATED COMPETITION: From John Wells Davidson, ed., *A Crossroads of Freedom: The 1912 Campaign Speeches of Woodrow Wilson* (New Haven, 1956), pp. 167–73, 346–53. Reprinted by permission of the editor.

do is for the government to take hold of monopoly and regulate it. If monopoly is not inevitable, then the thing for law to do is to break it up and prevent its forming again. I believe that monopoly can be broken up. If I didn't believe it, I would know that all the roads of free development were shut in this country.

The reason I say that this campaign depends upon that proposition is this: I understand the leaders of the third party, for example, to have a great many attractive things in their program. Nevertheless, they start with this proposition: that the big combinations which now control business in this country are inevitable, and that the best we can do is to establish an industrial commission which will take charge of them and see to it that they are good to us. I deny the fundamental proposition. I deny that these big combinations are inevitable. And I can prove that they were not inevitable by the processes by which they were established.

. . . The object of these combinations that have been formed in our time is to shut competition out and to get control of the market by seeing to it that there is no successful competition such as will bring prices down. The most conspicuous example of it is the Steel Trust.

There was one particular set of factories, or rather of mills, which the gentlemen who first put their heads together to set up this would-be monopoly found that it was most difficult to deal with. There was one man in the United States who knew how to manufacture steel rails so cheaply and had such a genius for the organization of business upon an economic scale and for its development by the discovery of finer and finer devices for cheapening the production that nobody else in the United States could compete with his brains in that particular line. His name was Andrew Carnegie. When the Steel Trust came to be formed Andrew Carnegie didn't care to come into it. Why should he come into it? He could undersell every man of them. There wasn't any reason why he should wish to come in when the market was his already for the asking. And they had to pay him—I have forgotten how many times—I think it was four times the value of his plant and of his business in order to get him out of the way; and they had to pay a number of other gentlemen, other independent mills and independent business in this field, very much more than their business was known to be worth in order to get them to come into the combination. It wasn't worth their while in view of their already established success to come into this combination unless they were paid so much more than their business was worth that they were willing to give the business up.

Then what happened? They made a combination upon which they issued securities to the amount representing, let's say, four times the value of Mr. Carnegie's business and several times the value of other businesses which they had absorbed. Then they based the new price of steel on the interest they had to pay on those securities, didn't they?

In other words, they are making us pay for steel on the most uneconomic and inefficient basis that can be imagined. And when these gentlemen say that these big combinations are necessary for economy and efficiency, the only answer I can think of that meets the suggestion is: Rats! Go and tell all that to the Marines. Go and tell that to somebody that doesn't even read the daily newspapers. Don't venture to tell it to anybody who knows the circumstances by which these combinations were made and the diligence with which these gentlemen have seen to it that understandings with regard to price should not be broken.

Why would anybody desire to break the understanding because it was possible to sell cheaper and capture the market? And these men were interested in seeing that nobody would sell cheaper and capture the market when it was possible for the man who had brains, exercised economy and ingenuity, and knew how to assemble the parts of his plant at any time he chose, to make steel cheaper and undersell them.

These combinations were made not for efficiency but to control and keep up the price. They were meant to control the domestic market, and just so soon as you make it possible to compete with these gentlemen you'll see a very great change in their business. I don't want to put them out of business. I simply want to make them attend to business. I want to make sure that steel and everything else that illustrates my subject is made as cheaply and as well as possible in America, and that profits and the successes of enterprise are not founded upon anything else but brains and success.

But the gentlemen of the third party say: "You are very much more mistaken. It may be that many inequities were practiced in the establishing of these things, but they were built up. And now they have become a constituted and necessary part of our modern business and the only thing we can do is to regulate them, is to regulate the memberships, is to legalize the thing that ought never to have been done and need never to have been done, and to see to it through a government agency, through a government commission, that they treat us kindly; that they don't impose upon us; that they are gentle in the market; that they don't do anybody any more harm; that they are shot through with the kindliness of Christianity."

Now, I don't expect to convert the trusts by any special means of evangelization. Moreover, when you have set up a government that has the right to create a commission of that sort, what temptation, I would like to have you tell me, have you added to the present almost overwhelming temptations of politics? If the President of the United States can through a commission guide the business of the United States, soon the businessmen of the United States who are interested in these combinations will put forth greater ingenuity and endeavor than ever to capture the Presidency of the United States. Ah, gentlemen, don't deceive yourselves. If men control business, then business will seek to control men. The only salvation for this country is that law shall control business. Now here is the parting of the ways.

You say, "Well, if we are not going to legalize the trusts and control them, what are we going to do?" Well, haven't you observed how the trusts were built up? You say, "Are you going to return by law to the old-fashioned competition?" I say, "No." It is the old-fashioned competition that enabled these men to build up these combinations, because the old-fashioned competition used in the new way was this: Here is a man with some personal capital, or with some personal credit at the local bank, and he tries to set out in a little business. Here in another city is a great combination of men with millions of money at their back who come there and say: "You are a mighty little fellow and you can't come into this thing. We don't want any interlopers here. You have got only your little local market. Very well, we will cut into your little local market and sell at a loss, sell at a figure that you can't possibly sell at because everywhere else in the United States we will sell at a profitable figure, meet our losses in your locality, and we will put you out of business." That is not a fictitious, hypothetical case. That thing has happened by scores and hundreds of instances all over the United States. Now, that is competition, but what sort of competition is it?

The alternative to regulating monopoly is to regulate competition: to say that to go into a community and sell below cost for no other purpose—for it can't be the purpose of profit—for no other purpose than to squeeze out a competitor shall be an offense against the criminal law of the United States, and anybody who attempts it will have to answer at the bar of a criminal tribunal. It won't make any difference whether he is big or little, he will have to answer at that tribunal; for we have been having trials and investigations by Congress, and we know the processes of unrestricted competition by which these men have accomplished the setting up of their monopolies. If we don't know how to stop them, then the lawyers of this country have lost their ingenuity and their intelligence. . . .

We shall be getting on the inside of a lot of the big business of the United States. And I venture to say that with the proper kind of legal advice you and I could easily sit down together and stop these things overnight. That is what I call the regulation of competition, saying: "Oh, yes, up to a certain point you can use your great power, a giant against a pigmy. But let me warn you that if you put that pigmy out of business, the pigmy will prove bigger than you are. He will stay out of the penitentiary and you will go in."

Choose your course then, gentlemen, on the fifth of November. Adopt the great trusts into the family and depend upon your government to make them be good, or else take the course by which it will be impossible for them to live by anything except economy and brains. Let your government patronize them, or else put them on their mettle and let them survive, as all honest business ought to be able to survive, in the open competition of the market.

"The Only Way to Dispel Fear," Speech at Lincoln, Nebraska, October 5, 1912

. . . .

Now, we are not going to discuss tonight the sympathies, the susceptibilities, the enthusiasms of the several men who are seeking your suffrages for President of the United States. I am perfectly ready to believe and will admit for the sake of argument that Mr. Roosevelt's heart and soul are committed to that part of the third-term program which contains those hopeful plans of human betterment in which so many noble men and women in this country have enlisted their sympathies and their energies.

I am not here to criticize anybody who has been drawn to that party because of that part of the program. But I want to call their attention to the fact that you can't have a program that you can carry out through a resisting and unsuitable medium, and that the thing that it is absolutely necessary for every candid voter to remember with regard to the third party is that the means of government, the means of getting the things that this country needs, are exactly the same on that side that they are on the side where Mr. Taft seeks the suffrages of the country. Because, while the party of Mr. Taft says in its platform that monopoly ought not to exist, the section of the Republican party that is following Mr. Roosevelt subscribes to the statement that monopoly ought to be adopted by the law, and by regulation should be the governing force in the development of American industry. So that all that the third party asks of the monopolists is that they should cooperate, and the only hope of a program of human uplift from that party is that the monopolists will cooperate.

Have you got any hopes in that direction? Don't you know what the Republican party has provided you with up to this time? I have taken special pains to clear from my own mind, at any rate, the Republican conception of government. That conception is that the people cannot organize their opinion in such fashion as to control their own government. And that, therefore, it is necessary constantly to consult those whose material interests in the development of the country are larger than anybody else's, and then through the hands of these trustees administer the government, not through the people but for the people. I am perfectly ready to believe—knowing some of the men concerned as I do, I must believe—that a great many men engaged in the promotion of monopoly in this country really wish to see the United States prosperous, and really desire to adopt the means that will make it prosperous. But they are not willing to let anybody else yield the means of prosperity except themselves. I wonder at the frame of mind which makes them believe that they are the trustees of political discretion in this country, but I am willing to admit for the sake of argument that that is their candid and deliberate judgment.

What we have to fight, therefore, is not a body of deliberate enemies, it may be, but a body of mistaken men. And what I want to point out to you is that Mr. Roosevelt subscribes to the judgment of these mistaken men as to the influences which should govern America. That is the serious part of it. Mr. Roosevelt's judgment has been captured. Mr. Roosevelt's idea of the way in which the industries of this country ought to be controlled has been captured. He does not propose to set us free. He proposes to use monopoly in order to make us happy. And the project is one of those projects which all history cries out against as impossible.

The Democratic platform is the only platform which says that private monopoly is indefensible and intolerable, and any man who does not subscribe to that opinion does not know the way to set the people of the United States free, and to serve humanity. All that Mr. Roosevelt is asking you to do is to elect him president of the board of trustees. I do not care how wise, how patriotic the trustees may be, I have never heard of any group of men in whose hands I am willing to put the liberties of America in trust. And, therefore, I am not in this campaign engaged in doubting any man's motives, I merely want to point out that these gentlemen are not proposing the methods of liberty but are proposing the methods of control. A control amongst a free people is intolerable.

I have been very much interested the last day or two in having described to me the industries of some of these smaller western cities. I know in Indiana, for example, town after town was pointed out to me that still has the American characteristic, in which there are factories upon factories owned by men who live in the place—independent enterprises still unabsorbed by the great economic combinations which have become so threateningly inhuman in our economic organization—and it seems to me that these are outposts and symbols of the older and freer America. And after I had traveled through that series of towns and met the sturdy people that live in them, I entered in the city of Gary, which is a little way outside of Chicago, and realized that I had come from the older America into the newer America. But this was a town owned and built by a single monopolistic corporation. And I wondered which kind of America the people of America, if they could see this picture as I saw it, would choose?

Which do you want? Do you want to live in a town patronized by some great combination of capitalists who pick it out as a suitable place to plant their industry and draw you into their employment? Or do you want to see your sons and your brothers and your husbands build up business for themselves under the protection of laws which make it impossible for any giant, however big, to crush them and put them out of business, so that they can match their wits here in the midst of a free country with any captain of industry or merchant of finance to be found anywhere in the world, and put every man who now assumes to control and promote monopoly upon his mettle to beat them at initiative, at economy, at the organization of business, and the cheap production of salable goods? Which do you want?

Why, gentlemen, America is never going to submit to monopoly. America is never going to choose thralldom instead of freedom. Look what there is to decide! There is the tariff question. Can the tariff question be decided in favor of the people of the United States so long as the monopolies are the chief counselors at Washington? There is the great currency question. You know how difficult it is to move your crops every year. And I tremble, I must frankly tell you, to think of the bumper crops that are now coming from our fields, because they are going to need enormous bodies of cash to move them. You have got to get that cash by calling in your loans and embarrassing people in every center of commercial activity, because there isn't cash enough under our inelastic currency to lend itself to this instrumentality. And are we going to settle the currency question so long as the government of the United States listens only to the counsel of those who command the banking situation in the United States? You can't solve the tariff, you can't solve the currency question under the domination which is proposed by one branch of the Republican party and tolerated by the other.

Then there is the great question of conservation. What is our fear about conservation? The hands that will be stretched out to monopolize our forests, to pre-empt the use of our great power-producing streams, the hands that will be stretched into the bowels of the earth to take possession of the great riches that lie hidden in Alaska and elsewhere in the incomparable domain of the United States are the hands of monopoly. And is this thing merely to be regulated? Is this thing to be legalized? Are these men to continue to stand at the elbow of government and tell us how we are to save ourselves from the very things that we fear? You can't settle the question of conservation while monopoly exists if monopoly is close to the ears of those who govern. And the question of conservation is a great deal bigger than the question of saving our forests and our mineral resources and our waters. It is as big as the life and happiness and strength and elasticity and hope of our people.

The government of the United States has now to look out upon her people and see what they need, what should be done for them. Why, gentlemen, there are tasks waiting the government of the United States which it cannot perform until every pulse of that government beats in unison with the needs and the desires of the whole body of the American people. Shall we not give the people access of sympathy, access of counsel, access of authority to the instrumentalities which are to be indispensable to their lives? . . .

Fear is abroad in free America. There are men who dare not undertake certain business enterprises because they know that they would be crushed. There are men who dare not speak certain opinions because they know that they would be boycotted in influential circles upon which their credit and their advancement in their business depends.

Do you suppose that it is singular that men should rise up and fight through half a generation as your own champions have fought in order to dispel that fear? The only way to dispel fear is to bring the things that you are afraid of out in the open and challenge them there to meet the great moral force of the people of the United States. So that if these gentlemen will come out and avow their purposes, they will destroy all possibility of realizing those purposes. . . .

America is as rich, not as Wall Street, not as the financial centers in Chicago and St. Louis and San Francisco; [but] it is as rich as the people that make its centers rich. And if those people hesitate in their enterprise, cowering in the face of power, hesitate to originate designs of their own, then the very foundations which make these places abound in wealth are dried up at the source; so that by setting the little men of America free you are not damaging the giants. You are merely making them behave like human beings. . . .

It may be that certain things will happen, for monopoly in this country is carrying a body of water such as no body of men ought to be asked to carry. And when by regulated competition—that is to say, fair competition, competition that fights fair—they are put upon their mettle, they will have to economize in their processes of business and they can't economize unless they drop that water. I do not know how to squeeze the water out but they will get rid of it, if you will put them on their mettle. They will have to get rid of it, or those of us who don't carry tanks will outrun them in the race. Put all the business of America upon the footing of economy and efficiency, and then let the race be to the strongest and the efficient.

So that our program is a program of prosperity, only it is a program of prosperity that is a little more pervasive [than] the present program—and pervasive prosperity is more fruitful than that which is narrow and restrictive. . . .

4] Congress Legislates

Wilson and the slogans of the New Freedom triumphed at the polls. During 1913, Wilson devoted his attention to banking reform and tariff reform. But, on January 20, 1914, following the passage of the Federal Reserve Act and the Underwood Tariff, he went before Congress to explain his program for trust control. In September and October of 1914, Congress passed the Federal Trade Commission Act and the Clayton Antitrust Act. One month later, Wilson announced that the reform movement had accomplished its purposes and was now complete. "We have only to look back ten years or so," he observed, "to realize the deep perplexities and dangerous ill-humors out of which we have at last issued, as if from a bewildering fog, a noxious miasma." *

THE FEDERAL TRADE COMMISSION ACT
September 26, 1914

. . . .

BE IT ENACTED . . . That a commission is hereby created and established, to be known as the Federal Trade Commission (hereafter referred to as the commission), which shall be composed of five commissioners, who shall be appointed by the President, by and with the advice and consent of the Senate. Not more than three of the commissioners shall be members of the same political party. . . .

SEC. 3. That upon the organization of the commission and election of its chairman, the Bureau of Corporations and the officers of Commissioner and Deputy Commissoner of Corporations shall cease to exist; and all pending investigations and proceedings of the Bureau of Corporations shall be continued by the commission. . . .

SEC. 5. That unfair methods of competition in commerce are hereby declared unlawful.

The commission is hereby empowered and directed to prevent persons, partnerships, or corporations, except banks, and common carriers subject to the Acts to regulate commerce, from using unfair methods of competition in commerce.

Whenever the commission shall have reason to believe that any such person, partnership, or corporation has been or is using any unfair method of competition in commerce, . . . it shall issue and serve upon such person, partnership, or corporation a complaint stating its charges in that respect, and containing a notice of a hearing upon a day and at a place therein fixed at least thirty days after the service of said complaint. The person, partnership, or corporation so complained of shall have the right to appear at the place and time so fixed and show cause why an order should not be entered by the com-

---

* CONGRESS LEGISLATES: From the Federal Trade Commission Act, *The Statutes at Large of the United States of America* (Washington, 1915), XXXVIII, part 1, 717–22; and the Clayton Antitrust Act, *Ibid.*, XXXVIII, 730–34, 738.

mission requiring such person, partnership, or corporation to cease and desist from the violation of the law so charged in said complaint. . . . If upon such hearing the commission shall be of the opinion that the method of competition in question is prohibited by this Act, it shall make a report in writing in which it shall state its findings as to the facts, and shall issue and cause to be served on such persons, partnership, or corporation an order requiring such person, partnership, or corporation to cease and desist from using such method of competition. . . .

SEC. 6. That the commission shall also have power—

(a) To gather and compile information concerning and to investigate from time to time the organization, business, conduct, practices, and management of any corporation engaged in commerce, excepting banks and common carriers subject to the Act to regulate commerce, and its relation to other corporations and to individuals, associations, and partnerships.

(b) To require . . . corporations engaged in commerce, excepting banks, and common carriers subject to the Act to regulate commerce, . . . to file with the commission in such form as the commission may prescribe annual or special, or both annual and special, reports or answers in writing to specific questions, furnishing to the commission such information as it may require as to the organization, business, conduct, practices, management, and relation to other corporations, partnerships, and individuals of the respective corporations filing such reports. . . .

(c) Whenever a final decree has been entered against any defendant corporation in any suit brought by the United States to prevent and restrain any violation of the antitrust Acts, to make investigation, . . . of the manner in which the decree has been or is being carried out, . . . it shall be its duty to make such investigation. It shall transmit to the Attorney General a report embodying its findings and recommendations as a result of any such investigation, and the report shall be made public in the discretion of the commission.

(d) Upon the direction of the President or either House of Congress to investigate and report the facts relating to any alleged violations of the antitrust Acts by any corporation.

(e) Upon the application of the Attorney General to investigate and make recommendations for the readjustment of the business of any corporation alleged to be violating the antitrust Acts in order that the corporation may thereafter maintain its organization, management, and conduct of business in accordance with law.

(f) To make public from time to time such portions of the information obtained by it hereunder, except trade secrets and names of customers, as it shall deem expedient in the public interest; and to make annual and special reports to the Congress and to submit therewith recommendations for additional legislation; and to provide for the publication of its reports and decisions in such form and manner as may be best adapted for public information and use.

(g) From time to time to classify corporations and to make rules and regulations for the purpose of carrying out the provisions of this Act.

The Clayton Antitrust Act
October 15, 1914

. . . .

Sec. 2. That it shall be unlawful for any person engaged in commerce, in the course of such commerce, either directly or indirectly to discriminate in price between different purchasers of commodities . . . where the effect of such discrimination may be to substantially lessen competition or tend to create a monopoly in any line of commerce: . . .

Sec. 3. That it shall be unlawful for any person engaged in commerce, in the course of such commerce, to lease or make a sale or contract for sale of goods . . . or fix a price charged therefor, or discount from, or rebate upon, such price, on the condition, . . . that the lessee or purchaser thereof shall not use or deal in the goods . . . of a competitor or competitors of the lessor or seller, where the effect of such lease, sale, or contract for sale or such condition, agreement, or understanding may be to substantially lessen competition or tend to create a monopoly in any line of commerce. . . .

Sec. 6. That the labor of a human being is not a commodity or article of commerce. Nothing contained in the antitrust laws shall be construed to forbid the existence and operation of labor, agricultural, or horticultural organizations, instituted for the purposes of mutual help, and not having capital stock or conducted for profit, or forbid or restrain individual members of such organizations from lawfully carrying out the legitimate objects thereof; nor shall such organizations, or members thereof, be held or construed to be illegal combinations or conspiracies in restraint of trade, under the antitrust laws.

Sec. 7. That no corporation engaged in commerce shall acquire, directly or indirectly, the whole or any part of the stock or other share capital of another corporation engaged also in commerce, where the effect of such acquisition may be to substantially lessen competition . . .

Sec. 8. That from and after two years from the date of the approval of this Act no person shall at the same time be a director or other officer or employee of more than one bank, banking association or trust company, organized or operating under the laws of the United States, either of which has deposits, capital, surplus, and undivided profits aggregating more than $5,000,000; and no private banker or person who is a director in any bank or trust company, organized and operating under the laws of a State, having deposits, capital, surplus, and undivided profits aggregating more than $5,000,000, shall be eligible to be a director in any bank or banking association organized or operating under the laws of the United States. . . .

That from and after two years from the date of the approval of this Act no person at the same time shall be a director in any two or more corporations, any one of which has capital, surplus, and undivided profits aggregating more than $1,000,000, engaged in whole or in part in commerce, other than banks, banking associations, trust companies and common carriers subject to the Act to regulate commerce, approved February fourth, eighteen hundred and eighty-seven, if such corporations are or shall have been theretofore, by virtue of their business and location of operation, competitors . . .

SEC. 10. That after two years from the approval of this Act no common carrier engaged in commerce shall have any dealings in securities, supplies, or other articles of commerce, or shall make or have any contracts for construction or maintenance of any kind, to the amount of more than $50,000, in the aggregate, in any one year, with another corporation, firm, partnership or association when the said common carrier shall have upon its board of directors or as its president, manager, or as its purchasing or selling officer, or agent in the particular transaction, any person who is at the same time a director, manager, or purchasing or selling officer of, or who has any substantial interest in, such other corporation, firm, partnership, or association, unless and except such purchases shall be made from, or such dealings shall be with, the bidder whose bid is the most favorable to such common carrier, to be ascertained by competitive bidding under regulations to be prescribed by rule or otherwise by the Interstate Commerce Commission. . . .

SEC. 20. That no restraining order or injunction shall be granted by any court of the United States, or a judge or the judges thereof, in any case between an employer and employees or between employers and employees, or between employees, or between persons employed and persons seeking employment, involving, or growing out of, a dispute concerning terms or conditions of employment, unless necessary to prevent irreparable injury to property, or to a property right, of the party making the application, for which injury there is no adequate remedy at law. . . .

CONCLUSION

THE Federal Trade Commission Act and the Clayton Antitrust Act represent the progressive era's final solution, in so far as it can be measured by legislation, to the disturbances created in American life by the emergence of the modern corporation. That solution was not, however, a clear one. The Clayton Act, with its prohibition of business practices tending "to substantially lessen competition" or "to create a monopoly," was consonant with the philosophy of the New Freedom and the attempt to control the trusts by restoring competition. But the Federal Trade Commission Act established a central federal agency to investigate and regulate the activities of large corporations which did not differ greatly from that proposed by Roosevelt and the Progressive party.

The ambiguity inherent in the passage of the two laws was reflected in the thinking of Wilson himself and in the subsequent record of his administration. By the end of 1914 Wilson had come to place his faith considerably more in the Federal Trade Commission Act than in the Clayton Act. During the succeeding years Wilson sought, in various ways, to pacify the business community, particularly by his appointments to the Federal Trade Commission and the Federal Reserve Board. His administration undertook more antitrust prosecutions than had Roosevelt's, but fewer than had Taft's. In 1916 Wilson vigorously supported the Webb Bill (passed in 1918 as the Webb-Pomerene Act), which amended the antitrust laws so as to allow American export manufacturers to combine for the purposes of selling abroad.

But the passage of the Federal Trade Commission Act and the Clayton Antitrust Act and the subsiding of the discussion of 1910–14 did mark the end of the issue of the trusts per se as a major concern of the American people. Particular questions having to do with the regulation of corporate activities were to come up in the future, especially during the period of the New Deal. But the fundamental question of the admissibility or inadmissibility of the large corporation in American life, which, in the last analysis, lay at the root of the trust problem during the progressive era, was not again a serious issue. Despite the unresolved ambiguity in their attitude, which, in fact, has never entirely disappeared, Americans gradually came to accept the large corporation as an inevitable accompaniment of modern economic conditions. In the words of John Dewey, "we do not solve" our problems; "we get over them."

STUDY QUESTIONS

1] What do the government and Standard Oil briefs reveal about the circumstances that gave rise to the modern corporation?

2] On what grounds did the government rest its charges of conspiracy and monopoly? On what grounds did Standard Oil deny the charge? Is the difference between the two one of fact or of the interpretation of fact?

3] How did the rise of the modern corporation affect the position and interests of different groups in American society?

4] On what did the witnesses called by the Senate Interstate Commerce Committee agree? On what did they disagree? Which do you think more significant, the area of agreement, or the area of disagreement?

5] Whose policy was more in accord with the realities of American economic life, Roosevelt's or Wilson's? Whose policy was more in accord with basic American values and attitudes? Is it possible to conceive of a policy that accords with both *realities* and *values?*

RECOMMENDED READINGS

PRIMARY SOURCES

Chicago Conference on Trusts (Chicago, 1900).

"Control of Corporations, Persons, and Firms Engaged in Interstate Commerce: Report of the Committee on Interstate Commerce, United States Senate," *Senate Reports*, No. 1326, 62 Cong., 3 Sess., 2 vols. (Washington, 1913).

CROLY, HERBERT. *The Promise of American Life* (New York, 1909).

DAVIDSON, JOHN WELLS, ed. *A Crossroads of Freedom: The 1912 Campaign Speeches of Woodrow Wilson* (New Haven, 1956).

"Hearings Before the Committee on Investigation of the United States Steel Corporation," *House Reports*, No. 1127, 62 Cong., 2 Sess., 8 vols. (Washington, 1912).

INDUSTRIAL COMMISSION. *Final Report*, 19 vols. (Washington, 1900–02), Vols. I, II, XIII.

LLOYD, HENRY DEMAREST. *Wealth Against Commonwealth* (New York, 1894).

MOODY, JOHN. *The Truth About the Trusts* (New York, 1904).

"Report of the Committee . . . to Investigate the Concentration of Control of Money and Credit," *House Reports*, No. 1593, 62 Cong., 3 Sess., 3 vols. (Washington, 1913).

ROOSEVELT, THEODORE. *The New Nationalism* (New York, 1911).

The Trust Problem: Replies of 16,000 Representative Americans to a Questionnaire Sent Out by Department on Regulation of Industrial Corporations of the National Civic Federation (New York, 1912).

WALLING, WILLIAM ENGLISH. *Socialism As It Is* (New York, 1912).

WEYL, WALTER. *The New Democracy* (New York, 1912).

SECONDARY SOURCES

CHANDLER, ALFRED D., JR. "The Beginnings of Big Business in American Industry," *Business History Review*, XXXIII, No. 1 (Spring, 1959).

De Witt, Benjamin Parke. *The Progressive Movement* (New York, 1915).

Goldman, Eric F. *Rendezvous With Destiny* (New York, 1952).

Hays, Samuel P. *The Response to Industrialism, 1885–1914* (Chicago, 1957).

Hofstadter, Richard. *The Age of Reform* (New York, 1955).

Jones, Eliot. *The Trust Problem in the United States* (New York, 1921).

Link, Arthur S. *Woodrow Wilson and the Progressive Era, 1910–1917* (New York, 1954).

Mowry, George E. *The Era of Theodore Roosevelt, 1900–1912* (New York, 1958).

Nye, Russell. *Midwestern Progressive Politics* (East Lansing, Mich., 1951).

Thorelli, Hans B. *The Federal Antitrust Policy* (Baltimore, 1955).

World War I:
Wilson and the Peace
of Versailles,
1919

ERNEST R. MAY

HARVARD UNIVERSITY

CONTENTS

CHRONOLOGY

1918

JANUARY 8	Wilson announces the Fourteen Points.
FEBRUARY 11	Wilson adds four principles.
SEPTEMBER 27	Regarding an Austro-Hungarian armistice intimation, Wilson outlines the five particulars of peace.
OCTOBER 6	Germany sues for an armistice on the basis of Wilson's points and principles.
NOVEMBER 5	The European allies agree that the peace will be governed by Wilson's points and principles.
NOVEMBER 5	Congressional elections give Republicans 239–193 majority in House and 49–47 majority in Senate.
NOVEMBER 11	The armistice.

1919

JANUARY 12	The Council of Ten meets in Paris.
JANUARY 18	First plenary session of the Paris Peace Conference.
FEBRUARY 14	Wilson presents a completed draft of the Covenant of the League of Nations and then departs for a brief visit to the United States.
MARCH 4	Lodge prints a "round robin" resolution saying the Covenant in its present form is unacceptable; it is signed by forty-eight senators.
MARCH 14	Wilson returns to Paris.
MARCH 24	Council of Four created.
MARCH–APRIL	Council of Four debates reparations, postwar German frontiers, and issues affecting Japan and Italy.
APRIL 7	Wilson reported preparing to re-embark for the United States and abandon the conference.
APRIL 23	Wilson's public statement on Fiume.
APRIL 24	Orlando deserts the conference.
APRIL 28	Revised text of the Covenant adopted.
APRIL 30	Settlement of the Shantung issue.
MAY 6	German treaty completed.
JUNE 2	Austrian treaty completed.
JUNE 28	Germans sign treaty at Versailles; Wilson sails for the United States.
JULY 10	Treaty formally laid before the Senate.
AUGUST– SEPTEMBER	Prolonged hearings on the treaty by the Senate Foreign Relations Committee.
SEPTEMBER 4	Wilson sets out on a nationwide speaking tour.
SEPTEMBER 25	Wilson collapses at Pueblo, Colorado.
OCTOBER 4	Wilson suffers a severe stroke.
NOVEMBER 19	Treaty defeated in the Senate.

1920

MARCH 13	Treaty revived in the Senate and defeated again.

INTRODUCTION

O N APRIL 2, 1917, Woodrow Wilson appeared before a joint session of Congress. Speaking with more than usual solemnity, he touched on his two-year struggle to dissuade Imperial Germany from using submarines against American ships and ships carrying American passengers; recited how that battle had been lost when, at the end of January, the Germans had decreed unrestricted submarine warfare; reminded his hearers that the United States had then severed diplomatic relations and moved to arm its merchantmen; and then announced regretfully that armed neutrality had been found ineffectual. Therefore, he asked, "with a profound sense of the solemn and even tragical character of the step," that Congress declare war.

He did not stop there. Going on to say that the object of the war would not be merely to punish the Germans for their transgressions, he declared:

We are glad, now that we see the facts with no veil of false pretense about them, to fight thus for the ultimate peace of the world and for the liberation of its peoples, the German peoples included: for the rights of nations great and small and the privilege of men everywhere to choose their way of life and of obedience. The world must be made safe for democracy.

These were noble words. But so were those uttered in other nations at war, including Germany, for orators in wartime have to be heard above the roar of cannon. And Wilson nearly always spoke with high-flown phrases. He was the son of a Presbyterian minister, accustomed from youth to the rhythms of the King James testaments and the cadences of the pulpit. Before turning to politics, he had been a teacher of political science and a college president, and, despite his success first as governor of New Jersey and then in the White House, he retained characteristics of the academic. With a long ascetic face and rimless spectacles perched on a thin nose, he looked the part. It was by no means certain that his war message was more than a sermon or a lecture.

As the war went on, however, he made it increasingly plain that he meant what he said. On January 8, 1918, he set forth the "program of the world's peace . . . , the only possible program," in fourteen points:

1. Open covenants of peace, openly arrived at. . . .
2. Absolute freedom of navigation upon the seas, . . . alike in peace and war. . . .
3. The removal, so far as possible, of all economic barriers and the establishment of an equality of trade conditions among all . . . nations. . . .
4. Adequate guarantees given and taken that national armaments will be reduced to the lowest points consistent with domestic safety.
5. A free, open-minded, and absolutely impartial adjustment of all colonial claims, based upon a strict observance of the principle that . . . the interests of the populations concerned must have equal weight with the equitable claims of the government whose title is to be determined.

6. The evacuation of all Russian territory and such a settlement of all questions affecting Russia as will secure . . . for her an unhampered and unembarrassed opportunity for the independent determination of her own political development and national policy. . . .

7. Belgium . . . must be evacuated and restored. . . .

8. All French territory should be freed and the invaded portions restored, and the wrong done to France by Prussia in 1871 in the matter of Alsace-Lorraine . . . should be righted. . . .

9. A readjustment of the frontiers of Italy should be effected along clearly recognizable lines of nationality.

10. The peoples of Austria-Hungary . . . should be accorded the freest opportunity of autonomous development.

11. Rumania, Serbia, and Montenegro should be evacuated; occupied territories restored; Serbia accorded free access to the sea; and the relations of the several Balkan states to one another determined by friendly counsel along historically established lines of allegiance and nationality. . . .

12. The Turkish portions of the present Ottoman Empire should be assured a secure sovereignty, but the other nationalities which are now under Turkish rule should be assured an undoubted security of life and an absolutely unmolested opportunity of autonomous development. . . .

13. An independent Polish state should be erected which should include the territories inhabited by indisputably Polish populations, which should be assured a free and secure access to the sea. . . .

14. A general association of nations must be formed under specific covenants for the purpose of affording mutual guarantees of political independence and territorial integrity to great and small states alike.

Earl Balfour, the British Foreign Secretary, subsequently termed these points "admirable but very abstract." On the other hand, Sir Harold Nicolson, a disciple of Balfour's and a lifelong student of diplomacy, describes them in *Peacemaking, 1919* as "precise to the point of recklessness."

They were added to or embellished by later utterances. On February 11, 1918, Wilson announced four "principles" which were to govern the peace:

First, that each part of the final settlement must be based upon the essential justice of that particular case and upon such adjustments as are most likely to bring a peace that will be permanent.

Second, that peoples and provinces are not to be bartered about from sovereignty to sovereignty as if they were mere chattels or pawns in a game, even the great game, now forever discredited, of the balance of power; but that

Third, every territorial settlement involved in this war must be made in the interest and for the benefit of the populations concerned . . . ; and

Fourth, that all well defined national aspirations shall be accorded the utmost satisfaction that can be accorded them without introducing new or perpetuating old elements of discord and antagonism. . . .

On September 27, 1918, commenting on an Austro-Hungarian overture for an armistice, he set forth five "particulars" of his program:

First, the impartial justice meted out must involve no discrimination between those to whom we wish to be just and those to whom we do not wish to be just. . . .

Second, no special or separate interest of any single nation or any group of nations can be made the basis of any part of the settlement which is not consistent with the common interest of all;

Third, there can be no leagues or alliances or special covenants or understandings within the general and common family of the League of Nations.

Fourth, and more specifically, there can be no special, selfish economic combinations within the League. . . .

Fifth, all international agreements and treaties of every kind must be made known in their entirety to the rest of the world.

Before the war came to an end, the whole world thus knew that the President of the United States had, if not a program, at least a vision of the new world order that peace should bring.

Moreover, the war ended with both the defeated and the victorious nations having agreed to pursue this vision. Concluding that they could fight no longer, the Germans appealed to Wilson to arrange an armistice, offering to accept his points and principles "as a basis for the peace negotiations." Before agreeing, Wilson demanded that they accept them as bases for the peace, understanding that negotiations would merely concern their application. The Germans consented. Meanwhile, Wilson had sent to Paris his alter ego, the sly, discreet honorary colonel from Texas, Edward M. House. There, by employing the threat of a separate peace, House extorted a similar concession from the Allies. They insisted only on stating reservations about "freedom of navigation" and about reserving their prerogative to make a levy on the defeated nations to pay for damage done civilians and their property. As of Armistice Day, November 11, 1918, the understanding was clear and universal that the eventual peace treaties were to be written according to Wilsonian ideals.

To work out the multifarious details of these treaties, representatives of the victorious nations gathered in Paris in January, 1919. Delegations from the United States, Britain, France, Italy, Japan, and the lesser victors met in plenary session. The work of the conference was meanwhile performed by commissions and committees on which sat individual delegates and some of the hundreds of experts who accompanied the delegations. The power of decision lay with an inner group: from January 18 to March 23, with a Council of Ten, composed of two representatives each from the United States, Britain, France, Italy, and Japan; from March 24 to June 28, with a Council of Four, the members of which were Wilson and the premiers of Britain, France, and Italy; afterward, with a Council of Five, comprising usually foreign ministers. When commission or committee recommendations won approval from the Ten, the Four, or the Five, acceptance at plenary sessions was a mere formality.

Even in the Council of Four, however, there were gradations. From beginning to end, Wilson held more power than any other individual. Not only did the pre-armistice agreements commit the other negotiators to follow his guidance, but elements in public opinion in all the Allied states supported his principles. In Italy, for example, his portrait decorated cottage walls like an icon, and a reporter overheard a peasant voicing fear lest the President name an American Protestant as Pope. This loyalty and reverence extended to many of the young experts in the Allied delegations. Wilson, in a sense, embodied the hopes of all men who believed that a better world could be built upon the ruins left by the war.

But Wilson was far from omnipotent. While he spoke for men's dreams, Georges Clemenceau of France spoke for their experience. Seventy-eight years old in 1919, he had seen the Germans invade France in 1870 as well as in 1914. His newspapers had been the critics of cabinet after cabinet; he had become famous as the "breaker of governments"; he knew how weak France was in relation to her German neighbor. Sitting at the council table, wearing a little black skullcap, his heavy eyelids often closed, a bushy mustache covering his mouth, his eczema-infected hands clothed in white gloves, he rumbled epigrammatic objections to all points and principles that threatened France's future security. "Moses gave us ten commandments and we broke them," he once said; "President Wilson gives us fourteen points and we shall see."

Instead of the even-handed justice of which Wilson had spoken, Clemenceau wanted a conqueror's peace. He desired maximum reparations from the Germans—enough to weaken Germany as well as assist the recovery of France. He wanted Germany's frontiers stripped so that she would lose the left bank of the Rhine and have on her eastern border a large and strong Poland—*"une Pologne grande et forte, très forte,"* as his Foreign Minister, Stephen Pichon, once said. And Clemenceau's voice was not one which Wilson and the others could ignore. In the first place, it spoke with comparative moderation. The army and ultranationalists in the French assembly demanded more than he; if he were humbled, they might control France; and such a France would be a shaky pillar under the peace. In the second place, Clemenceau's voice was that of the nation which, on the Allied side, had spent the most blood in the war. Over four million young Frenchmen had died or suffered wounds so that their children might live in safety, and this was an argument to which neither Wilson nor any other had a ready reply.

But the British Prime Minister, David Lloyd George, also spoke with authority. His nation had had 2,750,000 casualties and, until America's belated intervention, had largely financed the Allied cause. Alone among the Four, moreover, Lloyd George could claim with assurance to speak for his people. Clemenceau had been put in office by the assembly; France had held no elections since before the war. Wilson, though re-elected in 1916, had appealed for a Democratic Congress in 1918 and failed; majorities in both the House and Senate had gone to Republicans. Lloyd George, on the other hand, had called a general election immediately after the war and had his coalition returned with large majorities. That, coupled with the fact that cooperation from Britain and the Dominions would be indispensable for a durable peace, gave him a voice almost equal to Clemenceau's.

During the war, Lloyd George had made idealistic speeches. Indeed, his Caxton Hall address of January 4, 1918, so resembled Wilson's Fourteen Points message as to produce contemporary speculation about a secret Anglo-American understanding. But Lloyd George actually had a number of reservations concerning Wilson's principles. One of his campaign leaders in the general election had spoken of squeezing the German orange "till the pips squeak," and the popular response to this slogan had been such as to put the

Prime Minister more in Clemenceau's camp than Wilson's on the question of German reparations. Owing to his responsibility to the Dominions, he also had reason to question the fifth of Wilson's Fourteen Points. Some of the Dominion governments did not want a "free, open-minded, and absolutely impartial adjustment of all colonial claims": Australia wished to annex German New Guinea and German islands south of the equator; the Union of South Africa desired German Southwest Africa in fee simple. The British government itself wanted the fulfillment of a secret agreement with France that assigned it control of the Lebanon and Persia, and both Lloyd George's cabinet and its predecessor had entered into other secret treaties and conventions that were at variance with some of Wilson's precepts. Despite the pre-armistice compact, Lloyd George envisioned the peace in terms differing from Wilson's, and he was in a position to insist that the President compromise with him.

The various secret treaties introduced other complications. Italy had entered the war in 1915 after heated public debate in which the issue was whether she could get more by being a neutral than by becoming a belligerent. Her government had chosen the latter course only after having its *sacro egoismo* appeased by the Allies in a secret treaty that promised Italy the Tyrol, where the inhabitants were mainly Austro-German, and the Trieste region, where the population came mainly from the nationalities now fused in the new state of Yugoslavia. The fulfillment of this contract would entail serious compromises with Wilsonian principles. Yet Premier Vittorio Orlando, the fourth member of the Council of Four, insisted that it be carried out in full. At the same time, he appealed to the ideal of self-determination in order to claim additionally the city of Fiume, where an Italian population was surrounded by Yugoslavs. The logical contradictions in the Italian position proved a trial and torment to the negotiators.

So did the position of the Japanese. They had entered the war in 1914 in order to take possession of German islands north of the equator and a German leasehold in the Shantung province of China. They had no intention of abandoning these properties, and their delegates in Paris said calmly that if Japan's title were not ratified, they would not sign the treaty. They also said, moreover, that if President Wilson were such an idealist as he pretended to be, he should have no objection to including in the charter for his projected League of Nations a declaration about racial equality. Though a Georgian by birth and a Virginian by upbringing, Wilson could not gainsay this proposal, but, remembering the number of Southerners and advocates of immigration restriction in the Senate, neither could he accept it. Like the question of Italy's frontiers, the Shantung issue embarrassed the effort to write a perfect peace.

To mention these outstanding points of controversy is but to brush the surface. The negotiators in Paris were surrounded by claimants representing the lesser powers, new states of central and eastern Europe, emergent nationalities of the Middle East, Africa, and Asia, and spokesmen for such causes as disarmament, temperance, and woman suffrage. The din of their own bevies of experts was sometimes deafening. The whole atmosphere of the conference, as Nicolson recalls it, was that of "riot in a parrot house." Amid it, three men, two in their late fifties and one nearly eighty, sat day after day trying to forge agreements that would leave a world at peace for generations yet unborn.

This was their high object, only occasionally obscured by selfish wrangling. The issue in Paris was whether ideals, emotionally perceived, could be worked and molded into the precise language of a general international agreement. A second issue was whether their creation, however perfect or imperfect, could command the popular support necessary to make it work. In Paris the talk turned mainly on French or British or Italian public opinion. In the end, the most important question proved to be whether or not the whole compact could win approval from the United States Senate. The outcome of the debates, first in Paris and then in Washington, influenced the lives of all men who lived afterward.

DOCUMENTS

1] Were the German Colonies to Be Treated as Spoils of War?

> When the conference got under way, Wilson insisted successfully that the Covenant of the League of Nations should be an integral part of the peace treaty and that its framing should be the first item of business. Despite the press of other affairs, he took the chairmanship of the Commission on the League of Nations, which was charged with drafting the Covenant. But it proved impossible to draw up this document without reaching some agreement on the disposition of the former German colonies.*

[TWELFTH MEETING OF THE COUNCIL OF TEN, JANUARY 30, 1919]

PRESIDENT WILSON said that in order that the field of discussion should be defined as clearly as possible perhaps it would be better to begin with a clear statement of what was the mind of those who proposed a trusteeship by the League of Nations through the appointment of mandatories. The basis of this idea was the feeling which had sprung up all over the world against further annexation. Yet, if the Colonies were not to be returned to Germany (as all were agreed), some other basis must be found to develop them and to take care of the inhabitants of these backward territories. It was with this object that the idea of administration through mandatories acting on behalf of the League of Nations arose. This idea would be most distinctly illustrated by an example. The case of the South West Africa would be found a most favourable instance to make a clear picture. South West Africa had very few inhabitants, and those had been so maltreated, and their numbers had been so reduced under German administration, that the whole area was open to development that could not yet be determined. Therefore, either it must be attached to its nearest neighbour and so establish what would seem a natural union with South Africa, or some institution must be found to carry out the ideas all had in mind, namely, the development of the country for the benefit of those already in it, and for the advantage of those who would live there later.

This he assumed to be the principle: it was not intended to exploit any people; it was not intended to exercise arbitrary sovereignty over any people.

The purpose was to serve the people in undeveloped parts, to safeguard them against abuses such as had occurred under German administration and such

---

* WERE THE GERMAN COLONIES TO BE TREATED AS SPOILS OF WAR?: Minutes of the Twelfth and Seventeenth Meetings of the Council of Ten, January 27, January 30. From U.S. Department of State, *Papers Relating to the Foreign Relations of the United States: Paris Peace Conference*, 1919 (Washington, 1942–47), III, 740–43, 785–89, 792.

as might be found under other administrations. Further, where people and territories were undeveloped, to assure their development so that, when the time came, their own interests, as they saw them might qualify them to express a wish as to their ultimate relations—perhaps lead them to desire their union with the mandatory power. . . .

If any nation could annex territory which was previously a German Colony, it would be challenging the whole idea of the League of Nations. Under the League of Nations they were seeking to lay down a law which would rally the whole world against an outlaw, as it had rallied against Germany during the last war. Should a nation attempt to take from a mandatory the country entrusted to it, such nation would become an outlaw. When any nation became an outlaw, all nations should rise up against it, and treat it as such. If they had any confidence in the League of Nations there was not the slightest danger that anyone else except the mandatory power could take possession of any colony entrusted to it, such as New Guinea, because all the other nations would be pledged, with the United States in the lead, to take up arms for the mandatory. . . .

GENERAL BOTHA [of the Union of South Africa] said that he did not wish to go over the ground which had been traversed by his colleagues last week. German South West Africa, as everybody knew, was part and parcel of South Africa. It was a piece of land cut out of the Union. The Eastern and Southern frontiers of German South West Africa was merely lines drawn on a map.

[SEVENTEENTH MEETING OF THE COUNCIL OF TEN, JANUARY 30, 1919]

1. M. CLEMENCEAU said that it was intended that morning to continue the exchange of views on the question of the disposal of the German Colonies.

Mr. LLOYD GEORGE said that he had circulated a document to each of the representatives of the Great Powers. That document did not represent the real views of the Colonies; but it had been accepted by them as an attempt at a compromise. Great Britain had deliberately decided to accept the principle of a mandatory; but that decision had not been wholly accepted by the Dominions. The Dominions, however, were prepared to accept the conclusions reached in the document as a compromise, because they fully realized that there could be no greater catastrophe than for the delegates to separate without having come to a definite decision. It had been decided to accept the doctrine of a mandatory for all conquests in the late Turkish Empire and in the German Colonies. But three classes of mandates would have to be recognized, namely:—

Firstly: Mandates applicable to countries where the population was civilized but not yet organized—where a century might elapse before the people could be properly organized. For example, Arabia. In such cases it would be impossible to give full self-government and at the same time prevent the various tribes or units from fighting each other. It was obvious that the system to be applied to these territories must be different from that which would have to be applied to cannibal colonies, where people were eating each other.

Secondly: Mandates applicable to tropical Colonies situated a long way from the country of the possible mandatory. In other words, territories which did not form an integral part of any particular mandatory country. For example,

New Guinea. In these Colonies the full principle of a mandatory would be applied, including the "open door."

Thirdly: Mandates applicable to countries which formed almost a part of the organization of an adjoining power, who would have to be appointed the mandatory. . . .

2. President WILSON said that . . . to take the document circulated by the Prime Minister of Great Britain, he considered it to be a very gratifying paper. It made a long stride towards the composition of their differences, bringing them to within an easy stage of final agreement. . . .

The difficulty with which they were faced was not to satisfy the Powers in that Room (France, the United Kingdom, Italy and America), but to satisfy the disturbed communities of the world, mostly on the other side of the Rhine. It would be difficult to harness these communities to any kind of arrangement. It would be impossible to drive them tandem; they must be driven abreast. Mr. Lloyd George was disturbed with regard to the number of troops which had to be maintained in different parts of the world—troops which could not be withdrawn until Peace was signed. Even if an understanding could be reached with another country to replace these troops, the world would ask "Are you exchanging territories before peace is made?" For instance, it had been suggested that America should act as a mandatory. The people of America would be most disinclined to do so. He himself had succeeded in getting the people of America to do many things, and he might succeed in getting them to accept this burden also. But even if it was suggested that American troops should occupy Constantinople, or Mesopotamia, it was evident that they could not do so as they were not at war with Turkey. Therefore, it would, in his opinion, be extremely unwise to accept any form of mandate until they knew how it was intended to work.

To return to the immediate subject, could they take a clean sheet, and say that Australia, for example, would accept a mandate about New Guinea? How would that mandate be exercised . . . ? He had been accused of being a hopeless Idealist, but as a matter of fact he never accepted an ideal until he could see its practical application. The practical application was always the more difficult. Mandatories might work unsatisfactorily under one programme, whilst they might work well under another. Therefore no one should accept the scheme unless it was shown how it was going to work. The mandatory system was not intended to satisfy merely the interests of the mandatory Power but to care for, protect and develop the people for whom it was intended. Consequently to hand over distinguishable people to a mandatory in perpetuity and to say: "You never shall have a voice in your future; you are finally disposed of," would be contrary to the principles of that Conference and contrary to the principles of self-determination accepted by it. . . . But, whilst accepting the paper of Mr. Lloyd George as a precursor of agreement, it did not constitute a rock foundation, as the League of Nations had not yet been fixed, on which this superstructure would rest.

. . . The Great Powers had agreed that the League of Nations should form an integral part of the Peace Treaty. Therefore, it would not be accepted by itself, and to make the document presented by Mr. Lloyd George valid, they were bound to complete a preliminary peace. He thought that could be done in a few weeks. Disinterested students had been studying territorial questions on documentary evidence of every kind, working like scholars and basing their conclusions on acknowledged facts as far as they were ascertainable. If a map of Europe were produced showing the limits of the territories to be created, based on historical, racial and economic facts, the Great Powers could then sit down to consider these suggestions and give weight to those points of view, such as expediency, natural antagonisms, etc., which played no part in scholarly wisdom. They could then arrive at a conclusion quickly and be able to conclude the preliminary peace, and the League of Nations would thereby be established without the haunting element of conjecture. In every instance the mandate should fit the case as the glove fits the hand. In conclusion, accepting the document presented by Mr. Lloyd George as practically clearing away all prospects of serious differences he thought they should build upon this agreement the solid foundations which would carry this super-structure. . . .

M. Clemenceau enquired what subject should next be placed on the agenda now that Mr. Lloyd George's resolutions had been accepted. From what had been said it would appear that everything depended on a decision being reached regarding the constitution of the League of Nations, consequently, the meeting would be bound to wait until the League of Nations had been established, and it would be obviously useless to discuss the claims of the Roumanians, Yugo-Slavs and others. If he had correctly interpreted what had been said that morning he felt compelled to make serious formal reservations. In his opinion it would be impossible to establish a League of Nations which was not to be a common organism of defence, but an organism to deal with all the world. Furthermore, if this new constitution for the whole world was to be produced in eight days he was bound to feel some anxiety.

2] Teeth for the League?

In the Commission on the League of Nations, however, Wilson had to do battle with the French members, Léon Bourgeois and François Larnaude, who there insisted that the proposed organization should be one really capable of enforcing the peace.*

Mr. Bourgeois. . . . read the following note, and asked that it be inserted in the minutes:

. . . .

"According to the Draft which has just been adopted . . . , even in case of an unanimous agreement, if a Power, acting in bad faith, and being the pos-

---

* teeth for the league?: Minutes of the Eighth Meeting of the Commission on the League of Nations, February 11, 1919. From David Hunter Miller, *The Drafting of the Covenant* (New York, 1928), II, 290–91, 293–94, 296–97.

sessor of the thing in dispute, refuses to abide by the judgment of the arbitrators or the decision of the Executive Committee, the League of Nations is not legally bound to ensure the fulfilment of the decree. In view of the necessary consequences, it is imperative that stronger provisions be introduced in order to protect a State acting in good faith against a State which is acting in bad faith.

"Otherwise it would happen that nations faithful to their international obligations would suffer as the result of an organisation effective in appearance, but in reality a trap for nations of good faith.

"Our Commission certainly does not want this, and indeed it would be too much in conflict with the principles of justice so forcibly expressed by President Wilson.

"I feel all the more impelled to offer these observations now for the reason that since we have been working here a trend of opinion has developed revealing a spirit of uneasiness to which I must call your attention.

"Our colleagues representing Great Britain and the United States have very justly called attention to the serious consideration which they must give to the public opinion of their nations, and to the necessity that their Governments should not be involved in sacrifices beyond those which are at the same time demanded and delimited by the very principles of the League of Nations.

"In the presence of these evidences of uneasiness, shall we not together examine carefully the articles which we adopted at the time of the first reading? In this way we can make whatever changes are necessary in order to secure the unqualified approval of the public opinion of our respective countries. . . ."

President WILSON. We must make a distinction between what is possible and what is not. No nation will consent to control. As for us Americans, we cannot consent to control because of our Constitution. We must do everything that is possible to ensure the safety of the world. Some plan must be worked out by which every country shall have a sufficient force, first, to maintain its national security, secondly, to contribute to international safety.

It may be admitted that France should maintain a force proportionately more considerable than other nations, on account of the geographical risk that has been mentioned, but as to the construction of an unified military machine in time of peace, that is quite another question. This war made apparent the absolute necessity of the unity of command, and this unity of command constituted an immense advantage which had a decisive influence on the very issue of the war, but the unity of command only became possible because of the immediate and imminent danger which threatened civilisation. To propose to realise unity of command in time of peace, would be to put forward a proposal that no nation would accept. The Constitution of the United States forbids the President to send beyond its frontiers the national forces. If the United States maintained an army, there would always be a certain inevitable delay in sending it to the States where it might be required. And it is possible that the Germans may gather together once more their military power. If the militarist madness has not been destroyed in Germany by this war, a new menace may threaten us, but this menace will not develop suddenly. The economic condition of Germany will make that impossible.

As for us, if we organise from now onwards an international army, it would appear that we were substituting international militarism for national militarism. Some eminent Frenchmen have already told me that they would not accept what the American Constitution forbids me to accept. I know how France has suffered, and I know that she wishes to obtain the best guarantees possible before she enters the League, and everything that we can do in this direction we shall do, but we cannot accept proposals which are in direct contradiction to our Constitution.

The argument which has been most employed against the League of Nations in America, is that the army of the United States would be at the disposal of an international council, that American troops would thus be liable to be ordered to fight at any moment for the most remote of causes and this prospect alarms our people. There is therefore no other course open to us but to accept some system compatible at once with our Constitution and with the views of our public opinion. . . .

Mr. LARNAUDE. Several nations which have taken part in this war are afraid of having made sacrifices in vain. The protection which results from the existence of a League of Nations will perhaps become a guarantee of safety, but within what period of time? Perhaps within a hundred years. By that time the militarist spirit will no doubt have disappeared, but at the present moment we are emerging from a terrible war. Can it be thought that we shall pass immediately from the state of intensive militarism in which we live to a state of practical disarmament?

To-day we are in a period of transition. We must have national contingents always ready to reassure the States within the League. The sacrifice which is asked of each State will be negligible beside this. The idea of an international force is bound up with the very idea of the League of Nations, unless one is content that the League should be a screen of false security.

President WILSON. It must not be supposed that any of the members of the League will remain isolated if it is attacked, that is the direct contrary of the thought of all of us. We are ready to fly to the assistance of those who are attacked, but we cannot offer more than the condition of the world enables us to give.

Mr. LARNAUDE. If the Treaty of Peace gives us absolute guarantees that Germany will be virtually disarmed, and will not be able to build up her armaments again, then we shall feel safer.

Mr. BOURGEOIS. The dilemma has been put to us in the following manner: Is France prepared to enter into a League of Nations such as is defined in the Covenant, that is to say, without the organisation of an international army, or would she prefer to stand alone?

We must equally call your attention to the fact that we are ourselves disposed to submit to the corresponding obligations, that is to say, to our armies, and our military preparations being controlled by the League. Other nations say they cannot consent to this control. Nevertheless, there can be no rule of justice and of safety among the different nations of the world if every State can at its will prepare an attack. Opposition to the essential principles of the League of Nations does not therefore come from our side.

President WILSON. The only method by which we can achieve this end lies in our having confidence in the good faith of the nations who belong to the League. There must be between them a cordial agreement and good will. Take a new State which is going to enter this League, Poland. We have confidence in Poland, we hope that she will co-operate willingly in our efforts, and that she will take the necessary measures to secure her safety, and also to make the principles of the League respected. I therefore ask the French Delegation to consider this question again, for I think that any control, by whatever name it may be called, will be too offensive to be adopted. All that we can promise, and we do promise it, is to maintain our military forces in such a condition that the world will feel itself in safety. When danger comes, we too will come, and we will help you, but you must trust us. We must all depend on our mutual good faith.

3] Danger Signals from Home

By February 14, 1919, a draft Covenant had been completed, and Wilson presented it to a plenary session of the conference, saying, "a living thing is born." He then sailed for a short visit to his homeland, where he discovered opposition to the Covenant that was even more alarming than what he had encountered in Paris. Republican senators were irritated that the President had taken with him to Paris no conspicuous figures from their party and no representatives of the Foreign Relations Committee. They bared their vexation by putting into the *Congressional Record* a resolution terming the Covenant, in its present form, unacceptable. Since this document was signed by forty-eight senators, more than enough to block ratification of the final treaty, Wilson was put on notice that the Covenant would have to be amended. As he returned to Paris, he received from the Democratic leader of the Senate the following advice.*

A NUMBER of republican Senators who signed Lodge's manifesto on the league of nations constitution will, in my opinion, vote for it nevertheless if it is a part of the peace treaty. A still larger number will give it support if certain amendments are made. The following I would mention as likely to influence votes in the order given:

First, a reservation to each high contracting party of its exclusive control over domestic subjects.

Second, a reservation of the Monroe doctrine.

Third, some provision by which a member of the league can, on proper notice, withdraw from membership. . . .

I wish you a safe journey.

* DANGER SIGNALS FROM HOME: Gilbert M. Hitchcock to Woodrow Wilson, March 4, 1919. From Ray Stannard Baker, *Woodrow Wilson and the World Settlement* (New York, 1923), III, 174. Reprinted by permission of Doubleday & Co., Inc., and Mrs. Rachel Baker Napier.

4] Amending the Covenant

Resignedly, Wilson reconvened the League of Nations Commission in order to insert the necessary amendments into the Covenant. The first that he brought forward followed the sense of Hitchcock's third suggestion.*

WITH reference to his amendment, which read as follows:—

"After the expiration of ten years from the ratification of the Treaty of Peace, of which this Covenant forms a part, any State member of the League may, after giving one year's notice of its intention, withdraw from the League, provided all its international obligations and all its obligations under this Covenant shall have been fulfilled at the time of its withdrawal."

President Wilson stated that he thought that if the League were successful it would be morally impossible for a State to withdraw.

Mr. Larnaude said that the world demanded something definite: the essence of the idea of the League was that it was to be a permanent thing. The placing of a ten years' time limit would give the idea that the success of the League was not hoped for.

President Wilson said that he had no idea of limiting the duration of the League, but sovereign States could not permanently be bound. . . .

Mr. Larnaude was not convinced. He stated that for some time past national sovereignty had been a fiction. He wanted not to make a Treaty on the old lines, but to strike out on new lines and provide a substitute for the old order of international relations. He thought that the giving of notice by a Great Power would throw the League into confusion. If a League were to be established at all, the foundation should be firm.

President Wilson said that he did not entertain the smallest fear that any State would take advantage of the proposed clause. Any State which did so would become an outlaw. The sovereignty of their own country was the fetish of many public men. If they entered into a permanent arrangement they would feel that they were surrendering this sovereignty. America valued her sovereignty more highly than most nations. Americans would have to be assured that they were not giving up the sovereignty of their State. He thought that the clause would have no practical effects, while its omission might have very serious results. It was necessary to avoid such consequences by making concessions to existing prejudice and thus avoiding risks. The time would come when men would be just as eager partisans of the sovereignty of mankind as they were now of their own national sovereignty. He himself would be in a very awkward position if the amendment was not passed, since in the earlier sessions of the Commission he alone had been anti-secessionist, and had reluctantly acquiesced in the opinion of the Commission that the right to withdraw should exist. No State would have a moral right to withdraw. States

* AMENDING THE COVENANT: Minutes of the Thirteenth Meeting of the Commission on the League of Nations, March 26, 1919. From David Hunter Miller, *The Drafting of the Covenant* (New York, 1928), II, 357–59.

would have a legal right, that was all that he proposed to admit. He was afraid that the Senate would not agree to come in if the right to withdraw did not somewhere exist. He had frequently stated this understanding in America.

5] The Question of French Security Mounts

> Wilson had rejected French proposals for giving teeth to the League of Nations. Now he was asking in the League Commission that they accept amendments to the Covenant while, at the same time, he was encountering in the Council of Four Clemenceau's pleas for a peace that would give security to France.*

[MEETING OF THE COUNCIL OF FOUR, MARCH 27, 1919]

President WILSON.—I hope you are in agreement in principle with Mr. Lloyd George on the moderation which it is necessary to display toward Germany. We do not want to and we cannot destroy her: our greatest mistake would be to give them powerful reasons for one day wanting to take their revenge. Excessive conditions would sow the certain seed of war.

Everywhere we have to modify frontiers and alter national sovereignties. There is nothing which carries more danger, for these changes controvert long established habits, changing the very life of peoples at the same time that they touch their emotions. It is necessary to avoid giving our enemies even the impression of injustice. I do not fear in the future wars launched through secret conspiracies of governments but rather conflicts engendered by the discontent of populations. If we make ourselves guilty of working injustice, such discontent is inevitable, with the consequences which will follow. Hence our desire to act with moderation and equity. . . .

M. CLEMENCEAU.—I have said . . . that I am entirely in agreement with Mr. Lloyd George and President Wilson on the manner of dealing with Germany; we do not wish to abuse our victory; we must deal with the people with caution and fear provoking an uprising of the national conscience. . . .

I appreciate the precept of President Wilson, which I accept, but which I cannot apply to the Germans without introducing a certain reservation. The Germans must not, says President Wilson, be given a sense of injustice. All right, but that which we here will find just, in this room, will not necessarily be accepted as such by the Germans. . . .

The Germans are a servile people who must have force to support an argument. Napoleon said before dying: "Nothing is permanent which is not founded on force." I am not sure of that, for it suffices to look at the great nations of Europe and the United States themselves in order to arouse doubts.

---

* THE QUESTION OF FRENCH SECURITY MOUNTS: Minutes of Sessions of the Council of Four, March 27, March 28, 1919. From Paul Mantoux, *Les délibérations du Conseil des Quatre (24 mars–28 juin 1919)* (Paris, 1955), I, 41–45, 68–72. Translations by Ernest R. May. Reprinted by permission of the Centre National de la Recherche Scientifique.

That which is true is that force cannot establish anything solid unless it is at the service of justice. It is necessary to do everything in order to be just toward the Germans; but as for persuading them that we are just toward them, that is another matter. I believe that we can act so as to spare the world for a long time a German aggression; but the German spirit will not change so quickly. . . .

Observe that no one in Germany makes a distinction between the just and the unjust exigencies of the Allies. There is no stronger resistance than that which manifests itself against the attribution of Danzig to Poland. Nevertheless, in order to repair the historic crime committed against the Polish nation, we are obliged, in restoring that nation to life, to give it the means of survival. We cannot forget the crimes committed by Germany in particular against Poland. . . .

After the great effort and the greatest sacrifice of blood which history has ever seen, we cannot compromise the result of our victory. The League of Nations is offered to us as a means of giving us the security of which we have need: I accept this means; but if the League of Nations cannot give military sanction to its orders, it will be necessary to find that sanction somewhere else. I might observe that, on the sea, that sanction is all ready: Germany no longer has a navy. We need an equivalent on the land. I have not prejudged the possible means. I beg you to understand my state of mind, as I make an effort to understand yours. America is far away, protected by the ocean. England could not be invaded, even by Napoleon himself. You are, both the one and the other, secure; we are not.

[MEETING OF THE COUNCIL OF FOUR, MARCH 28, 1919]

President WILSON.—The question which rises here rises in other parts of Europe, in the region of Danzig, at Teschen, where the debate between Czechs and Poles recalls in many respects this problem of the Saar. Mr. Lloyd George said the other day: if you try to establish frontiers according to historic or strategic—and I would add: economic—considerations, there will be no limit to the claims. It is necessary for us to hold to the principles which we have put forward, and, in that way, we will not do injury to France.

M. CLEMENCEAU.—Maybe, but still it is necessary that this should be the opinion of France.

President WILSON.—There is no nation more intelligent than the French nation. If you will let me explain frankly my position, I have no fear of your verdict. Doubtless, if they should see that we do not apply the same principle everywhere, the French would not accept a solution which seems to them unfavorable; but if we show them that we do our best to act justly everywhere where comparable problems present themselves, the sense of justice which is in the heart of the French people will rise to answer me: "You are right." I have such a high conception of the spirit of the French nation that I believe it will always accept a principle founded on justice and applied with even-handedness.

Annexation by France of these regions does not have sufficient historic basis.

Part of this territory has not been French for twenty-two years; the rest has been separated from France for more than a hundred years. The map of Europe is covered, I know, with old injustices which cannot all be made right. That which is just is to assure France the compensation which is due her for the loss of her coal mines and at the same time to give the region of the Saar the guarantees of which it has need for the use of its own fuel. If we do that, we will do all which can be reasonably asked of us.

M. CLEMENCEAU.—I note the words and the excellent intentions of President Wilson. He sets aside sentiment and memory: it is for that reason that I have to state a reservation about that which has just been said. The President of the United States misunderstands the basis of human nature. The fact of the war cannot be forgotten. America did not see this war at first hand during its first three years; we, during this time, lost a million and a half men. We have no more labor. Our English friends, who have lost less than we, but enough to have also suffered much, will understand me.

Our trials have created in this country a profound desire for the recompense which is due us; and this is not only material reparation: the need for moral reparation is no less great. The doctrines which have just been invoked, if they were interpreted in all their rigor, would deny us even Alsace-Lorraine. In reality, the Saar and Landau are part of Lorraine and of Alsace. . . .

You wish to render justice to the Germans. Do not believe that they will ever forgive us; they will seek nothing but an occasion for revenge; nothing will destroy the rage of those who wanted to establish their domination over the world and who believe that they were so near success. . . .

I respect your sentiment, which is very honorable. Your role is great. But you go contrary to your aim. You will not sow hatred; but you will arouse bitterness and regret. That is why there must be a peace which is not mathematical, but which takes account of emotion.

You are ready to do justice to us from the economic point of view; I thank you. But economic necessities are not all. The history of the United States is a glorious history, but short. A hundred years for you is a very long period; for us, it is nothing. I have known men who have seen Napoleon with their own eyes. We have our conception of history which is not the same as yours.

I ask you simply to think on that which I have just said when you are alone and to ask yourself in conscience if it does not contain some particle of truth.

President WILSON.—I thank you for the very fine words you have pronounced; I feel all their gravity. I do not have excessive confidence in my own personal judgment. But I wish, before terminating this discussion, to return to one single point.

I believe with you that emotion is the most powerful force which exists in the world. Someone said to me once: "Intelligence is the sovereign of the world." I replied: "If so, it is a sovereign which reigns but which does not govern."

There is today throughout the world a passion for justice. Some of the injuries and even some of the crimes which have been committed have been inspired by a false idea of what is just. The emotion which has brought together in combat peoples from all parts of the world is the feeling that they were fighting together for justice. It is for that reason that I have been able to say sometimes that we here represent less the states than the opinion of the world. This enthusiastic aspiration for just solutions will change into cynical skepticism if there is any impression that we depart from the rules of justice which we have announced. . . . What I seek is not to deviate from the path along which presses this great impulse of the world for justice. I do not wish to do anything which would allow it to be said of us: "They profess grand principles; but they have made exceptions everywhere, whether on account of sentiment or on account of national interest, where they wanted to deviate from the rule."

I beg your pardon for having spoken thus. It is painful to me to oppose you: I could not do otherwise without failing in my duty.

6] Reparations Debated by the Council of Four

> While the American amendments to the Covenant were still being debated in the League Commission, the problem of reparations also came before the Council of Four.*

[MEETING OF THE COUNCIL OF FOUR, MARCH 30, 1919]

Mr. LLOYD GEORGE read the attached memorandum, and handed copies round:

"1. The loss and damage to which the Allied and Associated Governments and their nationals have been subjected as a direct and necessary consequence of the war, imposed upon them by the aggression of the enemy states by land, air and sea, is upwards of £30,000,000,000.

"2. Notwithstanding the indisputable claim of the Allied and Associated Governments to full compensation, they recognise that the financial and economic resources of the enemy states are not unlimited and that it will therefore, so far as they can judge, be impracticable for the enemy states to make complete reparation.

"3. The Allied and Associated Governments, however, require that the enemy states should at least make good, at whatever cost to themselves, the value of the material damage done and of the personal losses and injuries, including those to the civilian dependents of combatants which the enemy states have caused.

"4. Each of the Allied and Associated Powers ought to receive from Germany a just reparation in respect of the death and disablement or permanent injury to health directly caused to any of its subjects by hostilities or by operations of war, whether on sea or land or in the air, or by the acts of enemy forces, populations or authorities in occupied, invaded or enemy territory. For

* REPARATIONS DEBATED BY THE COUNCIL OF FOUR: Minutes of Sessions of the Council of Four, March 30, April 7, 1919. From Foreign Relations: Paris Peace Conference, 1919 (Washington, 1942–47), V, 16–17, 19, 44–45.

each Power interested this reparation may always be measured by the rate of pensions or allowances now established in its territories."

Article 1. President Wilson did not like the mention of the sum of £30,-000,000 [£30,000,000,000]. He suggested that the first few articles should be re-drafted so as to commence as follows:—

"Recognizing the central fact that the loss and damage to which the Allied and Associated Governments and their nations have been subjected as a direct and necessary consequence of the War is so colossal, that it would be impracticable for the enemy States to make complete reparation," &c., &c. . . .

[MEETING OF THE COUNCIL OF FOUR, APRIL 7, 1919]

THE Supreme Council had before them a revised edition of the clauses on reparation . . .

Clause 1, as finally approved, reads as follows:—

"The Allied and Associated Governments affirm and the Enemy States accept the responsibility of the Enemy States for causing all the loss and damage [to] which the Allied and Associated Governments and their nationals have been subjected as a consequence of the war imposed upon them by the aggression of the Enemy States." . . .

In the course of the discussion, Mr. LLOYD GEORGE pointed out that it was necessary somewhere in the document for the reasons to appear why the Allies could accept less than the whole cost of the war. This phrase had not been put in for the benefit of the Germans but to enable M. CLEMENCEAU and himself to justify to the French and British peoples their acceptance of less than the whole cost of the war. . . .

After an adjournment Clause 2 was agreed to in the following form:

"The Allied and Associated Powers recognise that the financial resources of the Enemy States are not adequate, after taking into account permanent diminutions of such resources which will result from other Treaty Clauses, to make complete reparation for all such loss and damage. The Allied and Associated Governments, however, require, and the German Government undertakes, that she will make compensation for all damage done to the civilian population of the Allied or Associated Powers and to their property by her aggression by land, by sea, and from the air as defined in the annexed schedule.["]

7] Clemenceau Stakes a Claim to the Saar

Clemenceau took the position that France needed and deserved not only reparations payments but also recompense in kind for the raw materials of which German occupying forces had robbed her during the war years. He asked that the Saar basin be made over in some fashion to France. Though peopled largely with Germans and German-controlled for over a hundred years, this small territory north of Lorraine was rich in coal and iron, and its possession would enable France not only to rebuild her metals industries but also perhaps to be sure of industrial supremacy over a recovered Germany.*

President WILSON.—I have read the three projects presented by the British delegation on the question of the Saar. All three imply a renunciation by Germany of sovereignty over the Saar basin. In my opinion, this prejudges the result of the plebiscite which is to take place fifteen years after the signing of the peace. . . .

Moreover, as I have already said very frankly, I am fearful of a solution of this kind for reasons of principle. I do not wish, however, to stand rigidly by the letter of the principle if it is possible to arrive at a reasonable solution. What I reject is an accord which prejudges the result of the plebiscite.

I propose that Germany be required for fifteen years to leave this region under the administration of a commission named by the League of Nations and responsible to it. . . . In effect, the sovereignty of Germany would be suspended for a period of fifteen years, and at the end of that period the population would decide its future for itself by a plebiscite. . . .

M. CLEMENCEAU.—I realize that German sovereignty would be suspended and the administration confided to the League of Nations. But in that case, why should the League of Nations not give a mandate to France?

Mr. LLOYD GEORGE.—I would observe that all the economic life of the region would already be in the hands of France.

President WILSON.—I seek with all my power a solution which will satisfy you and satisfy me. . . . I cannot return to the United States and say to the American people: "We have, upon consideration, found it convenient to go back on our word." I would be answered that we had made engagements under the terms of the armistice and the declarations that we made at the time when it was signed.

I ask you to help me find a path in your direction. I have gone a long way to meet you; don't make it impossible for me to assist you as much as I can. . . .

M. CLEMENCEAU.—Would it be possible, in your system, to get rid of the Prussian officials?

President WILSON.—The commission would have complete powers. . . .

M. CLEMENCEAU.—I foresee a satisfactory accord on this basis.

8] Defining the Monroe Doctrine

One obvious reason for the President's conciliatory attitude was the fact that he still had not won approval for all the necessary amendments to the Cove-

* CLEMENCEAU STAKES A CLAIM TO THE SAAR: Minutes of the Council of Four, April 9, 1919. From Paul Mantoux, *Conseil des Quatre* (Paris, 1955), I, 203–04, 206–07. Translation by Ernest R. May. Reprinted by permission of the Centre National de la Recherche Scientifique.

nant. One relating to the Monroe Doctrine was brought to a vote in the League Commission on April 10.*

President WILSON proposed the following amendment . . .

"Nothing in this Covenant shall be deemed to affect the validity of international engagements such as Treaties of arbitration or regional understandings like the Monroe Doctrine for securing the maintenance of peace."

.   .   .   .

Mr. Larnaude was anxious to have a clear definition of the Monroe Doctrine. Every time liberty had been threatened, either in America or in Europe, the United States had either acted upon the Doctrine or had reserved the right to intervene. If an European war occurred in which the interests of the United States were imperilled, the Monroe Doctrine would not prevent her from taking part. Did President Wilson's amendment consecrate or change this policy . . . ?

President Wilson replied in the negative. The Covenant provided that the members of the League should mutually defend one another in respect of their political and territorial integrity. The Covenant was therefore the highest possible tribute to the Monroe Doctrine. It adopted the principle of the Monroe Doctrine as a world doctrine. It was an international acceptance of the principle by which the United States had said that it would protect the political independence and territorial integrity of other American States. The Commission should study, not theoretical interpretations which had been placed upon the Monroe Doctrine, but actions of the United States which had been taken thereunder.

His colleagues in America had asked him whether the Covenant would destroy the Monroe Doctrine. He had replied that the Covenant was nothing but a confirmation and extension of the doctrine. He had then been asked whether, if this were so, there would be any objection to making a specific statement to that effect in the text. It was by way of concession to this reasonable request that he was asking the Commission to state definitely something which was already implied. . . .

Mr. Larnaude thought that it would certainly be very unfortunate if the Monroe Doctrine should be interpreted to mean that the United States could not participate in any settlement of European affairs decided upon by the League. . . .

President Wilson said that should the Monroe Doctrine in future be interpreted in a manner prejudicial to the peace of the world, the League of Nations would be there to deal with it. . . .

Mr. Larnaude thought that if it was not inconsistent with the terms of the Covenant, it was unnecessary to refer to it. What was unnecessary might be dangerous. Relying on the special mention of the Monroe Doctrine in the Covenant, the United States might some day assert that this doctrine forbade some act of intervention decided upon by the other members of the League.

---

* DEFINING THE MONROE DOCTRINE: Minutes of the Fourteenth Meeting of the Commission on the League of Nations, April 10, 1919. From David Hunter Miller, *The Drafting of the Covenant* (New York, 1928), II, 369–72, 374.

President Wilson again assured Mr. Larnaude that if the United States signed this document they would be solemnly obliged to render aid in European affairs, when the territorial integrity of any European State was threatened by external aggression. . . .

Mr. Larnaude said that he had no doubt that the United States would come again to the help of Europe if it were threatened by absolutism. Future wars might not, however, be wars of liberation. They might be economic in origin. The question was, therefore, whether the United States would come to the help of France should she be engaged in a struggle with a country which happened to be quite as liberal as herself. . . .

President Wilson asked why Mr. Larnaude asked this question when America promised to come to the rescue of France, as she did by signing the Covenant. Was it conceivable that he wanted the United States alone of the signatories of the Covenant to say that she would not repudiate her obligations under that Covenant? Did she wish to stop her signing the Covenant? . . .

The amendment was then adopted.

9] A Covenant of Equal Races?

As Wilson secured the amendments he required, he encountered the Japanese proposal for a declaration on racial equality. This embarrassing proposition forced him into highhanded action.*

BARON MAKINO asked . . . that, after the words "relations between Nations" in the Preamble, the following clause should be inserted: "by the endorsement of the principle of the equality of Nations and the just treatment of their nationals."

Lord Robert Cecil regretted that he was not in a position to vote for this amendment although he was personally entirely in accord with the idea advanced by the Japanese Delegation. The British Government realised the importance of the racial question, but its solution could not be attempted by the Commission without encroaching upon the sovereignty of States members of the League. . . .

Viscount Chinda replied to the objections raised by Lord Robert Cecil. He pointed out that the Japanese Delegate had not broached the question of race or immigration. He asked for nothing more than the principle of equality of nations and the just treatment of their nationals. . . . Japanese public opinion was so strongly behind this amendment that he asked the Commission to put it to the vote. If the amendment were rejected, it would be an indication to Japan that the equality of members of the League was not recognised and, as a consequence, the new organisation would be most unpopular. The formula which he proposed was of great importance, and the national aspirations of

* A COVENANT OF EQUAL RACES?: Minutes of the Fifteenth Meeting of the Commission on the League of Nations, April 11, 1919. From David Hunter Miller, *The Drafting of the Covenant* (New York, 1928), II, 389–92.

Japan were depending upon its adoption. Public opinion in Japan was very much concerned over this question and certain people had even gone so far as to say that Japan would not become a member of the League of Nations unless she were satisfied on this point.

Mr. Orlando supported the Japanese amendment. . . .

Mr. Bourgeois agreed with Mr. Orlando. . . .

Mr. Larnaude remarked that . . . it would be difficult not to adopt the principle of equality of nations as it was now proposed. . . .

President Wilson felt that the greatest difficulty lay in controversies which would be bound to take place outside the Commission over the Japanese proposal, and that in order to avoid these discussions it would perhaps be wise not to insert such a provision in the Preamble. The equality of nations was a fundamental principle of the League of Nations. It was the spirit of the Covenant to make a faithful attempt to place all nations upon a footing of equality, in the hope that the greater nations might aid the lesser in advantageous ways. Not only did the Covenant recognise the equality of States, but it laid down provisions for defending this equality in case it should be threatened.

Baron Makino said that he did not wish to continue an unprofitable discussion, but in these matters he was representing the unqualified opinion of the Government of Japan. Therefore he could not avoid the necessity of asking the Commission to make a definite decision in this matter and he had the honour of asking his fellow-members to vote upon the question of the insertion of his amendment in the Preamble.

A vote was taken and eleven votes out of seventeen were recorded in favour of the amendment.

President Wilson declared that the amendment was not adopted inasmuch as it had not received the unanimous approval of the Commission.

Mr. Larnaude called attention to the fact that a majority had voted in its favour.

President Wilson admitted that a majority had so voted, but stated that decisions of the Commission were not valid unless unanimous, and the Japanese amendment had not received unanimous support. There was only one case where a decision of the majority had prevailed, and that was in the case of determining the Seat of the League. In that case it had been necessary to accept the opinion of the majority inasmuch as no other procedure was possible if the question was to be decided at all. In the present instance there was, certainly, a majority, but strong opposition had manifested itself against the amendment and under these circumstances the resolution could not be considered as adopted. . . .

10] Fiume and Shantung Versus the Covenant

With the precious Covenant amended and now almost complete, the President could breathe more easily and, when Orlando raised the Fiume issue, revert to the strict principles he had enunciated earlier. Though the Italian

Premier could plead that the population of this important Adriatic port was two-thirds Italian and should be Italy's by right of national self-determination, Wilson could reply that the hinterland was ten-to-one Yugoslav, that the eleventh of the fourteen points had promised the south Slav state "free access to the sea," and that Fiume was almost the only good harbor readily accessible to her.

At the same time, however, the Japanese raised the Shantung question. In 1895 Japan had taken this populous north-coast peninsula from China but had been forced to return it by pressure from the great powers. Immediately afterward, Germany and Britain had seized ports on the peninsula and Russia had taken other territory that the Japanese had been compelled to give up. When war broke out in Europe in 1914, Japan seized the opportunity to regain control of Shantung. Though she could not claim the area under any of the principles announced by Wilson, she held possession, and, if her title was not recognized, the Japanese representatives in Paris, unlike the Italians, had the option of refusing to sign the treaty.*

[MEETING OF THE COUNCIL OF FOUR, APRIL 13, 1919]

President WILSON.—We are concerned now to see if we can set a date for the convocation of the German plenipotentiaries. Mr. Orlando, with whom I have talked, wishes that no final decision should be taken on this subject until we have arrived at agreement in principle on the Italian questions.

M. ORLANDO.—It would be practically impossible for me to agree. The impression would be disastrous in Italy if I told my compatriots that, five months after the conclusion of the armistice, all the French questions were adjusted while there was not even accord in principle on the Italian questions. I am very reasonable, and I do not ask that the latter should be completely adjusted before the convocation of the German plenipotentiaries; I ask only that solutions in principle should be fixed. That could be done, if there is no serious disagreement among us, in forty-eight hours. . . .

M. CLEMENCEAU.—Do you speak of all the questions that interest Italy or only that of Fiume and the Dalmatian coast?

M. ORLANDO.—That is the most important. . . .

President WILSON.—May I speak out loud the thoughts that are in my mind? The difficulty in which Mr. Orlando finds himself is real: it is the same which preoccupies Mr. Lloyd George in England and M. Clemenceau in France. It is to give satisfaction to a public opinion which is badly informed and which grows uneasy. This problem is not a stranger to me. In America, too, people ask: "What are you doing? What is your attitude? What goes on in the meetings between you and the three statesmen who visit you every day?" Undoubtedly it is time to answer. I will be obliged for my part to do it in writing; you have the advantage of being able to speak directly to your assemblies. . . .

We should do what is necessary to press actively the examination of the

* FIUME AND SHANTUNG VERSUS THE COVENANT: Minutes of Sessions of the Council of Four, April 13, 1919. From Paul Mantoux, *Conseil des Quatre* (Paris, 1955), I, 237, 242. Translation by Ernest R. May. Reprinted by permission of the Centre National de la Recherche Scientifique. Minutes of Sessions of the Council of Four, April 19, April 21, April 22, April 30, 1919. From *Foreign Relations: Paris Peace Conference, 1919* (Washington, 1942–47), V, 80–88, 90–91, 93, 106–11, 126–27, 135–36, 363–65.

Italian question without neglecting the last touches on the preliminaries of peace with Germany.

[MEETING OF THE COUNCIL OF FOUR, APRIL 19, 1919]

M. ORLANDO said that he would consider the whole question of Italian claims from the point of view of the resolutions taken by the Supreme Council on other questions. He recognised that there was one Power represented there to-day, namely, the United States of America, which had not taken any part in the Treaty concluded with Italy by France and Great Britain. Consequently, he proposed at the moment to deal with the subject on the hypothesis that no engagements existed. Italy had formulated three definite and distinct claims. He believed these to be in conformity with the general principles which had been adopted by the Supreme Council in dealing with the Peace Treaty. Consequently, he proposed to make a comparison between the principles underlying Italian claims and the general principles on which the Treaty of Peace was being based.

Italy's first claim related to her desire for union with the territories on the Italian side of the natural frontiers of Italy. . . .

The second point, M. Orlando continued, related to Fiume. Italy considered that the question of Fiume depended on general frontiers fixed for her. The historic frontier line of Italy passed along the water-shed of the mountains and came down to the sea on the Gulf of Quarnero and would embrace Fiume. For Fiume Italy appealed to the principle of self determination of the people. He referred to a historical fact that was insufficiently remembered, that Fiume itself had, before the conclusion of the Armistice, expressed a desire for incorporation in Italy. On the 18th October, 1918, the deputies of Fiume had in the Hungarian Chamber stated that as the Austro-Hungarian Empire was in a state of dissolution, Fiume being a free city demanded union with Italy. Hence Italy was in the presence of a question that had not been raised in the first instance by Italians, and there was a general demand that the declaration by Fiume should be supported. One objection that might be raised was that the principle of self determination was not applicable to a small community. It might be urged, also, that Fiume was not a part of Italy. Nevertheless, Fiume could not be considered as an isolated unit. The principle of self determination ought to apply just as much to little peoples as to great nations, particularly where there was a historical claim. . . .

Italy's third claim, M. Orlando continued related to Dalmatia and the Islands off the coast—and he would mention here that the case of the Islands applied also to Istria with which must be considered the large Islands of Cherso and Lussin which were largely Italian in character.

Italy's claims here were of a strategic order. . . . The eastern shores of the Adriatic with their covering Islands and high coast commanding the Adriatic; even if the Naval Forces on the Italian side were reduced to the lowest limits necessary for policing the seas, there would always be the possibility of ships setting out from these recesses reaching and bombarding the Italian coast and then returning with little or no damage behind the screen of Islands. . . .

The strategic argument, however, was not the only one on which Italy based her claims. There was a national question as well. In the course of those conversations it had been stated that historical claims must not be allowed to possess a decisive influence. He, himself, recognized that. There were, however, cases where history must exercise a deep influence. Since historic days right down to the Treaty of Campo Formio [of 1797] Dalmatia had been connected with Italy—first as part of the Roman Empire, subsequently as part of Venice. . . . There still remained in Dalmatia a flourishing Italianism. Was it possible, he asked, after all the sacrifices of the war for Italy to see this Italianism devoted to destruction[?] What Italy demanded was only a small part of Dalmatia leaving to Yugo-Slavia Spalato, Ragusa and Gattaro. He considered that this was a very modest demand, and he only asked that the existing agreement in regard to Dalmatia should be adhered to.

President WILSON recalled that it had been agreed that he should confer with M. Orlando and through him with his colleagues and he would now state the substance of what he had said. His Italian friends would bear witness that throughout the conversations he had insisted on the same point of view. It had been his privilege as the spokesman of the Associated Powers to initiate the negotiations for peace. The bases of the Peace with Germany had then been clearly laid down. It was not reasonable—and he thought his Italian friends would admit this—to have one basis of Peace with Germany and another set of principles for the Peace with Austria-Hungary, Bulgaria and Turkey. He must assume that the principles in each case would be the same. The whole question resolved itself into this: we were trying to make peace on an entirely new basis and to establish a new order of international relations. At every point the question had to be asked whether the lines of the settlement would square with the new order. No greater question had ever been asked in any negotiations. No body of statesmen had ever before undertaken to make such a settlement. There was a certain claim of argument which must be brushed aside, namely, the economic and strategic argument. Within certain limits he agreed that natural boundaries such as existed in the cases of Spain or Scandinavia (which M. Orlando had referred to) must be taken into consideration. The whole course of life in these regions was determined by such natural boundaries. . . . The slope of the mountains not only threw the rivers in a certain direction but tended to throw the life of the people in the same direction. These, however, were not strategic nor economic arguments. On these grounds he felt no difficulty in assenting to that part of the Italian claims included in M. Orlando's first point. Nature had swung a great boundary round the north of Italy. It included Trieste and most of the Istrian Peninsula on which Pola lies. He had no great difficulty there in meeting the Italian views.

Outside of these, however, further to the South all the arguments seemed to him to lead the other way. A different watershed was reached. Different racial units were encountered. There were natural associations between the peoples and this brought him to the question of Fiume.

From the first it had seemed to him plain that on the side of the Alps on which Fiume lay there was not only a difficult but an entirely new problem. Hitherto Fiume had been linked up with the policy of the Austro-Hungarian

Empire. That Empire had been governed by men who were in spirit very similar to the former rulers of Germany and who had been more or less under their domination. In fact they had become their instruments. If the Austro-Hungarian Empire had not gone to pieces the question could not have been difficult to deal with. Now, however, it had disappeared. Hence part of the wisdom of the present situation seemed to build up new States linked in their interest for the future with the new order. These States must indeed become partners in the new order and not be regarded as States under suspicion but as linked in the new international relationship. M. Orlando would remember that at the time that we were trying to detach the Jugo-Slavs from Austria we spoke of them as friends. We could not now speak of them as enemies. By separating from Austria-Hungary they had become connected with the new and disconnected from the old policy and order. M. Orlando had argued the case of Fiume as though it were purely an Italian and Jugo-Slav interest. Fiume was undoubtedly important to Jugo-Slavia whatever the proportion of the Jugo-Slav trade to the whole might be. But above all its importance was that of an international port serving Roumania, Hungary, and Czecho-Slovakia. The Italian population at Fiume was not connected with Italy by intervening Italian population. Hence, to unite it with Italy would be an arbitrary act, so inconsistent with the principles on which we were acting that he for one could not concur in it. . . .

[MEETING OF THE COUNCIL OF FOUR, APRIL 21, 1919]

President WILSON reported a conversation he had had that morning with Baron Makino and Count Chinda. He had made the suggestion . . . that all claims in the Pacific should be ceded to the Allied and Associated Powers as trustees leaving them to make fair and just dispositions. He had, at the same time, reminded the Japanese Delegates that it had been understood that Japan was to have a mandate for the islands in the north Pacific although he had made a reserve in the case of the island of Yap, which he himself considered should be international. He had suggested that, similarly, in the case of Kiau-Chau, where there was a definite Treaty relating to Kiau-Chau and Shantung, Japan should place the question in the hands of the 5 powers. He had asked whether there could not be some modification of the Treaty with the consent of both parties. The Powers had no right to force Japan but they had the right to try and persuade her to make some agreement with China on the subject. The Japanese had been very stiff about it. They had said that they would return Kiau-Chau to China. . . . They insisted that Germany should resign the whole of her interests in Kiau-Chau to the Japanese and that the Powers should trust Japan to carry out her bargain with China.

Mr. LLOYD GEORGE asked why Japan should have a different treatment in regard to Kiau-Chau to what other Powers had in respect to German colonies.

President WILSON said the reason was because in the Treaty it had been made clear that the transfer was to precede the retrocession of the territory to China.

Mr. LLOYD GEORGE suggested that it ought to be ceded by the League of Nations. . . .

President WILSON said that to be perfectly fair to the Japanese he thought they would interpret this as a challenge of their good faith. He had put it to the Japanese representatives that the peace of the Far East depended more on Chino-Japanese relations than on anything else. China was full of riches. It was clearly to the advantage of Japan to take the most generous position towards China and to show herself as a friend. The interest of the world in China was the "open door." The Japanese had assented and expressed benevolent intentions.

[MORNING MEETING OF THE COUNCIL OF FOUR, APRIL 22, 1919]

President WILSON said that he had already taken the liberty of describing as well as he could to M. Clemenceau and Mr. Lloyd George what happened in his conversation with Baron Makino and Viscount Chinda. Their minds, therefore, were in the midst of the subject. He had laid what was in his own mind before all present. He did not know what was the impression formed by Mr. Lloyd George and M. Clemenceau.

Mr. LLOYD GEORGE said that so far as Great Britain was concerned they were in the same position towards Japan as towards Italy. They had a definite engagement with Japan, as recorded in the Note of the British Ambassador at Tokio, dated 16th February, 1917. Hence, so far as Great Britain was concerned, there was a definite engagement. The only doubt he felt was as to whether the ultimate destination of Kiauchau was a matter for inclusion in the Treaty with Germany. . . .

Viscount CHINDA . . . asked if it was merely proposed to postpone this question: to put it in abeyance? The Japanese Delegation were under an express order for the case that the question was not settled. The Japanese Government had a duty to perfom to China in this matter, and they could not carry out their obligation to China unless Kiauchau was handed over to them. The Japanese Delegates were under an express instruction from their Government that unless they were placed in a position to carry out Japan's obligation to China, they were not allowed to sign the Treaty.

[MEETING OF THE COUNCIL OF FOUR, APRIL 30, 1919]

IN reply to questions by President Wilson—the Japanese Delegates declared that:—

"The policy of Japan is to hand back the Shantung Peninsula in full sovereignty to China retaining only the economic privileges granted to Germany and the right to establish a settlement under the usual conditions at Tsingtao. The owners of the Railway will use special Police only to ensure security for traffic. They will be used for no other purpose. The Police Force will be composed of Chinese, and such Japanese instructors as the Directors of the Railway may select will be appointed by the Chinese Government." . . .

The Articles . . . relative to Shantung Province were approved.

11] The Treaty Is Completed

Wilson held his ground against the demand for Fiume. He also joined his Allied colleagues in standing fast against German proposals for changes in the treaty presented them. On June 28 a reluctant German delegation signed it, and that evening Wilson departed for home to seek its ratification by the Senate. The document had 440 articles and ran to over two hundred pages, but debate in the United States was to turn on the territorial provisions benefiting France and Poland, the Shantung clause, the reparations articles, and the following sections of Part I, the Covenant of the League of Nations.*

ARTICLE 1

. . . .

ANY FULLY self-governing State, Dominion, or Colony . . . may become a Member of the League. . . .

Any Member of the League may, after two years' notice of its intention so to do, withdraw from the League, provided that all its international obligations and all its obligations under this Covenant shall have been fulfilled at the time of its withdrawal.

. . . .

ARTICLE 3

. . . .

At meetings of the Assembly each Member of the League shall have one vote. . . .

. . . .

ARTICLE 8

The Members of the League recognise that the maintenance of peace requires the reduction of armaments to the lowest point consistent with national safety and the enforcement by common action of international obligations.

The Council, taking account of the geographical situation and circumstances of each State, shall formulate plans for such reduction for the consideration and action of the several Governments. . . .

After these plans shall have been adopted by the several Governments, the limits of armaments therein fixed shall not be exceeded without the concurrence of the Council.

. . . .

* THE TREATY IS COMPLETED: Text of the Treaty of Versailles. From *The Treaties of Peace, 1919–1923* (New York, 1924), I, 10–11, 14, 17, 18–20.

ARTICLE 10

The Members of the League undertake to respect and preserve as against external aggression the territorial integrity and existing political independence of all Members of the League. In case of any such aggression or in case of any threat or danger of such aggression the Council shall advise upon the means by which this obligation shall be fulfilled.

ARTICLE 11

Any war or threat of war, whether immediately affecting any of the Members of the League or not, is hereby declared a matter of concern to the whole League, and the League shall take any action that may be deemed wise and effectual to safeguard the peace of nations. In case any such emergency should arise the Secretary General shall on the request of any Member of the League forthwith summon a meeting of the Council.

It is also declared to be the friendly right of each Member of the League to bring to the attention of the Assembly or of the Council any circumstance whatever affecting international relations which threatens to disturb international peace or the good understanding between nations upon which peace depends.

ARTICLE 12

The Members of the League agree that if there should arise between them any dispute likely to lead to a rupture, they will submit the matter either to arbitration or to inquiry by the Council. . . .

. . . .

ARTICLE 15

If there should arise between Members of the League any dispute likely to lead to a rupture, which is not submitted to arbitration in accordance with Article 13, the Members of the League agree that they will submit the matter to the Council. . . .

If the dispute between the parties is claimed by one of them, and is found by the Council, to arise out of a matter which by international law is solely within the domestic jurisdiction of that party, the Council shall so report, and shall make no recommendation as to its settlement. . . .

ARTICLE 16

Should any Member of the League resort to war in disregard of its covenants . . . , it shall *ipso facto* be deemed to have committed an act of war against all other Members of the League, which hereby undertake immediately to subject it to the severance of all trade or financial relations, the prohibition of all intercourse between their nations and the nationals of the covenant-breaking State, and the prevention of all financial, commercial, or personal intercourse between the nationals of the covenant-breaking State and the nationals of any other State, whether a Member of the League or not.

It shall be the duty of the Council in such case to recommend to the several Governments concerned what effective military, naval, or air force the Members of the League shall severally contribute to the armed forces to be used to protect the covenants of the League. . . .

. . . .

ARTICLE 19

The Assembly may from time to time advise the reconsideration by Members of the League of treaties which have become inapplicable and the consideration of international conditions whose continuance might endanger the peace of the world.

. . . .

ARTICLE 21

Nothing in this Covenant shall be deemed to affect the validity of international engagements, such as treaties of arbitration or regional understandings like the Monroe doctrine, for securing the maintenance of peace.

ARTICLE 22

To those colonies and territories which as a consequence of the late war have ceased to be under the sovereignty of the States which formerly governed them and which are inhabited by peoples not yet able to stand by themselves under the strenuous conditions of the modern world, there should be applied the principle that the well-being and development of such peoples form a sacred trust of civilisation and that securities for the performance of this trust should be embodied in this Covenant.

The best method of giving practical effect to this principle is that the tutelage of such peoples should be entrusted to advanced nations . . . and that this tutelage should be exercised by them as Mandatories on behalf of the League.

The character of the mandate must differ according to the stage of development of the people, the geographical situation of the territory, its economic condition, and other similar circumstances. . . .

There are territories, such as South-West Africa and certain of the South Pacific Islands, which, owing to the sparseness of their population, or their small size, or their remoteness from the centres of civilisation, or their geographical contiguity to the territory of the Mandatory, and other circumstances, can be best administered under the laws of the Mandatory as integral portions of its territory. . . .

12] Lodge States the Case Against Ratification

Though the American public seemed in general to approve the document that Wilson brought home, opposition continued among Republicans in the Senate. A majority on the Foreign Relations Committee favored either rejecting the treaty or attaching serious amendments or reservations prior to ratification. Henry Cabot Lodge, now the chairman of that committee, summarized nearly all the arguments of this group in an eloquent speech in the Senate on August 12, 1919.*

TURN TO the preamble of the covenant of the league of nations now before us, which states the object of the league. It is formed "in order to promote international cooperation and to achieve international peace and security by the acceptance of obligations not to resort to war, by the prescription of open, just, and honorable relations between nations, by the firm establishment of the understandings of international laws as the actual rule of conduct among governments and by the maintenance of justice and a scrupulous respect for all treaty obligations in the dealings of organized peoples with one another."

No one would contest the loftiness or the benevolence of these purposes. Brave words, indeed! They do not differ essentially from the preamble of the treaty of Paris, from which sprang the Holy Alliance. But the covenant of this league contains a provision which I do not find in the treaty of Paris, and which is as follows:

The assembly may deal at its meetings with any matter within the sphere of action of the league or affecting the peace of the world.

There is no such sweeping or far-reaching provision as that in the treaty of Paris, and yet able men developed from that treaty the Holy Alliance, which England, and later France were forced to abandon and which, for 35 years, was an unmitigated curse to the world. England broke from the Holy Alliance and the breach began three years after it was formed, because English statesmen saw that it was intended to turn the alliance—and this league is an alliance—into a means of repressing internal revolutions or insurrections. There was nothing in the treaty of Paris which warranted such action, but in this covenant of the league of nations the authority is clearly given in the third paragraph of article 3, where it is said:

The assembly may deal at its meetings with any matter within the sphere of action of the league or affecting the peace of the world.

No revolutionary movement, no internal conflict of any magnitude can fail to affect the peace of the world. The French Revolution, which was wholly internal at the beginning, affected the peace of the world to such an extent that it brought on a world war which lasted some 25 years. Can anyone say that our Civil War did not affect the peace of the world? At this very moment,

* LODGE STATES THE CASE AGAINST RATIFICATION: From the *Congressional Record*, 66 Cong., 1 Sess., pp. 3779–84.

who would deny that the condition of Russia, with internal conflicts raging in all parts of that great Empire, does not affect the peace of the world and therefore come properly within the jurisdiction of the league? "Any matter affecting the peace of the world" is a very broad statement which could be made to justify almost any interference on the part of the league with the internal affairs of other countries. . . . If Europe desires such an alliance or league with a power of this kind, so be it. I have no objection, provided they do not interfere with the American Continents or force us against our will but bound by a moral obligation into all the quarrels of Europe. If England, abandoning the policy of Canning, desires to be a member of a league which has such powers as this, I have not a word to say. But I object in the strongest possible way to having the United States agree, directly or indirectly, to be controlled by a league which may at any time, and perfectly lawfully and in accordance with the terms of the covenant, be drawn in to deal with internal conflicts in other countries, no matter what those conflicts may be. We should never permit the United States to be involved in any internal conflict in another country, except by the will of her people expressed through the Congress which represents them.

With regard to wars of external aggression on a member of the league, the case is perfectly clear. There can be no genuine dispute whatever about the meaning of the first clause of article 10. In the first place, it differs from every other obligation in being individual and placed upon each nation without the intervention of the league. Each nation for itself promises to respect and preserve as against external aggression the boundaries and the political independence of every member of the league. . . . In article 10 the United States is bound on the appeal of any member of the league not only to respect but to preserve its independence and its boundaries, and that pledge, if we give it, must be fulfilled.

There is to me no distinction whatever in a treaty between what some persons are pleased to call legal and moral obligations. A treaty rests and must rest, except where it is imposed under duress and securities and hostages are taken for its fulfillment, upon moral obligations. No doubt a great power impossible of coercion can cast aside a moral obligation if it sees fit and escape from the performance of the duty which it promises. The pathway of dishonor is always open. I for one, however, cannot conceive of voting for a clause of which I disapprove because I know it can be escaped in that way. Whatever the United States agrees to, by that agreement she must abide. Nothing could so surely destroy all prospects of the world's peace as to have any powerful nation refuse to carry out an obligation, direct or indirect, because it rests only on moral grounds. Whatever we promise we must carry out to the full, "without mental reservation or purpose of evasion." To me any other attitude is inconceivable. Without the most absolute and minute good faith in carrying out a treaty to which we have agreed, without ever resorting to doubtful interpretations or to the plea that it is only a moral obligation, treaties are worthless. The greatest foundation of peace is the scrupulous observance of every promise, express or implied, of every pledge, whether it can be described as legal or moral. No vote should be given to any clause in any treaty or to any treaty except in this spirit and with this understanding.

I return, then, to the first clause of article 10. It is, I repeat, an individual obligation. It requires no action on the part of the league, except that in the second sentence the authorities of the league are to have the power to advise as to the means to be employed in order to fulfill the purpose of the first sentence. But that is a detail of execution, and I consider that we are morally and in honor bound to accept and act upon that advice. The broad fact remains that if any member of the league suffering from external aggression should appeal directly to the United States for support the United States would be bound to give that support in its own capacity and without reference to the action of other powers, because the United States itself is bound, and I hope the day will never come when the United States will not carry out its promises. If that day should come, and the United States or any other great country should refuse, no matter how specious the reasons, to fulfill both in letter and spirit every obligation in this covenant, the United States would be dishonored and the league would crumble into dust, leaving behind it a legacy of wars. If China should rise up and attack Japan in an effort to undo the great wrong of the cession of the control of Shantung to that power, we should be bound under the terms of article 10 to sustain Japan against China, and a guaranty of that sort is never involved except when the question has passed beyond the stage of negotiation and has become a question for the application of force. I do not like the prospect. It shall not come into existence by any vote of mine.

Article 11 carries this danger still further, for it says:

Any war or threat of war, whether immediately affecting any of the members of the league or not, is hereby declared a matter of concern to the whole league, and the league shall take any action that shall be deemed wise and effectual to safeguard the peace of nations.

"Any war or threat of war" means both external aggression and internal disturbance, as I have already pointed out in dealing with article 3. "Any action" covers military action, because it covers action of any sort or kind. Let me take an example, not an imaginary case, but one which may have been overlooked because most people have not the slightest idea where or what a King of the Hedjaz is. The following dispatch appeared recently in the newspapers:

"HEDJAZ AGAINST BEDOUINS.

"The forces of Emir Abdullah recently suffered a grave defeat, the Wahabis attacking and capturing Kurma, east of Mecca. Ibn Savond is believed to be working in harmony with the Wahabis. A squadron of the royal air force was ordered recently to go to the assistance of King Hussein."

Hussein I take to be the Sultan of Hedjaz. He is being attacked by the Bedouins. . . . Under article 10, if King Hussein appealed to us for aid and protection against external aggression affecting his independence and the boundaries of his Kingdom, we should be bound to give that aid and protection and to send American soldiers to Arabia. It is not relevant to say that this is unlikely to occur; that Great Britain is quite able to take care of King Hussein, who is her fair creation, reminding one a little of the Mosquito King, a monarch once developed by Great Britain on the Mosquito Coast of Central America. The fact that we should not be called upon does not alter the right which the King of Hedjaz possesses to demand the sending of American troops to Arabia in order to preserve his independence against the assaults of the Wahabis or Bedouins. I am unwilling to give that right to King Hussein, and this illustrates the point which is to me the most objectionable in the league as it stands; the right of other powers to call out American troops and American ships to go to any part of the world, an obligation we are bound to fulfill under the terms of this treaty. I know the answer well—that of course they could not be sent without action by Congress. Congress would have no choice if acting in good faith, and if under article 10 any member of the league summoned us, or if under article 11 the league itself summoned us, we should be bound in honor and morally to obey. There would be no escape except by a breach of faith, and legislation by Congress under those circumstances would be a mockery of independent action. Is it too much to ask that provision should be made that American troops and American ships should never be sent anywhere or ordered to take part in any conflict except after the deliberate action of the American people, expressed according to the Constitution through their chosen representatives in Congress?

Let me now briefly point out the insuperable difficulty which I find in article 15. It begins: "If there should arise between members of the league any dispute likely to lead to a rupture." "Any dispute" covers every possible dispute. It therefore covers a dispute over tariff duties and over immigration. Suppose we have a dispute with Japan or with some European country as to immigration. I put aside tariff duties as less important than immigration. This is not an imaginary case. Of late years there has probably been more international discussion and negotiation about questions growing out of immigration laws than any other one subject. It comes within the definition of "any dispute" at the beginning of article 15. In the eighth paragraph of that article it is said that "if the dispute between the parties is claimed by one of them, and is found by the council to arise out of a matter which, by international law, is solely within the domestic jurisdiction of that party, the council shall so report and shall make no recommendation as to its settlement." . . . I wish somebody would point out to me those provisions of international law which make a list of questions which are hard and fast within the domestic jurisdiction. No such distinction can be applied to tariff duties or immigration, nor indeed finally and conclusively to any subject. . . .

An immigration dispute or a dispute over tariff duties, met by the procedure set forth in article 15, comes before the assembly of delegates for a decision by what is practically a majority vote of the entire assembly. That is something to which I do not find myself able to give my assent. So far as immigration is concerned, and also so far as tariff duties, although less important, are concerned, I deny the jurisdiction. There should be no possibility of other nations deciding who shall come into the United States, or under what conditions they shall enter. The right to say who shall come into a country is one of the very highest attributes of sovereignty. If a nation cannot say without appeal who shall come within its gates and become a part of its citizenship it has ceased to be a sovereign nation. It has become a tributary and a subject nation, and it makes no difference whether it is subject to a league or to a conqueror. . . . We and we alone must say who shall come into the United States and become citizens of this Republic, and no one else should have any power to utter one word in regard to it.

Article 21 says:

"Nothing in this covenant shall be deemed to affect the validity of international engagements, such as treaties of arbitration or regional understandings like the Monroe doctrine for securing the maintenance of peace."

The provision did not appear in the first draft of the covenant, and when the President explained the second draft of the convention in the peace conference he said:

"Article 21 is new."

And that was all he said. No one can question the truth of the remark, but I trust I shall not be considered disrespectful if I say that it was not an illuminating statement. The article was new, but the fact of its novelty, which the President declared, was known to everyone who had taken the trouble to read the two documents. We were not left, however, without a fitting explanation. The British delegation took it upon themselves to explain article 21 at some length, and this is what they said:

"Article 21 makes it clear that the covenant is not intended to abrogate or weaken any other agreements, so long as they are consistent with its own terms, into which members of the league may have entered or may hereafter enter for the assurance of peace. Such agreements would include special treaties for compulsory arbitration and military conventions that are genuinely defensive.

"The Monroe doctrine and similar understandings are put in the same category. They have shown themselves in history to be not instruments of national ambition, but guarantees of peace. The origin of the Monroe doctrine is well known. It was proclaimed in 1823 to prevent America from becoming a theater for intrigues of European absolutism. At first a principle of American foreign policy, it has become an international understanding, and it is not illegitimate for the people of the United States to say that the covenant should recognize that fact.

"In its essence it is consistent with the spirit of the covenant, and, indeed, the principles of the league, as expressed in article 10, represent the extension to the whole world of the principles of the doctrine, while, should any dispute as to the meaning of the latter ever arise between the American and European powers, the league is there to settle it."

The explanation of Great Britain received the assent of France. . . .

Says M. Lausanne, editor of the *Matin* and a chief spokesman for M. Clemenceau—

". . . If the league takes in the world, then Europe must mix in the affairs of America; if only Europe is included, then America will violate of necessity her own doctrine by intermixing in the affairs of Europe."

It has seemed to me that the British delegation traveled a little out of the precincts of the peace conference when they undertook to explain the Monroe doctrine and tell the United States what it was and what it was not proposed to do with it under the new article. That, however, is merely a matter of taste and judgment. Their statement that the Monroe doctrine under this article, if any question arose in regard to it, would be passed upon and interpreted by the league of nations is absolutely correct. There is no doubt that this is what the article means. The statement of M. Lausanne is equally explicit and truthful, but he makes one mistake. He says, in substance, that if we are to meddle in Europe, Europe cannot be excluded from the Americas. He overlooks the fact that the Monroe doctrine also says:

"Our policy in regard to Europe, which was adopted at an early stage of the wars which have so long agitated that quarter of the globe, nevertheless remains the same, which is not to interfere in the internal concerns of any of the powers."

The Monroe doctrine was the corollary of Washington's neutrality policy and of his injunction against permanent alliances. It reiterates and reaffirms the principle. We do not seek to meddle in the affairs of Europe and keep Europe out of the Americas. It is as important to keep the United States out of European affairs as to keep Europe out of the American Continents. Let us maintain the Monroe doctrine, then, in its entirety, and not only preserve our own safety, but in this way best promote the real peace of the world. Whenever the preservation of freedom and civilization and the overthrow of a menacing world conqueror summon us we shall respond fully and nobly, as we did in 1917. He who doubts that we could do so has little faith in America. But let it be our own act and not done reluctantly by the coercion of other nations, at the bidding or by the permission of other countries.

Let me now deal with the article itself. . . . The Monroe doctrine is described as a "regional understanding" whatever that may mean. The boundaries between the States of the Union, I suppose, are "regional understandings," if anyone chooses to apply to them that somewhat swollen phraseology. But the Monroe doctrine is no more a regional understanding than it is an "international engagement." The Monroe doctrine was a policy declared by President Monroe. Its immediate purpose was to shut out Europe from interfering with the South American Republics, which the Holy Alliance designed to do. It was stated broadly, however, as we all know, and went much further than that. It was, as I have just said, the corollary of Washington's declaration against our interfering in European questions. It was so regarded by Jefferson at the time and by John Quincy Adams, who formulated it, and by President Monroe, who declared it. It rested firmly on the great law of self-preservation, which is the basic principle of every independent State.

It is not necessary to trace its history or to point out the extensions which it has received or its universal acceptance by all American statesmen without regard to party. All Americans have always been for it. They may not have known its details or read all the many discussions in regard to it, but they knew that it was an American doctrine and that, broadly stated, it meant the exclusion of Europe from interference with American affairs and from any attempt to colonize or set up new States within the boundaries of the American Continent. I repeat it was purely an American doctrine, a purely American policy, designed and wisely designed for our defense. It has never been an "international engagement." No nation has ever formally recognized it. It has been the subject of reservation at international conventions by American delegates. It has never been a "regional understanding" or an understanding of any kind with anybody. It was the declaration of the United States of America, in their own behalf, supported by their own power. They brought it into being, and its life was predicated on the force which the United States could place behind it. Unless the United States could sustain it it would die. The United States has supported it. It has lived—strong, efficient, respected. It is now proposed to kill it by a provision in a treaty for a league of nations.

The instant that the United States, who declared, interpreted, and sustained the doctrine, ceases to be the sole judge of what it means, that instant the Monroe doctrine ceases and disappears from history and from the face of the earth. I think it is just as undesirable to have Europe interfere in American affairs now as Mr. Monroe thought it was in 1823, and equally undesirable that we should be compelled to involve ourselves in all the wars and brawls of Europe. The Monroe doctrine has made for peace. Without the Monroe doctrine we should have had many a struggle with European powers to save ourselves from possible assault and certainly from the necessity of becoming a great military power, always under arms and always ready to resist invasion from States in our near neighborhood. In the interests of the peace of the world it is now proposed to wipe away this American policy, which has been a bulwark and a barrier for peace. . . .

Another point in this covenant where change must be made in order to protect the safety of the United States in the future is in article 1, where withdrawal is provided for. This provision was an attempt to meet the very general objection to the first draft of the league, that there was no means of getting out of it without denouncing the treaty; that is, there was no arrangement for the withdrawal of any nation. As it now stands it reads that—

Any member of the league may, after two years' notice of its intention to do so, withdraw from the league, provided that all its international obligations, and all its obligations under this covenant shall have been fulfilled at the time of its withdrawal.

The right of withdrawal is given by this clause, although the time for notice, two years, is altogether too long. Six months or a year would be found, I think, in most treaties to be the normal period fixed for notice of withdrawal. But whatever virtue there may be in the right thus conferred is completely nullified by the proviso. The right of withdrawal cannot be exercised until all the international obligations and all the obligations of the withdrawing nations have been fulfilled. The league alone can decide whether "all international obligations and all obligations under this covenant" have been fulfilled, and this would require, under the provisions of the league, a unanimous vote so that any nation desiring to withdraw could not do so, even on the two years' notice, if one nation voted that the obligations had not been fulfilled. Remember that this gives the league not only power to review all our obligations under the covenant but all our treaties with all nations for every one of those is an "international obligation."

Are we deliberately to put ourselves in fetters and be examined by the league of nations as to whether we have kept faith with Cuba or Panama before we can be permitted to leave the league? This seems to me humiliating to say the least. The right of withdrawal, if it is to be of any value whatever, must be absolute, because otherwise a nation desiring to withdraw could be held in the league by objections from other nations until the very act which induces the nation to withdraw had been completed; until the withdrawing nation had been forced to send troops to take part in a war with which it had no concern and upon which it did not desire to enter. It seems to me vital to the safety of the United States not only that this provision should be eliminated and the right to withdraw made absolute but that the period of withdrawal should be much reduced. . . .

I have dwelt only upon those points which seem to me most dangerous. There are, of course, many others, but these points, in the interest not only of the safety of the United States but of the maintenance of the treaty and the peace of the world, should be dealt with here before it is too late. Once in the league the chance of amendment is so slight that it is not worth considering. Any analysis of the provisions of this league covenant, however, brings out in startling relief one great fact. Whatever may be said, it is not a league of peace; it is an alliance, dominated at the present moment by five great powers, really by three, and it has all the marks of an alliance. The development of international law is neglected. The court which is to decide disputes brought before it fills but a small place. The conditions for which this league really provides with the utmost care are political conditions, not judicial questions, to be reached by the executive council and the assembly, purely political bodies without any trace of a judicial character about them. Such being its machinery, the control being in the hands of political appointees whose votes will be controlled by interest and expedience, it exhibits that most marked characteristic of an alliance—that its decisions are to be carried out by force. Those articles upon which the whole structure rests are articles which provide for the use of force; that is, for war. This league to enforce peace does a great deal for enforcement and very little for peace. It makes more essential provisions looking to war than to peace, for the settlement of disputes.

Article 10 I have already discussed. There is no question that the preservation of a State against external aggression can contemplate nothing but war. In article 11, again, the league is authorized to take any action which may be necessary to safeguard the peace of the world. "Any action" includes war. We also have specific provisions for a boycott, which is a form of economic warfare. The use of troops might be avoided but the enforcement of a boycott would require blockades in all probability, and certainly a boycott in its essence is simply an effort to starve a people into submission, to ruin their trade, and, in the case of nations which are not self-supporting, to cut off their food supply. The misery and suffering caused by such a measure as this may easily rival that caused by actual war. Article 16 embodies the boycott and also, in the last paragraph, provides explicitly for war. We are told that the word "recommends" has no binding force; it constitutes a moral obligation, that is all. But it means that if we, for example, should refuse to accept the recommendation, we should nullify the operation of article 16 and, to that extent, of the league. It seems to me that to attempt to relieve us of clearly imposed duties by saying that the word "recommend" is not binding is an escape of which no nation regarding the sanctity of treaties and its own honor would care to avail itself.

The provisions of article 16 are extended to States outside the league who refuse to obey its command to come in and submit themselves to its jurisdiction; another provision for war.

Taken altogether, these provisions for war present what to my mind is the gravest objection to this league in its present form. We are told that of course nothing will be done in the way of warlike acts without the assent of Congress. If that is true, let us say so in the covenant. But as it stands there is no doubt whatever in my mind that American troops and American ships may be ordered to any part of the world by nations other than the United States, and that is a proposition to which I for one can never assent. It must be made perfectly clear that no American soldiers, not even a corporal's guard, that no American sailors, not even the crew of a submarine, can ever be engaged in war or ordered anywhere except by the constitutional authorities of the United States. . . . I believe that we do not require to be told by foreign nations when we shall do work which freedom and civilization require. I think we can move to victory much better under our own command than under the command of others. Let us unite with the world to promote the peaceable settlement of all international disputes. Let us try to develop international law. Let us associate ourselves with the other nations for these purposes. But let us retain in our own hands and in our own control the lives of the youth of the land. Let no American be sent into battle except by the constituted authorities of his own country and by the will of the people of the United States.

Those of us, Mr. President, who are either wholly opposed to the league or who are trying to preserve the independence and the safety of the United States by changing the terms of the league and who are endeavoring to make the league, if we are to be a member of it, less certain to promote war instead of peace, have been reproached with selfishness in our outlook and with a desire to keep our country in a state of isolation. So far as the question of isolation goes, it is impossible to isolate the United States. I well remember the time, 20 years ago, when eminent Senators and other distinguished gentlemen who were opposing the Philippines and shrieking about imperialism, sneered at the statement made by some of us, that the United States had become a world power. I think no one now would question that the Spanish War marked the entrance of the United States into world affairs to a degree which had never obtained before. It was both an inevitable and an irrevocable step, and our entrance into the war with Germany certainly showed once and for all that the United States was not unmindful of its world responsibilities. We may set aside all this empty talk about isolation. Nobody expects to isolate the United States or to make it a hermit Nation, which is a sheer absurdity. But there is a wide difference between taking a suitable part and bearing a due responsibility in world affairs and plunging the United States into every controversy and conflict on the face of the globe. By meddling in all the differences which may arise among any portion or fragment of humankind we simply fritter away our influence and injure ourselves to no good purpose. We shall be of far more value to the world and its peace by occupying, so far as possible, the situation which we have occupied for the last 20 years and by adhering to the policy of Washington and Hamilton, of Jefferson and Monroe, under which we have risen to our present greatness and prosperity. The fact that we have been separated by our geographical situation and by our consistent policy from the broils of Europe has made us more than any one thing capable of performing the great work which we performed in the war against Germany, and our disinterestedness is of far more value to the world than our eternal meddling in every possible dispute could ever be.

Now, as to our selfishness. I have no desire to boast that we are better than our neighbors, but the fact remains that this Nation in making peace with Germany had not a single selfish or individual interest to serve. All we asked was that Germany should be rendered incapable of again breaking forth, with all the horrors incident to German warfare, upon an unoffending world, and that demand was shared by every free nation and indeed by humanity itself. For ourselves we asked absolutely nothing. We have not asked any government or governments to guarantee our boundaries or our political independence. We have no fear in regard to either. We have sought no territory, no privileges, no advantages, for ourselves. That is the fact. It is apparent on the face of the treaty. I do not mean to reflect upon a single one of the powers with which we have been associated in the war against Germany, but there is not one of them which has not sought individual advantages for their own national benefit. I do not criticize their desires at all. The services and sacrifices of England and France and Belgium and Italy are beyond estimate and beyond praise. I am glad they should have what they desire for their own welfare and safety. But they all receive under the peace territorial and commercial benefits. We are asked to give, and we in no way seek to take. Surely it is not too much to insist that when we are offered nothing but the opportunity to give and to aid others we should have the right to say what sacrifices we shall make and what the magnitude of our gifts shall be. In the prosecution of the war we gave unstintedly American lives and American treasure. When the war closed we had 3,000,000 men under arms. We were turning the country into a vast workshop for war. We advanced ten billions to our allies. We refused no assistance that we could possibly render. All the great energy and power of the Republic were put at the service of the good cause. We have not been ungenerous. We have been devoted to the cause of freedom, humanity, and civilization everywhere. Now we are asked, in the making of peace, to sacrifice our sovereignty in important respects, to involve ourselves almost without limit in the affairs of other nations, and to yield up policies and rights which we have maintained throughout our history. We are asked to incur liabilities to an unlimited extent and furnish assets at the same time which no man can measure. I think it is not only our right but our duty to determine how far we shall go. Not only must we look carefully to see where we are being led into endless disputes and entanglements, but we must not forget that we have in this country millions of people of foreign birth and parentage.

Our one great object is to make all these people Americans so that we may call on them to place America first and serve America as they have done in the war just closed. We cannot Americanize them if we are continually thrusting them back into the quarrels and difficulties of the countries from which they came to us. We shall fill this land with political disputes about the troubles and quarrels of other countries. We shall have a large portion of our people voting not on American questions and not on what concerns the United States but

dividing on issues which concern foreign countries alone. That is an unwhole-
some and perilous condition to force upon this country. We must avoid it. We
ought to reduce to the lowest possible point the foreign questions in which we
involve ourselves. Never forget that this league is primarily—I might say overwhelmingly—a political organization, and I object strongly to having the
politics of the United States turn upon disputes where deep feeling is aroused
but in which we have no direct interest. It will all tend to delay the Ameri-
canization of our great population, and it is more important not only to the
United States but to the peace of the world to make all these people good
Americans than it is to determine that some piece of territory should belong
to one European country rather than to another. For this reason I wish to
limit strictly our interference in the affairs of Europe and of Africa. We have
interests of our own in Asia and in the Pacific which we must guard upon our
own account, but the less we undertake to play the part of umpire and thrust
ourselves into European conflicts the better for the United States and for the
world. . . .

I am as anxious as any human being can be to have the United States render
every possible service to the civilization and the peace of mankind, but I am
certain we can do it best by not putting ourselves in leading strings or subject-
ing our policies and our sovereignty to other nations. The independence of the
United States is not only more precious to ourselves but to the world than any
single possession. Look at the United States to-day. We have made mistakes in
the past. We have had shortcomings. We shall make mistakes in the future
and fall short of our own best hopes. But none the less is there any country today on the face of the earth which can compare with this in ordered liberty,
in peace, and in the largest freedom? I feel that I can say this without being
accused of undue boastfulness, for it is the simple fact, and in making this
treaty and taking on these obligations all that we do is in a spirit of unselfishness and in a desire for the good of mankind. But it is well to remember that
we are dealing with nations every one of which has a direct individual interest
to serve and there is grave danger in an unshared idealism. Contrast the United
States with any country on the face of the earth to-day and ask yourself whether
the situation of the United States is not the best to be found. I will go as far as
anyone in world service, but the first step to world service is the maintenance
of the United States. You may call me selfish if you will, conservative or reactionary, or use any other harsh adjective you see fit to apply, but an American
I was born, an American I have remained all my life. I can never be anything
else but an American, and I must think of the United States first, and when I
think of the United States first in an arrangement like this I am thinking of
what is best for the world, for if the United States fails the best hopes of mankind fail with it. I have never had but one allegiance—I cannot divide it now.
I have loved but one flag and I cannot share that devotion and give affection
to the mongrel banner invented for a league. Internationalism, illustrated by
the Bolshevik and by the men to whom all countries are alike provided they
can make money out of them, is to me repulsive. National I must remain, and
in that way I, like all other Americans, can render the amplest service to the
world. The United States is the world's best hope, but if you fetter her in
the interests and quarrels of other nations, if you tangle her in the intrigues of

Europe, you will destroy her power for good and endanger her very existence. Leave her to march freely through the centuries to come as in the years that have gone. Strong, generous, and confident, she has nobly served mankind. Beware how you trifle with your marvelous inheritance, this great land of ordered liberty, for if we stumble and fall, freedom and civilization everywhere will go down in ruin. . . .

No doubt many excellent and patriotic people see a coming fulfillment of noble ideals in the words "league for peace." We all respect and share these aspirations and desires, but some of us see no hope, but rather defeat, for them in this murky covenant. For we, too, have our ideals, even if we differ from those who have tried to establish a monopoly of idealism. Our first ideal is our country, and we see her in the future, as in the past, giving service to all her people and to the world. Our ideal of the future is that she should continue to render that service of her own free will. She has great problems of her own to solve, very grim and perilous problems, and a right solution, if we can attain to it, would largely benefit mankind. We would have our country strong to resist a peril from the West, as she has flung back the German menace from the East. We would not have our politics distracted and embittered by the dissensions of other lands. We would not have our country's vigor exhausted or her moral force abated by everlasting meddling and muddling in every quarrel, great and small, which afflicts the world. Our ideal is to make her ever stronger and better and finer, because in that way alone, as we believe, can she be of the greatest service to the world's peace and to the welfare of mankind.

13] Liberals Move Against the Treaty

Lodge and his colleagues succeeded in delaying action on the treaty. Meanwhile, sentiment against it grew—among German-Americans who felt their fatherland had been unfairly treated, Italian-Americans resentful about Fiume, Sinophiles angered by the Shantung clauses, conservatives more and more alarmed by what Lodge and others prophesied, and liberals disillusioned by Wilson's compromises. The changing attitudes of the latter are illustrated by the following editorials from the *New Republic*, a weekly edited by Walter Weyl, Herbert Croly, and Walter Lippmann, which had previously been staunch in support of the President.*

[May 10, 1919]

THE TREATY IS READY

A PEACE will be signed. It will not be in all the essentials the kind of peace which was promised to the world while the exaltation of the war was at its height. There is small evidence at Paris of any profound conviction that a new order of international affairs has been inaugurated. The treaty will show at

* LIBERALS MOVE AGAINST THE TREATY: From the *New Republic*, XIX (May 10, 1919), 35; (May 24, 1919), 100–02. Reprinted by permission.

many points the marks of compromise and abatement. It is possible that too much has been conceded. But now within a few days a practical decision must be made and the issue will be between rejection and acceptance of the Treaty and the Covenant. For those who believe that liberal progress depends at this time upon a restoration of industry and normal conditions, who believe that a convulsion wide as the continent would prostrate Europe for decades, there is a strong presumption in favor of accepting the peace. Acknowledging its faults, accepting its disappointments, men who hoped for a better outcome can yet count two clear gains. The nations have agreed to compulsory conference, and they have legally made the causes of war a subject of inquiry by all the members of the League. This is something to build upon. There is here the possibility of growth. The peoples of the world can with these instruments correct errors that may have been made at Paris and complete what Paris has left undone.

[May 24, 1919]

PEACE AT ANY PRICE

THERE are many of our fellow countrymen both in the East and in the West whose sense of justice and fair-dealing is outraged by the treaty, but who cannot quite decide to place themselves in open and uncompromising opposition to it. Their state of mind is analogous to that of those Americans in August, 1914, whose consciences were troubled by the wanton violence of the German invasion of Belgium, but who did not know how as American citizens they could assume effective responsibility for defeating the monster of militant imperialism.

To Americans who share this . . . state of mind, we should like to address an appeal. They are in danger now of committing a mistake similar to that which their fellow countrymen committed in the fall of 1914. During the early months of the war the majority of uneasy Americans compromised with their consciences. They usually became definitely pro-Ally in opinion, but they were mentally unprepared for war, and they considered it unnecessary to consider any method, short of an actual declaration of war, which would bring American political influence and economic power to the support of democratic Europe. In an analogous spirit Americans who are deeply troubled by the proposed treaty of peace are feeling for a way out which does not imply outspoken and uncompromising opposition. Just as four and one-half years ago they shrank from breaking down the traditional aloofness of this country from European political and military controversies, so now they shrink from parting company with their recent companions in arms. The bonds forged by their fight against a common enemy are hard to break. If they reject the treaty they are afraid of looking to themselves and to their European friends like quitters. They are longing for peace and are tempted to accept it at any price.

Yet if they connive at this treaty they will, as liberal and humane American democrats who seek by social experiment and education to render this country more worthy of its still unredeemed national promise, be delivering themselves into the hands of their enemies, the reactionaries and the revolutionists. The future of liberal Americanism depends upon a moral union between democracy and nationalism. Such a union is compromised so long as nationalism remains competitive in policy, exclusive in spirit and complacently capitalist in organization. Liberals all over the world have hoped that a war, which was so clearly the fruit of competition and imperialist and class-bound nationalism, would end in a peace which would moralize nationalism by releasing it from class bondage and exclusive ambitions. The Treaty of Versailles does not even try to satisfy these aspirations. Instead of expressing a great recuperative effort of the conscience of civilization, which for its own sins has sweated so much blood, it does much to intensify and nothing to heal the old and ugly dissensions between political nationalism and social democracy. In so far as its terms are actually carried out, it is bound to provoke the ultimate explosion of irreconcilable warfare. It weaves international animosities and the class conflict into the very fabric of the proposed new system of public law. The European politicians who with American complicity have hatched this inhuman monster have acted either cynically, hypocritically or vindictively, and their handiwork will breed cynicism, hypocrisy or vindictiveness in the minds of future generations. The moral source of the political life of modern nations remains polluted.

The authors of the Treaty of Versailles are the victims of the blind interests and the imperious determinism of an inhumane class economy. They admit in private conversation the diseased nature of their own offspring. "Even conservative opinion in Europe," says William Allen White, "is frankly cynical about Germany's fulfillment of the terms imposed. They are too severe for Germany to live under for a generation. . . . They practically exterminate her as a nation." Why, then, did they do it? Why do they propose to terminate a war, fought in part to vindicate the sacredness of public treaties, by compelling the vanquished enemy to sign a bond which they know he cannot fulfill? The answer is not pleasant. They do this thing because they themselves are the unconscious servants of the cupidity and the vindictiveness which infect the psychology of an inhumane and complacent capitalist society. They crave at any cost the emotional triumph of imposing on the German nation the ultimate humiliation of solemnly consenting to its own abdication as a self-governing and self-respecting community. To satisfy this craving they are so far as possible depriving the German people by public law of the status of economic citizens with rights which other nations are bound to respect. Thus they are deliberately raising the question of working-class solidarity. They are defying the community of interest and the feeling of brotherhood which unites the socially alert workers of all the European peoples. They are subsidizing the growth of class-conscious and class-bound proletarian internationalism dominated by the conviction of the incorrigible inhumanity of a capitalist national economy. They are demonstrating by example what a perfidious protectorate nationalism exercises over the common human interests of all peoples.

The Socialists are fully alive to this deeper and less obvious meaning of the treaty. They will flourish it as a complete vindication of the Marxian dogma that, as long as capitalism prevails, war necessarily operates as the instrument of class aggrandizement and popular exploitation. The treaty proposes the exploitation of the German people only, but an international organization whose chief object it is to profit by the exploitation of a subject people can survive only through the exploitation and deception of its own workers. The treaty is, consequently, greeted as a declaration of a class war by organized society against the proletariat of all nations. It is condemned as a final exposure of the hypocrisy and inhumanity of a national economy. Hitherto, in spite of all their propaganda and of the grievances of the wage-earning class, the Socialists have never persuaded the workers to believe in the need of a class war, or to undermine the popular confidence in nationalism. Now, as they believe, their class enemies have provided them with an unanswerable demonstration, and they are looking forward jubilantly to the inevitable revolution. . . .

In our opinion the Treaty of Versailles subjects all liberalism and particularly that kind of liberalism which breathes the Christian spirit to a decisive test. Its very life depends upon the ability of the modern national state to avoid the irreconcilable class conflict to which, as the Socialists claim, capitalism condemns the future of society. In the event of such a conflict, liberalism is ground, as it is being ground in Russia, between the upper and lower millstones of reaction and revolution. The treaty in so far as it commits the national democracies to a permanent policy of inhumane violence does weave this conflict into the fabric of international law. It is the most shameless and, we hope, the last of those treaties which, while they pretend to bring peace to a mortified world, merely write the specifications for future revolution and war. It presents liberalism with a perfect opportunity of proving whether or not it is actually founded in positive moral and religious conviction. If a war which was supposed to put an end to war culminates without strenuous protest by humane men and women in a treaty of peace which renders peace impossible, the liberalism which preached this meaning for the war will have committed suicide. That such a protest on the part of national liberals may not have much immediate success in defeating the ratification of the treaty is not essential. The Treaty of Versailles, no matter under what kind of compulsion it is ratified by the nations, is impossible of execution and will defeat itself. But it is essential that the ratification should not take place with the connivance of the sincerely liberal and Christian forces in public opinion. . . .

The calamity of the war descended on the western nations because of the existence of one crying weakness in western civilization. The organized Christian nations could never agree upon an effective method of subordinating the exercise of political and economic power to moral and humane purposes. Many liberals have hoped that at the end of the war the enlightened conscience of the western people would arise and exert itself to cure this weakness. The Treaty of Versailles is damned because it does nothing to moralize the future exercise of political and economic power. On the contrary, it conceives the victors who exercise the power as possessing only rights and the vanquished who have lost the power as possessing only duties. The powerful are permitted to abuse it as much as they please, and, in their relations to the defeated Hungary, Austria, Russia and Germany they are encouraged and licensed to abuse it. . . . The treaty does not embody either the spirit or method even of punitive justice. What it does embody and strain to the breaking point is the pagan doctrine and spirit of retaliation. What it treats with utter ignorance is the Christian doctrine of atonement and redemption. At a crisis in the history of civilization, the rulers of the victorious Christian states conclusively demonstrate their own contemptuous disbelief in the practical value of Christian moral economy.

Just as the acceptance of the Treaty of Versailles without protest will undermine the moral foundation of nationalism and menace civilization with an uncontrollable class conflict, so its defeat or discredit will clearly and emphatically testify to a formative connection between religion and morals and economics and politics. It would begin the cure of the spiritual anarchy in western civilization which the recent war and the proposed peace both exemplify. It would constitute the first step in the moral preparation of the western democracies for a League of Nations. For the possibility of any vital League of Nations does not depend, as so many liberals seem to suppose, on the ratification of the treaty. It depends on the rejection of the treaty. The League is not powerful enough to redeem the treaty. But the treaty is vicious enough to incriminate the League. It would convert the League into the instrument of competitive imperialist nationalism whose more disinterested members would labor in vain to mould it into a cooperative society. Liberal democrats cannot honestly consent to peace on the proposed terms. If it was wrong when confronted by the imperialist aggression of Germany to tolerate peace by conniving at such an attack, it is equally wrong when confronted by a treaty which organizes competitive imperialism into an international system to pay so high a price for the ending of the war. This above all others is the time and the occasion to repudiate the idea of peace at any price, to reject immediate peace at the price of permanent moral and economic warfare.

14] Wilson Defends the League

In order to check this drift against the treaty and, if possible, to stir up public pressure in favor of ratification, the President set out upon a nationwide speaking tour. His appearance in Omaha on September 8, 1919, was one of the high points of that swing round the circle.*

Mr. Chairman, My Fellow Citizens:

I never feel more comfortable in facing my fellow citizens than when I can realize that I am not representing a peculiar cause, that I am not speaking for a single group of my fellow citizens, that I am not the representative of a party but the representative of the people of the United States. I went across the water with that happy consciousness, and in all the work that was done on the other side of the sea, where I was associated with distinguished Americans of both political parties, we all of us constantly kept at our heart the feeling that we were expressing the thoughts of America, that we were working for the things that America believed in. I have come here to testify that this treaty contains the things that America believes in.

I brought a copy of the treaty along with me, for I fancy that, in view of

---

* WILSON DEFENDS THE LEAGUE: From Albert Shaw, ed., *The Public Papers of Woodrow Wilson* (New York, 1924), II, 803–16.

the criticisms you have heard of it, you thought it consisted of only four or
five clauses. Only four or five clauses out of this volume are picked out for
criticism. Only four or five phrases in it are called to your attention by some
of the distinguished orators who oppose its adoption. Why, my fellow citizens,
this is one of the great charters of human liberty, and the man who picks out
the flaws that are in it, for there are flaws in it—forgets the magnitude of the
thing, forgets the majesty of the thing, forgets that the counsels of more than
twenty nations combined and were rendered unanimous in the adoption of
this great instrument. Let me remind you of what everybody admits who has
read the document. Everybody admits that it is a complete settlement of the
matters which led to this war, and that it contains the complete machinery
which provides that they shall stay settled.

You know that one of the greatest difficulties in our own domestic affairs
is unsettled land titles. Suppose that somebody were mischievously to tamper
with the land records of the State of Nebraska, and that there should be a
doubt as to the line of every farm. You know what would happen in six
months. All the farmers would be sitting on their fences with shotguns. Litigation would penetrate every community, hot feeling would be generated, contests not only of lawyers, but contests of force, would ensue. Very well, one
of the interesting things that this treaty does is to settle the land titles of Europe, and to settle them in this way, on the principle that every land belongs
to the people that live on it. This is actually the first time in human history
that that principle was ever recognized in a similar document, and yet that
is the fundamental American principle. The fundamental American principle
is the right of the people that live in the country to say what shall be done
with that country. We have gone so far in our assertions of popular right that
we not only say that the people have a right to have a government that suits
them, but that they have a right to change it in any respect at any time. Very
well, that principle lies at the heart of this treaty.

There are peoples in Europe who never before could say that the land they
lived in was their own, and the choice that they were to make of their lives
was their own choice. I know there are men in Nebraska who come from that
country of tragical history, the now restored Republic of Poland, and I want
to call your attention to the fact that Poland is here given her complete resti-
tution; and not only is she given the land that formerly belonged to the Poles,
but had been permitted to remain under other sovereignties. She is given those
lands on a principle that all our hearts approve of. Take what in Europe they
call High Silesia, the mountainous, the upper, portions of the district of Silesia.
The very great majority of the people in High Silesia are Poles, but the Germans contested the statement that most of them were Poles. We said, "Very
well, then, it is none of our business; we will let them decide. We will put
sufficient armed forces into High Silesia to see that nobody tampers with the
processes of the election, and then we will hold a referendum there, and those
people can belong either to Germany or to Poland, as they prefer, and not as
we prefer." And wherever there was a doubtful district we applied the same
principle, that the people should decide and not the men sitting around the
peace table at Paris. When these referenda are completed the land titles of
Europe will be settled, and every country will belong to the people that live

on it to do with what they please. You seldom hear of this aspect of this treaty, my fellow citizens.

You have heard of the council that the newspaper men call the "big four." We had a very much bigger name for ourselves than that. We called ourselves the "supreme council of the principal allied and associated powers," but we had no official title, and sometimes there were five of us instead of four. Those five represented, with the exception of Germany, of course, the great fighting nations of the world. They could have done anything with this treaty that they chose to do, because they had the power to do it, and they chose to do what had never been chosen before, to renounce every right of sovereignty in that settlement to which the people concerned did not assent. That is the great settlement which is represented in this volume.

And it contains, among other things, a great charter of liberty for the workingmen of the world. For the first time in history the counsels of mankind are to be drawn together and concerted for the purpose of defending the rights and improving the conditions of working people—men, women, and children —all over the world. Such a thing as that was never dreamed of before, and what you are asked to discuss in discussing the League of Nations is the matter of seeing that this thing is not interfered with. There is no other way to do it than by a universal League of Nations, and what is proposed is a universal League of Nations. Only two nations are for the time being left out. One of them is Germany, because we did not think that Germany was ready to come in, because we felt that she ought to go through a period of probation. She says that she made a mistake. We now want her to prove it, by not trying it again. She says that she has abolished all the old forms of government by which little secret councils of men, sitting nobody knew exactly where, determined the fortunes of that great nation and, incidentally, tried to determine the fortunes of mankind; but we want her to prove that her constitution is changed and that it is going to stay changed; and then who can, after those proofs are produced, say "No" to a great people 60,000,000 strong, if they want to come in on equal terms with the rest of us and do justice in international affairs? I want to say that I did not find any of my colleagues in Paris disinclined to do justice to Germany. But I hear that this treaty is very hard on Germany. When an individual has committed a criminal act, the punishment is hard, but the punishment is not unjust. This nation permitted itself, through unscrupulous governors, to commit a criminal act against mankind, and it is to undergo the punishment, not more than it can endure, but up to the point where it can pay it must pay for the wrong that it has done.

But the things prescribed in this treaty will not be fully carried out if any one of the great influences that brought that result about is withheld from its consummation. Every great fighting nation in the world is on the list of those who are to constitute the League of Nations. I say every great nation, because America is going to be included among them, and the only choice, my fellow citizens, is whether we will go in now or come in later with Germany; whether we will go in as founders of this covenant of freedom or go in as those who are admitted after they have made a mistake and repented.

I wish I could do what is impossible in a great company like this. I wish I could read that covenant to you, because I do not believe, if you have not read it yourself and have only listened to certain speeches that I have read, that you know anything that is in it. Why, my fellow citizens, the heart of that covenant is that there shall be no war. To listen to some of the speeches that you may have listened to or read, you would think that the heart of it was that it was an arrangement for war. On the contrary, this is the heart of that treaty: The bulk of it is concerned with arrangements under which all the members of the League—that means everybody but Germany and dis-membered Turkey—agree that they never will go to war without first having done one or other of two things—either submitted the question at issue to arbitration, in which case they agree absolutely to abide by the verdict, or, if they do not care to submit it to arbitration, submitted it to discussion by the council of the League of Nations, in which case they must give six months for the discussion and wait three months after the rendering of the decision, whether they like it or not, before they go to war. They agree to cool off for nine months before they yield to the heat of passion which might otherwise have hurried them into war.

If they do not do that, it is not war that ensues; it is something that will interest them and engage them very much more than war; it is an absolute boycott of the nation that disregards the covenant. The boycott is automatic, and just as soon as it applies, then this happens: No goods can be shipped out of that country; no goods can be shipped into it. No telegraphic message may pass either way across its borders. No package of postal matter—no letter —can cross its borders either way. No citizen of any member of the League can have any transactions of any kind with any citizen of that nation. It is the most complete isolation and boycott ever conceived, and there is not a nation in Europe that can live for six months without importing goods out of other countries. After they have thought about the matter for six months, I predict that they will have no stomach for war.

All that you are told about in this covenant, so far as I can learn, is that there is an Article X. I will repeat Article X to you; I think I can repeat it verbatim, the heart of it at any rate. Every member of the League promises to respect and preserve as against external aggression—not as against internal revolution—the territorial integrity and existing political independence of every other member of the League, and if it is necessary to enforce this promise—I mean, for the nations to act in concert with arms in their hands to enforce it —then the council of the League shall advise what action is necessary. Some gentlemen who doubt the meaning of English words have thought that ad-vice did not mean advice, but I do not know anything else that it does mean, and I have studied English most of my life and speak it with reasonable cor-rectness. The point is this: The council can not give that advice without the vote of the United States, unless it is a party to the dispute; but, my fellow citizens, if you are a party to the dispute you are in the scrap anyhow. If you are a party, then the question is not whether you are going to war or not, but merely whether you are going to war against the rest of the world or with the rest of the world, and the object of war in that case will be to defend that central thing that I began by speaking about. That is the guaranty of the land titles of the world which have been established by this treaty. Poland, Czecho-slovakia, Roumania, Jugoslavia—all those nations which never had a vision of independent liberty until now—have their liberty and independence guaranteed to them. If we do not guarantee them, then we have this interesting choice: I hear gentlemen say that we went into the recent war because we were forced into it, and their preference now is to wait to be forced in again. They do not pretend that we can keep out; they merely pretend that we ought to keep out until we are ashamed not to go in.

This is the covenant of the League of Nations that you hear objected to, the only possible guaranty against war. I would consider myself recreant to every mother and father, every wife and sweetheart in this country, if I consented to the ending of this war without a guaranty that there would be no other. You say, "Is it an absolute guaranty?" No; there is no absolute guaranty against human passion; but even if it were only 10 per cent. of a guaranty, would not you rather have 10 per cent. guaranty against war than none? If it only creates a presumption that there will not be war, would you not rather have that presumption than live under the certainty that there will be war? For, I tell you, my fellow citizens, I can predict with absolute certainty that within another generation there will be another world war if the nations of the world do not concert the method by which to prevent it.

But I did not come here this morning, I remind myself, so much to expound the treaty as to talk about these interesting things that we hear about that are called reservations. A reservation is an assent with a big but. We agree —but. Now, I want to call your attention to some of these buts. I will take them, so far as I can remember the order, in the order in which they deal with clauses of the League itself.

In the first article of the covenant it is provided that a nation can withdraw from the League on two years' notice, provided at the time of its withdrawal, that is to say, at the expiration of the two years, it has fulfilled all its international obligations and all its obligations under the covenant. Some of our friends are very uneasy about that. They want to sit close to the door with their hands on the knob, and they want to say, "We are in this thing but we are in it with infinite timidity; we are in it only because you overpersuaded us and wanted us to come in, and we are going to try this thing every now and then and see if it is locked, and just as soon as we see anything we don't like, we are going to scuttle." Now, what is the trouble? What are they afraid of? I want you to put this to every man you know who makes this objection, what is he afraid of? Is he afraid that when the United States withdraw it will not have fulfilled its international obligations? Is he willing to bring that indictment against this beloved country? My fellow citizens, we never did fail to fulfill an international obligation and, God guiding and helping us, we never will. I for one am not going to admit in any connection the slightest doubt that, if we ever choose to withdraw, we will then have fulfilled our obligations. If I make reservations, as they are called, about this, what do I do? This covenant does not set up any tribunal to judge whether we have fulfilled our obligations at that time or not. There is only one thing to restrain us, and that is the opinion of mankind. Are these gentlemen such poor patriots that they are afraid that the United States will cut a poor figure in the opinion of mankind? We have always been at pains to earn the respect of mankind, and we shall always be at pains to retain it. I for one am too proud as an American to say that any doubt will ever hang around our right to withdraw upon the condition of the fulfillment of our international obligations.

They do not like the way in which the Monroe Doctrine is mentioned. Well, I would not stop on a question of style. The Monroe Doctrine is adopted. It is swallowed, hook, line, and sinker, and, being carefully digested into the central organism of the whole instrument, I do not care what language they use about it. The language is entirely satisfactory so far as I understand the English language. That puzzles me, my fellow citizens. The English language seems to have got some new meaning since I studied it that bothers these gentlemen. I do not know what dictionaries they resort to. I do not know what manuals of conscience they can possibly resort to. The Monroe Doctrine is expressly authenticated in this document, for the first time in history, by all the great nations of the world, and it was put there at our request.

The fourth matter that they are concerned about is domestic questions, so they want to put in a reservation enumerating certain questions as domestic questions which everybody on both sides of the water admits are domestic questions. That seems to me, to say the least, to be a work of supererogation. It does not seem to me necessary to specify what everybody admits, but they are so careful—I believe the word used to be "meticulous"—that they want to put in what is clearly implied in the whole instrument. "Well," you say, "why not?" Well, why not, my fellow citizens? The conference at Paris will still be sitting when the Senate of the United States has acted upon this treaty. Perhaps I ought not to say that so confidently. No man, even in the secrets of Providence, can tell how long it will take the United States Senate to do anything, but I imagine that in the normal course of human fatigue the Senate will have acted upon this treaty before the conference in Paris gets through with the Austrian treaty and the Bulgarian treaty and the Turkish treaty. They will still be there on the job. Now—every lawyer will follow me in this —if you take a contract and change the words, even though you do not change the sense, you have to get the other parties to accept those words. Is not that true? Therefore every reservation will have to be taken back to all the signatories of this treaty, and I want you to notice that that includes Germany. We will have to ask Germany's consent to read this treaty the way we understand it. I want to tell you that we did not ask Germany's consent with regard to the meaning of any one of those terms while we were in Paris. We told her what they meant and said, "Sign here." Are there any patriotic Americans who desire the method changed? Do they want me to ask the assembly at Weimar if I may read the treaty the way it means but in words which the United States Senate thinks it ought to have been written in? You see, reservations come down to this, that they want to change the language of the treaty without changing its meaning and involve all the embarrassments. Because, let me say, there are indications—I am judging not from official dispatches but from the newspapers—that people are not in as good a humor over in Paris now as they were when I was there, and it is going to be more difficult to get agreement from now on than it was then. After dealing with some of those gentlemen I found that they were as ingenious as any American in attaching unexpected meanings to plain words, and, having gone through the mill on the existing language, I do not want to go through it again on changed language.

I must not turn away from this great subject without adverting to one particular in the treaty itself, and that is the provision with regard to the transfer of certain German rights in the Province of Shantung, China, to Japan. I have frankly said to my Japanese colleagues in the conference, and therefore I can without impropriety say it here, that I was very deeply dissatisfied with that part of the treaty. But, my fellow citizens, Japan agreed at that very time, and as part of the understanding upon which those clauses were put into the treaty, that she would relinquish every item of sovereignty that Germany had enjoyed to China, and that she would retain only what other nations have elsewhere in China, certain economic concessions with regard to the railway and the mines, which she was to operate under a corporation and subject to the laws of China. As I say, I wish she could have done more. But suppose, as some have suggested, that we dissent from that clause in the treaty. You can not sign all of the treaty but one part, my fellow citizens. It is like the President's veto. He can not veto provisions in a bill. He has got either to sign the bill or veto the bill. We can not sign the treaty with the Shantung provision out of it, and if we could, what sort of service would we be doing to China?

Let us state the facts with brutal frankness. England and France are bound by solemn treaty, entered into before the conference at Paris, before the end of the war, to give Japan what she gets in this treaty in the Province of Shantung. They can not in honor withdraw from that promise. They can not consent to a peace treaty which does not contain those provisions with regard to Shantung. England and France, therefore, will stand behind Japan, and if we are not signatories to the treaties and not parties she will get all that Germany had in Shantung, more than she will get under the promises which she made to us, and the only way we can get it away from her is by going to war with Japan and Great Britain and France. Does that look like a workable proposition? Is that doing China a service? Whereas, if we do accept this treaty, we are members of the League of Nations, China is a member of the League, and Japan is a member of the League, and under that much-criticized Article X Japan promises and we guarantee that the territorial integrity and political independence of China will be respected and preserved. That is the way to serve China. That is the only possible way in the circumstances to serve China.

Therefore we can not rewrite this treaty. We must take it or leave it, and gentlemen, after all the rest of the world has signed it, will find it very difficult to make any other kind of treaty. As I took the liberty of saying the other night, it is a case of "put up or shut up." The world can not breathe in the atmosphere of negations. The world can not deal with nations who say, "We won't play!" The world can not have anything to do with an arrangement in which every nation says, "We will take care of ourselves." Is it possible, my fellow citizens—is it possible, for the sinister thing has been suggested to me—that there is a group of individuals in this country who have conceived it as desirable that the United States should exercise its power alone, should arm for the purpose, should be ready for the enterprise, and should dominate the world by arms? There are indications that there are groups of citizens in this country who do not find that an unpalatable program. Are we going to substitute for Pan Germanism a sinister Pan Americanism? The thing is inconceivable. It is hideous. No man dare propose that in plain words to any American audience anywhere. The heart of this people is pure. The heart of this people is true. This great people loves liberty. It loves justice. It would rather have liberty and justice than wealth and power. It is the great idealistic force of history, and the idealism of America is what has made conquest of the spirits of men.

I said just now at the opening that I was happy to forget on a campaign like this what party I belonged to, and I hope that you will not think that I am recalling what party I belong to if I say how proud I have been to stand alongside of Senator Hitchcock in this fight. I would be just as glad to stand by Senator Norris if he would let me. I refer to Senator Hitchcock because I know this is his home town and because of my personal regard for him, and because I wanted to make it the preface to say I want to be the brother and comrade and coworker of every man who will work for this great cause. It heartens me when I find, as I found in Des Moines and I find here, that there are more Republicans on the committees that meet me than Democrats. That may be in proportion to the population, but nevertheless I judge from what I see of these gentlemen that they are, at any rate, very favorable specimens and that I can take it for granted, because of what I see in my dealing with them, that they do represent some of the permanence and abiding influences of great communities like this. Why, the heart of America beats in these great prairies and on these hillsides. Sometimes in Washington you seem very far away. The voices that are most audible in Washington are not voices that anybody cares to listen to for very long, and it is refreshing to get out among the great body of one's fellow citizens and feel the touch of hand and the contact of shoulder and the impulse of mass movement which is going to make spiritual conquest of the world.

15] The Senate Maintains Its Reservations

Wilson had never been altogether well, and toward the end of his speaking tour he approached the point of physical collapse. He was ordered back to Washington by his doctor. Soon afterward he suffered a paralytic stroke and for some time was almost wholly incapacitated. He had given his lieutenants in the Senate orders to oppose any amendments or reservations, and, though astute observers predicted that the treaty could not pass without reservations, he left these instructions unchanged. On November 19, 1919, the treaty came up for a vote. The following reservations, which were brought up and voted upon individually, were proposed.*

1. The reservations adopted are hereby made a part and condition of this resolution of ratification, which ratification is not to take effect or bind the

* THE SENATE MAINTAINS ITS RESERVATIONS: From the *Congressional Record*, 65 Cong., 1 Sess., pp. 8767–803.

United States until the said reservations and understandings adopted by the Senate have been accepted by an exchange of notes as a part and a condition of this resolution of ratification by at least three of the four principal Allied and Associated Powers, to wit, Great Britain, France, Italy, and Japan.

2. The United States so understands and construes Article 1 that in case of notice of withdrawal from the league of nations, as provided in said article, the United States shall be the sole judge as to whether all its international obligations and all its obligations under the said covenant have been fulfilled, and notice of withdrawal by the United States may be given by a concurrent resolution of the Congress of the United States.

3. The United States assumes no obligation to preserve the territorial integrity or political independence of any other country or to interfere in controversies between nations—whether members of the league or not—under the provisions of Article 10, or to employ the military or naval forces of the United States under any article of the treaty for any purpose, unless in any particular case the Congress, which, under the Constitution, has the sole power to declare war or authorize the employment of the military or naval forces of the United States, shall by act or joint resolution so provide.

4. No mandate shall be accepted by the United States under Article 22, Part I, or any other provision of the treaty of peace with Germany, except by action of the Congress of the United States.

5. The United States reserves to itself exclusively the right to decide what questions are within its domestic jurisdiction and declares that all domestic and political questions relating wholly or in part to its internal affairs, including immigration, labor, coastwise traffic, the tariff, commerce, the suppression of traffic in women and children and in opium and other dangerous drugs, and all other domestic questions, are solely within the jurisdiction of the United States and are not under this treaty to be submitted in any way either to arbitration or to the consideration of the council or of the assembly of the league of nations, or any agency thereof, or to the decision or recommendation of any other power.

6. The United States will not submit to arbitration or to inquiry by the assembly or by the council of the League of Nations, provided for in said treaty of peace, any questions which in the judgment of the United States depend upon or relate to its long-established policy, commonly known as the Monroe Doctrine; said doctrine is to be interpreted by the United States alone and is hereby declared to be wholly outside the jurisdiction of said League of Nations and entirely unaffected by any provision contained in the said treaty of peace with Germany.

7. The United States withholds its assent to Articles 156, 157, and 158, and reserves full liberty of action with respect to any controversy which may arise under said articles between the Republic of China and the Empire of Japan.

8. The Congress of the United States will provide by law for the appointment of the representatives of the United States in the assembly and the council of the league of nations, and may in its discretion provide for the participation of the United States in any commission, committee, tribunal, court, council, or conference, or in the selection of any members thereof and for the appointment of members of said commissions, committees, tribunals, courts, councils, or con-

ferences, or any other representatives under the treaty of peace, or in carrying out its provisions, and until such participation and appointment have been so provided for and the powers and duties of such representatives have been defined by law, no person shall represent the United States under either said league of nations or the treaty of peace with Germany or be authorized to perform any act for or on behalf of the United States thereunder, and no citizen of the United States shall be selected or appointed as a member of said commissions, committees, tribunals, courts, councils, or conferences except with the approval of the Senate of the United States.

9. The United States understands that the reparation commission will regulate or interfere with exports from the United States to Germany, or from Germany to the United States, only when the United States by Act or Joint Resolution of Congress approves such regulation or interference.

10. The United States shall not be obligated to contribute to any expenses of the League of Nations, or of the Secretariat, or of any commission, or committee, or conference, or other agency, organized under the League of Nations or under the treaty or for the purpose of carrying out the treaty provisions, unless and until an appropriation of funds available for such expenses shall have been made by the Congress of the United States.

11. If the United States shall at any time adopt any plan for the limitation of armaments proposed by the council of the league of nations under the provisions of Article 8, it reserves the right to increase such armaments without the consent of the council whenever the United States is threatened with invasion or engaged in war.

12. The United States reserves the right to permit in its discretion, the nationals of a covenant-breaking State, as defined in Article 16 of the covenant of the league of nations, residing within the United States or in countries other than that violating said Article 16, to continue their commercial, financial, and personal relations with the nationals of the United States.

13. Nothing in Articles 296, 297, or in any of the annexes thereto [canceling debts to German nationals] or in any other article, section, or annex of the treaty of peace with Germany shall, as against citizens of the United States, be taken to mean any confirmation, ratification, or approval of any act otherwise illegal or in contravention of the rights of citizens of the United States.

14. The United States withhold its assent to Part XIII (Articles 387 to 427, inclusive) unless Congress by Act or Joint Resolution shall hereafter make provision for representation in the organization established by said Part XIII [the International Labor Organization], and in such event the participation of the United States will be governed and conditioned by the provisions of such Act or Joint Resolution.

CONCLUSION

Loyal to their invalid chief, most of the Democrats in the Senate voted against these reservations. They were joined by a minority, largely Republican, that opposed ratification in any form. The treaty with reservations thus went down to defeat. Hitchcock then asked for a vote on the treaty without reservations, and most of the Republicans, as well as the irreconcilable foes of the treaty, united in killing it in that form as well. Through the winter, Democrats and moderate Republicans labored for a compromise. But Wilson remained practically immovable; Lodge and the Republican leadership obstructed rather than furthered a solution. Consequently, on March 13, 1920, when the treaty was brought up for a second time, it lost again. Many prominent figures, including former President Taft and former Secretary of State Elihu Root, continued to call for participation in the League, and Republican Presidential candidate Warren Harding spoke vaguely of a substitute "association of nations." So far as the United States was concerned, however, the treaty and the Covenant were in fact dead.

Few episodes in American history have excited so much recrimination. Historians and publicists in later years damned Wilson for compromising at Versailles and blamed him and the other peacemakers for many of the world's subsequent troubles. Others charged these tragic events to Lodge and the senators who rejected Wilson's handiwork, saying that they had caused America to shirk its responsibility for maintaining the peace.

But all these accusations and counteraccusations rest on hypotheses about what might have been. The serious student of history knows such speculation to be idle. His task is to understand what men did and why. The selections in this chapter are only fragments, but they may perhaps give the reader some compassion for those who in 1919 had the awful responsibility of making peace for the world and some comprehension of the fears as well as the hopes of those days.

STUDY QUESTIONS

1] One historian has written as follows of Wilson at the Paris Peace Conference: "A careful study of the record reveals an extraordinary consistency in Wilson's fight for his program under overwhelming difficulties, as well as a high degree of political intelligence in translating the abstract principle of his program into concrete details of application." Do you agree or disagree? Discuss.

2] The treaty was opposed both by "liberals," such as the editors of the *New Republic*, and by "conservatives," such

as Senator Lodge. On what did each group base its objections? Was there merit in either position?

3] In defending the treaty in his Omaha speech, was Wilson
entirely honest in replying to Lodge's objections? Were
there discrepancies between what he said in public in the
United States and what he had said behind closed doors
in Paris?

4] Why did Wilson stand steadfastly against the Senate
reservations? Did they seriously damage the peace or
change the treaty? Would it have been better for the
United States and the world for Wilson to have accepted
the reservations in their final form?

RECOMMENDED READINGS

PRIMARY SOURCES

BAKER, RAY STANNARD, AND WILLIAM E. DODD, eds. *The Public Papers of Woodrow Wilson*, 6 vols. (New York, 1925–27).

KEYNES, JOHN MAYNARD. *The Economic Consequences of the Peace* (New York,
1920).

LANSING, ROBERT. *The Peace Negotiations: A Personal Narrative* (Boston, 1921).

LLOYD GEORGE, DAVID. *Memoirs of the Peace Conference*, 2 vols. (New Haven,
1939).

LODGE, HENRY CABOT. *The Senate and the League of Nations* (New York, 1925).

MANTOUX, PAUL. *Les délibérations du Conseil des Quatre (24 mars–28 juin 1919)*,
2 vols. (Paris, 1955).

MILLER, DAVID HUNTER. *The Drafting of the Covenant*, 2 vols. (New York,
1923).

SEYMOUR, CHARLES, ed. *The Intimate Papers of Colonel House*, 4 vols. (Boston,
1926–28).

U.S. CONGRESS. *Congressional Record*, 65 Cong., 1 Sess.

U.S. DEPARTMENT OF STATE. *Papers Relating to the Foreign Relations of the
United States: The Paris Peace Conference, 1919*, 13 vols. (Washington,
1942–47).

SECONDARY SOURCES

ADLER, SELIG. *The Isolationist Impulse* (New York, 1957).

BAILEY, THOMAS A. *Woodrow Wilson and the Great Betrayal* (New York, 1945).

————. *Woodrow Wilson and the Lost Peace* (New York, 1944).

BAKER, RAY STANNARD. *Woodrow Wilson and the World Settlement*, 3 vols.
(New York, 1922).

BIRDSALL, PAUL. *Versailles: Twenty Years After* (New York, 1941).

BLUM, JOHN M. *Woodrow Wilson and the Politics of Morality* (Boston, 1956).

FLEMING, DENNA F. *The United States and the League of Nations, 1918–1920*
(New York, 1932).

GARRATY, JOHN A. *Henry Cabot Lodge: A Biography* (New York, 1953).

KING, JERE C. *Foch vs. Clemenceau* (Cambridge, Mass., 1960).

LINK, ARTHUR S. *Wilson the Diplomatist* (Baltimore, 1957).

McCALLUM, RONALD B. *Public Opinion and the Last Peace* (London, 1944).

NICOLSON, HAROLD. *Peacemaking, 1919* (New York, 1939).

NOBLE, G. BERNARD. *Policies and Opinions at Paris, 1919* (New York, 1935).

TEMPERLEY, HAROLD W. V. *A History of the Peace Conference of Paris*, 6 vols. (London, 1920–24).

The Depression Crisis and the Emergence of the Welfare State, 1932–1935

ALFRED D. CHANDLER, JR.

MASSACHUSETTS INSTITUTE OF TECHNOLOGY

CONTENTS

CHRONOLOGY

1932

FEBRUARY 2 Reconstruction Finance Corporation established.
NOVEMBER 8 Roosevelt defeats Hoover—popular vote: 27,821,857 to 15,761,841.

1933

MARCH 9–JUNE 16 The "Hundred Days."
MARCH 9 Emergency Banking Relief Act enacted.
MAY 12 Agricultural Adjustment Act enacted.
MAY 12 Federal Emergency Relief Act enacted.
MAY 18 Tennessee Valley Authority Act enacted.
JUNE 16 National Industrial Recovery Act enacted.

1934

JANUARY 30 Gold Reserve Act enacted.
APRIL 2 Cotton Control Act enacted.
MAY–JULY Keynes visits United States.
JUNE 6 Securities Exchange Act enacted.
JUNE 8 Roosevelt outlines long-term plans to Congress.
JUNE 28 Tobacco Control Act enacted.
JUNE 30 National Resources Board appointed.
NOVEMBER 6 Democrats gain ten seats in Senate and ten in House.

1935

JANUARY 4 Roosevelt's annual message to Congress recommending legislation for the "Second New Deal."
APRIL 8 WPA created.
MAY 27 NIRA invalidated by Supreme Court.
JUNE 7 National Resources Committee created.
JULY 5 National Labor Relations Act enacted.
AUGUST 14 Social Security Act enacted.

INTRODUCTION

ONLY THE nation's great wars have directly affected more Americans than did the great depression of the 1930's. And where war for all its tragedies often brought excitement, challenges, and expansion of personal energies and national resources, economic depression meant only stagnation, frustration, and unused energies and resources. The great depression began with the dramatic stock-market crash in October, 1929. Overnight, fortunes were wiped out. Then followed the inexorable descent of production, profits, salaries, wages, and employment. In a little over two years the depression had sliced national production in half and left more than twelve million unemployed. The nation's businesses, which reported profits totaling $8.3 billion in 1929, recorded a net loss of $1.3 billion in 1931. Those who still had jobs lived in perpetual fear of losing them. Those whose businesses still showed a profit lived in dread of bankruptcy.

These fears had a shattering effect on many basic beliefs. Most Americans firmly believed that hard work, thrift, technological innovation, and careful investment assured an expanding economy and, thus, the economic security of the individual. Yet, in spite of continued innovation and investment, half the nation's vast industrial plant and complex technological equipment stood idle while millions of men searched futilely for work. Savings disappeared when the neighborhood bank closed its doors. Years of regular work ended suddenly and incomprehensibly with unemployment. For many Americans such experiences shook their confidence in themselves, in their economy, and even in their beliefs. To others it called for developing new concepts and new methods to permit the survival of the old values. To still others the clear challenge made them cling more tenaciously to their inherited ways and economic beliefs.

As those who still had jobs and businesses became more apprehensive, those without them grew more despairing. As the depression deepened, the mood of men changed when they could find no work in a land of great factories and shops and went hungry in a land of bountiful harvests. Anger followed initial unbelief and doubt, only to be replaced by an often numbing desperation. The shock at being unable to find the work they so urgently needed would often turn to anger at the economic system and the men who managed it. John Steinbeck caught this feeling in his novel, *The Grapes of Wrath* (1939):

> And the companies, the banks worked at their own doom and they did not know it. The fields were fruitful, and starving men moved on the roads. The granaries were full and the children of the poor grew up rachitic, and the pustules of pellagra swelled on their sides. . . . On the highways the people moved like ants and searched for work, for food. And the anger began to ferment.

By the third winter of the depression, malnutrition and a growing sense of futility had seeped into much of the anger. More often than not, apathy and utter helplessness began to take its place. But whatever their mood, men without work looked constantly to their government to provide some security and some hope.

The full impact of the depression on American ideas and institutions came only after the election of Franklin D. Roosevelt in November, 1932. Taking office the following March, Roosevelt began to turn the nation's energies to meet the crises of the depression far more effectively than had his predecessor. In developing policies of relief, recovery, and reform, his administration produced answers to long-standing issues and problems. The farmers obtained government control of prices and production, which many had come to consider even before 1929 as the only practical solution to the overproduction that had been plaguing agriculture since the end of World War I. Labor won government support of collective bargaining for which it had been fighting for more than a generation. Finance, the power industry, and communications came to be regulated by commissions similar to those created earlier to supervise railroads, commerce, and other branches of trade.

As significant as the fulfillment of earlier reforms was the growth of brand-new governmental functions. Under Roosevelt, the national state undertook for the first time the responsibility of assuring its citizens a minimum of security against the vicissitudes inherent in a commercial, industrial, and increasingly urban society. And for the first time it began to develop coherent, long-term economic policies and plans necessary to maintain the stability of an advanced economy. Before the depression, very few voices called for the federal government to assume these responsibilities. Even the states had made only a feeble start toward social security. A number had established pensions for the aged, but before 1932 no state had set up a program for unemployment insurance. During the 1920's, the federal government's responsibility for maintaining economic stability had been even less discussed in Congress or in the press than its obligations for social security. With the coming of the depression, however, the federal government quickly took on these basic functions of a modern welfare state. It began to provide a minimum of economic security to the individual citizen, and it accepted the responsibility for maintaining the stability of the national economy on which such security must ultimately rest.

The welfare state was slow in coming to the United States, primarily because the country enjoyed continuing solid economic growth, interrupted only by two very brief recessions, from the late 1890's until 1929. This prolonged prosperity was based on the coming of great new industries—electrical, automotive, and chemical—and the rapid growth of cities and their suburbs (urban population rose from 30.2 million in 1900 to 69.0 million in 1930). The building of these industries required heavy capital investment and, in turn, provided a host of new jobs and new sources of profits, salaries, and wages. Moreover, these industries became huge new markets for many of the leading older trades, particularly petroleum, rubber, steel, and nonferrous metals, and so further expanded investment, jobs, and income. Furthermore, the growth of the city, the suburb, and the use of the automobile stimulated a far-reaching boom in private construction of homes, buildings, and highways. The net result was an impressive increase in the nation's over-all income. Total annual income from private production rose from $13.8 billion in 1899 to $55.5 billion in 1919 and to $65.7 in 1928.

For all this solid growth, the American economy in the 1920's had critical weaknesses. One was the existence of large, unprofitable industries—including textiles, bituminous coal, clothing, and, above all, agriculture. These businesses differed from the more prosperous ones in that they were made up of many small, highly competitive units that were unable to adjust output to demand as could the great corporations that dominated the steel, electrical, automobile, chemical, petroleum, rubber, and other key trades. Severe competition in those industries not yet dominated by big business brought repeated cuts in prices, wages, salaries, and profits.

Other serious flaws in the economy of the 1920's were an uneven distribution of wealth and an unstable and still only partially regulated national credit structure. In 1929, 42.4 per cent of American families had an income of less than $1500 a year, while the 24,000 families with incomes of over $100,000 each had a total income three times as great as the total income of the 5.8 million poorest families. This maldistribution of income and wealth had a double-barreled effect. It placed a real limit on the possible consumption of the products of the nation's ever growing industrial plant. At the same time, the wealthy tended to invest their surplus income in what was becoming, given the limited size of the market, an unnecessary expansion of plant and facilities. Or else they spent their funds on luxuries or speculative ventures. Not surprisingly then, automobile production leveled off in the mid-twenties with an output of approximately four million passenger cars a year, even though the industry's factories had the capacity for producing six million. In the mid-1920's, too, the construction boom leveled off and so did other capital goods industries. Demand was maintained until 1929 largely through the extension of credit. Excessive credit also permitted continued investment in capital goods and increasing speculation on the stock market. Loans from banks to stock brokers for speculative purposes rose from about three billion dollars in 1927 to over eight billion in 1929.

In October, 1929, the "great bull market" collapsed. With the crash, credit dried up. Without credit, demand plummeted. As demand disappeared, profits, salaries, and wages dropped and men were laid off. With the contraction of the nation's income came a further shrinkage in demand, which, in turn, meant lower wages, salaries, and profits and more unemployed. The downward spiral was more vicious after 1929 than in the extended depressions of the nineteenth century just because the country had become transformed into an urban and industrial one. In the earlier depressions, the majority of the population, still living on farms, could keep busy growing crops and eke out a living with relatively little cash. Without a cash income, the city dweller literally had nothing. Moreover, by the 1930's many more farmers were tenants, sharecroppers, and even hired laborers than they were in earlier years. As such they were almost as dependent on regular income as the urban worker.

As more and more men lost their means of earning a cash income, they had to turn to local private charities or public agencies for food, clothing, and shelter. Yet the depression was quickly drying up the sources of funds for both private and public relief. As municipal and state tax receipts dropped and the wealthier had fewer funds available for charity, the demand grew increasingly stronger for federal moneys to provide direct relief for the unemployed. Even the richest communities found themselves without adequate funds to assist the distressed. As the crisis of the depression spread, the call for federal action went even further. The national government, more and more citizens insisted, must act energetically to stop the decline and set the economy on the road to recovery.

Herbert Hoover, who had been President only seven months when the stock market collapsed, moved towards federal action with the greatest reluctance. His profound distrust of governmental power reflected both the values he had learned as a boy in Iowa and his later experiences—as an engineer in foreign lands, as the administrator who provided food to starving civilians in Europe during and after World War I, and as the Secretary of Commerce from 1921 until 1928. The government should provide assistance and advice to individuals and private enterprises, but it must not attempt to control, plan, or direct their activities. Centralization of authority and concentration of power necessary for such control would threaten, Hoover believed, fundamental American ways and values. Before the great depression, the majority of his countrymen undoubtedly agreed with him.

In providing relief for the unemployed, Hoover pinned his hopes on voluntary local associations, particularly combined charities in the form of "community chests." These private activities obviously had to be backed by local public aid. State and municipal funds paid for three-fourths of the nation's relief in 1929 and four-fifths of it by 1932. To coordinate the activities of community chests, cities, and states, Hoover created the Emergency Committee on Employment. But this organization did little more than advise and exhort. Throughout Hoover's term, relief continued to be financed locally. Only in 1932 did the federal government lend, but not give, funds to states and municipalities to help them meet relief bills.

Hoover was somewhat less hesitant in using federal funds to try to stop the decline of prices, wages, and output. Under the Agricultural Marketing Act, passed in June, 1929, he had the government purchase commodities on the open market in order to maintain prices. But without some means of controlling agricultural production, the attempt proved futile. In 1930, he brought industrial and labor leaders together to get them to agree voluntarily not to reduce wages or lay off men. But again continuing competition for decreasing markets and fewer jobs made this effort also futile. As early as 1930 Hoover spent $700 million on public buildings, roads, and river and harbor improvements. Finally in December, 1931, he proposed the creation of a large government lending agency, the Reconstruction Finance Corporation, which during 1932 lent more than $1.5 billion to bolster the finances of local and state governments, banks, insurance companies, railroads, and other private enterprises. These federal loans went, where possible, to "self-liquidating" projects, that is, to those like toll bridges and power plants that could pay for themselves. Hoover, while using the federal government to combat the depression, had no intention of having it play a continuing role in maintaining economic stability.

Hoover's opponent in the election of 1932, had much less fear than his rival of expanding the functions of government to insure the security of the individual citizen. As governor of New York Franklin D. Roosevelt had done as much as any state executive to aid the unemployed. As Presidential candidate, he not only called for direct federal relief, but insisted that the welfare of the individual had become "the positive duty of the Federal Government" when and if the states could not carry on the burden. Such a duty, he suggested, included the provision of adequate housing and medical care as well as the establishment of old-age benefits, compulsory unemployment insurance, and the provision of jobs through publicly financed projects for housing, slum clearance, and the like.

In advocating the enlargement of the welfare activities of the federal government, Roosevelt did not believe he was rejecting essential American beliefs. "This seeking for a greater measure of welfare and happiness," he wrote after he became President, "does not indicate a change in values. It is rather a return to values lost in the course of our economic development and expansion." The challenge facing Americans, he insisted, was to adjust existing ways and institutions to meet the underlying needs of an urban, industrial nation that the depression had so starkly revealed. Only in this way could the older values be maintained or even saved. Hoover disagreed completely. Roosevelt's proposals were, he maintained, based on alien philosophies that, if adopted, would destroy the unique American system.

By 1932 many Americans had become convinced that survival of old values called for a more drastic change in the role of the federal government than even Roosevelt was proposing. Plans for security of the individual were in themselves not enough, for such security depended fundamentally on the nation's over-all economic health. Academicians, such as Raymond Moley, Adolf A. Berle, Jr., and Rexford G. Tugwell of Columbia University, who advised Roosevelt both before and after he became President, believed that economic recovery and stability could come only through centralized coordination and control. Continued competition and exposure to the natural forces of the market meant continuing disaster. Their views were strongly seconded by progressive Republicans, including Donald Richberg, General Hugh Johnson, Harold Ickes, and Senator Robert La Follette, Jr., who fully supported General Johnson's belief that: "For good or evil, we are entering a managed economy. . . . It is not a question of whether we shall have a managed economy, but of who shall manage it. . . . The rout of laissez-faire is rampant throughout the world." Labor's leaders too, such as Sidney Hillman, and its political supporters, such as Senator Robert F. Wagner, agreed that centralized federal control must replace decentralized competitive chaos. Even leading industrialists, including the presidents of General Electric and the United States Chamber of Commerce, had reached these same convictions. During the campaign, Roosevelt himself, however, never made an unqualified commitment to securing recovery and maintaining stability through centralized federal planning and control.

When Roosevelt took office in March, 1933, after a sweeping victory in the November elections, many of these advocates of centralized direction were among his closest advisers. They helped work out the proposals and legislation that made the first hundred days of the administration so memorable. These proposals, which came in quick succession, dramatized the new, flexible, imaginative, and innovative assault the federal government was making on the depression. The attack restored the confidence of most Americans who now felt that the crisis could be met without fundamentally altering basic institutions and values.

Roosevelt acted first to meet a banking crisis. He did so by assuring the country that the banking system was sound, by having the RFC expand its loans to distressed financial institutions, and by providing federal insurance of bank deposits. To give immediate relief to the unemployed, he recommended the passage of the Civilian Conservation Corps Act, which offered jobs to 250,000 young men in constructive outdoor work, and the creation of the Federal Emergency Relief Administration, to provide the states with outright grants rather than loans for meeting the costs of relief. The formation of the Tennessee Valley Authority expanded the activities of the government-owned plants on the Tennessee River and in time provided a model for the government planning of a geographical region. In early June, Congress created the Home Owners Loan Corporation, authorized to issue $2 billion in bonds to refinance home mortgage debts. Shortly afterwards, Congress approved the Emergency Railroad Transportation Act.

The two most important pieces of legislation during the first hundred days were, however, the Agricultural Adjustment Act and the National Industrial Recovery Act. The first aimed at restoring the purchasing power of farmers by increasing prices through restricting production. The government was to pay benefits, or "rents," to farmers for not planting or producing corn, wheat, cotton, tobacco, hogs, and dairy products. Funds for these payments came from taxes on processors of specified farm goods. Besides providing further for the refinancing of farm mortgages through federal land banks, the act also permitted the President to devalue the dollar. Under this provision Roosevelt attempted to raise prices and stimulate foreign trade by going off the gold standard. After a short and futile period of experimenting with the value of the dollar, Roosevelt, acting under the provisions of the Gold Revenue Act of January, 1934, fixed its gold content at 59.06 cents. Of more significance in providing the federal government with the means to regulate the economy than this currency legislation was the passage of the Banking Act of 1935, which empowered the Federal Reserve Board to regulate interest rates.

The National Industrial Recovery Act, passed June 16, had two parts. The first set up the National Recovery Administration (NRA) and the second the Public Works Administration (PWA). To the act's framers, particularly Johnson, Richberg, and Moley, each agency would be a supplement to the other. PWA was to expand purchasing power by building roads, dams, bridges, and public buildings. This would not only provide employment on the projects themselves but also, by creating demands for steel, trucks and so forth, bring work to Pittsburgh and Detroit. The NRA was to support prices and raise wages by restricting production and competition through codes or trade agreements to be drawn up by representatives of the producers, workers, and consumers in each industry or trade. The act further guaranteed labor the right of collective bargaining. The expectation was that the rapid reactivation of the capital-goods industries by the PWA would expand the market quickly

NIRA

1) NRA
2) PWA

enough to absorb increased labor costs arising under the NRA and so prevent a rise in prices. Johnson saw the two agencies as part of a "giant organ through which he could play on the economy of the country."

Roosevelt, however, viewed the Recovery Act as more of an emergency measure to get the people back to work than as a grand scheme for a managed economy. He preferred to keep the two agencies completely independent of one another. Johnson, assisted by Richberg, took over the administration of the NRA, while Harold Ickes became head of the PWA. Ickes moved slowly. By taking great care to assure the usefulness and proper cost of each project, he helped to assure the long-term value of his agency. This policy, however, deprived Johnson of the rapid expansion of the capital-goods sector of the economy. Once the PWA did begin to spend funds, most economists agree that it became an important factor in bringing economic recovery.

The economic benefits of the NRA, economists also agree, were far more uncertain. Wages rose but—so did prices. Codes drawn up largely by industrialists were bound to be more beneficial to themselves than to labor or the consumer. As recovery came, these businessmen resented the paper work involved and the continued possibility of outside control. Labor union membership expanded rapidly, but union leaders were distressed because much of this growth came through the expansion of company-controlled unions and also because of the difficulty in enforcing the labor provisions of the act. By the time the Supreme Court declared the NRA unconstitutional in May, 1935, the act had relatively few supporters.

The AAA had a stronger backing, even though in 1934 it had to abandon the voluntary system of allotments for cotton and tobacco and had to place taxes on all farmers who exceeded their quotas. Planning and administering the production of a few basic agricultural commodities was, of course, far less complex than estimating prices, production, and wages for myriads of industrial enterprises. Moreover, neither the farmers nor government officials saw any realistic alternative way to maintain agricultural prices.

During 1934 protests against centralized planning mounted both within and without the Roosevelt administration. Not only were industrialists and labor leaders becoming increasingly dissatisfied with the NRA, but many New Dealers were convinced that the Richberg type of planning ran counter to older beliefs, the tested experience of market competition and decentralized economic decision-making. Many, including the President, had always expected that private enterprise would manage most of the nation's economy and decide the allocation of its resources once the crisis of the depression had been met. While these men saw little chance of altering agricultural policy, some found viable alternatives to the difficulties created by the NRA type of industrial control in the concepts of the distinguished British economist, John Maynard Keynes.

To Keynes, the critical task facing the American government was the development of policies "to hasten the return of normal [business] enterprise." Keynes was convinced that unemployment was the critical problem and that unemployment resulted from a lack of investment demand. As he was further convinced that private business enterprise could not provide this investment, he urged heavy government spending to assure new jobs and so increase consumption. Thus, when funds were invested in capital goods, the availability of money would increase, or multiply, through the cumulative effect of increased individual spending. His proposals were straightforward. Forget the balanced budget. Reduce taxes. Spend larger amounts with more wisdom. Concentrate spending on housing, railroads, and utilities. Such capital investment would have a "multiplier effect" comparable to that provided by the coming of the great new industries after 1900. This sort of investment could be further encouraged, Keynes added, by lowering interest rates and by effective management of the currency.

In the ensuing arguments between the spenders and the planners, President Roosevelt never committed himself fully to either side. His fundamental concern remained, as it had been before 1932, the assurance of a minimum of economic security to the individual citizen. To achieve this end he was willing to try many means. He always liked to experiment and improvise. As he emphasized in 1932: "It is common sense to take a method and try it. If it fails, admit it frankly and try another. But above all try something." The realities of economics, politics, and constitutional law did, however, eventually turn the President more and more to a Keynesian type of program.

In June, 1934, Roosevelt told Congress that the immediate crisis of the depression had been met and that the government must now turn to providing long-term security for the individual. This required first of all better housing; old-age, unemployment, and health insurance; and benefits to dependent mothers and children. Since individual security depended ultimately on the effective use of national resources, Roosevelt proposed drawing up a set of long-range objectives and plans for their use. As a first step he suggested the formation of a National Resources Board to take an inventory of the country's human and physical resources.

In the following January, Roosevelt repeated these aims in his annual message to Congress. He further proposed a great, coordinated program for attacking the continuing problem of unemployment. For although national income and productivity had been rising since the summer of 1933, the number of jobless still remained over eleven million at the end of 1934 (see Table). Roosevelt, therefore, urged that the responsibility for the unemployable be returned to states and local communities. The federal government would concentrate on employing those who wanted work by setting up large-scale projects that would add to the wealth of the nation and not compete with private enterprise. Costs of the work, totaling $4.8 billion, were to be covered by loans and not by taxes. The Supreme Court decision later in the year declaring the NRA unconstitutional did not affect the PWA, which continued to carry out still more extensive projects such as power-generating facilities, highways, and major public buildings. From 1935 on, spending through the PWA and the new Works Progress Administration (WPA), rather than planning through an NRA, became the New Deal's approach to the problem of economic recovery.

The demagogic demands of Senator Huey Long and Dr. Francis E. Townsend for massive government handouts to the poor and the aged hastened the passage of the legislation Roosevelt requested. In April, Congress passed the Emergency Relief Appropriations Act, which provided funds and the agency (the WPA) to carry out the President's plans for the unemployed. In August, it enacted the nation's first social security act in much the same form as Roosevelt had proposed in January. So by the summer of 1935 the federal government had fully accepted the responsibilities of a modern welfare state. It assured the individual of social security benefits as a cushion against economic disaster and it offered him employment. While the government still had to provide this employment, it hoped through spending and fiscal policies to regulate the economy so that private rather than public enterprise could supply the jobs.

Not all Americans were pleased by the federal government's new responsibilities. Businessmen whose profits returned with economic recovery were concerned by the increased costs and taxes the new legislation would bring. Financiers were shocked at the thought of increasing the national debt through deficit spending. To these and others, the New Deal's economic plans and policies appeared to violate the conventional lessons of economic experience and the canons of common sense. These same conservatives remained skeptical of the need for federally supported social security. Many still dreamed of returning to a society where local and private agencies had the responsibility for the security of the individual and where the market alone, without government interference, regulated the economy. No one expressed his views more precisely and more sincerely than former President Herbert Hoover, who throughout the 1930's continued to be the most powerful and respected voice of conservatism within and without the Republican party. Yet for all these remonstrances the welfare state was here to stay. After 1935 the more significant arguments concerned how the federal government should provide for the economic security of the individual rather than whether it should carry this responsibility. The question was no longer whether to have a welfare state, but of how to manage it.

DOCUMENTS

1] Crisis Looms in the Country

> In the grim year of 1932 crops were plentiful, but hunger stalked the land. The poverty of the city only intensified that of the country. Oscar Ameringer, an Oklahoma City newspaper editor, described this cruel paradox of "appalling overproduction on the one side and the staggering underconsumption on the other side" before a Congressional committee in February, 1932.*

Mr. AMERINGER. My name is Oscar Ameringer. I am editor of the American Guardian and former editor of the American Miner. I live in Oklahoma City, Okla.

I may say that I am a representative of the country at large. During the last four months I have visited more than 20 States in my capacity as a newspaper man and an observer of prevailing conditions. Now, the witnesses that have preceded me have told you about a deplorable condition among the unemployed. They have told you of exhausted city treasuries and exhausted charity funds. They have told you about rising needs and falling incomes. They have told you about mothers being emaciated and not being able to give milk to their offspring. They have told you about infants being fed for months on flour and water. You have heard the young miner from Pennsylvania tell about conditions in his section of the country. You have heard the young miner from the State of West Virginia tell of conditions in his country. Both of these men have served their country trying to make the country safe for democracy. . . .

During the last three months I have visited, as I have said, some 20 States of this wonderfully rich and beautiful country. Here are some of the things I heard and saw: In the State of Washington I was told that the forest fires raging in that region all summer and fall were caused by unemployed timber workers and bankrupt farmers in an endeavor to earn a few honest dollars as fire fighters. The last thing I saw on the night I left Seattle was numbers of women searching for scraps of food in the refuse piles of the principal market of that city. A number of Montana citizens told me of thousands of bushels of wheat left in the fields uncut on account of its low price that hardly paid for the harvesting. In Oregon I saw thousands of bushels of apples rotting in the orchards. Only absolute flawless apples were still salable, at from 40 to 50 cents a box containing 200 apples. At the same time, there are millions of children who, on account of the poverty of their parents, will not eat one apple this winter.

While I was in Oregon the Portland Oregonian bemoaned the fact that

---

* CRISIS LOOMS IN THE COUNTRY: Testimony of Oscar Ameringer in Hearings on Unemployment. From Subcommittee of the Committee on Labor of the House of Representatives, *Unemployment in the United States, Hearings Before a Subcommittee of the House Committee on Labor,* H.R. 8088, 72 Cong., 1 Sess. (Washington, 1932), pp. 97–99.

thousands of ewes were killed by the sheep raisers because they did not bring enough in the market to pay the freight on them. And while Oregon sheep raisers fed mutton to the buzzards, I saw men picking for meat scraps in the garbage cans in the cities of New York and Chicago. I talked to one man in a restaurant in Chicago. He told me of his experience in raising sheep. He said that he had killed 3,000 sheep this fall and thrown them down the canyon, because it cost $1.10 to ship a sheep, and then he would get less than a dollar for it. He said he could not afford to feed the sheep, and he would not let them starve, so he just cut their throats and threw them down the canyon.

The roads of the West and Southwest teem with hungry hitchhikers. The camp fires of the homeless are seen along every railroad track. I saw men, women, and children walking over the hard roads. Most of them were tenant farmers who had lost their all in the late slump in wheat and cotton. Between Clarksville and Russellville, Ark., I picked up a family. The woman was hugging a dead chicken under a ragged coat. When I asked her where she had procured the fowl, first she told me she had found it dead in the road, and then added in grim humor, "They promised me a chicken in the pot, and now I got mine."

In Oklahoma, Texas, Arkansas, and Louisiana I saw untold bales of cotton rotting in the fields because the cotton pickers could not keep body and soul together on 35 cents paid for picking 100 pounds. The farmers cooperatives who loaned the money to the planters to make the crops allowed the planters $5 a bale. That means 1,500 pounds of seed cotton for the picking of it, which was in the neighborhood of 35 cents a pound. A good picker can pick about 200 pounds of cotton a day, so that the 70 cents would not provide enough pork and beans to keep the picker in the field, so that there is fine staple cotton rotting down there by the hundreds and thousands of tons.

As a result of this appalling overproduction on the one side and the staggering underconsumption on the other side, 70 per cent of the farmers of Oklahoma were unable to pay the interests on their mortgages. Last week one of the largest and oldest mortgage companies in that State went into the hands of the receiver. In that and other States we have now the interesting spectacle of farmers losing their farms by foreclosure and mortgage companies losing their recouped holdings by tax sales.

The farmers are being pauperized by the poverty of industrial populations and the industrial populations are being pauperized by the poverty of the farmers. Neither has the money to buy the product of the other, hence we have overproduction and underconsumption at the same time and in the same country.

I have not come here to stir you in a recital of the necessity for relief for our suffering fellow citizens. However, unless something is done for them and done soon, you will have a revolution on hand. And when that revolution comes it will not come from Moscow, it . . . will bear the label "Laid in the U.S.A." and its chief promoters will be the people of American stock. . . .

2] And in the City

Without cash to buy the barest necessities of life, the unemployed in the city subsisted through locally financed bread lines, soup kitchens, and relief payments. By the autumn of 1932, even the largest American towns and cities were no longer able to find funds to meet relief costs. Ewan Clague, director of research of Philadelphia's Community Council, told of the resulting situation in one great seaboard city in an article entitled: "When Relief Stops What Do They Eat?" *

PEOPLE do not starve to death when relief stops; they just starve, with the margin by which life persists maintained by the pity of their neighbors and by a sort of scavenging on the community.

Relief stopped in Philadelphia on June 25. For months fifty-two thousand destitute families had been receiving modest grocery orders and a little milk. Their rent was unpaid, their credit and their borrowing power exhausted. Most of them were absolutely dependent for existence on the food orders supplied through state funds administered by the Committee for Unemployment Relief. Then there were no more funds, and relief—except for a little milk for half-sick children, and a little Red Cross flour—was suddenly discontinued. And Philadelphia asked itself what was happening to these fifty-two thousand families. There were no reports of people starving in the streets, and yet from what possible source were fifty-two thousand families getting enough food to live on?

It was a fair question and the Community Council, with the cooperation of ten settlements and the social-service departments of six hospitals, set out to find the answer by a special study of four hundred families who had been without relief for a period varying from ten to twenty-five days. The families selected were known to the settlements or hospitals in some other than a relief capacity. They were not picked out as the worst cases, but as fairly typical of the fifty-two thousand.

The count of the four hundred families showed a total of 2464 persons. There were two single persons living alone and a few couples, but there was one household of fifteen persons, two of fourteen and three of thirteen. The great majority ranged from five to eight persons per family. In 254 of the families were children of five years or under, many others had older children only, so that the proportion of families with no children at all was comparatively small. There were many mothers with very young babies and a number of pregnant women.

In their effort to discover how these 2464 human beings were keeping themselves alive the investigators inquired into the customary sources of family maintenance, earnings, savings, regular help from relatives, credit and, last but not least, the neighbors.

Some current income in the form of wages was reported by 128 families,

---

* AND IN THE CITY: Ewan Clague, "When Relief Stops What Do They Eat?" From *Survey*, LXVIII (November 15, 1932), 583–85.

though the amounts were generally small and irregular, two or three dollars a week perhaps, earned on odd jobs, by selling knickknacks on the street or by youngsters delivering papers or working nights. In only a handful of cases did the income exceed $10 a week. The great bulk was below $7 a week and for the whole 128 the average wage income was only $4.16 a week. And 272 families of the four hundred had no earnings whatsoever.

Savings were an even more slender resource. Only fifty-four families reported savings and most of these were nothing more than small industrial insurance policies with little or no cash surrender value, technically an asset, actually an item of expense. This does not mean that these families had not had savings— take for instance the Baker family, father, mother and four children. They had had $1000 in a building and loan association which failed. They had had more than $2000 in a savings bank, but the last cent had been withdrawn in January 1931. They had had three insurance policies, which had been surrendered one by one. Both the father and the oldest son were tuberculous, the former being at the moment an applicant for sanitarium care. This family, intelligent, clean, thrifty and likeable—one of thousands at the end of their rope, had had savings as a resource even a year ago—but not now.

The same situation, it was found, prevailed in regard to regular help from relatives. In the early stages of the depression a large proportion of relief families could count on this help in some form. But of our four hundred families only thirty-three reported assistance from kinsfolk that could be counted on, and this assistance was slender indeed: a brother paid the rent to save eviction, a brother-in-law guaranteed the gas and electric bills, a grandmother, working as a scrubwoman put in a small sum each week. Most of the relatives it was found were so hard-pressed that it was all they could do to save themselves. As a matter of fact many relatives had moved in with the families and were recorded as members of the household.

In the absence of assets or income the next line of defense is credit. But most of the four hundred families were bogged down in debt and retained only a vestige of credit. Take the item of rent or building and loan payments: 349 of the families were behind—some only a month or two, some for a year, a few for two or three years, with six months as the average for the group. The total indebtedness for rent amounted to about $41,000 an average of $120.78. A few landlords had grown impatient and evictions had resulted, but on the whole the contribution of the landlords of Philadelphia to unemployment relief in the form of unpaid rent has been very substantial. Nearly three fourths of the families reported debts other than rent, with their credit to grocers, milkmen, coal dealers and so on used to the limit. At least two thirds of the families owed for gas or electricity or both, but these items rarely ran above $5 since the companies cut off the supply at about that level of indebtedness. Few grocers' bills ran beyond $50—the bulk ranged from $1 to $25. Occasionally the grocers were unwilling to risk very much and the non-payment of very small bills stopped further credit. Milk bills were less frequent and seldom amounted to as much as $15. Other types of debts were varied in character. Substantial money loans from friends or loan companies amounting to $100, $200 or even $300 were occasionally noted. Overdue instalments on furniture were frequent, a few cases of debts for taxes, water rents, furniture storage and doctors were mentioned. One family reported owing $5 to the church.

In numbers the outstanding debts were to grocers and other food retailers though the amounts averaged smaller than any other type of indebtedness. The outstanding feature of the loans was their size—an average of $160 each, whether friendly or commercial. It is surprising that families were able to borrow such sums on what was obviously unsubstantial prospect of repayment. The reasons were, probably, that relatives and sometimes friends were more or less compelled by duty to carry the family, that the loans were a hangover from previous prosperity and that notes undoubtedly had endorsers so that the lending concerns were pressing other persons for payment. In any case this group of families had small chance for any further loans, commercial or friendly.

For an instance of how the load of debt mounted up consider the Beccaria family. Threatened with a second eviction, behind in gas and electricity bills, they owed $45 to the grocer and $112 to the baker, this latter item having accumulated over two years. They owed $45 to a downtown department store, $200 to a brother, $150 to a cousin and a 6 percent commercial loan of $300. Their troubles were complicated by a variety of health problems which were not improving under a diet of bread, potatoes and spaghetti.

Thus, then, the picture of the four hundred families shaped itself: generally no income, such as there was slight, irregular and undependable; shelter still available so long as landlords remained lenient; savings gone; credit exhausted.

But what of food, the never ending, ever pressing necessity for food? In this emergency the outstanding contribution has been made by neighbors. The poor are looking after the poor. In considerably more than a third of the four hundred families the chief source of actual subsistence when grocery orders stopped was the neighbors. The supply was by no means regular or adequate but in the last analysis, when all other resources failed the neighbors rallied to tide the family over a few days. Usually it was leftovers, stale bread, meat bones for soup, a bowl of gravy. Sometimes the children are asked in for a meal. One neighbor sent two eggs a day regularly to a sick man threatened with tuberculosis. This help was the more striking since the neighbors themselves were often close to the line of destitution and could illy spare the food they shared. The primitive communism existing among these people was a constant surprise to the visitors. More than once a family lucky enough to get a good supply of food called in the entire block to share the feast. There is absolutely no doubt that entire neighborhoods were just living from day to day sharing what slight resources any one family chanced to have. Without this mutual help the situation of many of the families would have been desperate.

THE FAMILIES rustled for themselves as much as they could. A common source of supply for one group was the docks where fruit and vegetables for market are sorted. Children and adults hung around the stalls and snatched at anything that was out. Occasionally they were able to make off with good produce but the police were watchful and such enterprise was often disastrous. Street begging was only occasionally resorted to, said the investigators, likewise the petty thieving of milk and groceries from doorsteps. There is little doubt however that gifts of food from grocers, reported by a considerable number of families, were usually obtained by a form of begging. Children, it seems, had the habit of going to a store and by pleading hunger inducing the grocer to give them a little food. Children ran errands for grocers, watched pushcarts, did anything in exchange for fruit or vegetables. The myriad ways in which a family, its entire attention concentrated on food, just food, succeeded in obtaining it constitutes abundant evidence of the ingenuity and perseverance of these people.

As a result of all these efforts, what did these families have? What meals did they get and of what did these meals consist? About 8 percent of the total number were subsisting on one meal a day. Many more were getting only two meals a day, and still others were irregular, sometimes one meal, sometimes two, occasionally by great good fortune, three. Thirty-seven percent of all families were not getting the normal three meals a day.

When the content of these meals is taken into consideration the facts are still more alarming. Four families had absolutely no solid food whatever—nothing but a drink, usually tea or coffee. Seventy-three others had only one food and one drink for all meals, the food in many cases being bread made from Red Cross flour. Even in the remaining cases, where there were two or three articles of food, the diets day after day and week after week consisted usually of bread, macaroni, spaghetti, potatoes, with milk for the children. Many families were getting no meat and very few vegetables. Fresh fruits were never mentioned, although it is possible that the family might pick these up in the streets occasionally.

These diets were exceedingly harmful in their immediate effects on some of the families where health problems are present. In a number of cases the children are definitely reported on a hospital diagnosis as anemic. Occasionally the adults are likewise affected. The MacIntyre family for instance: these two older people have an adopted child eight years of age. The husband is a bricklayer by trade and the wife can do outside housework. They have had occasional odd jobs over the past year but have been very hard pressed. For the three meals immediately preceding the visit they reported the menus as follows: dinner, previous day, bread and coffee; breakfast, bread and coffee; lunch, corn, fish, bread and coffee; one quart of milk for the little girl for the entire three meals.

Also their health problems were serious. The wife has had several operations, the husband is a possible tuberculosis case, and the child is underweight. All three have been receiving medical attention from a hospital for the past three years. The little girl has been nervous, has fainted at times, and is slightly deformed from rickets. Being undernourished, she needs cod liver oil, milk, oranges and the food which was possible only when the family was on relief. She went to camp for two weeks and returned up to weight and in good spirits. But relief was cut off while she was away and she came back to meals of milk, coffee and bread. In the short time at home she had become fretful and listless, refusing to take anything but milk. This whole family promised to be in serious health difficulties if their situation were long continued.

The Bakers, the Beccarias, the MacIntyres and the other 397 families visited did not starve to death when relief stopped. They kept alive from day to day, catch-as-catch can, reduced for actual subsistence to something of the status of a stray cat prowling for food, for which a kindly soul occasionally sets out a plate of table scraps or a saucer of milk. What this does to the innate dignity of the human soul is not for this writer to discuss. What it does to the bodies and the social attitudes of adults and children is something that we shall know more and more about for years to come. And these four hundred families were, remember, a fair sampling of fifty-two thousand from whom relief was withdrawn. What happened to the four hundred happened in greater or less degree to the fifty-two thousand, and will happen again if the exigencies of the winter should force another discontinuance of food orders.

3] "The Need for National Assistance"

A leading economist, Sumner H. Slichter, professor of business economics at Harvard University, explained why the desperately needed relief funds had dried up in Philadelphia and so many other American municipalities. He gave this testimony in January, 1933, before a Congressional committee that was studying a bill to provide direct federal financial assistance for unemployment relief.*

The CHAIRMAN. Doctor Slichter, will you give your full name and address and your present occupation in the Harvard School to the reporter, for the record?

Professor SLICHTER. My name is Sumner H. Slichter, and I am professor of business economics, Harvard Business School.

The CHAIRMAN. The committee would be grateful to you, Doctor Slichter, if you would, in your own way, comment upon the economic consequences and implications of the unemployment problem. We will then ask you any questions that occur to us.

Professor SLICHTER. Mr. Chairman, the need for national assistance, by this time, has become so self-evident that it would seem to me to be a waste of your time for me to offer anything along that line.

The CHAIRMAN. Unfortunately, however, we do not find that to be the generally accepted opinion.

Professor SLICHTER. The tax base of the local communities is a somewhat narrow one. About nine-tenths of their income is derived from real estate taxation, and the difficulty, or one of the difficulties, with that base is that a man is liable for taxes simply because he owns the title to the real estate, quite regardless of whether or not he has any income from the real estate.

Senator COSTIGAN. Or able to pay it?

Professor SLICHTER. Yes, or from any other source.

* "THE NEED FOR NATIONAL ASSISTANCE": Testimony of Sumner H. Slichter. From Subcommittee of the Committee on Manufactures, United States Senate, *Federal Aid for Unemployment Relief, Hearings*, 72 Cong., 2 Sess. (Washington, 1933), pp. 124–27.

The result one could predict without much difficulty is a steadily rising ratio of delinquent taxes throughout the country. In fact, delinquency ratios of from 20 to 30 per cent are not unusual.

The income from real estate, itself, of course, has gone down. It is one of the slower incomes to fall; but it is a fairly conservative generalization, I should say, to estimate that the rentals, in most places, are down about 20 per cent, in some cases more, and in some cases less.

Of course, the real estate owner bears a double burden in the case of unemployment, because it is almost the universal rule that relief agencies do not pay rent, except on eviction, and then they only pay for a month or two. In other words, there is a more or less national moratorium on rents, in so far as the unemployed are concerned.

The older the depression gets, the more unsatisfactory becomes this narrow base of public revenue. The private agencies have been compelled to conserve their resources, and to withdraw from the strictly unemployment field. They started out to help out the unemployed, more or less, but the burden became too great; and in order to conserve the permanent part of their work, they had to withdraw.

I made a compilation not long ago of some community chest drives for 1932 and 1933, and this covers 44 cities.

In 1932, the community chests in these cities raised about $24,900,000. This goal for 1933 is $23,100,000. That, of course, means that the burden on public relief funds is increasing. . . .

The bill, as drafted, provides that part of the appropriation shall be distributed on the basis of the population of the States, but that "no State shall receive more than two-thirds of the amount made available by it or its subdivisions."

Now, if I interpret this correctly, the cities of a State and the private agencies might be making available $10,000,000, and the State would then have the right, assuming its population were sufficient, to receive up to $6,667,000, under the bill. Under these conditions it seems to me that there is danger that some States might make no appropriations at all. In other words, some States might fall back on this Federal aid, obtained because the cities and charitable organizations within the State made appropriations.

That would be unfortunate, not primarily because the States should be such an important source of help, but because, in order to get the best administration through the States' machinery, some of the money should be the States' money. Consequently, I venture the suggestion that the States be required, in order to share in the appropriation on the basis of population, to make reasonable appropriations of their own funds.

After all, I think only eight States have made appropriations. These eight include some of the largest industrial States, such as the States of New York, New Jersey, Pennsylvania, and Illinois, but on the whole, the States have been the most delinquent bodies in helping the unemployment relief in the country; and if the proper administrative machinery is to be created, the States must help provide it. In order for that machinery to function most effectively the States should be spending some of their own money. . . .

The CHAIRMAN. Yes; if I get your point, Doctor Slichter, it is that this should be based upon the principle of joint cooperation between the Federal Government and the States, such as we have had in connection with other Federal aid projects—a matching of funds and a participation in administrative function by both State and Federal Governments?

Professor SLICHTER. Yes; the unemployment problem is so far flung and it varies so greatly in the different parts of the country, that some decentralization of the overseeing machinery is necessary, and that machinery ought not to get its money solely from Washington. Yet it seems to me, as the bill stands, there is the possibility of a State, which had done nothing, receiving, under the two-thirds provision, a really substantial sum, simply because some of its cities have done a great deal. . . .

4] Roosevelt Calls for Federal Responsibility

By the fall of 1932, such national assistance had become a major political issue. Franklin Delano Roosevelt, the governor of New York and Democratic candidate for President, stressed that the federal government should take responsibility for relief. Beyond this it should assure some sort of minimum security to citizens caught by industrial and economic forces over which they had no control. He outlined his views in a radio campaign address on October 13, 1932.*

I AM SPEAKING to you from my desk in the Executive Mansion in Albany of a subject which is not in the narrower sense of the word political, but which, because it is connected with Government, vitally affects the life of almost every man, woman and child in the United States.

I cannot, of course, answer the hundreds of questions which come to me in every mail, but a letter signed by ten of the leading social welfare workers permits me to use their questions as a text for the expression of certain great basic principles which are vital to us in this time of stress.

The first question asks my position in relation to the duty of the Federal and State and local Governments to provide funds and aid for the relief of those who are out of work.

The problem therein outlined is one which is very real in every section of the country, as I have good reason to know. This was accentuated by what I saw and heard on my recent trip to the Pacific Coast.

Let me answer it by laying down what I believe to be certain cardinal principles.

In the first place, even in an ideal community where no one is out of work, there would always be the need of welfare work conducted through the churches, through private charity and by local government—the need for

* ROOSEVELT CALLS FOR FEDERAL RESPONSIBILITY: Radio Campaign Address (October 13, 1932). From Samuel I. Rosenman, ed., *The Public Papers and Addresses of Franklin D. Roosevelt: The Genesis of the New Deal, 1928–1932* (New York, 1938), pp. 786–94. Reprinted by permission of Random House, Inc.

clinics and hospitals and vocational training, the need for the care of the aged, for care of mental cases and for care of the crippled.

Such communities where there is no unemployment are almost utopian, for even in times of prosperity there are always some unemployed—people who want to work but can find no work.

The first principle I would lay down is that the primary duty rests on the community, through local government and private agencies, to take care of the relief of unemployment. But we then come to a situation where there are so many people out of work that local funds are insufficient.

It seems clear to me that the organized society known as the State comes into the picture at this point. In other words, the obligation of Government is extended to the next higher unit.

I practice what I preach. In 1930 the State of New York greatly increased its employment service and kept in close touch with the ability of localities to take care of their own unemployed. But by the summer of 1931 it became apparent to me that actual State funds and a State-supervised system were imperative.

I called a special session of the Legislature and they appropriated a fund of $20,000,000 for unemployment relief, this fund to be reimbursed to the State through the doubling of our income taxes. Thus the State of New York became the first among all the States to accept the definite obligation of supplementing local funds where these local funds were insufficient.

The administration of this great work has become a model for the rest of the country. Without setting up any complex machinery or any large overhead, the State of New York is working successfully through local agencies, and in spite of the fact that over a million people are out of work and in need of aid in this one State alone, we have so far met at least the bare necessities of the case.

This past spring the Legislature appropriated another $5,000,000 and on November 8 the voters will pass on a $30,000,000 bond issue to tide us over this winter and at least up to next summer.

Finally, let me come to the last step in the statement of the principle. I am very certain that the obligation extends beyond the States and to the Federal Government itself if and when it becomes apparent that States and communities are unable to take care of the necessary relief work.

It may interest you to have me read a short quotation from my message to the Legislature in 1931:

"What is the State? It is the duly constituted representative of an organized society of human beings, created by them for their mutual protection and well being. One of the duties of the State is that of caring for those of its citizens who find themselves the victims of such adverse circumstances as make them unable to obtain even the necessities of mere existence without the aid of others.

"In broad terms, I assert that modern society, acting through its Government, owes the definite obligation to prevent the starvation or the dire want of any of its fellow men and women who try to maintain themselves but cannot. To these unfortunate citizens aid must be extended by the Government—not as a matter of charity, but as a matter of social duty."

That principle which I laid down in 1931, I reaffirm. I not only reaffirm it, I go a step further and say that where the State itself is unable successfully to fulfill this obligation which lies upon it, it then becomes the positive duty of the Federal Government to step in to help.

In the words of our Democratic national platform, the Federal Government has a "continuous responsibility for human welfare, especially for the protection of children." That duty and responsibility the Federal Government should carry out promptly, fearlessly and generously.

It took the present Republican Administration in Washington almost three years to recognize this principle. I have recounted to you in other speeches, and it is a matter of general information, that for at least two years after the crash, the only efforts made by the national Administration to cope with the distress of unemployment, were to deny its existence.

When finally this year, after attempts at concealment and minimizing had failed, it was at last forced to recognize the fact of suffering among millions of unemployed, appropriations of Federal funds for assistance to States were finally made.

I think it is fair to point out that a complete program of unemployment relief was on my recommendation actually under way in the State of New York over a year ago, and that in Washington relief funds in any larger volume were not provided until this Summer and at that they were pushed through at the demand of Congress rather than through the leadership of the President of the United States.

At the same time, I have constantly reiterated my conviction that the expenditures of cities, States and the Federal Government must be reduced in the interest of the Nation as a whole. I believe that there are many ways in which such reduction of expenditures can take place, but I am utterly unwilling that economy should be practiced at the expense of starving people.

We must economize in other ways, but it shall never be said that the American people have refused to provide the necessities of life for those who, through no fault of their own, are unable to feed, clothe and house themselves. The first obligation of Government is the protection of the welfare and well-being, indeed the very existence of its citizens.

So much for that.

The next question asks my attitude toward appropriations for public works as an aid to unemployment. I am perfectly clear as to the principles involved in this case also.

From the long-range point of view it would be advisable for Governments of all kinds to set up in times of prosperity what might be called a nest egg to be used for public works in times of depression. That is a policy which we should initiate when we get back to good times.

But there is the immediate possibility of helping the emergency through appropriations for public works. One question, however, must be answered first, because of the simple fact that these public works cost money.

We all know that Government treasuries, whether local or State or Federal, are hard put to it to keep their budgets balanced, and in the case of the Federal Treasury thoroughly unsound financial policies have made its situation not exactly desperate, but at least threatening to future stability, if the policies of the present Administration are continued.

All public works, including Federal, must be considered from the point of view of the ability of the Government treasury to pay for them. There are two ways of paying for public works.

One is by the sale of bonds. In principle such bonds should be issued only to pay for self-sustaining projects or for structures which will without question have a useful life over a long period of years.

The other method of payment is from current revenues, which in these days means in most cases added taxes. We all know that there is a very definite limit to the increase of taxes above the present level.

From this point, therefore, I can go on and say that if funds can be properly provided by the Federal Government for increased appropriations for public works, we must examine the character of these public works. I have already spoken of that type which is self-sustaining. These should be greatly encouraged.

The other type is that of public works which are honestly essential to the community. Each case must rest on its own merits. It is impossible, for example, to say that all parks or all playgrounds are essential. One may be and another may not be.

If a school, for instance, has no playground, it is obvious that the furnishing of a playground is a necessity to the community. But if the school already has a playground and some people seek merely to enlarge it, there may be a very definite question as to how necessary that enlargement is.

Let me cite another example. I am much interested in providing better housing accommodations for the poor in our great cities. If a slum area can be torn down and new modern buildings put up, I should call that almost a human necessity, but on the other hand, the mere erection of new buildings in some other part of the city while allowing the slums to remain raises at once a question of necessity. I am confident that the Federal Government working in cooperation with States and cities can do much to carry on increased public works and along lines which are sound from the economic and financial point of view.

Now I come to another question. I am asked whether I favor a system of unemployment insurance reserves made compulsory by the States, supplemented by a system of federally coordinated State employment offices to facilitate the reemployment of jobless workers.

The first part of the question is directly answered by the Democratic platform, which advocates unemployment insurance under State laws.

This is no new policy for me. I have advocated unemployment insurance in my own State for some time, and indeed last year six Eastern Governors were my guests at a conference which resulted in the drawing up of what might be called an ideal plan of unemployment insurance.

This type of insurance is not a cure-all, but it provides at least a cushion to mitigate unemployment in times of depression. It is sound if, after starting it, we stick to the principle of sound insurance financing. It is only where Governments, as in some European countries, have failed to live up to these sound principles that unemployment insurance has been an economic failure.

As to the coordinated employment offices, I can only tell you that I was for the bills sponsored by Senator Wagner of my own State and passed by the Congress. They created a nationally coordinated system of employment offices operated by the individual States with the advisory cooperation of joint boards of employers and employees.

To my very great regret this measure was vetoed by the President of the United States. I am certain that the Federal Government can, by furnishing leadership, stimulate the various States to set up and coordinate practical, useful systems.

These first three questions which I have discussed related to the relief of those who are unemployed, and it is perhaps logical that the next two questions should relate to children, because we know that unemployment works a great hardship on the young people of the coming generation.

I certainly favor the continuance of the fine work which has been done by the Children's Bureau in Washington, but at the same time we must not forget that the Federal Government through several other agencies is constantly working for the welfare of children.

Attempts have been made to cut the appropriations for child welfare work. It seems to me that this is the last place in which we should seek to economize. I cannot agree with the member of President Hoover's Cabinet who suggests that this depression is not altogether a bad thing for our children.

You and I know the appalling fact that malnutrition is one of the saddest by-products of unemployment. The health of these children is being affected not only now but for all the rest of their lives.

Furthermore, a depression takes thousands of children away from schools and puts them to work to help the family income. They are underpaid and only too often work under conditions which, physically and morally, are often dangerous. It is well to remember, too, that the use of these untrained children in industry keeps many adults out of employment and has the effect of cutting down wages below a decent living standard.

These are only a few of the many reasons why the Federal Government must continue to act as an agency to disseminate information about child welfare and to encourage State and local governments to raise their standards to the highest possible levels.

The last question relates to keeping children in school to the age of sixteen. I am in favor of that. Furthermore, I go along with the thought that we must increase vocational education for those children who otherwise would not receive adequate training. . . .

The Federal Government, without in any way taking away the right and the duty of the several States to manage their own educational affairs, can act as a clearing house of information and as an incentive to higher standards.

But the Federal Government has had no continuing policy for dealing with problems of public health and social welfare. In this as in other activities a multiplicity of unrelated agencies has been developed hit-or-miss to deal with aspects of the same problem. The result has been waste of men and money and a more costly and less efficient service than we should have.

The Administration has done nothing to reorganize this or other branches of the Federal Government, in spite of campaign promises at the last three

Presidential elections. I propose to inaugurate a definite long-range plan for dealing with all phases of public health and welfare, which are a proper concern of the Federal Government.

May I add that in the State of New York during the past four years we have accomplished definite and practical results by coordinating and planning the work of the State?

I cite as a simple example the public health program, which is a part of my Administration. It has been referred to in other States as the most important contribution to practical public health work during this generation. And all of this we have taken out of politics.

The same principles can and should be applied to the health and welfare work of the Federal Government.

In closing, will you let me make an appeal to the entire country—an appeal with all my heart, with all my mind and with all my soul—to let nothing interfere with the duty and obligation of coming forward as individuals and as groups to the support of the unemployed and their dependents during the coming winter. . . .

5] Hoover Warns of the Consequences of the Proposed New Deal

> During 1932 Hoover greatly increased the loan of federal funds to financially shaky states and municipalities and to near-bankrupt private corporations. Nevertheless, he remained convinced that the responsibility for relief and for the economic security and welfare of the individual citizen must be left to local, voluntary groups. Renominated by the Republicans for the Presidency, he warned of the dangers of centralizing such activities in Washington in a campaign speech delivered at New York's Madison Square Garden on October 31, 1932.*

THIS CAMPAIGN is more than a contest between two men. It is more than a contest between two parties. It is a contest between two philosophies of government.

We are told by the opposition that we must have a change, that we must have a new deal. It is not the change that comes from normal development of national life to which I object, but the proposal to alter the whole foundations of our national life which have been builded through generations of testing and struggle, and of the principles upon which we have builded the nation. The expressions our opponents use must refer to important changes in our economic and social system and our system of government, otherwise they are nothing but vacuous words. And I realize that in this time of distress many of

---

* HOOVER WARNS OF THE CONSEQUENCES OF THE PROPOSED NEW DEAL: "The Consequences of the Proposed New Deal." From Herbert Hoover, *Addresses upon the American Road, 1933–1938* (New York, 1938), pp. 1–7. Reprinted by permission of Herbert Hoove..

our people are asking whether our social and economic system is incapable of that great primary function of providing security and comfort of life to all of the firesides of our 25,000,000 homes in America, whether our social system provides for the fundamental development and progress of our people, whether our form of government is capable of originating and sustaining that security and progress.

This question is the basis upon which our opponents are appealing to the people in their fears and distress. They are proposing changes and so-called new deals which would destroy the very foundations of our American system.

Our people should consider the primary facts before they come to the judgment—not merely through political agitation, the glitter of promise, and the discouragement of temporary hardships—whether they will support changes which radically affect the whole system which has been builded up by a hundred and fifty years of the toil of our fathers. They should not approach the question in the despair with which our opponents would clothe it.

Our economic system has received abnormal shocks during the last three years, which temporarily dislocated its normal functioning. These shocks have in a large sense come from without our borders, but I say to you that our system of government has enabled us to take such strong action as to prevent the disaster which would otherwise have come to our Nation. It has enabled us further to develop measures and programs which are now demonstrating their ability to bring about restoration and progress.

We must go deeper than platitudes and emotional appeals of the public platform in the campaign, if we will penetrate to the full significance of the changes which our opponents are attempting to float upon the wave of distress and discontent from the difficulties we are passing through. We can find what our opponents would do after searching the record of their appeals to discontent, group and sectional interest. We must search for them in the legislative acts which they sponsored and passed in the Democratic-controlled House of Representatives in the last session of Congress. We must look into measures for which they voted and which were defeated. We must inquire whether or not the Presidential and Vice-Presidential candidates have disavowed these acts. If they have not, we must conclude that they form a portion and are a substantial indication of the profound changes proposed.

And we must look still further than this as to what revolutionary changes have been proposed by the candidates themselves.

We must look into the type of leaders who are campaigning for the Democratic ticket, whose philosophies have been well known all their lives, whose demands for a change in the American system are frank and forceful. I can respect the sincerity of these men in their desire to change our form of government and our social and economic system, though I shall do my best tonight to prove they are wrong. . . .

I may say at once that the changes proposed from all these Democratic principles and allies are of the most profound and penetrating character. If they are brought about this will not be the America which we have known in the past.

Let us pause for a moment and examine the American system of government, of social and economic life, which it is now proposed that we should alter. Our system is the product of our race and of our experience in building a nation to heights unparalleled in the whole history of the world. It is a system peculiar to the American people. It differs essentially from all others in the world. It is an American system.

It is founded on the conception that only through ordered liberty, through freedom to the individual, and equal opportunity to the individual will his initiative and enterprise be summoned to spur the march of progress.

It is by the maintenance of equality of opportunity and therefore of a society absolutely fluid in freedom of the movement of its human particles that our individualism departs from the individualism of Europe. We resent class distinction because there can be no rise for the individual through the frozen strata of classes and no stratification of classes can take place in a mass livened by the free rise of its particles. Thus in our ideals the able and ambitious are able to rise constantly from the bottom to leadership in the community.

This freedom of the individual creates of itself the necessity and the cheerful willingness of men to act co-operatively in a thousand ways and for every purpose as occasion arises; and it permits such voluntary co-operations to be dissolved as soon as they have served their purpose, to be replaced by new voluntary associations for new purposes.

There has thus grown within us, to gigantic importance, a new conception. That is, this voluntary co-operation within the community. Co-operation to perfect the social organizations; co-operation for the care of those in distress; co-operation for the advancement of knowledge, of scientific research, of education; for co-operative action in the advancement of many phases of economic life. This is self-government by the people outside of Government; it is the most powerful development of individual freedom and equal opportunity that has taken place in the century and a half since our fundamental institutions were founded.

It is in the further development of this co-operation and a sense of its responsibility that we should find solution for many of our complex problems, and not by the extension of government into our economic and social life. The greatest function of government is to build up that co-operation, and its most resolute action should be to deny the extension of bureaucracy. We have developed great agencies of co-operation by the assistance of the Government which promote and protect the interests of individuals and the smaller units of business. The Federal Reserve System, in its strengthening and support of the smaller banks; the Farm Board, in its strengthening and support of the farm co-operatives; the Home Loan banks, in the mobilizing of building and loan associations and savings banks; the Federal land banks, in giving independence and strength to land mortgage associations; the great mobilization of relief to distress, the mobilization of business and industry in measures of recovery, and a score of other activities are not socialism—they are the essence of protection to the development of free men.

The primary conception of this whole American system is not the regimentation of men but the co-operation of free men. It is founded upon the conception of responsibility of the individual to the community, of the responsibility of local government to the State, of the State to the national Government.

It is founded on a peculiar conception of self-government designed to maintain this equal opportunity to the individual, and through decentralization it brings about and maintains these responsibilities. The centralization of government will undermine responsibilities and will destroy the system.

Our Government differs from all previous conceptions, not only in this decentralization, but also in the separation of functions between the legislative, executive, and judicial arms of government, in which the independence of the judicial arm is the keystone of the whole structure.

It is founded on a conception that in times of emergency, when forces are running beyond control of individuals or other co-operative action, beyond the control of local communities and of States, then the great reserve powers of the Federal Government shall be brought into action to protect the community. But when these forces have ceased there must be a return of State, local, and individual responsibility. . . .

When the political and economic weakness of many nations of Europe, the result of the World War and its aftermath, finally culminated in collapse of their institutions, the delicate adjustments of our economic and social life received a shock unparalleled in our history. No one knows that better than you of New York. No one knows its causes better than you. That the crisis was so great that many of the leading banks sought directly or indirectly to convert their assets into gold or its equivalent with the result that they practically ceased to function as credit institutions; that many of our citizens sought flight for their capital to other countries; that many of them attempted to hoard gold in large amounts. These were but indications of the flight of confidence and of the belief that our Government could not overcome these forces.

Yet these forces were overcome—perhaps by narrow margins—and this action demonstrates what the courage of a nation can accomplish under the resolute leadership in the Republican Party. And I say the Republican Party because our opponents, before and during the crisis, proposed no constructive program; though some of their members patriotically supported ours. Later on the Democratic House of Representatives did develop the real thought and ideas of the Democratic Party, but it was so destructive that it had to be defeated, for it would have destroyed, not healed.

In spite of all these obstructions we did succeed. Our form of government did prove itself equal to the task. We saved this Nation from a quarter of a century of chaos and degeneration, and we preserved the savings, the insurance policies, gave a fighting chance to men to hold their homes. We saved the integrity of our Government and the honesty of the American dollar. And we installed measures which today are bringing back recovery. Employment, agriculture, business—all of these show the steady, if slow, healing of our enormous wound.

I therefore contend that the problem of today is to continue these measures and policies to restore this American system to its normal functioning, to repair the wounds it has received, to correct the weaknesses and evils which would defeat that system. To enter upon a series of deep changes to embark upon this inchoate new deal which has been propounded in this campaign would be to undermine and destroy our American system. . . .

[Mr. Hoover then described the specific nature of the future changes that he attributed to his opponents: a departure from a system of life that had proven highly successful in the past, a huge increase in government expenditures, inflation, changes in the Supreme Court, the government undertaking the generation of electrical power beyond that incidental to irrigation and flood control, the expansion of bureaucratic power, and a drift toward socialism.]

6] "A Nationally Planned Economy Is the Only Salvation"

Roosevelt's sweeping victory in November, 1932, meant that the federal government would have a greater responsibility for the economic welfare and security of the individual citizen. Yet the means to carry out this commitment remained long in dispute. Most of Roosevelt's original set of advisers firmly believed that such security could not come merely from federal relief funds, or even from old-age, unemployment, and health insurance benefits. Genuine security depended on economic recovery and this, in turn, depended on effective centralized planning. On January 12, 1933, Donald Richberg, who was shortly to become a top administrator in the NRA, explained these views to a congressional committee on unemployment relief.*

Mr. RICHBERG. My name is Donald R. Richberg, counsel for the Railway Labor Executives Association. I am speaking in behalf of the association which represents the 21 standard railroad labor organizations. I do not think it is necessary, probably, to go into any details concerning the membership of that association.

The CHAIRMAN. When this committee held hearings a little over a year ago on unemployment and its relief, you appeared in the same representative capacity and gave the committee interesting information concerning the situation in the transportation industry. The committee would be very grateful to you if you would proceed, in your own way, to recapitulate, in so far as you think necessary, the data you gave us previously, bringing it down to date, and give us any additional information which you think would be helpful in the consideration of this general subject.

Mr. RICHBERG. Mr. Chairman, I have prepared a brief statement which is rather an outline of what I would like to present to the committee and I might proceed to follow that outline and explain it and answer any questions you see fit to ask.

It was almost exactly one year ago when I testified before this committee,

* "A NATIONALLY PLANNED ECONOMY IS THE ONLY SALVATION": Testimony of Donald Richberg. From Subcommittee of the Committee on Manufactures, United States Senate, Federal Aid for Unemployment Relief, Hearings, 72 Cong., 2 Sess. (Washington, 1933), pp. 448–56.

in behalf of the organized railway employees, urging the passage of a similar bill. To-day the need for Federal relief is far greater and more desperate. . . .

In giving whole-hearted support to this bill the railway employees, however, must also make clear their position, that this is only a pitifully small measure of relief to meet unavoidable demands and to alleviate acute distress. We would point out that Congress must not be satisfied merely with assisting public and private relief agencies to prevent wholesale starvation and intolerable physical distress. The object of Federal relief should not be merely to prevent masses of the people from choosing between suicide and revolution.

Now, this is our position which I feel should be made very clear in this case in connection with our whole-hearted support of this bill as urgently needed, knowing the distressing conditions existing throughout the country and the absence of any very adequate relief—and by "adequate" I refer to the extent to which it goes. We want to make our position in the handling of this practical problem quite clear.

First. To limit Federal relief to emergency aid for the destitute is to carry on a policy of gradually pauperizing the Nation. The persistent reduction of the living standards of more than one-fourth of our population to mere subsistence, is creating an army of submerged workers who, by competitive labor, will drag the entire body of manual workers down to lower and lower levels.

I want to give a very unpleasant example of that which has come to my attention in the last few days, without particularizing to attack a particular railroad. But one of the great railroad systems of this country, because they can obtain labor now for 90 cents a day, is using labor on that wage scale for construction purposes, although they ordinarily handle their maintenance-of-way work with their maintenance-of-way forces. The maintenance-of-way forces, men who get the enormous sum of 35 cents an hour, are too expensive for the economy of railroad purposes; therefore, this particular railroad is building new construction work with labor paid at the rate of 90 cents a day.

There are many instances of this sort of the driving down of the level of living by this constant competition of low-paid labor.

I might give another example, that we have had a great deal of difficulty with, and that is, for example, in the Pullman service. In order to save the wages of Pullman conductors, the Pullman Co., is adopting, as an emergency measure, putting Pullman porters in charge of cars instead of conductors, because by doing that, they have only to add $5 a month to the wages of the Pullman porter. Therefore you have substituted an underpaid porter, supported largely by tips, for a previously self-supporting individual.

Those are just two examples that came particularly to my attention. In regard to the employment of cheap labor on the railroads the instances I have named are not exceptional.

The CHAIRMAN. Are you apprehensive that the conditions may be extended and become more aggravated?

Mr. RICHBERG. That is perfectly evident, and if you consider the possible transfer of work from the shops of railroads to outside contractors who may not be required to maintain a respectable wage scale, all we have to do is to go back to 1921, when that became almost the universal practice of the railroads of the country, to contract out the work and thus evade the wage scales they were paying, by agreements, to their employees. We know from sad and very bitter experience just how this competition of underpaid labor breaks down the whole wage scale.

The result is that the fiber of the Nation is being steadily weakened; self-respect, courage, and initiative are being destroyed in millions of homes by years of idleness, malnutrition, and despair. We must check this national degradation at any cost. To continue present industrial competition in reducing the standards of American living, and present competition in reducing the standards of charitable relief—and I think you have a great deal of testimony on that—and present competition in reducing quality or quantity of necessary public services, is simply to engage in competitive suicide. That we are engaged in it, anyone can see; and certainly we are getting a demonstration of what it means in this country to-day.

Second. It has been demonstrated to be futile to utilize national credit and to mortgage the future in order to try to support, temporarily, property values which can only be supported by employed workers earning decent livelihoods on the farms, and the cities, and on the highways.

If time permitted and I had the ability, I could expand that particular proposition into a volume. It seems to me that is one thing that has been made overwhelmingly clear during the years of the depression. You can not maintain property values and security values except by maintaining the earnings of the workers. Out of the earnings of the workers must be taken the interest paid on capital and all the returns that create property values; and when you are constantly cutting down the earnings of the workers, you are cutting down property values, and you can not maintain them by constantly borrowing money to maintain interest payments. It is a hopeless proposition, and I think all of the operations of the Government have demonstrated that it is hopeless. Huge sums of money have been loaned the railroads in order to protect their financial situation, but what is the result? With declining revenue, they are getting into worse and worse condition all the time, and all that is happening is that they are sinking deeper and deeper into the mire of debt.

Third. Our national credit should be used to mobilize, and to bring about the utilization of, our natural resources, our man power, and our industrial facilities, so as to provide compensatory employment for all those capable of self-support.

Fourth. While not advocating the permanent socialization of business or property, we believe that an emergency governmental control is now as essential to the national welfare as it would be in a time of war.

In other words, we see no way of checking this constant competition for lower standards and the constant degradation of the standard of living except by a governmental control to establish common standards. It is exactly the same type of problem I have been testifying to this morning before a subcommittee of the Committee on Interstate Commerce, in the way of pensions. One railroad can not maintain a decent system of pensions unless its competitors maintain it. If one railroad throws out upon the public its unemployed in old age——

The CHAIRMAN. It throws that cost on society.

Mr. RICHBERG. Yes; and someone must bear it, and such a railroad is in unfair competition with the railroad attempting to meet the problem.

Senator CUTTING. How far would you extend governmental control of that kind?

Mr. RICHBERG. Practically as far as necessary to put the employees to work by whatever means were necessary.

In a word, it seems to me that by a concerted national effort, such a mobilization as we have had in time of war, it would not be at all impossible by the utilization of Government credit to put factories into operation to bring the unemployed industrial workers back to work, to bring the products of the farm to those workers, and, by bringing up the prices of commodities on the farms so that a decent living would be had by the agricultural workers, to bring about that exchange of products, the lack of which at the present time seems to indicate the absolute insanity of the whole system.

Of course, we have talked much during the last few years about the absurdity of surpluses on the farms, surplus productive power in the factories, and surplus transportation facilities, and no ability to put these people to work—but we have made no concerted effort to do so.

Senator CUTTING. You realize there is, of course, a strong urge for governmental retrenchment at this time?

Mr. RICHBERG. There is.

Senator COSTIGAN. Not only that, we have not succeeded in bringing the surplus food and the unemployed people together.

Mr. RICHBERG. We absolutely have not; and it is difficult for me to understand that particular policy—I can understand the necessity for the elimination of waste and duplication of effort, but I can not understand the policy of throwing out of employment hundreds and thousands of workers and then turning around and appropriating money to help meet the problem of the unemployed. I am frankly out of sympathy with the proposals of some of these "economy" organizations.

Senator CUTTING. Do you not think at times it is necessary for the Government to extend its activities?

Mr. RICHBERG. It is necessary for the Government to extend its activities; and just as in time of war you issue bonds and borrow against the future to protect the future of the Nation, so if you can not raise, by taxation, the funds to carry through such a program, you can raise it by borrowing against the future. Of course, the minute you start the wheels of machinery moving, the minute commodity prices begin to rise, the entire taxation problem you are discussing begins to disappear, because then the sources of Government revenue open up.

Senator CUTTING. In other words, it would be easier to balance the Budget in years of prosperity than in years of depression?

Mr. RICHBERG. Absolutely.

Senator COSTIGAN. And the raising of funds in the manner you suggest does not really involve unbalancing the Budget?

Mr. RICHBERG. As far as I can see, it will be impossible for us to balance the Budget as long as we are going downhill. I do not believe it is possible to balance a budget while sliding downhill. Your revenues are diminishing and you can not increase your economy without accentuating the speed of the descent.

Senator COSTIGAN. A bond issue is not properly chargeable against the Budget, is it?

Mr. RICHBERG. That is not my understanding of it. It is not a means of raising revenue. It surely is not the method in normal accounting. If you think of it in a broader way and think of it as the raising of capital for the benefit of the whole Nation for the future, any such expenditures should not be charged as current expenditures.

Fifth. The last point I have listed is that we advocate a civil mobilization under civil authority to organize our resources for national defense against the destructiveness of present uncontrolled economic forces.

The kindergarten arguments of those in high places, who are still waiting for economic disease to cure itself, merit only contempt. Frankly, I can not differentiate between a great economic crisis such as we are facing, or a vast epidemic, or anything of that sort, and the menace of war.

Public physicians who urged us to let an epidemic run its course would be universally condemned. Economic illness is primarily man made and can be cured by the use of human intelligence or aggravated by human timidity and folly.

I do not pretend to be an economist in the sense of one having a series of university degrees in such subjects to my credit, but I have long been a student of political economy and a student of the law, and it seems to me quite obvious that our economic conditions are all man made. This is a kind of social structure and business structure which we have built up in which we live. It is not a creation of Providence—something found in the world; it is not a natural product; it is man made and if it is not working correctly, it is subject to correction by the men who made it. The idea of saying that the system is going badly and therefore we must wait until it begins to go rightly is a type and kind of logic I can not follow. It is simply our own system that is not going rightly. It is as though a man whose office gets in such a mess that he can not do business, should then sit down and say, "If I wait long enough it will straighten itself out and everything will be all right."

That is the whole situation, as I see it, in regard to our economic conditions. We created society and created, by law, the corporate forms of activities which permit this tremendous mass organization of our resources and therefore permit mass destructive policies. All these factors in our system are man created and certainly the remedy for them lies in new systems——

Senator COSTIGAN. In your last statement, do you want to go on record as favoring a nationally planned economy?

Mr. RICHBERG. A nationally planned economy is the only salvation of our present situation and only hope for the future in the complications of modern life.

To conclude what I have to say, definitely in behalf of the organizations I represent, I want to say that we indorse this bill to provide for the relief of immediate and acute distress, in the hope that through such relief opportunity may be given, even at this late hour, for the development of a program of economic recovery by public officials who have faith in planning for recovery. I say "at this late hour" because of assuming that we still have an opportunity to plan in the midst of order and comparative social regularity.

We trust that such a program may be devised in confidence; that it will not be sabotaged by those who administer it—which I think is a very important part of the program. We hope that such a program may be made effective before too large a percentage of the people have been starved into either hopeless resignation or desperate revolt.

I would like to say there that the menace, as much as any other, to the future is not merely the danger of revolt, but the danger of destruction of character and confidence and faith of the people until they are unable to adopt and carry forward real programs for their salvation.

The patience of the American people with leaders who are either unable or unwilling to lead has been astounding; but it can not be everlasting. There are many signs that if the lawfully constituted leadership does not soon substitute action for words, a new leadership, perhaps unlawfully constituted, will arise and act. We commend this bill as a better means of preserving law and order than machine guns and tear gas.

I would like to say, in amplification of what I said concerning leadership, that I am not referring merely to political leadership. I am referring to industrial leadership and I am referring particularly to the field of labor leadership; in other words, there is a demand in every avenue of life to-day for a leadership that will really lead.

The present leadership is a result of the system which has built up what we call lawfully constituted authority, but we find everywhere that the system is breaking down and showing cracks and there is a rise of irregularly constituted leaders. You see that demonstrated in the tax strikes; in the efforts to prevent foreclosure of farm mortgages. We can find that exactly in the same way in labor organizations where internal rifts develop. In every avenue of our public life I think that condition is developing.

7] "To Put People Back to Work"

Richberg soon had an opportunity to play a significant role in national economic planning. After meeting the immediate banking crisis of March, 1933, Roosevelt and his advisers turned to working out their programs for industry and agriculture. Strong advocates of national planning, including Moley, Richberg, Johnson, and Senator Wagner, had a hand in drafting the basic legislation for industry. The resulting National Industrial Recovery Act not only reflected their views but also the demands of both industry and labor— and the continuing cry for an expanded public works program as well. Businessmen had been urging Congress to give legal sanctions to "codes of fair competition" drawn up by trade associations in many industries during the 1920's. These codes provided for the exchange of information, improvement of marketing methods, setting of fair trade practices, establishment of standards and grades, and even the determination of prices. Labor called for a shorter working week as a way to spread around available work and so increase employment.

The final bill provided that in each industry trade associations or other spokesmen of business, assisted by representatives of labor and of the consumer, were to draw up fair competition codes, which were to have the force of law and were to take precedence over possible conflicting antitrust laws. The codes were also to set minimum wages and maximum hours. Section 7a of the act guaranteed labor the right of collective bargaining. After the NIRA was declared unconstitutional, this section became the basis for the National Labor Relations Act of 1935, which did so much to encourage the rapid growth of unions.

Richberg, Johnson, and the others completed drafting the bill on May 15. After a month of debate Congress passed it. In the following statement, which he made as he signed the bill, Roosevelt emphasized its fundamental importance.*

THE LAW I have just signed was passed *to put people back to work,* to let them buy more of the products of farms and factories and start our business at a living rate again. This task is in two stages; first, to get many hundreds of thousands of the unemployed back on the payroll by snowfall and, second, to plan for a better future for the longer pull. While we shall not neglect the second, the first stage is an emergency job. It has the right of way.

The second part of the Act gives employment through a vast program of public works. Our studies show that we should be able to hire many men at once and to step up to about a million new jobs by October 1st, and a much greater number later. We must put at the head of our list those works which are fully ready to start now. Our first purpose is to create employment as fast as we can, but we should not pour money into unproved projects.

We have worked out our plans for action. Some of the work will start tomorrow. I am making available $400,000,000 for State roads under regulations which I have just signed, and I am told that the States will get this work under way at once. I have also just released over $200,000,000 for the Navy to start building ships under the London Treaty.

In my Inaugural I laid down the simple proposition that nobody is going to starve in this country. It seems to me to be equally plain that no business which depends for existence on paying less than living wages to its workers has any right to continue in this country. By "business" I mean the whole of commerce as well as the whole of industry; by workers I mean all workers, the white collar class as well as the men in overalls; and by living wages I mean more than a bare subsistence level—I mean the wages of decent living.

Throughout industry, the change from starvation wages and starvation employment to living wages and sustained employment can, in large part, be made by an industrial covenant to which all employers shall subscribe. It is greatly to their interest to do this because decent living, widely spread among our 125,000,000 people, eventually means the opening up to industry of the richest market which the world has known. It is the only way to utilize the so-called excess capacity of our industrial plants. This is the principle that makes this one of the most important laws that ever has come from Congress

* "TO PUT PEOPLE BACK TO WORK": Presidential statement on the NIRA (June 16, 1933). From Samuel I. Rosenman, ed., *The Public Papers and Addresses of Franklin D. Roosevelt: The Year of Crisis,* 1933 (New York, 1938), pp. 251–56. Reprinted by permission of Random House, Inc.

because, before the passage of this Act, no such industrial covenant was possible.

On this idea, the first part of the Act proposes to our industry a great spontaneous cooperation to put millions of men back in their regular jobs this summer. The idea is simply for employers to hire more men to do the existing work by reducing the workhours of each man's week and at the same time paying a living wage for the shorter week.

No employer and no group of less than all employers in a single trade could do this alone and continue to live in business competition. But if *all* employers in each trade now band themselves faithfully in these modern guilds—without exception—and agree to act together and at once, none will be hurt and millions of workers, so long deprived of the right to earn their bread in the sweat of their labor, can raise their heads again. The challenge of this law is whether we can sink selfish interest and present a solid front against a common peril.

It is a challenge to industry which has long insisted that, given the right to act in unison, it could do much for the general good which has hitherto been unlawful. From today it has that right.

Many good men voted this new charter with misgivings. I do not share these doubts. I had part in the great cooperation of 1917 and 1918 and it is my faith that we can count on our industry once more to join in our general purpose to lift this new threat and to do it without taking any advantage of the public trust which has this day been reposed without stint in the good faith and high purpose of American business.

But industry is challenged in another way. It is not only the slackers within trade groups who may stand in the path of our common purpose. In a sense these groups compete with each other, and no single industry, and no separate cluster of industries, can do this job alone for exactly the same reason that no single employer can do it alone. In other words, we can imagine such a thing as a *slacker industry*.

This law is also a challenge to labor. Workers, too, are here given a new charter of rights long sought and hitherto denied. But they know that the first move expected by the Nation is a great cooperation of all employers, by one single mass-action, to improve the case of workers on a scale never attempted in any Nation. Industries can do this only if they have the support of the whole public and especially of their own workers. This is not a law to foment discord and it will not be executed as such. This is a time for mutual confidence and help and we can safely rely on the sense of fair play among all Americans to assure every industry which now moves forward promptly in this united drive against depression that its workers will be with it to a man.

It is, further, a challenge to administration. We are relaxing some of the safeguards of the anti-trust laws. The public must be protected against the abuses that led to their enactment, and to this end, we are putting in place of old principles of unchecked competition some new Government controls. They must, above all, be impartial and just. Their purpose is to free business, not to shackle it; and no man who stands on the constructive, forward-looking side of his industry has anything to fear from them. To such men the opportunities for individual initiative will open more amply than ever. Let me make it clear, however, that the anti-trust laws still stand firmly against monopolies that restrain trade and price fixing which allows inordinate profits or unfairly high prices.

If we ask our trade groups to do that which exposes their business, as never before, to undermining by members who are unwilling to do their part, we must guard those who play the game for the general good against those who may seek selfish gains from the unselfishness of others. We must protect them from the racketeers who invade organizations of both employers and workers. We are spending billions of dollars and if that spending is really to serve our ends it must be done quickly. We must see that our haste does not permit favoritism and graft. All this is a heavy load for any Government and one that can be borne only if we have the patience, cooperation, and support of people everywhere.

Finally, this law is a challenge to our whole people. There is no power in America that can force against the public will such action as we require. But there is no group in America that can withstand the force of an aroused public opinion. This great cooperation can succeed only if those who bravely go forward to restore jobs have aggressive public support and those who lag are made to feel the full weight of public disapproval.

As to the machinery, we shall use the practical way of accomplishing what we are setting out to do. When a trade association has a code ready to submit and the association has qualified as truly representative, and after reasonable notice has been issued to all concerned, a public hearing will be held by the Administrator or a deputy. A Labor Advisory Board appointed by the Secretary of Labor will be responsible that every affected labor group, whether organized or unorganized, is fully and adequately represented in an advisory capacity and any interested labor group will be entitled to be heard through representatives of its own choosing. An Industrial Advisory Board appointed by the Secretary of Commerce will be responsible that every affected industrial group is fully and adequately represented in an advisory capacity and any interested industrial group will be entitled to be heard through representatives of its own choosing. A Consumers Advisory Board will be responsible that the interests of the consuming public will be represented and every reasonable opportunity will be given to any group or class who may be affected directly or indirectly to present their views.

At the conclusion of these hearings and after the most careful scrutiny by a competent economic staff the Administrator will present the subject to me for my action under the law.

I am fully aware that wage increases will eventually raise costs, but I ask that managements give first consideration to the improvement of operating figures by greatly increased sales to be expected from the rising purchasing power of the public. That is good economics and good business. The aim of this whole effort is to restore our rich domestic market by raising its vast consuming capacity. If we now inflate prices as fast and as far as we increase wages, the whole project will be set at naught. We cannot hope for the full effect of this plan unless, in these first critical months, and, even at the expense of full initial profits, we defer price increases as long as possible. If we can thus start a strong, sound, upward spiral of business activity, our industries will have little doubt of black-ink operations in the last quarter of this year. The pent-up demand of this people is very great and if we can release it on so broad a front, we need not fear a lagging recovery. There is greater danger of too much feverish speed. . . .

Between these twin efforts—public works and industrial re-employment—it is not too much to expect that a great many men and women can be taken from the ranks of the unemployed before winter comes. It is the most important attempt of this kind in history. As in the great crisis of the World War, it puts a whole people to the simple but vital test:—*"Must we go on in many groping, disorganized, separate units to defeat or shall we move as one great team to victory?"*

8] "Toward Planned Harvests"

The Agricultural Adjustment Act, signed May 13, aimed at restoring prosperity to American farmers by raising prices of basic commodities—cotton, wheat, corn, hogs, tobacco, dairy products, and rice—to a level that "would give agricultural commodities a purchasing power equivalent to the purchasing power of agricultural commodities in the base period, August 1909–July 1914," a period of high farm prices. The farmers, who were to be paid for not raising these crops, were to obtain their expanded income from government payments as well as from increased prices resulting from a decreased supply. Because the bill was not passed until after the spring planting season, one of Agricultural Adjustment Administration's first acts was to authorize the plowing under of one-fourth of the young cotton crop and the slaughter of six million little pigs. Such deliberate destruction at a time when men so badly needed food and clothing drew bitter comments from critics of the New Deal. To explain these measures and to describe the goals and methods of his agency, Chester C. Davis, the AAA's director of production, wrote the following comments in the autumn of 1933 in an article entitled "Toward Planned Harvests." Davis, a former farm editor and Montana state commissioner of agriculture, had long been an advocate of increased intervention by the federal government in agriculture.

The AAA was, like the NIRA, ultimately declared unconstitutional. The Supreme Court ruled that the tax on processors, which was used to provide the funds for the benefit payments, was invalid. But unlike the NIRA, the Agricultural Adjustment Administration was quickly revived and its powers and scope of activities broadened by legislation passed in 1936 and 1938 that dropped the offending tax provisions.*

.   .   .   .

THE FARM ACT, passed by the Congress on May 10, last, gave the Secretary of Agriculture and an Adjustment Administrator, representing the President, broad permissive powers to induce active agricultural planning among the farmers themselves. The Agricultural Adjustment Administration was set up in the Department of Agriculture. George N. Peek of Illinois, who throughout the twelve years of American agriculture's post-war depression, had fought for

* "TOWARD PLANNED HARVESTS": Chester C. Davis, "Toward Planned Harvests." From the *Review of Reviews*, LXXXVIII (December, 1933), 20–21.

better farm prices, and a better balance between rural and urban spending power, was named Chief Administrator. The attack of the Agricultural Adjustment Administration upon surplus plantings of wheat, corn, cotton, and tobacco is essentially the domestic allotment plan fortified by provision for a variety of other necessary adjustments. The Act provides for an adjustment of debts, and authorizes an adjusted dollar if need be. It allows auxiliary maneuvers to clear surpluses from the top of the pile, as well as from direct attack from underneath in the soundest manner possible—not planting them. Our recent relief purchases of butter, the induced export of northwestern wheat, and present efforts to feed other surpluses direct to the unemployed, are examples of auxiliary maneuvers.

Devices of this nature are of dubious value if employed alone. The operation, if successful, raises prices temporarily. The raised price induces a greater sowing. The great sowing wrecks the price. But if under your entire structure of farm prices you put a solid basis of controlled sowing, and planned national harvests, then stabilization and induced exports, within the limits of well-defined world agreements, become not only defensible but promising means of meeting temporary emergencies. In the future we shall probably employ stabilization and induced shipments to level off regional and national crop excesses and deficiencies, due to the weather, from year to year.

In this article I wish to speak principally of our foundation effort: a voluntary, coöperative control of volume output, organized from the ground up, and conducted principally by the farmers themselves. But the fact that this coöperation is induced by processing taxes, which redistribute buying power to people at the grass roots, long deprived; and the fact that we are attacking not only disorganized food production, but disorganized distribution should at least be mentioned.

AGRICULTURE first felt the present depression in 1920. With agriculture prostrate at the end of 1932, and with the cities sharing in the depression, at last, many distribution margins remained as wide as in 1929. Between 1929 and 1933 city incomes fell one-third; farm income, already low, fell two-thirds; but distribution spreads stayed wide. It is informing to note that of the fifteen leading corporations in point of earnings in 1932 nine dealt in food or tobacco.

Industry and the distribution trades in general, like agriculture in general, are overextended, sprawling, struggling more or less helplessly amid insane duplications of effort and blind, destructive competition. Unlike agriculture, industry and the distributing trades have been putting too little money into prices for raw materials and into wages. Wealth has become overcentralized, too narrowly circulated. Business has stacked up too much of a pile in excess plant, dividends, and interest payments. The New Deal proposes, for the sake of all, that money be put forth more freely in farm prices and city wages, to breed again. The great effort is to start money moving from the bottom up, and to reorganize both production and distribution so as to avoid recurring economic paralysis which, under laissez-faire, has been the price of progress.

In the field of agricultural distribution we have chosen at first to move rather slowly, feeling our way. The Act gives us mandate to seek first more orderly distribution, by marketing agreements voluntarily entered into by the trades. If voluntary agreements do not suffice, we can issue revokable licenses. By voluntary agreement we have obtained from the leading tobacco companies a farm price on flue-cured tobacco 40 per cent. above the figure that was being paid them when the Governors of certain southern states were closing markets last summer. Milk, which provides about a quarter of all American farm income, presents production and distribution problems that have given us much concern. The situation is enormously complicated, and varies widely by regions. Only recently have we succeeded in getting marketing agreements that give the farmer more money without running up the price to the consumer. We shall proceed in that direction, using the power to license wherever necessary; but we shall never put the milk business on a satisfactory basis until we introduce decisive measures of production control.

PRODUCTION adjustment efforts so far have been directed against the crops of which, in consequence of closing European markets, we have towering export surpluses. We have had to work fast, taking these crops as they came along. Time so forced our hand on cotton that we had to take it out as it ripened. I hope we shall never again have to destroy part of a standing crop, but the urgency was so great in the South this year that our emergency campaign there was justified. Another year of 5-cent cotton would stifle the whole program of national recovery. We are lending 10 cents a pound on cotton now.

We took out 10½ million acres of ripening cotton, a quarter of the 1933 crop, and seeded 110 million dollars in new spending power in the cotton South. It was rough work, but the crisis in the South has eased. The plows of those cotton farmers struck at the roots of their trouble and turned those roots to the sky. Now we are launching a program to plant not the usual 40 million acres but only 25 million for 1934 harvest.

This year's wheat campaign was more thoroughly organized. There was time. With world accord, we have signed about four-fifths of America's commercial wheat acreage for a three-year acreage adjustment, with a 15 per cent. pro-rata reduction in 1934. In 1450 counties more than a half million wheat growers have formed county wheat production control associations to administer this huge coöperative undertaking from the ground up. We shall displace 8 million acres from American wheat lands in 1934, and distribute around 100 million dollars in adjustment payments.

Because of the intricate interrelation of corn and hog prices, the 350 million dollar adjustment program that we now are launching in the Corn Belt is beset with peculiar difficulties. The rough stab that we were forced to take at the problem last summer, with an induced slaughter of little pigs and sows, was a stopgap at best. The present plan attacks the base of the difficulty by the sounder means of agrarian birth control. We are striving now for permanent effect. Somewhere between 10 and 15 million acres now planted to corn are surplus acres. We shall seek to reduce corn planting about one-fifth and hog farrowing about one-quarter in the next three years.

Let me say at this point that all our plans are elastic. If an unforeseen world condition should require us to increase rather than to decrease agricultural output, our newly mobilized production control machinery could immediately be turned the other way, with a premium put upon expanding, not upon restricting acreage.

FIFTEEN million acres less cotton next year, 8 million acres taken out of wheat, 10 million or more acres no longer given over to surplus cornland: these figures begin to mount up. Add minor displacements of tobacco and rice acreage already agreed upon, the figure exceeds 33 million acres, more than the entire cultivated area of Japan proper, taken out of key crops—and turned to other uses.

To what other uses? That is a pressing question nowadays, not only here in Washington, but on every farm in the land. You cannot move one piece on the vast agricultural checkerboard without altering in the end the entire design. One move compels another.

The land taken out of cotton, wheat, corn, and tobacco is being fallowed and rested, or sown, speaking generally, to non-competitive soil-building crops. That generally means grass. The dairymen are inclined to resist the tendency (mistakenly, I believe; as dairy cows are preëminently efficient in transforming grass into proteins); but the tendency of our present programs seems increasingly back in the direction we came from far too hastily: back to grass.

There are many reasons for this. The land needs a rest. The people who have overworked it need rest also. Women and children of the farm family especially have been driven often far too hard without reward. Grassland culture is less laborious, and life upon grasslands is pleasanter than life in a skinned, high-pressure farming area as a rule. Land in grass does not wash away. But the most immediate and pressing cause of retreat from high-pressure farming toward a more pastoral, yet modern, economy is this: It takes three or four times as much land to feed a cow on grass as it does to grow grain and feed high-pressure feed mixtures. Livestock on grass, with supplemental rations, will not produce as much of meat or milk as livestock pressed into high production by grain feeding. But we have too much milk and meat as it is; and food produced on a grassland economy over wider areas is much more cheaply produced.

The open country is not only a place to grow things; it is a place to live; and much land pleasant to live upon is unfit to farm. As we put our lands in order from the standpoint of economical production we shall gradually accomplish also a reordering of all America as a place to live. Not only crops will move; people will move; and we shall see, I think, a widespread intermingling of those ways of life we now think of separately as rural and urban. . . .

9] Keynes Poses Alternatives to Centralized Planning

By the summer of 1934, the high hopes of the planners had somewhat dimmed. In agriculture, planning for a few basic crops presented relatively few difficulties. But even here voluntary methods of control through subsidies were proving inadequate. In industry, the fashioning and administering of codes for many, many complex and interrelated industries became an extremely difficult task. Some of those New Dealers who were seeking alternatives to the Richberg type of planning listened attentively to the suggestions of John Maynard Keynes, the celebrated British economist.*

THESE are a few notes on the New Deal by one who has come here on a brief visit of pure inquisitiveness—made under the limitations of imperfect knowledge, but gaining, perhaps, from the detachment of a birdseye view.

My purpose is to consider the prospects rather than the past—taking the legislation of this Congress for granted and examining what might be done on the basis thus given. I am in sympathy with most of the social and reforming aims of this legislation; and the principal subject of these notes is the problem of consolidating economic and business recovery.

For this reason, I have not much to say about NRA. I doubt if this measure is either such an advantage to recovery or such a handicap as its advocates and its critics suppose. It embodies some important improvements in labor conditions and for obtaining fair trade practices. But I agree with the widespread opinion that much of it is objectionable because of its restrictionist philosophy which has a proper place in agricultural adjustment today but not in American industry, and because of its excessive complexity and regimentation.

In particular, it would be advisable to discard most of the provisions to fix prices and to forbid sales below an alleged, but undefinable, cost basis. Nevertheless, its net effect on recovery can easily be overestimated either way.

I find most Americans divided between those who believe that higher wages are good because they increase purchasing power and those who believe that they are bad because they raise costs. But both are right, and the net result of the two opposing influences is to cancel out. The important question is the proper adjustment of relative wage rates. Absolute wage rates are not of primary importance in a country where their effect on foreign trade has been offset by exchange devaluation.

The case for AAA, on the other hand, is much stronger. For the farmer has had to shoulder more than his share of the trouble and also has more lasting difficulties ahead of him than industry has. AAA is organizing for the farmer the advisable measure of restriction which industry long ago organized for itself. Thus the task which AAA is attempting is necessary though difficult; whereas some part of what NRA seems to be aiming at is not only impracticable but unnecessary.

I see the problem of recovery, accordingly, in the following light: How soon will normal business enterprise come to the rescue? What measures can be taken to hasten the return of normal enterprise? On what scale, by which expedients and for how long is abnormal government expenditure advisable in the meantime? For this, I think, is how the administration should view its task.

I see no likelihood that business, of its own initiative, will invest in durable goods on a sufficient scale for many months to come. There are several reasons for this.

* KEYNES POSES ALTERNATIVES TO CENTRALIZED PLANNING: From the New York *Times* (June 10, 1934). Reprinted by permission of the New York *Times* and the estate of John Maynard Keynes.

In the first place, the important but intangible state of mind, which we call business confidence, is signally lacking. It would be easy to mention specific causes of this, for some of which the administration may be to blame. Probably the most important is the menace of possible labor troubles. But the real explanation, in my judgment, lies deeper than the specific causes. It is to be found in the perplexity and discomfort which the business world feels from being driven so far from its accustomed moorings into unknown and uncharted waters.

The business man, who may be adaptable and quick on his feet in his own particular field, is usually conservative and conventional in the larger aspects of social and economic policy. At the start he was carried away, like other people, by the prevailing enthusiasm—without being converted at bottom or suffering a sea-change. Thus, he has easily reverted to where he was. He is sulky and bothered; and, with the short memory characteristic of contemporary man, even begins to look back with longing to the good old days of 1932.

This atmosphere of disappointment, disillusion and perplexity is nothing to wonder at. I doubt if it could have been avoided without undue concession to conventional ideas. But it is not incurable. The mere passage of time for business to work out its new bearings and recover its equanimity should do much. If the President could convince business men that they know the worst, so to speak, and can settle down to adjust themselves to a known situation, that might hasten matters. Above all, the actual experience of gradually improving conditions might work wonders.

In the second place, there are still serious obstacles in the way of reopening the capital market to large-scale borrowing for new investment; particularly, the high cost of borrowing to those who need loans most and the attitude of the finance houses to the Securities Act, though I consider that they should accept the amended act as workable.[1]

Moreover, many types of durable goods are already in sufficient supply, so that business will not be inclined to repair or modernize plant until a stronger demand is being experienced than can be met with existing plant; to which should be added the excessively high cost of building relatively to rents and incomes.

None of these obstacles can be overcome in a day or by a stroke of the pen. The notion that, if the government would retire altogether from the economic field, business, left to itself, would soon work out its own salvation, is, to my mind, foolish; and, even if it were not, it is certain that public opinion would allow no such thing. This does not mean that the administration should not be assiduously preparing the way for the return of normal investment enterprise. But this will unavoidably take time. When it comes, it will intensify and maintain a recovery initiated by other means. But it belongs to the second chapter of the story and not to the first.

I conclude, therefore, that, for six months at least, and probably a year, the measure of recovery to be achieved will mainly depend on the degree of the

---

1 On June 6, Roosevelt had signed the Securities Exchange Act, which set up the Securities and Exchange Commission to regulate the issue, sale, and exchange of stocks, bonds, and other securities.

direct stimulus to production deliberately applied by the administration. Since I have no belief in the efficacy for this purpose of the price and wage-raising activities of NRA, this must chiefly mean the pace and volume of the government's emergency expenditure. . . .

. . . the aggregate emergency expenditure is now declining. If it is going to decline to $200,000,000 monthly, much of the ground already gained will probably be lost. If it were to rise to $400,000,000 monthly, I should be quite confident that a strong business revival would set in by the Autumn.

So little divides a retreat from an advance. Most people greatly underestimate the effect of a given emergency expenditure, because they overlook the multiplier—the cumulative effect of increased individual incomes, because the expenditure of these incomes improves the incomes of a further set of recipients and so on. Four hundred million dollars monthly is not much more than 11 per cent of the national income; yet it may, directly and indirectly, increase the national income by at least three or four times this amount. Thus the difference between a monthly emergency expenditure of $400,000,000, financed out of loans and not out of taxation, which would represent a mere redistribution of incomes, and a $100,000,000 expenditure, may be, other things being equal, to increase the national money income by 25 to 30 per cent. . . .

This brings me to my agenda for the President:

1. Sufficient appropriations should be obtained before Congress adjourns to provide the necessary ammunition. I believe that this has been obtained.

2. A small office should be set up to collate the spending programs, both realized and prospective, of the various emergency organizations, to compare estimates with results and to report to the President weekly.

3. If the volume or pace of prospective estimates appear to be deficient, the emergency organization should be instructed to report urgently on further available projects. Housing and the railroads appear to offer the outstanding opportunities. The new housing bill is brilliantly conceived and if it is operated vigorously may prove to be a measure of the first importance. Drought relief may be an unexpectedly large factor in the coming months.

4. Meanwhile active preparations should be on foot to make sure that normal enterprise will take the place of the emergency programs as soon as possible. Much progress has already been made with the problem of remedying the widespread and paralyzing loss of liquidity. But that task must still be carried on.

5. With the Securities Act and the Stock Exchange Act carried into law, the battle is over and the time has come for sincere efforts on both sides to establish co-operative and friendly relations between the commission which will work the acts and the leading financial interests. For it is vital to reopen the capital market.

6. Continuous pressure should be exerted by the Treasury and the Federal Reserve System to bring down the long-term rate of interest. . . .

7. To an Englishman the high level of building costs in this country appears to be scandalous, both of building materials and of direct labor. They must be more than 50 per cent above, and perhaps double, what they are in England. So long as the volume of work remains as low as it is now, these high costs do not mean high incomes to producers. Thus, no one benefits. It is of the first

importance for the administration to take whatever steps are in its power to reduce unit costs in these industries against an undertaking to increase the volume of business sufficiently to maintain and probably to increase actual earnings. This might involve a national program of building working-class houses to rent, which would be, in itself, a great benefit. The measure of recovery now enjoyed in England is largely due to the activity of house building.

8. Either by skill or by good fortune the United States has arrived at what seems to me an excellent currency policy. It was right to devalue. It is right to have a value for the dollar currently fixed in terms of gold. It is prudent to keep a discretionary margin to allow future changes in the gold value of the dollar, if a change in circumstances makes this advisable. But all these measures have been carried fully far enough. Thus there would be no risk, in my judgment, if the President were to make it plain that he has now successfully attained his objects, so far as they can be attained by monetary policy, and that, henceforth, a wise spending policy and a gradual but obstinate attack on high interest rates through the agency of the Federal Reserve System and otherwise will occupy the foreground of the economic program.

9. A word as to the budget. Expenditures fall into three classes: the normal expenditure of administration, relief expenditures and capital expenditures represented by valuable assets and obligations. The first two classes should, probably, be balanced by revenue by 1936. But it would be a disastrous error, and an instrument of strong deflation, to attempt to cover capital expenditure out of current revenue. At present, the public mind is apt to be confused, because relief and capital expenditure are linked together indiscriminately as emergency expenditure. . . .

If, in conclusion, I may give for what they are worth the impressions of a brief visit to Washington, I believe that there is much devoted and intelligent work in progress there, and that the fittest ideas and the fittest men are tending to survive. In many parts of the world the old order has passed away. But, of all the experiments to evolve a new order, it is the experiment of young America which most attracts my own deepest sympathy. For they are occupied with the task of trying to make the economic order work tolerably well, while preserving freedom of individual initiative and liberty of thought and criticism.

The older generation of living Americans accomplished the great task of solving the technical problem of how to produce economic goods on a scale adequate to human needs. It is the task of the younger generation to bring to actual realization the potential blessings of having solved the technical side of the problem of poverty. The central control which the latter requires involves an essentially changed method and outlook. The minds and energies which have found their fulfillment in the achievements of American business are not likely to be equally well adapted to the further task. That must be, as it should be, the fulfillment of the next generation.

The new men will often appear to be at war with the ideas and convictions of their seniors. This cannot be helped. But I hope that these seniors will look as sympathetically as they can at a sincere attempt—I cannot view it otherwise —to complete, and not to destroy, what they themselves have created.

10] Lippmann Advocates Keynes-like Policies

> Walter Lippmann, noted newspaper columnist, emphasized the constitutional and ideological, as well as the administrative, advantages of deficit spending, a managed currency, and controlled interest rates. He stressed the value of such a program, which he termed "reflation," in his New York *Herald Tribune* column of June 8, 1935, written shortly after the Supreme Court declared the NRA unconstitutional.*

PERHAPS the worst thing about N.R.A. was that in respect both to recovery and to reform it took the country up a blind alley.

It has been attacked as a tyranny. This would have been an important charge had N.R.A. not been breaking down because it could not be enforced. It had been attacked as a brake upon recovery. This was, I believe, true in 1933–34, but, since the thing lost momentum and above all since the genuine recovery measures have begun to take effect, it ceased some months ago to be very important. But as a diversion of energy and attention from the crucial to the trivial, from major policy to minor meddlesomeness, it continues to confuse a large body of opinion and, it would seem, the Administration itself. . . .

. . . Now N.R.A. was administered on the theory that if by fiat and by agreement you could stop wage and price cutting in one industry after another, you could stop it entirely.

N.R.A. tried to stop the water from running through the sieve by plugging each hole in the sieve.

That was and is beyond human power. To attempt it required a detailed intervention in every factory and store. But no act of Congress could define that intervention. Because no act of Congress could define just how each hole in the sieve was to be plugged, blanket power had to be delegated to the President. Because the President could not decide how to plug each hole he had, in turn, to delegate blanket power to General Johnson. Because General Johnson could not decide how to plug all the holes, he had to delegate blanket powers to the code authorities. The net result was that several thousand private business men were making and enforcing Federal laws, and the courts and the Department of Justice were entangled in the preposterous effort to send men to jail because they had violated laws which no one known to the Constitution had had any part in framing.

To this state of affairs the Supreme Court unanimously put an end. . . .

Now, of course, if the only way that the Federal government can deal with a depression is by plugging each hole in the sieve, then it is powerless. But the New Dealers who are wringing their hands because they have been forbidden to do something which they could not do if they were permitted, are exhibiting a curious lack of understanding of the social order which they would like to

* LIPPMANN ADVOCATES KEYNES-LIKE POLICIES: From the New York *Herald Tribune* (June 8, 1935), in Walter Lippmann, *Interpretations, 1933–1935* (New York, 1936), pp. 286–90. Reprinted with permission of The Macmillan Company from *Interpretations, 1933–1935* by Walter Lippmann. Copyright, 1936, by Walter Lippmann.

manage. They do not seem to understand it any better than their conservative opponents, who seem to think that a modern state cannot and need not and should not go beyond issuing bulletins to tell bankers and business men what wonderful fellows they are. Both of them assume that there is no form of social control except to plug the holes in the sieve. The only difference between the so-called left-wing New Dealers and the die-hard conservatives is that the New Dealers want to try it, though it is impossible, whereas the conservatives do not want to try it, even if it were possible.

For a central government the only effective method of general social control—the only constitutional method—is not to plug the individual holes in the sieve but to control the flow of the water. . . .

These measures, to describe them in a catchword, are measures of reflation rather than of regimentation. In substance they amount to this: That the major effort of recovery has been devoted not to helping this or that victim of the depression by laws, subsidies, and what not, but to restoring the balance of prices and augmenting the whole purchasing power of the community.

Thus in all countries where there is recovery, there has been depreciation or revaluation. In all countries where there has been recovery, there has been a central bank and Treasury policy to increase bank reserves, to increase bank deposits and to lower the long-term rate of interest. In all countries where there is recovery, there has been some kind of government stimulus to promote expenditure. In almost all countries where there is recovery, in most countries where recovery is far advanced, there have been deliberate government deficit expenditures financed by loans to augment the general purchasing power of the community.

If anything has been demonstrated in this depression which can be relied upon as a guide to policy, it is that reflation—not planning, not regimentation, and not laissez-faire—is the remedy for this depression. When you think of it, it would be strange if it had not been demonstrated. For it stands to reason that if some deflation is the remedy for inflation, then some inflation must be the remedy for deflation. . . .

Now, a reflation policy—and reflation can mean either the contraction or the expansion of general purchasing power—is indisputably within the province of the Federal government. It is secure beyond challenge in the constitutional power to regulate the value of money, and in the right invincibly established by precedents originating in the Republican Party to spend money for public works. This power, effectively and wisely used, is the fundamental power necessary to regulate a modern economy. The power to fix the wages paid for killing chickens is negligible [1] and would be totally unnecessary, and would not even be desired, if the great power to stablize the total purchasing power of the nation were properly used. . . .

Moreover, this power to reflate—to control the value of money and the total volume of money, to increase or decrease total national purchasing power by expenditure and retrenchment, by taxation and by deficit financing—is a power that can be exercised without destroying the federal character of the

---

[1] A reference to *Schecter Poultry Corporation* v. *U.S.*, the case in which the Court invalidated the NIRA.

American government. For a central government can reflate without ruining local sovereignty: a reflation policy affects only the general purchasing power of the whole nation, and can be administered without detailed intervention in each man's affairs. But it cannot regiment the individual industries of the nation without a dictatorship and a bureaucracy that would be intolerable to a nation habituated to freedom.

11] Roosevelt Outlines the "Second New Deal"

> Roosevelt would not commit himself fully to either the Keynesian or the Richberg programs. His primary concern remained one of assuring individual Americans a minimum of economic security. Yet administrative, economic, and constitutional realities turned him away from centralized planning and control. His annual message to Congress on January 4, 1935, outlined what has often been called the Second New Deal. The following selection from that message clearly indicates his objectives and the means by which he wished to achieve them.*

. . . .

I RECALL to your attention my message to the Congress last June in which I said: "among our objectives I place the security of the men, women and children of the Nation first." That remains our first and continuing task; and in a very real sense every major legislative enactment of this Congress should be a component part of it.

In defining immediate factors which enter into our quest, I have spoken to the Congress and the people of three great divisions:

1. The security of a livelihood through the better use of the national resources of the land in which we live.
2. The security against the major hazards and vicissitudes of life.
3. The security of decent homes.

I am now ready to submit to the Congress a broad program designed ultimately to establish all three of these factors of security—a program which because of many lost years will take many future years to fulfill.

A study of our national resources, more comprehensive than any previously made, shows the vast amount of necessary and practicable work which needs to be done for the development and preservation of our natural wealth for the enjoyment and advantage of our people in generations to come. The sound use of land and water is far more comprehensive than the mere planting of trees, building of dams, distributing of electricity or retirement of sub-marginal land. It recognizes that stranded populations, either in the country or the city, cannot have security under the conditions that now surround them.

---

* ROOSEVELT OUTLINES THE "SECOND NEW DEAL": Annual Message to Congress (January 5, 1935). From Samuel I. Rosenman, ed., *The Public Papers and Addresses of Franklin D. Roosevelt: The Court Disapproves, 1935* (New York, 1938), pp. 17–23. Reprinted by permission of Random House, Inc.

To this end we are ready to begin to meet this problem—the intelligent care of population throughout our Nation, in accordance with an intelligent distribution of the means of livelihood for that population. A definite program for putting people to work, of which I shall speak in a moment, is a component part of this greater program of security of livelihood through the better use of our national resources.

Closely related to the broad problem of livelihood is that of security against the major hazards of life. Here also, a comprehensive survey of what has been attempted or accomplished in many Nations and in many States proves to me that the time has come for action by the national Government. I shall send to you, in a few days, definite recommendations based on these studies. These recommendations will cover the broad subjects of unemployment insurance and old age insurance, of benefits for children, for mothers, for the handicapped, for maternity care and for other aspects of dependency and illness where a beginning can now be made.

The third factor—better homes for our people—has also been the subject of experimentation and study. Here, too, the first practical steps can be made through the proposals which I shall suggest in relation to giving work to the unemployed.

Whatever we plan and whatever we do should be in the light of these three clear objectives of security. We cannot afford to lose valuable time in haphazard public policies which cannot find a place in the broad outlines of these major purposes. In that spirit I come to an immediate issue made for us by hard and inescapable circumstance—the task of putting people to work. In the spring of 1933 the issue of destitution seemed to stand apart; today, in the light of our experience and our new national policy, we find we can put people to work in ways which conform to, initiate and carry forward the broad principles of that policy.

The first objectives of emergency legislation of 1933 were to relieve destitution, to make it possible for industry to operate in a more rational and orderly fashion, and to put behind industrial recovery the impulse of large expenditures in Government undertakings. The purpose of the National Industrial Recovery Act to provide work for more people succeeded in a substantial manner within the first few months of its life, and the Act has continued to maintain employment gains and greatly improved working conditions in industry.

The program of public works provided for in the Recovery Act launched the Federal Government into a task for which there was little time to make preparation and little American experience to follow. Great employment has been given and is being given by these works.

More than two billions of dollars have also been expended in direct relief to the destitute. Local agencies of necessity determined the recipients of this form of relief. With inevitable exceptions the funds were spent by them with reasonable efficiency and as a result actual want of food and clothing in the great majority of cases has been overcome.

But the stark fact before us is that great numbers still remain unemployed.

A large proportion of these unemployed and their dependents have been forced on the relief rolls. The burden on the Federal Government has grown with great rapidity. We have here a human as well as an economic problem.

When humane considerations are concerned, Americans give them precedence. The lessons of history, confirmed by the evidence immediately before me, show conclusively that continued dependence upon relief induces a spiritual and moral disintegration fundamentally destructive to the national fibre. To dole out relief in this way is to administer a narcotic, a subtle destroyer of the human spirit. It is inimical to the dictates of sound policy. It is in violation of the traditions of America. Work must be found for able-bodied but destitute workers.

The Federal Government must and shall quit this business of relief.

I am not willing that the vitality of our people be further sapped by the giving of cash, of market baskets, of a few hours of weekly work cutting grass, raking leaves or picking up papers in the public parks. We must preserve not only the bodies of the unemployed from destitution but also their self-respect, their self-reliance and courage and determination. This decision brings me to the problem of what the Government should do with approximately five million unemployed now on the relief rolls.

About one million and a half of these belong to the group which in the past was dependent upon local welfare efforts. Most of them are unable for one reason or another to maintain themselves independently—for the most part, through no fault of their own. Such people, in the days before the great depression, were cared for by local efforts—by States, by counties, by towns, by cities, by churches and by private welfare agencies. It is my thought that in the future they must be cared for as they were before. I stand ready through my own personal efforts, and through the public influence of the office that I hold, to help these local agencies to get the means necessary to assume this burden.

The security legislation which I shall propose to the Congress will, I am confident, be of assistance to local effort in the care of this type of cases. Local responsibility can and will be resumed, for, after all, common sense tells us that the wealth necessary for this task existed and still exists in the local community, and the dictates of sound administration require that this responsibility be in the first instance a local one.

There are, however, an additional three and one half million employable people who are on relief. With them the problem is different and the repsonsibility is different. This group was the victim of a nation-wide depression caused by conditions which were not local but national. The Federal Government is the only governmental agency with sufficient power and credit to meet this situation. We have assumed this task and we shall not shrink from it in the future. It is a duty dictated by every intelligent consideration of national policy to ask you to make it possible for the United States to give employment to all of these three and one half million employable people now on relief, pending their absorption in a rising tide of private employment.

It is my thought that with the exception of certain of the normal public building operations of the Government, all emergency public works shall be united in a single new and greatly enlarged plan.

With the establishment of this new system we can supersede the Federal Emergency Relief Administration with a coordinated authority which will be charged with the orderly liquidation of our present relief activities and the substitution of a national chart for the giving of work.

This new program of emergency public employment should be governed by a number of practical principles.

(1) All work undertaken should be useful—not just for a day, or a year, but useful in the sense that it affords permanent improvement in living conditions or that it creates future new wealth for the Nation.

(2) Compensation on emergency public projects should be in the form of security payments which should be larger than the amount now received as a relief dole, but at the same time not so large as to encourage the rejection of opportunities for private employment or the leaving of private employment to engage in Government work.

(3) Projects should be undertaken on which a large percentage of direct labor can be used.

(4) Preference should be given to those projects which will be self-liquidating in the sense that there is a reasonable expectation that the Government will get its money back at some future time.

(5) The projects undertaken should be selected and planned so as to compete as little as possible with private enterprises. This suggests that if it were not for the necessity of giving useful work to the unemployed now on relief, these projects in most instances would not now be undertaken.

(6) The planning of projects would seek to assure work during the coming fiscal year to the individuals now on relief, or until such time as private employment is available. In order to make adjustment to increasing private employment, work should be planned with a view to tapering it off in proportion to the speed with which the emergency workers are offered positions with private employers.

(7) Effort should be made to locate projects where they will serve the greatest unemployment needs as shown by present relief rolls, and the broad program of the National Resources Board should be freely used for guidance in selection. Our ultimate objective being the enrichment of human lives, the Government has the primary duty to use its emergency expenditures as much as possible to serve those who cannot secure the advantages of private capital.

Ever since the adjournment of the 73d Congress, the Administration has been studying from every angle the possibility and the practicability of new forms of employment. As a result of these studies I have arrived at certain very definite convictions as to the amount of money that will be necessary for the sort of public projects that I have described. I shall submit these figures in my budget message. I assure you now they will be within the sound credit of the Government.

The work itself will cover a wide field including clearance of slums, which for adequate reasons cannot be undertaken by private capital; in rural housing of several kinds, where, again, private capital is unable to function; in rural electrification; in the reforestation of the great watersheds of the Nation; in an intensified program to prevent soil erosion and to reclaim blighted areas; in improving existing road systems and in constructing national highways designed to handle modern traffic; in the elimination of grade crossings; in the extension and enlargement of the successful work of the Civilian Conservation

Corps; in non-Federal works, mostly self-liquidating and highly useful to local divisions of Government; and on many other projects which the Nation needs and cannot afford to neglect.

This is the method which I propose to you in order that we may better meet this present-day problem of unemployment. Its greatest advantage is that it fits logically and usefully into the long-range permanent policy of providing the three types of security which constitute as a whole an American plan for the betterment of the future of the American people. . . .

12] The President Defines a Program for Social Security

Roosevelt followed his annual message of 1935 with others that spelled out his proposals in more detail. Among the most important was the message on social security that he sent to Congress on January 17. On August 14, Congress passed the nation's first social security act, substantially as Roosevelt had recommended it.*

To the Congress:

IN ADDRESSING you on June 8, 1934, I summarized the main objectives of our American program. Among these was, and is, the security of the men, women, and children of the Nation against certain hazards and vicissitudes of life. This purpose is an essential part of our task. In my annual message to you I promised to submit a definite program of action. This I do in the form of a report to me by a Committee on Economic Security, appointed by me for the purpose of surveying the field and of recommending the basis of legislation. . . .

The detailed report of the Committee sets forth a series of proposals that will appeal to the sound sense of the American people. It has not attempted the impossible, nor has it failed to exercise sound caution and consideration of all of the factors concerned: the national credit, the rights and responsibilities of States, the capacity of industry to assume financial responsibilities and the fundamental necessity of proceeding in a manner that will merit the enthusiastic support of citizens of all sorts.

It is overwhelmingly important to avoid any danger of permanently discrediting the sound and necessary policy of Federal legislation for economic security by attempting to apply it on too ambitious a scale before actual experience has provided guidance for the permanently safe direction of such efforts. The place of such a fundamental in our future civilization is too precious to be jeopardized now by extravagant action. It is a sound idea—a sound ideal. Most of the other advanced countries of the world have already adopted it and their experience affords the knowledge that social insurance can be made a sound and workable project.

Three principles should be observed in legislation on this subject. First, the

* THE PRESIDENT DEFINES A PROGRAM FOR SOCIAL SECURITY: Message to Congress (January 17, 1935). From Samuel I. Rosenman, ed., *The Public Papers and Addresses of Franklin D. Roosevelt: The Court Disapproves, 1935* (New York, 1938), pp. 43–46. Reprinted by permission of Random House, Inc.

system adopted, except for the money necessary to initiate it, should be self-sustaining in the sense that funds for the payment of insurance benefits should not come from the proceeds of general taxation. Second, excepting in old-age insurance, actual management should be left to the States subject to standards established by the Federal Government. Third, sound financial management of the funds and the reserves, and protection of the credit structure of the Nation should be assured by retaining Federal control over all funds through trustees in the Treasury of the United States.

At this time, I recommend the following types of legislation looking to economic security:

1. Unemployment compensation.

2. Old-age benefits, including compulsory and voluntary annuities.

3. Federal aid to dependent children through grants to States for the support of existing mothers' pension systems and for services for the protection and care of homeless, neglected, dependent, and crippled children.

4. Additional Federal aid to State and local public-health agencies and the strengthening of the Federal Public Health Service. I am not at this time recommending the adoption of so-called "health insurance," although groups representing the medical profession are cooperating with the Federal Government in the further study of the subject and definite progress is being made.

With respect to unemployment compensation, I have concluded that the most practical proposal is the levy of a uniform Federal payroll tax, 90 percent of which should be allowed as an offset to employers contributing under a compulsory State unemployment compensation act. The purpose of this is to afford a requirement of a reasonably uniform character for all States co-operating with the Federal Government and to promote and encourage the passage of unemployment compensation laws in the States. The 10 percent not thus offset should be used to cover the costs of Federal and State administration of this broad system. Thus, States will largely administer unemployment compensation, assisted and guided by the Federal Government. An unemployment compensation system should be constructed in such a way as to afford every practicable aid and incentive toward the larger purpose of employment stabilization. This can be helped by the intelligent planning of both public and private employment. It also can be helped by correlating the system with public employment so that a person who has exhausted his benefits may be eligible for some form of public work as is recommended in this report. Moreover, in order to encourage the stabilization of private employment, Federal legislation should not foreclose the States from establishing means for inducing industries to afford an even greater stabilization of employment.

In the important field of security for our old people, it seems necessary to adopt three principles: First, noncontributory old-age pensions for those who are now too old to build up their own insurance. It is, of course, clear that for perhaps 30 years to come funds will have to be provided by the States and the Federal Government to meet these pensions. Second, compulsory contributory annuities which in time will establish a self-supporting system for those now young and for future generations. Third, voluntary contributory annuities by which individual initiative can increase the annual amounts received in old age. It is proposed that the Federal Government assume one-half of the cost of the old-age pension plan, which ought ultimately to be supplanted by self-supporting annuity plans.

The amount necessary at this time for the initiation of unemployment compensation, old-age security, children's aid, and the promotion of public health, as outlined in the report of the Committee on Economic Security, is approximately $100,000,000.

The establishment of sound means toward a greater future economic security of the American people is dictated by a prudent consideration of the hazards involved in our national life. No one can guarantee this country against the dangers of future depressions but we can reduce these dangers. We can eliminate many of the factors that cause economic depressions, and we can provide the means of mitigating their results. This plan for economic security is at once a measure of prevention and a method of alleviation.

We pay now for the dreadful consequence of economic insecurity—and dearly. This plan presents a more equitable and infinitely less expensive means of meeting these costs. We cannot afford to neglect the plain duty before us. I strongly recommend action to attain the objectives sought in this report.

13] Hoover Condemns All National Economic Planning

> Many Americans saw little difference between the policies proposed by Richberg, Keynes, or Roosevelt himself. Moreover they did not believe that planning of any type would necessarily bring economic security to the individual citizen. Few men expressed these views more clearly than former President Hoover in an address he made in New York City on November 16, 1935, entitled "The Consequences of 'Economic Planning' and Some Remedies for It." *

. . . .

I RECENTLY made an address upon the New Deal Spending, Debts, and their Consequences. I purpose on this occasion to discuss what the New Deal calls "National Planning," the expenditures it imposes on the people, its consequences, and some remedies that it requires. This old and respected phrase "National Planning" has been disclosed to have powerful meanings. You might think that meant blueprints. But this sort of "National Planning" includes political management of money, credit, farming, industry, morals, and the more abundant life. Two years ago the phrase more frequently used was "Planned Economy." But as that has become so obviously "Planned Extravagance," it has been less used in these last few months. Even "National Planning" is threatened with ejection by a still newer glittering phrase, the "Third Economy." I trust it is not so expensive as the others.

Let me say at once that I am not here criticizing all the measures taken in

* HOOVER CONDEMNS ALL NATIONAL ECONOMIC PLANNING: "The Consequences of 'Economic Planning' and Some Remedies for It." From Herbert Hoover, *Addresses upon the American Road, 1933-1938* (New York, 1938), pp. 75-86. Used by permission of Charles Scribner's Sons. Copyright 1938 by Edgar Rickard.

Washington. Whatever is good should be continued. Republics must go forward, not backward, but if they would go forward they must promptly discard the bad. I am here discussing those measures which threaten to impoverish the nation.

There are two different groups of opponents of the New Deal sort of "National Planning" or "Planned Economy." One group holds that it is a deliberate plan for centralizing authority to a point where we the people can be made to do what starry-eyed young men in Washington think is good for us—whether it is good for us or not. This group believes "Planned Economy" is the American name for the European diseases which have infected us for the past three years. They feel these catchwords cloak that incarnate passion for power, the insidious end of which is the destruction of liberty and the rise of the regimented state.

The other group of opponents hold that the new "National Planning" is an attempt of a collegiate oligarchy to sanctify by a phrase a muddle of unco-ordinated reckless adventures in government—flavored with unctuous claims to monopoly in devotion to their fellow men. These opponents believe "National Planning" has neither philosophy nor consistency of action.

My own conclusion is that the new "National Planning" contains any or all these elements, depending upon which New Dealer is doing the Planning for the day.

Any of these views could be confirmed by the writings of a dozen charter members of the New Deal who have now turned against the order. They could be substantiated by the writings of many who remain in it.

I do not intend on this occasion to elaborate the philosophy of "Planned Economy." It is neither conservative, liberal, nor common sense. Nor do I propose on this occasion to discuss its Constitutional aspects. There are nests of Constitutional termites at work.

I shall simply inquire whether we ought to want this sort of "Economic Planning" and its invisible costs. It has unfolded itself through some scores of new bureaus of the Federal Government. I will not take your time to enumerate all the alphabetical agencies. I may say, however, there are only four letters of the alphabet not now in use by the Administration in Washington. When we establish the Quick Loans Corporation for Xylophones, Yachts, and Zithers, the alphabet of our fathers will be exhausted. But of course the New Russian alphabet has thirty-four letters.

We have now had three years in which to appraise the work of these agencies. They are no longer in the aurora borealis stage, with all its excitement and false promises of light. We emerge from illusion into the daylight of practical experience.

There is one consistency in all this new "National Planning," or "Planned Economy," or "Third Economy." Every branch of these plans has the habit of carefree scattering of public money. They are haunted by no old ghost of a balanced budget. But "National Planning" thinks in phrases and slogans rather than the exactitude of the cash register. We now know that in addition to increased taxes after four years of it the bill of increased taxpayers' liabilities will be about $14,000,000,000. If they have a cash register it certainly has an astronomical keyboard.

The obvious hope of this new "National Plan" is that by creating bank credit they can avoid adding more burdens on the poor and the economic middle class—until after the election.

These are, however, only the visible expenditures imposed on the people. The taxes of today and their sure increase in the future if these policies are not stopped are but a small part of even the money cost of "National Planning." And let no one be deluded. It is the farmer, the worker, as well as the business man, who pay the invisible costs, just as they pay the bulk of the tax assessments.

I may give you a few examples.

Judged by works and not by words, another consistency in this sort of "Economic Planning" is to limit competition and restrict production—the essence of monopoly. They have given us planned scarcity—upon which civilization always degenerates—in the place of economic plenty, upon which America has grown great. It is the more abundant life—without bacon.

One of the wheel-horses of the "National Planning"—that is the NRA—was thought to have been killed by the Supreme Court. That decision has not yet been claimed as part of the new "National Planning," although every day men are getting jobs because of it. But we are now promised a resurrection of this dead. The price of it was and will be in every household budget.

The new "National Planning" is building vast projects—perhaps useful to our grandchildren. We have to pay the cost of interest and maintenance until they come of age. This is also the New Deal door by which the government rushes into business in competition with its own citizens. The citizen loses because he cannot compete with government bookkeeping and the pipe line into the treasury. Few of these projects were even mentioned until after blank checks were drawn by Congress. This method of planning avoids exhaustion from Congressional debate—and takes the limit off spending.

The new "National Planning" of relief shifted its administration from local and state authorities to a political bureaucracy centralized at Washington. That has resulted not only in stupendous waste but in the creation of a great group of permanent dependents. It has added nothing to the security and care of those deserving in distress except—expense. And we are destroying the self respect and the responsibility of self government by turning the treasury into a national grab bag. Our national ideals get little of a lift from the general attitude, "If we don't get ours some one else will."

The new "National Planning" of taxes, currency, credit, and business has raised and will continue to raise the cost of living to the farm housewife, the worker's housewife, and all other housewives. It is a deduction from economic and social security of the poor—it is not a more abundant life. It erodes the purchasing power of wages. It gives birth to strikes and inflames class conflict. During the depression years of the last Administration the loss of man days from strikes and lockouts averaged about 5,000,000 per year. During this Administration it has averaged a loss of about 18,000,000 man days per year. These gigantic losses appear in the worker's budget, not in the treasury.

The new "Economic Planning" has included repudiation of government covenants, which raises somber questions of government morals and honor. In any event it devalued the dollar by 41 per cent. It gave us the gift of "Managed Currency." As potent devices for destroying confidence these have merit. Through politically managed credit it has brought us to the threshold of devastating inflation. The stock market is already peeking into that Bluebeard's cave. . . .

There are morals in that story. But there is something of far more present importance in that story than postmortem moralizing. Despite that bitter experience the new National Planners, to finance their huge spending and other purposes, have desperately resorted to the same inflation of bank credits. They, however, apparently do not believe in homeopathic doses. The dose of that same poison now injected into our national bloodstream by the New Deal is already three or four times as great as that of 1927.

They say also it can be controlled. But will the politically controlled Reserve system prove any more successful? Stated in its mildest form, this is gambling with the fate of a nation. Should these controls fail, this democracy will not survive the shock.

And "National Planning" was supposed to shake us free from vicious speculation and money changers. Of this you can be sure. Instability of currencies and inflation of credit are the green pastures upon which the speculator grows fat. He is the sole beneficiary from instability. The costs of that instability do not appear in the government budget, yet they appear in every honest business. They add to the price of every commodity.

And here the "National Planning" collides with itself. Of what value are old age pensions, or unemployment insurance, savings for old age, or any other beneficent effort under the scourge of devaluation and inflation?

I will not tire you with further examples of these invisible costs which far exceed even the torrent of government spending. There are scores more.

We can express government expenses in figures. But no mortal man can compute the costs, the burdens, and dangers imposed upon 120,000,000 people by these actions. Its cost in national impoverishment far exceeds even taxes. Its losses will be larger than the national debt.

It is a time for plain speaking and blunt statement of some fundamental principles upon these monetary and fiscal questions. And let me speak to you in old-fashioned language. When I was a boy in Iowa I learned some very simple truths about finance. I learned that money does not grow on trees; it must be earned. I learned that the first rule of a successful career is to keep expenditures within the means of paying them. I learned that the keeping of financial promises is the first obligation of an honorable man. And I learned that the man who borrows without intent to repay is headed for bankruptcy or disgrace or crime. These may be platitudes, but they are still truths.

As I have increased in years and in opportunity to study the affairs of governments, I have made a very simple but vital observation. That is that a government should have in financial matters the same standards that an honorable man has. A government must realize that money must be earned before it is spent, that a nation's word in finance must be sacredly kept, that a nation is immoral if it repudiates its obligations or inflates its mediums of exchange or borrows without regard to posterity; and, finally, that a nation which violates these simple principles will, like a man, end in dishonor and disaster. A government cannot expect financial honor in its people unless it maintains honor itself. A large part of the world's misery in all ages has come from the acts of government that ignored these principles and entered upon policies of reckless spending and debasement and repudiation.

Our country shows hopeful signs of recovery despite great hindrances. That convalescence should be speeded and made secure. We should no longer tolerate financial policies that prolong unemployment, that create fear and distrust and uncertainty, that slowly but surely undermine the industrial structure on which the living of the whole nation depends. We should no longer tolerate a money system that is not a money system, but a hodge-podge of promiscuous ingredients that not even the Administration will attempt to name, define, or defend. We should no longer tolerate gambling in the future of a nation with the dice of inflation. We should no longer tolerate a financial policy that does not balance the budget.

The American citizen wants to know whether his savings are to be confiscated. The plain man wants to know whether his little life insurance policy is going to be worth anything at his death. The housewife wants to know whether her husband's wages are going to buy food for his family.

There is a way to settle all these questions. That way is through abandonment of present financial and fiscal policies and return to sound policies. Do you wish a constructive fiscal program?

The waste of taxpayers' money on unnecessary public works should end.

The administration of relief should be turned over to local authorities. Federal expenditures for relief should be confined to cash allowances to these authorities to the extent that they are unable to provide their own funds.

The spending for visionary and un-American experiments should be stopped.

This horde of political bureaucracy should be rooted out.

The provision of the Constitution requiring that expenditures shall only be in accordance with appropriations actually made by law should be obeyed. And they should be made for specific purposes.

The budget should be balanced, not by more taxes, but by reduction of follies.

The futile purchases of foreign silver should be stopped.

The gold standard should be re-established, even on the new basis.

The act authorizing the President to inflate the currency should be repealed.

The administration should give and keep a pledge to the country that there will be no further juggling of the currency and no further experiments with credit inflation.

Confidence in the validity of promises of the government should be restored.

The nation seeks for solution of its many difficulties. It is groping for security from economic storms and from individual poverty. But economic security, social security, or any other security cannot be found without first restoring these primary policies of government.

These matters are no abstractions. They are not theoretical questions of academic debate. They are the invisible forces which surround every American fireside. They determine the happiness of every American home. In their rightful direction lies the safety of these homes and the fruition of their hopes. They determine the welfare of our children and the progress of our nation.

TABLE

Economic Statistics, 1929–1958 *

	GNP (billions in unadjusted dollars)	GNP (billions in 1958 prices)	National Income (billions)	Gross National Debt (billions)	Interest Paid on Debt †		Corporate Profits (billions)		Total Unemployed (thousands)	Unemployment as Per cent of Civilian Labor Force	
					total	per cent of federal expenditures	before taxes	after taxes			
1929	104.4	201.0	87.8	16.3	.7	20.6	9.6	8.3	1,550	3.2	1929
1930	91.1	182.0	75.7	16.0	.7	19.2	3.3	2.5	4,340	8.7	1930
1931	76.3	168.3	59.7	17.8	.6	17.1	-.8	-1.3	8,020	15.9	1931
1932	58.5	143.1	42.5	20.8	.6	12.9	-3.0	-3.4	12,060	23.6	1932
1933	56.0	139.5	40.2	24.0	.7	14.9	.2	-.4	12,830	24.9	1933
1934	65.0	152.9	49.0	31.5	.8	11.3	1.7	1.0	11,340	21.7	1934
1935	72.5	168.3	57.1	35.1	.8	12.6	3.1	2.2	10,610	20.1	1935
1936	82.7	191.7	64.9	39.1	.7	8.8	5.7	4.3	9,030	16.9	1936
1937	90.8	202.5	73.6	41.9	.9	11.2	6.2	4.7	7,700	14.3	1937
1938	85.2	192.8	67.6	44.4	.9	13.6	3.3	2.3	10,390	19.0	1938
1939	91.1	208.8	72.8	47.6	.9	10.6	6.4	5.0	9,480	17.2	1939
1940	100.6	227.0	81.6	50.9	1.0	11.5	9.3	6.5	8,120	14.6	1940
1941	125.8	264.1	104.7	64.3	1.1	8.4	17.0	9.4	5,560	9.9	1941
1942	159.1	299.4	137.7	112.5	1.2	3.7	20.9	9.5	2,660	4.7	1942
1943	192.5	335.7	170.3	170.1	1.8	2.3	24.6	10.5	1,070	1.9	1943
1944	211.4	360.0	182.6	232.1	2.6	2.7	23.3	10.4	670	1.2	1944
1945	213.6	354.1	181.2	278.7	3.6	3.7	19.0	8.3	1,040	1.9	1945
1946	210.7	312.2	180.9	259.5	4.7	7.8	22.6	13.4	2,270	3.9	1946
1947	234.3	311.8	198.2	257.0	5.0	12.7	29.5	18.2	2,142	3.6	1947
1948	259.4	323.7	223.5	252.9	5.2	15.8	32.8	20.3	2,064	3.4	1948
1949	258.1	324.0	217.7	257.2	5.3	13.5	26.2	15.8	3,395	5.5	1949
1950	284.6	351.6	241.9	256.7	5.8	14.5	40.0	22.1	3,142	5.0	1950
1951	329.0	379.6	279.3	259.5	5.6	12.7	41.2	18.7	1,879	3.0	1951
1952	347.0	393.3	292.4	267.4	5.9	9.0	35.9	16.1	1,673	2.7	1952
1953	365.4	411.1	305.6	275.2	6.5	8.8	37.0	16.7	1,602	2.5	1953
1954	363.1	403.2	301.8	278.8	6.4	9.4	33.5	16.0	3,230	5.0	1954
1955	397.5	435.4	330.2	280.8	6.4	9.9	42.5	21.0	2,654	4.0	1955
1956	419.2	446.1	349.4	276.7	6.8	10.2	43.0	21.0	2,551	3.8	1956
1957	440.3	452.1	364.0	275.0	7.2	10.3	41.2	20.2	2,936	4.3	1957
1958	436.7	436.7	359.6	283.0	7.8 ‡	—	—	—	5,198 (Mar.)	7.7 (Mar.)	1958

* All data, unless otherwise indicated, are from *The Economic Report of the President, 1959* (Washington, 1959).
† Data for 1929–45 from *Historical Statistics of the United States 1789–1945* (Washington, 1949); data for 1946–58 from *Statistical Abstract of the United States, 1958* (Washington, 1958).
‡ Estimated.

CONCLUSION

HOOVER's arguments had a genuine appeal, for they invoked many inherited beliefs and values. Yet the realities of a modern, industrialized urban economy, and the polity it required, militated against any return to the older definition of the role of government as an impartial "referee" in the economy. As time passed, fewer and fewer people seriously suggested that the federal government be relieved of its responsibilities to provide minimum economic security to the individual through welfare benefits and through the assurance of some type of employment.

In the years after 1935, political arguments continued over how the federal government should best carry out these responsibilities. Social security was extended, with relatively little debate, to persons not included in the 1935 act. In the more extended controversy over the means of assuring employment, the Keynesian proposals won out. The recession of 1938 helped convince the President of the value of a spending program. In 1936, believing economic recovery was assured, Roosevelt cut government spending. Quickly, national income and production dropped, and when he renewed government expenditures they rose again (see Table). Spending, however, failed to bring full employment. The reason, Keynes told Roosevelt, was that not enough funds had been injected into the economy. The Second World War emphatically demonstrated the validity of these views. The vast wartime expenditures, far exceeding anything Keynes proposed, quickly brought full employment and set the economy off on a decade of growth and prosperity unparalleled in American history.

In 1945, however, the nation's leaders had their eyes more on the possibility of a postwar recession than on the vast, pent-up demand created by wartime spending. As a result, Congress passed the Employment Act of 1946, which declared "that it is the continuing policy and responsibility of the Federal Government . . . to promote maximum employment, production, and purchasing power." This responsibility was reaffirmed by Dwight D. Eisenhower, the first Republican President since Herbert Hoover, in the initial report of his economic advisers to Congress in 1953. During the Eisenhower administration, Republicans effectively applied Keynesian techniques to maintaining economic stability and also extended the scope of social security. In the 1950's, the welfare state had as few responsible opponents as it had proponents in the 1920's. The crisis of the depression had made the difference.

STUDY QUESTIONS

1] What was the nature of Roosevelt's commitment to economic planning by the federal government? How did he, Hoover, Richberg, Lippmann, and Keynes differ regard-

ing the way market competition was expected to help
maintain the nation's economic health?

2] On what basic American values did Roosevelt, Hoover,
Richberg, Lippmann, and Davis agree? How have such
values shaped the role of the federal government in maintaining economic security and stability?

3] Of the methods of economic control proposed by Richberg, Hoover, and Keynes, why were those of the last
accepted by later Democratic and Republican administrations? Since Congress has made no serious move since the
depression to relieve the federal government of its responsibilities for maintaining economic stability and security, why are arguments about the welfare state similar
to those made by Herbert Hoover still heard today?

4] How did the depression of the 1930's differ from previous
depressions in American history, and why did it call forth
a different response from the federal government?

RECOMMENDED READINGS

PRIMARY SOURCES

HOOVER, HERBERT. *Addresses upon the American Road, 1928–1932* (New York,
1933).
————. *Addresses upon the American Road, 1933–1938* (New York, 1938).
————. *The Challenge to Liberty* (New York, 1934).
————. *The Memoirs of Herbert Hoover: The Great Depression, 1929–1941*
(New York, 1952).
ICKES, HAROLD L. *The Autobiography of a Curmudgeon* (New York, 1943).
————. *Back to Work: The Story of the PWA* (New York, 1935).
————. *The Secret Diary of Harold L. Ickes,* 3 vols. (New York, 1953–54).
JOHNSON, HUGH S. *The Blue Eagle from Egg to Earth* (New York, 1935).
LIPPMANN, WALTER. *Interpretations, 1933–1935* (New York, 1936).
————. *The Method of Freedom* (New York, 1934).
————. *The New Imperative* (New York, 1935).
MOLEY, RAYMOND. *After Seven Years* (New York, 1939).
RAUCH, BASIL, ed. *Franklin D. Roosevelt: Selected Speeches, Messages, Press Con-
ferences, and Letters* (New York, 1957).
ROSENMAN, SAMUEL I., ed. *The Public Papers and Addresses of Franklin D.
Roosevelt,* 9 vols. (New York, 1938–41).
SHANNON, DAVID A. *The Great Depression* (Englewood Cliffs, N.J., 1959).

SECONDARY SOURCES

AGEE, JAMES. *Let Us Now Praise Famous Men,* with photographs by Walker
Evans (Boston, 1941, 1960).
BLUM, JOHN M. *From the Diaries of Henry Morgenthau* (Boston, 1959).
BURNS, JAMES MACGREGOR. *The Lion and the Fox* (New York, 1956).

DOUGLAS, PAUL H. *Social Security in the United States* (New York, 1936).

EPSTEIN, ABRAHAM. *Insecurity, A Challenge to America* (New York, 1938).

FREIDEL, FRANK. *Franklin D. Roosevelt*, 3 vols. (Boston, 1952, 1954, 1956).

MACMAHON, ARTHUR W., ET AL. *The Administration of Federal Work Relief* (Washington, 1941).

MITCHELL, BROADUS. *Depression Decade: From New-Era Through New Deal, 1929–1941* (New York, 1947).

PERKINS, DEXTER. *The New Age of Franklin Roosevelt, 1932–1945* (Chicago, 1957).

PERKINS, FRANCES. *The Roosevelt I Knew* (New York, 1946).

RAUCH, BASIL. *The History of the New Deal: 1932–1938* (New York, 1944).

SCHLESINGER, ARTHUR M., JR. *The Age of Roosevelt*, 3 vols. (Boston, 1957, 1959, 1960).

SHERWOOD, ROBERT E. *Roosevelt and Hopkins* (New York, 1948).

TUGWELL, REXFORD G. *The Democratic Roosevelt* (New York, 1957).

WECTER, DIXON. *The Age of the Great Depression, 1929–1941* (New York, 1948).

World War II: Roosevelt and Intervention, 1940–1941

JAMES MacGREGOR BURNS
JANET THOMPSON BURNS

CONTENTS

CHRONOLOGY

1939

SEPTEMBER 1 German troops invade Poland.
SEPTEMBER 3 Great Britain and France declare war on Germany.
NOVEMBER 4 Repeal of Arms Embargo and authorization of "cash and carry."

1940

APRIL 9 Germany attacks Denmark and Norway.
MAY 10 Germany begins massive attack through Belgium, Holland, and Luxembourg toward France.
JUNE 22 France capitulates to Germany.
SEPTEMBER 3 Roosevelt announces destroyer deal.
SEPTEMBER 16 Selective Service Act passed.
SEPTEMBER 27 Tripartite Pact between Germany, Italy, and Japan.
OCTOBER 28 Italy invades Greece.
NOVEMBER 5 Roosevelt elected to third term.

1941

MARCH 11 Lend-Lease Bill becomes law.
MAY 21 American merchantman *Robin Moor* sunk in South Atlantic.
JUNE 22 German troops invade Russia.
AUGUST 14 Announcement of Churchill–Roosevelt meeting and Atlantic Charter.
SEPTEMBER 4 Attack on the U.S.S. *Greer*.
OCTOBER 16 Resignation of "moderate" Konoye Cabinet in Japan.
NOVEMBER 17 Repeal of restrictive provisions of Neutrality Act.
NOVEMBER 26 United States–Japanese negotiations break down.
DECEMBER 7 Japan attacks Pearl Harbor.
DECEMBER 8 Congress declares state of war exists with Japan.
DECEMBER 11 Germany declares itself as being in state of war with the United States.

INTRODUCTION

A T TEN minutes before three on the morning of September 1, 1939, a ringing telephone next to his bed awakened President Franklin D. Roosevelt. It was the American ambassador to France, calling from Paris:

"Who is it?"
"This is Bill Bullitt, Mr. President."
"Yes, Bill."
"Tony Biddle has just got through from Warsaw, Mr. President. Several German divisions are deep in Polish territory, and fighting is heavy. Tony said there were reports of bombers all over the city. Then he was cut off . . ."
"Well, Bill, it's come at last. God help us all."

World War II had come at last. The nation was more shocked than surprised. For several years war clouds had been thickening over Europe and the Far East as Italy, Germany, and Japan had forged their arms and overcome weaker nations in their paths. But now the question for Americans was sharper than ever—What would be the role of the United States? Should it stay completely clear of the conflict? Should it intervene with all its strength on the side of those nations opposing aggression? Or should it find some middle ground, such as "all aid to the Allies short of war." Could it do any of these things?

On certain of such questions American public opinion was quite definite, on others confused. The overwhelming majority of Americans wanted to keep out of the war in Europe. Still affected by the disillusionment following World War I, by a host of antiwar novels and tracts, by widespread charges that we had been tricked into the First World War through the machinations of evil munitions makers and greedy bankers, the American people had vowed that this time "Uncle Sam must stay at home." But on matters closely related to these, Americans were unsure or divided. For one thing, they were pessimistic about the chances of the United States staying out of the war. Secondly, almost half of them, according to a poll taken during the first weeks of hostilities, believed that America should send troops to help Britain and France if these nations were in danger of being defeated. Two students of this period have summed it up: "We were not really blind to the grave implications for ourselves of the German invasion of Poland; nevertheless, we steadfastly shrank from facing the issues."

The neutralist attitudes of most Americans were strongly represented in Congress. Earlier in the decade the national legislature had passed measures to prevent the United States from doing those things that Americans widely believed had caused our entrance into the first war: loans to warring states and trafficking in arms were forbidden; the President was first allowed and later required to keep Americans off belligerent ships; and under the "cash-and-carry" provision warring nations could buy only such commodities as the

President authorized, and only by "paying on the barrelhead" and carrying off the goods in their own vessels. Some Americans argued that this neutrality actually was not a true neutrality, because it played into the hands of Hitler and others who knew they could commit acts of aggression without American opposition. But Congress as a whole was strongly committed to its neutrality legislation at the time war broke out. Indeed, a few weeks before, Congress had refused Roosevelt's request to repeal the provision requiring an arms embargo in the event of war—a provision that would be clearly to Hitler's advantage if war came.

And what about the President? His views were mixed. He had already come to feel that the neutrality measures, which he had signed without great enthusiasm, were positive disadvantages to him in discouraging aggression. His basic sympathies lay strongly with the Allies, on whose behalf, as well as his own country's, he had labored twenty years earlier, during World War I, as Woodrow Wilson's Assistant Secretary of the Navy. He loathed Hitler and all his works. On the other hand, Roosevelt was highly sensitive to the strong neutralist and isolationist feelings in Congress and among the people. Because of these political obstacles to purposeful action, because of the unpredictability of the military and diplomatic situation (for example, the sudden making of a nonaggression pact by Hitler and Stalin on the eve of war's outbreak), and because of his own bent for practical, opportunistic tactics, the President had no long-range plan or strategy but was operating from day to day and from crisis to crisis.

On September 3, a few hours after Britain and France declared war on Germany, the President said to the people in a "fireside chat" that when peace has been broken anywhere, the peace of all countries everywhere is in danger. The nation would remain a neutral nation, he said, but he could not ask that every American remain neutral in thought as well. Soon afterward the President convened Congress in special session to repeal the embargo provisions. The legislators finally did so, despite passionate oratory on Capitol Hill against the "war hounds of Europe" who would drag us into war. But Congress still insisted on "cash and carry" and the other neutrality provisions.

Once Poland was conquered in a blitzkrieg, hostilities quieted down during late fall and winter of 1939–40, to a point where some American isolationists were calling it scornfully a "phony war." The lull was not to last long. In April Hitler suddenly invaded Denmark and Norway. In May he smashed through Holland and Belgium into France. Winston Churchill, elevated to Prime Minister during the crisis, informed Roosevelt that the Low Countries and France were doomed and Britain would soon be attacked. Amid this "hurricane of events," as he called it, Roosevelt acted boldly. He asked Congress for almost a billion dollars for greater defense, including at least fifty thousand planes a year. This request was cheered by Congress; but the burning question was help for the Allies. The French—until Hitler's forces inundated them —and Churchill pleaded for direct and immediate aid. By August hundreds of Stukas and Messerschmidts were roaring down on British convoys, radar stations, and airfields. German barges were moving down the coasts of Europe to the ports of northern France. A Nazi invasion of Britain seemed imminent; Churchill desperately needed military aid, especially destroyers.

Roosevelt wanted to give Britain "all aid short of war." What did the electorate want? The public had tended to be pessimistic and even panicky after the Nazi march to the Channel; but then it had steadied down. Most Americans wanted to help Britain—but how much was not clear. Most Americans clearly still wanted to stay out of the war, even if Britain was in great danger. The isolationist bloc in Congress seemed unmoved by Allied defeats. The press was divided, as usual; newspapers like the New York *Times* and the New York *Herald Tribune* were demanding that Roosevelt take more forthright action; while the Chicago *Tribune* and other isolationist organs interpreted any Presidential move to aid Britain as a step designed to plunge us directly into war.

But beyond all this, by late summer, 1940, Roosevelt was facing a highly uncertain political situation at home. He himself had been renominated in July, despite substantial opposition in his party to a third term, and on a Democratic party platform promise stating: "We will not participate in foreign wars, and we will not send out Army, naval or air forces to fight in foreign lands outside of the Americas, except in case of attack." In a dramatic contest, Wendell Willkie had won the nomination of the Republican party, which in its platform had proclaimed simply: "The Republican party is firmly opposed to involving this nation in foreign war." Although basically an "internationalist" Republican, Willkie was pointing up this promise by pledging again and again that if elected President he would ". . . never send an American boy to fight in any European war," and implying that his rival's promise of no involvement could not be trusted.

Finally, there were some powerful pressure groups at work. William Allen White, famous editor of the Emporia, Kansas, *Gazette* and long a progressive Republican, had organized the Committee to Defend America by Aiding the Allies. Composed of highly influential editors, teachers, ministers, and the like, and organized into active groups in many communities, the Committee urged the country to become the nonbelligerent ally of Britain. A host of isolationist groups sprang up to publicize a contrary view. Both sides—but especially the latter—were represented eloquently in Congress.

In this highly charged political atmosphere President Roosevelt faced the issue of quick and decisive aid to Britain. Churchill desperately pleaded for destroyers to counter the looming Nazi invasion. "Mr. President," he said, ". . . in the long history of the world this is a thing to do *now*." What could Roosevelt do? Congress would support sending destroyers to Britain only if the Navy certified that they were useless for national defense, and the Navy, of course, wanted to keep its forces as intact as possible. On the other hand, key members of his Cabinet were pressing for action; among them were the two Republican members whom Roosevelt had appointed on the eve of the Republican convention, Henry L. Stimson and Frank Knox. And always there was the crucial question of the November election only a few weeks ahead. Roosevelt asked William Allen White to talk with his fellow Republican, Wendell Willkie, and to see whether the Republican nominee would support the sending of destroyers. White found Willkie to be personally in favor of *legislation* to send destroyers but unwilling to take a public stand, for he did not dare provoke the Congressional isolationists in his own party. Clearly,

Congress would either oppose sending destroyers or approve it only after a long debate—when it might be too late.

Only one course was possible—simple executive action. Some internationalist-minded lawyers, including Dean Acheson, later Secretary of State under Harry Truman, were contending that the President could act under existing legislation. Knox had also suggested another idea that might help break the log jam—why not trade the destroyers for military bases on British possessions in the Americas? Giving up hope that he could get action from Congress, Roosevelt now seized eagerly on the idea. It would solve his political problem, he felt, because people would say (in Roosevelt's later words), "My God, the old Dutchman and Scotchman in the White House has made a good trade."

But Roosevelt knew, too, that Congress would "raise hell about this," as he said to a secretary while working on a draft of the agreement. He was right. Following the President's announcement of the deal of September 3, 1940, the St. Louis *Post-Dispatch* published an advertisement in leading newspapers: "Mr. Roosevelt today committed an act of war. He also became America's first dictator. . . . Of all sucker real estate deals in history, this is the worst. . . ." A howl of indignation rose from Capitol Hill. Willkie endorsed the trade but denounced the bypassing of Congress, which he was soon calling "the most dictatorial and arbitrary act of any President in the history of the United States."

As the Presidential campaign roared toward a finish, Willkie intensified his efforts to picture Roosevelt as an irresponsible warmonger. "If his promise to keep our boys out of foreign wars is no better than his promise to balance the budget," he said, "they're already almost on the transports." The President seemed all the more vulnerable to attack because he had sponsored passage of the Selective Service Act, which became law in mid-September, and which meant that the President would preside conspicuously at draft ceremonies just before the election.

Having taken his daring plunge on the destroyer deal, and facing Willkie's accusations of warmongering, Roosevelt played a cautious game in the last weeks of the campaign. He found it necessary to give "this most solemn assurance: There is no secret treaty, no secret obligation, no secret commitment, no secret understanding in any shape or form, direct or indirect, with any other Government, or any other nation in any part of the world, to involve this nation in any way or for any other purpose." He charged Republican leaders with "playing politics with national defense"—with opposing defense measures in the past but now accusing the administration of unpreparedness. In Boston, at the height of the campaign, he declared: "I have said this before, but I shall say it again and again and again: Your boys are not going to be sent into any foreign wars." It was the flattest pledge that Roosevelt had yet made, and his advisers had urged him beforehand to add the usual qualifying phrase at the end, "except in case of attack." But this time, bending to the fury of Willkie's attack, he did not. "It's not necessary," he had said to his aides. "If we're attacked it's no longer a foreign war."

Probably the President's promises to the people helped him measurably in achieving a decisive victory over Willkie early in November. But the nature of the campaign tended to blur any value the outcome might have had in indicating what the voters wanted—except that America must be kept out of the war. To be sure, Roosevelt's promises of staying out had not been quite so definite as Willkie's; moreover, both men had favored extensive aid to Hitler's foes, so evidently the electorate approved such aid. But how much aid? What kind—both military and economic? How—in our own vessels or the enemy's? And with what risks—aid even at the danger of being drawn into a shooting war? The election settled none of these questions. They were to be settled by developments over which the American people would have little control.

As in the past, these events were initiated chiefly by Germany, Italy, and Japan. Late in September, 1940, these three powers had joined in a treaty respecting one another's "leadership" in their geographical spheres and guaranteeing to come to one another's assistance if attacked by a nation not then at war. Italy, which had come into the war following Hitler's triumphs earlier in the year, attacked Greece and drove into Egypt. The Japanese were pressing south, especially into Indochina. British shipping losses in the Atlantic were mounting ominously. And Hitler, in telling the German people in December, 1940, that the war was a struggle to the death between the democratic and totalitarian worlds, one of which must "break asunder," was proclaiming in effect that his fight was against all democracies, not merely the European ones.

In the postelection lull, meantime, administration officials were meeting all kinds of difficulties in trying, within the law, to help Britain maintain her lifeline to the United States. As 1941 approached, it was becoming clear that Britain needed massive aid far beyond the fifty destroyers sent under the "deal." Stimson and many other officials believed that the United States must squarely face up to the situation. For a time Roosevelt seemed to temporize; then, at the end of the year, he acted. In a fireside chat he stated that while there was risk in any course the nation took, the chances of getting into war were far less if the United States did all it could to support nations defending themselves against attack by the Axis: "If we acquiesce in their defeat, submit tamely to an Axis victory, [we] wait our turn to be the object of attack in another war later on." The answer? "We must be the great arsenal of democracy." Roosevelt proposed that the President be empowered to lend or lease equipment to nations whose defense he considered necessary to the security of the nation. He was trying, as he had said somewhat earlier, to get rid of the "silly, foolish, old dollar sign."

This time, however, there could be no simple Presidential action, as in the case of the destroyers; the President must have the moral, legislative, and political support of Congress in undertaking such a grave step. In January the Lend-Lease Bill—entitled "An Act Further to Promote the Defense of the United States"—was introduced into Congress. The effect was once again to split the country wide apart. Anti-interventionists greeted the measure as the most drastic step yet on the road to war. A recently formed isolationist organization, America First, aroused opposition throughout the country. Such eminent Americans as Charles Lindbergh, former ambassador to Great Britain Joseph P. Kennedy, and the renowned historian and political scientist Charles A. Beard, testified strongly against the bill. One Democratic senator branded the bill as the "New Deal's 'triple A' foreign policy—to plow under every fourth American boy." Despite sharp opposition throughout the country, however, it became evident that the bill had powerful support. Many newspapers backed it; the polls indicated that those favoring assistance to Britain even at the risk of involvement in war had risen to about seventy per cent; and Congress, after a long debate, convincingly endorsed the President's bill by a 60–31 vote in the Senate and a 317–71 vote in the House, with a substantial number of Republicans in both houses supporting the measure.

Of all the administration actions that brought the United States more closely into the world balance, the Lend-Lease Act was the most momentous. "It was more than an abandonment of neutrality," historian Thomas A. Bailey has said, "for neutrality had already been abandoned; it was an unofficial declaration of war on the Axis—or rather a belated recognition of the fact that the Axis had officially or unofficially declared war on all the democracies." It represented a historic commitment by Congress as well as the President to the proposition that America must give Britain all aid short of war. But would it be "short of war"? Roosevelt publicly maintained that it could and would be, but events were to dictate otherwise.

For Lend-Lease turned out to be a major link in the events leading to a shooting war. Those events came pell-mell during 1941. In the spring Hitler smashed southeastward, forcing Rumania, Hungary, and Bulgaria into the Axis camp, overrunning Yugoslavia, and bailing out the Italians in Greece. The United States seized scores of Axis ships in American ports, and jailed hundreds of seamen for attempted sabotage. Berlin and Rome hotly protested, but in vain. In April Roosevelt signed an agreement with the Danish "government-in-exile" under which the United States occupied Greenland for defensive purposes, without impairing Denmark's sovereignty after the war. The Nazi-controlled regime in Copenhagen denounced the action. In May the President appealed directly to the French people, urging them not to support the Vichy government. A few days later came the news that the Germans had shelled and sunk a neutral passenger ship in the South Atlantic, injuring some of the hundred American passengers. Shortly thereafter Nazi glider-borne troops captured the vital island of Crete.

Roosevelt was responding to events rather than leading public opinion. Late in May, 1941, however, he went on the air to announce the issuance of a proclamation of an unlimited national emergency. Noting that the Axis was sinking ships two times as fast as Britain and the United States combined could replace them, and that Brazil was only seven hours from Europe, he said: "We insist upon the vital importance of keeping Hitlerism away from any point of attack in the world which could be used and would be used as a base of attack against the Americas." A few days later word was flashed to Washington that the Germans had sunk an American freighter, the *Robin Moor*, in what seemed to be a deliberate attack—the first such attack that the Nazis had made. Roosevelt promptly froze all Italian and German assets in the United States. Italy and Germany froze American assets in turn. Then Washington asked Germany to close all its consulates in the United States, and Berlin made the same demand of Washington. The chain of events was tightening.

And now a momentous event was close at hand. Late in June, 1941, Hitler, despairing of the possibilities of a successful assault on the British fortress, suddenly turned on his recent ally, Russia. Americans were now divided between their general hostility to Russia and its form of government and the sudden necessity of working with Russia against a nation that was now the common foe of both. Roosevelt, although still opposing the Russian form of dictatorship equally with the German, stated that the immediate threat to American security was the Nazis. He quickly made loans available to Stalin; he unfroze Soviet credits; and, most important, he did not invoke the Neutrality Act, with the result that supplies could be transported to Soviet ports in American bottoms. Washington even brought pressure to bear on Finland to induce that country, once the idol of America because it had paid its war debt to us and later resisted Russian aggression, to withdraw from a new struggle it was waging against the Russians with Hitler's backing.

But it was with Britain that America was forging its closest ties, and in August, 1941, Roosevelt and Churchill met secretly on British and American warships off Newfoundland to concert their strategy. In proclaiming the Atlantic Charter, the two leaders stated war aims that were highly reminiscent of the Fourteen Points proclaimed by Woodrow Wilson twenty-three years before. "Their countries seek no aggrandizement," the two leaders stated. ". . . They respect the right of all people to choose the form of government under which they will live. . . . They will endeavor . . . to further the enjoyment of all states, great or small, victor or vanquished, of access . . . to the trade and to the raw materials of the world. . . . They desire to bring about the fullest collaboration between all Nations" for social security and economic welfare.

Anti-interventionists greeted with indignation Roosevelt's role in the Atlantic Conference. What business did he have discussing such matters with the head of a state already at war? demanded the Chicago *Tribune*. Yet, the isolationist opposition to intervention seemed to be less effective than earlier. By and large, Roosevelt was allowing events to influence the people, and the "propaganda of the deed" was proving more significant than the "propaganda of the word." As usual, public opinion tended to be mixed; action by the President—interpreted for the people as only he could do it—seemed to shift public opinion in his favor. But he still had to reckon with opposition in Congress, and in mid-August the House of Representatives threw a scare into the administration when it extended selective service by only one vote.

Events continued to dominate Roosevelt's course. Late in the summer the American destroyer *Greer*, while en route to Iceland, learned from the British of a German submarine, and trailed it for several hours, meanwhile notifying the British of its position; the submarine fired two torpedoes at the destroyer, missing it; the destroyer then depth-bombed the submarine, with unknown results. The United States and Germany were in active combat. The incident had been inevitable, for some time earlier in the summer the President had decided to convoy lend-lease goods as far as Iceland. Following the *Greer* incident Roosevelt went farther, stating that from then on American patrols would defend the freedom of the seas by striking first at all Axis raiders operating within American defense areas. A few weeks later he asked Congress to repeal the "crippling provisions" of the Neutrality Act of 1939 so that the nation could uphold the freedom of the seas.

While matters in the Atlantic had reached the stage of a shooting war, crisis was also brewing in the Far East. Tokyo renewed its diplomatic offensive in Indochina. When the helpless French government yielded, Roosevelt ordered the freezing of all Japanese assets in the United States, and Tokyo responded with a similar order against American assets. This action brought to a climax a year of deepening hostility between the two nations, beginning with diplomatic protests against Japanese aggression, restrictions on (in effect) the export of scrap metal, oil, and gasoline to Japan and ending with loans to China. Furthermore, all these actions by the United States had stemmed, in turn, from years of strong American opposition to Japanese aggression against China and other Asiatic nations, which was symbolized by Secretary of State Henry Stimson's nonrecognition of the Japanese conquest of Manchuria ten years earlier.

In October, 1941, even the Konoye Cabinet seemed too "soft" for Japanese militarists; it was replaced by a new government headed by the fire-breathing general Hideki Tojo. The Far Eastern deadlock was now tighter than ever; Tokyo was willing to compromise with Washington only if its long-planned expansion in the Far East was accepted, while Roosevelt wanted agreement with Japan in the Far East only if the integrity of China could be protected.

Tokyo now undertook a double game. On the one hand, it dispatched a special envoy to assist its ambassador in Washington in presenting Japan's "last proposals." On the other hand, the militarists planned that as soon as these negotiations broke down—as they must unless Washington retreated from its stand—Tokyo would decide for war. Fruitless negotiations followed; late in November Tokyo offered to move Japanese troops from southern to northern Indochina if Washington ended its economic offensive against Japan, and once peace was restored in East Asia Tokyo would undertake not to make any armed advances into southeastern Asia and the South Pacific (but this pledge did not extend to China). A few days later Washington made its reply; in exchange for economic concessions from the United States, Japan must withdraw her armed forces from Indochina and China and join a multilateral nonaggression pact to guarantee East Asian nations against aggression. Each side privately rejected the other's demands; an irresistible force faced an immovable object.

Crises were piling up now on the far shores of both the Atlantic and Pacific. In mid-October a German submarine badly damaged the U.S. destroyer *Kearny*, with the loss of eleven sailors; two weeks later another destroyer, the *Reuben James*, was torpedoed with much heavier loss of life. These developments speeded up Congressional action to amend the Neutrality Act of 1939 so that the President could arm American ships, with the Congress abandoning "storm-cellar neutrality" in mid-November. By the end of the month intelligence reports were indicating that the Japanese planned to attack, though it was not known where. Hearing that Tokyo was massing troops in Indochina for an invasion of Thailand, Roosevelt sent a message to Emperor Hirohito appealing for peace. Negotiations were still going on in Washington with the Japanese representatives.

But these actions were now meaningless, for the Japanese carriers had received their orders to attack the American naval and army base in Honolulu, and they were already steaming southeast toward Oahu. On Sunday, December 7, Roosevelt had just finished eating lunch when the telephone rang. It was Navy Secretary Frank Knox.

"Hello, Frank."

"Mr. President, it looks as though the Japanese have attacked Pearl Harbor."

"No!"

DOCUMENTS

1] The Campaign of 1940: "No Involvement in Foreign Wars"

> The Presidential campaign of 1940 was dominated by the holocaust of events in Europe. The two major parties met in national convention while Americans were still trying to adjust themselves to the fall of France and the Nazi air attack on Great Britain. In nominating Wendell L. Willkie for President, the Republicans chose a man who was an internationalist compared to Republican Congressional leaders, such as House leader Joseph W. Martin, Senator Robert A. Taft of Ohio, and even Willkie's own running mate, Senator Charles McNary of Oregon. Both candidates took positions in favor of aid to beleaguered Britain, and Roosevelt's destroyer deal became a vital episode in the campaign. The campaign speeches of the two candidates show their tendency to avoid sharp differences over the specifics of foreign policy and to cater to the strong feeling among the electorate against involvement in the war. That Roosevelt was eager to follow a bipartisan foreign policy and to win over internationalist elements of the Republican party is evident from his dealings with William Allen White, the famous editor of the Emporia *Gazette* and leader of the Committee to Defend America by Aiding the Allies.*

A] THE PARTY PLATFORMS DECLARE AGAINST WAR

DEMOCRATIC

THE AMERICAN people are determined that war, raging in Europe, Asia and Africa, shall not come to America.

We will not participate in foreign wars, and we will not send our army, naval or air forces to fight in foreign lands outside of the Americas, except in case of attack. We favor and shall rigorously enforce and defend the Monroe Doctrine.

The direction and aim of our foreign policy has been, and will continue to be, the security and defense of our own land and the maintenance of its peace. . . .

Weakness and unpreparedness invite aggression. We must be so strong that no possible combination of powers would dare to attack us. We propose to provide America with an invincible air force, a navy strong enough to pro-

---

* THE CAMPAIGN OF 1940: "NO INVOLVEMENT IN FOREIGN WARS": From K. H. Porter and D. B. Johnson, eds., *National Party Platforms, 1840–1956* (Urbana, Ill., 1956), pp. 382, 390; Ms., Franklin D. Roosevelt Library, Hyde Park, N.Y., reprinted by permission of the library; New York *Times* (August 18 and October 31, 1940); Samuel I. Rosenman, ed., *The Public Papers and Addresses of Franklin D. Roosevelt: War—and Aid to Democracies* (New York, 1941), pp. 375–81; *Ibid.*, pp. 499–509, reprinted by permission of The Macmillan Co.

tect all our seacoasts and our national interests, and a fully-equipped and mech-
anized army. . . .

To make America strong, and to keep America free, every American must
give of his talents and treasure in accordance with his ability and his country's needs. We must have democracy of sacrifice as well as democracy of opportunity.

REPUBLICAN

THE REPUBLICAN PARTY is firmly opposed to involving this nation in foreign war.

We are still suffering from the ill effects of the last World War. . . .

The Republican Party stands for Americanism, preparedness and peace. We
accordingly fasten upon the New Deal full responsibility for our unpreparedness and for the consequent danger of involvement in war.

We declare for the prompt, orderly and realistic building of our national
defense to the point at which we shall be able not only to defend the United
States, its possessions, and essential outposts from foreign attack, but also efficiently to uphold in war the Monroe Doctrine. To this task the Republican
Party pledges itself when entrusted with national authority. In the meantime
we shall support all necessary and proper defense measures proposed by the
Administration in its belated effort to make up for lost time; but we deplore
explosive utterances by the President directed at other governments which
serve to imperil our peace; and we condemn all executive acts and proceedings which might lead to war without the authorization of the Congress of
the United States.

B] ROOSEVELT PLANS THE DESTROYER DEAL

THE WHITE HOUSE, Aug. 2, 1940, 9:37 P.M.

MEMORANDUM:

At Cabinet meeting, in afternoon, long discussion in regard to devising ways
and means to sell directly or indirectly fifty or sixty World War old destroyers
to Great Britain. It was the general opinion, without any dissenting voice, that
the survival of the British Isles under German attack might very possibly depend on their getting these destroyers.

It was agreed that legislation to accomplish this is necessary.

It was agreed that such legislation if asked for by me without any preliminaries would meet with defeat or interminable delay in reaching a vote.

It was agreed that the British be approached through Lord Lothian to find
out if they would agree to give positive assurance that the British Navy, in the
event of German success in Great Britain, would not under any conceivable
circumstances fall into the hands of the Germans, and that if such assurances
could be received and made public, the opposition in the Congress would be
greatly lessened. I suggested that we try to get further assurance from the
British that the ships of their Navy would not be sunk, but would sail for
North American or British Empire ports where they would remain afloat and
available.

It was agreed that I would call up William Allen White, who has recently talked with Willkie on this subject; ask White to come to Washington at once to see Hull, Knox and Stimson and after that to see me; then returning to see Willkie and seek to get, with Willkie's approval, the support of Joe Martin and Charlie McNary for such a plan. It was agreed that if this procedure went through successfully that I would, at once, send a definite request to the Congress for the necessary legislation.

I stressed the point that in all probability the legislation would fail if it had substantially unanimous Republican opposition—and that the crux of the matter lay in the vote of the Republican minority in each house. I stressed the importance of having the issue acted on without regard to party politics in any way.

At 8:30 P.M., I talked with William Allen White, who was in Estes Park, Colorado; explained the above to him and asked him to come East.

He told me that he was sure that Willkie's attitude in the matter was the same as mine. I explained to him that that was wholly insufficient, and that Willkie's attitude was not what counted, but that the Republican policy in Congress was the one essential.

White told me he would get in touch with Willkie and let me know at the earliest possible moment.

F.D.R.

c] Willkie Takes His Stand

[Speech of August 17, 1940]

. . . .

In the foreign policy of the United States, as in its domestic policy, I would do everything to defend American democracy and I would refrain from doing anything that would injure it.

We must not permit our emotions—our sympathies or hatreds—to move us from that fixed principle.

For instance, we must not shirk the necessity of preparing our sons to take care of themselves in case the defense of America leads to war. I shall not undertake to analyze the legislation on this subject that is now before Congress, or to examine the intentions of the administration with regard to it. I concur with many members of my party, that these intentions must be closely watched. Nevertheless, in spite of these considerations, I cannot ask the American people to put their faith in me, without recording my conviction that some form of selective service is the only democratic way in which to secure the trained and competent manpower we need for national defense.

Also, in the light of my principle, we must honestly face our relationship with Great Britain. We must admit that the loss of the British fleet would greatly weaken our defense. This is because the British fleet has for years controlled the Atlantic, leaving us free to concentrate in the Pacific. If the British fleet were lost or captured, the Atlantic might be dominated by Germany, a power hostile to our way of life, controlling in that event most of the ships and shipbuilding facilities of Europe.

This would be a calamity for us. We might be exposed to attack on the Atlantic. Our defense would be weakened until we could build a navy and air force strong enough to defend both coasts. Also, our foreign trade would be profoundly affected. That trade is vital to our prosperity. But if we had to trade with a Europe dominated by the present German trade policies, we might have to change our methods to some totalitarian form. This is a prospect that any lover of democracy must view with consternation.

The objective of America is in the opposite direction. We must, in the long run, rebuild a world in which we can live and move and do business in the democratic way.

The President of the United States recently said: "We will extend to the opponents of force the material resources of this nation, and at the same time we will harness the use of those resources in order that we ourselves, in the Americas, may have equipment and training equal to the task of any emergency and every defense."

I should like to state that I am in agreement with these two principles, as I understand them—and I don't understand them as implying military involvement in the present hostilities. As an American citizen I am glad to pledge my wholehearted support to the President in whatever action he may take in accordance with these principles.

But I cannot follow the President in his conduct of foreign affairs in this critical time. There have been occasions when many of us have wondered if he is deliberately inciting us to war. I trust that I have made it plain that in the defense of America, and of our liberties, I should not hesitate to stand for war. But like a great many other Americans I saw what war was like at first hand in 1917. I know what war can do to demoralize civil liberties at home. And I believe it to be the first duty of a President to try to maintain peace.

But Mr. Roosevelt has not done this. He has dabbled in inflammatory statements and manufactured panics. Of course, we in America like to speak our minds freely, but this does not mean that at a critical period in history our President should cause bitterness and confusion for the sake of a little political oratory. The President's attacks on foreign powers have been useless and dangerous. He has courted a war for which the country is hopelessly unprepared—and which it emphatically does not want. He has secretly meddled in the affairs of Europe, and he has even unscrupulously encouraged other countries to hope for more help than we are able to give.

"Walk softly and carry a big stick" was the motto of Theodore Roosevelt. It is still good American doctrine for 1940. Under the present administration the country has been placed in the false position of shouting insults and not even beginning to prepare to take the consequences.

But while he has thus been quick to tell other nations what they ought to do, Mr. Roosevelt has been slow to take the American people into his confidence. He has hesitated to report facts, to explain situations, or to define realistic objectives. The confusion in the nation's mind has been largely due to this lack of information from the White House. . . .

And in this tragedy let us find our lesson. The foreign policy of the United States begins right here in our own land. The first task of our country in its international affairs is to become strong at home. We must regain prosperity, restore the independence of our people, and protect our defensive forces. If that is not done promptly we are in constant danger. If that is done no enemy on earth dare attack us. I propose to do it.

We must face a brutal, perhaps, a terrible fact. Our way of life is in competition with Hitler's way of life.

This competition is not merely one of armaments. It is a competition of energy against energy, production against production, brains against brains, salesmanship against salesmanship.

In facing it we should have no fear. History shows that our way of life is the stronger way. From it has come more wealth, more industry, more happiness, more human enlightenment than from any other way. Free men are the strongest men.

But we cannot just take this historical fact for granted. We must make it live. If we are to out-distance the totalitarian powers, we must arise to a new life of adventure and discovery. We must make a wider horizon for the human race. It is to that new life that I pledge myself.

I promise, by returning to those same American principles that overcame German autocracy once before, both in business and in war, to out-distance Hitler in any contest he chooses in 1940 or after. And I promise that when we beat him, we shall beat him on our own terms, in our own American way.

[Speech of October 30, 1940]

. . . The world across the ocean is in flames. New wars and formidable alliances of force against democracy are the order of the day. Freedom abroad has fallen before the onslaught of the aggressor. Only on the small island of Britain does it hold out.

We in America are left almost alone. Ours is the duty to hold fast the great traditions of democracy. . . .

One-man rule always leads to the road to war. . . .

By the third-term candidate's own record, we know that during the last many years he disregarded the repeated warnings of his own diplomatic and military experts. Yet from 1933 until 1939 he made no adequate move toward giving the United States modernized defense.

In this threatening year of 1940, in January, he requested an increase in the defense budget of only $250,000,000. He said that, despite contrary expert opinion, that amount was sufficient.

But a few months after he expressed that opinion, he was forced to ask Congress for more. After that he had to go back to Congress four times. . . .

In protecting America, the maintenance of peace in the Western Hemisphere will be my objective. The President must be dedicated to the objective of peace in our part of the world.

Aid to Britain to the limits of prudence for our own safety is essential to that objective.

I have given you my pledge many times over: I will work for peace. We are against sending our boys into any war other than the defense of our own country.

The third-term candidate has also pledged himself to peace. . . .

I ask you whether his pledge for peace is going to last any longer than his pledge for sound money [in 1932].

On the basis of his past performance with pledges to the people, you may expect we will be at war by April, 1941, if he is elected. . . .

D] ROOSEVELT ANNOUNCES THE DESTROYER DEAL: PRESS CONFERENCE ON BOARD PRESIDENT'S TRAIN EN ROUTE TO WASHINGTON, D.C., SEPTEMBER 3, 1940

The PRESIDENT: Hello, good people, how are you? This was an easy trip for you, an awfully easy trip with no news. Why, there is old Fred [Mr. Essary]. Fred, who let you come?

Q. [Mr. Essary] I did not ask anybody's permission. I just came.

The PRESIDENT: You just came. Gosh, I am glad that somebody got up to give the lady [Miss Fleeson] a seat. Fred, you have become a trouper again; it is all right.

Q. [Mr. Essary] So I have.

The PRESIDENT: Sit on the floor, Felix [Mr. Belair]; you are too big to stand up.

Q. This is the first train Press Conference since Germany moved into Denmark.

The PRESIDENT: I guess that's right.

Q. We had a big talk with you at that time about Iceland and Greenland.

The PRESIDENT: You are learning geography. There was another Press Conference where we talked about the Celebes Islands. (*Laughter*)

Q. We were clear to the Cocos before we knew. (*Laughter*)

The PRESIDENT: I have today nothing for you as news from here, although I have something for you for your own information. It is a Washington story that will be out there in twenty-two minutes, so the story will come from Washington. I cannot add to it, but you ought to know about it because you will probably get all kinds of flashes. "For God's sake, get some news." Well, there isn't any news.

In twenty minutes there is going to the Congress tne following message, which I am going to read from the only copy I have, which is a rough copy, so there is no use taking it down.

Mr. EARLY: The text will be released there [in Washington].

The PRESIDENT: It is probably the most important thing that has come for American defense since the Louisiana Purchase. [Turning to Mr. Essary] That goes back before you and me.

Q. [Mr. Essary] That is quite far.

The PRESIDENT: How far? About 1803?

Q. [Mr. Essary] About.

The PRESIDENT: (*reading*)

"TO THE CONGRESS OF THE UNITED STATES:

"I transmit herewith for the information of the Congress notes exchanged between the British Ambassador at Washington and the Secretary of State on September 2, 1940."

—in other words, that is yesterday—(*Reading*)

"under which this Government has acquired the right to lease naval and air bases in Newfoundland, and in the islands of Bermuda, the Bahamas, Jamaica, St. Lucia—"

Q. [interposing] What is that last one?
The PRESIDENT: St. Lucia.
Q. How do you spell it?
The PRESIDENT: S-t. L-u-c-i-a, period. Now, I am not fooling on those. These are real places. (*Laughter*) [The President continued reading]

"—Trinidad, and Antigua, and in British Guiana—"

Get out the map. We haven't even got an atlas on board. That is terrible. (*Reading*)

"—also a copy of an opinion of the Attorney General dated August 27, 1940, regarding my authority to consummate this arrangement." . . .
"The right to bases in Newfoundland and Bermuda are gifts—generously given and gladly received."

Mind you, all these places being mentioned are what they call Crown Colonies.
Q. Are these ninety-nine-year leases, Mr. President?
The PRESIDENT: Yes. (*Reading*)

"The other bases mentioned have been acquired in exchange for fifty of our over-age destroyers."

Q. This is breaking out of Washington? (*Laughter*)
The PRESIDENT: This is breaking out of Washington. This is not a Press Conference; just a little information conference.
Q. No connection between those bases and the destroyers?
Q. Which of the bases are being leased?
The PRESIDENT: They are all ninety-nine years, but Newfoundland and Bermuda are gifts. In other words, there is no exchange in relation to them.
Q. No *quid pro quo*?
The PRESIDENT: No *quid pro quo* on those at all. You see the point? . . .
Q. The release clause applies also to the two gifts?
The PRESIDENT: Yes. (*Reading*)

"This is not inconsistent in any sense with our status of peace. Still less is it a threat against any nation. It is an epochal and far-reaching act of preparation for continental defense in the face of grave danger.
"Preparation for defense is an inalienable prerogative of a sovereign state.

Under present circumstances this exercise of sovereign right is essential to the maintenance of our peace and safety. This is the most important action in the reinforcement of our national defense that has been taken since the Louisiana Purchase. Then, as now, considerations of safety from overseas attack were fundamental.

"The value to the Western Hemisphere of these outposts of security is beyond calculation. Their need has long been recognized by our country, and especially by those primarily charged with the duty of charting and organizing our own naval and military defense. They are essential to the—"

a lot more geography for you—(*Reading*)

"protection of the Panama Canal, Central America, the Northern portion of South America, The Antilles, Canada, Mexico, and our own Eastern and Gulf Seaboards. Their consequent importance in hemispheric defense is obvious. For these reasons I have taken advantage of the present opportunity to acquire them."

That is all.

Q. Mr. President, when will the destroyers be sent to Great Britain?

The PRESIDENT: Oh, some of them are—I don't know; reasonably soon.

Q. Would it be a fair assumption to say that some are on the way?

The PRESIDENT: No, I would not say that.

Q. Will the British send crews over to take the destroyers?

The PRESIDENT: I don't know; I don't know.

Q. Where are the destroyers now?

The PRESIDENT: I don't know.

Q. Mr. President, does this require Senate ratification?

The PRESIDENT: Listen: (*reading*)

"I transmit herewith for the information of the Congress—"

these notes and the opinion. And, at the end, I say (*reading*)

"For these reasons I have taken advantage of the present opportunity to acquire them."

Q. Mr. Jackson's opinion?

The PRESIDENT: It is all over; it is all done. . . .

Q. How close is the formula that you have used to make this public to the procedure President Monroe used in announcing the Monroe Doctrine? Wasn't there an exchange of correspondence?

The PRESIDENT: I think that was employed too.

Q. An exchange of correspondence?

The PRESIDENT: Of course there was no mutuality in the Monroe Doctrine. There is mutuality here.

This has to be for background—it is for your own information, historical, without attribution. In about—I cannot give you the exact dates—about 1803, Napoleon was at war with Great Britain. France was a belligerent, and we were scared pink because France had bought from Spain the whole of the Louisiana Territory, and especially the mouth of the Mississippi. That was the important thing to our defense. France had a very weak army down there in Louisiana. I think they had one regiment, something like that, for the whole of the Territory. We were scared to death that there might be, as an outcome of the Napoleonic wars, some threat or some danger of some power going in there and going up the valley to connect up with Canada, the back part of Canada, thereby confining the States practically to this side of the Mississippi.

There was an awful lot of discussion about it and everybody was yelling, "For God's sake protect us," all over the country, "by acquiring, if you can, this mouth of the Mississippi." Of course in those days they, none of them, realized what they were getting with the Louisiana Purchase, that they were getting that tremendous back country that went clear up to Montana, but they saw it primarily from the standpoint of the mouth of the Mississippi and the control of the main stem of the Mississippi.

So Jefferson sent Monroe and Chancellor Robert R. Livingston over to Paris—

Q. [interposing] One of your relatives, wasn't he?

The PRESIDENT: Relative, yes. He was my wife's great grandfather. (*Laughter*)

And they went to Paris and negotiated with Napoleon, who was a belligerent, fighting Great Britain at the time. In fact, he was fighting over most of Europe. They made this deal for the purchase of the whole thing from Napoleon for a price of—as I remember it—what was it, $15,000,000?

Q. Yes, sir.

The PRESIDENT: And Napoleon, at the same time, verbally agreed that a portion of that money would be spent over here in buying certain naval supplies and certain food supplies that he needed over there for the continuation of his wars. The contract was signed over there in Paris, Monroe and, I think, Livingston hopped the first sail boat they could, and came back to Washington, and announced that the thing had been done. Thereupon there ensued a long session in the Cabinet and every other place, as to whether such a thing could be done. You see, there was nothing said about it in the Constitution.

Q. I thought Jefferson did it—made the Louisiana Purchase?

The PRESIDENT: But it was Monroe and Livingston who made the actual purchase. They brought back a signed contract to him. He said, "Fine; I accept it," and then there ensued this discussion in the early days when the Constitution had never been tried out very much. There wasn't anything in the Constitution about it, and to put the thing up to Congress would have involved a delay. Now, the main thing was to put our hands on it, to take it, to get it; and Jefferson thereupon, as soon as word came from the two commissioners, proceeded to take over Louisiana. It was a *fait accompli*. He got the opinion of the Attorney General that he could do it without a treaty, do it for the national defense as Commander-in-Chief, and do it as President, as well, in an obvious emergency.

And, later on, he asked, not the Senate but he asked the Appropriations Committee of the House to please appropriate $15,000,000 to him as an item in an appropriation bill, which was done. There was never any treaty, there was never any two-thirds vote in the Senate, and today Louisiana is about one-third of the whole of the United States.

And we are going back a hundred—about a hundred and thirty-seven years
—for our historical precedent and authority. It is a very interesting thing.

Q. Did Mr. Jackson, in setting up his opinion saying that you had authority
to do that, set forth the Louisiana Purchase as a historical precedent?

The PRESIDENT: I think that is mentioned in it. . . .

E] ROOSEVELT ASSAILS THE REPUBLICAN LEADERSHIP:
ADDRESS AT MADISON SQUARE GARDEN, NEW YORK
CITY, OCTOBER 28, 1940

NO CAMPAIGN can possibly be complete without this great Garden meeting.

I have had a very wonderful day in New York, in all five boroughs. But,
as you know, I have had an anxious day too, because three or four times during the day I have had to be in touch with the Department of State and with
the Secretary of State, Cordell Hull, because, unfortunately, it seems that another war has broken out on the other side of the ocean. I am quite sure that
all of you will feel the same sorrow in your hearts that I feel—sorrow for the
Italian people and the Grecian people, that they should have been involved
together in conflict.

Tonight, for the second time, I take up the public duty—the far from disagreeable duty—of answering major campaign falsifications with facts.

Last week in Philadelphia, which is supposed to be the City of Brotherly
Love, but isn't always, I nailed the falsehood about some fanciful secret treaties
to dry on the barn door. I nailed that falsehood and other falsehoods the way
when I was a boy up in Dutchess County we used to nail up the skins of foxes
and weasels. And, incidentally, I think it was a kinsman of mine, about thirty
years ago, who invented the term, "weasel words."

Tonight I am going to nail up the falsifications that have to do with our
relations with the rest of the world and with the building up of our Army,
our Navy and our air defense. It is a very dangerous thing to distort facts
about things like that, because if repeated over and over again, it is apt to
create a sense of fear and doubt in the minds of some of the American people.

I now brand as false the statement being made by Republican campaign
orators, day after day and night after night, that the rearming of America is
slow, that it is hamstrung and impeded, that it will never be able to meet
threats from abroad. Those are the whisperings of appeasers.

That particular misstatement has a history. It came into the world last June,
just about the time of the Republican National Convention. Before that, the
responsible Republican leaders had been singing an entirely different song.
For almost seven years the Republican leaders in the Congress kept on saying that I was placing too *much* emphasis on national defense.

And now today these men of great vision have suddenly discovered that
there is a war going on in Europe and another one in Asia. And so, now, always with their eyes on the good old ballot box, they are charging that we
have placed too *little* emphasis on national defense.

But, unlike them, the printed pages of the Congressional Record cannot be
changed or suppressed at election time. And based on that permanent record

of their speeches and their votes, I make this assertion—that if the Republican leaders had been in control of the Congress of the United States during the past seven years, the important measures for our defense would not now be law: and the Army and Navy of the United States would still be in almost the same condition in which I found them in 1933.

Remember, I am making those charges against the responsible political leadership of the Republican Party. But there are millions—millions and millions —of patriotic Republicans who have at all times been in sympathy with the efforts of this Administration to arm the nation adequately for purposes of defense. . . .

When the first World War broke out, we were pretty weak, but by the end of it we were one of the strongest naval and military powers in the world. When this Administration first came into office fifteen years later, we were one of the weakest.

As early as 1933 the storm was gathering in Europe and in Asia. Year by year I reported the warnings of danger from our listening posts in foreign lands. But I was only called "an alarmist" by the Republican leadership, and by the great majority of the Republican newspapers of the country.

Year by year I asked for more and more defense appropriations. In addition, I allocated hundreds of millions of dollars for defense work from relief funds. The C.C.C. helped, the Public Works helped—as was understood by the Congress when the money was voted by them.

Today our Navy is at a peak of efficiency and fighting strength. Ship for ship, man for man, it is as powerful and efficient as any single navy that ever sailed the seas in history. But it is not as powerful as combinations of other navies that might be put together in an attack upon us. Our Army and our air forces are now at the highest level that they have ever been in peacetime. But in the light of existing dangers they are not great enough for the absolute safety of America at home.

While this great, constructive work was going forward, the Republican leaders were definitely and beyond peradventure of doubt trying to block our efforts toward national defense. They not only voted against these efforts; but they stated time and again through the years that they were unnecessary and extravagant, that our armed strength was sufficient for any emergency.

I propose now to indict these Republican leaders out of their own mouths— these leaders who now disparage our defenses—with what they themselves said in the days before this election year, about how adequate our defenses already were.

Listen to this for instance:

The facts are that we have the largest and most powerful Navy we ever had, except for two years after the World War, and the greatest air forces we ever had and a match for any nation.

Now, who do you suppose made that statement a little over two years ago? It was not I. It was not even a member of this Administration. It was the ranking Republican member of the House Committee on Foreign Affairs, Republican leader, Hamilton Fish.

And now listen to the only living ex-President of the United States. He said in that same year, two years ago:

We shall be expending nine hundred million dollars more than any nation on earth. We are leading in the arms race.

And now listen to Republican leader Senator Vandenberg, also speaking at that time. He said that our defense expenditures had already brought us "an incomparably efficient Navy"; and he said further, "I rise in opposition to this super-super Navy bill. I do not believe it is justified by any conclusive demonstration of national necessity."

And now listen to what Republican leader Senator Taft—the runner-up for the Republican Presidential nomination this year—said this past February, 1940:

The increase of the Army and Navy over the tremendous appropriations of the current year seems to be unnecessary if we are concerned solely with defense.

There is the record on that; the permanent crystal clear record. Until the present political campaign opened, Republican leaders, in and out of the Congress shouted from the housetops that our defenses were fully adequate.

Today they proclaim that this Administration has starved our armed forces, that our Navy is anemic, our Army puny, our air forces piteously weak.

Yes, it is a remarkable somersault.

I wonder if the election could have something to do with it. . . .

Not only in their statements but in their votes is written their record of sabotage of this Administration's continual efforts to increase our defenses to meet the dangers that loomed ever larger and larger upon the horizon.

For example, deeply concerned over what was happening in Europe, I asked the Congress in January, 1938, for a naval expansion of twenty per cent—forty-six additional ships and nine hundred and fifty new planes.

What did the Republican leaders do when they had this chance to increase our national defense almost three years ago? You would think from their present barrage of verbal pyrotechnics (*laughter*), that they rushed in to pass that bill, or that they even demanded a larger expansion of the Navy.

But, ah! my friends, they were not in a national campaign for votes then.

In those days they were trying to build up a different kind of political fence. . . .

On the radio these Republican orators swing through the air with the greatest of ease; but the American people are not voting this year for the best trapeze performer.

The plain fact is that when that naval bill I was speaking about was submitted to the Congress, the Republican leaders jumped in to fight it.

Who were they? There was the present Republican candidate for Vice President, Senator McNary. There were Senator Vandenberg and Senator Nye. And there was the man who would be the Chairman of the House Committee on Foreign Affairs, Congressman Fish.

The first thing they did was to try to eliminate the battleships from the bill. The Republicans in the House voted sixty-seven to twenty against building them; and in the Senate, where they had a much smaller number, the Republicans voted seven to four against building them. . . .

I say that the Republican leaders played politics with defense in 1938 and 1939. I say that they are playing politics with our national security today.

Turn another page:

The Republican campaign orators and leaders are all now yelling "me too" on help to Britain. But this fall they had their chance to vote to give aid to Britain and other democracies—and they turned it down.

This chance came when I recommended that the Congress repeal the embargo on the shipment of armaments and munitions to nations at war, and permit such shipment on a "cash-and-carry basis." It is only because of the repeal of the embargo law that we have been able to sell planes and ships and guns and munitions to victims of aggression.

But how did the Republicans vote on the repeal of that embargo?

In the Senate the Republicans voted fourteen to six against it. In the House the Republicans voted one hundred and forty to nineteen against it.

The Act was passed by Democratic votes but it was over the opposition of the Republican leaders. And just to name a few, the following Republican leaders, among many others, voted against the Act: Senators McNary, Vandenberg, Nye and Johnson; now wait, a perfectly beautiful rhythm—Congressmen Martin, Barton and Fish.

Now, at the eleventh hour, they have discovered what we knew all along—that overseas success in warding off invasion by dictatorship forces means safety to the United States. It means also continued independence to those smaller nations which still retain their independence. And it means the restoration of sovereignty to those smaller nations which have temporarily lost it. As we know, one of the keystones of American policy is the recognition of the right of small nations to survive and prosper.

Great Britain and a lot of other nations would never have received one ounce of help from us—if the decision had been left to Martin, Barton and Fish. . . .

This record of Republican leadership—a record of timidity, of weakness, of short-sightedness—is as bad in international as in military affairs.

It is the same record of timidity, of weakness, of short-sightedness which they showed in domestic affairs when they were in control before 1933.

But the Republican leaders' memories seem to have been short, in this, as in some other matters. And by the way—who was it said that an elephant never forgets?

It is the same record of timidity, of weakness and of short-sightedness that governed the policy of the confused, reactionary governments in France and England before the war.

That fact was discovered too late in France.

It was discovered just in time in England.

Pray God that, having discovered it, we won't forget it either.

For eight years our main concern, as you know and as the nation knows, has been to look for peace and the preservation of peace.

Back in 1935, in the face of growing dangers throughout the world, your

Government undertook to eliminate certain hazards which in the past had led us into war.

By the Neutrality Act of 1935, and by other steps:

We made it possible to prohibit American citizens from traveling on vessels belonging to countries at war. Was that right?

We made it clear that American investors, who put their money into enterprises in foreign nations, could not call on American warships or American soldiers to bail out their investments. Was that right?

We made it clear that we would not use American armed forces to intervene in affairs of the sovereign republics to the south of us. Was that right?

We made it clear that ships flying the American flag could not carry munitions to a belligerent; and that they must stay out of war zones. Was that right?

In all these ways we made it clear to every American, and to every foreign nation that we would avoid becoming entangled through some episode beyond our borders.

Those were measures to keep us at peace. And through all the years since 1935, there has been no entanglement and there will be no entanglement. . . .

I am asking the American people to support a continuance of this type of alternative, realistic fight for peace. The alternative is to risk the future of the country in the hands of those with this record of timidity, weakness and shortsightedness or to risk it in the inexperienced hands of those who in these perilous days are willing recklessly to imply that our boys are already on their way to the transports. . . .

2] Lend-Lease: "Aid to the Allies Short of War"

The War in Europe widened in the fall of 1940. Italy assaulted Greece; and Germany, giving up plans for a sea invasion of Britain, laid plans for new offensives to the south and east. Most serious at the moment, the Battle of the Atlantic was going against Britain as the Nazis sought to destroy her sea lines of communication with the United States and the Commonwealth. With the election behind him, Roosevelt could now plan a bigger, more sustained program of aid. His sweeping proposal for Lend-Lease, presented in a general way in his annual message of January 6, 1941, and more specifically by members of his Cabinet to Congressional committees, aroused the intense opposition of isolationists in both parties. Some of the sharpest encounters took place in the hearings before the Senate's Committee on Foreign Relations, between administration representatives and the Republican senators who for years had been leading that party's isolationist wing. Final passage of the Lend-Lease Act, on March 11, 1941, altered the world balance of power, for it proved decisive to Britain and was later extended to Soviet Russia and other Allied nations.

The isolationist campaign against American involvement in the war intensified rather than lessened at that time. The center of that campaign was the America First Committee. Colonel Charles A. Lindbergh, Jr., who had testified against the Act during the hearings earlier in the year, was by April the man around whom the most passionate isolationist sentiment clung. An authentic national hero as a result of his solo flight to Paris in 1927, Lindbergh was Roosevelt's most formidable opponent in radio address. On April 23, 1941, in a speech broadcast nationally and given before a mammoth rally of the America First Committee in New York City, he delivered the most measured statement of the isolationist position.*

A] THE PRESIDENT ADDRESSES CONGRESS: ANNUAL
MESSAGE, JANUARY 6, 1941

I ADDRESS YOU, the Members of the Seventy-seventh Congress, at a moment unprecedented in the history of the Union. I use the word "unprecedented," because at no previous time has American security been as seriously threatened from without as it is today.

Since the permanent formation of our Government under the Constitution, in 1789, most of the periods of crisis in our history have related to our domestic affairs. Fortunately, only one of these—the four-year War Between the States— ever threatened our national unity. Today, thank God, one hundred and thirty million Americans, in forty-eight States, have forgotten points of the compass in our national unity.

It is true that prior to 1914 the United States often had been disturbed by events in other Continents. We had even engaged in two wars with European nations and in a number of undeclared wars in the West Indies, in the Mediterranean and in the Pacific for the maintenance of American rights and for the principles of peaceful commerce. But in no case had a serious threat been raised against our national safety or our continued independence.

What I seek to convey is the historic truth that the United States as a nation has at all times maintained clear, definite opposition, to any attempt to lock us in behind an ancient Chinese wall while the procession of civilization went past. Today, thinking of our children and of their children, we oppose enforced isolation for ourselves or for any other part of the Americas.

That determination of ours, extending over all these years, was proved, for example, during the quarter century of wars following the French Revolution.

While the Napoleonic struggles did threaten interests of the United States because of the French foothold in the West Indies and in Louisiana, and while we engaged in the War of 1812 to vindicate our right to peaceful trade, it is nevertheless clear that neither France nor Great Britain, nor any other nation, was aiming at domination of the whole world.

In like fashion from 1815 to 1914—ninety-nine years—no single war in Europe or in Asia constituted a real threat against our future or against the future of any other American nation.

Except in the Maximilian interlude in Mexico, no foreign power sought to establish itself in this Hemisphere; and the strength of the British fleet in the Atlantic has been a friendly strength. It is still a friendly strength.

---

* LEND-LEASE: "AID TO THE ALLIES SHORT OF WAR": From Samuel I. Rosenman, ed., *The Public Papers and Addresses of Franklin D. Roosevelt: The Call to Battle Stations* (New York, 1950), pp. 663–72, reprinted by permission of Harper & Bros.; Committee on Foreign Relations of the U.S. Senate, *Hearings*, 77 Cong., 1 Sess. (Washington, January–February, 1941), *passim*; New York *Times* (April 24, 1941).

Even when the World War broke out in 1914, it seemed to contain only small threat of danger to our own American future. But, as time went on, the American people began to visualize what the downfall of democratic nations might mean to our own democracy.

We need not overemphasize imperfections in the Peace of Versailles. We need not harp on failure of the democracies to deal with problems of world reconstruction. We should remember that the Peace of 1919 was far less unjust than the kind of "pacification" which began even before Munich, and which is being carried on under the new order of tyranny that seeks to spread over every continent today. The American people have unalterably set their faces against that tyranny.

Every realist knows that the democratic way of life is at this moment being directly assailed in every part of the world—assailed either by arms, or by secret spreading of poisonous propaganda by those who seek to destroy unity and promote discord in nations that are still at peace.

During sixteen long months this assault has blotted out the whole pattern of democratic life in an appalling number of independent nations, great and small. The assailants are still on the march, threatening other nations, great and small.

Therefore, as your President, performing my constitutional duty to "give to the Congress information of the state of the Union," I find it, unhappily, necessary to report that the future and the safety of our country and of our democracy are overwhelmingly involved in events far beyond our borders.

Armed defense of democratic existence is now being gallantly waged in four continents. If that defense fails, all the population and all the resources of Europe, Asia, Africa and Australasia will be dominated by the conquerors. Let us remember that the total of those populations and their resources in those four continents greatly exceeds the sum total of the population and the resources of the whole of the Western Hemisphere—many times over.

In times like these it is immature—and incidentally, untrue—for anybody to brag that an unprepared America, single-handed and with one hand tied behind its back, can hold off the whole world.

No realistic American can expect from a dictator's peace international generosity, or return of true independence, or world disarmament, or freedom of expression, or freedom of religion—or even good business.

Such a peace would bring no security for us or for our neighbors. "Those, who would give up essential liberty to purchase a little temporary safety, deserve neither liberty nor safety."

As a nation, we may take pride in the fact that we are soft-hearted; but we cannot afford to be soft-headed.

We must always be wary of those who with sounding brass and a tinkling cymbal preach the "ism" of appeasement.

We must especially beware of that small group of selfish men who would clip the wings of the American eagle in order to feather their own nests.

I have recently pointed out how quickly the tempo of modern warfare could bring into our very midst the physical attack which we must eventually expect if the dictator nations win this war.

There is much loose talk of our immunity from immediate and direct invasion from across the seas. Obviously, as long as the British Navy retains its power, no such danger exists. Even if there were no British Navy, it is not probable that any enemy would be stupid enough to attack us by landing troops in the United States from across thousands of miles of ocean, until it had acquired strategic bases from which to operate.

But we learn much from the lessons of the past years in Europe—particularly the lesson of Norway, whose essential seaports were captured by treachery and surprise built up over a series of years.

The first phase of the invasion of this Hemisphere would not be the landing of regular troops. The necessary strategic points would be occupied by secret agents and their dupes—and great numbers of them are already here, and in Latin America.

As long as the aggressor nations maintain the offensive, they—not we—will choose the time and the place and the method of their attack.

That is why the future of all the American Republics is today in serious danger.

That is why this Annual Message to the Congress is unique in our history.

That is why every member of the Executive Branch of the Government and every member of the Congress faces great responsibility and great accountability.

The need of the moment is that our actions and our policy should be devoted primarily—almost exclusively—to meeting this foreign peril. For all our domestic problems are now a part of the great emergency.

Just as our national policy in internal affairs has been based upon a decent respect for the rights and the dignity of all our fellow men within our gates, so our national policy in foreign affairs has been based on a decent respect for the rights and dignity of all nations, large and small. And the justice of morality must and will win in the end.

Our national policy is this:

First, by an impressive expression of the public will and without regard to partisanship, we are committed to all-inclusive national defense.

Second, by an impressive expression of the public will and without regard to partisanship, we are committed to full support of all those resolute peoples, everywhere, who are resisting aggression and are thereby keeping war away from our Hemisphere. By this support, we express our determination that the democratic cause shall prevail; and we strengthen the defense and the security of our own nation.

Third, by an impressive expression of the public will and without regard to partisanship, we are committed to the proposition that principles of morality and considerations for our own security will never permit us to acquiesce in a peace dictated by aggressors and sponsored by appeasers. We know that enduring peace cannot be bought at the cost of other people's freedom.

In the recent national election there was no substantial difference between the two great parties in respect to that national policy. No issue was fought out on this line before the American electorate. Today it is abundantly evident that American citizens everywhere are demanding and supporting speedy and complete action in recognition of obvious danger. . . .

I . . . ask this Congress for authority and for funds sufficient to manufacture additional munitions and war supplies of many kinds, to be turned over to those nations which are now in actual war with aggressor nations.

Our most useful and immediate role is to act as an arsenal for them as well as for ourselves. They do not need man power, but they do need billions of dollars worth of the weapons of defense.

The time is near when they will not be able to pay for them all in ready cash. We cannot, and we will not, tell them that they must surrender, merely because of present inability to pay for the weapons which we know they must have.

I do not recommend that we make them a loan of dollars with which to pay for these weapons—a loan to be repaid in dollars.

I recommend that we make it possible for those nations to continue to obtain war materials in the United States, fitting their orders into our own program. Nearly all their matériel would, if the time ever came, be useful for our own defense.

Taking counsel of expert military and naval authorities, considering what is best for our own security, we are free to decide how much should be kept here and how much should be sent abroad to our friends who by their determined and heroic resistance are giving us time in which to make ready our own defense.

For what we send abroad, we shall be repaid within a reasonable time following the close of hostilities, in similar materials, or, at our option, in other goods of many kinds, which they can produce and which we need.

Let us say to the democracies: "We Americans are vitally concerned in your defense of freedom. We are putting forth our energies, our resources and our organizing powers to give you the strength to regain and maintain a free world. We shall send you, in ever-increasing numbers, ships, planes, tanks, guns. This is our purpose and our pledge."

In fulfillment of this purpose we will not be intimidated by the threats of dictators that they will regard as a breach of international law or as an act of war our aid to the democracies which dare to resist their aggression. Such aid is not an act of war, even if a dictator should unilaterally proclaim it so to be.

When the dictators, if the dictators, are ready to make war upon us, they will not wait for an act of war on our part. They did not wait for Norway or Belgium or the Netherlands to commit an act of war.

Their only interest is in a new one-way international law, which lacks mutuality in its observance, and, therefore, becomes an instrument of oppression.

The happiness of future generations of Americans may well depend upon how effective and how immediate we can make our aid felt. No one can tell the exact character of the emergency situations that we may be called upon to meet. The Nation's hands must not be tied when the Nation's life is in danger. . . .

Certainly this is no time for any of us to stop thinking about the social and economic problems which are the root cause of the social revolution which is today a supreme factor in the world.

For there is nothing mysterious about the foundations of a healthy and strong democracy. The basic things expected by our people of their political and economic systems are simple. They are:

Equality of opportunity for youth and for others.

Jobs for those who can work.

Security for those who need it.

The ending of special privilege for the few.

The preservation of civil liberties for all.

The enjoyment of the fruits of scientific progress in a wider and constantly rising standard of living.

These are the simple, basic things that must never be lost sight of in the turmoil and unbelievable complexity of our modern world. The inner and abiding strength of our economic and political systems is dependent upon the degree to which they fulfill these expectations. . . .

In the future days, which we seek to make secure, we look forward to a world founded upon four essential human freedoms.

The first is freedom of speech and expression—everywhere in the world.

The second is freedom of every person to worship God in his own way—everywhere in the world.

The third is freedom from want—which, translated into world terms, means economic understandings which will secure to every nation a healthy peacetime life for its inhabitants—everywhere in the world.

The fourth is freedom from fear—which, translated into world terms, means a world-wide reduction of armaments to such a point and in such a thorough fashion that no nation will be in a position to commit an act of physical aggression against any neighbor—anywhere in the world.

That is no vision of a distant millennium. It is a definite basis for a kind of world attainable in our own time and generation. That kind of world is the very antithesis of the so-called new order of tyranny which the dictators seek to create with the crash of a bomb.

To that new order we oppose the greater conception—the moral order. A good society is able to face schemes of world domination and foreign revolutions alike without fear.

Since the beginning of our American history, we have been engaged in change—in a perpetual peaceful revolution—a revolution which goes on steadily, quietly adjusting itself to changing conditions—without the concentration camp or the quick-lime in the ditch. The world order which we seek is the cooperation of free countries, working together in a friendly, civilized society.

This nation has placed its destiny in the hands and heads and hearts of its millions of free men and women; and its faith in freedom under the guidance of God. Freedom means the supremacy of human rights everywhere. Our support goes to those who struggle to gain those rights or keep them. Our strength is our unity of purpose.

To that high concept there can be no end save victory.

B] THE FOREIGN RELATIONS COMMITTEE CONSIDERS LEND-LEASE

Secretary STIMSON.[1] . . . Let me try to answer here suggestions which I can only answer in the broadest terms in an open session. But let me answer the suggestions which are being made that the situation of Great Britain is so hopeless that there is no use to try to help her. The world situation today is certainly serious not only from Britain's standpoint but from our own. For the first time in modern history the United States is confronted by a nation with an overwhelming army, including an overwhelming air force, and with the possibility of getting control of the Atlantic. As opposed to this threat, the United States has a one-ocean fleet and that fleet in the Pacific; and a vulnerable Panama Canal. Such a situation can easily become critical if British sea power in the Atlantic is lost. Such a disaster would involve not only the security of the North Atlantic but the security of the South Atlantic and South America as well. If these things should happen, our own safety would not easily or quickly be retrieved. It would be an indefinitely lasting result. With the British Isles in German control, the great preponderance of the shipbuilding capacity of the world will be indefinitely in the hands of the Axis powers.

I have been told on the best information that I can get, that after the fall of the British Isles, if that takes place, that preponderance would be as high as or higher than 7 to 1 in comparison with our own.

The control of the great trade routes of the seas would be in the hands of nations whose ways of life and methods of trade are contrary to our own, and there would be little hope of soon regaining that control. The defense of this hemisphere, under such circumstances, would present most difficult problems. The interests of South America would naturally follow the direction of the control of those trade routes and would certainly be heavily influenced if Spain were in the hands of a hostile power.

On the other hand, if the control of the seas and of the air remain in our hands and in the hands of those friendly to our Nation and to our methods of life, the threat of the Axis powers is gone. Germany has a great and strong army but it is spread out very thin and already in Italy and in Roumania and in Norway we begin to hear the creaks of the strain under which the German power is laboring. Japan has a large and strong army but that is spread out even thinner than the army of Germany, and for a long time the economic situation of Japan has been strained. Italy is already in serious straits. On the other hand, England's morale remains unimpaired. From all our reports it is as strong as ever and her successes in North Africa have been inspiring to her morale. Granted that Britain survives the crisis of this coming summer (and the passage of this bill will go far to stiffen the morale necessary for her to survive that crisis), the probability of an ultimate solution in favor of the democracies would, in my opinion, be very great. I can say stronger than "very great." I think it would be very preponderant.

1 Secretary of War Henry L. Stimson, formerly Secretary of State in Hoover's Cabinet.

Without sea power and with the control of the air against them, the armies of the Axis Powers cannot indefinitely hold even the European world in subjection. Sooner or later the inevitable reaction against such slavery will come and, in my opinion, when it once starts it will come with a speed which our defeatists have far underestimated.

It is said by critics of the bill that it confers powers upon the President to act contrary to the canons of international law. The Secretary of State answered that argument very fully in his hearing before the House. He pointed out that in the world today aggressor nations had, by their threats and actions in violation of international law, produced a situation where a law-abiding nation could not defend itself against their lawless action if it permitted itself to be shackled by rules which they disregard. He pointed out with great clarity and reason that in such a situation the law of self-defense justified freedom of action on the part of the victims of the aggressor nations. . . .

Senator LA FOLLETTE.[2] Now, coming back to this question of convoys, and the fact that prior to the time you entered the Cabinet you advocated the convoying of munitions and other matériel of war, do you see any objection to the inclusion of an amendment in this bill prohibiting such convoying?

Secretary STIMSON. Well, Senator, I do not think that such a position would be germane to the bill.

Senator LA FOLLETTE. That might be a theoretical objection, but it could not be an effective objection in the Senate, because we have no rule of germaneness. As I recall your testimony, you made a statement that you objected to or would regard as unfortunate such an amendment?

Secretary STIMSON. Well, I do regard it as unfortunate.

Senator LA FOLLETTE. For the benefit of our record, would you amplify it?

Secretary STIMSON. No one can tell what will happen in the course of a war, going on as the war in Europe is today, and getting nearer and nearer to this country in its effects, as it is today; and it was for that reason, as I see it, that the President was made the Commander in Chief of the Army and the Navy and vested with full and, so far as the Constitution is concerned, unrestricted powers over the movements of the Army and the Navy.

Now, that was a grant of power which you doubtless favor. You have been a member of this learned body for a long time and have read much history. That was a power which was given by the framers of the Constitution, who had served, many of them, in the Revolutionary War and had witnessed the difficulties that diversity of power had given to the conduct of that war and the difficulties that primarily the Commander in Chief, General Washington, had with, as I remember it—I am speaking from recollection—committees of the Continental Congress, who tried to dictate the movements of his forces.

So that it was evidently put in there for the purpose of meeting these difficulties that these wise gentlemen had known by experience, and that is the interpretation that has been given to it ever since. And I think that for the Congress now to introduce a provision which, if only by implication, sought to fetter a power which has existed untrammeled for over 150 years would be a

2 Robert M. La Follette, Jr., of Wisconsin, son of "Fighting Bob" La Follette and, like his father, a progressive and an isolationist.

very unfortunate thing, even if it was a provision which had no power or efficacy at all. It would stand there as record of perhaps misapprehension, which
does not conduce to the unity of the Nation in such a situation as we have
today.

Senator LA FOLLETTE. Well, you would have no doubt, would you, Mr. Secretary, that if we did convoy defense articles, as described in this bill, to Great
Britain, let us say, as an example, we would actually be in the war?

Secretary STIMSON. I have no such assurance.

Senator LA FOLLETTE. You would not be sure of that?

Secretary STIMSON. It is all speculation, both by you and by me.

Senator LA FOLLETTE. With a bill of this nature I have to do some speculating.

Secretary STIMSON. So do I. . . .

Senator GILLETTE.[3] I want to say that nobody appreciates any more than I
do your attitude as a member of a party other than my own and the thorough
American way in which you approached this. But may I read to you this, and
then you may make such comment as you choose or you may make none, if
you choose, that is, so far as I am concerned.

The American people went to the polls last November and the two political
parties spoke on this matter, and so far as an issue could be drawn it was drawn
on this subject at that time. I am quoting from the Democratic platform.

We pledge to extend to those people [speaking of the democracies] all of the
material aid at our command, consistent with law and not inconsistent with the
interests of our own national defense.

I call your attention that the law on the statute books at that time was the
neutrality law.

The Republican platform stated:

Our sympathies have been profoundly stirred by the invasion of unoffending
countries. We favor the extension to all peoples fighting for liberty or whose liberty
is threatened of such aid as shall not be in violation of international law or inconsistent with the requirements of our own national defense.

I call your attention to the fact of the only word that changes the meaning.
In one case they said "consistent with law," and in the other "consistent with
international law."

I am not going to ask you any question. But so far as the platforms drew an
issue there was substantial agreement that we should extend aid consistent with
law and not inconsistent with our national defense.

If you care to make any comment, you may make it. If not, all right.

Secretary STIMSON. So far as "consistent with international law" is concerned,
I have already treated that in my testimony. So far as consistency with the
neutrality statute is concerned, I simply say that in months or years after those
declarations were made, with changes in the fortunes of the world, not to make
a modification of some of the legislation then standing would be to put a
shackle on the safety of the United States. Since you have gone into the plat-

3 Guy Gillette, Democratic senator from Iowa and a leading isolationist.

forms of the two parties last summer, I say further that, unless my memory is very much at fault, both of the candidates who were in nomination and subject to election for the office of President, did express themselves directly in favor of aid to Great Britain.

. . . .

Dr. NIEBUHR.[4] . . . If Nazi tyranny establishes its supremacy in Europe and makes all trade with the continent subject to its decrees, penetrates into South America through economic and political and cultural pressure, and challenges us in the Orient through its allies and satellites, we would be faced with the alternatives of either conniving with this tyranny or spending more billions than have yet been envisaged to challenge it. Connivance would mean, among other things, participation in world trade on Nazi terms.

The Nazi unification of Europe would combine the conditions of slavery with the efficiency of a technical civilization for the first time in history. We have known slavery before and we know what the efficiency of modern industry is. But we have never had these two together. To compete with this combination in world trade would mean to debase our living standards to the level of slave labor, an achievement which is obviously impossible without destroying the democratic instruments by which our workers would rightly resist the debasement of their living standards.

It is difficult to understand why those who are not willing that we spend a comparatively small sum in aid of the nations which are resisting totalitarianism are quite willing that we spend many more billions preparing for the eventuality of facing the totalitarian powers alone. It is difficult to understand because first of all our defense would require many more billions than now contemplated; secondly it might prove ineffective, no matter what the cost; and finally we would be strongly tempted by the very enormity of the cost to write off our present expenditures and decide to come to terms with the Nazis. The forces in our national life which even now counsel such a course would certainly become more formidable and bolder. It is difficult not to be a defeatist, when one envisages the enormity of the task which would confront us and remembers that the very victory of the Nazis would rob us of some of the moral and spiritual resources which we still possess in our will to resist.

Beyond the problem of our national interest is the larger problem of the very quality of our civilization, with its historic liberties and standards of justice, which the Nazis are sworn to destroy. No nation can be unmindful of its obligations to a civilization of which it is a part, even though no nation is able to think of these obligations in terms disassociated from its national interest. If we should define the present struggle in Europe as merely a clash between rival imperialisms, it would merely mean that a strange combination of cynicism and abstract idealism had so corrupted the commonsense moral insights of a people that we could no longer distinguish between right and wrong. History never presents us with choices of pure good against pure evil. But the Nazis have achieved something which is so close to the very negation

4 Reinhold Niebuhr, noted theologian, author, and internationalist.

of justice that if we cannot recognize it and react to it with a decent sense of moral indignation, we would prove ourselves incapable of preserving the heritage of our western culture. Fortunately the various tests of public opinion prove that the common people have not lost this moral capacity, however much some intellectuals and religious idealists may be confused.

The Nazis have declared their intention of annihilating the Jewish race. This maniacal fury against a great race goes beyond anything previously known in the category of race prejudice. They have also declared their intention of subordinating the other nations of Europe to the dominion of a master race. In the case of Poland and Czechoslovakia their policy goes to the length of systematically destroying the whole fabric of the national life of these unhappy nations so that, were the Nazis to control Europe only for a decade, they would destroy some of these nations beyond hope of reconstruction. Other subordinate nations would fare slightly better, if they allowed themselves to be used as compliant instruments of Nazi tyranny.

Nor ought we forget that the Nazis are intent upon destroying the religious and cultural heritages of western Christendom, that they have debased all culture so that truth has been made a prostitute of power, and that violation of solemn undertakings, corruption of leaders in subordinate nations and every strategy in the arsenal of deception has been combined by them with a strategy of cruelty and terror in a new and terrible total policy of tyrannical imperialism. Should they succeed it might be impossible to rescue the western world for decades from a cruel dominion which maintained itself by a monopoly of violence for war and a monopoly of technical skills for peacetime.

In resisting such a tyranny we are fortunate that we still have the possibility of making our contribution in terms which are moderate compared with the cost in life and treasure which European nations must bear.

. . . A recurring motif of Greek tragedy is the tendency of men to become the prisoners of a fate which they try too desperately to avoid. These insights of Aeschylus and Sophocles have relevance for our own day. Nations which try to eliminate every risk of war with too great a caution may face the horror of war the more certainly. Indeed, there must be many nations in Europe today who have reason to meditate ruefully upon the futility of what may be termed hysterical caution.

Democracies must be vigilant of their liberties. But if they do not also trust themselves by trusting their leaders, so that they can match the speed of tyrannies, they may awake to discover that they have, as some anxious mothers have done, smothered what they highly prized by guarding it too frantically. . . .

The CHAIRMAN. Are there any questions? Senator Johnson.

Senator JOHNSON [5] of California. Is it your belief that the bill will keep us out of war?

Dr. NIEBUHR. I should hope so, Senator. I do not think that anybody could guarantee it. I should think the bill offers us a better opportunity to keep out of war than anything else I know.

---

5 Hiram Johnson, veteran California progressive, one of the "irreconcilables" in the fight against the League of Nations.

Senator JOHNSON of California. But, even if it did not have that effect, you would still be in favor of it, would you not?

Dr. NIEBUHR. Yes, I would. As I said in my statement, I believe one has to take some risks or involve one's self in even greater risks.

Senator JOHNSON of California. So that you would be willing to go into war with Hitler?

Dr. NIEBUHR. I would want to know what the circumstances and conditions are. I would rather cross that bridge when I came to it.

Senator JOHNSON of California. But it has no terrors for you at all?

Dr. NIEBUHR. Yes; it has. War has terrors for me.

Senator JOHNSON of California. Really? Really? I did not think so.

Dr. NIEBUHR. Well, I do not see how any human being could be without a terror of war. I think we all have to face this proposition, whether a war is the worst terror we can conceive, and I am frank to say that I am not certain that it is, and if I were certain that it was I do not see how I could assume any responsible attitude toward any political question, because there is no political question that does not have to face ultimately the problem of possibility of war, if we decide there are some things we want to maintain at all costs. . . .

Senator CLARK [6] of Missouri. Doctor, you are a man of the cloth—do you consider that your profession as a clergyman would prevent your entering into a war, about which you speak so complacently, if we were to have a war?

Dr. NIEBUHR. No; it does not, Senator. I do not believe in clerical exemption.

Senator CLARK of Missouri. I am very glad to hear you say that, in view of the fact you were speaking so very complacently about the United States engaging in war.

You were 25 years old when the last war started, were you not?

Dr. NIEBUHR. Yes.

Senator CLARK of Missouri. Where did you put in your time during the time that the United States was engaged in war?

Dr. NIEBUHR. I put my time in as chairman of the Wartime Commission of my denomination, working with soldiers in the camps.

Senator CLARK of Missouri. You were a minister during that time?

Dr. NIEBUHR. Yes, sir.

Senator CLARK of Missouri. You never wore the uniform of the United States during that period, did you?

Dr. NIEBUHR. I did not; no, sir.

Senator CLARK of Missouri. That is all.

. . . .

STATEMENT OF HON. FRANK KNOX.[7]

. . . I reiterate here my belief that the chief question that confronts us is whether we shall now take steps to keep Europe's wars in Europe, or shall drift along and permit those wars to be transferred to the Americas. We need time

6 Champ Clark, veteran Missouri Democrat.

7 Secretary of the Navy Frank Knox, an Illinois Republican and publisher of the Chicago *Daily News*.

to get ready to meet out at sea a strong, aggressive Germany, if we are to keep the fighting away from the lands of this hemisphere. You may remember that in my statement before the House committee I gave a comparative table of naval tonnage which might oppose us, both in the immediate future and over the next several years, if Britain does not survive Germany's attack. I would not have you draw the implication from my statement and from those figures that I fear that the United States will not fully realize in time the danger that confronts them. But they have no time to waste, and must act at once.

In public speeches I have warned the American people that if Britain is defeated, we ought then to be fully prepared to repel attempts by Germany to seize bases on this side of the Atlantic. Germany would use these bases either to attack us directly, or else first to establish herself solidly in South America. Many of our people and many of the speakers who have opposed giving ample aid to Great Britain apparently believe it fantastic to think that there is any real danger of invasion. I disagree with such people, and believe that a victorious Germany would move over to this hemisphere just as soon as she could accumulate the strength to do so, and certainly very soon unless we now take the steps to check her career of reckless aggression.

Admiral General Raeder, chief of the German Navy, recently made a speech to the shipyard workers in Bremen. The significant portion of his speech to the United States was a promise that after the war Germany would have—I quote—

A fleet developed and enlarged to a size befitting a world power, and overseas naval bases where there would be plenty of work of all kinds.

There can be little doubt as to German ambitions for world sea power in the event of victory.

The existence of the British Navy and a balance of power in Europe have operated to give us military security against aggressions from that region. For many years we actually have had the benefits of a two-ocean Navy, instead of only the one-ocean Navy that flies the American flag. The defeat of Great Britain would definitely carry with it the destruction of the British Fleet, or would transfer it to German hands to be used against us when Germany has trained German naval personnel to operate it.

Even were there no danger of invasion, and I may say that I believe building up our Navy and our Army in the way we are now doing will give us the means to defeat invasion, provided we have the time to complete our plans I repeat, even if there were no danger of invasion, I ask the committee whether they can face calmly the prospect of all of Europe completely dominated by the Hitler regime? The question to decide is, would we rather see Europe dominated by a democratic system, or would we rather see Europe dominated by a Hitler system? What would be our relative positions under those very different sets of circumstances? If the Hitler system is victorious, can any of us imagine that we can return freely to the ways of peace which we have known in the past? For my part, I believe that so long as the Hitler system endures we will be forced to maintain a tremendous Navy and a very large Army in order to continue any sort of national existence. I well realize the sacrifices that our people will have to make to maintain their liberties in such a world, and I believe that we should now do everything that we can do to keep the British Commonwealth of Nations from being overcome by this terrible new system of government that has arisen in Germany. For myself, I prefer to live in a world governed by a victorious democracy rather than by a victorious Hitler.

Suppose, contrary to my own view, we concentrate our full effort on building up our own ships, and troops, and aircraft, and stand aside and accept the chance of a complete German victory over Britain. As I understand their arguments, that is the course that the opponents of the lend-lease plan would have this Government pursue. I am ready to admit that we might be able to arm ourselves so heavily that it would become impossible for the Axis Powers to bring their military power directly against us across the seas and to defeat us here in our own territory. The costs of such armaments would be great, and they would bear very heavily upon our people. But let us admit, for the sake of the argument, that we could bear these burdens, and that we could build up the fleets and armies we would need to fend off a direct invasion: Would we, then, be safe from Axis attack?

I say that no, decidedly, we would not be safe. The Nazi method is plain to all, and it is to win by any means, direct or indirect. . . .

Senator NYE.[8] . . . do you still feel that there is a large action now for repeal of the Neutrality Act?

Secretary KNOX. I do. I have been against it from the start. I opposed it when it was proposed. I opposed it when it came up for revision. I was for its repeal then. I supported its amendment.

Senator NYE. You would repeal it, among other reasons, for a restoration of that alleged right that was ours as to freedom upon the high seas?

Secretary KNOX. Do you call freedom of the seas an alleged right?

Senator NYE. In wartime.

Secretary KNOX. You do?

Senator NYE. Yes.

Secretary KNOX. I do not. That is where you and I differ. We have gone to war for it, you know. There isn't anything anywhere in international law against it.

Senator NYE. We fought at least two wars in the name of "freedom of the seas."

Secretary KNOX. That is right. Do you disapprove of those wars? Do you think they were mistakes? Do you think those wars were mistakes?

Senator NYE. Do I hold that those wars were mistakes?

Secretary KNOX. To achieve the freedom of the seas?

Senator NYE. I am not testifying now.

Secretary KNOX. If they were good enough to fight for then they ought to be pretty good now.

8 Gerald P. Nye, Republican senator from North Dakota, who had chaired the famed munitions investigation, 1934–36, that contributed to the neutrality legislation of the 1930's.

Senator NYE. Having fought for it twice and not having it now——

Secretary KNOX. I should certainly repeal the Neutrality Act. And I know that it is within the powers of the President to keep our vessels out of the war zone, if he wants to. We do not need the Neutrality Act.

Senator NYE. Having gone to war for that cause and having failed twice, after having failed to win freedom of the seas, shall we do it again?

Secretary KNOX. We certainly ought to keep our freedom of the seas, yes. I do not admit that we failed twice. I admit that we won twice. The seas were free when we finished the last war on that subject.

Senator NYE. Mr. Secretary, supposing we were to go to war again in defense of the freedom of the seas——

Secretary KNOX. Perhaps we will have to some time.

Senator NYE [continuing]. What probability is there that we can ever have freedom of the seas mentioned in the peace agreements?

Secretary KNOX. You know, if the Nazis destroy the British Isles and with it the British Fleet, the next war we will be into will be for the freedom of the seas.

Senator NYE. I take it, from what you have testified to previously, that if we are in it by that time we are not going to have a Chinaman's chance, if I may use the expression.

But you do believe in our jealously preserving whatever may be our rights and so-called freedom of the seas?

Secretary KNOX. I do, with never a waiver. . . .

Senator NYE. How dangerous or how large is the chance of attack upon the United States in the event the worst should happen to Great Britain, Mr. Secretary?

Secretary KNOX. Well, that is all purely speculative. I do not know. I would hazard as my judgment that it would not come directly on us, anyway. It would come indirectly.

Senator NYE. I did not catch that.

Secretary KNOX. I said I would just hazard a guess that it would come indirectly rather than directly.

Senator NYE. In an economic way, perhaps?

Secretary KNOX. Beginning that way, south of us.

Senator NYE. I shall come back to that again, but, for the purpose of the record now, may I call your attention to a statement appearing in the New York *Times* of September 4, 1940, which reports a statement of September 3 issued by you at Salt Lake City. [Reading:]

Navy base exchange rare and unusual transaction. United States would gain bases from which observation planes would operate in a 500-mile radius, thus making it "impossible for a surprise attack on America."

Now, assuming, Mr. Secretary, that we are going to have time to fortify these new bases that we have access to, do you feel we would have accomplished a complete protection against a surprise attack against America?

Secretary KNOX. Against surprise, yes.

Senator NYE. Against a surprise attack?

Secretary Knox. On North America.

Senator Nye. Well, your quotation, as you were quoted, said America. I was about to ask you whether you meant to include South America and Central America.

Secretary Knox. No; North America. These bases protect us against an approach against the North American coast.

Senator Nye. On May 12, 1940, a Chicago *Daily News* editorial spoke as follows:

> In the way of preventive measures there is no longer much we can do in Europe beyond what we are doing in facilitating the sale of supplies to the Allies.

You have altered your opinion in that regard, have you?

Secretary Knox. No, not necessarily; only in the mode by which the supplies are transferred. All of us assumed at that time that the British resources would be available to pay for the supplies they were getting as they were at that time. Then we were confronted with a new situation when we discovered that they had run out of dollar exchange and had to have some help in some other way. Hence this bill.

Senator Nye. Mr. Secretary, did you have any hand whatever in the drafting of this lend-lease bill?

Secretary Knox. I saw it before it was introduced, but I did not handle the drafting.

Senator Nye. Did anybody in the Navy Department have any hand in it?

Secretary Knox. No.

Senator Nye. Were you consulted as concerns its purposes?

Secretary Knox. Yes.

Senator Nye. As you have testified, the bill is presented, of course, because of what is considered a very serious emergency?

Secretary Knox. Correct.

Senator Nye. You do feel that the emergency is very serious?

Secretary Knox. Very.

Senator Nye. I could not be other than so impressed from listening to your testimony, Mr. Secretary.

Might it be, Mr. Secretary, that we have magnified or had magnified for the benefit of our minds, whatever the emergency might be to the end that there might be expedition of certain legislation?

Secretary Knox. Well, I can easily understand how men occupying the position that you do would feel that. I do not think so.

Senator Nye. You have felt, have you not, that it has often been true that emergencies have been created in the interest of accomplishing some purpose that was rather indirect?

Secretary Knox. Yes; on both sides.

Senator Nye. On both sides. You have known times when you felt very strongly that the so-called drums of emergency were being beaten to the end that there could be larger powers accomplished for an executive, have you not?

Secretary Knox. Not in this emergency; no, sir.

Senator Nye. Not in this emergency?

Secretary KNOX. I feel very deeply that this is a real one. It is impossible to exaggerate its gravity.

Senator NYE. I am quoting now.

It is a disturbing quality, but Mr. Roosevelt seems to delight in catching people off guard.

Secretary KNOX. When was this written?

Senator NYE. Just a moment [continuing reading]:

One technique is to beat the drums of emergency and try to force legislation "now"; the other technique is to slip something across quietly. The inevitable result is that he has engendered a feeling that he has to be watched—and watched continuously.

Does that have a familiar ring to it, Mr. Secretary?

Senator CONNALLY.[9] Mr. Chairman, I want to intervene. The Secretary asked when this was written, and the Senator declined to give him that information. I think that is an unfair method of interrogation. I want to insist that he be advised of the information he asked for.

Senator NYE. Very well. The publication of this particular statement was in 1938.

Secretary KNOX. I thought so.

Senator JOHNSON of California. Get an answer to your question.

Secretary KNOX. You know, Senator, I am not a bit ashamed of having been a Republican all my life. I am not ashamed of it now. But I am not functioning as a Republican now.

Senator NYE. Nor am I.

Secretary KNOX. Thanks. That is fine. I do not think any of us should.

Senator NYE. You do not feel that an emergency has been created and magnified to the end that there could be a hurrying and a speeding of this legislation that is pending at the present time?

Secretary KNOX. No, sir; and, on the contrary, I think we are awfully slow in meeting this crisis. Perfectly vital time right now is being lost. . . .

c] LINDBERGH CALLS FOR AMERICA FIRST

THERE ARE many viewpoints from which the issues of this war can be argued. Some are primarily idealistic. Some are primarily practical. One should, I believe, strive for a balance of both. But, since the issues that can be covered in a single address are limited, tonight I shall discuss the war from a viewpoint which is primarily practical. It is not that I believe ideals are unimportant, even among the realities of war; but if a nation is to survive in a hostile world, its ideals must be backed by the hard logic of military practicability. If the outcome of war depended upon ideals alone, this would be a different world than it is today.

9 Tom Connally, Democratic senator from Texas.

I know I will be severely criticized by the interventionists in America when I say we should not enter a war unless we have a reasonable chance of winning. That, they will claim, is far too materialistic a standpoint. They will advance again the same arguments that were used to persuade France to declare war against Germany in 1939. But I do not believe that our American ideals, and our way of life, will gain through an unsuccessful war. And I know that the United States is not prepared to wage war in Europe successfully at this time. We are no better prepared today than France was when the interventionists in Europe persuaded her to attack the Siegfried Line.

I have said before, and I will say again, that I believe it will be a tragedy to the entire world if the British Empire collapses. That is one of the main reasons why I opposed this war before it was declared, and why I have constantly advocated a negotiated peace. I did not feel that England and France had a reasonable chance of winning. France has now been defeated: and, despite the propaganda and confusion of recent months, it is now obvious that England is losing the war. I believe this is realized even by the British Government. But they have one last desperate plan remaining. They hope that they may be able to persuade us to send another American Expeditionary Force to Europe and to share with England militarily, as well as financially, the fiasco of this war.

I do not blame England for this hope, or for asking for our assistance. But we now know that she declared a war under circumstances which led to the defeat of every nation that sided with her from Poland to Greece. We know that in the desperation of war England promised to all these nations armed assistance that she could not send. We know that she misinformed them, as she has misinformed us, concerning her state of preparation, her military strength, and the progress of the war.

In time of war, truth is always replaced by propaganda. I do not believe we should be too quick to criticize the actions of a belligerent nation. There is always the question whether we, ourselves, would do better under similar circumstances. But we in this country have a right to think of the welfare of America first, just as the people in England thought first of their own country when they encouraged the smaller nations of Europe to fight against hopeless odds. When England asks us to enter this war, she is considering her own future, and that of her empire. In making our reply, I believe we should consider the future of the United States and that of the Western Hemisphere.

It is not only our right, but it is our obligation as American citizens to look at this war objectively and to weigh our chances for success if we should enter it. I have attempted to do this, especially from the standpoint of aviation; and I have been forced to the conclusion that we cannot win this war for England, regardless of how much assistance we send.

I ask you to look at the map of Europe today and see if you can suggest any way in which we could win this war if we entered it. Suppose we had a large army in America, trained and equipped. Where would we send it to fight? The campaigns of the war show only too clearly how difficult it is to force a landing, or to maintain an army, on a hostile coast.

Suppose we took our Navy from the Pacific, and used it to convoy British shipping. That would not win the war for England. It would, at best, permit her to exist under the constant bombing of the German air fleet. Suppose we had an air force that we could send to Europe. Where could it operate? Some of our squadrons might be based in the British Isles; but it is physically impossible to base enough aircraft in the British Isles alone to equal in strength the aircraft that can be based on the Continent of Europe.

I have asked these questions on the supposition that we had in existence an Army and an air force large enough and well enough equipped to send to Europe; and that we would dare to remove our Navy from the Pacific. Even on this basis, I do not see how we could invade the Continent of Europe successfully as long as all of that Continent and most of Asia is under Axis domination. But the fact is that none of these suppositions are correct. We have only a one-ocean Navy. Our Army is still untrained and inadequately equipped for foreign war. Our air force is deplorably lacking in modern fighting planes because most of them have already been sent to Europe.

When these facts are cited, the interventionists shout that we are defeatists, that we are undermining the principles of democracy, and that we are giving comfort to Germany by talking about our military weakness. But everything I mention here has been published in our newspapers, and in the reports of congressional hearings in Washington. Our military position is well known to the governments of Europe and Asia. Why, then, should it not be brought to the attention of our own people?

I say it is the interventionist in America, as it was in England and in France, who gives comfort to the enemy. I say it is they who are undermining the principles of democracy when they demand that we take a course to which more than 80 per cent of our citizens are opposed. I charge them with being the real defeatists, for their policy has led to the defeat of every country that followed their advice since the war began. There is no better way to give comfort to an enemy than to divide the people of a nation over the issue of foreign war. There is no shorter road to defeat than by entering a war with inadequate preparation. Every nation that has adopted the interventionist policy of depending on some one else for its own defense has met with nothing but defeat and failure.

When history is written, the responsibility for the downfall of the democracies of Europe will rest squarely upon the shoulders of the interventionists who led their nations into war uninformed and unprepared. With their shouts of defeatism, and their disdain of reality, they have already sent countless thousands of young men to death in Europe. From the campaign of Poland to that of Greece, their prophecies have been false and their polices have failed. Yet these are the people who are calling us defeatists in America today. And they have led this country, too, to the verge of war.

There are many such interventionists in America, but there are more people among us of a different type. That is why you and I are assembled here tonight. There is a policy open to this nation that will lead to success—a policy that leaves us free to follow our own way of life, and to develop our own civilization. It is not a new and untried idea. It was advocated by Washington.

It was incorporated in the Monroe Doctrine. Under its guidance, the United States has become the greatest nation in all the world.

It is based upon the belief that the security of a nation lies in the strength and character of its own people. It recommends the maintenance of armed forces sufficient to defend this hemisphere from attack by any combination of foreign powers. It demands faith in an independent American destiny. This is the policy of the America First Committee today. It is a policy not of isolation, but of independence; not of defeat, but of courage. It is a policy that led this nation to success during the most trying years of our history, and it is a policy that will lead us to success again.

We have weakened ourselves for many months, and still worse, we have divided our own people by this dabbling in Europe's wars. While we should have been concentrating on American defense we have been forced to argue over foreign quarrels. We must turn our eyes and our faith back to our own country before it is too late. And when we do this, a different vista opens before us. Practically every difficulty we would face in invading Europe becomes an asset to us in defending America. Our enemy, and not we, would then have the problem of transporting millions of troops across the ocean and landing them on a hostile shore. They, and not we, would have to furnish the convoys to transport guns and trucks and munitions and fuel across three thousand miles of water. Our battleships and our submarines would then be fighting close to their home bases. We would then do the bombing from the air and the torpedoing at sea. And if any part of an enemy convoy should ever pass our navy and our air force, they would still be faced with the guns of our coast artillery and behind them the divisions of our Army.

The United States is better situated from a military standpoint than any other nation in the world. Even in our present condition of unpreparedness no foreign power is in a position to invade us today. If we concentrate on our own defenses and build the strength that this nation should maintain, no foreign army will ever attempt to land on American shores.

War is not inevitable for this country. Such a claim is defeatism in the true sense. No one can make us fight abroad unless we ourselves are willing to do so. No one will attempt to fight us here if we arm ourselves as a great nation should be armed. Over a hundred million people in this nation are opposed to entering the war. If the principles of democracy mean anything at all, that is reason enough for us to stay out. If we are forced into a war against the wishes of an overwhelming majority of our people, we will have proved democracy such a failure at home that there will be little use fighting for it abroad.

The time has come when those of us who believe in an independent American destiny must band together and organize for strength. We have been led toward war by a minority of our people. This minority has power. It has influence. It has a loud voice. But it does not represent the American people. During the last several years I have traveled over this country from one end to the other. I have talked to many hundreds of men and women, and I have letters from tens of thousands more, who feel the same way as you and I.

Most of these people have no influence or power. Most of them have no means of expressing their convictions, except by their vote which has always been against this war. They are the citizens who have had to work too hard at their daily jobs to organize political meetings. Hitherto, they have relied upon their vote to express their feelings; but now they find that it is hardly remembered except in the oratory of a political campaign. These people—the majority of hardworking American citizens, are with us. They are the true strength of our country. And they are beginning to realize, as you and I, that there are times when we must sacrifice our normal interests in life in order to insure the safety and the welfare of our nation.

Such a time has come. Such a crisis is here. That is why the America First Committee has been formed—to give voice to the people who have no newspaper, or newsreel, or radio station at their command, to give voice to the people who must do the paying, and the fighting, and the dying if this country enters the war.

Whether or not we do enter the war rests upon the shoulders of you in this audience, upon us here on this platform, upon meetings of this kind that are being held by Americans in every section of the United States today. It depends upon the action we take, and the courage we show at this time. If you believe in an independent destiny for America, if you believe that this country should not enter the war in Europe, we ask you to join the America First Committee in its stand. We ask you to share our faith in the ability of this nation to defend itself, to develop its own civilization, and to contribute to the progress of mankind in a more constructive and intelligent way than has yet been found by the warring nations of Europe. We need your support, and we need it now. The time to act is here. I thank you.

3] Presidential Leadership Toward Further Intervention

In the spring and summer of 1941, the United States became increasingly committed to the giving of aid to the Allies and to helping to move that aid through the Nazi blockade. Every one of President Roosevelt's steps set off bursts of opposition. Skillfully using his press conferences as a means of shaping public opinion, the President was often at his most engaging—and most annoying—in his semiweekly encounters with the press. He was forthright in denouncing "business as usual" attitudes and war profiteering in American industry, but he was less than candid in speaking to the American public of the risks that were being run in the Atlantic by the gradual exten sion of a system of hemispheric patrol into virtually a system of convoy to Britain. Late in the summer of 1941, after the Nazi invasion of the Soviet Union, the President met with Prime Minister Churchill at sea, and together they issued the Atlantic Charter. The Charter, widely endorsed by anti-Axis nations, proclaimed no radical, new war aims. In many respects, it was a restatement of what had been put before the previous generation in Wilson's Fourteen Points. But the conferences on board British and American men-of-war was a brilliant example of the President's ability to dramatize his leadership and to supplement the "propaganda of the word" with the "propaganda of the deed." Public opinion charts show how events more than speeches influenced support in the United States for interventionist actions.*

A] ROOSEVELT SPARS WITH THE PRESS: PRESS CONFERENCE, APRIL 25, 1941

The PRESIDENT: Steve [Early] says there isn't anything—any formality, or anything to talk about today.

Q. Mr. President, three strong speeches were made yesterday by three Cabinet officers—

The PRESIDENT: (*interposing*) Three?

Q. Yes, Secretary Hull, Secretary Knox, and Secretary Wickard.

The PRESIDENT: Oh, is that so?

Q. (*continuing*) About possible advances in foreign policy, and greater aid and more initiative, etc. Would you comment, sir, on this?

The PRESIDENT: I think they speak for themselves pretty clearly and for the great majority of the American people.

Q. And also for you, sir?

The PRESIDENT: Yes, yes.

Q. Mr. President, the newspapers this morning generally seem to regard these speeches as indicating that it may soon be necessary to resort to an extended use of the Navy in protecting the "bridge of ships." Would you consider that a fair interpretation of the speeches?

The PRESIDENT: I don't think that we had better talk about interpretations. I think we had better confine ourselves to facts, and I am sorry, but I have to make a liar out of a lot of people—some of them in this room. What—I will tell you how.

In September, 1939, about a year and a half ago, the whole subject of hemisphere defense came up, as we know. And at that time, because of the conditions surrounding the outbreak of the war—in other words, a complete failure to adhere to international law, a surprise invasion, which was followed by other surprise attacks on peaceful Nations—at that time there was instituted by the Western Hemisphere what is known as a *patrol,* and that patrol extended on all sides of the hemisphere as necessary at the time. Of course, nobody here knows geography. People said it was 300 miles off-shore. It wasn't. It was a patrol that was carried out partly by the American Navy, partly by other American ships, off what was then considered a reasonable limit, depending on where it was. A lot of very careless people called it 300 miles. If you went over to the eastern shore of Maryland, you would have found for the past year and a half that that patrol was extended a thousand miles out to sea at that point. It was maintained as a patrol for such distances as seemed advisable, in view of the conditions at the time. That patrol has been extended

---

* PRESIDENTIAL LEADERSHIP TOWARD FURTHER INTERVENTION: From Samuel I. Rosenman, ed., *The Public Papers and Addresses of Franklin D. Roosevelt: The Call to Battle Stations* (New York, 1950), pp. 132–38; *Ibid.,* pp. 175–80; *Ibid.,* pp. 314–15; *Ibid.,* pp. 337–41. Reprinted by permission of Harper & Bros.

from time to time in different places. Some places it has been pulled in, depending entirely on the conditions and the locations on any given duty. That was a patrol. It was not a convoy.

I think some of you know what a horse looks like. I think you also know what a cow looks like. If, by calling a cow a horse for a year and a half, you think that that makes the cow a horse, I don't think so. Now, that's pretty plain language. You can't turn a cow into a horse by calling it something else; calling it a horse it is still a cow. Now this is a patrol, and has been a patrol for a year and a half, still is, and from time to time it has been extended, and is being extended, and will be extended—the patrol—for the safety of the Western Hemisphere.

Q. Could you tell us, sir, how far it may possibly go?

The PRESIDENT: That is exactly the question I hoped you would ask. As far on the waters of the seven seas as may be necessary for the defense of the American hemisphere.

Q. Mr. President—

Q. (interposing) Will there be any extension of its functions?

The PRESIDENT: No, no.

Q. Could you define its functions?

The PRESIDENT: Its function is protection of the American hemisphere.

Q. By belligerent means?

The PRESIDENT: Protection of the American hemisphere.

Q. Mr. President, does that include the protection of shipping, that is—

The PRESIDENT: (interposing) Protection of the American hemisphere.

Q. Mr. President, just what—

The PRESIDENT: (interposing) Now you can't—. Just what? What do you mean, just what? [No answer] The point of it is the protection of the American hemisphere, and will be so used as it has been for the past year and a half. Now I can't tell you what is going to happen.

Q. Mr. President, can you tell us the difference between a patrol and a convoy?

The PRESIDENT: You know the difference between a cow and a horse?

Q. Yes, I know the difference.

The PRESIDENT: All right, there is just as much difference. Just exactly as much difference.

Q. Is there more patrolling against—

The PRESIDENT: The point is the protection of the merchant convoy—the escorting of merchant ships in a group to prevent an act of aggression against that group of merchant ships under escort. A patrol is a reconnaissance—I think that is the word—of certain areas of ocean to find out whether there is any possibly aggressive ship within that area, or areas, or the whole of the ocean, which might be coming toward the Western Hemisphere, or into the Western Hemisphere.

Now one thing that will occur to you as being, just as you say, a rule of common sense—back there in 1939 the area of the patrol on the Atlantic was nearer, because there didn't seem to be any danger of an attack on places like Bermuda or Newfoundland, or Greenland, or Trinidad, or Brazil. The events, however, in the later period of the war show that such attack is more possible today than it was then. We have, incidentally, some rather valuable American lives and American property at various points that we didn't have in 1939. Again Greenland, Newfoundland, Bermuda, Newfoundland, Bermuda, and the obligation that we have under the Monroe Doctrine for the protection of Canada against any other non-American Nation. That's old stuff. Then you have got other islands, the Bahamas, Antigua, and all the West Indies, Trinidad, British Guiana, which were not an American possession a year and a half ago. Today they are. Those bases, those points—

Q. (interposing) Mr. President—

The PRESIDENT: *(continuing)* It's a little bit like what I was talking about to one of the Senators over the telephone today. He happened to come from the West, and it's rather a good simile. In the old days a wagon train across the plains—of course it had its immediate guard around it, that was perfectly true—but it didn't go—it didn't move across the plains unless it got reports from a long ways—200 to 300 miles off. It was not felt safe to wait until the Indians got two miles away before you saw them. It was advisable, if possible, to find out if the Indians were 200 miles away.

Q. Mr. President—

The PRESIDENT: *(interposing)* I think the simile probably is a useful one.

Q. Mr. President, if this patrol should discover some apparently aggressive ships headed toward the Western Hemisphere, what would it do about it?

The PRESIDENT: Let me know. (*Loud laughter*)

Q. Mr. President, has this Government any idea of escorting convoys?

The PRESIDENT: No, no, and that, I am afraid, will be awfully bad news to some of you.

Q. Is there any better plan?

The PRESIDENT: What?

Q. Has it any better system?

The PRESIDENT: Well, you remember Mr. Bairnsfather. [English cartoonist in World War I, whose celebrated character Old Bill said to his worried friend in a shell-hole, "If you know a better 'ole, go to it."]

Q. Mr. President, to some of us who read those speeches of the Cabinet officers, they seem to be concerned about the delivery of aid to Britain. How does this tie in with that?

The PRESIDENT: I don't know, it's a new one on me. . . .

Q. Mr. Secretary, could you tell us—(*Loud laughter*) could you tell us whether these patrol ships have any instructions as to the action they should take, in the event there was an attack in nearby—

The PRESIDENT: *(interposing)* I can't tell you where they are because the next question would be just where are they, and just where are they going tomorrow. You see?

Q. Mr. President, does this extension of patrol involve any revision of the so-called Pan-American Security Zone?

The PRESIDENT: No, no.

Q. No connection?

The PRESIDENT: No.

Q. Mr. President, are we doing anything special, with any—

The PRESIDENT: (*interposing*) Just an extension. After all, it's just what has been going on for a year and a half. Now, that will answer all your questions. . . .

CONSTANTINE BROWN: Mr. President, last week you said that people in this country are not quite aware of the gravity of the situation. Would you care to amplify that a little bit?

The PRESIDENT: I don't think so, Constantine, without some further thought about it beforehand. Perhaps I could put it as one little thought to throw out.

There are people in this country, I am sorry to say I can't recognize any faces here, but some in this room—who are adopting a rather curious attitude, which I should say hadn't been thought through. These people say out of one side of the mouth, "No, I don't like it, I don't like dictatorship," and then out of the other side of the mouth, "Well, it's going to beat democracy, it's going to defeat democracy, therefore I might just as well accept it." Now, I don't call that good Americanism. I am not mentioning any names but that attitude is held by a minority in this country. It's just the same way—I read an editorial on Monday, or something like that the other day—which said in effect, Why, we have always had conquerors all through the history of the world, and Alexander the Great who tried to conquer all the known world, he was not satisfied to stay at home—where was it, Macedonia?—he went out and tried to conquer lots of people he never saw before, just to add to his empire. He was not satisfied with his own people, his own flesh and blood.

And there was another fellow called Caesar. He was not satisfied with the Rome of his day, and went out to conquer the whole of Europe and North Africa, and the Near East, and so forth and so on. And then there were, according to this mentality—there were two other conquerors—one was Cromwell, who conquered England, and the other one was George Washington, who conquered America. (*Laughter*) Now, any mentality that lumps George Washington and Cromwell with Caesar and Napoleon—oh, yes, Napoleon—Napoleon and Alexander the Great—well, all I can say is I am awfully sorry that people with those mentalities are in such high places that they can write or talk at all. It's just dumb.

Now, coming back to this mythical person in our midst who takes the attitude that dictatorships are going to win anyway, I think that is almost equally dumb, because I am "agin" them, and everybody else in this country—the overwhelming majority are "agin" them. We will fight for the democratic process, and that's all. We are willing to fight for the democratic process. I don't want to lie down and say, "Dictatorship is inevitable. We have got to do the best we can. We have got to make our peace. We have got to yield to the demands of the dictatorship because it has the military might to win." I don't think along those lines, and neither do you. . . .

If you go back to the roster of the Army in the Civil War—we called on people there from liberty-loving people on both sides—both the Confederates and the North; and from outside this country we had people fighting for us because they believed in it. On the other hand, the Confederacy and the North let certain people go. In other words, in both armies there were—what shall

I call them?—there were Vallandighams [Ohio's Clement L. Vallandigham, leader of the "Copperheads" in the Civil War].

Well, Vallandigham, as you know, was an appeaser. He wanted to make peace from 1863 on because the North "couldn't win." Once upon a time there was a place called Valley Forge and there were an awful lot of appeasers that pleaded with Washington to quit, because he "couldn't win." Just because he "couldn't win." See what Tom Paine said at that time in favor of Washington keeping on fighting!

Q. Yes.

The PRESIDENT: It's worth reading.

Q. Wasn't it, "These are the times that try men's souls?"

The PRESIDENT: Yes, that particular paragraph. . . .

B] ROOSEVELT DENOUNCES "BUSINESS AS USUAL": PRESS CONFERENCE, MAY 23, 1941

(This press conference was held especially for editors of business magazines and papers.)

Mr. WOOTON [Mr. Paul Wooton, President of National Conference of Business Paper Editors]: Mr. President, I thought that since you have this group here, and behind these men are several hundred thousands of readers, that you might like to say just the sort of editorial they could write, or what kind of an article they might run, that would be most helpful in forwarding the defense program. They are all anxious to do something constructive, and they go to the key men in industry in the papers, and if you have any thought at all that would be helpful along that line, I know they would appreciate it.

The PRESIDENT: I think you can't overstress the seriousness of the present situation. I think it does need stressing, because we all know that this world situation, if it goes the wrong way—the Axis powers win—it is going to hit business far more than any one thing that has ever hit them. It will hit them far worse than a mere ending of all of these emergency orders, because it will mean that you will get "put in a vise," not by our own volition, or the volition of all the democratic Nations that have an economy that is somewhat similar to ours. We will get "put in a vise," a "strait jacket," by the Axis powers; and I don't think that the seriousness of that situation can be overestimated. I think it ought to be played up all the time. And furthermore, that if we are going to meet the situation as it develops, and as it is becoming increasingly serious, that we have got to quit all this silly business of "business as usual." The Nations that are actually at war certainly are not conducting "business as usual," and the more we help to defeat the control of the world by dictatorships, the less "business as usual" we are going to have.

It means giving up, of course, on the part of the American public, and therefore of the manufacturers of the country—the businessmen of the country—a great many things which were all very nice and pleasant in our normal lives, and substitute for them the things that are necessary to carry on this aid to the democracies that we are giving at the present time.

Well, it is going to hit a lot of people, sure, but you can't eat your cake and have it too. That is the message to give to the American people: "You can't eat your cake and have it too." If you do one thing you have got to go all out for it. If you are going to do the other thing—lie down and take it on the chin—it will be putting us in a strait jacket that we won't get out of for one hundred years. I think that should be told quite frankly to the public.

After all, the country *can* get on without a great many things that it uses normally. Is it worth while to give up certain things in order to carry through an effort to survive, or isn't it? We know that there is a very great lack of understanding at the present time of the seriousness of the world situation as it affects us. You take, for example, a great deal of this perfectly well-intended publicity has been stupid. I begged them when they started the so-called Aid to Britain movement—I said, "You know there are an awful lot of people in this country that don't personally 'give a continental' about Aid to Britain, but on the other hand, if you tell the whole sentence you get people to understand."

What is the whole sentence? "America First Through Aid to Britain." Now that's a very different thing; that tells the truth. You are working for America first, because England today is holding the line and is doing practically all the fighting. Now the real sentence is, "Let us keep America going by giving aid to Britain while we are arming ourselves," and that is the thought to get across. And I think you can all help tremendously to make people realize the seriousness of the situation, and eliminate a lot of the perfectly silly prejudices that exist today because of wrong slogans—literally, the wrong slogans.

I suppose, for example, that if there is any person in the United States who happens to be the leader of the America First movement, it is the unfortunate fellow who happens to have the responsibility—who happens to be President of the United States. He is the leader of the America First movement. Now these other fellows jumped, and nobody's printed the fact that they have grabbed off something that does not belong to them. . . .

Well I think—I think that, taking it by and large, business as a whole is going along awfully well in this whole thing, and we are having very, very few complaints.

I was talking the other day to one of those people who had been largely responsible for the great effort of 1917 and 1918, and there were three of the fairly top people who were running the war production of the country, which began, mind you, not until the day we got into the war in 1917. There had been a certain amount done in the way of orders from the British and the French before we got into the war, but the great volume of orders came after we got into the war with no preparation for it. To these three people I asked the straight question: "How does the speed of our present production effort, on a relative basis, compare with the speed from the sixth of April, 1917, to the sixth of April, 1918?" And all three of them—although they are not in this year responsible for this production as they were then—all three of them said, "You are way ahead of what had been done in the first year of the World

War." I said, "How far?" They agreed about three months ahead in the first twelve months of effort. Well, now, that is quite a record to have that admitted by three fellows who were responsible for the 1917 effort.

Mr. Wooton: It certainly is.

The President: I think that is a pretty good compliment to pay to American business. I really do.

Mr. Wooton: And that is the text of these editorials that industry by and large is doing—

The President: (*interposing*) Yes.

Mr. Wooton:—a breath-taking job.

The President: That's right. . . .

c] Roosevelt and Churchill Issue the Atlantic Charter, August 14, 1941

The President of the United States and the Prime Minister, Mr. Churchill, representing His Majesty's Government in the United Kingdom, have met at sea.

They have been accompanied by officials of their two Governments, including high-ranking officers of their military, naval, and air services.

The whole problem of the supply of munitions of war, as provided by the Lend-Lease Act, for the armed forces of the United States and for those countries actively engaged in resisting aggression has been further examined.

Lord Beaverbrook, the Minister of Supply of the British Government, has joined in these conferences. He is going to proceed to Washington to discuss further details with appropriate officials of the United States Government. These conferences will also cover the supply problems of the Soviet Union.

The President and the Prime Minister have had several conferences. They have considered the danger to world civilization arising from the policies of military domination by conquest upon which the Hitlerite Government of Germany and other Governments associated therewith have embarked, and have made clear the steps which their countries are respectively taking for their safety in the face of these dangers.

They have agreed upon the following joint declaration:

The President of the United States of America and the Prime Minister, Mr. Churchill, representing His Majesty's Government in the United Kingdom, being met together, deem it right to make known certain common principles in the national policies of their respective countries on which they base their hopes for a better future of the world.

First, their countries seek no aggrandizement, territorial or other;

Second, they desire to see no territorial changes that do not accord with the freely expressed wishes of the peoples concerned;

Third, they respect the right of all peoples to choose the form of government under which they will live; and they wish to see sovereign rights and self-government restored to those who have been forcibly deprived of them;

Fourth, they will endeavor, with due respect for their existing obligations, to further the enjoyment by all states, great or small, victor or vanquished, of access, on equal terms, to the trade and to the raw materials of the world which are needed for their economic prosperity;

Fifth, they desire to bring about the fullest collaboration between all Nations in the economic field with the object of securing, for all, improved labor standards, economic advancement, and social security;

Sixth, after the final destruction of the Nazi tyranny, they hope to see established a peace which will afford to all Nations the means of dwelling in safety within their own boundaries, and which will afford assurance that all the men in all the lands may live out their lives in freedom from fear and want;

Seventh, such a peace should enable all men to traverse the high seas and oceans without hindrance;

Eighth, they believe that all of the Nations of the world, for realistic as well as spiritual reasons, must come to the abandonment of the use of force. Since no future peace can be maintained if land, sea, or air armaments continue to be employed by Nations which threaten, or may threaten, aggression outside of their frontiers, they believe, pending the establishment of a wider and more permanent system of general security, that the disarmament of such Nations is essential. They will likewise aid and encourage all other practicable measures which will lighten for peace-loving peoples the crushing burden of armaments.

d] ROOSEVELT ANSWERS SOME CRITICS: PRESS CONFERENCE, AUGUST 22, 1941

Q. Good morning, Mr. President.

The PRESIDENT: Good morning. How is everybody? . . . I don't think there is any news.

Oh yes there is too. I entirely forgot. I heard about and read that speech by Senator Byrd, giving figures on defense production, and I sent it to the War Department to ask for a check on the figures, and the War Department said that most unfortunately all of the figures, except on planes, are completely inaccurate, and somebody—unfortunately—has misled the Senator. But the War Department for obvious reasons can't give out the exact figures, but they gave me certain illustrations on things that they said it's all right to make public, which illustrations are examples of all of the other cases—of figures to use, except airplanes.

The Senator said that not a single tank had gone to England. Actually, we have turned over to the British hundreds of tanks of modern design produced during the last year. Some of these tanks, as we all know, are in Egypt, and the papers have had various stories on the excellence of their performance. They are with the British in Egypt.

In the case of anti-aircraft guns, the Senator said the program provides for an average monthly delivery of only four 90-mm. guns a month during the balance of this year. The program actually calls for a monthly delivery of 61 for the four remaining months of this year, and the War Department believes that they will be met. In other words, there is a certain difference between the figure 4 and the figure 61.

And another example is the 37-mm. anti-tank gun. The Senator said that these guns will be produced only at the rate of 15 a month. Actual production in July was 72. August production will be 160, September 260, and October 320.

Q. What was the Senator's figure on that, sir?

The PRESIDENT: Fifteen. There seems to be a certain discrepancy between the figure 15 and the figures that I have just given. Even if you add a zero to 15 you would still be way below the actual numbers. Fourth, the Senator said that only fifteen 81-mm. mortars will be produced in the immediate months ahead. In July there were actually, instead of 15, there were 221 produced, and in August the figure is 340.

Q. Excuse me, Mr. President, what type of gun was that?

The PRESIDENT: Eighty-one-mm. mortar—now you know as much as I do— and the figures for September and October will be even larger than 340, so there would seem to be somewhat of a difference between the figure 15 and the figure 340. The figures, of course, on the airplanes, are substantially correct, except that he said that the production of military planes progressively declined in the months of June and July, which is not strictly true. The number of training planes increased and the others remained steady—the military planes, because there were certain changes in design, and the testing of the new design to meet lessons that were learned this spring. . . . But the fact that remains—that statement as a whole in every single item, except planes, was full of discrepancies that ran just as high as those discrepancies which the War Department says it's all right to mention. . . .

Q. Mr. President, Congressman Fish and Dr. MacCracken of Vassar both addressed recent American First rallies, and Fish has pointed out—has gotten to the point now where he was quoted as saying that if Germany should lose, why America—America would suffer through loss of markets and buying power.

The PRESIDENT: If Germany loses?

Q. Yes.

The PRESIDENT: So, he thinks we wouldn't lose if Germany won. (*He laughs*) I don't think any comment that could be printed is necessary.

Q. Of course, Dr. MacCracken has taken the point of view that—

The PRESIDENT: (*interposing*) You know, once upon a time there was a fellow—this you might use only as background—there was a fellow who had a great deal more information and was a much more reasoning person than any of the people—I won't say Fish or MacCracken—it's obvious whom I am talking about. His name is Senator Borah—in many ways a very great statesman, and certainly with experience and information that was far better than most of the speakers. And he was the gentleman who in July, 1939—the famous conference upstairs—after the Secretary of State, who had still more information than he had, said that, "From our information we really believed regretfully that a war would break out that year," turned to the Secretary of State and said, "I am sorry, Mr. Secretary, my information is better than yours. There will be no war this year." And yet he had been on the Foreign Relations

Committee and everything else, and had been there for years and years—nearly forty years. In the Senate he certainly had far more information than any of these people that are going around making speeches today; and of course his error has become a classic.

Q. Walter Lippmann says that these Senators—the Foreign Relations groups—are people that got us into trouble over a long period of years.

The PRESIDENT: Yes, and a good many other people have got us in trouble over a period of years.

Q. Mr. Fish is on the Foreign Affairs Committee of the House. Maybe that qualifies him to make a few errors.

The PRESIDENT: I think—off the record—that is probably correct. (*Laughter*) . . .

Q. Mr. President, have you heard directly from Mr. Stalin on the proposal of the three-party conference on [Lend-Lease] supplies?

The PRESIDENT: You have all the stuff.

Q. Have you got to the point yet, sir, of naming your commission?

The PRESIDENT: Not yet.

Q. How soon?

The PRESIDENT: I don't know. The time hasn't been set.

Q. Mr. President—

The PRESIDENT: (*continuing*) The State Department is taking it up all the time. . . .

Q. Mr. President, on this production matter, do you feel that over-all the production has been satisfactory from a military point of view?

The PRESIDENT: It has never been satisfactory.

Q. But it has not lagged behind the program?

The PRESIDENT: Behind estimates? In some things it is ahead of estimates, and some things behind. Of course, that is on the assumption always that the original estimates were right. There is always the human possibility that they were too low. And there is the possibility in some other cases that they were too high. But on the actual estimates the averages were up too. I don't think anybody has asked Mr. Knudsen in the last two or three months. I should think somebody ought to ask him. You remember he talked about airplanes and gave the figure of 85 percent of the estimates. Quite a long while ago. And what his present estimate is, I don't know, but pretty close to the estimate. The original estimate I think was 1,500 planes in—first of July, and they were up to 1,465 as I remember it at that time. That is a monthly production. . . .

E] PUBLIC OPINION ON AMERICAN POLICY AND
THE WAR *

[The charts that constitute this section follow on pages 448 and 449.]

* Reprinted by special permission from the copyrighted article by Hadley Cantril, "Opinion Trends in World War II: Some Guides to Interpretation," *Public Opinion Quarterly*, Volume 12, 1948, pages 36–37.

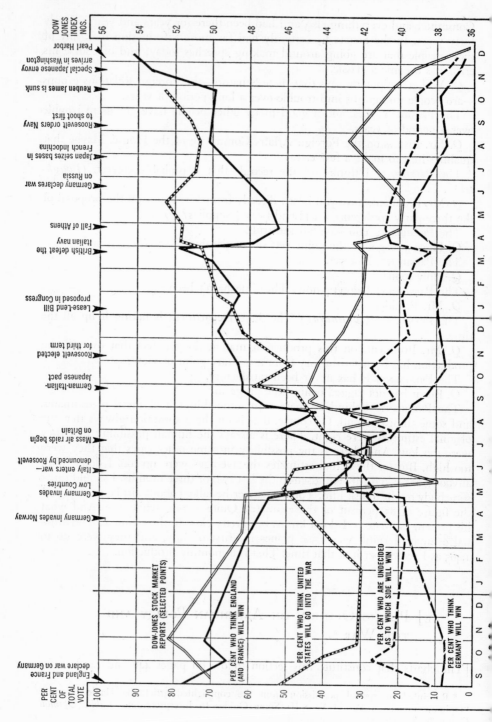

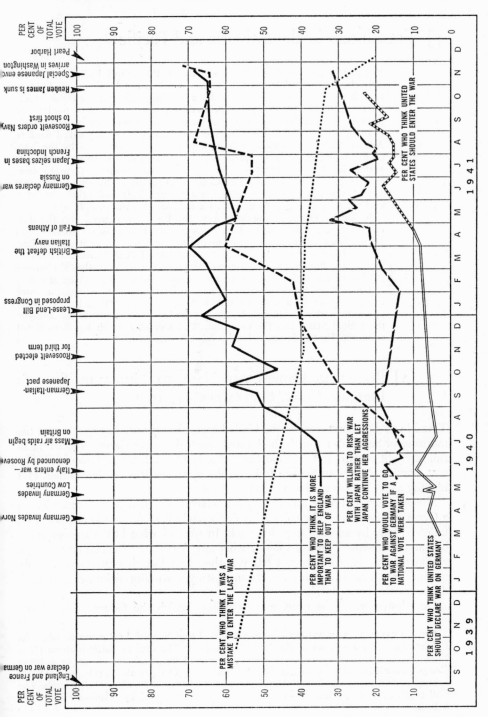

4] Encounters in the Atlantic and Pacific

With an increasing commitment to defend the British lifeline across the Atlantic, the United States was bound to risk armed conflict with German fleet units. Following the attack by a German submarine on the U.S.S. *Greer,* on September 4, 1941, the President, in a fireside chat, tried to explain to America his concept of the nation's traditional role in maintaining freedom of the seas. At this time the country was exposing a naked flank to Axis aggression, for American ships were unarmed, as required by the Neutrality Act of 1939. In October, 1941, he asked Congress to revise the act, authorizing the arming of merchant vessels and permitting them to carry their cargoes to belligerent ports. Congress complied in November, but only against vigorous opposition from Ohio Senator Taft and other anti-interventionists, who saw the measure as a final step on the road to war.

In the fall of 1941, Americans were also becoming alarmed over the drift of events across the Pacific. In a desperate effort to stave off conflict with Japan, Roosevelt made a personal appeal to the Emperor; but it was too late, for the Japanese fleet was already steaming toward Pearl Harbor. Within an hour of the President's call for a declaration of war on December 8, Congress passed the resolution. There were no desenting votes in the Senate and only one in the House. Three days later, on December 11, Germany declared itself as being in a state of war with the United States, and Congress promptly, without a dissenting vote, resolved that "the state of war between the United States and the Government of Germany which has been thrust upon the United States is hereby formally declared." *

A] Roosevelt Orders the Navy to "Shoot on Sight": Fireside Chat, September 11, 1941

The Navy Department of the United States has reported to me that on the morning of September fourth the United States destroyer *Greer,* proceeding in full daylight toward Iceland, had reached a point southeast of Greenland. She was carrying American mail to Iceland. She was flying the American flag. Her identity as an American ship was unmistakable.

She was then and there attacked by a submarine. Germany admits that it was a German submarine. The submarine deliberately fired a torpedo at the *Greer,* followed later by another torpedo attack. In spite of what Hitler's propaganda bureau has invented, and in spite of what any American obstructionist organization may prefer to believe, I tell you the blunt fact that the German submarine fired first upon this American destroyer without warning, and with deliberate design to sink her.

Our destroyer, at the time, was in waters which the Government of the

---

* ENCOUNTERS IN THE ATLANTIC AND PACIFIC: From Samuel I. Rosenman, ed., *The Public Papers and Addresses of Franklin D. Roosevelt: The Call to Battle Stations* (New York, 1950), pp. 384–92; *Ibid.,* pp. 406–11, reprinted by permission of Harper & Bros.; *Congressional Record,* 77 Cong., 1 Sess. (Washington, October 28, 1941), pp. 8278–84; Samuel I. Rosenman, ed., *The Public Papers and Addresses of Franklin D. Roosevelt: The Call to Battle Stations,* pp. 511–13; *Ibid.,* pp. 14–15, reprinted by permission of Harper & Bros.

United States had declared to be waters of self-defense—surrounding outposts of American protection in the Atlantic.

In the North of the Atlantic, outposts have been established by us in Iceland, in Greenland, in Labrador and in Newfoundland. Through these waters there pass many ships of many flags. They bear food and other supplies to civilians; and they bear matériel of war, for which the people of the United States are spending billions of dollars, and which, by Congressional action, they have declared to be essential for the defense of our own land.

The United States destroyer, when attacked, was proceeding on a legitimate mission.

If the destroyer was visible to the submarine when the torpedo was fired, then the attack was a deliberate attempt by the Nazis to sink a clearly identified American warship. On the other hand, if the submarine was beneath the surface of the sea and, with the aid of its listening devices, fired in the direction of the sound of the American destroyer without even taking the trouble to learn its identity—as the official German communiqué would indicate—then the attack was even more outrageous. For it indicates a policy of indiscriminate violence against any vessel sailing the seas—belligerent or non-belligerent.

This was piracy—piracy legally and morally. It was not the first nor the last act of piracy which the Nazi Government has committed against the American flag in this war. For attack has followed attack.

A few months ago an American flag merchant ship, the *Robin Moor,* was sunk by a Nazi submarine in the middle of the South Atlantic, under circumstances violating long-established international law and violating every principle of humanity. The passengers and the crew were forced into open boats hundreds of miles from land, in direct violation of international agreements signed by nearly all Nations including the Government of Germany. No apology, no allegation of mistake, no offer of reparations has come from the Nazi Government.

In July, 1941, an American battleship in North American waters was followed by a submarine which for a long time sought to maneuver itself into a position of attack. The periscope of the submarine was clearly seen. No British or American submarines were within hundreds of miles of this spot at the time, so the nationality of the submarine is clear.

Five days ago a United States Navy ship on patrol picked up three survivors of an American-owned ship operating under the flag of our sister Republic of Panama—the *S.S. Sessa.* On August seventeenth, she had been first torpedoed without warning, and then shelled, near Greenland, while carrying civilian supplies to Iceland. It is feared that the other members of her crew have been drowned. In view of the established presence of German submarines in this vicinity, there can be no reasonable doubt as to the identity of the flag of the attacker.

Five days ago, another United States merchant ship, the *Steel Seafarer,* was sunk by a German aircraft in the Red Sea two hundred and twenty miles south of Suez. She was bound for an Egyptian port.

So four of the vessels sunk or attacked flew the American flag and were clearly identifiable. Two of these ships were warships of the American Navy.

In the fifth case, the vessel sunk clearly carried the flag of our sister Republic of Panama.

In the face of all this, we Americans are keeping our feet on the ground. Our type of democratic civilization has outgrown the thought of feeling compelled to fight some other Nation by reason of any single piratical attack on one of our ships. We are not becoming hysterical or losing our sense of proportion. Therefore, what I am thinking and saying tonight does not relate to any isolated episode.

Instead, we Americans are taking a long-range point of view in regard to certain fundamentals and to a series of events on land and on sea which must be considered as a whole—as a part of a world pattern.

It would be unworthy of a great Nation to exaggerate an isolated incident, or to become inflamed by some one act of violence. But it would be inexcusable folly to minimize such incidents in the face of evidence which makes it clear that the incident is not isolated, but is part of a general plan.

The important truth is that these acts of international lawlessness are a manifestation of a design which has been made clear to the American people for a long time. It is the Nazi design to abolish the freedom of the seas, and to acquire absolute control and domination of these seas for themselves.

For with control of the seas in their own hands, the way can obviously become clear for their next step—domination of the United States—domination of the Western Hemisphere by force of arms. Under Nazi control of the seas, no merchant ship of the United States or of any other American Republic would be free to carry on any peaceful commerce, except by the condescending grace of this foreign and tyrannical power. The Atlantic Ocean which has been, and which should always be, a free and friendly highway for us would then become a deadly menace to the commerce of the United States, to the coasts of the United States, and even to the inland cities of the United States.

The Hitler Government, in defiance of the laws of the sea, in defiance of the recognized rights of all other Nations, has presumed to declare, on paper, that great areas of the seas—even including a vast expanse lying in the Western Hemisphere—are to be closed, and that no ships may enter them for any purpose, except at peril of being sunk. Actually they are sinking ships at will and without warning in widely separated areas both within and far outside of these far-flung pretended zones.

This Nazi attempt to seize control of the oceans is but a counterpart of the Nazi plots now being carried on throughout the Western Hemisphere—all designed toward the same end. For Hitler's advance guards—not only his avowed agents but also his dupes among us—have sought to make ready for him footholds and bridgeheads in the New World, to be used as soon as he has gained control of the oceans.

His intrigues, his plots, his machinations, his sabotage in this New World are all known to the Government of the United States. Conspiracy has followed conspiracy. . . .

To be ultimately successful in world mastery, Hitler knows that he must get control of the seas. He must first destroy the bridge of ships which we are building across the Atlantic and over which we shall continue to roll the implements of war to help destroy him, to destroy all his works in the end. He must wipe out our patrol on sea and in the air if he is to do it. He must silence the British Navy.

I think it must be explained over and over again to people who like to think of the United States Navy as an invincible protection, that this can be true only if the British Navy survives. And that, my friends, is simple arithmetic.

For if the world outside of the Americas falls under Axis domination, the shipbuilding facilities which the Axis powers would then possess in all of Europe, in the British Isles, and in the Far East would be much greater than all the shipbuilding facilities and potentialities of all of the Americas—not only greater, but two or three times greater—enough to win. Even if the United States threw all its resources into such a situation, seeking to double and even redouble the size of our Navy, the Axis powers, in control of the rest of the world, would have the manpower and the physical resources to outbuild us several times over.

It is time for all Americans, Americans of all the Americas to stop being deluded by the romantic notion that the Americas can go on living happily and peacefully in a Nazi-dominated world.

Generation after generation, America has battled for the general policy of the freedom of the seas. And that policy is a very simple one—but a basic, a fundamental one. It means that no Nation has the right to make the broad oceans of the world at great distances from the actual theater of land war unsafe for the commerce of others.

That has been our policy, proved time and time again, in all our history.

Our policy has applied from the earliest days of the Republic—and still applies—not merely to the Atlantic but to the Pacific and to all other oceans as well.

Unrestricted submarine warfare in 1941 constitutes a defiance—an act of aggression—against that historic American policy. . . .

No act of violence, no act of intimidation will keep us from maintaining intact two bulwarks of American defense: First, our line of supply of matériel to the enemies of Hitler; and second, the freedom of our shipping on the high seas.

No matter what it takes, no matter what it costs, we will keep open the line of legitimate commerce in these defensive waters.

We have sought no shooting war with Hitler. We do not seek it now. But neither do we want peace so much, that we are willing to pay for it by permitting him to attack our naval and merchant ships while they are on legitimate business.

I assume that the German leaders are not deeply concerned, tonight or any other time, by what we Americans or the American Government say or publish about them. We cannot bring about the downfall of Nazism by the use of long-range invective.

But when you see a rattlesnake poised to strike, you do not wait until he has struck before you crush him.

These Nazi submarines and raiders are the rattlesnakes of the Atlantic. They are a menace to the free pathways of the high seas. They are a challenge to our sovereignty. They hammer at our most precious rights when they attack ships of the American flag—symbols of our independence, our freedom, our very life.

It is clear to all Americans that the time has come when the Americas themselves must now be defended. A continuation of attacks in our own waters, or in waters that could be used for further and greater attacks on us, will inevitably weaken our American ability to repel Hitlerism.

Do not let us be hair-splitters. Let us not ask ourselves whether the Americas should begin to defend themselves after the first attack, or the fifth attack, or the tenth attack, or the twentieth attack.

The time for active defense is now.

Do not let us split hairs. Let us not say: "We will only defend ourselves if the torpedo succeeds in getting home, or if the crew and the passengers are drowned."

This is the time for prevention of attack.

If submarines or raiders attack in distant waters, they can attack equally well within sight of our own shores. Their very presence in any waters which America deems vital to its defense constitutes an attack.

In the waters which we deem necessary for our defense, American naval vessels and American planes will no longer wait until Axis submarines lurking under the water, or Axis raiders on the surface of the sea, strike their deadly blow—first.

Upon our naval and air patrol—now operating in large number over a vast expanse of the Atlantic Ocean—falls the duty of maintaining the American policy of freedom of the seas—now. That means, very simply, very clearly, that our patrolling vessels and planes will protect all merchant ships—not only American ships but ships of any flag—engaged in commerce in our defensive waters. They will protect them from submarines; they will protect them from surface raiders.

This situation is not new. The second President of the United States, John Adams, ordered the United States Navy to clean out European privateers and European ships of war which were infesting the Caribbean and South American waters, destroying American commerce.

The third President of the United States, Thomas Jefferson, ordered the United States Navy to end the attacks being made upon American and other ships by the corsairs of the Nations of North Africa.

My obligation as President is historic; it is clear. It is inescapable.

It is no act of war on our part when we decide to protect the seas that are vital to American defense. The aggression is not ours. Ours is solely defense.

But let this warning be clear. From now on, if German or Italian vessels of war enter the waters, the protection of which is necessary for American defense, they do so at their own peril.

The orders which I have given as Commander in Chief of the United States Army and Navy are to carry out that policy—at once.

The sole responsibility rests upon Germany. There will be no shooting unless Germany continues to seek it.

That is my obvious duty in this crisis. That is the clear right of this sovereign

Nation. This is the only step possible, if we would keep tight the wall of defense which we are pledged to maintain around this Western Hemisphere.

I have no illusions about the gravity of this step. I have not taken it hurriedly or lightly. It is the result of months and months of constant thought and anxiety and prayer. In the protection of your Nation and mine it cannot be avoided.

The American people have faced other grave crises in their history—with American courage, and with American resolution. They will do no less today.

They know the actualities of the attacks upon us. They know the necessities of a bold defense against these attacks. They know that the times call for clear heads and fearless hearts.

And with that inner strength that comes to a free people conscious of their duty, and conscious of the righteousness of what they do, they will—with Divine help and guidance—stand their ground against this latest assault upon their democracy, their sovereignty, and their freedom.

B] ROOSEVELT CALLS FOR ARMING THE MERCHANT SHIPS: ADDRESS TO CONGRESS, OCTOBER 9, 1941

IT IS OBVIOUS to all of us that world conditions have changed violently since the first American Neutrality Act of 1935. The Neutrality Act of 1939 was passed at a time when the true magnitude of the Nazi attempt to dominate the world was visualized by few persons. We heard it said, indeed, that this new European war was not a real war, and that the contending armies would remain behind their impregnable fortifications and never really fight. In this atmosphere the Neutrality Act seemed reasonable. But so did the Maginot Line.

Since then—in these past two tragic years—war has spread from continent to continent; very many Nations have been conquered and enslaved; great cities have been laid in ruins; millions of human beings have been killed, soldiers and sailors and civilians alike. Never before has such widespread devastation been visited upon God's earth and God's children.

The pattern of the future—the future as Hitler seeks to shape it—is now as clear and as ominous as the headlines of today's newspapers.

Through these years of war, we Americans have never been neutral in thought. We have never been indifferent to the fate of Hitler's victims. And, increasingly, we have become aware of the peril to ourselves, to our democratic traditions and institutions, to our country, and to our hemisphere.

We have known what victory for the aggressors would mean to us. Therefore, the American people, through the Congress, have taken important and costly steps to give great aid to those Nations actively fighting against Nazi-Fascist domination.

We know that we could not defend ourselves in Long Island Sound or in San Francisco Bay. That would be too late. It is the American policy to defend ourselves wherever such defense becomes necessary under the complex conditions of modern warfare.

Therefore, it has become necessary that this Government should not be handicapped in carrying out the clearly announced policy of the Congress and of the people. We must face the truth that the Neutrality Act requires a complete reconsideration in the light of known facts.

The revisions which I suggest do not call for a declaration of war any more than the Lend-Lease Act called for a declaration of war. This is a matter of essential defense of American rights.

In the Neutrality Act are various crippling provisions. The repeal or modification of these provisions will not leave the United States any less neutral than we are today, but will make it possible for us to defend the Americas far more successfully, and to give aid far more effectively against the tremendous forces now marching toward conquest of the world.

Under the Neutrality Act, we established certain areas as zones of combat into which no American flag ships could proceed. Hitler proclaimed certain far larger areas as zones of combat into which any neutral ship, regardless of its flag or the nature of its cargo, could proceed only at its peril. We know now that Hitler recognizes no limitation on any zone of combat in any part of the seven seas. He has struck at our ships and at the lives of our sailors within the waters of the Western Hemisphere. Determined as he is to gain domination of the entire world, he considers the entire world his own battlefield.

Ships of the United States and of other American Republics continue to be sunk, not only in the imaginary zone proclaimed by the Nazis in the North Atlantic, but also in the zoneless South Atlantic.

I recommend the repeal of section 6 of the Act of November 4, 1939, which prohibits the arming of American flag ships engaged in foreign commerce.

The practice of arming merchant ships for civilian defense is an old one. It has never been prohibited by international law. Until 1937 it had never been prohibited by any statute of the United States. Through our whole history American merchant vessels have been armed whenever it was considered necessary for their own defense.

It is an imperative need now to equip American merchant vessels with arms. We are faced not with the old type of pirates but with the modern pirates of the sea who travel beneath the surface or on the surface or in the air destroying defenseless ships without warning and without provision for the safety of the passengers and crews.

Our merchant vessels are sailing the seas on missions connected with the defense of the United States. It is not just that the crews of these vessels should be denied the means of defending their lives and their ships. . . .

There are other phases of the Neutrality Act to the correction of which I hope the Congress will give earnest and early attention. One of these provisions is of major importance. I believe that it is essential to the proper defense of our country that we cease giving the definite assistance which we are now giving to the aggressors. For, in effect, we are inviting their control of the seas by keeping our ships out of the ports of our own friends.

It is time for this country to stop playing into Hitler's hands, and to unshackle our own.

A vast number of ships are sliding into the water from American shipbuilding ways. We are lending them to the enemies of Hitlerism and they are carrying food and supplies and munitions to belligerent ports in order to withstand Hitler's juggernaut.

Most of the vital goods authorized by the Congress are being delivered. Yet many of them are being sunk; and as we approach full production requiring the use of more ships now being built it will be increasingly necessary to deliver American goods under the American flag.

We cannot, and should not, depend on the strained resources of the exiled Nations of Norway and Holland to deliver our goods nor should we be forced to masquerade American-owned ships behind the flags of our sister Republics.

I earnestly trust that the Congress will carry out the true intent of the Lend-Lease Act by making it possible for the United States to help to deliver the articles to those who are in a position effectively to use them. In other words, I ask for Congressional action to implement Congressional policy. Let us be consistent.

I would not go back to the earlier days when private traders could gamble with American life and property in the hope of personal gain, and thereby embroil this country in some incident in which the American public had no direct interest. But, today, under the controls exercised by the Government, no ship and no cargo can leave the United States, save on an errand which has first been approved by governmental authority. And the test of that approval is whether the exportation will promote the defense of the United States.

I cannot impress too strongly upon the Congress the seriousness of the military situation that confronts all of the Nations that are combating Hitler.

We would be blind to the realities if we did not recognize that Hitler is now determined to expend all the resources and all the mechanical force and manpower at his command to crush both Russia and Britain. He knows that he is racing against time. He has heard the rumblings of revolt among the enslaved peoples—including the Germans and Italians. He fears the mounting force of American aid. He knows that the days in which he may achieve total victory are numbered.

Therefore, it is our duty, as never before, to extend more and more assistance and ever more swiftly to Britain, to Russia, to all peoples and individuals fighting slavery. We must do this without fear or favor. The ultimate fate of the Western Hemisphere lies in the balance. . . .

We intend to maintain the policy of protecting the freedom of the seas against domination by any foreign power which has become crazed with a desire to control the world. We shall do so with all our strength and all our heart and all our mind.

c] Senator Taft Speaks for the Opposition

THE ADOPTION of the joint resolution now before the Senate would be direct authority from the Congress to the President to carry on an undeclared war against Germany, Italy, and Japan on all the oceans of the world and in all the ports into which seagoing ships may sail. If the Members of the Senate intend to keep their pledges to the people of the United States, pledges made by themselves, by their leaders, and by their parties, they can only vote "No" on the pending measure.

I intend today to present only one proposition, that the adoption of the resolution is equivalent to authorizing war. I recognize that there are many who feel that war is justified. There is every reason why they should support the resolution. I myself am convinced that the entry of the United States into the present war would be unwise and useless and destructive in the end to our own people and our own Government.

The time given to the opponents of the pending measure, particularly those not on the Committee on Foreign Relations, has been so short that I have been unable to prepare my remarks on the general question, which is the real issue before us today, whether we should go to war; but there still seem to remain some remnants of the argument which was advanced when the lease-lend bill was before Congress, that this is in fact a move for peace. There are still in the President's statement, the message proposing the legislation, these words:

The revisions which I suggest do not call for a declaration of war any more than the Lend-Lease Act called for a declaration of war.

Technically, the President is correct. They do not call for a declaration of war. But the suggestion given to the people that we may remain at peace and still adopt this resolution is one which apparently has impressed some members of the public, and apparently is going to be a reason given by some of those who vote for the pending resolution for their support of it.

Mr. President, I cannot understand the position of those Senators. Those who have read the President's speeches, and those who heard his speech last night, can hardly doubt that he is proposing that the United States carry on an undeclared naval war, and that in the passage of this resolution he is asking Congress for authority for him to carry on such a war.

The repeal of sections 2 and 3 of the Neutrality Act would mean the dispatch of American ships into British ports through the submarine blockade of the Germans. It cannot be doubted that many of those ships would be sunk, and that many Americans would be drowned. It cannot be doubted that that would be the first result of our vote here to repeal the Neutrality Act, and authorize Americans and American ships, not only authorize them, but perhaps order them, to proceed into the battlefields of Europe.

It was just such sinkings and such deaths which took us into the World War. It is an almost inevitable cause of complete war. It is probably more likely to be so now than it was in the World War, because now these ships would be invariably carrying contraband manufactured by the United States and shipped by us to the British in order to enable them to carry on war against Germany. There could hardly be any doubt in the mind of any German commander as to any such ship that it would be carrying contraband.

It is only because of the provisions of the Neutrality Act which we are asked to repeal that we are not at war today.

As the Senator from Michigan [Mr. VANDENBERG] pointed out, that is not really a neutrality act but an act to keep the United States out of war, and it has up to this time accomplished its purpose. If it had been carried out in good faith, there would be little danger of war today, instead of great danger of war.

After all, it is common sense. Regardless of international law, regardless of history, two great nations today are at war, and the actual battlefields of that war are the waters which surround Great Britain. There is no other battlefield between the English and the Germans except that battlefield into which we now are going to send our ships and our men. No neutral can venture into a battlefield without danger to its property and its citizens, and danger of becoming involved in war. Human nature being what it is, incidents involving American ships and American citizens are likely to lead to war, and because of the death of 11 men, or of 100 men, millions may be sent to slaughter.

It seems common sense to say that in the interest of all of us, Americans shall keep away from battlefields far from our own land. But more than anything else, the actual experience of the World War, the inevitable result of shipping contraband to a belligerent nation through such a zone, is conclusive proof of what will happen if we repeal this law.

1. THE ARMS EMBARGO POLICY

Mr. President, I wish to review briefly the various foreign policies that this country has adopted since I have been a Member of the Senate. When I came here in 1939 the arms embargo was in effect. It prohibited the shipment of munitions of any kind to any belligerent nation. It was an extreme measure. Personally I did not favor it, and I voted for its repeal, because I felt that a policy of arms embargo—absolute refusal to permit anybody to come here and buy arms—was for the benefit of the strong nation, the nation which built up a great war-like force, and against the weak nation. But I voted for repeal of the measure principally because it was accompanied by provisions which reinstated in the law the cash-and-carry provisions of the former act which had then expired, and which were no longer in effect. If we had not enacted that law American ships could have gone through the war zone to Great Britain, unless they were actually carrying contraband.

2. THE CASH-AND-CARRY POLICY UNANIMOUSLY ADOPTED 2 YEARS AGO

We adopted then the policy No. 2, the cash-and-carry policy. That was just 2 years ago, and there are few Senators here who did not vote for that measure, or at least of the Senators who are likely to vote for the pending measure there are very few who did not vote for the establishment of that cash-and-carry policy. I myself believe it was a sound policy. I believe it was the policy which has kept us out of war. I believe that the policy of saying that any persons may come here if they please and purchase goods, provided the title is transferred to them before the goods leave here, provided they pay for the goods, and provided they carry them away in their own ships, is the policy which is sound, and is the only policy which ever will keep the United States out of European wars.

Mr. President, I should like to call attention to the fact that by the pending joint resolution nearly all the Senators are being asked to reverse the position which they took at that time, for those who voted for the repeal of the arms embargo and those who voted against it were unanimous in the belief that the establishment of the cash-and-carry policy was the best method of keeping the United States out of war. The record is full of statements which bear out that conclusion.

I should like to read what the President himself said in the campaign of 1940 about the neutrality law, in which he took credit for setting up this cash-and-carry system. He said at Madison Square Garden:

By the Neutrality Act of 1935, and by other steps: We made it possible to prohibit American citizens from traveling on vessels belonging to countries at war. Was that right? We made it clear that American investors who put their money into enterprises in foreign nations could not call on American warships or soldiers to bail out their investments. Was that right?

The President went on:

We made it clear that ships flying the American flag could not carry munitions to a belligerent, and that they must stay out of war zones. Was that right?
In all these ways—

The President said:

we made it clear to every American, and to every foreign nation, that we would avoid becoming entangled through some episode beyond our borders. These were measures to keep us at peace. And through all the years of war since 1935, there has been no entanglement, and there will be no entanglement.

That was the statement of the President of the United States just about a year ago. That certainly was a pledge to the people of the United States that he intended to pursue the policy for which he was claiming credit.

The President today, by asking for the repeal of this law, is repudiating his promise made to the American people, and no future historian will question my statement.

There are plenty of Senators here who took very much the same position in favor of the establishment of the cash-and-carry policy, and I think it only fair to remind them what they said at that time. The senior Senator from North Carolina [Mr. BAILEY] said this during the debate 2 years ago on the arms embargo:

I will say that the chief motive that induced me to give my allegiance to the cause of supporting the pending joint resolution was precisely the proposition to withdraw from the waters of the earth our ships, whereby there might be incidents that would arouse our people and change them from their blessed state of desire for peace into a state of contention as to our rights, and finally, into a possible disposition to assert them, go forth in our strength, and pay the price.

This is still the Senator from North Carolina [Mr. BAILEY] speaking:

We are not going to get into this war. It is a European war. It is not our war. . . . If we were to get into it I should think we were the greatest pack of fools history ever recorded.

Today, Senators, we are that pack of fools.
The majority leader, the Senator from Kentucky [Mr. BARKLEY], said:

The law which we are now proposing would have prevented these attacks upon, and losses of, property and lives, because both property and lives would have been withheld from the regions of danger resulting in their destruction or attack on them. The law we are proposing will keep American ships and American cargoes and American sailors and American travelers out of present regions of danger.

The majority leader said that if this law had been in effect during the World War we would not have become involved in the World War. . . .

Mr. President, we are asked to repudiate the reasons which we then gave. I think there is only one argument to be made in answer to the arguments I have quoted from Senators who spoke at that time. That is the argument that now the time has come to go to war. Any Senator who wishes to go to war may well vote for the joint resolution. Otherwise I cannot see how Senators can explain their votes or in any way make them consistent with what they said 2 years ago, and what they necessarily pledged themselves to support when they ran for reelection—if they did—in 1940, and what their parties pledged for them at that time.

3. AID TO BRITAIN—SHORT OF WAR

Cash-and-carry was policy No. 2. Then we gradually adopted a third policy —perhaps only a modification of the second. For purposes of convenience I shall call it policy No. 3. After the downfall of France and the disaster at Dunkerque we added to the cash-and-carry policy the theory of aid to Britain short of war. That was the policy that prevailed during the entire election campaign of 1940. I do not know exactly what that aid to Britain implied. It was necessarily vague; but at the time it seemed to me very clearly to imply that we would organize our industry so that we could build tanks, airplanes, and every other kind of war material and make it available to be bought by the British.

Let me say that we could have done nothing at that time or since that would have been of more aid to the British than that one thing. That was the thing which Mr. Willkie emphasized in his campaign. That the thing to help the British was production of materials. Yet during that whole period we took practically no steps toward efficient organization of American industry. There was a Council of National Defense, made up of seven men, each one independent, without a chairman, each one reporting to the President. The machinery was so cumbersome that the moment the election was over it was changed and another form of organization was attempted. Production of materials was the meaning of aid to Britain; and I think it is fairly clear that that is what aid to Britain meant to the candidates and to the parties.

The Democratic platform said this about aid to Britain:

In self-defense and in good conscience, the world's greatest democracy cannot afford heartlessly or in a spirit of appeasement to ignore the peace-loving and liberty-loving peoples wantonly attacked by ruthless aggressors.

We pledge to extend to these peoples all the material aid at our command consistent with law and not inconsistent with the interests of our own national self-defense, all to the end that peace and international good faith may yet emerge triumphant.

"Consistent with law," I suppose, meant the neutrality law. There was not the slightest suggestion that that law was to be repealed, and presumably the pledge meant that aid must be consistent with the neutrality law.

The Republican platform was approximately the same. With respect to aid to Britain it said:

We favor the extension to all peoples fighting for liberty, or whose liberty is threatened, of such aid as shall not be in violation of international law or inconsistent with the requirements of our own national defense.

There never was a suggestion at anytime during that campaign that the policy of aid to Britain short of war meant anything but what it said—aid to Britain short of war. There was nothing that indicated or in any way implied an intention to repeal the neutrality law. In fact, Mr. Roosevelt and Mr. Willkie went far to make it clear that they were going to keep away from Europe altogether. Those were the pledges they gave to the American people. Those pledges have been frequently quoted here. President Roosevelt said:

To every man, woman, and child in the Nation I say this: Your President and your Secretary of State are following the road to peace. We are arming ourselves not for any foreign war. We are arming ourselves not for any purpose of conquest or intervention in foreign disputes. I repeat again that I stand on the platform of our party.

Mr. Willkie went a little further. At Cleveland on October 2, 1940, he said:

The American people do not want war. They have no idea whatever of joining in any conflict, whether on the Atlantic or the Pacific. They are determined to keep America at peace. In this determination I stand with them. I am for keeping out of war. I am for peace for America. We must not rashly move. Any man who involves us in the risk of war betrays his country.

Policy No. 3 was the policy of aid to Britain short of war. If either of those gentlemen had advocated the repeal of the Neutrality Act he would have signed his own political death warrant. The other man would have won in that election, because the people wanted the pledge of peace. They would have repudiated any man who had said, "We will repeal the Neutrality Act and take our chance of war." I am afraid they would even have repudiated any man who had said, "In this aid to Britain I intend to remove the cash provisions of the Neutrality Act and give Britain $13,000,000,000." I do not think any candidate could have made such a statement and carried the suffrage of the American people. Such action was not part of that policy.

If that policy had been administered with fairness and in good faith and if we had in fact tried to aid Britain short of war, the policy would have worked. We could have kept out of the difficulty in which we now find ourselves. We could have built up our production much faster. We could have gone on. We certainly could have been 6 months or perhaps a year ahead of where we are now, and Britain and Russia might have had the material which they need and which they do not now have. That kind of aid to Britain would have been more effective than the repeal of the Neutrality Act and the substitution of American ships going to Britain for British ships going to Britain.

4. THE LEASE-LEND POLICY DID NOT AUTHORIZE DELIVERY

That policy was an effective and reasonable policy and one that could have been successfully carried out. But the President was determined to go on, and so he came to foreign policy No. 4. Each policy was a step closer to war. He proposed the lease-lend bill. The lease-lend bill, of course, repealed the cash provisions of the Neutrality Act. It had not been mentioned before the campaign or during the campaign. There was not even a proposal to extend credits to Britain. I do not say that we should not have changed our policy and extended credits to Britain, but the lease-lend policy was still a policy that might have been administered without taking us into war. When that bill passed I said—and I now believe—that we gave authority to the President to take us into war if he should see fit to do so. But it was a policy that did not necessarily involve us in war.

There has been much talk to the effect that we must pass the pending measure to carry out the policy of the Lease-Lend Act, but the policy of the Lease-Lend Act never involved the idea of delivery of materials to England.

It is true that the Lease-Lend Act repealed the "cash" end of the cash-and-carry policy, but it did not repeal the "carry" end of that policy; and, after all, it was the "carry" end of the policy that was primarily dangerous in respect to involving us in war. That was the point on which practically every one spoke. That was the thing which practically got us into the World War, and that was the important end of the cash-and-carry policy.

The President himself, even in his message asking for the passage of the lease-lend bill, simply said:

I also ask this Congress for authority and for funds sufficient to manufacture additional munitions and war supplies of many kinds, to be turned over to those nations which are now in actual war with aggressor nations.

. . . .

I recommend that we make it possible for those nations to continue to obtain war materials in the United States. . . .

He did not say anything about delivering materials.

The lease-lend policy is a perfectly understandable policy. It is a policy of standing on the line of the Atlantic and Pacific Oceans, of defending ourselves, of building up a defense sufficiently strong so that no one will attack us, and then saying to the rest of the world, "We are not going to be concerned with your problems; but if any man is attacked unjustly, if any man is attacked by an aggressor, he may come here and get all the arms he needs with which to defend himself against that aggression."

That is the essence of the lease-lend policy. Of course, we remember the debates on the floor of the Senate as to whether that policy in any way involved a delivery policy. The distinguished Senator who was then chairman of the Foreign Relations Committee [Mr. GEORGE], who certainly spoke for the administration in that regard, said this:

I do not think the word "transfer" means anything else in the family and group of words here used except the transfer of title, or the right of possession, or the right of use. I cannot conceive of it meaning anything else. Now, if there is anything else in the bill that gives rise to the worry that the distinguished Senator from Wyoming has that deliveries might be made in danger areas, war zones, in places where we have forbidden our own ships to go, where the President has proclaimed they should not go, I should like to have the benefit of the Senator's statement about it. But if it arises out of the word "transfer," I frankly must say that we can give it no construction except the one that I think every one should give it as a realist. As found in the family of words it partakes of kinship to all of them. When you say "sell or lease," you are talking about titles, and the right of possession, and the right of use, and nothing else, so far as I can see.

But if there is some other provision in the bill that seems to give rise to a fear that the President of the United States will undertake to deliver defense articles in a zone of great danger—

Just exactly what he himself has done since that time, I may say—

where even our own merchant ships cannot go, then, as a realist, I do not understand it. I do not understand it any more, may I say to the Senator from Wyoming, than the argument that has been heard here that somebody has a design upon all the social legislation that labor and the workers of America now enjoy under a President who brought those social benefits; who has stood and constantly fought for those social benefits.

The Senator from Maine [Mr. White], who is a member of the Foreign Relations Committee, said the same thing:

The chief criticism of this paragraph seems to arise from an alleged doubt as to the meaning of the word "transfer." Some see in this word an authorization to "transport" defense articles in American vessels in disregard of the present Neutrality Act. I see no merit in this criticism. It is not the intent of the legislation.

Of course, the word "transfer" was amended by inserting the word "title," so that it became clear that it could not possibly mean delivery; and there was contained in the policy written into the bill in so many words the provision that it should not be taken to authorize convoys of lease-lend material or otherwise—a policy which apparently is now being pursued without legislative authority. There was written into the bill the provision that section 3, regarding merchant ships in war zones, should not be in any way repealed—a provision which it is now proposed to repeal, with the Lend-Lease Act urged as justification. It was expressly provided that American troops should not be sent out of this country; but they have been sent out of this country, into Iceland—out of the Western Hemisphere and into the war zones of Europe.

Mr. President, that was the lease-lend policy. . . .

If that policy had been administered in good faith, we would not today be in danger of war. It could have been so administered. It gave cause for war, but under the circumstances that exist in the world there is no reason to suppose that what we are doing under the Lease-Lend Act could finally have involved us in the European war unless the President chose to exercise to a greater extent than he actually has the powers contained in that act.

Mr. Lucas. Mr. President, will the Senator yield for one question?

Mr. Taft. I yield to the Senator from Illinois.

Mr. Lucas. Did I correctly understand the Senator to say a few moments ago that under the Lease-Lend Act the President really has power to take us into the European war?

Mr. Taft. I think under the Lease-Lend Act he has power to do a good many things. I always thought he could have sent the whole fleet over to

Gibraltar, for instance, and could have combined it with the British Fleet. There are various things that I think he could have done that would have involved us in the World War for which he would have had authority. The particular things he has done relating to the war zones of Europe I do not think he had any power to do under the Lease-Lend Act.

Mr. Lucas. But there is no question in the Senator's mind that under the Lend-Lease Act the President of the United States would have had the right, had he wanted to do so, to send the American Fleet into Singapore or Gibraltar or any other place, to join it with the British Fleet, and thereby have America involved in the present European war?

Mr. Taft. I so stated at the time the lease-lend bill was passed and I think that is true. I was most hopeful that the President would not exercise those powers. He has chosen to exercise other powers that I do not think he had.

Mr. Lucas. And the truth of the matter is that the President of the United States has not followed the theory that the Senator from Ohio has stated he could have followed. He has been overly cautious in doing just the opposite.

Mr. Taft. On the contrary, he has pursued a policy which is leading directly and necessarily to war, and he is justifying that policy on the basis of the Lease-Lend Act. I do not happen to think that the particular things he has done, like sending troops to Iceland, which inevitably involves us in the probability of war, like his convoying of vessels, like his orders to "shoot at sight," are in any way justified by the Lease-Lend Act; but they are acts which he justifies on the basis of the Lease-Lend Act and which inevitably are leading rapidly to war.

Mr. Lucas. Mr. President, will the Senator further yield at that point?

Mr. Taft. I further yield to the Senator from Illinois.

Mr. Lucas. With all due deference to the able Senator from Ohio, it is difficult for me to follow his argument, in view of the statement he made that under the Lease-Lend Act the President of the United States has all the authority that is necessary to involve this country in war, and yet, on the other hand, he does not pursue that policy; but the Senator from Ohio says, on the other hand, he is gradually leading us to war, step by step. If he has the power, and if he is the type of warmonger that many persons in this country say he is, it seems to me, under the Senator's own statement and under his construction of the Lend-Lease Act, that he would have had us in this war a long, long time ago.

Mr. Taft. I have not said he is a warmonger, but I have said he is leading us steadily toward war and that he intends us to get into war; that that is his purpose; but he is in no hurry about it. We are not ready for war; but I say that every step he has taken has been a step toward war.

5. THE POLICY OF UNDECLARED NAVAL WAR, BEGUN BY THE PRESIDENT WITHOUT AUTHORITY, WOULD BE RATIFIED BY THE REPEAL OF THE NEUTRALITY ACT

Mr. President, the next step, policy No. 5, is that of undeclared naval war. That is a step beyond the Lease-Lend Act. It is a step which we have partially taken. I think we have taken it without authority of law, but the President has certainly moved toward an undeclared naval war. The incident of the

Kearny is to some extent war. Today, however, we have the opportunity of passing on the question whether we are going to step from the lease-lend policy, under which other nations come to this country, to a policy of undeclared naval war on the two oceans of the world and in every port into which a seagoing ship may go. If we refuse to repeal the Neutrality Act, there is a probability that the President will withdraw from that policy, but if we pass the pending measure, if we repeal the neutrality law, we confirm, ratify, and approve everything the President has done and everything he has said. We approve the occupation of Iceland; we approve the orders to shoot on sight; we approve the patrolling and convoying American vessels, not only in the somewhat restricted areas where they have been patrolling and convoying, but all the way to the ports of Great Britain; for the only reason that the convoy has not extended to the ports of Great Britain is the fact that the American merchant ships, even if convoyed, cannot go into the war zones of Europe. We do not know that that step itself has not been taken.

The policy of undeclared naval war, it seems to me, is not a very effective policy of aiding Britain. There has not been any destruction of any great percentage of lease-lend goods or any other goods; there is not any evidence that the British have not got enough ships of their own. They have something like, so far as I can figure, three times as many ships as the Americans have; and there is plenty of neutral shipping. It is a little difficult to see how they are going to be benefited by American merchant ships sailing to England instead of neutral or British merchant ships sailing to England.

The Senator from Michigan yesterday pointed out that arming ships is of no great assistance to the ships. It is very doubtful, indeed, whether it will save any merchant ships or whether it will do any good to the British.

But there is not any question that the adoption of policy No. 5 is a policy of war, a policy of war which every party in this country has denied that it wishes to adopt, and which every Senator has denied that he wishes to adopt. It cannot be long, in my opinion, after that policy is adopted before we have policy No. 6, the policy of complete war, including the sending of troops to Europe or to Africa or to Asia. It is almost impossible to engage in a partial war. If there is actual shooting; if every day there are engagements between American war vessels and German war vessels; if American sailors are killed day by day, certainly the American people are going to feel that they are fully at war; that it is our war.

They had thought up to now that it was a question of aiding Britain, but once it is our own war there is no stopping short of anything which may be necessary to defeat the enemy; and that necessarily includes an A.E.F. It happened in the World War. The record of President Wilson shows without question that when we went into that war he expected to fight a naval war; he did not intend to send any troops to Europe. It was about 3 months before he was persuaded to change his mind; before he saw, as we can now see, that a nation cannot engage in an undeclared naval war unless it is prepared to do everything in the world to win that war. That means necessarily the sending of an A.E.F. to Europe. We are getting there. In the World War we first sent a detachment of engineers. They were the first units. Just as President Wilson was persuaded to send a token unit to Europe, and they were reviewed by the King, so this week we read that the King and Queen reviewed 100 Americans who are in the C.T.C., and about 12 naval lieutenants, officers of the American Navy, who were standing up in parade before the King of England.

We have seen this week a demand for doubling the tank program and doubling the airplane program. What possible use is that going to have except for an American expeditionary force? We have the demand now from the British generals for such a force. Such a force probably is not contemplated for a year or more, but what else can be the purpose of this tank program? We have ordered tanks for 3,000,000 men already. Why double the tank program unless we are looking forward to an A.E.F.? If we pass this joint resolution, we should look forward to an A.E.F., and will have to prepare to win the war which we would vote if we adopted this resolution.

If we go ahead now and abandon the policy of cash and carry, if we proceed to vote to authorize American vessels to carry on this war all the way over to the shores of Germany, then I say that the next step, which is the last step of complete war, is on our threshold.

A naval war is bound to be indecisive. It may be that the President hopes that we may win the war against Hitler without sending our troops; but even he cannot feel confident of any such result, and when for 6 months or 12 months there has been a completely indecisive result, the cry will grow louder and louder that we must finish this war; and the way the war can be finished is by sending perhaps a million men to Africa and later on two or three million men to Europe. There is no other way by which Hitler can be crushed. . . .

6. EVERY POLICY HAS BEEN ADMINISTERED WITH AN EVIDENT DESIRE TO TAKE THIS COUNTRY INTO WAR

Mr. President, I would feel less confident of the inevitable result if it had not been true that all the steps which have been taken seem to have tended so steadily toward war that any reasonable man must conclude that they were intended to tend toward war. I have pointed out how one policy after another could have been administered without taking us into war, without taking the next step. There was no popular pressure for any such step, and yet every step was followed by one more step, by one more evidence that the administration itself is really desiring a policy of complete war with Germany. Otherwise, how could the President permit the remarks which have been made by members of his Cabinet? We have had Mr. Knox declaring war not only on Hitler but also on Japan, we have had Mr. Stimson declaring war, and Mr. Ickes declaring war. Certainly no responsible President could permit members of his Cabinet to make speeches advocating war unless he was, at least, contemplating such a policy or unless, at least, that policy was agreeable to him. To my mind, if he does not repudiate those statements, it is impossible for him to avoid the just charge that he himself is stimulating the policy of war. We had an 8-point declaration by which the United States and Great Britain, or at least, the President of the United States and His Majesty's Government in Great Britain, entered into an agreement which was somewhat vague in its terms but which was interpreted by Mr. Churchill shortly afterwards; and the

President has never in any way modified or repudiated the statement of Mr. Churchill.

Mr. Churchill said this in his speech:

You will, perhaps, have noticed that the President of the United States and the British representative, in what is aptly called the Atlantic charter, have jointly pledged their countries to the final destruction of the Nazi tyranny. That is a solemn and grave undertaking. It must be made good. It will be made good. And, of course, many practical arrangements to fulfill that purpose have been and are being organized and set in motion.

Mr. Churchill says that the President has pledged his country "to the final destruction of the Nazi tyranny." No reasonable man can interpret those words to mean anything except an intention to go to war. There is no other way to crush the Nazi tyranny.

Mr. Churchill further said:

The United States and Great Britain do not now assume that there will never be any more war again. On the contrary, we—

That is, the United States and Great Britain—

intend to take ample precaution to prevent its renewal in any period we can foresee, by effectively disarming the guilty nations while remaining suitably protected ourselves.

"While effectively disarming the guilty nations"—Germany, Italy, and Japan. I do not see how those words can be interpreted in any way except as an intention to go to war.

Mr. Willkie, the Senator from New Hampshire [Mr. Bridges], and others advocate in effect a war policy, and they are the persons who have forced the consideration of this amendment here. The Senator from Florida [Mr. Pepper], the Senator from Oklahoma [Mr. Lee], and the Senator from Rhode Island [Mr. Green] in effect proposed the pending amendment. Every one of them is for war. They admit the logical conclusion from their acts. They admit that this policy must necessarily lead to war. . . .

Mr. President, the whole approach of the administration today seems to be one of war. I think it is fair to say—at least, the impression given from the newspapers is—that the administration welcomes every incident which may possibly lead to war. Those incidents are not reported in the usual way. They are announced by the President at a press conference. They are sent out to the world as something by which, on the whole, the Government is delighted. The story of the *Greer* was told by the President, it seems to me, in such a way as deliberately to incite more feeling than was justified by the actual event which occurred. He said, for instance:

Our destroyer at the time was in waters which the Government of the United States had declared to be waters of self-defense, surrounding outposts of American protection in the Atlantic. The United States destroyer, when attacked, was proceeding on a legitimate mission.

As a matter of fact, the facts which came out much later before a committee, when the public had forgotten the *Greer,* show that it was in the neighborhood of a submarine of which it was told by a British destroyer which was also there; that after it had located the submarine a British plane came and dropped four depth bombs; and that the *Greer* then turned off its course and chased the submarine for 3 hours and 20 minutes, zig-zagging in the way that a vessel would zigzag if it were going to attack a submarine. Whether or not the submarine was justified in finally shooting a torpedo, whether or not it thought this was a joint British-American attack, certainly the President's report of the incident was made in such a way as deliberately to incite the American people. No man who sincerely desired peace would have failed to state the actual circumstances.

I do not know what happened to the *Kearny*. We still do not know for certain; but it seems almost certain that the *Kearny* was engaged in convoying, not American ships, but British and neutral ships, from this country. But the President did not so advise the American people.

Mr. Tobey. Mr. President, will the Senator yield?

Mr. Taft. I yield to the Senator from New Hampshire.

Mr. Tobey. I was not here during the time the hearings were conducted before the Committee on Foreign Relations; but I should like to ask some member of the committee, the Senator from Michigan [Mr. Vandenberg] or some other member, whether Admiral Stark did not definitely testify that the *Kearny* was convoying ships.

Mr. Johnson of California. He did.

Mr. Tobey. Further, when he was asked, as I read the testimony in the New York Times, what was the nationality of those ships, whether American or British, he could not remember, or he declined to answer. Which was it?

Mr. Johnson of California. The story went off the record at that point; but we had sufficient on the record to establish that the *Kearny* was convoying ships then.

Mr. Tobey. And certainly, beyond peradventure, Admiral Stark knew whether it was convoying American ships or British ships, did he not?

Mr. Johnson of California. Oh, certainly; certainly.

Mr. Taft. Mr. President, I may say that convoying was proposed last spring, but there was so much opposition to convoys that authority to convoy never was specifically presented to Congress. Apparently without such presentation we now have the United States engaged in convoying. But the point I wanted to make is that the whole intention of the administration, every indication that a reasonable man can draw from its acts, is that it intends to go into war; and certainly, if we pass this resolution, and the administration has such an intention, we are going very shortly to become involved in war.

7. WE ARE NOT ALREADY SO FAR AT WAR THAT WE CANNOT EASILY WITHDRAW IF
CONGRESS REFUSES TO REPEAL NEUTRALITY

There is no argument made today that, after all, we are already at war, and therefore we should not hesitate to go on and vote authority to conduct war. The power to declare war rests solely in the United States Congress. If the President can declare or create an undeclared naval war beyond our power to act upon, the Constitution might just as well be abolished. The Constitution deliberately gave to the representatives of the people the power to declare war, to pass on the question of war and peace, because that was something which kings had always done, which they had done against the interests of the people themselves, and which the founders of the Constitution thought the people ought to determine. It is true there have been one or two acts of war; but if Congress will refuse to repeal the Neutrality Act, I do not believe those acts of war can be continued. I do not believe the President is prepared to defy the express action of the Congress. Up to date he has not purported to do so. He has only claimed a power which I do not think he has. I stated on the floor of the Senate that I did not think he had the power to send American troops to Iceland, because Iceland was not in the Western Hemisphere, and it was already in the war zone. There was already there a British garrison. We have undertaken a joint defense of Iceland together with the British, who are actually at war with Germany. We can withdraw from Iceland. If we are sending convoys—as we are sending them—we can stop the policy of convoying vessels to Great Britain.

I do not think we are at war. I think the people who say we are at war now will find that when war actually comes it will be something very different. There will be long casualty lists, a constant series of battles, constant incitement of the people to war, gradually building up a bigger and bigger Army, until it is big enough to undertake a trip to Europe.

8. THE PRESIDENT IS ATTEMPTING TO DECLARE WAR WITHOUT AUTHORITY FROM CONGRESS

Mr. President, the speech of the President last night seems to me an extraordinary speech, because in effect it makes it plain that he has personally declared war on Germany. That certainly is a power which he does not have.

It seems to me that he has admitted publicly that he has tricked the American people. While talking of peace, even while Senate leaders here talk of amending the Neutrality Act as a measure of defense, President Roosevelt announces that he has already done what he could to plunge the Nation into a shooting war. He has given unqualified corroboration to those who have sought to convince the American people by methods which are leading them down the road to war. While constantly repeating pledges of peace, he now informs us, "The shooting has started." He says, "Very simply and very bluntly we are pledged to pull our own oar in the destruction of Hitler."

By what authority does the President make that statement? Who gave the pledge? Unless the President is willing to admit that he has assumed final unconstitutional and dictatorial powers, then his statement that such a pledge has been given is not worth the paper it is written on, for only Congress can give such a pledge.

Mr. Roosevelt says that our Navy has been instructed to shoot on sight. There is no stated limitation on those orders. By what authority does Mr. Roosevelt send American youths to war—and that is what he is doing with the boys in the Navy—to prowl the ocean in quest of offensive warfare? Only Congress can constitutionally order our ships and our boys into an offensive war. Does Mr. Roosevelt contend, then, that he has assumed Hitlerian authority over the United States?

We have the President in effect admitting every charge made against him, that he was working toward war while promising peace, that he did intend to disregard Congress and the Constitution, and follow the course of dictatorship to an undeclared war.

There is just a shadow of substance to the claim that he can conduct war in defense of the United States. But defense has been stretched so thin that it cannot much longer be called anything like defense. We had first the defense of the United States. When we undertook a defense program, that is what everyone thought it meant, defense of continental United States, and the islands around it on this side of the Atlantic Ocean.

The next thing proposed was defense by seizing Iceland, and Dakar, and points in Europe. It used to be said in the British Government of the nineteenth century that if they would permit the British Navy to establish a base on the moon to defend themselves against the sun, they would certainly do so—a policy which England has pursued for many years, but which our Nation has never seen fit to consider.

Certainly the seizure of Iceland and Dakar is not defense of the United States. It is an aggressive policy of defending the sea lanes to Great Britain. It is the defense of Great Britain, not of the United States.

The next position of the President was that we would shoot at any place where we found a German vessel in our defense waters. What our defense waters are he did not say. Apparently our defense waters extend to Iceland and well beyond. If we enact the pending measure, of course, our defense waters are going to be every ocean and every port in the entire world, in Asia, Africa, Europe, or Australia.

The message on this measure finally contains the statement that we must fight in defense of American rights. Although we have seen fit to say that one of those rights, like the sending of our ships into belligerent ports, is a right we desire to give up, now the President says we should stand on that right, and precipitate the very kind of a conflict which brought on the World War.

9. CONCLUSION

Mr. President, we have to consider here the question whether we will approve a policy of undeclared naval war, whether we will give approval to the President, who has shown his desire to forward that war, who has constantly worked toward developing the war spirit in the United States, who apparently, under every reasonable conclusion from his speeches, is in favor of outright war—whether we shall vote here to authorize such a war.

If we do vote to authorize war, then I say that Congress will never again debate the question of war. By the time we come to a formal declaration of war, so much actual warfare will have taken place that while I should vote against such a declaration for the purpose of the record, I certainly would not seriously attempt to combat the effort to take us into a declared war at that time.

Do we wish to keep our pledges to the people of the United States, pledges which practically every Senator here has made? There is no difference between the conditions today and the conditions during the campaign of 1940. If anything, conditions today do not justify war as much as did conditions at that time. At that time Great Britain was being nightly bombarded, the general feeling was that it might be successfully invaded at any moment. France had fallen. Hitler had spread over a great part of Europe, and it was obvious that he could spread over all the rest of Europe. There is no substantial difference between the conditions now and what the conditions were in 1940, when we gave our pledge. Possibly public opinion has changed, possibly it has not, but in the Senate we must decide this question on the basis of our own principles, and I say that no man who gave his pledge that we should keep out of war, who gave his pledge to do everything he could to keep the United States out of war, in November 1940 can today vote for the pending resolution without repudiating that pledge.

d] Roosevelt Appeals to Emperor Hirohito, December 6, 1941

Almost a century ago the President of the United States addressed to the Emperor of Japan a message extending an offer of friendship of the people of the United States to the people of Japan. That offer was accepted, and in the long period of unbroken peace and friendship which has followed, our respective Nations, through the virtues of their peoples and the wisdom of their rulers, have prospered and have substantially helped humanity.

Only in situations of extraordinary importance to our two countries need I address to Your Majesty messages on matters of state. I feel I should now so address you because of the deep and far-reaching emergency which appears to be in formation.

Developments are occurring in the Pacific area which threaten to deprive each of our Nations and all humanity of the beneficial influence of the long peace between our two countries. Those developments contain tragic possibilities.

The people of the United States, believing in peace and in the right of Nations to live and let live, have eagerly watched the conversations between our two Governments during these past months. We have hoped for a termination of the present conflict between Japan and China. We have hoped that a peace of the Pacific could be consummated in such a way that nationalities of many diverse peoples could exist side by side without fear of invasion; that unbearable burdens of armaments could be lifted for them all; and that all peoples would resume commerce without discrimination against or in favor of any Nation.

I am certain that it will be clear to Your Majesty, as it is to me, that in seeking these great objectives both Japan and the United States should agree to eliminate any form of military threat. This seemed essential to the attainment of the high objectives.

More than a year ago Your Majesty's Government concluded an agreement with the Vichy Government by which five or six thousand Japanese troops were permitted to enter into Northern French Indo-China for the protection of Japanese troops which were operating against China further north. And this spring and summer the Vichy Government permitted further Japanese military forces to enter into Southern French Indo-China for the common defense of

French Indo-China. I think I am correct in saying that no attack has been made upon Indo-China, nor that any has been contemplated.

During the past few weeks it has become clear to the world that Japanese military, naval, and air forces have been sent to Southern Indo-China in such large numbers as to create a reasonable doubt on the part of other Nations that this continuing concentration in Indo-China is not defensive in its character.

Because these continuing concentrations in Indo-China have reached such large proportions and because they extend now to the southeast and the southwest corners of that peninsula, it is only reasonable that the people of the Philippines, of the hundreds of islands of the East Indies, of Malaya, and of Thailand itself are asking themselves whether these forces of Japan are preparing or intending to make attack in one or more of these many directions.

I am sure that Your Majesty will understand that the fear of all these peoples is a legitimate fear inasmuch as it involves their peace and their national existence. I am sure that Your Majesty will understand why the people of the United States in such large numbers look askance at the establishment of military, naval, and air bases manned and equipped so greatly as to constitute armed forces capable of measures of offense.

It is clear that a continuance of such a situation is unthinkable.

None of the peoples whom I have spoken of can sit either indefinitely or permanently on a keg of dynamite.

There is absolutely no thought on the part of the United States of invading Indo-China if every Japanese soldier or sailor were to be withdrawn therefrom.

I think that we can obtain the same assurance from the Governments of the East Indies, the Governments of Malaya, and the Government of Thailand. I would even undertake to ask for the same assurance on the part of the Government of China. Thus a withdrawal of the Japanese forces from Indo-China would result in the assurance of peace throughout the whole of the South Pacific area.

I address myself to Your Majesty at this moment in the fervent hope that Your Majesty may, as I am doing, give thought in this definite emergency to ways of dispelling the dark clouds. I am confident that both of us, for the sake of the peoples not only of our own great countries but for the sake of humanity in neighboring territories, have a sacred duty to restore traditional amity and prevent further death and destruction in the world.

E] ROOSEVELT CALLS FOR A DECLARATION OF WAR: ADDRESS TO CONGRESS, DECEMBER 8, 1941

YESTERDAY, December 7, 1941—a date which will live in infamy—the United States of America was suddenly and deliberately attacked by naval and air forces of the Empire of Japan.

The United States was at peace with that Nation and, at the solicitation of Japan, was still in conversation with its Government and its Emperor looking toward the maintenance of peace in the Pacific. Indeed, one hour after Japanese air squadrons had commenced bombing in the American Island of Oahu, the

Japanese Ambassador to the United States and his colleague delivered to our Secretary of State a formal reply to a recent American message. And while this reply stated that it seemed useless to continue the existing diplomatic negotiations, it contained no threat or hint of war or of armed attack.

It will be recorded that the distance of Hawaii from Japan makes it obvious that the attack was deliberately planned many days or even weeks ago. During the intervening time the Japanese Government has deliberately sought to deceive the United States by false statements and expressions of hope for continued peace.

The attack yesterday on the Hawaiian Islands has caused severe damage to American naval and military forces. I regret to tell you that very many American lives have been lost. In addition American ships have been reported torpedoed on the high seas between San Francisco and Honolulu.

Yesterday the Japanese Government also launched an attack against Malaya.

Last night Japanese forces attacked Hong Kong.

Last night Japanese forces attacked Guam.

Last night Japanese forces attacked the Philippine Islands.

Last night the Japanese attacked Wake Island.

And this morning the Japanese attacked Midway Island.

Japan has, therefore, undertaken a surprise offensive extending throughout the Pacific area. The facts of yesterday and today speak for themselves. The people of the United States have already formed their opinions and well understand the implications to the very life and safety of our Nation.

As Commander in Chief of the Army and Navy I have directed that all measures be taken for our defense.

But always will our whole Nation remember the character of the onslaught against us.

No matter how long it may take us to overcome this premeditated invasion, the American people in their righteous might will win through to absolute victory.

I believe that I interpret the will of the Congress and of the people when I assert that we will not only defend ourselves to the uttermost but will make it very certain that this form of treachery shall never again endanger us.

Hostilities exist. There is no blinking at the fact that our people, our territory, and our interests are in grave danger.

With confidence in our armed forces—with the unbounding determination of our people—we will gain the inevitable triumph—so help us God.

I ask that the Congress declare that since the unprovoked and dastardly attack by Japan on Sunday, December 7, 1941, a state of war has existed between the United States and the Japanese Empire.

CONCLUSION

DEBATE over intervention came to a sudden end with the Japanese assault on Pearl Harbor. Senators and representatives who had considered an attack on the United States impossible became interventionists overnight. For the balance of the war debate centered on the question of how best to attain victory, not on the responsibility for United States involvement in World War II. But after the successful conclusion of the war, and especially as the new peace and the fruits of victory seemed endangered by rising tensions between the United States and Soviet Russia, the old question began to be debated again. Did the American people ever have a chance to decide calmly and intelligently what their role in the European war should be? Was Roosevelt the evil genius of American intervention, or a leader caught in the grip of irresistible forces? Had he actually precipitated an unnecessary war by bringing the United States in "through the back door" in the Pacific?

As the United States settled into the "cold war" with Russia during the 1950's, the old question of intervention took on wider implications. Would it have been better to let the two tyrannies, Nazi and Bolshevik, "fight it out," perhaps leaving both exhausted? Had the United States unwittingly strengthened communism by vanquishing Nazism and leaving a void in Central Europe that the Russians quickly filled? Some argued that such questions were "Monday-morning quarterbacking," that people and their leaders had neither twenty-twenty insight nor foresight, that the best they could have done was to deal with threats to national security from whatever quarter they might have arisen and to ally the United States with any other forces that could have assisted in the immediate crisis. The new debate over interventionism took many other forms, as Americans once again had to concert themselves with other peoples against a new imperialism that showed much of the purposefulness and ruthlessness of the old. The debate over intervention, in short, never really died away, for once again, in the 1960's, Americans face the stern question of what sacrifices a free nation must steel itself to make in the face of clear threats to its survival.

STUDY QUESTIONS

1] Did the Presidential campaign of 1940 present the American electorate with clear alternatives and with a definite understanding of the foreign policy each candidate would follow if elected?

2] Do you believe Roosevelt secretly felt that the United States was inevitably going to be involved in the conflict? If you do, can you justify the methods he used—for example, his insistence that intervention made war *less* likely, his refusal to get too far ahead of public opinion, his apparent lack of candor on certain incidents, such as the *Greer?*

3] Which arguments of the isolationists, which arguments of the interventionists, have been best vindicated by later events? Which least?

4] Was it more the events themselves, or more the leaders' interpretation and exploitation of the events, that caused the United States to become increasingly involved in the war?

RECOMMENDED READINGS

PRIMARY SOURCES

CANTRIL, HADLEY, ed. *Public Opinion, 1945–1946* (Princeton, 1951).

JONES, S. S., ET AL., eds. *Documents on American Foreign Relations, 1938–50,* 12 vols. (Boston, 1939–51), Vols. for 1938–41.

ROOSEVELT, ELLIOT, ed. *FDR: His Personal Letters,* 4 vols. (New York, 1947, 1950).

ROSENMAN, SAMUEL I., ed. *The Public Papers and Addresses of Franklin D. Roosevelt,* 13 vols. (New York, 1938–50).

U.S. CONGRESS. Committee on Foreign Relations of the U.S. Senate, *Hearings on Neutrality,* 76 Cong., 1 Sess., 20 pts. (1939).

————. Committee on Foreign Relations of the U.S. Senate, *Hearings on S. 275,* 77 Cong., 1 Sess. (January–February, 1941).

————. *Congressional Record,* 76 Cong., 2 Sess.; 77 Cong., 1 Sess. (Washington, 1940–41).

SECONDARY SOURCES

ADLER, SELIG. *The Isolationist Impulse* (New York, 1957).

BEARD, CHARLES A. *American Foreign Policy in the Making, 1932–40* (New Haven, 1946).

————. *President Roosevelt and the Coming of the War 1941* (New Haven, 1948).

CHURCHILL, WINSTON. *The Gathering Storm* (Boston, 1948).

FEIS, HERBERT. *The Road to Pearl Harbor* (Princeton, 1950).

HULL, CORDELL. *The Memoirs of Cordell Hull,* 2 vols. (New York, 1948).

ICKES, HAROLD L. *The Secret Diary of Harold L. Ickes, III, The Lowering Clouds, 1939–1941* (New York, 1954).

JOHNSON, WALTER. *The Battle Against Isolation* (Chicago, 1944).

LANGER, WILLIAM L., AND S. EVERETT GLEASON. *The World Crisis and American Foreign Policy,* 2 vols. (New York, 1952–53).

Democracy Fights a Limited War: Korea, 1950–1953

SAMUEL P. HUNTINGTON

COLUMBIA UNIVERSITY

CONTENTS

4] The Greater Debate: Soldiers and Politicians
   a] MacArthur Addresses Congress
                    (*Congressional Record*, 82 Cong., 1 Sess.)

   b] General Bradley Replies for the Administration
                    (MacArthur Hearings)

   c] A Republican Congressman Demands a "Program for Korea"
                    (*Congressional Record*, 82 Cong., 2 Sess.)

   d] Eisenhower Promises to Go to Korea
                    (New York *Times*, October 25, 1952)

CHRONOLOGY

1949

JUNE 29   American combat forces leave Korea.

1950

JUNE 25   North Koreans invade South Korea.

JUNE 25–30   UN Security Council calls on members to assist South Korea. President Truman orders American forces to help repel invasion.

AUGUST 5   North Korean advance halted.

SEPTEMBER 15   American forces land at Inchon.

OCTOBER 1   South Koreans cross 38th parallel.

OCTOBER 7   American troops cross 38th parallel. UN General Assembly urges that "all appropriate steps be taken to ensure conditions of stability throughout Korea."

OCTOBER 15   President Truman and General MacArthur confer at Wake Island.

OCTOBER 14–16   Chinese forces first enter Korea.

OCTOBER 26–   South Korean troops reach Yalu. Extensive fighting

NOVEMBER 7   occurs between UN forces and Chinese forces. UN forces withdraw to Chongchon River.

NOVEMBER 24   MacArthur launches "end the war" offensive.

NOVEMBER 28   Chinese begin counteroffensive.

DECEMBER 15   Chinese reach 38th parallel.

DECEMBER 24   UN forces complete evacuation from Hungnam.

1951

JANUARY 4   Communists recapture Seoul.

JANUARY 25   Ridgway launches UN counteroffensive.

MARCH 15   UN forces re-enter Seoul.

APRIL 11   President Truman relieves General MacArthur.

APRIL 19   MacArthur addresses Congress.

MAY 13–   Senate committees hold MacArthur Hearings.
JUNE 27

JUNE 23   Soviet Ambassador Malik proposes truce in Korea.

JULY 10   Truce negotiations begin at Kaesong.

1952

OCTOBER 24   Eisenhower promises "I shall go to Korea."

NOVEMBER 4   Eisenhower defeats Stevenson for the Presidency.

DECEMBER 2–5   Eisenhower visits Korea as President-elect.

1953

JULY 27   Korean armistice signed.

INTRODUCTION

I do not think we could fight another Korea and not use all the resources necessary to win the war. . . . I do not think the American people would be in favor of another one like that.

THESE WORDS from Secretary of Defense Charles Wilson in 1953 expressed a prevailing viewpoint. Scholars have termed the Korean War the "most unpopular war" in American history. Yet, five years after the war was over, the administration to which Mr. Wilson had belonged was openly admitting that the United States might have to fight other wars comparable to the Korean War. Undoubtedly the Korean War was, as Robert Osgood has stated, "the single most significant event" in American strategy after World War II. Certainly it was the most traumatic event. It was twentieth-century America's first limited war. It was also the United Nations' first war in the name of collective security. It gave rise to bitter disputes between the government in Washington and its commanders in the Far East and came to a head in the dramatic firing of the country's most dramatic general. While the most active phase of the war lasted just a year, for two more years fighting continued on the battlefield while American and Communist negotiators fought over the terms of a truce. The war aims of the administration and its conduct of the war became the subjects of intense and often acrimonious domestic political conflict. For the first time since 1864 the conduct of a war was the major issue in a Presidential election. In the Korean War many traditional American political ideas and practices came into direct conflict with the new requirements of national security in an age of cold war and atom bombs.

In the course of the nineteenth and twentieth centuries, Americans developed a distinctive approach to the problems of war and peace. A century of isolation ending in two world wars had given rise to the idea that fundamental differences existed between war and peace. In peacetime, foreign policy was the province of the diplomats, large military forces were unneeded and even dangerous, harmony existed among nations. If this harmony were disrupted by an aggressive or totalitarian power, the country must mobilize its energies to remove the source of the evil. War was justified only to defend moral principles against immoral ones. Americans came to view wars as crusades against a clearly identifiable evil; hence the purpose of war had to be the complete defeat of the enemy, and the conduct of war should be guided by the military needs of victory, unsullied by extraneous political considerations. At the close of World War II General Marshall rejected British suggestions that the Western armies occupy Prague and Berlin before the Russians did. "I would be loath to hazard American lives for purely political purposes," Marshall declared. "The single objective," he argued, "should be quick and complete victory." "In war there is no substitute for victory," said General MacArthur at the climax of the Korean War.

Up until August 6, 1945, the day when the first atomic bomb was used in combat at Hiroshima, the twentieth century was an age in which total war dominated international affairs. But as George Kennan observed in 1954, "the day of total wars has passed, and . . . from now on limited military operations are the only ones that could conceivably serve any coherent purpose." The Korean War marked this change. A local war from the start, five months later it became a limited war in the sense that goals and means were deliberately restricted. As the first limited war between major powers in the nuclear era, many experts see it as the prototype of future conflicts. When the major states possess bombs with the explosive power of fifteen million tons of TNT, what other type of war can nations fight? Although it antedated the "balance of terror," the Korean War is directly relevant to the problems of the balance of terror. The question is: can the United States, given its traditions and governmental system, successfully employ such "limited military operations" on behalf of a "coherent purpose"? Or are its options restricted to appeasement and retreat, on the one hand, and thermonuclear Armageddon, on the other? The Korean War posed many of the dilemmas that democracy will face in the remainder of the twentieth century.

The roots of the Korean War lie in the decisions and the confusion of World War II. Two decades of aggression culminated, in 1910, in the formal annexation of Korea by Japan. At the Cairo Conference in December, 1943, the United States, Great Britain, and China proclaimed that "in due course Korea shall become free and independent," and the Soviet Union supported this policy at the time of its declaration of war on Japan, on August 8, 1945. When two days later Japan offered to surrender, the military exigencies of the hectic last weeks of the war led to an *ad hoc* arrangement in which the Soviet forces accepted the surrender of Japanese forces north of the 38th parallel in Korea, while the Americans accepted the surrender south of the parallel. At that time no high-ranking American thought of the parallel as a line permanently dividing the country. The American goal was the creation of a democratic government for a unified and independent Korea. But for two years negotiations between the American and Soviet generals and diplomats failed to bring agreement on the unification of the two occupation zones. Faced with this stalemate, the United States referred the problem to the United Nations. In November, 1947, the UN General Assembly created a UN Temporary Commission on Korea to supervise elections for a Korean national assembly that would draft a constitution for a new Korean government. The Soviets refused to allow the commission to operate in North Korea. In South Korea, elections were held, a constitution was drawn up, further elections were held, and on August 15, 1948, the new government of the Republic of Korea was established. Meanwhile, in the North, the Soviets proceeded to organize the Democratic People's Republic, which claimed to be the legitimate government of the entire peninsula. The division of Korea, which had begun in 1945 as a temporary military arrangement, had by 1949 become an established political fact.

Beginning in September, 1947, the Joint Chiefs of Staff argued that the United States had little strategic interest in Korea and pressed for the withdrawal of American forces. The creation of the new government, the withdrawal of Soviet troops from North Korea at the end of 1948, and the 1949 reductions in the American defense budget led to the departure of the last American combat forces from Korea in June, 1949. At that time the President of the Republic of Korea, Syngman Rhee, unsuccessfully urged the United States to make a positive commitment to come to the defense of Korea if it were attacked by another power. Other actions of the American government seemed to indicate that it did not attach much value to Korea. Congress delayed approval of economic assistance for the new country. First General MacArthur, American military commander in the Far East, then Secretary of State Dean Acheson, and then Senator Connally, chairman of the Senate Foreign Relations Committee, stated that Korea lay outside the American "defensive perimeter" in the Far East. Given all these indications and cues— the withdrawal of troops, the refusal to make a specific commitment to defend South Korea, the hesitancy about giving South Korea aid, the statements by our officials—what is surprising is not the Communist attack on South Korea but the United States response to that attack.

At about ten o'clock in the evening of Saturday, June 24, the Secretary of State in Washington phoned the President in Independence, Missouri: "Mr. President, I have very serious news. The North Koreans have invaded South Korea." Almost immediately the President made up his mind that the United States could not permit the invasion to go unopposed. Flying back to Washington the next day, he recalled Manchuria, Ethiopia, Austria—little countries that whetted the appetites of aggressive powers in the 1930's.

I remembered how each time the democracies failed to act it had encouraged the aggressors to keep going ahead. Communism was acting in Korea just as Hitler, Mussolini, and the Japanese had acted ten, fifteen, and twenty years ago. . . . If this was allowed to go unchallenged it would mean a third world war, just as similar incidents had brought on the second world war.

That Sunday the United Nations Security Council met in emergency session. Because the Soviet Union was boycotting the Security Council in protest against its refusal to seat Communist China, no Soviet delegate was present to veto the United States resolution, which called for a cease-fire and the withdrawal of North Korean forces and asked the member states to render "every assistance" in carrying out the resolution. Sunday evening the President met with his aides in Washington and authorized the use of American air and naval forces to evacuate American nationals from Korea. Twenty-four hours later, as the situation continued to deteriorate, he authorized air and naval assistance to South Korea, directed American naval forces to prevent any assault by the Chinese Communists on Formosa, and requested Chiang Kai-shek not to launch attacks from Formosa against the Chinese mainland. The next day, Tuesday, June 27, the President informed Congressional leaders of these actions and publicly announced them at noon. That evening the UN Security Council passed another American-sponsored resolution calling upon its members to "furnish such assistance to the Republic of Korea as may be necessary to repel the armed attack and to restore international peace and security in the area." Meanwhile, the North Koreans continued their rapid advance. Early in the morning of Friday, June 30, MacArthur reported to the Pentagon that if the situation was to be saved, American ground forces were necessary. At 5 A.M. Secretary of the Army Frank Pace awoke the President and reported this information to him. The President authorized MacArthur to fly in an American regimental combat team from Japan. Later that morning MacArthur was authorized to employ his other troops in Japan to halt the North Korean advance. The United States was now fully committed to the defeat of the North Korean invasion.

Virtually no prominent American challenged the President's actions. Senator Taft, Republican leader in the Senate, attacked the wisdom of previous American policy in the Far East and the constitutionality of the President's failure to obtain formal Congressional approval, but not the wisdom of what he had done. As MacArthur struggled to stem the Communist advance in July, the people, Congress, and the administration were united on the need to repel the aggressor. Here was a direct and unambiguous challenge. It was met, for the moment, with a direct, unambiguous, and united response.

The United States was not alone in Korea. Eventually, fifteen other members of the United Nations contributed military forces to fight alongside the South Koreans and the Americans. Apart from the British Commonwealth forces, these were hardly more than token contributions. Nevertheless, their presence dramatized the fact that this was a United Nations war against aggression and in behalf of the principle of collective security.

So long as the issue was in doubt, the war aims could be vague. By mid-summer, however, the lines had been stabilized about the Pusan beachhead in southern South Korea. Additional American forces were moving to the Far East. The time had come for the United Nations to assume the offensive. On September 15 General MacArthur launched amphibious landings at Inchon, near Seoul, coupled with an offensive from the Pusan beachhead to catch the North Korean armies in a gigantic pincer movement. The peaceful unification of North and South Korea had been a long-standing objective of both the United Nations and the United States. The issue now was: should UN armies seize the opportunity to achieve this goal through military means? In the enthusiasm of victory no other course seemed sensible. Why should the UN forces stop on an artificial parallel and allow the North Koreans to reorganize their forces and perhaps to prepare a new invasion?

On September 11, before the offensive began, the President of the National Security Council authorized MacArthur to send his troops into North Korea, *provided* that there was "no indication or threat of entry of Soviet or Chinese Communist elements in force. . . ." On October 1 United Nations forces crossed the parallel. Six days later the UN General Assembly implicitly endorsed the military move northward.

The critical issue now became the intentions of the Chinese Communists. What were their goals and would these goals lead them to intervene in the war? Was their object to forestall an American invasion of Manchuria? To prevent Western forces from reaching the Yalu? To insure a buffer zone in North Korea between the UN forces and the Chinese border? To preserve in being a North Korean Communist government and party? To protect the territorial integrity of North Korea? Even today doubt remains as to just exactly what fears, motives, and interests the Chinese Communists had. Repeatedly, however, in the first half of October, Chinese government officials warned that they would not sit idly by while the UN armies headed for their border. In the middle of the month Chinese troops began to move into North Korea and in the last week of October they engaged the UN forces in combat. Then, during the first week in November, the extended UN forces were withdrawn to a more defensible line and the Chinese broke off contact. At this point the Chinese had, as Allen Whiting put it, crossed the Yalu, but they had not crossed the Rubicon. Full-scale fighting between Chinese and American forces was possible but not necessary, depending upon the interests of their governments and the movements of the troops.

Throughout this period the American government imposed restrictions on military operations in the vicinity of the Chinese border. Such restrictions were the first timid movements toward turning the Korean War from a local war into a limited war. They were resisted by General MacArthur and they probably had little effect on the Chinese. Conceivably, a complete halt of the UN advance northward at the narrow waist of Korea might have forestalled major offensive action by the Chinese. Certainly it would have placed the UN military forces in a much better position to resist such an offensive. Despite the evidence of Chinese interest, however, optimism ran high both at MacArthur's headquarters in Tokyo and in Washington. At his Wake Island conference with President Truman on October 15, MacArthur assured the President that Chinese Communist intervention posed no threat to his command. Soon after the conference, MacArthur rejected suggestions from the Joint Chiefs of Staff that he stop his forces on the highlands south of the Yalu. Instead he launched his final "win the war" offensive on November 24. Four days later the Chinese launched their offensive against the widely dispersed UN forces. The UN advance quickly turned into a rout.

Up to this point the difference on strategy between headquarters in Tokyo and Washington had been on relatively minor or peripheral matters; the full-scale intervention of the Chinese Communists brought about a complete cleavage. MacArthur's reaction to the defeat of his forces was that the UN was now fighting an "entirely new war" with Communist China. Within Korea, he believed, Communist China could easily defeat the existing UN forces. To secure victory over Communist China the war had to be expanded outside Korea. Specifically, MacArthur suggested a blockade of the Chinese coast, the bombing of Chinese industries, the use of Chinese Nationalist troops in Korea, and the launching of an attack on mainland China from Formosa. The government in Washington, however, was interested in limiting, rather than extending, its commitment in the Far East. It was much more concerned with the danger in Europe. If the Communists could launch aggression in Korea, they could also launch aggression in Germany. Allied military strength in western Europe was pitifully inadequate. (When asked what the Soviets needed in order to reach the Pyrenees, one Allied officer reportedly answered, "Shoes!") The Truman administration, consequently, was rushing American reinforcements to NATO. The last thing it wanted was a general war in the Far East. As long as some hope remained of keeping a foothold in Korea, the United States refused to sanction any expansion of the war outside Korea.

In December and January the Chinese forces pushed south. The 38th parallel was crossed; Seoul was recaptured. Under the firm leadership of Lieutenant General Matthew B. Ridgway, however, the UN ground forces brought the Chinese advance to a halt by the end of January. Once it became evident that the UN was not going to be driven out of Korea, MacArthur's recommendations lost their urgency and their rationale. The possibility of winning a limited victory within Korea rendered unnecessary these proposals for winning a bigger victory outside Korea.

Ridgway's success in stemming the Chinese advance and in preparing a new UN offensive northward raised again, in March, the same issues that the Inchon landing had raised the previous September. This time the policy of the government was markedly different. As the UN armies advanced northward, American officials, in cooperation with the Allied governments, prepared an offer to negotiate a cease-fire. On March 24, MacArthur attempted to forestall this offer by demanding the full surrender of the Chinese Communist armies.

It was this action that precipitated MacArthur's recall by President Truman, and it was this recall that dramatized the willingness of the government to accept a restoration of the prewar border. In April and May, as the furor over MacArthur's dismissal raged in the United States, the lines of battle in Korea ebbed and flowed. A Chinese spring offensive was stopped, and a counteroffensive by the UN forces shifted the fighting north of the 38th parallel. The United States government refused, however, to approve plans for deep amphibious landings on North Korea that were designed to encircle and destroy the Chinese forces. Its aim now was to apply sufficient pressure to produce a truce but to do no more than that. On June 23 Soviet Ambassador Malik indicated the willingness of the Communists to begin truce negotiations. On July 10 the truce talks began at Kaesong in Korea.

Negotiations lasted for two years. The Democratic administration in Washington was caught in a dilemma. Communist demands were such that only strong, sustained military pressure would have brought about a quick truce agreement acceptable to the United States, and to achieve this would have cost the commitment of more military forces and the loss of more American lives. A new all-out offensive would reawaken the doubts of our Allies in Europe and of our supporters in the UN. It would also reopen the dangers of Russian intervention. Thus, the administration could not achieve its limited goal of a truce reflecting the status quo ante bellum without employing means that would suggest to its enemies, its allies, and its domestic public that its real goal was either to unify Korea by force or to overthrow the Chinese Communist government. As the war dragged on into 1952, public resentment and frustration mounted and increasingly sharp political attacks were launched against the administration. To its domestic critics, the government seemed committed to an indefinite, agonizing struggle in the bleak hills of Korea that it lacked either the will to win through military action or the skill to end by diplomatic negotiation.

It was perhaps predictable that the Korean War would become a hotly contested issue in the Presidential election of 1952. At the start of his campaign, Republican candidate Dwight Eisenhower seemed reluctant to make political capital out of Korea. He would not assume, he declared, "a Messiah role on peace." As the campaign progressed, however, the Korean War figured more and more prominently in his speeches. In January, 1952, only twenty-five per cent of the public had thought the war the most important issue confronting the United States. In the heat of the campaign, the figure rose to thirty-four per cent in September and to over fifty per cent in October, when Eisenhower made his dramatic promise to go to Korea if elected President. By election day sixty per cent of the public thought the war was the principal issue in the Presidential contest, and ninety per cent thought it was one of the top three issues.

The termination of the war became the foremost goal of the Eisenhower administration in 1953. The new administration "unleashed" Chiang Kai-shek's forces for an attack on the Chinese mainland, though Chiang obviously did not have the strength to deliver. It announced a build-up of the South Korean military forces, along with shifts of American units to the Far East. Administration officials spoke of expanding the war to mainland China if a truce agreement was not speedily reached. But on March 28 the Chinese Communists indicated their willingness to resume the truce negotiations that had been suspended the previous autumn. In part, the new Communist attitude was probably due to the military actions of the new administration. In part, also, it was probably a result of the death of Stalin on March 5, 1953. Despite the efforts of Syngman Rhee to sabotage the negotiations, agreements were quickly reached on the remaining issues concerning the disposition of prisoners of war. On July 27, 1953, the truce was formally signed.

DOCUMENTS

1] The Uncertainties of Success: American Goals and Chinese Intervention

A] WASHINGTON CLARIFIES GOALS, DISCOUNTS INTERVENTION

> The landing at Inchon, in September, 1950, changed the character of the Korean War overnight. Military success posed two new problems. What should be the goals of the United States (and the United Nations) with respect to North Korea? What were the probabilities of Chinese Communist intervention in the war? To consider questions of this magnitude, Congress had created the National Security Council, which, in 1950, included the President, Vice-President, Secretary of State, Secretary of Defense, and other officials concerned with defense policy. Here President Truman, in a passage from his memoirs, describes how he and the National Security Council weighed the problems presented by the Korean War.*

THE DECISION to take the offensive in Korea made it necessary to consider on a high policy level what our subsequent course of action should be. This was done in National Security Council discussions which finally resulted in a policy statement that I approved on September 11, 1950.

The National Security Council recommended that our course of action would be influenced by three factors: action by the Soviet Union and the Chinese Communists, consultation with friendly members of the United Nations, and the risk of general war.

General MacArthur was to conduct the necessary military operations either to force the North Koreans behind the 38th parallel or to destroy their forces. If there was no indication or threat of entry of Soviet or Chinese Communist elements in force, the National Security Council recommended that General MacArthur was to extend his operations north of the parallel and to make plans for the occupation of North Korea. However, no ground operations were to take place north of the 38th parallel in the event of Soviet or Chinese Communist entry.

A Joint Chiefs' directive based on this recommendation, which I approved, was sent to General MacArthur on September 15.

September 15 was D-Day at Inchon. The 1st Marine Division and the Army's 7th Infantry Division went ashore there and established a bridgehead. Then

---

* WASHINGTON CLARIFIES GOALS, DISCOUNTS INTERVENTION: From Harry S. Truman, *Memoirs*, II, *Years of Trial and Hope* (New York, 1956), pp. 359–62. Copyright 1956, Time, Inc. Reprinted by permission of Time, Inc.

these two units, comprising the X Corps commanded by Major General Almond, moved toward Seoul in order to free the Korean capital of the enemy. Resistance was fanatical, but on September 28 the liberation of the city was complete, and on September 29 Syngman Rhee moved his government back. Earlier, on September 26, a juncture had been effected between elements of the 1st Cavalry Division of the Eighth Army, which had broken out of the Pusan perimeter, and 7th Infantry Division troops from the Inchon area. The enemy was disorganized and badly shaken. . . .

I had already given approval to new instructions which the Joint Chiefs of Staff had transmitted to MacArthur on September 27, in which he was told that his military objective was "the destruction of the North Korean Armed Forces." In attaining this objective he was authorized to conduct military operations north of the 38th parallel in Korea, provided that at the time of such operation there had been no entry into North Korea by major Soviet or Chinese Communist forces, no announcement of an intended entry, and no threat by Russian or Chinese Communists to counter our operations militarily in North Korea. He was also instructed that under no circumstances were any of his forces to cross the Manchuria or U.S.S.R. borders of Korea, and, as a matter of policy, no non-Korean ground forces were to be used in the provinces bordering on the Soviet Union or in the area along the Manchurian border. Similarly, support of his operations north or south of the 38th parallel by air or naval action against Manchuria or against U.S.S.R. territory was specifically ruled out.

The directive further instructed the Far East commander the action he should take in the event of Soviet entry into the conflict or entry by the Chinese Communists. It read:

"In the event of the open or covert employment of major Chinese Communist units south of the 38th parallel, you should continue the action as long as action by your forces offers a reasonable chance of successful resistance." . . .

On October 2 MacArthur reported that Republic of Korea Army units were operating north of the 38th parallel, that progress was rapid, and that there seemed little enemy resistance. On October 3 the State Department received a number of messages which all reported the same thing: The Chinese Communists were threatening to enter the Korean conflict. Chou En-lai, now the Foreign Minister of the Chinese Communist regime, had called in the Indian Ambassador to Peiping, K. M. Panikkar, and had told him that if United Nations forces crossed the 38th parallel China would send in troops to help the North Koreans. However, this action would not be taken if only South Koreans crossed the 38th parallel.

This message was at once transmitted to General MacArthur.

Similar reports had been received from Moscow, Stockholm, and New Delhi. However, the problem that arose in connection with these reports was that Mr. Panikkar had in the past played the game of the Chinese Communists fairly regularly, so that his statement could not be taken as that of an impartial observer. It might very well be no more than a relay of Communist propaganda. There was also then pending in the Political and Security Committee of the General Assembly of the United Nations a resolution recommending that all appropriate steps be taken to insure stability throughout all of Korea. This resolution, if adopted, would be a clear authorization for the United Nations commander to operate in North Korea. The key vote on the resolution was due the following day, and it appeared quite likely that Chou En-lai's "message" was a bald attempt to blackmail the United Nations by threats of intervention in Korea.

The possibility of Chinese intervention in Korea, however, could not be discounted, and I therefore instructed the Joint Chiefs of Staff to prepare a directive to General MacArthur to cover such an eventuality. The Joint Chiefs submitted their recommendation to me through the Secretary of Defense, George C. Marshall, who had succeeded Louis Johnson on September 21, and I approved the following message to General MacArthur:

"In light of the possible intervention of Chinese Communist forces in North Korea the following amplification of our directive [of September 25] is forwarded for your guidance:

"'Hereafter in the event of the open or covert employment anywhere in Korea of major Chinese Communist units, without prior announcement, you should continue the action as long as, in your judgment, action by forces now under your control offers a reasonable chance of success. In any case you will obtain authorization from Washington prior to taking any military action against objectives in Chinese territory.'"

This directive was sent to General MacArthur on October 9. In the meantime, however, I had reached another decision. I wanted to have a personal talk with the general. . . .

b] The View from Peking

According to President Truman, K. M. Panikkar, the Indian ambassador to the Chinese Communist government, was not an "impartial observer" because he "had in the past played the game of the Chinese Communists fairly regularly." Here is Mr. Panikkar's account of his dealings with the Peking officials.*

The situation in Korea changed all of a sudden by the American landings at Inchon. There were great rejoicings in the western camp in China, and if the Chinese on their part were bitterly disappointed they showed no signs of it. When the northern lines began to be rolled up and the Americans and their allies were shouting of victory, my thoughts were all on Taiwan, for I felt that if the Americans were able to carry everything before them in Korea they might be tempted to encourage Chiang to attack the mainland and thus precipitate a world war. The situation seemed altogether confused. There were rumours of large-scale troop movements from the Peking area to the north, and a western Military Attaché told me that he had information that a con-

---

* THE VIEW FROM PEKING: From K. M. Panikkar, *In Two Chinas* (London, 1955), pp. 107–10. Reprinted by permission of George Allen & Unwin, Ltd.

tinuous stream of troop trains was passing Tientsin. It was when things were in this state of uncertainty that General Nieh Yen-jung, the acting Chief of Staff who was also the Military Governor of Peking, with the inoffensive title of mayor, came to dine with me on the 25th of September. General Nieh, with his round face and shaven head, gives one the impression of a Prussian officer. But he is a pleasant-spoken man, friendly and ready to discuss matters with an air of frankness. After the dinner the conversation turned to Korea. General Nieh told me in a quiet and unexcited manner that the Chinese did not intend to sit back with folded hands and let the Americans come up to their border. This was the first indication I had that the Chinese proposed to intervene in the war. I was taken aback a little by this statement, all the more impressive because it was said in a quiet and pleasant tone, as if he were telling me that he intended to go shooting the next day. I asked him whether he realized in full the implications of such an action. He replied: "We know what we are in for, but at all costs American aggression has to be stopped. The Americans can bomb us, they can destroy our industries, but they cannot defeat us on land."

I tried to impress on him how destructive a war with America would be; how the Americans would be able to destroy systematically all the industries of Manchuria and put China back by half a century, how China's coastal towns would be exposed to bombardment and how even the interior could be bombed. He only laughed. "We have calculated all that," he said. "They may even drop atom bombs on us. What then? They may kill a few million people. Without sacrifice a nation's independence cannot be upheld." He gave some calculations of the effectiveness of atom bombs and said: "After all, China lives on the farms. What can atom bombs do there? Yes, our economic development will be put back. We may have to wait for it."

This conversation left me very depressed. The next morning I had some news which added greatly to that depression. After the general had left my house, my first secretary A. K. Sen had stayed for a time with me to enable us to compare notes. He left at about a quarter-past eleven but found that a curfew had been clamped on Peking and all traffic had been stopped. He was, however, escorted by a security officer to the Legation street but could not get back to his hotel. He was nevertheless able to see troop formations and trucks moving towards the railway station. Perhaps this was part of the general troop movements towards the Manchurian border. . . .

At midnight on the 2nd of October, after I had been asleep for an hour and a half, I was awakened by my steward with the news that Chen Chia-kang the Director of the Asian Affairs of the Foreign Ministry, was waiting for me in the drawing-room. I hastily put on my dressing-gown and went downstairs, not knowing what it could be which had brought so important an officer at midnight to my house. Chen was very apologetic about the lateness of the hour but added that the matter was most important and that the Prime Minister desired to see me immediately at his residence. I said I would be ready to accompany him in ten minutes and went upstairs to dress. When my wife heard that I was going out in the company of a Foreign Office official at that unusual time she was uncertain whether she was awake and witnessing my arrest and deportation or seeing a nightmare. It took me some time to persuade her that it was not usual to kidnap ambassadors and in my case she need not lose even a wink of sleep for fear that the Chinese would do any personal harm to me.

We left my house at twenty minutes past midnight. The streets were practically deserted and the clear October air in Peking added serenity to the silence of the night. Though I had guessed from the beginning that the reason for this sudden call was something connected with Korea, I was bursting with impatience to know what the matter actually was. Was it that Chou En-lai had fresh proposals that he desired to be communicated to Nehru? Was it to let me know that war had already started? Anyway I decided to wait and not to try and get an inkling from Chen. So we conversed about the magnificence of the celebrations of the previous day and the order and discipline which marked the proceedings. At 12.30 I was with Premier Chou En-lai at his official residence.

Though the occasion was the most serious I could imagine, a midnight interview on questions affecting the peace of the world, Chou En-lai was as courteous and charming as ever and did not give the least impression of worry or nervousness or indeed of being in any particular hurry. He had the usual tea served and the first two minutes were spent in normal courtesies, apology for disturbing me at an unusual hour, etc. Then he came to the point. He thanked Pandit Nehru for what he had been doing in the cause of peace, and said no country's need for peace was greater than that of China, but there were occasions when peace could only be defended by determination to resist aggression. If the Americans crossed the 38th parallel China would be forced to intervene in Korea. Otherwise he was most anxious for a peaceful settlement, and generally accepted Pandit Nehru's approach to the question. I asked him whether he had already news of the Americans having crossed the borders. He replied in the affirmative but added that he did not know where they had crossed. I asked him whether China intended to intervene, if only the South Koreans crossed the parallel. He was emphatic: "The South Koreans did not matter but American intrusion into North Korea would encounter Chinese resistance."

I returned home at 1.30 where my first secretary and cypher assistant were waiting. A telegram conveying the gist of the conversation with my own appreciation of the situation went the same night to New Delhi. . . .

c] TRUMAN AND MACARTHUR MEET

The Chief of State and the Far Eastern commander met briefly at Wake Island on October 15. MacArthur saw little purpose to the meeting but still was cordial to the President. The general's aides believed the meeting was designed to identify the President and *his* party with MacArthur and *his* victory, in order to help the Democrats in the Congressional elections three weeks away. Truman and MacArthur first had a private talk, apparently devoted largely to Philippine problems! They were then joined by their advisers in a discussion primarily concerned with the postwar reconstruction of Korea. Some attention was given, however, to the possibility of Chinese intervention.*

THE FOLLOWING were at the table: The President; General of the Army Douglas MacArthur; Admiral Arthur W. Radford, commander in chief, United States Pacific Fleet; Ambassador John Muccio; Secretary of the Army Frank Pace; Col. A. L. Hamblen; Ambassador at Large Philip C. Jessup; General of the Army Omar N. Bradley; Assistant Secretary of State Dean Rusk; Mr. W. Averell Harriman.

The conference opened at 0736.

The President asked General MacArthur to state the rehabilitation situation with reference to Korea.

General MACARTHUR. It cannot occur until the military operations have ended. I believe that formal resistance will end throughout North and South Korea by Thanksgiving. There is little resistance left in South Korea—only about 15,000 men—and those we do not destroy, the winter will. We now have about 60,000 prisoners in compounds.

In North Korea, unfortunately, they are pursuing a forlorn hope. They have about 100,000 men who were trained as replacements. They are poorly trained, led, and equipped, but they are obstinate and it goes against my grain to have to destroy them. They are only fighting to save face. Orientals prefer to die rather than to lose face.

. . . The North Koreans are making the same mistake they have made before. They have not deployed in depth. When the gap is closed the same thing will happen in the north as happened in the south.

It is my hope to be able to withdraw the Eighth Army to Japan by Christmas. That will leave the X Corps, which will be reconstituted, composed of the Second and Third Divisions and UN detachments. I hope the United Nations will hold elections by the first of the year. Nothing is gained by military occupation. All occupations are failures. [The President nodded agreement.] After elections are held I expect to pull out all occupying troops. Korea should have about 10 divisions with our equipment, supplemented by a small but competent Air Force and also by a small but competent Navy. If we do that, it will not only secure Korea but it will be a tremendous deterrent to the Chinese Communists moving south. This is a threat that cannot be laughed off. Again I emphasize the fact that the military should get out the minute the guns stop shooting and civilians take over. Korea is a land of poverty. . . .

The PRESIDENT. What are the chances for Chinese or Soviet interference?

General MACARTHUR. Very little. Had they interfered in the first or second months it would have been decisive. We are no longer fearful of their intervention. We no longer stand hat in hand. The Chinese have 300,000 men in Manchuria. Of these probably not more than 100,000 to 125,000 are distributed along the Yalu River. Only 50,000 to 60,000 could be gotten across the Yalu

---

* TRUMAN AND MACARTHUR MEET: From General Omar N. Bradley, ed., *Substance of Statements Made at Wake Island Conference on October 15, 1950* (Washington, 1951), pp. 1, 5.

River. They have no Air Force. Now that we have bases for our Air Force in Korea, if the Chinese tried to get down to Pyongyang there would be the greatest slaughter.

D] BOMBING THE BRIDGES

> The entry of Chinese forces into Korea in mid-October confronted the United States government with a new challenge, made all the more confusing by the fact that after about ten days of scattered fighting the Chinese broke off contact with the UN forces. In the proposals that MacArthur made to deal with this new situation and in the Washington reaction described by President Truman can be seen the germs of the conflict that full-scale Chinese intervention was to make a full-scale reality.*

THE FIRST report came from the headquarters of the X Corps in the Wonsan sector of North Korea. Prisoners captured on October 26 and later days had been identified as Chinese and, on interrogation, proved to be members of organized Chinese units. The prisoners stated that their units had crossed the Yalu River on October 16, only one day after General MacArthur had assured me on Wake Island that if any Chinese were to enter Korea they would face certain disaster but that he did not expect them to try anything that foolish. I asked the Joint Chiefs of Staff to obtain an up-to-date estimate of the situation from General MacArthur. This was MacArthur's answer, received on November 4:

"It is impossible at this time to authoritatively appraise the actualities of Chinese Communist intervention in North Korea. Various possibilities exist based upon the battle intelligence coming in from the front:

"First, that the Chinese Communist Government proposes to intervene with its full potential military forces, openly proclaiming such course at what it might determine as an appropriate time; second, that it will covertly render military assistance, but will, so far as possible, conceal the fact for diplomatic reasons; third, that it is permitting and abetting a flow of more or less voluntary personnel across the border to strengthen and assist the North Korean remnants in their struggle to retain a nominal foothold in Korea; fourth, that such intervention, as exists, has been in the belief that no UN forces would be committed in the extreme northern reaches of Korea except those of South Korea. A realization that such forces were insufficient for the purpose may well have furnished the concept of salvaging something from the wreckage.

"The first contingency would represent a momentous decision of the gravest international importance. While it is a distinct possibility, and many foreign experts predict such action, there are many fundamental logical reasons against it and sufficient evidence has not yet come to hand to warrant its immediate acceptance.

* BOMBING THE BRIDGES: From Harry S. Truman, *Memoirs*, II, *Years of Trial and Hope* (New York, 1956), pp. 373–78, 380. Copyright 1956, Time, Inc. Reprinted by permission of Time, Inc.

"The last three contingencies, or a combination thereof, seem to be most likely condition at the present moment.

"I recommend against hasty conclusions which might be premature and believe that a final appraisement should await a more complete accumulation of military facts."

Thus General MacArthur warned against any hasty action and specifically discounted the possibility that the intervention of the Chinese Communists was a "new war." It came as something of a shock, therefore, when within two days he began to sound the alarm.

I was in Kansas City on November 6; it was the day before election, and as usual I planned to cast my ballot in Independence. That morning I received an urgent call from Dean Acheson. The Secretary of State was calling from a conference in Washington with the Under Secretary of Defense, Robert Lovett, and the matter before them was of such importance that they felt an immediate decision was necessary.

This was the situation and developments as Acheson reported to me over the telephone. Under Secretary of Defense Lovett had come to his office, Acheson said, at ten o'clock to tell him that a message had just been received from the Air Force commander in the Far East, Lieutenant General Stratemeyer. MacArthur had ordered a bombing mission to take out the bridge across the Yalu River from Sinuiju (Korea) to Antung (Manchuria). Ninety B-29's were scheduled to take off at one o'clock Washington time to take part in this mission. Lovett had told Acheson that from an operational standpoint he doubted whether the results to be achieved would be important enough to outweigh the danger of bombing Antung or other points on the Manchurian side of the river.

Assistant Secretary of State Dean Rusk pointed out that we had a commitment with the British not to take action which might involve attacks on the Manchurian side of the river without consultation with them. He also told Mr. Lovett that the State Department had presented MacArthur's report on Chinese Communist intervention to the United Nations and that an urgent meeting of the Security Council had been requested. At this meeting we would try to get a resolution adopted calling on the Chinese Communists to cease their activities in Korea; this was necessary in order to maintain U.N. support for any further action to be taken. Mr. Rusk also mentioned the danger of involving the Soviets, especially in the light of the mutual-assistance treaty between Moscow and Peiping.

Acheson went on to say that Lovett and he had agreed that this air action ought to be postponed until we had more facts about the situation there. Lovett then called Marshall, who agreed that the attack was unwise unless there was some mass movement across the river which threatened the security of our troops. Then Lovett called the Air Force Secretary, Mr. Finletter, and instructed him to tell the Joint Chiefs what Mr. Rusk had set forth and to tell them that he (Lovett) and Acheson both felt that this action should be postponed until they were able to get a decision from me.

I told Acheson that I would approve this bombing mission only if there was an immediate and serious threat to the security of our troops. Acheson said that nothing had been heard from MacArthur since his last report, and that report had contained no statement of any further movements across the river but had spoken only of reserves on the Chinese side. I told Acheson that we would have to find out why MacArthur suddenly found this action necessary and told him to have Lovett issue instructions accordingly.

The Joint Chiefs of Staff carried out my instructions in a message that went out at eleven-forty Washington time, only an hour and twenty minutes before the planes were to take off from their Japanese bases. In the message that was sent, MacArthur was advised that consideration was urgently being given to the Korean situation at the governmental level. He was informed that there was a commitment not to take action affecting Manchuria without consultation with the British, and that until further orders all bombing of targets within five miles of the Manchurian border should be postponed. Meanwhile, he should forward his estimate of the situation and his reasons for ordering the bombing of the Yalu River bridges.

This was MacArthur's reply:

6 November 50

Men and material in large force are pouring across all bridges over the Yalu from Manchuria. This movement not only jeopardizes but threatens the ultimate destruction of the forces under my command. The actual movement across the river can be accomplished under cover of darkness and the distance between the river and our lines is so short that the forces can be deployed against our troops without being seriously subjected to air interdiction. The only way to stop this reinforcement of the enemy is the destruction of these bridges and the subjection of all installations in the north area supporting the enemy advance to the maximum of our air destruction. Every hour that this is postponed will be paid for dearly in American and other United Nations blood. The main crossing at Sinuiju was to be hit within the next few hours and the mission is actually being mounted. Under the gravest protest that I can make, I am suspending this strike and carrying out your instructions. What I had ordered is entirely within the scope of the rules of war and the resolutions and directions which I have received from the United Nations and constitutes no slightest act of belligerency against Chinese territory, in spite of the outrageous international lawlessness emanating therefrom. I cannot overemphasize the disastrous effect, both physical and psychological, that will result from the restrictions which you are imposing. I trust that the matter be immediately brought to the attention of the President as I believe your instructions may well result in a calamity of major proportion for which I cannot accept the responsibility without his personal and direct understanding of the situation. Time is so essential that I request immediate reconsideration of your decision pending which complete compliance will of course be given to your order.

General Bradley read this message to me over the phone. There were grave dangers involved in a mass bombing attack on a target so close to Manchuria and to Soviet soil. An overly eager pilot might easily bring about retaliatory moves; damaged planes might be forced to land in territory beyond our control. But since General MacArthur was on the scene and felt so strongly that this was of unusual urgency, I told Bradley to give him the "go-ahead."

This was the message sent MacArthur by the Joint Chiefs:

"The situation depicted in your message (of November 6) is considerably changed from that reported in last sentence your message (of November 4) which was our last report from you. We agree that the destruction of the Yalu bridges would contribute materially to the security of the forces under your command unless this action resulted in increased Chinese Communist effort and even Soviet contribution in response to what they might well construe as an attack on Manchuria. Such a result would not only endanger your forces but would enlarge the area of conflict and U.S. involvement to a most dangerous degree.

"However in view of first sentence your message (of November 6) you are authorized to go ahead with your planned bombing in Korea near the frontier including targets at Sinuiju and Korean end of Yalu bridges provided that at time of receipt of this message you still find such action essential to safety of your forces. The above does not authorize the bombing of any dams or power plants on the Yalu River.

"Because of necessity for maintaining optimum position with United Nations policy and directives and because it is vital in the national interests of the U.S. to localize the fighting in Korea it is important that extreme care be taken to avoid violation Manchurian territory and airspace and to report promptly hostile action from Manchuria.

"It is essential that we be kept informed of important changes in situation as they occur and that your estimate as requested in our [message of November 6] be submitted as soon as possible."

On this day, November 6, General MacArthur issued a communiqué in Tokyo in which he announced that his forces were now faced by a new and fresh army backed up by large reserves and adequate supplies within easy reach of the enemy but beyond the limits of the present sphere of military action.

The Central Intelligence Agency also now supplied me with an estimate of the situation based on their sources of information. It reported that there might be as many as two hundred thousand Chinese Communist troops in Manchuria and that their entry into Korea might stop the United Nations advance and actually force the United Nations forces to withdraw to defensive positions farther south. The estimate concluded by pointing to one inescapable fact: With their entry into Korea, the Chinese Communists had staked not only some of their forces but also their prestige in Asia. It had to be taken into account that they knew what risks they were taking; in other words, that they were ready for general war.

General MacArthur's estimate of the situation arrived in two messages on November 7. In the first of these messages MacArthur referred back to his initial appraisal (of November 4) of the Chinese intervention and concluded that he had been confirmed in his belief that this was not a full-scale intervention by the Chinese Communists. He conceded the possibility that the intervening forces might be reinforced to "a point rendering our resumption of advance impossible and even forcing a movement in retrograde." He was planning, he said, again to assume the initiative in order to take "accurate measure . . . of enemy strength." And he went on to say: "I deem it essential to execute the bombing of the targets under discussion as the only resource left to me to prevent a potential buildup of enemy strength to a point threatening the safety of the command. This interdiction of enemy lines of advance within Korea is so plainly defensive that it is hard to conceive that it would cause an increase in the volume of local intervention or, of itself, provoke a general war.

"The inviolability of Manchuria and Siberia has been a cardinal obligation of this headquarters from the beginning of hostilities and all verified hostile action therefrom is promptly reported. The destruction of hydroelectric installation has never been contemplated. Complete daily situation reports will continue to be furnished you as heretofore."

The second message from MacArthur read:

7 November 50

Hostile planes are operating from bases west of the Yalu River against our forces in North Korea. These planes are appearing in increasing numbers. The distance from the Yalu to the main line of contact is so short that it is almost impossible to deal effectively with the hit and run tactics now being employed. The present restrictions imposed on my area of operation provide a complete sanctuary for hostile air[craft] immediately upon their crossing the Manchuria-North Korean border. The effect of this abnormal condition upon the morale and combat efficiency of both air and ground troops is major.

Unless corrective measures are promptly taken this factor can assume decisive proportions. Request instructions for dealing with this new and threatening development.

Every military commander and every civilian official in the government is, of course, entitled to his views. Indeed, we would have a poor government if we expected all our public servants to be of one mind and one mind alone. I valued the expression of MacArthur's opinions, and so did the Joint Chiefs. There was never any question about my high regard for MacArthur's military judgment. But as President I had to listen to more than military judgments, and my decisions had to be made on the basis of not just one theater of operations but of a much more comprehensive picture of our nation's place in the world.

We were in Korea in the name and on behalf of the United Nations. The "unified command" which I had entrusted to Douglas MacArthur was a United Nations command, and neither he nor I would have been justified if we had gone beyond the mission that the United Nations General Assembly had given us.

There was no doubt in my mind that we should not allow the action in Korea to extend into a general war. All-out military action against China had to be avoided, if for no other reason than because it was a gigantic booby trap.

The Central Intelligence Agency's estimate of the situation was that the Russians were not themselves willing to go to war but that they wanted to involve us as heavily as possible in Asia so that they might gain a free hand in Europe.

I asked the Joint Chiefs of Staff to give their views on the military significance of the Chinese Communists' intervention in Korea. This is what they recommended:

"1. Every effort should be expended as a matter of urgency to settle the problem of Chinese Communist intervention in Korea by political means, preferably through the United Nations, to include reassurances to the Chinese Communists with respect to our intent, direct negotiations through our Allies and the Interim Committee with the Chinese Communist Government, and by any other available means.

"2. Pending further clarification as to the military objectives of the Chinese Communists and the extent of their intended commitments, the missions assigned to the Commander in Chief, United Nations Command, should be kept under review, but should not be changed.

"3. The United States should develop its plans and make its preparations on the basis that the risk of global war is increased."

General Marshall, as Secretary of Defense, concurred in these conclusions.

At a meeting on November 9 the National Security Council held a full discussion of these views of the Joint Chiefs and of the general problems created by the Chinese intervention. I was unable to attend this meeting but was given a report of the proceedings afterward. . . .

When Secretary Acheson summarized this discussion, he pointed out that it was agreed that General MacArthur's directive should not now be changed and that he should be free to do what he could in a military way, but without bombing Manchuria. At the same time, the State Department would seek ways to find out whether negotiations with the Chinese Communists were possible, although one problem was that we lacked any direct contacts with the Peiping regime through diplomatic channels.

The situation in Korea, it should be pointed out, was not the only instance of a new aggressiveness on the part of Communist China. There was evidence that the Communist rebel forces in Indo-China were receiving increasing aid and advice from Peiping. Also, in the last days of October, Communist China had moved against the ancient theocracy of Tibet.

We were seeing a pattern in Indo-China and Tibet timed to coincide with the attack in Korea as a challenge to the Western world. It was a challenge by the Communists alone, aimed at intensifying the smoldering anti-foreign feeling among most Asian peoples.

Our British allies and many statesmen of Europe saw in the Chinese moves a ruse to bring to a halt American aid in the rebuilding of Europe. They knew that nothing had hurt world Communism worse than the policy of the United States: aid to Greece and Turkey, the Marshall Plan, the decision to hold fast in Berlin, the North Atlantic Treaty Organization. The Kremlin could never communize Europe as long as that policy was followed and the United States stood ready to back it. The first commandment of Soviet foreign policy has always been to divide the enemies of the Soviet Union, and the unity that United States leadership had created in Europe was the most important target for world Communism's attack.

I had no intention of allowing our attention to be diverted from the unchanging aims and designs of Soviet policy. I knew that in our age, Europe, with its millions of skilled workmen, with its factories and transportation network, is still the key to world peace. . . .

E] The Chinese Intervene: Washington Takes
a Cautious Line

The Chinese launched a massive attack on November 28, and Truman had
the news by phone at 6:15 A.M. His staff was not informed at that hour.
John Hersey, who was writing a *New Yorker* profile of the President at the
time, happened to attend the regular White House staff meeting the morning the news arrived. The meeting started promptly at ten. Besides the President, there were twelve men in the room. Asking each aide in turn what he
had for the President's attention, Truman responded to each situation put
to him with deliberation and no trace of rush. The circuit of his aides took
some time. It was apparent, as it proceeded, that while the President brought
his mind to bear on whatever matter was raised, his attention was held by
some pressing concern within his privacy. When the questions were over,
he paused for a moment, and then, as Hersey reports it, said simply and
solemnly,

> We've got a terrific situation on our hands. General Bradley called me at
> six-fifteen this morning. He told me that a terrible message had come
> from General MacArthur. MacArthur said there were two hundred and
> sixty thousand Chinese troops against him out there. He says he has to
> go over to the defensive. It's no longer a question of a few so-called volun-
> teers. The Chinese have come in with both feet.

Continuing, the President noted what he had done by telephone before ten
o'clock and closed the meeting after making clear who was to be told what,
and when and how.
Once the full scope of the enemy offensive was evident, MacArthur dispatched to Washington the first of many requests for new measures to counter
the Chinese Communists. As the following excerpt from Truman's *Memoirs*
makes clear, however, the concerns and priorities of the officials in Washington differed markedly from those of the theater commander.*

By that time a new point of disagreement had come up between General
MacArthur and the defense chiefs. On November 28 General MacArthur had
reported that he was changing his plans from the offensive to the defensive
as provided for in the directives which he had been given. In his message on
this subject he made the statement that "we face an entirely new war. . . ."
His message said, "The resulting situation presents an entire new picture
which broadens the potentialities to world embracing consideration beyond the
sphere of decision by the theatre commander. This command has done everything humanly possible within its capabilities but is now faced with conditions
beyond its control and its strength."
On the following day General MacArthur submitted a recommendation
that we go back and take up the offer made seven months earlier by Chiang
Kai-shek of thirty-three thousand Chinese Nationalist troops for Korea. At
that time he himself had advised against using these troops. His recommendation now was, of course, in line with his view that the Korean action had

---

* THE CHINESE INTERVENE: WASHINGTON TAKES A CAUTIOUS LINE: From Harry S.
Truman, *Memoirs*, II, *Years of Trial and Hope* (New York, 1956), pp. 384–88. Copyright
1956, Time, Inc. Reprinted by permission of Time, Inc.

become a war with Communist China. I instructed the Joint Chiefs of Staff, after a lengthy conference in which State Department and Defense Department took part, to call MacArthur's attention to the international implication of his recommendation, and the following message was sent on November 29 by the Joint Chiefs of Staff:

"Your proposal is being considered. It involves world-wide consequences. We shall have to consider the possibility that it would disrupt the united position of the nations associated with us in the United Nations, and have us isolated. It may be wholly unacceptable to the commonwealth countries to have their forces employed with Nationalist Chinese. It might extend hostilities to Formosa and other areas. Incidentally, our position of leadership in the Far East is being most seriously compromised in the United Nations. The utmost care will be necessary to avoid the disruption of the essential Allied line-up in that organization."

Of course the situation in Korea was the subject of many long and anxious discussions in my office. The future of our policy, not only in Asia, but in Europe as well, was at stake, and we spent a good deal more time searching for the answers to the tremendous problems before us than merely worrying over General MacArthur's lack of discretion.

On November 28, when the bad news from Korea had changed from rumors of resistance into certainty of defeat, I called a special meeting of the National Security Council. My own first knowledge of the extent of damage that the Chinese were inflicting on our troops had come at six-fifteen that morning, when General Bradley had telephoned me a cable report from General MacArthur. General Bradley and the Chiefs of Staff had been in session all the day before, examining the situation, and they felt that while it was serious they were doubtful that it was as much a catastrophe as our newspapers were leading us to believe.

General Bradley, however, stressed the danger that might arise if the Communists decided to use their air potential. It was our information that there were at least three hundred bombers on fields in nearby Manchuria. These bombers could hurt us badly, both by attacks on the airlift and by surprise raids on our closely jammed planes on Korean fields. Despite these facts, General Bradley said that the Joint Chiefs of Staff did not believe that General MacArthur should be authorized to bomb airfields in Manchuria.

I asked if there was any way to lessen the damage we might suffer from a sudden air attack by the Chinese Communists, and General Vandenberg said there was none, short of moving our planes back to Japan. This, of course, would mean a considerable slowing up of our own military operations.

I asked Secretary of Defense Marshall for his comments on the situation, and he reported that the civilian heads of the services, too, had been in conference all day as a result of the developments in Korea. They had talked over what new requirements this would place on the procurement and supply of both men and matériel. A second military supplemental budget estimate was ready, and it was Marshall's opinion, as he had made clear to me earlier that day, that it ought to be sent over to Congress at once. I was therefore able to inform the meeting that the Budget Director had already been instructed by me on this point.

General Marshall then talked about the diplomatic aspects of the situation, saying he thought it essential for the United States to go along with the United Nations approach to the Korean question, even if going along with the United Nations meant some difficult problems for us. He said that he felt it essential for us to keep a unanimity of approach in the U.N. He was emphatic on one point, on which he said the three service Secretaries agreed as the most important: that we should not get ourselves involved either individually or with the United Nations in a general war with China. Marshall said he did not think it was likely that the U.N. would get us "in such a fix," but he thought we should recognize that there were some people at home who seemed to want all-out action against China.

Bradley said this reflected the Joint Chiefs' thinking too. If we allowed ourselves to be pulled into a general war with China, it would be impossible to continue the build-up of forces in Europe. Secretary Pace added that it was important that everyone in the room understand that we had only the 82nd Airborne Division available at home and that the National Guard units that had been called into federal service would not be ready for combat until the middle of March. . . .

There was discussion then of the number of replacements MacArthur would need and what we might be able to send him. General Collins said he thought that a line could be held in Korea. The X Corps in the east was in a precarious position but probably could be pulled back to safety.

I asked Dean Acheson then to comment on the situation from his point of view, and the Secretary of State began with the statement that the events of the last few hours had moved us very much closer to the danger of general war. There had always been evidence of some Chinese participation in Korea, of course, but now we had an open, powerful, offensive attack. He said that we needed to bear in mind that the Soviet Union was behind every one of the Chinese and North Korean moves and that we had to think of all that happened in Korea as world matters. We should never lose sight of the fact that we were facing the Soviet Union all around the world.

Of course, Acheson continued, if we openly accused the Soviet Union of aggression, the United Nations would be demolished. If we came out and pointed a finger at the Soviet Union, it would serve no purpose, because we could do nothing about it. To make the accusation, however, and then to do nothing about it would only weaken our world position. If we proposed action against the Kremlin, on the other hand, we might find ourselves alone, without allies.

As for the Chinese Communists, Acheson went on, we ought to draw a line and not try to walk both sides of the street. There was no use denying that they were fighting us, so we had better stir up trouble for them. There were a number of ways in which that could be done besides playing with Chiang.

As for the conflict in Korea, the Secretary of State was of the opinion that we should find some way to end it. If we went into Manchuria and bombed the airfields there with any degree of success, "Russia would cheerfully get in it." We had banked our entire foreign policy on the idea of keeping Russia contained, and we had succeeded in repulsing her attempts to break out. If we allowed the Russians now to trap us inside their perimeter, however, we would run the risk of being sucked into a bottomless pit. There would be no end to it, and it would bleed us dry. The Russians had tried to lure us into traps time and again. This one differed only in being bigger than the earlier ones.

Averell Harriman, who took part in the meeting, said that we ought to give careful attention to the mood of the free world. We had to maintain our leadership, and the immediate appointment of a supreme commander for the NATO powers would prove that. The free nations would stick with us if they felt sure that we were going to stick with them.

I said that it would be easier to convince the free world if some of our press were not so anxious to prove the contrary. Three of our biggest publishers, I think, were dividing our people and leading the world to believe that the American people had no confidence in their government. The campaign of vilification and lies and distortion of facts in so many of our papers was the greatest asset the Soviets had.

I told the National Security Council that I had thought at first that I ought to go before Congress and address a special session but that I did not now think this would be right. Korea was a United Nations matter, and our country should not make an individual approach to it. . . .

2] The Dilemmas of Defeat: MacArthur and Washington Debate Policy

> December, 1950, was a grim month. The UN forces were driven out of North Korea and the Communists reoccupied Seoul, capital of South Korea, on January 4. Throughout the first part of January, whether the UN forces would be able to maintain themselves in Korea remained in doubt. Such circumstances led to an extended exchange of messages between MacArthur and Washington. Washington wanted light on the military situation; MacArthur wanted an explicit policy; both wished to minimize their responsibility for the defeat that seemed so probable.*

A] JOINT CHIEFS OF STAFF TO MACARTHUR, DECEMBER 29, 1950

CHINESE Communists now appear, from estimates available, capable of forcing evacuation by forces of UN. By committing substantial United States forces

---

* THE DILEMMAS OF DEFEAT: MACARTHUR AND WASHINGTON DEBATE POLICY: From *Military Situation in the Far East, Hearings Before Committee on the Armed Services and Committee on Foreign Relations*, U.S. Senate, 82 Cong., 1 Sess. (1951), pp. 2179–80; Major General Courtney Whitney, *MacArthur, His Rendezvous with History* (New York, 1956), pp. 432–34, reprinted from *MacArthur, His Rendezvous with History* by Major General Courtney Whitney, by permission of Alfred A. Knopf, Inc., copyright 1955 by Time, Inc.; *Military Situation in the Far East, Hearings Before Committee on the*

which would place other commitments, including safety of Japan, in serious jeopardy, or by inflicting serious losses on him, enemy might be forced to abandon exercise of his capability. If with present UN strength successful resistance at some position in Korea without our incurring serious losses could be accomplished and apparent military and political prestige of Chinese Communists could be deflated, it would be of great importance to our national interests. In the face of increased threat of general war JCS believe commitment of additional United States ground forces in Korea should not be made, since our view is that major war should not be fought in Korea.

Not considered practicable to obtain at this time significant additional forces from other United Nations. Therefore in light of present situation your basic directive, of furnish to ROK assistance as necessary to repel armed attack and restore to the area security and peace, is modified. Your directive now is to defend in successive positions, subject to safety of your troops as your primary consideration, inflicting as much damage to hostile forces in Korea as is possible.

In view of continued threat to safety of Japan and possibility of forced withdrawal from Korea it is important to make advance determination of last reasonable opportunity for orderly evacuation. It appears here that if Chinese Communists retain force capability of forcing evacuation after having driven UN forces to rear it would be necessary to direct commencement of your withdrawal. Request your views on these conditions which should determine evacuation. You should consider your mission of defending Japan and limitation on troops available to you. Definite directive on conditions for initiation of evacuation will be provided when your views are received.

For the present this message which has been handled with ultimate security should be known only to your chief of staff and to Ridgway and his chief of staff.

B] MacArthur to the Joint Chiefs of Staff, December 30, 1950

Any estimate of relative capabilities in the Korean campaign appears to be dependent upon political-military policies yet to be formulated vis-à-vis Chinese military operations being conducted against our forces. It is quite clear now that the entire military resource of the Chinese nation, with logistic support from the Soviet, is committed to a maximum effort against the United Nations command. In implementation of this commitment a major concentration of Chinese force in the Korean-Manchurian area will increasingly leave China

Armed Services and Committee on Foreign Relations, U.S. Senate, 82 Cong., 1 Sess. (1951), pp. 332–33; Major General Courtney Whitney, *MacArthur, His Rendezvous with History* (New York, 1956), pp. 435–36, reprinted from *MacArthur, His Rendezvous with History* by Major General Courtney Whitney, by permission of Alfred A. Knopf, Inc., copyright 1955 by Time, Inc.; Harry S. Truman, *Memoirs*, II, *Years of Trial and Hope* (New York, 1956), pp. 435–36, copyright 1956, Time, Inc., reprinted by permission of Time, Inc.

vulnerable in areas whence troops to support Korean operations have been drawn. Meanwhile, under existing restrictions, our naval and air potential are being only partially utilized and the great potential of Chinese Nationalist force on Formosa and guerrilla action on the mainland are being ignored. Indeed, as to the former, we are preventing its employment against the common enemy by our own naval force.

Should a policy determination be reached by our government or through it by the United Nations to recognize the state of war which has been forced upon us by the Chinese authorities and to take retaliatory measures within our capabilities, we could: (1) blockade the coast of China; (2) destroy through naval gun fire and air bombardment China's industrial capacity to wage war; (3) secure reinforcements from the Nationalist garrison in Formosa to strengthen our position in Korea if we decided to continue the fight for that peninsula; and (4) release existing restrictions upon the Formosan garrison for diversionary action (possibly leading to counter-invasion) against vulnerable areas of the Chinese mainland.

I believe *that by the foregoing measures we could severely cripple and largely neutralize China's capability to wage aggressive war and thus save Asia from the engulfment otherwise facing it.* I believe furthermore that we could do so with but a small part of our overall military potential committed to the purpose. There is no slightest doubt but that this action would at once release the pressure upon our forces in Korea, whereupon determination could be reached as to whether to maintain the fight in that area or to affect a strategic displacement of our forces with the view to strengthening our defense of the littoral island chain while continuing our naval and air pressure upon China's military potential. I am fully conscious of the fact that this course of action has been rejected in the past for fear of provoking China into a major war effort, but we must now realistically recognize that China's commitment thereto has already been fully and unequivocably made and that nothing we can do would further aggravate the situation as far as China is concerned.

Whether defending ourselves by way of military retaliation would bring in Soviet military intervention or not is a matter of speculation. I have always felt that a Soviet decision to precipitate a general war would depend solely upon the Soviet's own estimate of relative strengths and capabilities with little regard to other factors. . . . If we are forced to evacuate Korea without taking military measures against China proper as suggested in your message, it would have the most adverse affect upon the people of Asia, not excepting the Japanese, *and a material reinforcement of the forces now in this theater would be mandatory if we are to hold the littoral defense chain against determined assault.*

Moreover, it must be borne in mind that evacuation of our forces from Korea under any circumstances would at once release the bulk of the Chinese forces now absorbed by that campaign for action elsewhere—quite probably in areas of far greater importance than Korea itself. . . .

I understand thoroughly the demand for European security and fully concur in doing everything possible in that sector, but not to the point of accepting defeat anywhere else—an acceptance which I am sure could not fail to insure later defeat in Europe itself. The preparations for the defense of Europe, however, by the most optimistic estimate are aimed at a condition of readiness two years hence. The use of forces in the present emergency in the Far East could not in any way prejudice this basic concept. To the contrary, it would ensure thoroughly seasoned forces for later commitment in Europe synchronously with Europe's own development of military resources.

So far as your tactical estimate of the situation in Korea is concerned, under the conditions presently implied, viz: no reinforcements, continued restrictions upon Chinese Nationalist action, no military measures against China's continental military potential, and the concentration of Chinese military force solely upon the Korean sector, would seem to be sound. The tactical plan of a successively contracting defense line south to the Pusan beachhead is believed the only possible way which the evacuation could be accomplished. In the execution of this plan it would not be necessary for you to make an anticipatory decision for evacuation until such time as we may be forced to that beachhead line.

c] Joint Chiefs of Staff to MacArthur, January 9, 1951

THIS replies to your recommendations:

Careful consideration still being given to measures of retaliation you suggested. Contribution to general situation resulting from drawing of Chinese Communists into Korea is fully appreciated.

The following points must be accepted on the basis of consideration of the over-all situation:

(*a*) Strengthening of our effort in Korea does not appear justified on the basis of any change in policy or other eventuality outside of Korea.

(*b*) United Nations concurrence would be necessary and, in particular, negotiations with the British would be required on the question of blockade. Hong Kong position and extent of Chinese Communist trade with British would be involved. Evacuation from Korea by our forces, or stabilization of our position in Korea, would be required before naval blockade of China coast could be undertaken.

(*c*) Decision of attack objectives in Communist China with naval and air forces must await attack outside of Korea on UN forces by Chinese Communists, since only in that eventuality could authorization be obtained.

(*d*) In view of probable greater usefulness elsewhere and unlikeliness of effect on Korean outcome which would be decisive, use in Korea of Chinese Nationalists from Formosa not favored.

(*e*) In event stabilization in Korea not feasible, security of Japan must be served by portion of the forces which may be evacuated from Korea. If stabilization in Korea without commitment of additional forces can be accomplished, deployment of two National Guard divisions partly trained may be expected.

(*f*) Intensification of economic blockade of Chinese trade being pressed.

d] MacArthur to the Joint Chiefs of Staff, January 10, 1951

In view of the self-evident fact that my command as presently constituted is of insufficient strength to hold a position in Korea and simultaneously protect Japan against external assault, strategic dispositions taken in the present situation must be based upon over-riding political policy establishing the relativity of American interests in the Far East. There is no doubt but that a beachhead line can be held by our existing forces for a limited time in Korea, but this could not be accomplished without losses. Whether such losses were regarded as "severe" or not would to a certain extent depend upon the connotation one gives the term. . . . The troops are tired from a long and difficult campaign, embittered by the shameful propaganda which has falsely condemned their courage and fighting quality in misunderstood retrograde maneuver, and their morale will become a serious threat to their battle efficiency unless the political basis on which they are asked to trade life for time is quickly delineated, fully understood and so impelling that the hazards of battle are cheerfully accepted.

The issue really boils down to the question whether or not the United States intends to evacuate Korea, and involves a decision of highest national and international importance, far above the competence of a theater commander guided largely by incidents affecting the tactical situation developing upon a very limited field of action. Nor is it a decision which should be left to the initiative of enemy action, which in effect would be the determining criteria under a reasonable interpretation of your message. My query therefore amounts to this: is it the present objective of United States political policy to maintain a military position in Korea indefinitely, for a limited time, or to minimize losses by the evacuation as soon as it can be accomplished?

e] The President Lays Down a Policy, January 13, 1951

When General Marshall brought me this message from MacArthur, I was deeply disturbed. The Far East commander was, in effect, reporting that the course of action decided upon by the National Security Council and by the Joint Chiefs of Staff and approved by me was not feasible. He was saying that we would be driven off the peninsula or, at the very least, suffer terrible losses. Events were to prove that he was wrong, but it was the proper procedure for him to voice his doubts and to ask for reconsideration of the Washington decision. I asked the National Security Council to meet in a special session on January 12 to discuss the MacArthur message and what should be done about it.

At this meeting I expressed the view that it was important to keep Mac-Arthur fully informed on political as well as military matters. We had done that all along. He had received copies of many important papers even though few, apparently, had really found their way to his desk. I would therefore send a personal message to General MacArthur bringing him up to date on our foreign policy. This was my message to MacArthur:

January 13, 1951

I want you to know that the situation in Korea is receiving the utmost attention here and that our efforts are concentrated upon finding the right decisions on this matter of the gravest importance to the future of America and to the survival of free peoples everywhere.

I wish in this telegram to let you have my views as to our basic national and international purposes in continuing the resistance to aggression in Korea. We need your judgment as to the maximum effort which could reasonably be expected from the United Nations forces under your command to support the resistance to aggression which we are trying rapidly to organize on a world-wide basis. This present telegram is not to be taken in any sense as a directive. Its purpose is to give you something of what is in our minds regarding the political factors.

1. A successful resistance in Korea would serve the following important purposes:

(a) To demonstrate that aggression will not be accepted by us or by the United Nations and to provide a rallying point around which the spirits and energies of the free world can be mobilized to meet the world-wide threat which the Soviet Union now poses.

(b) To deflate the dangerously exaggerated political and military prestige of Communist China which now threatens to undermine the resistance of non-Communist Asia and to consolidate the hold of Communism on China itself.

(c) To afford more time for and to give direct assistance to the organization of non-Communist resistance in Asia, both outside and inside China.

(d) To carry out our commitments of honor to the South Koreans and to demonstrate to the world that the friendship of the United States is of inestimable value in time of adversity.

(e) To make possible a far more satisfactory peace settlement for Japan and to contribute greatly to the post-treaty security position of Japan in relation to the continent.

(f) To lend resolution to many countries not only in Asia but also in Europe and the Middle East who are now living within the shadow of Communist power and to let them know that they need not now rush to come to terms with Communism on whatever terms they can get, meaning complete submission.

(g) To inspire those who may be called upon to fight against great odds if subjected to a sudden onslaught by the Soviet Union or by Communist China.

(h) To lend point and urgency to the rapid build-up of the defenses of the western world.

(i) To bring the United Nations through its first great effort on collective security and to produce a free-world coalition of incalculable value to the national security interests of the United States.

(j) To alert the peoples behind the Iron Curtain that their masters are bent upon wars of aggression and that this crime will be resisted by the free world.

2. Our course of action at this time should be such as to consolidate the great majority of the United Nations. This majority is not merely part of the organization but is also the nations whom we would desperately need to count on as allies in the event the Soviet Union moves against us. Further, pending the build-up of our national strength, we must act with great prudence in so far as extending the area of hostilities is concerned. Steps which might in themselves be fully justified and which might lend some assistance to the campaign in Korea would not be beneficial if they thereby involved Japan or Western Europe in large-scale hostilities.

3. We recognize, of course, that continued resistance might not be militarily possible with the limited forces with which you are being called upon to meet large Chinese armies. Further, in the present world situation, your forces must be preserved as an effective instrument for the defense of Japan and elsewhere. However, some of the important purposes mentioned above might be supported, if you should think it practicable, and advisable, by continued resistance from off-shore islands of Korea, particularly from Cheju-do, if it becomes impracticable to hold an important portion of Korea itself. In the worst case, it would be important that, if we must withdraw from Korea, it be clear to the world that that course is forced upon us by military necessity and that we shall not accept the result politically or militarily until the aggression has been rectified.

4. In reaching a final decision about Korea, I shall have to give constant thought to the main threat from the Soviet Union and to the need for a rapid expansion of our armed forces to meet this great danger.

5. I am encouraged to believe that the free world is getting a much clearer and realistic picture of the dangers before us and that the necessary courage and energy will be forthcoming. Recent proceedings in the United Nations have disclosed a certain amount of confusion and wishful thinking, but I believe that most members have been actuated by a desire to be absolutely sure that all possible avenues to peaceful settlement have been fully explored. I believe that the great majority is now rapidly consolidating and that the result will be an encouraging and formidable combination in defense of freedom.

6. The entire nation is grateful for your splendid leadership in the difficult struggle in Korea and for the superb performance of your forces under the most difficult circumstances.

[s] Harry S. Truman

General MacArthur had, as he had in previous wars, displayed splendid leadership. But I wanted him to accept, as a soldier should, the political decisions which the civil authorities of the government had determined upon.

3] The Conflict of Authorities: The President Chooses

a] MacArthur Counters the President

General Ridgway's success in stopping the Chinese advance at the end of January and his subsequent counteroffensive cut the ground out from under MacArthur's strategy. In February the Far Eastern commander declared that the UN forces would not be able to go north of the 38th parallel unless the war was expanded. By March, however, the UN armies were at the parallel and Washington was seeking ways of bringing the war to an end without further fighting.*

. . . Throughout the early months of 1951, Defense and State Department officials met repeatedly to plan possible courses of action in Korea and in Asia generally.

* MACARTHUR COUNTERS THE PRESIDENT: From Harry S. Truman, *Memoirs*, II, *Years of Trial and Hope* (New York, 1956), pp. 438–42. Copyright 1956, Time, Inc. Reprinted by permission of Time, Inc.

In March, as the tide of battle in Korea began to turn in our favor, both groups favored a new approach to a negotiated cease-fire. The reasoning was that, in the first place, since we had been able to inflict heavy casualties on the Chinese and were pushing them back to and beyond the 38th parallel, it would now be in their interest at least as much as ours to halt the fighting, and secondly, the invaders stood substantially ejected from the territory of the Republic of Korea.

The Department of State drew up a statement which they proposed I should issue. On March 19 Secretary Acheson, General Marshall, and the Joint Chiefs of Staff held a meeting at which they discussed this draft. They also agreed to inform General MacArthur that there was going to be a presidential announcement and to ask him to offer his recommendations.

I was just ending a brief vacation at the Little White House at Key West, Florida, where I kept in constant touch with Acheson and Marshall, when on March 20 the Joint Chiefs of Staff, carrying out the agreement of the preceding day, sent this message to General MacArthur:

"State Department planning a Presidential announcement shortly that, with clearing of bulk of South Korea of aggressors, United Nations now preparing to discuss conditions of settlement in Korea. United Nations feeling exists that further diplomatic efforts toward settlement should be made before any advance with major forces north of 38th parallel. Time will be required to determine diplomatic reactions and permit new negotiations that may develop. Recognizing that parallel has no military significance, State has asked Joint Chiefs of Staff what authority you should have to permit sufficient freedom of action for next few weeks to provide security for United Nations forces and maintain contact with enemy. Your recommendation desired."

In his reply the following day General MacArthur recommended that no additional restrictions be imposed on his command. He pointed out that, with the forces at his command and operating under the limitations which had been placed on him, it was not practicable for him to attempt to clear North Korea of the enemy and that he felt for that reason his current directive covered the situation quite well.

Following the receipt of MacArthur's reply, the Joint Chiefs of Staff again met with the Secretary of Defense and the State Department, and further details of the proposed presidential announcement were worked out. Furthermore, State Department officials met with the Washington representatives of the other nations that had troops in Korea in order to obtain their approval to the proposed draft.

This was the draft:

"I make the following statement as Chief Executive of the Government requested by the United Nations to exercise the Unified Command in Korea, and after full consultation with United Nations Governments contributing combat forces in support of the United Nations in Korea.

"United Nations forces in Korea are engaged in repelling the aggressions committed against the Republic of Korea and against the United Nations.

"The aggressors have been driven back with heavy losses to the general vicinity from which the unlawful attack was first launched last June.

"There remains the problem of restoring international peace and security in the area in accordance with the terms of the Security Council resolution of June 27, 1950. The spirit and principles of the United Nations Charter require that every effort be made to prevent the spread of hostilities and to avoid the prolongation of the misery and the loss of life.

"There is a basis for restoring peace and security in the area which should be acceptable to all nations which sincerely desire peace.

"The Unified Command is prepared to enter into arrangements which would conclude the fighting and ensure against its resumption. Such arrangements would open the way for a broader settlement for Korea, including the withdrawal of foreign forces from Korea.

"The United Nations has declared the policy of the world community that the people of Korea be permitted to establish a unified, independent and democratic state.

"The Korean people are entitled to peace. They are entitled to determine their political and other institutions by their own choice and in response to their own needs.

"The Korean people are entitled to the assistance of the world community in repairing the ravages of war—assistance which the United Nations is ready to give and for which it has established the necessary machinery. Its member nations have already made generous offers of help. What is needed is peace, in which the United Nations can use its resources in the creative tasks of reconstruction.

"It is regrettable that those who are opposing the United Nations in Korea have made so little response to the many opportunities which have been and continue to be afforded for a settlement in Korea.

"A prompt settlement of the Korean problem would greatly reduce international tension in the Far East and would open the way for the consideration of other problems in that area by the processes of peaceful settlement envisaged in the Charter of the United Nations.

"Until satisfactory arrangements for concluding the fighting have been reached, United Nations military action must be continued."

The thought behind this was that a suggestion of our willingness to settle, without any threats or recriminations, might get a favorable reply.

Unfortunately, the careful preparations were all in vain. The many hours spent to secure the approval of the other governments, the detailed discussions among diplomats and defense leaders became useless when on March 24 General MacArthur released a statement that was so entirely at cross-purposes with the one I was to have delivered that it would only have confused the world if my carefully prepared statement had been made.

What General MacArthur said was this:

"Operations continue according to schedule and plan. We have now substantially cleared South Korea of organized Communist forces. It is becoming increasingly evident that the heavy destruction along the enemy's lines of supply, caused by our round-the-clock massive air and naval bombardment, has left his troops in the forward battle area deficient in requirements to sustain his operations. This weakness is being brilliantly exploited by our ground forces. The enemy's human wave tactics have definitely failed him as our own forces have become seasoned to this form of warfare; his tactics of infiltration are but contributing to his piecemeal losses, and he is showing less stamina than our own troops under the rigors of climate, terrain and battle.

"Of even greater significance than our tactical successes has been the clear revelation that this new enemy, Red China, of such exaggerated and vaunted military power, lacks the industrial capacity to provide adequately many critical items necessary to the conduct of modern war. He lacks the manufacturing base and those raw materials needed to produce, maintain and operate even moderate air and naval power, and he cannot provide the essentials for successful ground operations, such as tanks, heavy artillery and other refinements science has introduced into the conduct of military campaigns. Formerly his great numerical potential might well have filled this gap but with the development of existing methods of mass destruction, numbers alone do not offset the vulnerability inherent in such deficiencies. Control of the seas and the air, which in turn means control over supplies, communications, and transportation, are no less essential and decisive now than in the past. When this control exists as in our case, and is coupled with an inferiority of ground fire power as in the enemy's case, the resulting disparity is such that it cannot be overcome by bravery, however fanatical, or the most gross indifference to human loss.

"These military weaknesses have been clearly and definitely revealed since Red China entered upon its undeclared war in Korea. Even under the inhibitions which now restrict the activity of the United Nations forces and the corresponding military advantages which accrue to Red China, it has been shown its complete inability to accomplish by force of arms the conquest of Korea. The enemy, therefore, must by now be painfully aware that a decision of the United Nations to depart from its tolerant effort to contain the war to the area of Korea, through an expansion of our military operations to its coastal areas and interior bases, would doom Red China to the risk of imminent military collapse. These basic facts being established, there should be no insuperable difficulty in arriving at decisions on the Korean problem if the issues are resolved on their own merits, without being burdened by extraneous matters not directly related to Korea, such as Formosa or China's seat in the United Nations.

"The Korean nation and people, which have been so cruelly ravaged, must not be sacrificed. This is a paramount concern. Apart from the military area of the problem where issues are resolved in the course of combat, the fundamental questions continue to be political in nature and must find their answer in the diplomatic sphere. Within the area of my authority as the military commander, however, it would be needless to say that I stand ready at any time to confer in the field with the commander-in-chief of the enemy forces in the earnest effort to find any military means whereby realization of the political objectives of the United Nations in Korea, to which no nation may justly take exceptions, might be accomplished without further bloodshed."

This was a most extraordinary statement for a military commander of the United Nations to issue on his own responsibility. It was an act totally disregarding all directives to abstain from any declarations on foreign policy. It was in open defiance of my orders as President and as Commander in Chief. This was a challenge to the authority of the President under the Constitution. It also flouted the policy of the United Nations.

By this act MacArthur left me no choice—I could no longer tolerate his insubordination.

In effect, what MacArthur was doing was to threaten the enemy with an ultimatum—intimating that the full preponderance of Allied power might be brought to bear against Red China. To be sure, he said that this would be a political decision, but considering his high office, the world would assume that he had advance knowledge that such a decision would be made.

This was certainly the immediate effect among our allies. From capitals all over the world came rush inquiries: What does this mean? Is there about to be a shift in American policy?

There was more involved than the fate of a prepared statement that the President of the United States had intended to make, or even than the diplomatic furor created by this "pronunciamento," as the Norwegian Ambassador called it when he inquired at the State Department what it meant. What was much more important was that once again General MacArthur had openly defied the policy of his Commander in Chief, the President of the United States. . . .

B] CONGRESSMAN MARTIN RELEASES A LETTER

The administration was slowly facing up to the "MacArthur problem." The final nudge was furnished by the Republican leader in the House of Representatives, Joseph W. Martin, Jr., of Massachusetts. On March 8 Martin had written MacArthur soliciting his views on the use of the Chinese Nationalist troops on Formosa "in the opening of a second Asiatic front to relieve the pressure on our forces in Korea." MacArthur replied on March 20. Martin held MacArthur's letter for two weeks and then, on April 5, arose on the floor of the House and read the letter into the Record, thereby precipitating the general's recall.*

Mr. MARTIN of Massachusetts. Mr. Chairman, the Speaker, for whom I have an affectionate regard and whose judgment I value, told us yesterday that because of the current massing of Communist troops in Korea and Manchuria, it is his "firm belief that we are in greater danger of an expanded war today than we have been at any time since the close of the World War in 1945."

Mr. RAYBURN said:

I think that we stand in the face of terrible danger and maybe the beginning of world war III.

It should be evident that the administration apparently has information which it has not imparted to the other Members of Congress and to the American people. We all know that we are in a critical period in our international relations. And that we must use every resource at our command and a maximum of wisdom if we are to survive. We have known that for some time; that is why we have the draft and are spending billions for armaments.

* CONGRESSMAN MARTIN RELEASES A LETTER: From the Congressional Record, 82 Cong., 1 Sess. (April 5, 1951), p. 3380.

Whether we are on the immediate brink of another world war, I cannot say.

But I do know this—because of adherence to policies long since proven disastrous, our State Department today is blocking the use of the fullest resources available to us.

I refer to the failure to employ the 800,000 anti-Communist Chinese troops on Formosa under the command of Generalissimo Chiang Kai-shek. I discussed this failure to use Formosan troops in a speech I delivered in Brooklyn on February 12, and I have reexamined this question in several speeches since.

Under the legislation we are considering here today, we contemplate calling up tens of thousands of additional American boys to hold the front in Korea, and for dispersal to Europe. We have had the testimony of General Eisenhower and the highest officers of the Pentagon concerning the European theater. The Congress unfortunately has not had the benefit of similar advice from our Far Eastern Command.

I want to say to this House that if we are closer to a third world war today than at any time since 1945 because of the current massing of Communist troops in Korea and Manchuria, then I think it is imperative for the safety of our Nation that we know completely and thoroughly the views of the Far Eastern Command, and at once. It is because of this belief I have decided to make public a letter that I received a week ago.

Several weeks ago I wrote General MacArthur a note and I enclosed a copy of my February 12 address. I wanted to make sure my views were not in conflict with what was best for America.

General MacArthur was kind enough to reply to my letter, and I wish at this time to read it to the House:

DEAR CONGRESSMAN MARTIN: I am most grateful for your note of the eighth forwarding me a copy of your address of February 12. The latter I have read with much interest, and find that with the passage of years you have certainly lost none of your old time punch.

My views and recommendations with respect to the situation created by Red China's entry into war against us in Korea have been submitted to Washington in most complete detail. Generally these views are well known and clearly understood, as they follow the conventional pattern of meeting force with maximum counter force as we have never failed to do in the past. Your view with respect to the utilization of the Chinese forces on Formosa is in conflict with neither logic nor this tradition.

It seems strangely difficult for some to realize that here in Asia is where the Communist conspirators have elected to make their play for global conquest, and that we have joined the issue thus raised on the battlefield; that here we fight Europe's war with arms while the diplomats there still fight it with words; that if we lose the war to communism in Asia the fall of Europe is inevitable, win it and Europe most probably would avoid war and yet preserve freedom. As you point out, we must win. There is no substitute for victory.

With renewed thanks and expressions of most cordial regard, I am,

Faithfully yours,

DOUGLAS MACARTHUR.

It is perfectly clear from General McArthur's words that he strongly favors the employment of the anti-Communist forces on Formosa. I wish to ask that if, as the general says, "The utilization of the Chinese forces on Formosa is in conflict with neither logic nor tradition," why in God's name are we not using them?

I think it is high time that the administration and the Pentagon came clean with the Congress and with the American people. Certainly if there is danger, the enemy knows it. Why hold it back from the American people? . . .

c] THE BRITISH EXPRESS ALARM

> MacArthur's letter to Representative Martin was directed as much against the administration's European allies as against the administration. The reaction in Europe was vigorous. The concern of the British government was reflected in a news report of April 8, which, as one historian put it, "may have been an official leak." *

BRITAIN ASKS UNITED STATES TO EXPLAIN
STRONG EXCEPTION TO MAC ARTHUR LETTER—FEAR OF CHANGES IN POLICY
(By Our Diplomatic Correspondent)

THE BRITISH Government has taken the strongest possible exception to General MacArthur's letter to Mr. Joseph Martin, the Republican Party leader, favouring the use of Nationalist Chinese troops from Formosa and interpreted as foreshadowing an extension of the war to the mainland of Asia.

Our Embassy in Washington has been asked to get a full explanation of how it is possible for such a statement, in complete variance with agreed policy, to be made by a serving officer.

The British had understood that the American Administration fully agreed with the policy of not extending the war far beyond the 38th Parallel unless military conditions made it essential. Now there is some doubt in Whitehall whether, in spite of the White House statement that there is no change in policy towards Formosa and the use of Nationalist troops, Mr. Truman and Mr. Acheson will be able to resist pressure for changes in policy from General MacArthur and his Republican Party adherents.

The reference by the Minister of State, Mr. Kenneth Younger, in a speech yesterday, to "such irresponsible statements as seem to come out at frequent intervals from highly placed quarters, without the authority of the United Nations, or indeed of any member Government," is regarded as a mild version of what the Cabinet really thinks about General MacArthur's statements.

It is also expected that Mr. Morrison will take the opportunity provided by numerous Parliamentary questions this week to make it clear how strongly the Government deprecates the intrusion of General MacArthur into politics.

AVOIDING CHECK TO OPERATIONS

The General's action is all the more galling because agreement between the British and American Governments over the question of crossing the 38th

* THE BRITISH EXPRESS ALARM: From the London *Observer*, April 8, 1951, in *Military Situation in the Far East, Hearings Before Committee on the Armed Services and Committee on Foreign Relations*, U.S. Senate, 82 Cong., 1 Sess. (1951), pp. 3193–94.

Parallel and over the importance of limiting the war in Korea had been virtually reached before General MacArthur sent his letter.

The consultations now going on in Washington on a declaration of United Nations aims in Korea have revealed differences between Britain and America, but only on questions of form and timing, not on any point of substance in future policy.

The main disagreement has been over the timing of any announcement. The British view is that a moderate statement now, during the lull, would seize the "psychological moment" of which the Foreign Secretary has spoken. The American view appears to be that it might hamper military operations to issue any statement at this moment when there are indications of a strong Chinese offensive. It is known that General MacArthur, who gave a warning of this offensive recently, strongly opposes issuing any such joint statement.

"IRRESPONSIBLE STATEMENTS" ON KOREA

Mr. Kenneth Younger, Minister of State, referred at a Labour conference in Cardiff yesterday to "natural differences of policy" between Britain and the United States.

He added: "Our biggest difference with the Americans is, of course, in our attitude towards China, and here I am bound to say that the Peking government have not done much to help us convince our American friends that we are right and they are wrong.

"We shall, however, persist in our efforts to give Communist China every chance to take her place in the world and in the United Nations.

"NOTHING HARMFUL

"People say that the door has been closed by our condemnation of the Chinese as aggressors. I doubt it. Their attitude depends much more on the military situation, otherwise why did they refuse the Indian cease-fire proposals before Christmas when no one had called them aggressors?

"United Nations aims in Korea have been made clear and there is nothing in them which the Chinese can regard as harmful to themselves.

"Neither we nor they should, therefore, be misled by such irresponsible statements as seem to come out at frequent intervals from highly placed quarters, without the authority of the United Nations, or indeed of any member Government."

On our "extremely bad" relations with Russia, Mr. Younger said: "I doubt whether the Soviet Government wants war, and I am certain the Soviet people do not. Many of the factors which drove previous dictators to war are lacking. Nor shall we exaggerate the strength of the Soviet bloc."

D] MACARTHUR IS FIRED

For four days President Truman consulted with his military and civilian advisers on how to handle MacArthur's latest challenge. The Secretaries of State and Defense and the Joint Chiefs of Staff all recommended that he should be relieved of his command. Having already come to that conclusion himself, Truman signed the appropriate orders at 3:15 P.M., on Monday, April 9. The administration planned to have them transmitted personally to MacArthur by Secretary of the Army Pace, who was then in Korea. On the evening of April 10, however, General Bradley learned that the Chicago *Tribune* was about to break the story. Washington newsmen were hurriedly summoned to a 1 A.M. White House news conference where they received the following documents.*

MESSAGE RELIEVING GENERAL MacARTHUR OF COMMAND, APRIL 10, 1951

I DEEPLY regret that it becomes my duty as President and Commander in Chief of the United States military forces to replace you as Supreme Commander, Allied Powers; Commander in Chief, United Nations Command; Commander in Chief, Far East; and Commanding General, United States Army, Far East.

You will turn over your commands, effective at once, to Lt. Gen. Matthew B. Ridgway. You are authorized to have issued such orders as are necessary to complete desired travel to such place as you select.

My reasons for your replacement will be made public concurrently with the delivery to you of the foregoing order, and are contained in the next following message.

STATEMENT OF THE PRESIDENT RELATIVE TO THE RELIEF OF GENERAL MacARTHUR, APRIL 10, 1951

WITH deep regret I have concluded that General of the Army Douglas Mac-Arthur is unable to give his wholehearted support to the policies of the United States Government and of the United Nations in matters pertaining to his official duties. In view of the specific responsibilities imposed upon me by the Constitution of the United States and the added responsibility which has been entrusted to me by the United Nations, I have decided that I must make a change of command in the Far East. I have, therefore, relieved General Mac-Arthur of his commands and have designated Lt. Gen. Matthew B. Ridgway as his successor.

Full and vigorous debate on matters of national policy is a vital element in the constitutional system of our free democracy. It is fundamental, however, that military commanders must be governed by the policies and directives issued to them in the manner provided by our laws and Constitution. In time of crisis, this consideration is particularly compelling.

General MacArthur's place in history as one of our greatest commanders is fully established. The Nation owes him a debt of gratitude for the distinguished and exceptional service which he has rendered his country in posts of great responsibility. For that reason I repeat my regret at the necessity for the action I feel compelled to take in his case.

* MACARTHUR IS FIRED: From *Military Situation in the Far East, Hearings Before Committee on the Armed Services and Committee on Foreign Relations*, U.S. Senate, 82 Cong., 1 Sess. (1951), pp. 3179–80.

4] The Greater Debate: Soldiers and Politicians

A] MacArthur Addresses Congress

In February, 1951, a "Great Debate" had taken place on a Republican-sponsored resolution in Congress attacking the administration's alleged right to send additional American troops to Europe without the prior consent of Congress. In this discussion the lines were fairly clearly drawn between isolationist, or Asia-oriented, Republicans and the Europe-oriented supporters of the administration. Hardly had the Great Debate come to an end when the firing of MacArthur precipitated what has been called the Greater Debate. Returning to the United States for the first time in fourteen years, the general was greeted by an ecstatic, cheering populace. He was invited to address a joint session of Congress, an honor more commonly accorded visiting Chiefs of State than cashiered generals. His address on April 19 was eloquent, dramatic, and, for his supporters, the true revelation. "We saw a great hunk of God in the flesh," exclaimed one congressman, "and we heard the voice of God." *

Mr. President, Mr. Speaker, distinguished Members of the Congress, I stand on this rostrum with a sense of deep humility and great pride; humility in the wake of those great American architects of our history who have stood here before me; pride in the reflection that this forum of legislative debate represents human liberty in the purest form yet devised. [Applause.]

Here are centered the hopes, and aspirations, and faith of the entire human race.

I do not stand here as advocate for any partisan cause, for the issues are fundamental and reach quite beyond the realm of partisan consideration. They must be resolved on the highest plane of national interest if our course is to prove sound and our future protected. I trust, therefore, that you will do me the justice of receiving that which I have to say as solely expressing the considered viewpoint of a fellow American. I address you with neither rancor nor bitterness in the fading twilight of life with but one purpose in mind, to serve my country. [Applause.]

The issues are global and so interlocked that to consider the problems of one sector oblivious to those of another is but to court disaster for the whole.

While Asia is commonly referred to as the gateway to Europe, it is no less true that Europe is the gateway to Asia, and the broad influence of the one cannot fail to have its impact upon the other.

There are those who claim our strength is inadequate to protect on both fronts, that we cannot divide our effort. I can think of no greater expression of defeatism. [Applause.] If a potential enemy can divide his strength on two fronts, it is for us to counter his effort.

The Communist threat is a global one. Its successful advance in one sector

---

* THE GREATER DEBATE: SOLDIERS AND POLITICIANS: From the *Congressional Record*, 82 Cong., 1 Sess. (April 19, 1951), pp. 4123–25.

threatens the destruction of every other sector. You cannot appease or otherwise surrender to communism in Asia without simultaneously undermining our efforts to halt its advance in Europe. [Applause.]

Beyond pointing out these general truisms, I shall confine my discussion to the general areas of Asia. Before one may objectively assess the situation now existing there, he must comprehend something of Asia's past and the revolutionary changes which have marked her course up to the present. Long exploited by the so-called colonial powers, with little opportunity to achieve any degree of social justice, individual dignity, or a higher standard of life such as guided our own noble administration of the Philippines, the peoples of Asia found their opportunity in the war just past to throw off the shackles of colonialism and now see the dawn of new opportunity and heretofore unfelt dignity and the self-respect of political freedom.

Mustering half of the earth's population and 60 percent of its natural resources these peoples are rapidly consolidating a new force, both moral and material, with which to raise the living standard and erect adaptations of the design of modern progress to their own distinct cultural environments. Whether one adheres to the concept of colonization or not, this is the direction of Asian progress and it may not be stopped. It is a corollary to the shift of the world economic frontiers, as the whole epi-center of world affairs rotates back toward the area whence it started. In this situation it becomes vital that our own country orient its policies in consonance with this basic evolutionary condition rather than pursue a course blind to the reality that the colonial era is now past and the Asian peoples covet the right to shape their own free destiny. What they seek now is friendly guidance, understanding, and support, not imperious direction [applause]; the dignity of equality, not the shame of subjugation. Their prewar standards of life, pitifully low, is infinitely lower now in the devastation left in war's wake. World ideologies play little part in Asian thinking and are little understood. What the peoples strive for is the opportunity for a little more food in their stomachs, a little better clothing on their backs, a little firmer roof over their heads, and the realization of a normal nationalist urge for political freedom. These political-social conditions have but an indirect bearing upon our own national security, but do form a backdrop to contemporary planning which must be thoughtfully considered if we are to avoid the pitfalls of unrealism.

Of more direct and immediate bearing upon our national security are the changes wrought in the strategic potential of the Pacific Ocean in the course of the past war. Prior thereto, the western strategic frontier of the United States lay on the littoral line of the Americas with an exposed island salient extending out through Hawaii, Midway, and Guam to the Philippines. That salient proved not an outpost of strength but an avenue of weakness along which the enemy could and did attack. The Pacific was a potential area of advance for any predatory force intent upon striking at the bordering land areas.

All this was changed by our Pacific victory. Our strategic frontier then shifted to embrace the entire Pacific Ocean which became a vast moat to protect us as long as we held it. Indeed, it acts as a protective shield for all of the Americas and all free lands of the Pacific Ocean area. We control it to the shores of Asia by a chain of islands extending in an arc from the Aleutians to the Marianas held by us and our free allies.

From this island chain we can dominate with sea and air power every Asiatic port from Vladivostok to Singapore and prevent any hostile movement into the Pacific. Any predatory attack from Asia must be an amphibious effort. No amphibious force can be successful without control of the sea lanes and the air over those lanes in its avenue of advance. With naval and air supremacy and modest ground elements to defend bases, any major attack from continental Asia toward us or our friends of the Pacific would be doomed to failure. Under such conditions the Pacific no longer represents menacing avenues of approach for a prospective invader—it assumes instead the friendly aspect of a peaceful lake. Our line of defense is a natural one and can be maintained with a minimum of military effort and expense. It envisions no attack against anyone nor does it provide the bastions essential for offensive operations, but properly maintained would be an invincible defense against aggression.

The holding of this littoral defense line in the western Pacific is entirely dependent upon holding all segments thereof, for any major breach of that line by an unfriendly power would render vulnerable to determined attack every other major segment. This is a military estimate as to which I have yet to find a military leader who will take exception. [Applause.]

For that reason I have strongly recommended in the past as a matter of military urgency that under no circumstances must Formosa fall under Communist control. [Applause.]

Such an eventuality would at once threaten the freedom of the Philippines and the loss of Japan, and might well force our western frontier back to the coasts of California, Oregon, and Washington.

To understand the changes which now appear upon the Chinese mainland, one must understand the changes in Chinese character and culture over the past 50 years. China up to 50 years ago was completely nonhomogeneous, being compartmented into groups divided against each other. The war-making tendency was almost nonexistent, as they still followed the tenets of the Confucian ideal of pacifist culture. At the turn of the century, under the regime of Chan So Lin, efforts toward greater homogeneity produced the start of a nationalist urge. This was further and more successfully developed under the leadership of Chiang Kai-shek, but has been brought to its greatest fruition under the present regime, to the point that it has now taken on the character of a united nationalism of increasingly dominant aggressive tendencies. Through these past 50 years, the Chinese people have thus become militarized in their concepts and in their ideals. They now constitute excellent soldiers with competent staffs and commanders. This has produced a new and dominant power in Asia which for its own purposes is allied with Soviet Russia, but which in its own concepts and methods has become aggressively imperialistic with a lust for expansion and increased power normal to this type of imperialism. There is little of the ideological concept either one way or another in the Chinese make-up. The standard of living is so low and the capital accumulation has been so thoroughly dissipated by war that the masses are desperate and avid to follow any leadership which seems to promise the alleviation of local stringencies. I have from the beginning believed that the Chinese

Communists' support of the North Koreans was the dominant one. Their interests are at present parallel to those of the Soviet, but I believe that the aggressiveness recently displayed not only in Korea, but also in Indochina and Tibet and pointing potentially toward the south, reflects predominantly the same lust for the expansion of power which has animated every would-be conqueror since the beginning of time. [Applause.]

The Japanese people since the war have undergone the greatest reformation recorded in modern history. With a commendable will, eagerness to learn, and marked capacity to understand, they have, from the ashes left in war's wake, erected in Japan an edifice dedicated to the primacy of individual liberty and personal dignity, and in the ensuing process there has been created a truly representative government, committed to the advance of political morality, freedom of economic enterprise and social justice. [Applause.] Politically, economically, and socially Japan is now abreast of many free nations of the earth and will not again fail the universal trust. That it may be counted upon to wield a profoundly beneficial influence over the course of events in Asia is attested by the magnificent manner in which the Japanese people have met the recent challenge of war, unrest, and confusion surrounding them from the outside, and checked communism within their own frontiers without the slightest slackening in their forward progress. I sent all four of our occupation divisions to the Korean battle front without the slightest qualms as to the effect of the resulting power vacuum upon Japan. The results fully justified my faith. [Applause.] I know of no nation more serene, orderly, and industrious—nor in which higher hopes can be entertained for future constructive service in the advance of the human race. [Applause.]

Of our former wards, the Philippines, we can look forward in confidence that the existing unrest will be corrected and a strong and healthy nation will grow in the longer aftermath of war's terrible destructiveness. We must be patient and understanding and never fail them, as in our hour of need they did not fail us. [Applause.] A Christian nation, the Philippines stand as a mighty bulwark of Christianity in the Far East, and its capacity for high moral leadership in Asia is unlimited.

On Formosa, the Government of the Republic of China has had the opportunity to refute by action much of the malicious gossip which so undermined the strength of its leadership on the Chinese mainland. [Applause.]

The Formosan people are receiving a just and enlightened administration with majority representation on the organs of government; and politically, economically, and socially appear to be advancing along sound and constructive lines.

With this brief insight into the surrounding areas I now turn to the Korean conflict. While I was not consulted prior to the President's decision to intervene in the support of the Republic of Korea, that decision from a military standpoint proved a sound one. [Applause.] As I say, a brief and sound one as we hurled back the invaders and decimated his forces. Our victory was complete and our objectives within reach when Red China intervened with numerically superior ground forces. This created a new war and an entirely new situation, a situation not contemplated when our forces were committed against the North Korean invaders, a situation which called for new decisions in the diplomatic sphere to permit the realistic adjustment of military strategy. Such decisions have not been forthcoming. [Applause.]

While no man in his right mind would advocate sending our ground forces into continental China—and such was never given a thought—the new situation did urgently demand a drastic revision of strategic planning if our political aim was to defeat this new enemy as we had defeated the old. [Applause.]

Apart from the military need as I saw it to neutralize sanctuary, protection given to the enemy north of the Yalu, I felt that military necessity in the conduct of the war made necessary:

First, the intensification of our economic blockade against China.

Second, the imposition of a naval blockade against the China coast.

Third, removal of restrictions on air reconnaissance of China's coastal areas and of Manchuria. [Applause.]

Fourth, removal of restrictions on the forces of the Republic of China on Formosa with logistical support of contribute to their effective operation against the Chinese mainland. [Applause.]

For entertaining these views all professionally designed to support our forces committed to Korea and bring hostilities to an end with the least possible delay and at a saving of countless American and Allied lives, I have been severely criticized in lay circles, principally abroad, despite my understanding that from a military standpoint the above views have been fully shared in the past by practically every military leader concerned with the Korean campaign, including our own Joint Chiefs of Staff. [Applause, the Members rising.]

I called for reinforcements, but was informed that reinforcements were not available. I made clear that if not permitted to utilize the friendly Chinese force of some 600,000 men on Formosa; if not permitted to blockade the China coast to prevent the Chinese Reds from getting succor from without; and if there were to be no hope of major reinforcements, the position of the command from the military standpoint forbade victory. We could hold in Korea by constant maneuver and at an approximate area where our supply advantages were in balance with the supply line disadvantages of the enemy, but we could hope at best for only an indecisive campaign, with its terrible and constant attrition upon our forces if the enemy utilized his full military potential. I have constantly called for the new political decisions essential to a solution. Efforts have been made to distort my position. It has been said in effect that I was a warmonger. Nothing could be further from the truth. I know war as few other men now living know it, and nothing to me is more revolting. I have long advocated its complete abolition as its very destructiveness on both friend and foe has rendered it useless as a means of settling international disputes. Indeed, on the 2d of September 1945, just following the surrender of the Japanese Nation on the battleship *Missouri,* I formally cautioned as follows:

"Men since the beginning of time have sought peace. Various methods through the ages have been attempted to devise an international process to prevent or settle disputes between nations. From the very start, workable methods were found insofar as individual citizens were concerned, but the mechanics of an instrumentality of larger international scope have never been successful. Military alliances, balances of power, leagues of nations, all in turn failed, leaving the only path to be by way of the crucible of war. The utter destructiveness of war now blots out this alternative. We have had our last chance. If we will not devise some greater and more equitable system, Armageddon will be at our door. The problem basically is theological and involves a spiritual recrudescence and improvement of human character that will synchronize with our almost matchless advances in science, art, literature, and all material and cultural developments of the past 2,000 years. It must be of the spirit if we are to save the flesh." [Applause.]

But once war is forced upon us, there is no other alternative than to apply every available means to bring it to a swift end. War's very object is victory— not prolonged indecision. [Applause.] In war, indeed, there can be no substitute for victory. [Applause.]

There are some who for varying reasons would appease Red China. They are blind to history's clear lesson. For history teaches with unmistakable emphasis that appeasement but begets new and bloodier war. It points to no single instance where the end has justified that means—where appeasement has led to more than a sham peace. Like blackmail, it lays the basis for new and successively greater demands, until, as in blackmail, violence becomes the only other alternative. Why, my soldiers asked of me, surrender military advantages to an enemy in the field? I could not answer. [Applause.] Some may say to avoid spread of the conflict into an all-out war with China; others, to avoid Soviet intervention. Neither explanation seems valid. For China is already engaging with the maximum power it can commit and the Soviet will not necessarily mesh its actions with our moves. Like a cobra, any new enemy will more likely strike whenever it feels that the relativity in military or other potential is in its favor on a world-wide basis.

The tragedy of Korea is further heightened by the fact that as military action is confined to its territorial limits, it condemns that nation, which it is our purpose to save, to suffer the devastating impact of full naval and air bombardment, while the enemy's sanctuaries are fully protected from such attack and devastation. Of the nations of the world, Korea alone, up to now, is the sole one which has risked its all against communism. The magnificence of the courage and fortitude of the Korean people defies description. [Applause.] They have chosen to risk death rather than slavery. Their last words to me were "Don't scuttle the Pacific." [Applause.]

I have just left your fighting sons in Korea. They have met all tests there and I can report to you without reservation they are splendid in every way. [Applause.] It was my constant effort to preserve them and end this savage conflict honorably and with the least loss of time and a minimum sacrifice of life. Its growing bloodshed has caused me the deepest anguish and anxiety. Those gallant men will remain often in my thoughts and in my prayers always. [Applause.]

I am closing my 52 years of military service. [Applause.] When I joined the Army even before the turn of the century, it was the fulfillment of all my boyish hopes and dreams. The world has turned over many times since I took the oath on the plain at West Point, and the hopes and dreams have long since vanished. But I still remember the refrain of one of the most popular barrack ballads of that day which proclaimed most proudly that—

"Old soldiers never die; they just fade away." And like the old soldier of

that ballad, I now close my military career and just fade away—an old soldier who tried to do his duty as God gave him the light to see that duty.
  Good-by.

B] GENERAL BRADLEY REPLIES FOR THE
ADMINISTRATION

> A few weeks after the general's address, the MacArthur Hearings began under the judicious chairmanship of the Southern Democratic leader, Senator Richard Russell of Georgia. The Senate committee heard testimony from MacArthur and virtually all the top officials of the executive branch concerned with foreign and military policy, except the President. Secretary of State Acheson and other civilian leaders of the administration, however, were not highly regarded in Congress. To rebut MacArthur, the administration relied heavily on the respect commanded in Congress by its principal military figures: General George C. Marshall, Secretary of Defense, and General Omar N. Bradley, chairman of the Joint Chiefs of Staff.*

General BRADLEY. Mr. Chairman and members of the committees, at the very outset, I want to make it clear that I would not say anything to discredit the long and illustrious career of Gen. Douglas MacArthur. We may have different views on certain aspects of our Government's military policy, but that is not unusual.

Certainly there have been no personal considerations in our differences of opinion. In matters of such great scope and of such importance many people have different ideas and might consequently recommend different courses of action.

As Chairman of the Joint Chiefs of Staff, I am one of the military advisers to the President, the Secretary of Defense, and the National Security Council. I pass on to them the collective advice and recommendations of the Joint Chiefs. When the Joint Chiefs of Staff express their opinion on a subject, it is from the military point of view, and is given with a full realizaton that considerations other than military may be overriding in making the final decision. The relative importance of the military aspect varies. In some cases it is greatly overshadowed by other considerations. In other cases, the military aspects may be the decisive ones.

When all of these aspects are considered the Government's policy is determined. As military men we then abide by the decision.

Before your interrogation on the details of our Government's policies in Korea and the Far East, I would like to ask myself this question: What is the great issue at stake in this hearing?

Principally I would say that you are trying to determine the course we should follow as the best road to peace. There are military factors which must

---

* GENERAL BRADLEY REPLIES FOR THE ADMINISTRATION: From *Military Situation in the Far East, Hearings Before Committee on the Armed Services and Committee on Foreign Relations,* U.S. Senate, 82 Cong., 1 Sess. (1951), pp. 729–33.

be evaluated before a sound decision can be made. At present the issue is obscured in the public mind by many details which do not relate to the task of keeping the peace and making America secure.

RISK OF GLOBAL WAR

The fundamental military issue that has arisen is whether to increase the risk of a global war by taking additional measures that are open to the United States and its allies. We now have a localized conflict in Korea. Some of the military measures under discussion might well place the United States in the position of responsibility for broadening the war and at the same time losing most if not all of our allies.

General MacArthur has stated that there are certain additional measures which can and should be taken, and that by so doing no unacceptable increased risk of global war will result.

The Joint Chiefs of Staff believe that these same measures do increase the risk of global war and that such a risk should not be taken unnecessarily. At the same time we recognize the military advantages that might accrue to the United Nations' position in Korea and to the United States position in the Far East by these measures. While a field commander very properly estimates his needs from the viewpoint of operations in his own theater or sphere of action, those responsible for higher direction must necessarily base their actions on broader aspects, and on the needs, actual or prospective, of several theaters. The Joint Chiefs of Staff, in view of their global responsibilities and their perspective with respect to the world-wide strategic situation, are in a better position than is any single theater commander to assess the risk of general war. Moreover, the Joint Chiefs of Staff are best able to judge our own military resources with which to meet that risk.

GLOBAL STRATEGY CONSIDERED

In order that all may understand the strategy which the Joint Chiefs of Staff believe the United States must pursue, I would like to discuss in broad terms this perspective in which we view our security problems.

As a background to our consideration of global strategy, we must realize that human beings have invented a great variety of techniques designed to influence other nations. Right now, nations are being subjected to persuasion by propaganda and coercion by force of arms. It is my conviction that broad and comprehensive knowledge of the strength, aims, and the policies of nations is basic to understanding the problem of security in a world of tension.

We must understand—as we conduct our foreign affairs and our military affairs—that while power and nationalism prevail, it is up to us to gain strength through cooperative efforts with other nations which have common ideals and objectives with our own. At the same time, we must create and maintain the power essential to persuasion, and to our own security in such a world. We must understand the role and nature, including the limitations, of this power if we are to exercise it wisely.

One of the great power potentials of this world is the United States of America and her allies. The other great power in this world is Soviet Russia and her satellites. As much as we desire peace, we must realize that we have two centers of power supporting opposing ideologies.

From a global viewpoint—and with the security of our Nation of prime importance—our military mission is to support a policy of preventing communism from gaining the manpower, the resources, the raw materials, and the industrial capacity essential to world domination. If Soviet Russia ever controls the entire Eurasian land mass, then the Soviet-satellite imperialism may have the broad base upon which to build the military power to rule the world.

PLAN OF KOREA, BERLIN, AND GREECE, AND TURKEY IN GLOBAL CONCEPT

Three times in the past 5 years the Kremlin-inspired imperialism has been thwarted by direct action.

In Berlin, Greece, and Korea, the free nations have opposed Communist aggression with a different type of action. But each time the power of the United States has been called upon and we have become involved. Each incident has cost us money, resources, and some lives.

But in each instance we have prevented the domination of one more area, and the absorption of another source of manpower, raw materials, and resources.

Korea, in spite of the importance of the engagement, must be looked upon with proper perspective. It is just one engagement, just one phase of this battle that we are having with the other power center in the world which opposes us and all we stand for. For 5 years this "guerrilla diplomacy" has been going on. In each of the actions in which we have participated to oppose this gangster conduct, we have risked world war III. But each time we have used methods short of total war. As costly as Berlin and Greece and Korea may be, they are less expensive than the vast destruction which would be inflicted upon all sides if a total war were to be precipitated.

CONCEPT OF LIMITED WAR IN KOREA

I am under no illusion that our present strategy of using means short of total war to achieve our ends and oppose communism is a guarantee that a world war will not be thrust upon us. But a policy of patience and determination without provoking a world war, while we improve our military power, is one which we believe we must continue to follow.

As long as we keep the conflict within its present scope, we are holding to a minimum the forces we must commit and tie down.

The strategic alternative, enlargement of the war in Korea to include Red China, would probably delight the Kremlin more than anything else we could do. It would necessarily tie down additional forces, especially our sea power and our air power, while the Soviet Union would not be obliged to put a single man into the conflict.

Under present circumstances, we have recommended against enlarging the war. The course of action often described as a "limited war" with Red China would increase the risk we are taking by engaging too much of our power in an area that is not the critical strategic prize.

Red China is not the powerful nation seeking to dominate the world. Frankly, in the opinion of the Joint Chiefs of Staff, this strategy would involve us in the wrong war, at the wrong place, at the wrong time, and with the wrong enemy.

ROLE OF JCS IN PLANNING POLICY

There are some other considerations which have tended to obscure this main issue. Some critics have not hesitated to state that the policy our Government is following, and its included strategy, is not that which has been recommended by the Joint Chiefs of Staff.

Statements have been made that the President, as Commander in Chief, and the Secretary of State and the Secretary of Defense, have a policy all their own, and that the Joint Chiefs of Staff have been overridden.

This is just not so. The Joint Chiefs of Staff have continually given their considered opinion—always from a military viewpoint—concerning our global capabilities and responsibilities and have recommended our present strategy in and for Korea. This has been the course of action which the Secretary of Defense and the Commander in Chief have adopted as far as practicable.

I pointed out earlier that many times the international policy considerations, including the views of our allies, are also considered and in some instances modify the course of action.

In other instances, even after the international considerations and the views of our allies have been considered, the proposed military strategy has not been altered.

Our over-all policy has been one of steadfast patience and determination in opposing Communist aggression without provoking unnecessarily a total war.

ADVISABILITY OF A "SHOWDOWN" NOW

There are many critics who have become impatient with this strategy and who would like to call for a show-down. From a purely military viewpoint, this is not desirable. We are not in the best military position to seek a show-down, even if it were the Nation's desire to forfeit the chances for peace by precipitating a total war.

Undoubtedly, this statement will be misconstrued by some critics who will say, "Why are the Joint Chiefs of Staff advertising the fact that we are not militarily in a position to have a show-down?"

I can assure those critics that with the methods we must pursue in a democracy in order to support a military establishment—including this present investigation of our strategy in the Far East—our capabilities are not unknown to the Communists.

They are apt students of military power, and fully realize that although we are not prepared to deliver any ultimatum, we could hurt them badly if they attacked us or our friends.

They also know that within our potential, and the strength of our allies, in the long run they could not win a war with a United States that is alert, and continuously prepared.

I would not be a proponent of any policy which would ignore the military facts and rush us headlong into a show-down before we are ready. It is true that this policy of armed resistance to aggression, which we pursue while we are getting stronger, often risks a world war. But so far we have taken these risks without disastrous results.

I think our global strategy is paying off and I see no reason to let impatience alter it in the Far East. Certainly the course of action we are pursuing has avoided a total war which could only bring death and destruction to millions of Americans, both in the United States and on the battlefield. Our present course of action has at the same time won us respect and admiration everywhere in the world, both inside and outside the iron curtain.

POSSIBLE RESULTS FROM ENLARGING WAR TO CHINA

There are also those who deplore the present military situation in Korea and urge us to engage Red China in a larger war to solve this problem. Taking on Red China is not a decisive move, does not guarantee the end of the war in Korea, and may not bring China to her knees. We have only to look back to the five long years when the Japanese, one of the greatest military powers of that time, moved into China and had almost full control of a large part of China, and yet were never able to conclude that war successfully. I would say that from past history one would only jump from a smaller conflict to a larger deadlock at greater expense. My own feeling is to avoid such an engagement if possible because victory in Korea would not be assured and victory over Red China would be many years away. We believe that every effort should be made to settle the present conflict without extending it outside Korea. If this proves to be impossible, then other measures may have to be taken.

In my consideration of this viewpoint, I am going back to the basic objective of the American people—as much peace as we can gain without appeasement.

NATURE OF APPEASEMENT FROM MILITARY VIEWPOINT

Some critics of our strategy say if we do not immediately bomb troop concentration points and airfields in Manchuria, it is "appeasement." If we do not immediately set up a blockade of Chinese ports—which to be successful would have to include British and Russian ports in Asia—it is "appeasement." These same critics would say that if we do not provide the logistical support and air and naval assistance to launch Chinese Nationalist troops into China it is "appeasement."

These critics ignore the vital questions:

Will these actions, if taken, actually assure victory in Korea?

Do these actions mean prolongation of the war by bringing Russia into the fight?

Will these actions strip us of our allies in Korea and in other parts of the world?

From a military viewpoint, appeasement occurs when you give up something, which is rightfully free, to an aggressor without putting up a struggle, or making him pay a price. Forsaking Korea—withdrawing from the fight unless we are forced out—would be an appeasement to aggression. Refusing to enlarge the quarrel to the point where our global capabilities are diminished, is certainly not appeasement but is a militarily sound course of action under the present circumstances.

c] A Republican Congressman Demands a "Program for Korea"

In the spring of 1951 many internationalist Republicans defended the President's firing of MacArthur, although criticizing the abrupt way in which it was handled. Similarly, many members of the opposition party endorsed the administration's efforts to arrive at a truce in Korea. Right-wing Republicans, however, were continuously critical of the administration. As the truce talks went on and on, comments such as those made by Representative B. Carroll Reece of Tennessee on May 16, 1952, seemed to strike a more and more responsive chord with the public at large.*

Mr. Reece of Tennessee. Mr. Speaker, it is time we faced the facts in Korea. More than a year ago General MacArthur was relieved from command. Since then our position in Korea has steadily deteriorated.

When he left Korea, the Red forces were suffering heavy losses, their supply position was precarious and their air support negligible. Had MacArthur been given a free hand, with air restrictions lifted, with Asiatic reinforcements made available, he would have given us a victory. We have this assurance from a number of responsible officers who have since returned from Korea.

But, Mr. Speaker, the State Department—of all people—has developed a new military strategy. It has decided that we will hold a line in Korea until someway, somehow, our enemy will naively conclude that the war is futile and then beg to come to honorable terms.

Cease-fire conversations have been going on nearly 10 months.

What has happened in the meanwhile?

Red strength has been increased enormously. We are outnumbered 2 or 3 to 1 on the ground; nearly 2 to 1 in aircraft; our Sabre jet fighter is outnumbered 5 to 1 by the Red MIG–15.

The Reds have recovered from their precarious supply position; in the cease-fire conversations we are confronted with stalling and lies; Red prisoners have kidnaped their commanding general.

But, Mr. Speaker, the alarming thing about this increased Red strength is not its actual present level, rather it is the fact that there is a constant and progressive increase. It is not only in Korea, it is in China also.

Airdromes, underground hangars, hard standings, runways, modern anti-aircraft are mushrooming up in critical areas in Korea, Manchuria, and China. Red submarines are being sighted in Korean waters.

For the Red forces Korea is a testing laboratory and back of this testing ground real inescapable, sinister power is being amassed.

A third of our entire defensive Air Force is tied down defending our ground

* A Republican Congressman demands a "program for korea": From the *Congressional Record*, 82 Cong., 2 Sess. (May 16, 1952), p. 5387.

forces; half of all American combat divisions are required in Korea and Japan; our allies continue with token forces only. We are not only sadly short of equipment in Korea; but we are so sadly short of ammunition that it is being rationed. Meanwhile, the American program of NATO support continues, so far as I know, on schedule. Our home defenses are sadly neglected.

Our defense and foreign-aid budgets have pushed us deep into deficit spending in spite of the fact that taxes are higher than during the war. The lives of American youth are completely disrupted. By 1954 every eligible lad will have been drafted into the military service.

Mr. Speaker, never before in all history has a first-rate power succeeded so effectively in the complete global diffusion of its entire military resources.

What every real American wants to know is: What is our program for Korea? How do we end Mr. Truman's war there? What is our long-range military program; where is it leading us?

Obviously, in Korea, there are three alternatives: Admit defeat and pull out; continue a war of attrition; reinforce and win.

The American people have a right to know what to expect. My reaction is if we do not intend to win, it is better to pull out and admit defeat than to continue the sacrifice of American lives and treasure with no hope of a military decision.

My further reaction is that so far as possible we should fight the Reds in Korea with our Asiatic allies. Gen. Chiang Kai-shek's troops could largely replace our ground forces. Eventually Chiang's troops should be able to hold the line in Korea and free our ground force from its 2-year-old, arduous assignment.

Our major effort could then be made in the air and on the sea where we are peculiarly qualified to be most effective.

The argument that the use of Chiang Kai-shek's troops would lead to war with Red China is fatuous. We are already at war with Red China.

While we followed Secretary Acheson's policy of "waiting for the dust to settle," we lost China.

Are we going to be foolish enough now, to continue Acheson's leadership of holding a line in a war of attrition while the Reds build up the striking potential to destroy us?

Mr. Speaker, I want to go on record as warning that the present drift of things in Korea could lead to a class "A" military debacle.

The American people have a right to definite assurance that if the Red forces should strike, American boys now in Korea will survive with minimum losses. Are we justified in our present allocation of strength for Europe—where there is no war—while our forces in Korea face a possible annihilation?

Mr. Speaker, if our administration and military leaders have answers to this Korean problem, the American people are entitled to those answers, now. If they do not have the answer, the Congress itself must take a hand.

D] EISENHOWER PROMISES TO GO TO KOREA

> As his campaign progressed, Eisenhower became more and more critical of
> the administration's conduct of the war. The climax came on October 24,
> at Detroit, when the Republican candidate declared that he would make a
> personal trip to Korea to see how the war could be ended.*

IN THIS anxious autumn for America, one fact looms above all others in our
people's mind. One tragedy challenges all men dedicated to the work of
peace. One word shouts denial to those who foolishly pretend that ours is not
a nation at war.

This fact, this tragedy, this word is: Korea.

A small country, Korea has been, for more than two years, the battleground
for the costliest foreign war our nation has fought, excepting the two world
wars. It has been the burial ground for 20,000 American dead. It has been another historic field of honor for the valor and skill and tenacity of American
soldiers.

All these things it has been—and yet one thing more. It has been a symbol—
a telling symbol—of the foreign policy of our nation.

It has been a sign—a warning sign—of the way the Administration has conducted our world affairs.

It has been a measure—a damning measure—of the quality of leadership we
have been given.

Tonight I am going to talk about our foreign policy and of its supreme symbol—the Korean war. I am not going to give you elaborate generalizations—but
hard, tough facts. I am going to state the unvarnished truth.

What, then, are the plain facts?

The biggest fact about the Korean war is this: It was never inevitable, it
was never inescapable, no fantastic fiat of history decreed that little South
Korea—in the summer of 1950—would fatally tempt Communist aggressors
as their easiest victim. No demonic destiny decreed that America had to be
bled this way in order to keep South Korea free and to keep freedom itself
self-respecting.

We are not mute prisoners of history. That is a doctrine for totalitarians, it is
no creed for free men.

There is a Korean war—and we are fighting it—for the simplest of reasons:
Because free leadership failed to check and to turn back Communist ambition
before it savagely attacked us. The Korean war—more perhaps than any other
war in history—simply and swiftly followed the collapse of our political defenses. There is no other reason than this: We failed to read and to outwit the
totalitarian mind.

I know something of this totalitarian mind. Through the years of World
War II, I carried a heavy burden of decision in the free world's crusade against
the tyranny then threatening us all. Month after month, year after year, I had

---

* EISENHOWER PROMISES TO GO TO KOREA: From the New York *Times* (October 25,
1952), p. 8.

to search out and to weigh the strengths and weaknesses of an enemy driven by the lust to rule the great globe itself.

World War II should have taught us all one lesson. The lesson is this: To vacillate, to hesitate—to appease even by merely betraying unsteady purpose—is to feed a dictator's appetite for conquest and to invite war itself.

That lesson—which should have firmly guided every great decision of our leadership through these later years—was ignored in the development of the Administration's policies for Asia since the end of World War II. Because it was ignored, the record of these policies is a record of appalling failure.

The record of failure dates back—with red-letter folly—at least to September of 1947. It was then that Gen. Albert Wedemeyer—returned from a Presidential mission to the Far East—submitted to the President this warning: "The withdrawal of American military forces from Korea would result in the occupation of South Korea by either Soviet troops or, as seems more likely, by the Korean military units trained under Soviet auspices in North Korea."

That warning and his entire report were disregarded and suppressed by the Administration.

The terrible record of these years reaches its dramatic climax in a series of unforgettable scenes on Capitol Hill in June of 1949. By then the decision to complete withdrawal of American forces from Korea—despite menacing signs from the North—had been drawn up by the Department of State. The decision included the intention to ask Congress for aid to Korea to compensate for the withdrawal of American forces.

This brought questions from Congress. The Administration parade of civilian and military witnesses before the House Foreign Affairs Committee was headed by the Secretary of State. He and his aides faced a group of Republican Congressmen both skeptical and fearful.

What followed was historic and decisive.

I beg you to listen carefully to the words that followed, for they shaped this nation's course from that date to this.

Listen, then:

First: Republican Congressman John Lodge of Connecticut asked "(do) you feel that the Korean Government is able to fill the vacuum caused by the withdrawal of the occupation forces?"

The Administration answered: "Definitely."

Second: A very different estimate of the risk involved came from Republican Congressman Walter Judd of Minnesota. He warned: "I think the thing necessary to give security to Korea at this stage of the game is the presence of a small American force and the knowledge (on the Soviet side) that attack upon it would bring trouble with us."

"I am convinced," Representative Judd continued, "that if we keep even a battalion there, they are not going to move. And if the battalion is not there"—listen now to his warning—"the chances are they will move within a year."

What a tragedy that the Administration shrugged off that so accurate warning!

Third: The Secretary of State was asked if he agreed that the South Koreans alone—and I quote—"will be able to defend themselves against any attack from the northern half of the country." To this the Secretary answered briskly: "We share the same view. Yes, sir."

Rarely in Congressional testimony has so much misinformation been compressed so efficiently into so few words.

Fourth: Republican Congressman Lodge had an incisive comment on all this. "That," he said, "is wishful thinking. . . . I am afraid it confesses a kind of fundamental isolationism that exists in certain branches of the Government, which I think is a very dangerous pattern. I think the presence of our troops there is a tremendous deterrent to the Russians."

Finally: This remarkable scene of the summer of 1949 ends with a memorable document. The minority report of five Republican members of the House Foreign Affairs Committee on July 26, 1949, submitted this solemn warning.

Listen to it:

"It is reliably reported that Soviet troops, attached to the North Korean puppet armies, are in position of command as well as acting as advisers. . . . This development may well presage the launching of a full-scale military drive across the Thirty-eighth Parallel.

"Our forces . . . have been withdrawn from South Korea at the very instant when logic and common sense both demanded no retreat from the realities of the situation."

The report continues: "Already along the Thirty-eighth Parallel aggression is speaking with the too-familiar voices of howitzers and cannons. Our position is untenable and indefensible.

"The House should be aware of these facts."

These words of eloquent, reasoned warning were spoken eleven months before the Korean war broke.

Behind these words was a fervent, desperate appeal. That appeal was addressed to the Administration. It begged at least some firm statement of American intention that might deter the foreseen attack.

What was the Administration answer to that appeal?

The first answer was silence—stubborn, sullen silence for six months.

Then, suddenly, came speech—a high Government official at long last speaking out on Asia. It was now January of 1950. What did he say? He said, "The United States Government will not provide military aid or advice to Chinese forces on Formosa."

Then, one week later, the Secretary of State announced his famous "defense perimeter"—publicly advising our enemies that, so far as nations outside this perimeter were concerned, "no person can guarantee these areas against military attack." Under these circumstances, it was cold comfort to the nations outside this perimeter to be reminded that they could appeal to the United Nations.

These nations, of course, included Korea. The armies of communism, thus informed, began their big build-up. Six months later they were ready to strike across the Thirty-eighth Parallel. They struck on June 25, 1950.

On that day, the record of political and diplomatic failure of this Administration was completed and sealed.

The responsibility for this record cannot be dodged or evaded. Even if not a single Republican leader had warned so clearly against the coming disaster, the responsibility for the fateful political decisions would still rest wholly with the men charged with making those decisions—in the Department of State and in the White House. They cannot escape that responsibility now or ever.

When the enemy struck, on that June day of 1950, what did America do? It did what it always has done in all its times of peril. It appealed to the heroism of its youth.

This appeal was utterly right and utterly inescapable. It was inescapable not only because this was the only way to defend the idea of collective freedom against savage aggression. That appeal was inescapable because there was now in the plight into which we had stumbled no other way to save honor and self-respect.

The answer to that appeal has been what any American knew it would be. It has been sheer valor—valor on all the Korean mountainsides that, each day, bear fresh scars of new graves.

Now—in this anxious autumn—from these heroic men there comes back an answering appeal. It is no whine, no whimpering plea. It is a question that addresses itself to simple reason. It asks: Where do we go from here? When comes the end? Is there an end?

These questions touch all of us. They demand truthful answers. Neither glib promises nor glib excuses will serve. They would be no better than the glib prophecies that brought us to this pass.

To these questions there are two false answers—both equally false. The first would be any answer that dishonestly pledged an end to war in Korea by any imminent, exact date. Such a pledge would brand its speaker as a deceiver.

The second and equally false answer declares that nothing can be done to speed a secure peace. It dares to tell us that we, the strongest nation in the history of freedom, can only wait—and wait—and wait. Such a statement brands its speaker as a defeatist.

My answer—candid and complete—is this:

The first task of a new administration will be to review and re-examine every course of action open to us with one goal in view: To bring the Korean war to an early and honorable end. That is my pledge, to the American people.

For this task a wholly new Administration is necessary. The reason for this is simple. The old Administration cannot be expected to repair what it failed to prevent.

Where will a new Administration begin?

It will begin with its President taking a simple, firm resolution. That resolution will be: To forego the diversions of politics and to concentrate on the job of ending the Korean war—until that job is honorably done.

That job requires a personal trip to Korea.

I shall make that trip. Only in that way could I learn how best to serve the American people in the cause of peace.

I shall go to Korea.

That is my second pledge to the American people.

Carefully, then, this new Administration, unfettered by past decisions and inherited mistakes, can review every factor—military, political and psychological—to be mobilized in speeding a just peace.

Progress along at least two lines can instantly begin. We can—first—step up the program of training and arming the South Korean forces. Manifestly, under the circumstances of today, United Nations forces cannot abandon that unhappy land. But just as troops of the Republic of Korea covet and deserve the honor of defending their frontiers, so should we give them maximum assistance to insure their ability to do so.

Then, United Nations forces in reserve positions and supporting roles would be assurance that disaster would not again strike.

We can—secondly—shape our psychological warfare program into a weapon capable of cracking the Communist front.

Beyond all this we must carefully weigh all interrelated courses of action. We will, of course, constantly confer with associated free nations of Asia and with the cooperating members of the United Nations. Thus we could bring into being a practical plan for world peace.

That is my third pledge to you.

As the next Administration goes to work for peace, we must be guided at every instant by that lesson I spoke of earlier. The vital lesson is this: To vacillate, to appease, to placate is only to invite war—vaster war—bloodier war. In the words of the late Senator [Arthur H.] Vandenberg, appeasement is not the road to peace; it is only surrender on the installment plan.

I will always reject appeasement.

And that is my fourth pledge to you.

A nation's foreign policy is a much graver matter than rustling papers and bustling conferences. It is much more than diplomatic decisions and trade treaties and military arrangements.

A foreign policy is the face and voice of a whole people. It is all that the world sees and hears and understands about a single nation. It expresses the character and the faith and the will of that nation. In this, a nation is like any individual of our personal acquaintance; the simplest gesture can betray hesitation or weakness, the merest inflection of voice can reveal doubt or fear.

It is in this deep sense that our foreign policy has faltered and failed.

For a democracy, a great election, such as this, signifies a most solemn trial. It is the time when—to the bewilderment of all tyrants—the people sit in judgment upon the leaders. It is the time when these leaders are summoned before the bar of public decision. There they must give evidence both to justify their actions and explain their intentions.

In the great trial of this election, the judges—the people—must not be deceived into believing that the choice is between isolationism and internationalism. That is a debate of the dead past. The vast majority of Americans of both parties know that to keep their own nation free, they bear a majestic responsibility for freedom through all the world. As practical people, Americans also know the critical necessity of unimpaired access to raw materials on other continents for our own economic and military strength.

Today the choice—the real choice—lies between policies that assume that responsibility awkwardly and fearfully—and policies that accept that responsibility with sure purpose and firm will. The choice is between foresight and blindness, between doing and apologizing, between planning and improvising.

In rendering their verdict, the people must judge with courage and with wisdom. For—at this date—any faltering in America's leadership is a capital offense against freedom.

In this trial, my testimony, of a personal kind, is quite simple. A soldier all my life, I have enlisted in the greatest cause of my life—the cause of peace.

I do not believe it a presumption for me to call the effort of all who have enlisted with me—a crusade.

I use that word only to signify two facts. First: We are united and devoted to a just cause of the purest meaning to all humankind. Second: We know that—for all the might of our effort—victory can come only with the gift of God's help.

In this spirit—humble servants of a proud ideal—we do soberly say: This is a crusade.

THE KOREAN WAR

MANCHURIA

U.S.S.R.

NORTH

[4] UNITED NATIONS FORCES,
NOVEMBER 24, 1950

Chongjin

Sinuiju

KOREA

[5]
CHINESE LAUNCH
ATTACK, NOVEMBER
26, 1950

Anju

Hamhung

Hungnam

[6] UNITED NATIONS
EVACUATION,
DECEMBER 12-24, 1950

Wonsan

Pyongyang

YELLOW

UNITED NATIONS PROPOSED LINE OF DEMARCATION

Pyonggang

[8] MILITARY LINE OF DEMARCATION
CEASE FIRE, JULY 27, 1953

Chorwon

Panmunjom

38TH
PARALLEL

Kaesong

[1] NORTH KOREANS ATTACK ACROSS
38th PARALLEL, JUNE 25, 1950

SEA OF

Seoul

Inchon

Han River

Wonju

[3] UNITED NATIONS
LANDING,
SEPTEMBER 15, 1950

[7] SOUTHERN LIMIT OF
CHINESE OFFENSIVE,
JANUARY, 1951

JAPAN

SOUTH

Naktong River

KOREA

[2] SOUTHERN LIMIT OF
NORTH KOREAN OFFENSIVE,
AUGUST, 1950

Chonju

Taegu

[3] UNITED NATIONS ATTACK,
SEPTEMBER 16, 1950

Kwangju

Pusan

KOJE-DO

SEA

JAPAN

PHASE I
North Korean Offensive
and Stalemate
June 25 – Sept. 15, 1950

PHASE II
United Nations Offensive
Sept. 15 – Nov. 25, 1950

PHASE III
Chinese Offensive
Nov. 26, 1950 – Jan. 24, 1951

PHASE IV
United Nations and Communist
Spring Offensive Drives
Jan. 25 – July 9, 1951

PHASE V
Stalemate, Truce Talks
July 10, 1951 – July 27, 1953

CONCLUSION

THE REPERCUSSIONS of the Korean War went far beyond the Presidential election of 1952. Seemingly a minor engagement in the cold war, its human costs alone were staggering. On the Communist side the casualties were between 1,500,000 and 2,000,000. Two to three million Korean civilians were killed during the war or died as a result of it. The principal cities of both North and South Korea were wholly or partially destroyed. American casualties numbered 142,000, of whom 33,000 were killed in action. The direct monetary cost of the war to the United States was probably higher than $20 billion. More significant, however, was a threefold increase in American defense expenditures largely as a result of Korea's witness to the dangers of Communist aggression. The nation, which had about 1,500,000 men under arms when the North Korean attack came, had a force of 3,600,000 two years later. Not only in Washington but in all the Western capitals, the Korean War led to a clearer definition of the Communist menace and of the military effort necessary to meet it. But only in the United States, where the pains and frustrations of Korea were most immediately felt, was the external menace of Communism used to whip the people into a frenzy over the alleged danger of Communists in their midst. The mania of McCarthyism rose with the Korean War and gradually subsided after its conclusion.

Who won the Korean War? The question will be debated for years to come. The United States failed to unify Korea. Supported by the Chinese Communists, the North Korean government survived. Yet its armies were decimated, and at the end of the war it controlled less territory than it had at the beginning. Communist China, of course, was not defeated. But the United States successfully repulsed aggression and, in cooperation with the United Nations, enforced the principle of collective security. For the remainder of the decade no other Communist government risked blatant aggression like that of North Korea. While this prompt American response in 1950 may have convinced the Communist powers that overt aggression was unprofitable, it may also have encouraged them to adopt the more ambiguous, subtle, and shifty forms of internal subversion and penetration, which are at least as difficult for the democracies to counter.

"A democracy," General George C. Marshall remarked in 1949, "cannot fight a Seven Years' War." The Korean War did not necessarily prove him wrong. The war was unpopular with the public and with the military commanders. For different reasons, it was unpopular with our allies. Nonetheless, for two and a half years an American administration was able to fight a war for limited goals and with limited means in a part of the world that very few Americans knew much about or cared much about. Despite MacArthur, the United States appeared to find in Korea a "substitute for victory." In an age when total victory is likely to mean total destruction, this was, perhaps, no small achievement.

STUDY QUESTIONS

1] Why did the United States decide to resist the aggression by North Korea? Did that decision prove to be right or wrong?

2] In what ways did the Korean War differ from every other war in which the United States had engaged? How do you account for these differences, and what were their implications for the American people?

3] Discuss the conflict between President Truman and General MacArthur. What were its causes? What were the issues at stake? What parallels, if any, can be found in earlier American history?

4] In what respects was the Korean War a "limited war" for the Koreans, the Communist Chinese, and other nations, as well as for the United States?

RECOMMENDED READINGS

PRIMARY SOURCES

BRADLEY, GENERAL OMAR N., ed. Substance of Statements Made at Wake Island Conference on October 15, 1950 (Washington, 1951).

CLARK, GENERAL MARK. From the Danube to the Yalu (New York, 1954).

HERSEY, JOHN. "Mr. President: Part II, Ten O'Clock Meeting," New Yorker (April 14, 1951).

JOY, ADMIRAL C. TURNER. How Communists Negotiate (New York, 1955).

RIDGWAY, GENERAL MATTHEW B. Soldier: The Memoirs of Matthew B. Ridgway (New York, 1956).

TRUMAN, HARRY S. Memoirs, II, Years of Trial and Hope (New York, 1956).

U.S. CONGRESS. Military Situation in the Far East, Hearings Before Committee on the Armed Services and Committee on Foreign Relations, U.S. Senate, 82 Cong., 1 Sess. (1951).

U.S. DEPARTMENT OF STATE. United States Policy in the Korean Conflict (Washington, 1951).

————. United States Policy in the Korean Crisis (Washington, 1950).

SECONDARY SOURCES

APPLEMAN, ROY L. United States Army in the Korean War: South to the Naktong, North to the Yalu (Washington, 1961).

BERGER, CARL. The Korean Knot: A Military-Political History (Philadelphia, 1957).

GEORGE, ALEXANDER L. "American Policymaking and the North Korean Aggression," World Politics, VII (January, 1955), 209–32.

GOODRICH, LELAND M. Korea: A Study of U.S. Policy in the United Nations (New York, 1956).

HIGGINS, TRUMBULL. Korea and the Fall of MacArthur: A Précis in Limited War (New York, 1960).

KINKEAD, EUGENE. *In Every War But One* (New York, 1959).

LICHTERMAN, MARTIN. "Korea: Problems in Limited War," in Gordon B. Turner and Richard D. Challener, eds., *National Security in the Nuclear Age: Basic Facts and Theories* (New York, 1960), pp. 31–56.

MARSHALL, S. L. A. *The River and the Gauntlet* (New York, 1953).

MILLIS, WALTER, WITH HARVEY C. MANSFIELD AND HAROLD STEIN. *Arms and the State: Civil-Military Elements in National Policy* (New York, 1958), chap. 7.

NEUSTADT, RICHARD E. *Presidential Power: The Politics of Leadership* (New York, 1960), chaps. 2 and 6.

OSGOOD, ROBERT E. *Limited War: The Challenge to American Strategy* (Chicago, 1957), chap. 8.

ROVERE, RICHARD H., AND ARTHUR M. SCHLESINGER, JR. *The General and the President* (New York, 1951).

SPANIER, JOHN W. *The Truman-MacArthur Controversy and the Korean War* (Cambridge, Mass., 1959).

WHITING, ALLEN A. *China Crosses the Yalu: The Decision to Enter the Korean War* (New York, 1960).

WHITNEY, MAJOR GENERAL COURTNEY. *MacArthur: His Rendezvous with History* (New York, 1956).

Historical Aids

HISTORICAL AIDS

TAKEN in its widest sense, history is the unreliable memory of the human race; it embraces everything that has happened in human experience. In a narrower sense, history is the *written* record of man's past. As a scholar's discipline or learned craft, as historians know and practice it, history is a method of thinking, learning, and writing. It is best studied and understood by gathering at first hand the facts of the past, evaluating their validity and reliability, critically selecting among them for relevance and significance, organizing that selection to convey meaning, and presenting the result in an independent and readable synthesis. The task calls for hard work on a sustained basis, for orderly and systematic thinking, for intellectual imagination, and for literary talent. Above all, it calls for careful evaluation of sources, towering skepticism toward every shred of evidence, and ability to work as dispassionately and objectively as is humanly possible—these are indispensable attributes of the historian. Because a critical and judicial mind is as essential for him as for the judge in the courtroom or the physicist in the laboratory, he must know how to distinguish facts from probabilities or possibilities. He must also develop a capacity for generalization and interpretation that is restricted by the evidence available to him. In short, the job of the historian demands complete intellectual honesty, an honesty that directs and informs an ability to function both as a discoverer of the past and an interpreter for the present.

Not the only way, but certainly the best way, to learn and appreciate history, as well as to insure that one is exposed to the best methods of learning what a liberal education can offer, is to act out the role of the historian to the extent that an undergraduate can. By participating in the process of understanding the nature and value of the sources, and by using them as the basis of his own writing of history, the student will not only learn far more effectively; the chances are enhanced that he will develop critical faculties that in the long run are more important in his education than the mere learning of the data.

The time required for sustained research in the gathering of facts from original or primary sources on a single topic is unfortunately not available to most students, even when the sources are at hand. *Major Crises in American History* therefore places before students a small but representative sampling of the source materials for a number of critical episodes in American history, which when read and understood will enable the student to write his own narratives and to make his own judgments about the events described. The book itself is but a point of departure, an immediate tool for the task. The bibliographical references to each chapter will guide students to additional materials, both primary and secondary in nature. But a variety of other tools will be necessary—guides to reference works, bibliographies, accounts of the technical apparatus used in historical writing, and statements of historical method and theories of history. The following list of books, chosen for students beginning the college study of American history, will prove of value.

The *Harvard Guide to American History*, by Oscar Handlin and five other distinguished Harvard historians (Cambridge, Mass.: The Belknap Press, 1955), is the most valuable single reference book. The first section is a series of essays and bibliographies on the nature of history, research methods, and literary presentation. It is organized under such headings as "Theories of Historical Interpretation," "Principles of Historical Criticism," "Methods of Note-Taking," "The Mechanics of Citation," and "History as a Literary Art." The second section is a list of materials and tools of history, such as maps, bibliographies, and guides to manuscript collections, government documents, newspapers, biographies, and encyclopedias. The rest of the book is an excellent bibliography of books and articles on American history organized by chronological topics from pre-Columbian times to "Social and Intellectual History, 1945–1953."

For a fuller treatment of the subjects covered by the first section of the *Harvard Guide*, refer to Homer Carey Hockett, *The Critical Method in Historical Research and Writing*, 3rd ed. (New York: Macmillan Co., 1955), or Jacques Barzun and Henry F. Graff, *The Modern Researcher* (New York: Harcourt, Brace & World, 1957). Hockett's book is a practical manual that places great stress on historical methodology, source materials, and the mechanics of writing. Barzun and Graff, who are more readable, stress history as a literary art and the means of effectively presenting the findings of one's research. Wood Gray's *Historian's Handbook: A Key to the Study and Writing of History* (Boston: Houghton Mifflin Co., 1959), is an inexpensive booklet that serves as a useful, although abbreviated, primer. *The Gateway to History*, by Allan Nevins (Boston: Little, Brown & Co., 1938), is a lively introduction to the nature and subject matter of history and its relations to biography, literature, and philosophy, by one of the greatest of American historians. Carl Becker's *Everyman His Own Historian* (New York: Appleton-Century-Crofts, 1935), is a series of provocative essays on relativism in history; the title essay is especially recommended. *Historians and Their Craft*, by Herman Ausubel (New York: Columbia University Press, 1950), is an interesting study of changing theories of history as revealed by an analysis of presidential addresses before the American Historical Association from 1884 to 1945. Edward Hallett Carr's *What Is History?* (New York: Alfred A. Knopf, 1962) passes in masterly and polemical review the major issues of modern historiography.

For interpretative introductions to the history of the writing of the history of the United States, consult Harvey Wish, *The American Historian: A Social-Intellectual History of the Writing of the American Past* (New York: Oxford University Press, 1960); Michael Kraus, *The Writing of American History* (Norman, Okla.: University of Oklahoma Press, 1953); and William T. Hutchinson, ed., *The Marcus W. Jernegan Essays in American Historiography* (Chicago: University of Chicago Press, 1937, paperback, 1962).

A *Guide to the Study of the United States of America*, edited by Roy Basler et al. (Washington: Library of Congress, 1960), is an excellent critical bibliography of secondary works on all aspects of the history of life in America, organized by subject matter. More advanced students will find indispensable

Philip M. Hamer, ed., *A Guide to Archives and Manuscripts in the United States* (New Haven: Yale University Press, 1961), which covers the manuscript holdings of more than thirteen hundred depositories in all the states. For the fullest bibliographical guide to articles and books on American history, one must consult, with considerable inconvenience, the *Writings on American History*, edited by Grace G. Griffin et al. in annual volumes since 1902. *The Index to the "Writings on American History," 1920–1940* (Washington: American Historical Association, 1956), facilitates the use of these volumes. Volume III of Robert E. Spiller et al., eds., *Literary History of the United States*, 3 vols. (New York: Macmillan Co., 1948), is a bibliography of the primary and secondary works in the field of literary history, including the writings of American statesmen. A *Bibliographical Supplement* to the same work, edited by Richard M. Ludwig, was published in 1959.

Richard B. Morris, ed., *Encyclopaedia of American History*, 2nd ed. (New York: Harper & Bros., 1961), is a reliable chronological and topical guide. Students should make a habit of consulting historical atlases. The best is still Charles O. Paullin's *Atlas of the Historical Geography of the United States* (Washington: Carnegie Institution, 1932). Others of value are James Truslow Adams and R. V. Coleman, eds., *Atlas of American History* (New York: Charles Scribner's Sons, 1943; and Clifford Lee Lord and Elizabeth H. Lord, *Historical Atlas of the United States* (New York: Holt, Rinehart & Winston, 1944).

An indispensable reference tool for biographical information is the *Dictionary of American Biography*, edited by Allen Johnson and Dumas Malone (New York: Charles Scribner's Sons, 1928–37), a monumental achievement of American historical scholarship in twenty-one volumes, including the Index volume. Harris E. Starr, ed., *Dictionary of American Biography: Supplement One*, published in 1944, and Robert Livingston Schuyler and Edward T. James, eds., *Supplement Two*, published in 1958, bring the project up to date by including biographies of persons who died after 1935.

There are a number of major scholarly journals in the field of American history with which students should make an effort to familiarize themselves. The leading ones are: *The American Historical Review, The Mississippi Valley Historical Review, The New England Quarterly, The William and Mary Quarterly, The Journal of Southern History, The Pacific Historical Review,* and *The Pennsylvania Magazine of History and Biography.* In addition, most state historical societies publish periodicals that cover, primarily, state and local history. Scholarly journals publish articles summarizing recent research and reinterpretation, book reviews, and bibliographies of current literature.